CONNECT

by experiencing history

Students will experience history in a variety of ways:

thinking about
SCIENCE & TECHNOLOGY

FIGURE 22.4 British Mark 1 Tank, 1916

The Invention of the Tank

Efforts to build movable protective devices for use as offensive weapons in warfare go back thousands of years. A modern form of these devices is the tank, a vehicle first developed during World War I. Trench warfare created a demand for an armored, self-propelled weapon that could bridge trenches, maneuver across the cratered battlefields of the western front, and enable the infantry to break through enemy lines to victory.

The British and French led efforts to develop this weapon. Manufacturers' early models were unreliable, and the tank's use on the battlefield was questionable—and sometimes led to outright failure. Too easily, the vehicles became mired and exposed in difficult terrain. Moreover, the heat and fumes that built up inside often made crews sick—and even lose consciousness. But the British and French inventors persisted, modifying the vehicle's design and tactical features. They eventually came up with a practical tank that used iron armor for defense, an internal combustion engine for power, caterpillar tracks for mobility, and cannons and machine guns for weapons.

The British first employed these practical tanks at the Battle of the Somme in 1916 but with only limited success. The photo in **Figure 22.4** shows the British Mark 1 tank spanning a trench at that battle. The tanks proved to be of greater effect during the last year of the war. However, because the slow-moving vehicles were vulnerable to artillery and antitank weapons, they required support from accompanying infantry and ground-attack aircraft.

As we will see in Chapter 24, the tank would become a much more potent and decisive weapon in World War II.

Connecting Science & Society

1. In what ways is the invention of a practical tank an example of the industrialization of warfare?
2. What role did inventors, producers, and the government, working together, play in the development of the tank?
3. How might an earlier development of a practical tank have altered the nature and course of World War I?

- With *Connect History*, students are no longer simply reading—they can also interact online with text activities, engaging in a visual, auditory, and hands-on experience.

- Through its narrative approach and its features, *The West in the World* emphasizes that history is not just a collection of facts but is created from the ongoing detective work of historians examining evidence from the past.

- "Thinking About" boxes—exploring primary source documents, geography, art, and (new to this edition) science and technology—involve students actively and analytically in the learning process, guiding them to approach documentary and material evidence in the ways that working historians do.

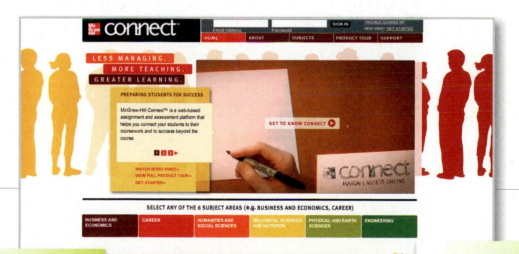

- *Connect History* helps students confirm what they know and learn what they don't know through interactive exercises and review questions.

- *Connect History* builds critical thinking skills by placing students in a "critical mission" and asking them to examine, evaluate, and analyze the data in order to support a point of view.

- *Connect History* includes tools for understanding maps and geography, exploring primary source documents, and writing a research paper (including how to document sources and avoid plagiarism).

THE WEST IN THE WORLD

Volume II: From 1600

THE WEST IN THE WORLD

Volume II: From 1600

FOURTH EDITION

Dennis Sherman
John Jay College
City University of New York

Joyce Salisbury
University of Wisconsin–Green Bay

McGraw Hill

Connect
Learn
Succeed™

Published by McGraw-Hill, an imprint of The McGraw-Hill Companies, Inc., 1221 Avenue of the Americas, New York, NY 10020. Copyright © 2011, 2008, 2006, 2004, 2001. All rights reserved. No part of this publication may be reproduced or distributed in any form or by any means, or stored in a database or retrieval system, without the prior written consent of The McGraw-Hill Companies, Inc., including, but not limited to, in any network or other electronic storage or transmission, or broadcast for distance learning.

This book is printed on acid-free paper.

1 2 3 4 5 6 7 8 9 0 DOW/DOW 9 8 7 6 5 4 3 2 1 0

ISBN: 978-0-07736760-2
MHID: 0-07-736760-X

Vice President Editorial: *Michael Ryan*
Editorial Director: *William R. Glass*
Publisher: *Christopher Freitag*
Sponsoring Editor: *Matthew Busbridge*
Marketing Manager: *Stacy Best Ruel*
Director of Development: *Rhona Robbin*
Developmental Editors: *Arthur Pomponio, Sylvia Mallory*
Editorial Coordinators: *Briana Porco, Jaclyn Mautone*
Senior Production Editor: *Carey Eisner*
Art Editor: *Robin Mouat*
Illustrator: *Patti Isaacs*
Design Manager: *Laurie Entringer*
Interior Designer: *Maureen McCutcheon*
Cover Designers: *Laurie Entringer and David Carlson, Gearbox*
Lead Photo Research Coordinator: *Alexandra Ambrose*
Photo Researcher: *Judy Mason*
Buyer II: *Sherry L. Kane*
Composition: *10.5/12 Goudy Old Style by Laserwords Private Limited*
Printing: *45# New Era Matte Thin, R.R. Donnelley & Sons*

Cover: Top: © Mike Agliolo/Corbis; Middle: New Walk Museum, Leicester City Museum Service, UK/Bridgeman Art Library; Bottom: © Digital Vision/Getty Images

Library of Congress Cataloging-in-Publication Data

Sherman, Dennis.
 The West in the world / Dennis Sherman, Joyce Salisbury. —4th ed.
  p. cm.
 Includes bibliographical references and index.
 ISBN-13: 978-0-07-736760-2 (v. 2 : alk. paper)
 ISBN-10: 0-07-736760-X (v. 2 : alk. paper)
 1. Civilization, Western—History—Textbooks. I. Salisbury, Joyce E. II. Title.
 CB245.S465 2011
 909'.09821—dc22

                                                                              2010037319

The Internet addresses listed in the text were accurate at the time of publication. The inclusion of a Web site does not indicate an endorsement by the authors or McGraw-Hill, and McGraw-Hill does not guarantee the accuracy of the information presented at these sites.

www.mhhe.com

Dennis Sherman

DENNIS SHERMAN is Professor of History at John Jay College, the City University of New York. He received his B.A. (1962) and J.D. (1965) degrees from the University of California at Berkeley and his Ph.D. (1970) from the University of Michigan. He was Visiting Professor at the University of Paris (1978–1979, 1985). He received the Ford Foundation Prize Fellowship (1968–1969, 1969–1970), a fellowship from the Council for Research on Economic History (1971–1972), and fellowships from the National Endowment for the Humanities (1973–1976). His publications include *A Short History of Western Civilization*, Eighth Edition (coauthor), *Western Civilization: Sources, Images, and Interpretations*, Seventh Edition, *World History: Sources, Images, and Interpretations*, Fourth Edition, a series of introductions in the Garland Library of War and Peace, several articles and reviews on nineteenth-century French economic and social history in American and European journals, and several short stories in literary reviews. He is the recipient of John Jay College's *"Outstanding Teacher of the Year"* award.

Joyce Salisbury

JOYCE SALISBURY is Professor Emerita of History at the University of Wisconsin–Green Bay, where she taught history to undergraduates for more than twenty years. She received a Ph.D. in medieval history from Rutgers University in New Jersey. She is a respected historian who has published many articles and has written or edited more than ten books, including the critically acclaimed *Perpetua's Passion: Death and Memory of a Young Roman Woman*, *The Blood of Martyrs: Unintended Consequences of Ancient Violence*, *The Encyclopedia of Women in the Ancient World*, and *The Greenwood Encyclopedia of Daily Life*, which won many awards for its creative organization and timely presentation of the material. In 2010, Salisbury published a second edition of her classic work on the history of attitudes toward animals: *The Beast Within: Humans and Animals in the Middle Ages*. Salisbury is an award-winning teacher who was named *"Professor of the Year for Wisconsin in 1991"* by CASE (Council for Advancement and Support of Education), a prestigious national organization. Since retiring from the University of Wisconsin–Green Bay, Salisbury has taught twice on Semester at Sea, a program sponsored by the University of Virginia that teaches students as they circumnavigate the world. Salisbury brought a global perspective to the history of Western civilization while teaching abroad, and this edition of the book has benefited from her interaction with students as they make sense of our twenty-first-century global civilization.

ABOUT THE AUTHORS

What's the best way to write an interesting, accessible, and accurate account of the West's complex history? This question confronts everyone who approaches this huge and important task. On the one hand, we believed strongly that different authors' perspectives would give readers a sense of the richness of the past. On the other hand, we wanted a seamless narrative that read like a good story. We decided that a careful, two-author collaboration would best enable us to achieve both goals. We brought our different backgrounds, research interests, and teaching experiences to the table. We talked over our ideas and read and struggled with one another's words. Throughout, we never lost sight of our goal: to bring the compelling history of the West in the world to students of the twenty-first century.

A NOTE FROM THE AUTHORS

Dennis Sherman

I was in the twelfth grade in west Los Angeles when I first realized I had a flair for history. Our teacher wisely gave us much latitude in selecting topics for two lengthy papers. I chose ancient Egypt (I liked the National Geographic visuals) as my first topic and Tasmania as the second. (I was the only one who seemed to know that Tasmania was an island below Australia.) Assembling the material and writing the papers just came easily to me, as did any questions our history teacher posed in class (though I was an otherwise fading-into-the-background student). I more or less blundered into different majors in college and then slid through law school (which taught me how to be succinct) before returning to history. At the beginning of my first semester of graduate school, I met my advisor, who asked me what courses I wanted to take. I ticked off four selections: History of South Asia; Nineteenth-Century Europe; Twentieth-Century America; and European Intellectual History. "You're a generalist," he said. Indeed I was. He wisely counseled me to narrow my focus. However, throughout my studies and professional career I have found the big picture—the forest rather than the trees—the most interesting aspect of history.

A few years later I moved to the front of the classroom and, never forgetting what it was like to be a student, found my heart in teaching. Teaching and writing about the sweep of Western civilization within the broadest possible context has remained my greatest interest over the years. That is why I have written this book with Joyce.

Joyce Salisbury

I grew up in Latin America (ten years in Brazil and five in Mexico). Through those years, I attended American schools filled with expatriates. There I studied a curriculum of Western culture, which in those days was equated with European history. But even as a young girl, I knew I wasn't getting the whole story. After all, we celebrated Mardi Gras (a Christian holiday) to an African drumbeat, and the national museum of Mexico was bursting with Napoleonic artifacts. I knew that the history and culture of the West was intimately tied to that of the rest of the world.

In the more than twenty years that I've been teaching Western civilization, I've brought this global perspective to the classroom, and now Dennis and I have brought it to this book. It is very satisfying to me to work with my students as we trace the unfolding history of the West and to see that all my students—with their own rich and varied cultural backgrounds—recognize their stories within the larger narrative. In Spring 2007 and Spring 2009, I had the opportunity to implement intensively my commitment to the integration of Western and global history: I signed on to the University of Virginia's Semester at Sea and had the wonderful experience of teaching Western civilization (as well as other courses) to students as we cruised around the world. This was indeed the opportunity to teach the West in the world!

BRIEF CONTENTS

CONTENTS

CHAPTER 23

CHAPTER 24

LIST OF PRIMARY SOURCE DOCUMENTS

THINKING ABOUT GEOGRAPHY

LIST OF MAPS

LIST OF FEATURES

Connect your students to history. Connect your students to the dramatic story of Western civilization. Connect your students to your course.

With *The West in the World*, Fourth Edition, students take an active, analytical approach to understanding history and historical change. They come to appreciate that history does not happen in isolation but rather is the consequence of a complex set of intersecting events, forces, and human actions among which there are cause-and-effect links that extend into the present day. As it compellingly tells the story of Western civilization, *The West in the World* encourages a critical examination and analysis of major events and themes, to promote student understanding and to uncover students' personal connections to the past.

HOW DOES *THE WEST IN THE WORLD*, FOURTH EDITION, ACHIEVE ITS PEDAGOGICAL GOALS?

The West in the World offers students broad and deep pedagogical support, including chapter previews, timelines, key dates boxes, margin notes, and critical thinking questions. In addition, the chapters feature a series of "Thinking About" selections with accompanying questions, focused on primary source documents, geography, science and technology, and works of art. The "Thinking About" examples encourage analytical thinking and active learning, as students read about, reflect on, and connect the events and themes of Western civilization to build an understanding of the past and an appreciation of history's influence on the present. In addition, new "Connect to Today" questions at the end of each chapter ask students to apply lessons from the past to today's issues.

With this edition, *The West in the World* also immerses students in *Connect History*, a new web-based assignment and assessment platform that includes a fully integrated e-book plus interactive quizzes and activities that make learning and studying both engaging and efficient.

HOW CAN *CONNECT HISTORY* HELP ENSURE THAT STUDENTS WILL COME TO CLASS PREPARED TO LEARN AND PREPARED FOR EXAMINATIONS?

A recent survey of professors by the *Chronicle of Higher Education* showed that 84 percent believe that their students are "unprepared" or only "somewhat prepared" to pursue a college degree. Through pre-tests and post-tests, map labeling, primary source activities, and a variety of question types, *Connect History* helps students determine what they know and do not yet know, guiding them to concentrate on their particular needs and to better prepare for class discussions, writing assignments, and examinations.

****

GOALS OF *THE WEST IN THE WORLD*, FOURTH EDITION

We have written the story of the West in a way that vividly reveals the complicated interactions and connections that distinguish it. Our primary goals have been to:

- **Tell the dramatic, diverse, and personal stories of Western Civilization.**

We showcase both the "art" and the "science" of history, as *The West and the World*'s engaging narrative of Western civilization (the "art") probes the events, individuals, ideas, and developments (the "science"). Students are drawn into the drama as they follow the evolution of Western culture from its earliest roots to the present day.

Building on a political framework, we integrate social history throughout the narrative. Our approach illuminates how individuals from *all* walks of life have shaped history—not just generals and political leaders or artistic and scientific geniuses.

- **Demonstrate the relationship between the West and the wider world.**

Historians use the term "Western civilization" to identify societies that seemed to share certain historical traditions and cultural traits. We present Western civilization as an ever-changing pattern of culture that originated in the ancient Middle East and spread westward through the Mediterranean lands, northward to Europe, and, in the sixteenth century, across the Atlantic.

To emphasize that the West did not progress in isolation, and to help students appreciate how the evolving West interacted with the rest of the world, we include **The World & the West** and **Global Connections** essays. What's more, throughout the narrative, we emphasize the importance of all interactions—economic, social, and cultural, as well as political—that have shaped Western civilization.

• *Create an accessible text of manageable length.*

The medium length of *The West in the World* is unusual for a history of Western civilization. Long accounts can overwhelm students in their level of detail and can make the assignment of supplementary readings difficult. Brief texts, while allowing time for additional reading, typically lack essential coverage and detail and make it a challenge for the authors to achieve the braided, nuanced narrative that history deserves. *The West in the World* is long enough to present a comprehensive, rich narrative but concise enough to give instructors the flexibility to use other sources and books as supplements.

A Note About the Dating System

The various civilizations across the world do not all use the same dating system. For example, the Hebrew calendar counts the Western year 3760 B.C.E. as year 1—which some consider to be when the world was created. Muslims use the date 622, the year that the Prophet fled from Mecca to Medina, as year 1 in their history. Furthermore, all cultures do not measure months on a solar calendar, which marks days based on the earth's revolution of the sun. Muslims, for instance, use a purely lunar calendar consisting of twelve lunar months in a year of 354 or 355 days. This tradition makes it particularly complicated to translate a date from the Islamic system to the Christian system.

Before the seventh century, people in the West (and in many other parts of the world) used dating systems based on rulers. That is, they might say "in the third year of the reign of Emperor Vespasian." Beginning in about the seventh century, many people in the West began to use a dating system that counts backward and forward from the birth of Christ, which Westerners consider year 1. Events that took place "Before Christ," designated as B.C., were counted backward from year 1. Thus something that happened 300 years before Christ's birth was dated 300 B.C. Events that took place after the birth of Christ were also dated from the hypothetical year 1 and were labeled A.D., which stands for the Latin *anno Domini*, meaning "in the year of our Lord."

In the twentieth century, many historians, scholars, and others who recognized that the West was not solely Christian wanted a dating designation that would apply more easily to non-Christians and that could be used more universally in a global context. They kept the same numerical system—counting backward and forward using the hypothetical date of Jesus' birth—but changed the designations. Now the common usage is "B.C.E.," which means "Before the Common Era," and "C.E.," meaning the "Common Era." We first adopted this system in the third edition of *The West in the World*, and we continue this practice in the fourth edition. The events described in the first four chapters all took place B.C.E. In Chapter 5, we have marked all dates with C.E., but because everything after that time is C.E., we then drop the designation.

Content changes for *The West in the World*, Fourth Edition

We have revised the narrative and the features throughout this fourth edition so as to keep the account up-to-date and in pace with the latest scholarly work. We have also made revisions in response to adopters' and reviewers' comments.

In all chapters, we have:

- Redesigned the maps and fine-tuned their content for enhanced clarity and pedagogical value.
- Rewritten and reformatted the critical thinking questions for the maps, biographies, and art to facilitate their use in the classroom and in individual study.
- Expanded and enriched the photo captions to increase their value as learning tools.
- Added a new section at the end of each chapter—"Connect to Today"—asking questions that help students connect what they have learned to current Western and world issues.
- Updated the suggested readings in the "Beyond the Classroom" section.

On a chapter-by-chapter basis, the significant changes include the following:

CHAPTER 1 THE ROOTS OF WESTERN CIVILIZATION: THE ANCIENT MIDDLE EAST TO THE SIXTH CENTURY B.C.E.

- New treatment of the lives and livelihoods of Paleolithic peoples
- New discussion of Paleolithic peoples' expression of symbolic thought through art, featuring a recent excavation of the earliest-known work of figurative sculpture
- New material on the Phoenicians' trade and industry and their impact on regional growth
- Expanded treatment of the Hittites' introduction of a new technology of warfare

CHAPTER 2 THE CONTEST FOR EXCELLENCE: GREECE, 2000–338 B.C.E.

- Extensive new material on the Greek architectural orders
- Expanded discussion of city-states beyond Athens and Sparta
- New information on Delos, shedding light on the growth of Athenian imperial ambitions

CHAPTER 3 THE POLEIS BECOME COSMOPOLITAN: THE HELLENISTIC WORLD, 336–150 B.C.E.

- Fresh discussion of the Greeks' achievements in applying theoretical science to practical applications
- New "Thinking About Science & Technology" feature on the invention of latitude and longitude

CHAPTER 4 PRIDE IN FAMILY AND CITY: ROME FROM ITS ORIGINS TO THE REPUBLIC, 753–44 B.C.E

- New material on the Etruscans, including a look at recent DNA studies of their origin
- Expanded examination of the government structure and social classes of the Roman Republic
- New account of Roman engineering genius as applied to the building of aqueducts across the Mediterranean world

CHAPTER 5 TERRITORIAL AND CHRISTIAN EMPIRES: THE ROMAN EMPIRE, 31 B.C.E–410 C.E.

- New, extended treatment of the praetorian guard
- New information on the Roman imperial government's finances and its considerable reliance on philanthropy
- Extended treatment of the fall of the Roman Empire, including new discussion of the invasions of the Goths and Visigoths
- More on the Wailing Wall and its symbolic significance
- Expanded examination of Constantine and his support of Christians

CHAPTER 6 A WORLD DIVIDED: WESTERN KINGDOMS, BYZANTIUM, AND THE ISLAMIC WORLD, ca. 376–1000

- New information on the discovery of a hoard of Anglo-Saxon gold and silver objects, ca. 675, excavated in 2009 in Staffordshire, England, and its confirmation of the accuracy of the accounts in *Beowulf*
- Expanded narrative on Muslim science, featuring a look at the invention of the mariner's astrolabe

CHAPTER 8 ORDER RESTORED: THE HIGH MIDDLE AGES, 1000–1300

- Revised section on medieval European peasants' use of windmills, incorporating details on recent excavations of tidal mills
- New "Thinking About Science & Technology" feature on windmills
- Substantial new discussion of Byzantium's external threats and disintegration on the eve of the crusades
- Expanded coverage of the Fourth Crusade

CHAPTER 9 THE WEST STRUGGLES AND EASTERN EMPIRES FLOURISH: THE LATE MIDDLE AGES, ca. 1300–1500

- New information on the Black Death, taking into account recent DNA studies
- Extended treatment of the Ottoman Turks' expansion, including a new look at their military structure
- Additional material on eastern Europe and the fall of the Byzantine Empire
- Expanded analysis of Russia and the impact of the Mongol legacy

CHAPTER 10 A NEW SPIRIT IN THE WEST: THE RENAISSANCE, ca. 1300–1640

- Revised introduction establishing the chapter's key theme of the transformative ideas of the Renaissance
- Extended treatment of the aftermath of the Great Schism and the influence of Pope Martin V, including his development of Rome as a seat of papal power
- New information on the expansion of the popes' territorial power
- Substantial new discussion and analysis of Renaissance music and the popularization of music in this era

CHAPTER 11 "ALONE BEFORE GOD": RELIGIOUS REFORM AND WARFARE, 1500–1648

- Increased coverage of John Calvin and his influence
- New analysis of Scotland's adherence to the firm Calvinism preached by John Knox and of the Scots Confession of 1560
- Expanded discussion of warfare in the Thirty Years' War
- New "Thinking About Science & Technology" feature on the invention of gunpowder

CHAPTER 12 FAITH, FORTUNE, AND FAME: EUROPEAN EXPANSION, 1450–1700

- Continued discussion of the impact of gunpowder and cannons, focused on explorations in the New World
- In-depth new treatment of Native Americans in North America, with examination of the cultures and livelihoods of southwestern, Mississippi Valley, and eastern tribes
- New account of the first European contacts with North America and their impact on native peoples in the form of rampant disease and devastating depopulation

CHAPTER 13 THE STRUGGLE FOR SURVIVAL AND SOVEREIGNTY: EUROPE'S SOCIAL AND POLITICAL ORDER, 1600–1715

- New material on the Ottomans' military defeat at the hands of Leopold and Sobieski and the subsequent stagnation and deterioration of the once-powerful Ottoman Empire

CHAPTER 15 COMPETING FOR POWER AND WEALTH: THE OLD REGIME, 1715–1789

- New narrative and analysis on the Ottoman Empire and the Middle East, including an examination of the empire's continuing decline
- New material on the institution of the monarchy, focusing on the emergence of a public sphere where individuals and groups exchanged information and ideas
- New analysis of France's celebration of the American Revolution as a triumph in France's own competition with its British rivals

CHAPTER 16 OVERTURNING THE POLITICAL AND SOCIAL ORDER: THE FRENCH REVOLUTION AND NAPOLEON, 1789–1815

- Increased coverage of Napoleon's invasion of Egypt and the consequences

CHAPTER 17 FACTORIES, CITIES, AND FAMILIES IN THE INDUSTRIAL AGE: THE INDUSTRIAL REVOLUTION, 1780–1850

- Updated material on England's Industrial Revolution

CHAPTER 19 NATIONALISM AND STATEBUILDING: UNIFYING NATIONS, 1850–1870

- Expanded treatment of the Ottoman Empire's struggles with the divisive forces of nationalism, highlighting the Ottomans' troubles with their North African and Balkan provinces as well as with their Russian neighbors

CHAPTER 20 MASS POLITICS AND IMPERIAL DOMINATION: DEMOCRACY AND THE NEW IMPERIALISM, 1870–1914

- Revised account of Western imperialism in Asia and Africa, emphasizing the advantages conferred by new ships, weapons, and finances
- New information on the Russian expansion that influenced Britain's imperialist strategy and of tensions between Russia and Britain in the 1880s.
- Extensive new narrative on the opening of Japan to trade and foreign presences and on the subsequent collapse of the Tokugawa shogunate

- Concise analysis of Japan's transformation from a feudal society with a preindustrial economy to a modern industrialized nation

CHAPTER 21 MODERN LIFE AND THE CULTURE OF PROGRESS: WESTERN SOCIETY, 1850–1914

- New "Thinking About Science & Technology" feature on universities and the professionalism of science

CHAPTER 22 DESCENDING INTO THE TWENTIETH CENTURY: WORLD WAR AND REVOLUTION, 1914–1920

- Extended coverage of the Ottoman Empire's attempts to reverse its decline
- New information on the 1918 flu pandemic and its ravages
- New account of the events leading up to the establishment of the republic of Turkey
- New material on Arab outrage in areas of North Africa and the Middle East owing to decisions of the Allied powers.
- Revised treatment of the course and consequences of World War I
- New "Thinking About Science & Technology" feature on the invention of the tank

CHAPTER 23 DARKENING DECADES: RECOVERY, DICTATORS, AND DEPRESSION, 1920–1939

- New material on Turkey focusing on Atatürk and his reforms and dictatorship
- Revised analysis of the appeal of Nazism and Nazi doctrine

CHAPTER 24 INTO THE FIRE AGAIN: WORLD WAR II, 1939–1945

- Revised treatment of the Holocaust
- New material on German society during World War II and citizens' knowledge of Hitler's Final Solution
- New analysis of developments in Eastern Europe

CHAPTER 26 INTO THE TWENTY-FIRST CENTURY: THE PRESENT IN PERSPECTIVE

- New text on Europeans' concerns about welcoming Turkey into the European Union and on the 2009 ratification of the Lisbon Treaty
- New material updating developments in the Middle East
- Revised, updated account of the political situation in Afghanistan and Pakistan
- New material on the recent U.S. financial crisis and economic recession and their global impacts
- Updated look at Russia's leadership and its internal and external political status
- New material on Barack Obama's election as president of the United States and its potential wider political impact
- New information on economic growth in Asia and worldwide
- New "Thinking About Science & Technology" feature on CERN—the European Organization for Nuclear Research
- All-new documents looking respectively at the end of the Cold War, the war in Afghanistan, and the Copenhagen Accord on climate change

Teaching the Art and Science

The powerful pedagogy of *The West in the World* features easy-to-use critical thinking tools that involve students actively in the quest for understanding the Western past—and that forge vital connections to the present and future.

The **Thinking About** series of boxes focuses on four key areas: primary source documents, geography, art, and, new to this edition, science and technology. All include critical thinking questions to help students connect with, understand, and apply the material.

thinking about
DOCUMENTS

DOCUMENT 4.2

Hannibal Triumphs at the Battle of Cannae

The Battle of Cannae, 216 B.C.E.

Rome
→ Advance ■ Infantry
→ Retreat ■ Cavalry

Carthage
→ Advance ■ Infantry
→ Retreat ■ Cavalry

Cannae   Cannae

The Carthaginians, led by Hannibal, were able to inflict the single greatest defeat of the Romans in the history of their empire. By feigning retreat and convincing the Romans that they were abandoning Cannae, the Carthaginian army was able to surround the Romans and defeat them without mercy. This defeat caused great alarm to the citizens of Rome, as it left them nearly defenseless.

FIGURE 4.9 The Battle of Cannae, 216 B.C.E.

The Roman historian Florus (ca. 70–ca. 140 C.E.) wrote History of the Romans, in which he recounted the long-remembered Battle of Cannae (216 B.C.E.), a turning point during the Second Punic War between Rome and Carthage. Military thinkers today still study Hannibal's winning battle strategy, but Florus notes Hannibal's mistake. Study Figure 4.9 to understand Hannibal's winning strategy.

The fourth and almost mortal wound of the Roman Empire was at Cannæ, an obscure village of Apulia; which, however, became famous by the greatness of the defeat, its celebrity being acquired by the slaughter of forty thousand men. Here the general, the ground, the face of heaven, the day, indeed, all nature conspired together for the destruction of the unfortunate army. For Hannibal, the most artful of generals, not content with sending pretended deserters among the Romans, who fell upon their rear as they were fighting, but having also noted the nature of the ground in those open plains, where the heat of the sun is extremely violent, the dust very great, and the wind blows constantly, and as it were stately, from the east, drew up his army in such a position that, while the Romans were exposed to all these inconveniences, he himself, having heaven, as it were, on his side, fought with wind, dust, and sun in his favor. Two vast armies, in consequence, were slaughtered till the enemy were satiated, and till Hannibal said to his soldiers, "Put up your swords." Of the two commanders, one escaped, the other was slain; which of them showed the greater spirit is doubtful. Paulus was ashamed to survive; Varro did not despair. Of the greatness of the slaughter the following proofs may be noticed: that the Aufidus was for some time red with blood; that a bridge was made of dead bodies, by order of

Hannibal, over the torrent of Vergellus, and that two *modii* of rings were sent to Carthage, and the equestrian dignity estimated by measure.

It was afterward not doubted but that Rome might have seen its last day, and that Hannibal, within five days, might have feasted in the Capitol, if—as they say that Adherbal, the Carthaginian, the son of Bomilcar, observed—"he had known as well how to use his victory as how to gain it." But at that crisis, as is generally said, either the fate of the city that was to be empress of the world, or his own want of judgment, and the influence of deities unfavorable to Carthage, carried him in a different direction. When he might have taken advantage of his victory, he chose rather to seek enjoyment from it, and, leaving Rome, to march into Campania and to Tarentum, where both he and his army soon lost their vigor, so that it was justly remarked that "Capua proved a Cannæ to Hannibal"; since the sunshine of Campania and the warm springs of Baiæ subdued—who could have believed it?—him who had been unconquered by the Alps and unshaken in the field.

SOURCE: Florus, History of the Romans, in The Great Events by Famous Historians, vol. II, ed. Rossiter Johnson (The National Alumni, 1905), pp. 186–187.

Analyze the Document

1. What are the tactics of ancient battles, and in what ways is Hannibal particularly skilled?

⬤ Thinking About Documents

thinking about
GEOGRAPHY

Habsburg Lands
Valois Lands
Ottoman Lands
→ Ottoman Attacks
▢ Boundary of the Holy Roman Empire
★ Battle Sites

MAP 11.1

Europe in 1526—Habsburg-Valois Wars

This map illustrates the political division of Europe in 1526 and highlights the Habsburg lands inherited by Charles V. It also shows the Ottoman Empire on Charles's borders.

Explore the Map

1. Why did the French king feel threatened by his powerful neighbor?

2. Why was Charles so concerned about the proximity of the Ottoman Empire?

3. Notice all the battles Charles fought. What might have been the impact of this warfare both on the people and on the emperor's ability to rule?

Thinking About Geography ⬤

# of Thinking Like a Historian

Thinking About Art ▶

thinking about
ART

FIGURE 10.12

Raphael, *School of Athens*, 1510–1511

Pope Julius II commissioned the painter Raphael to create a fresco for his library. The artist portrayed famous ancient philosophers, such as Euclid, Pythagoras, and Socrates, along with Plato and Aristotle in the center. Plato (looking remarkably like Leonardo da Vinci) is on the left, with his hand pointing in the air to remind viewers of the realm of ideas. He is speaking to [...], reminding [...] knowledge. [...] the right (in the

black hat) and a depiction of a brooding Michelangelo sitting in the center foreground, leaning his head on his hand.

Connecting Art & Society

1. Identify the following characteristics of the Renaissance in this image: individualism, appreciation of the classics, and perspective.

2. Why would the pope find the content of this fresco suitable subject matter for the papal library?

3. Why do you think Raphael included portraits of his artist contemporaries in the company of the philosophers?

thinking about
SCIENCE & TECHNOLOGY

FIGURE 26.14 The CERN Hadron Collider

CERN

What gives matter its mass? What makes up the invisible 96 percent of the universe? These are two of the fundamental research questions being investigated by the European Organization for Nuclear Research (CERN). Located in Switzerland but spilling over the border into France, this is the world's largest particle physics laboratory. Ideas for the international organization first surfaced in the 1940s. Finally established in 1954 by eleven Western European countries, CERN now includes twenty European member states and many more observer nations. The organization employs some 8,000 scientists who split their time between the main CERN site and hundreds of universities and national laboratories in their home countries. The dual goals of projects such as those conducted by CERN are to advance knowledge and, in doing so, to set the stage for later practical applications to life.

One of CERN's best-known achievements was the invention of the World Wide Web in 1989. Originally designed to enable scientists in different institutes and universities to share information, the Web was expanded to a world audience in 1993. CERN's new, extremely expensive Large Hadron Collider, shown in **Figure 26.14**, is a current worldwide scientific cooperation project. Sixteen miles in circumference and buried 300 yards underground, the massive collider will be used to study the subatomic world and the nature of the universe in all its vastness. Computers around the world will process information from the Collider experiments, which perhaps will lead to yet-unimagined applications.

CERN represents another extension of the connections among science, universities, and governments we examined in Chapter 21, as well as the growth of big science, discussed in Chapter 25.

Connecting Science & Society

1. In what ways does CERN represent big science?

2. What are some effects that the World Wide Web has had on peoples around the world?

3. Do you think that projects as costly as those undertaken by CERN can be justified only if they lead to practical applications such as the World Wide Web? Explain.

4. How might the rise of organizations such as CERN reflect globalization?

◀ **Thinking About Science & Technology**

The **Biography** feature spotlights the lives of men and women who embody major themes. Accompanying **Connecting People & Society** questions draw students into each individual's life and help them to link this personal experience to larger developments.

Biography ▶

The text demonstrates the complex relationship between Western and world history through **The World & the West** and **Global Connections** essays.

◀ Four essays titled **The World & the West** investigate what historians have considered the "West" and how the West related to the wider world in various periods. Featuring an accompanying map, each essay ends with **Thinking Globally** questions.

Global Connections essays reinforce the key idea that the West has always developed within a world context. Analytical **Making Connections** questions ask students to see the links between the events in the West and those in the wider world.

The West in the World *ensures student success through* **preview** *and* **review** *features and an exciting digital program,* **Connect History**.

The Struggle for Survival and Sovereignty

13

Europe's Social and Political Order, 1600–1715

"This poor country is a horrible sight," wrote the abbess of a French town in January 1649. "[I]t is stripped of everything. The soldiers take possession of the farms . . . there are no more horses . . . the peasants are reduced to sleeping in the woods . . . and if they only had enough bread to half satisfy their hunger, they would indeed count themselves happy." France had just emerged a victor from the Thirty Years' War (discussed in Chapter 11), only to find itself embroiled in a series of internal revolts. These revolts, like many others erupting throughout Europe, signaled new strains on European society from the bottom to the top of the traditional order.

For the vast majority—peasants who worked the fields—pressures came from powers outside their control. The landowning aristocracy required service and obedience; governmental officials demanded ever more taxes and military service; and the impersonal forces that most people attributed to luck, fate, or God brought bad weather, failed harvests, and plagues. Sometimes peasants fled their aristocratic masters or turned violently against isolated governmental officials. However, against the fates and well-armed soldiers, they were powerless.

For those at the top of society, the pressures came from central governments and monarchs. Kings, struggling with the increasingly heavy burdens of war and governance, chipped away at aristocratic independence year after year. They argued that "the royal power is absolute. . . . The prince [king] need render account of his acts to no one." Elites insisted that "our privileges and liberties are our right and due inheritance, no less than our very lands and goods." This contention between monarch and aristocrat sometimes broke out in violence, at other times led to compromises, and often severely strained the elite order.

These two struggles—the first faced by the vast majority on the bottom, the second by the dominant elites on top—colored the West's social and political life during the seventeenth and early eighteenth centuries. This chapter follows these intertwined conflicts in four areas—France, eastern Europe, England, and the Netherlands—where the story took different turns.

TIMELINE

Romanov Dynasty in Russia 1613-1917
Civil War in England 1642-1649
Stuart Dynasty in England 1603-1714
Russia's Time of Troubles 1584-1613
Thirty Years' War 1618-1648
Commonwealth in England 1649-1660
Bourbon Dynasty of France 1589-1792

1600 1610 1620 1630 1640 1650 1660 1700 1800 1900

PREVIEW

STRESSES IN TRADITIONAL SOCIETY
Learn about the growing problems in both lower and upper orders.

ROYAL ABSOLUTISM IN FRANCE
Trace the rise of the French monarchy from Henry IV to Louis XIV.

THE STRUGGLE FOR SOVEREIGNTY IN EASTERN EUROPE
Study the political fortunes of Prussia, Austria, Russia, and Poland.

THE TRIUMPH OF CONSTITUTIONALISM
Learn about the English civil war and the Republic of the Netherlands.

Each chapter begins with a high-interest **vignette** that forecasts the major themes and sets the historical stage. A **Timeline** covers the period as a whole and tracks the sequence of the events.

The chapter **Preview** highlights the main topic headings and states the learning focus for each major section.

REVIEW, ANALYZE, & CONNECT TO TODAY

REVIEW THE PREVIOUS CHAPTERS

Chapter 12—"Faith, Fortune, and Fame"—told how several European powers expanded overseas during the fifteenth, sixteenth, and seventeenth centuries and grew rich from the commerce. Chapter 13—"The Struggle for Survival and Sovereignty"—focused on how kings and nobles battled for power, the resolutions of those struggles, and their impact on the millions of people outside the elite.

1. Analyze how the expansion of Europe might have stimulated scientific research.

2. In what ways did the effort of monarchs to increase their power and create stability relate to the promotion of science and the desire for greater intellectual certainty?

ANALYZE THIS CHAPTER

Chapter 14—"A New World of Reason and Reform"—examines the changing intellectual foundations of the West.

1. List and analyze the differences between the new scientific views of the world and traditional medieval views.

How did standards for ascertaining the "truth" differ between these two perspectives?

2. Analyze the beliefs and motives of three central figures in the Scientific Revolution. What barriers did they have to overcome to present their views?

3. Do you think the Enlightenment merely popularized the Scientific Revolution, or did it accomplish something more?

4. In what ways did the Enlightenment threaten traditional views and authorities?

CONNECT TO TODAY

Think about the meaning of the Scientific Revolution and the values underlying the Enlightenment.

1. In what ways are our present-day assumptions about the physical universe and the workings of nature based on the ideas and discoveries of the Scientific Revolution?

2. What aspects of world politics today reflect Enlightenment values? What asp[ects of] global politics seem to be oppo[sed]

Review, Analyze, & Connect to Today questions at the end of each chapter ask students first to review the preceding chapters and to place the present chapter's history in the context of what has come before; second, to analyze developments in the current chapter; and third, to connect the ideas and developments discussed in the chapter at hand to present-day issues

Connect History provides students with a fully integrated e-book with highlighting and note-taking features, plus interactive quizzes and activities that make learning and studying engaging and efficient.

CH-13 LO-08:Analyze the English Civil War, the Commonwealth, and the restoratio

Question #4 (of 8)

4. value
10 points
Drag and drop the location names to the appropriate places on the map.

Marston Moor
Lichfield
Naseby
Newbury
Philiphaugh

Marston Moor
Naseby

Controlled by the Parliamentarians, Beginning of 1645
Controlled by the Royalists, Beginning of 1645
Conquered by the Parliamentarians, in 1645
Battle Site

Reset Help

Check My Work

FOR STUDENTS

ONLINE LEARNING CENTER

The Online Learning Center, at www.mhhe.com /sherman4e, provides a wide range of tools that will help students test their understanding of the book. It includes chapter summaries, learning objectives, interactive maps and glossary, and multiple choice and essay quizzes, as well as matching and identifying games.

PRIMARY SOURCE INVESTIGATOR ONLINE

McGraw-Hill's Primary Source Investigator (PSI), available online at www.mhhe.com/psi, is designed to support and enrich the text discussion in *The West in the World*, 4e. PSI gives instructors and students access to more than 650 primary and secondary sources including documents, images, maps, and videos. Students can use these resources to formulate and defend their arguments as well as further their understanding of the topics discussed in each chapter. All assets are also indexed alphabetically as well as by type, subject, place, and time period, allowing students and instructors to locate resources quickly and easily.

INVESTIGATIONS

The Investigation activities give students an opportunity to try their hand at historical analysis. Based on sources found in PSI, the modules ask students to evaluate multiple sources and formulate their own interpretation of an historical event, providing valuable skills for their own research.

RESEARCH AND WRITING CENTER

The online Research and Writing Center offers a guide to college success, plus general assistance for writing college papers, as well as specific tips for history papers. Topics include research, paragraph and argument creation, a comparison of style guides, information on plagiarism and source citation, and much more.

FOR INSTRUCTORS

ONLINE LEARNING CENTER

The Online Learning Center, at www.mhhe.com /sherman4e, contains several instructor tools including a link to the faculty guide on Primary Source Investigator (www.mhhe.com/psi), PowerPoint presentations for each chapter, and the computerized test bank. The instructor side of the OLC is password protected to prevent tampering. Please contact your local McGraw-Hill representative for details.

CLASSROOM PERFORMANCE SYSTEM (CPS)

The Classroom Performance System brings ultimate interactivity to *The West in the World*. CPS is a wireless response system that gives you immediate feedback from every student in the class. With CPS you can ask subjective and objective questions during your lecture, prompting every student to respond with his or her individual, wireless response pad, and providing you with instant results. A complete CPS Tutorial is available at www.einstruction.com.

VIDEOS

Created and narrated by Joyce Salisbury, this three-video collection illuminates the author's lectures on the Middle Ages with the sculpture and fine art of the times. Available to adopters through your local McGraw-Hill representative, this unique series contains a video on each of the following topics: medieval women, medieval Judaism, and medieval life. A wide range of videos on classic and contemporary topics in history is available through the Films for the Humanities and Sciences collection. Instructors can illustrate classroom discussion and enhance lectures by selecting from a series of videos that are correlated to complement *The West in the World*. Contact your local McGraw-Hill sales representative for further information.

PRIMARY SOURCE INVESTIGATOR ONLINE FACULTY GUIDE

The annotated Faculty Guide provides easy reference to all learning assets, both in the text and on PSI, available to instructors and students. Each chapter is accompanied by a rich list of resources, including PowerPoint slides, image bank, outline maps, book maps, and test bank questions, all keyed to the chapter. Resources are organized within chapters by A-heads to streamline lecture and assignment preparation. Icons allow users to quickly differentiate between text and PSI sources. Each asset is listed by title and includes a brief annotation.

In addition to assets, the Faculty Guide also includes a chapter overview, a list of themes, lecture strategies, teaching suggestions, suggestions for further reading, and chapter-specific film recommendations. These, too, are organized by chapter and A-head to make classroom implementation simple.

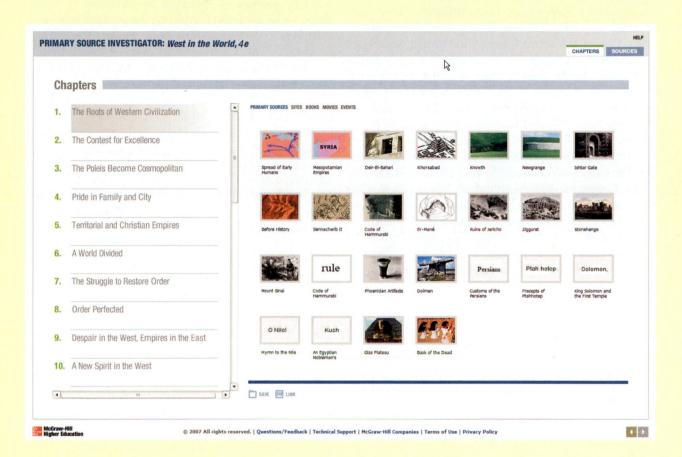

ACKNOWLEDGMENTS

We have nurtured this book through many drafts, and every page has benefited from the advice of numerous reviewers, some of whom we have gone back to several times. For their thoughtful comments and generous contribution of time and expertise, we would like to thank the following reviewers:

For the Fourth Edition

Karen A. Bartley, *University of Dayton*; Carl Boening, *Shelton State Community College*; Fred Boettcher, *Otero Junior College*; Robert Brennan, *Cape Fear Community College*; Robert J. Brown, *SUNY Finger Lakes Community College*; Tracy Nichols Busch, *Ferris State University*; Marie Therese Champagne, *University of West Florida*; Margaret Crowe, *Bridgewater State College*; Salvador Diaz, *Santa Rosa Junior College*; Martin F. Ederer, *Buffalo State College*; Natalie Kimbrough, *Community College of Baltimore County*; Janilyn Kocher, *Richland Community College*; Pamela Koenig, *Seminole State College*; Ilana Krug, *York College of Pennsylvania*; Mike Kugler, *Northwestern College*; Margaret H. Mahoney, *Bellarmine University*; Thomas Martin, *Sinclair Community College*; Ronald Palmer, *SUNY Jefferson Community College*; Elizabeth Propes, *Mesa State College*; Mark Edward Ruff, *Saint Louis University*; Steven Soper, *University of Georgia*; John F. Weinzierl, *Lyon College*; Steven Jay White, *Bluegrass Community and Technical College*; Julianna Wilson, *Pima Community College*; Sergei I. Zhuk, *Ball State University*

For the Third Edition

April Brooks, *South Dakota State University*; Daniel Patrick Brown, *Moorpark College*; Kathleen Carter, *High Point University*; Laura Cruz, *Western Carolina University*; Philip Daileader, *College of William and Mary*; Cassie Farrelly, *Fordham University*; Beth Fickling, *Coastal Carolina Community College*; Ginger Guardiola, *Colorado State University*; Jennifer Hedda, *Simpson College*; Barry Jackisch, *Gannon University*; Molly Johnson, *University of Alabama–Huntsville*; William Kinsella, *Northern Virginia Community College*; Todd Larson, *Xavier University*; Elizabeth Lehfeldt, *Cleveland State University*; William Lipkin, *Union County College*; Nancy Locklin, *Maryville College*; Karl Loewenstein, *University of Wisconsin–Oshkosh*; Michael Loughlin, *Ohio Northern University*; Jack Pesda, *Camden County College*; Penne Prigge, *Rockingham Community College*; Dana Sample, *University of Virginia's College at Wise*

For the Second Edition

Joseph Appiah, *Virginia Community College*; Douglas C. Baxter, *Ohio University*; Jonathan Bone, *William Paterson University*; Suzanne Bowles, *William Paterson University*; April Brooks, *South Dakota State University*; Katherine Clark, *University of Kansas*; Sandi Cooper, *City University of New York*; Florin Curta, *University of Florida*; Norman C. Delany, *Del Mar College*; David D. Flaten, *Plymouth State College*; Marsha L. Frey, *Kansas State University*; Bruce Garver, *University of Nebraska at Omaha*; Carla Hay, *Marquette University*; Holly Hurlburt, *Southern Illinois University*; Andrew Keitt, *University of Alabama at Birmingham*; Dave Kelly, *Colorado State University*; Jason Knirck, *Humboldt State University*; Mark W. McLeod, *University of Delaware*; Carol Menning, *University of Toledo*; Jeffrey Lee Meriwether, *Roger Williams University*; Zachary Morgan, *William Paterson University*; Michael Myers, *University of Illinois*; Max Okenfuss, *Washington University*; Jack Pesda, *Camden County College*; Dolores Davison Peterson, *Foothill College*; Paul Rempe, *Carroll College*; Harry Rosenberg, *Colorado State University*; Shawn Ross, *William Paterson University*; Glenn Sanders, *Oklahoma Baptist University*; Marc Schwarz, *University of New Hampshire*; David Stefanic, *Saint Mary's College*; Aliza Wong, *Texas Technical University*; Michael A. Zaccaria, *Cumberland County College*

For the First Edition

Edward Anson, *University of Arkansas*; William S. Arnett, *West Virginia University*; Richard Berthold, *University of New Mexico*; Robert Blackey, *California State University–San Bernardino*; Hugh Boyer, *Michigan Technical University*; Carol Bresnahan-Menning, *University of Toledo*; April Brooks, *South Dakota State University*; Nathan Brooks, *New Mexico State University*; Blaine T. Browne, *Broward Community College*; Donald Butts, *Gordon College*; Frederick Corney, *University of Florida*; Jeffrey Cox, *University of Iowa*; Florin Curta, *University of Florida*; Norman Delaney, *Del Mar College*; Robert Dise, *University of Northern Iowa*; Chris Drake, *Houston Community College–Northwest*; Lawrence G. Duggan, *University of Delaware*; Laird Easton, *California State University–Chico*; Gregory Elder, *Riverside Community College*; Nancy Erickson, *Erskine College*; Chiarella Esposito, *University of Mississippi*; Gary Ferngren, *Oregon State University*; Nancy Fitch, *California State University–Fullerton*; Elizabeth Lane Furdell, *University of North Florida*; Frank Garosi, *California State University–Sacramento*; Don Gawronski, *Mesa Community College*; Paul Goodwin, *University of Connecticut*; Anita Guerrini, *University of California–Santa Barbara*; Louis Haas, *Duquesne University*; Alice Henderson, *University of South Carolina–Spartanburg*; Jennifer Hevelone-Harper, *Gordon College*; Steven Hill, *Wake Technical Community College*; Laura J. Hilton, *Ohio State University*; Karen Holland, *Providence College*; David Hudson,

California State University–Fresno; Gary Johnson, *University of Southern Maine;* Jonathan G. Katz, *Oregon State University;* Andrew Keitt, *University of Alabama–Birmingham;* Charles Killinger, *Valencia Community College;* Lisa Lane, *Mira Costa College;* John Livingston, *University of Denver;* David Longfellow, *Baylor University;* Donna Maier, *University of Northern Iowa;* James I. Martin Sr., *Campbell University;* Carol Miller, *Tallahassee Community College;* Eileen Moore, *University of Alabama–Birmingham;* Frederick I. Murphy, *Western Kentucky University;* Max J. Okenfuss, *Washington University;* Michael Osborne, *University of California–Santa Barbara;* Jack Pesda, *Camden County College;* Russell Quinlan, *Northern Arizona University;* Patricia Ranft, *Central Michigan University;* Roger Reese, *Texas A&M University;* Harry Rosenberg, *Colorado State University;* Constance M. Rousseau, *Providence College;* Jay Rubenstein, *University of New Mexico;* Claire Sanders, *Texas Christian College;* Alan Schaffer, *Clemson University;* Daryl Schuster, *University of Central Florida;* Marc Schwarz, *University of New Hampshire;* David Shearer, *University of Delaware;* Arlene Sindelar, *University of Central Arkansas;* James Sisson, *Central Texas College;* Ronald D. Smith, *Arizona State University;* Saulius Suziedelis, *Millersville University of Pennsylvania;* Hunt Tooley, *Austin College;* Kevin Uhalde, *Northern Illinois University;* David Ulbrich, *Kansas State University;* Bruce Venarde, *University of Pittsburgh;* Charlotte Wells, *University of Northern Iowa;* Michael Wilson, *University of Texas–Dallas;* Robert Wise, *University of Northern Iowa;* Bill Wrightson, *American River College*

In addition to our reviewers and focus group participants, we would like to thank Matthew Busbridge, sponsoring editor; Rhona Robbin, director of development; Arthur Pomponio and Sylvia Mallory, developmental editors; Briana Porco, Carey Eisner, Robin Mouat, Laurie Entringer, Alexandra Ambrose, and the rest of the Fourth Edition team, whose efforts have made this a better book. Last, but certainly not least, we would like to thank the many professors who choose to use this text in their classrooms. It is they who will fulfill our hope for this text—that it will bring the past to life for many undergraduates and will perhaps awaken in them a love for history and an awareness that understanding the past is the key to our future.

CHARLES LEBRUN, *CHANCELLOR SEGUIER,* ca. 1670

Chancellor Pierre Seguier (1588–1672) was an ambitious courtier to the French king Louis XIV and a member of France's new nobility that earned position by service to the crown, the *noblesse de robe*. In this painting, Seguier's office is symbolized by the formal robes he wears, rather than by arms. Several well-dressed pages surround him, one holding an umbrella over his head as if he were a minor monarch. His face conveys a sense of pleased assurance with the position he has gained. Charles Lebrun (1619–1690), like several other leading artists of the day, served as painter to Louis XIV and for eighteen years created decorations for the king's Versailles palace.

The Struggle for Survival and Sovereignty

Europe's Social and Political Order, 1600–1715

"This poor country is a horrible sight," wrote the abbess of a French town in January 1649. "[I]t is stripped of everything. The soldiers take possession of the farms . . . there are no more horses . . . the peasants are reduced to sleeping in the woods . . . and if they only had enough bread to half satisfy their hunger, they would indeed count themselves happy." France had just emerged a victor from the Thirty Years' War (discussed in Chapter 11), only to find itself embroiled in a series of internal revolts. These revolts, like many others erupting throughout Europe, signaled new strains on European society from the bottom to the top of the traditional order.

For the vast majority—peasants who worked the fields—pressures came from powers outside their control. The landowning aristocracy required service and obedience; governmental officials demanded ever more taxes and military service; and the impersonal forces that most people attributed to luck, fate, or God brought bad weather, failed harvests, and plagues. Sometimes peasants fled their aristocratic masters or turned violently against isolated governmental officials. However, against the fates and well-armed soldiers, they were powerless.

For those at the top of society, the pressures came from central governments and monarchs. Kings, struggling with the increasingly heavy burdens of war and governance, chipped away at aristocratic independence year after year. They argued that "the royal power is absolute. . . . The prince [king] need render account of his acts to no one." Elites insisted that "our privileges and liberties are our right and due inheritance, no less than our very lands and goods." This contention between monarch and aristocrat sometimes broke out in violence, at other times led to compromises, and often severely strained the elite order.

These two struggles—the first faced by the vast majority on the bottom, the second by the dominant elites on top—colored the West's social and political life during the seventeenth and early eighteenth centuries. This chapter follows these intertwined conflicts in four areas—France, eastern Europe, England, and the Netherlands—where the story took different turns.

TIMELINE

Romanov Dynasty in Russia 1613–1917

Civil War in England 1642–1649

Stuart Dynasty in England 1603–1714

Commonwealth in England 1649–1660

Russia's Time of Troubles 1584–1613

Thirty Years' War 1618–1648

Bourbon Dynasty of France 1589–1792

1600 1610 1620 1630 1640 1650 1660 1700 1800 1900

STRESSES IN TRADITIONAL SOCIETY

"It is necessary that some command and others obey," explained a French judge and legal scholar in 1610. "Sovereign lords address their commands to the great; the great to the middling, the middling to the small, and the small to the people." This description captures the traditional social order that reigned in the West during the seventeenth century. Indeed, people took this order for granted. The structure was based on a hierarchy of ranks, and each rank, from nobility to peasantry, had its set status and occupations. Within each rank were subranks. For example, a hierarchy of titles and offices determined position among the nobility. Artisans divided themselves into masters, journeymen, and apprentices. Within the peasantry, landholders stood above laborers, and all looked down on serfs. Each rank distinguished itself through conventions, dress, duties, and etiquette. Finally, within all these ranks, position went hand in hand with family, itself ranked with men at the top, followed by women, and then children at the bottom.

Together the ranks made up the "body politic," with kings and nobles serving as the head and arms, and artisans and peasants as hands and feet. All worked together to perpetuate life as an organic whole. Everywhere, the church and religious sentiments sanctified this organic social hierarchy. Indeed, the social structure paralleled what Westerners saw as the larger, hierarchical order of the universe—the **Great Chain of Being.** In the Great Chain, everything—from God to the angels, humans, animals, and plants—existed in an ordered, permanent arrangement. During the seventeenth century, new forces tested the smooth running of this traditional society.

Mounting Demands on Rural Life

Facing new demands from many quarters, rural life declined. At the beginning of the century, life for most Europeans typically centered on small, self-sufficient villages that contained a few to a hundred families. A church or manor served as the center of communal activities. Strangers attracted intense scrutiny, and most authorities were local people whom everyone knew. When bad harvests, plagues, or war struck, the villagers received little help from the outside.

The majority of people lived in crowded one-room houses made of timber, thatch, and mud, with one or two narrow windows. At one end of the house stood a stone hearth used for light, cooking, and heat. Wood and peat, which fired the stove, were often in short supply, and the villagers struggled to stay warm during the winters. Grain, in the form of black bread and porridge, made up most meals, though in some areas meat, vegetables, fruits, and dairy products supplemented diets. A few treasured pots, pans, and utensils served all.

In **Figure 13.1,** Louis le Nain (1593–1648), a French artist known for his realistic paintings of peasant life, shows a farmyard scene in rural France. The faces of these people express a grimness; clearly they have known hard times and would endure difficulties again and again. Many seventeenth-century Europeans were poorer even than those in this painting. According to one observer in 1696, "They suffer from exposure: winter and summer, three-fourths of them are dressed in nothing but half-rotting tattered linen, and wear throughout the year wooden shoes and no other covering for the foot."

As in past centuries, the family functioned as both a social and an economic unit. Women and men married for practical as well as sentimental reasons. The land, wealth, skills, and position one held counted for much in a potential marriage partner. Husband, wife, and children lived together, and most marriages, whether happy or not, lasted until death. At various times, relatives, domestics, and laborers might live for a while in the household. Finally, although everyone worked together in the fields, men generally did the heaviest work, while women gardened, raised poultry, and supervised dairy producing.

The family

Fathers, older children, and other relatives might also participate with mothers in raising and socializing young children. Nevertheless, children were not considered at the center of family life, and girls were less valued than boys. Indeed, parents often sent children away to other households to work as apprentices, domestics, or laborers if they could earn more there. Infant mortality ran high; of the five or more children to whom a woman was likely to give birth, only two or three lived beyond 5 years. Parents valued and cared for their children, but in a time of grinding poverty, it is not surprising that parents also viewed children as either assets or liabilities in the struggle for survival; great emotional entanglements with them were risky.

The stresses on these common people are strikingly revealed by the population decreases that occurred during the first half of the seventeenth century. The devastation from the seemingly endless wars took many lives, especially in German lands. The old enemies—poverty, disease, and famine—also roared through these decades. Unusually severe winters—advancing glaciers marked the 1600s as part of the "little ice age"—froze rivers and fields, and wet summers destroyed crops. Suffering, malnutrition, illness, and, too often, death followed. "The staple dish here consists of mice, which the inhabitants hunt, so desperate are they from hunger," reported provincial officials in northern France in 1651. "They devour roots which the animals cannot eat . . . not a day passes but at least 200 people die of famine in the two provinces."

Population changes

Bad times also meant postponed marriages, fewer births, and an increase in the number of deaths among infants and children. Europeans already married late compared to the rest of the world. On average, men waited until their late 20s to wed; women, until their mid-20s. Sometimes so many people died, wandered away in search of food, or fled to the cities that whole villages were abandoned. Conditions improved a bit during the second half of the century, though only enough for the European population to maintain itself and perhaps grow slightly. Life expectancy, which varied by social class and region, was probably less than 30 years (in part because of high infant mortality).

New demands from central governments cut into traditional patterns of rural life. With every new outbreak of war, governmental officials intruded more and more into villages in search of army conscripts. People resisted, and for good reason. Military service took men out of the fields, increasing the burden on the women, children, and elderly who had to shoulder the men's share of the labor. Soldiers embroiled in nearby battles plundered what they could from the villages they passed.

Officials also came with new tax assessments, even though peasants already owed much to those above them. Traditional taxes to the government, tithes to the church, and rents to large landowners used up more than half of the already scant wealth peasants produced. **Figure 13.2**, a mid-seventeenth-century print, caustically depicts some of the peasants' grievances. On the left, the well-dressed noble sits authoritatively on his padded chair to receive the peasant ("thin as the noble's terrier"), who is bringing money in his right hand, fruits and vegetables in his left hand, and a sack

FIGURE 13.1

Louis le Nain, *The Cart*, 1641

This painting by Louis le Nain provides a glimpse of everyday life in rural France during the mid-seventeenth century. Here, women and children of varying ages stand on a cart or tend a few animals. One woman sits with her baby on the ground; another has slung a large pot over her back, perhaps in preparation for gathering water. In the background stands a modest house.

Connecting Art & Society

1. What does this painting reveal about how these people spend their time?

2. What roles do women and children play in this rural economy?

3. Considering his portrayal of the figures and details in this painting, what impression of rural life do you think the artist wanted to convey to viewers?

of wheat at his feet. Above the noble are a spider and a fly caught in its web. As the caption on the lower left states, "The noble is the spider and the peasant the fly." The noble says, "You must pay or serve." The peasant can only reply, "To all masters, all honors."

Peasants avoided collectors and hid what assets they could. In countless incidents, peasants and city dwellers across Europe rose against increasing taxes and attacked the hated collectors. In the 1630s, for example, French peasants rose against tax increases

Tax revolts

FIGURE 13.2 The Noble and the Peasant, seventeenth century This print starkly laments the lot of the poor peasant. Here he brings money and the fruits of his hard labor to the rich noble, who sits arrogantly in a padded chair.

and forced temporary concessions from local officials, only to have those victories reversed by the state. Farther south, in 1647, women demanding more bread led riots that swept through the city of Palermo in Spanish-occupied Italy. Rebels in the city chanted, "Down with taxes!" As in France, government forces eventually reversed early victories and crushed the revolt.

Other intrusions further eroded the traditional isolation that characterized rural life. Officials and merchants ventured more and more often to the countryside to buy grain for cities, creating food shortages in rural villages. Moreover, as members of the local nobility departed for capital cities and the king's court, new officials appeared and began administering affairs and rendering judgments in courts. For good or ill, villagers found themselves increasingly drawn into the web of national affairs.

Pressures on the Upper Orders

Monarchs faced pressures of their own, especially the demands of war. In the competition for territory and status, kings won by fielding ever-larger armies and mustering the resources needed to support them. During the seventeenth century, armies doubled and redoubled in size, as did the central governments that supported them (see Chapter 11). The costs of making war and supporting government increased accordingly. Governments devoted half or more of their income to the military, and monarchs desperate for money levied more and more taxes just to stay even. The ability to collect taxes could make or break a ruler. More than anything else, a king's unrelenting demands for more taxes sparked widespread resistance to his rule.

Competing centers of power added to the kings' problems. Independent town officials, church leaders, and provincial officials tried to hold on to their authority over local matters. Religious dissidents, for their part, guarded what independence they could. Finally, those who resented the royal tax collectors resisted the crown's reach. But the greatest threat to monarchical power came from aristocrats, who tried to retain as much of their social and economic dominance as possible. These nobles often challenged royal policies and decried royal "tyranny" as a violation of divine law. They guarded their traditional rights and local authority, and many of them refused to give up their tax exemptions. Should the crown falter, they stood ready to take back any powers they might have lost.

> Competing centers of power

Monarchs argued with, fought, and schemed against these forms of opposition. They justified their power as a divine right, because they represented God on earth, and surrounded themselves with compliant advisors and admirers. As Document 13.1 reveals, their favored supporters, such as France's court preacher and royal tutor Bishop Jacques-Bénigne Bossuet (1627–1704), backed them. Bossuet declared, "The whole state is included in him [the monarch], the will of all the people is enclosed within his own."

Yet the kings used more than words and "yes-men" in this power struggle. Bypassing representative institutions, they sent their royal law courts into the provinces as a way to extend their authority. Sometimes they appointed new local leaders to gain allies. Other times, they attracted aristocrats from the provinces to the royal court, thereby creating a power vacuum that they then filled with their own men. When great nobles resisted being turned into obedient officials, rulers often turned to the lesser nobility or members of the wealthy middle class—men such as Chancellor Seguier, whom we met in the opening of this chapter. Such royal servants received titles or land and were elevated to high office as compensation for their loyalty.

Women also became entwined in these struggles between monarchs and aristocrats. With the royal courts growing in size, many women became important friends and unofficial advisors to kings and influential aristocrats. They used their intelligence, wit, services, and advice to gain privileged positions in royal courts. There they won titles, offices, lands, money, and advantageous marriages for themselves and their families. Mothers encouraged their daughters

DOCUMENT 13.1

Bishop Bossuet Justifies Monarchical Absolutism

In their efforts to acquire as much power as possible, European monarchs and their supporters sought justifications for monarchical rights. One of the most explicit and influential justifications was written and preached by Jacques-Bénigne Bossuet (1627–1704), a French bishop and tutor to the son of Louis XIV. In the following excerpt from his Politics Drawn from the Very Words of Holy Scripture, *Bossuet argues for the divine right of kings.*

Article I

There are four characters or qualities essential to royal authority: First, royal authority is sacred; second, it is paternal; third, it is absolute; fourth, it is ruled by reason. . . .

Article II

Royal authority is sacred.

Proposition 1

God established kings as his ministers and rules peoples by them.

We have already seen that all power comes from God. "The prince," St. Paul adds, "is the minister of God to thee for good. But if thou do that which is evil, be afraid; for he beareth not the sword in vain; for he is the minister of God, a revenger to execute wrath upon him that doeth evil."

Thus princes act as ministers of God, and as his lieutenants on earth. It is by them that he exercises his rule. . . .

Proposition 2

The person of kings is sacred.

It thus appears that the person of kings is sacred and that to make an attempt on their lives is a sacrilege. . . .

The title of Christ is given to kings; and they are everywhere called christs, or the anointed of the lord. . . .

Proposition 3

The prince must provide for the needs of the people.

It is a royal right to provide for the needs of the people. He who undertakes it at the expense of the prince undertakes royalty: this is why it has been established. The obligation to care for the people is the foundation of all the rights that sovereigns have over their subjects. . . .

Article III

The royal authority is absolute.

. . . The prince is by his office the father of his people; he is placed by his grandeur above all petty interests; even more: all his grandeur and his natural interests are that the people shall be conserved, for once the people fail him he is no longer prince. There is thus nothing better than to give all the power of the state to him who has the greatest interest in the conservation and greatness of the state itself. . . .

Proposition 4

Kings are not by this above the laws. . . .

Kings therefore are subject like any others to the equity of the laws both because they must be just and because they owe to the people the example of protecting justice; but they are not subject to the penalties of the laws; or, as theology puts it, they are subject to the laws, not in terms of its coactive power but in terms of its directive power.

SOURCE: J.B. Bossuet, *Politics Drawn from the Very Words of Holy Scripture* (1709), in *Western Societies, A Documentary History,* vol. II, eds. Brian Tierney and Joan Scott (New York: McGraw-Hill, 1984), pp. 11–13.

Analyze the Document

1. What, according to Bossuet, are the nature and properties of royal authority?

2. How does Bossuet justify the various qualities of royal authority?

3. How absolute is the power of kings?

---

not to let good marriage opportunities pass by. "It is true that [the proposed groom] is some fifteen years older than you," wrote one aristocratic mother in 1622. "[B]ut . . . you are going to marry a man . . . who has spent his life honorably at court and at the wars and has been granted considerable payments by the king." Royal mistresses also achieved important positions in the king's household. Françoise d'Aubigné (Marquise de Maintenon), mistress (and, secretly, wife) of France's King Louis XIV, influenced court appointments and founded a royal school for the daughters of impoverished nobles in 1686. Some mistresses even persuaded kings to acknowledge their children as "royal bastards" and grant them titles and privileges.

This system of elevated royal authority has been called **royal absolutism** because the kings of the day commanded more loyalty, control, and resources than their predecessors had, and because they justified their right to rule as an absolute. However, no monarch gained true absolute power. Most people understood that even the strongest ruler, divinely ordained, was vaguely subject to tradition and law. As one seventeenth-century French jurist explained, the king's power "seems to place him above the law, . . . [but] his rank obliges him to subordinate his personal interests to the general good of the state." Further, with so many local centers of power, with scores of nobles who persisted in their independent

> Royal absolutism

ways, and with too much information to control, no king in this era could hope to dominate everything. Some monarchs even found themselves on losing ends of internal battles for power.

ROYAL ABSOLUTISM IN FRANCE

In western Europe, the efforts of French kings to maximize their power exemplified the development of royal absolutism. Building upon the work of predecessors who had enhanced the power of the monarchy, Louis XIV (r. 1643–1715) took personal control of the French monarchy in 1661. By then, France had supplanted Spain as the most powerful nation in Europe. Under Louis' long rule, royal absolutism reached its peak and inspired other monarchs to emulate his style.

Henry IV Secures the Monarchy

French absolutism had its immediate roots in the reign of Henry IV (r. 1589–1610). When Henry IV ascended the French throne in 1589, his country had endured several decades of wars between Protestants and Catholics, combined with conflicts between different political factions. Law and order had broken down, and powerful nobles had reasserted their authority. The finances of the central government lay in disarray, and French prestige abroad had sunk to a low level.

The talented, witty Henry, in his prime at 36, set out to change all this. He defused the religious turmoil by issuing the Edict of Nantes (see Chapter 11), which granted to Huguenots (French Protestants) religious toleration and control of some two hundred fortified cities and towns as a guarantee against future oppression. He appealed to the traditional nobility by developing an image as a cultured warrior-king who could be trusted to enforce the law. He catered to rich lawyers, merchants, and landowners by selling new governmental offices, which often came with ennoblement as well as prestige. This growing elite became known as the nobility of the robe because their robes of office, rather than the arms borne by the traditional nobility of the sword, represented their power (see p. 414). Many of these nobles gladly paid annual fees for the right to pass their offices on to heirs. For the peasantry, Henry suggested that prosperity should bring "a chicken in the pot of every peasant for Sunday dinner." Not surprisingly, Henry's authority and popularity soared.

With the help of his able, methodical administrator, the Duke of Sully (1560–1641), Henry also launched a comprehensive program of economic reconstruction. Agriculture and commerce benefited from the increased security of life and property brought by better law enforcement; from improved transportation facilitated by the repair of roads, bridges, and harbors; and from the freeing of trade, thanks to lower internal tariff barriers. The monarchy even subsidized and protected new industries that produced luxuries such as glass, porcelain, lace, silk, tapestries, fine leather, and textiles. Sully's efficient collection of taxes and administration of expenditures produced a rare budget surplus.

Henry also dreamed of making France secure from ambitious foreign states and of ensuring his country a supreme position in all of Europe. However, the powerful Spanish and Austrian Habsburgs on France's borders stood in his way. In 1610, he prepared to join his armies for a campaign against his rivals. Yet before he could set out, he was assassinated by a fanatic, and his plans died with him.

Richelieu Elevates Royal Authority

For several years after Henry's death, his Italian wife, Marie de Médicis (1573–1642), ruled as regent for their son, the young Louis XIII (r. 1610–1643). Marie kept opponents at arm's length but made little headway in strengthening the position of the monarchy. Then in 1624, one of her favorite advisors, Cardinal Richelieu (1585–1642), became chief minister and began exercising power from behind the throne. Having come from a minor noble family and possessing a keen intellect, the arrogant and calculating Richelieu handled the young king deftly and controlled others through a skillful blend of patronage and punishment. His twofold policy was to make royal power supreme in France and to maneuver France into a position of dominance in Europe. To Louis XIII, Richelieu promised "to ruin the Huguenot party, to abase the pride of the nobles, to bring back all your subjects to their

KEY DATES

THE POLITICS OF ABSOLUTISM

1533–1584	Reign of Ivan IV the Terrible in Russia
1589–1610	Reign of Henry IV in France
1640–1688	Reign of Frederick William in Prussia
1643–1715	Reign of Louis XIV in France
1648–1653	The Fronde in France
1683	Siege of Vienna by Ottoman forces
1685	Revocation of the Edict of Nantes in France
1688–1713	Reign of Frederick I in Prussia
1689–1725	Reign of Peter the Great in Russia
1713–1714	Peace of Utrecht
1721	Treaty of Nystad

duty, and to elevate your name among foreign nations to the point where it belongs."

With the royal army at his disposal, Richelieu boldly destroyed the castles of nobles who opposed the king; he disbanded their private armies and executed a number of the most recalcitrant among them. When Huguenot nobles in the southwest rebelled, Richelieu sent in the army and stripped the Huguenots of the special military and political privileges that Henry IV had granted them. Only their religious liberties remained intact. To dilute local centers of political power, the dynamic minister divided France into some thirty administrative districts, placing each under the control of a powerful *intendant*, who was an agent of the crown. He chose these *intendants* from the ranks of the middle class and recently ennobled people and shifted them around frequently, lest they become too sympathetic with their localities. Finally, Richelieu plunged France into the Thirty Years' War in Germany (see Chapter 11). His purpose was to weaken the Habsburgs, chief rivals of the French monarchs for European supremacy.

By the time of his death in 1642, Richelieu had firmly secured royal power in France and elevated France's position in Europe. Nevertheless, the imperious cardinal, having more than doubled taxes to promote his policies, had gained few friends. Far more French subjects rejoiced in his death than mourned his passing.

Mazarin Overcomes the Opposition

Richelieu was succeeded by his protégé, Cardinal Jules Mazarin (1602–1661). Louis XIII's death in 1643, a few months after that of his great minister, left the throne to Louis XIV, a child of 5. Mazarin, who began his career as a gambler and diplomat, played the same role in the early reign of Louis XIV and his regent, Anne of Austria (1601–1666), that Richelieu had played during the reign of Louis XIII.

Early on, Mazarin, Anne, and the child-king faced a series of wide-ranging, uncoordinated revolts that forced them to flee Paris. Known collectively as the **Fronde** (the name of a child's slingshot game, which implied that the participants were childish), these revolts stemmed primarily from French subjects' objections to high taxes and increasing royal power. Between 1648 and 1653, ambitious nobles, footloose soldiers returning from war, urban artisans, and even some peasants fought the monarchy and its supporters in what amounted to a civil war at times. Bad harvests added to the chaos and suffering: "People massacre each other daily with every sort of cruelty," wrote an observer in 1652. "The soldiers steal from one another when they have denuded everyone else . . . all the armies are equally undisciplined and vie with one another in lawlessness." Nobles conspired and shifted alliances for their own gains, resulting in growing disillusionment with their cause. Gaining support from city dwellers and peasants longing for peace, and shrewdly buying off one noble after another, Mazarin quashed the revolts by 1653. The crown gradually reasserted itself as the basis for order in France.

The Fronde was paralleled by other revolts during the 1640s in Spain, the Italian states, and, much more seriously, England. In each case, the catalysts included new taxes, the demand for more men and supplies for the military, and monarchies' efforts to acquire more power. In the Spanish provinces of Catalonia and Portugal, as well as in the Italian states of Naples and Sicily, rebels murdered tax officials, peasants took up arms, and local nobles joined the fray. Localities demanded and sometimes got concessions, but many of these victories proved short-lived when the crown reasserted its authority. As we will see, matters grew much worse in England. Taken together, these mid-century rebellions served as a warning to monarchs not to push unpopular policies too far—and to the aristocracy not to underestimate the power of the crown.

The Sun King Rises

Upon Mazarin's death in 1661, the 23-year-old Louis XIV finally stepped forward to rule in his own right. "Up to this moment I have been pleased to entrust the government of my affairs to the late Cardinal," he announced. "It is now time that I govern them myself." With his regal bearing and stolid build, young Louis fit the part well. His lack of intellectual brilliance was offset by a sharp memory, a sense of responsibility, and a capacity for tedious work. "One reigns only by dint of hard work," he warned his own son. Haunted by childhood memories of fleeing in terror across the tiled rooftops of Paris during the Fronde revolts, he remained determined to prevent further challenges from rebellious aristocrats. By his mother, Mazarin, and a succession of tutors, Louis had been convinced that he was God's appointed deputy for France. Supporting him was the most famous exponent of royal absolutism, Bishop Bossuet, who argued that the monarchy "is sacred, it is paternal, it is absolute, and it is subject to reason . . . the royal throne is not that of a man but the throne of God Himself." As Document 13.2 indicates, Louis XIV learned these lessons well. In words commonly attributed to Louis, "L'état, c'est moi" (I am the state).

However, Louis could not possibly perform all the functions of government personally. The great bulk of the details were handled by a series of councils and bureaus and administered locally by the *intendants*. Distrusting the traditional nobility, Louis instead usually appointed members of modest noble backgrounds

DOCUMENT 13.2

Louis XIV Describes Monarchical Rights and Duties

For many, France's Louis XIV embodied the nearly all-powerful king—at least in his glorious appearance and style, if not always in his deeds. Louis XIV probably wielded more power than any other seventeenth-century European monarch. In the following excerpts from his writings, he describes his view of kingship to his son.

Homage is due to kings, and they do whatever they like. It certainly must be agreed that, however bad a prince may be, it is always a heinous crime for his subjects to rebel against him. He who gave men kings willed that they should be respected as His lieutenants, and reserved to Himself the right to question their conduct. It is His will that everyone who is born a subject should obey without qualification. This law, as clear as it is universal, was not made only for the sake of princes: it is also for the good of the people themselves. It is therefore the duty of kings to sustain by their own example the religion upon which they rely; and they must realize that, if their subjects see them plunged in vice or violence, they can hardly render to their person the respect due to their office, or recognize in them the living image of Him who is all-holy as well as almighty.

It is a fine thing, a noble and enjoyable thing, to be a king. But it is not without its pains, its fatigues, and its troubles. One must work hard to reign. In working for the state, a king is working for himself. The good of the one is the glory of the other. When the state is prosperous, famous, and powerful, the king who is the cause of it is glorious; and he ought in consequence to have a larger share than others do of all that is most agreeable in life.

SOURCE: J.M. Thompson, *Lectures on Foreign History, 1494–1789* (Oxford: Blackwell, 1956), pp. 172–174.

Analyze the Document

1. In what ways, according to Louis XIV, should a king take steps to maintain his authority?

2. How does Louis justify the obedience owed to kings?

3. In what ways do these views support an alliance between church and state?

to the important offices of his government. Well supervised by the industrious king, the administrative machinery hummed along.

To raise his stature, Louis XIV initiated massive public-works projects that glorified him, his government, and his reign. His greatest architectural project was a new palace. Hating the tumult of Paris, with its streets teeming with commoners, he selected Versailles, 11 miles southwest of the city, as the new seat of government. There, as many as 35,000 workmen toiled for more than forty years to turn marshes and sand into Europe's most splendid palace and grounds.

Figure 13.3 shows Versailles in 1668. Over the next forty-three years, successive teams of workers added rear gardens and more than doubled the size of the buildings. This painting, which shows the roads, paths, and gardens of Versailles geometrically laid out, gives a sense of the scale of the project. In the foreground to the right, the royal coach, with its train of followers, arrives at the front gates. The exterior of Versailles was designed in long, horizontal, classic lines. The interior boasted a lavish baroque style with richly colored marbles, mosaics, inlaid woods, gilt, silver, silk, velvet, and brocade. Ceiling-to-floor windows and mirrors and crystal chandeliers holding thousands of candles illuminated the salons and halls. In terms of sheer capacity, the palace could house 5,000 people and serve thousands more visitors each day. It faced hundreds of acres of groves, walks, canals, pools, terraces, fountains, statues, flower beds, and clipped shrubs—all laid out in formal geometric patterns symbolizing the triumph of engineering over nature. So dazzling was this hallmark of royal absolutism that other European monarchs soon attempted to copy it.

Louis used Versailles, images of himself, and symbols to enhance his authority among the nobility and everyone else. "The peoples over whom we reign, being unable to apprehend the basic reality of things, usually derive their opinions from what they can see with their eyes," he explained. **Figure 13.4,** a painting by an anonymous seventeenth-century artist, shows Louis—in the center astride a white horse—as he rides into the gardens at Versailles. His favored courtiers throng around him, hoping to be seen by him and others more than to see him. Servants mingle in the crowd as well. Above is the king's chosen symbol, the sun, with its light radiating out. As Louis put it, "The symbol that I have adopted and that you see all around you represents the duties of a Prince . . . endlessly promoting life, joy and growth." It is "the most dazzling and most beautiful image of the monarch."

The Sun King finally moved to Versailles in 1682. Once established there, he lured the men and women of the nobility away from their local centers

FIGURE 13.3 Pierre Patel the Elder, View of Versailles, 1668 A royal procession enters the grounds of Versailles in this aerial view. The new geometrically ordered palace and grounds became a monument to Louis XIV's reign and French royal absolutism.

of power where they might make trouble and turned them into domesticated court "butterflies." He subjected them to a complex system of etiquette and favoritism that made every aspect of Louis' daily life the center of their concern. Court became a theater where those already in favor, as well as aspiring favorites, had to scheme for gifts, patronage, and position. Winners might secure lucrative rewards, and losers might spend themselves broke trying to stay in the race.

Despite the grandeur of Versailles, this glittering monument to royal absolutism had its critics. In her novel *The Princess of Clèves* (1678), the Countess de Lafayette complained that at Versailles "everybody was busily trying to better their position by pleasing, by helping, or by hindering somebody else." The court reportedly seethed with gossip, scandal, and intrigue. Critics such as Pierre Jurieu, a French Calvinist pastor who fled to Holland, lamented that the king "is the idol to which are sacrificed princes, great men and small, families, provinces, cities, finances and generally everything." Resentful nobles once proudly drawing high status from their lands

Versailles' critics

and lineage came to depend on the approval of and service to the king as the primary route to power. Many hard-toiling, heavily taxed French commoners also grumbled about living in the reflected glory of a pretentious monarch.

To enhance the glory of his court, Louis XIV subsidized and attracted to Versailles leading French artists and literary figures. The elegance, the sense of order, and the formalism of royalty all found expression in much of the literature of this **classical style** in French culture. Pierre Corneille (1606–1684), for example, wrote elegant plays modeled on the ancient Greek tragedies. Human beings' conflicts with their own nature and with the workings of fate and the universe furnished the plots. Even more exquisite were the perfectly rhymed and metered couplets of Jean Racine's (1639–1699) dramas. Finally, in his profound comedies, Jean-Baptiste Molière (1622–1673) satirized pompous scholars, social climbers, false priests, and quack physicians. Louis and his court had little to fear from this literature. On the contrary, they appreciated its formal order and laughed along with other audiences at its satire, which was

Classical literature

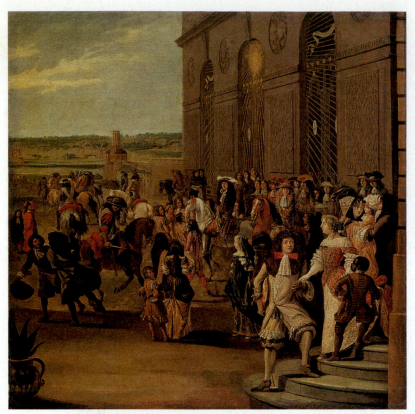

FIGURE 13.4 Louis XIV at Versailles, seventeenth century
In this painting by an unknown artist, Louis sits on a white horse surrounded by his courtiers at his Versailles palace. Above him radiates his adopted symbol, the sun.

reflected their wealth and power. Yet during the second half of the seventeenth century, classicism, with its emphasis on control and restraint, began to gain favor. The appealing paintings of French artists Claude Lorraine (1600–1682) and Nicolas Poussin (1594–1665) helped classicism win official approval in France. Both men spent much time in Italy, studying the Renaissance masters and the Italian landscape. **Figure 13.5** embodies their style. In this painting, Lorraine has framed the foreground figures with trees under a radiant sky. The Italian landscape is geometrically balanced, the figures are in classic dress, and the scene exudes calm and discipline. Here is an idyllic vision, a scene designed to elevate the minds of viewers. Compared to the baroque, the classical style shows a logic that echoed the sense of order pervading the Versailles court of the Sun King.

Versailles, the arts, and all other aspects of government cost money. Louis assigned the talented Jean-Baptiste Colbert (1619–1683) **Colbert** to manage his finances. An engine of efficiency, Colbert toiled endlessly, supervising the details of the French economy while also promoting culture by founding the Royal Academy of Sciences in 1666 and subsidizing the arts. In keeping with his bourgeois origins, he chose service to the king as his means of advancement. His family shared in his success, becoming ministers, gaining high offices in the church, marrying well, and securing top positions in the military.

Promoting mercantilistic economic policies (see Chapter 12), Colbert protected industries with high tariffs while subsidizing exports and new industries. To encourage France's growing empire and the commerce it generated, he built a large navy. Finally, Colbert worked to ensure a worldwide reputation for the uniformly high quality of French products. He subjected manufacturing to the most minute regulation and supervision: So many threads of such and such quality and color must go into every inch of this textile and that lace. Although Colbert's restrictive mercantilistic controls in the long run stifled initiative and economic change, French products earned wide acclaim for their quality. By his death in 1683, Colbert had balanced the budget and promoted relative prosperity despite Louis XIV's lavish expenditures.

During the following decades, however, Louis embarked on policies that undermined much of what Colbert had accomplished. The king's demands for religious conformity and his military ambitions ranked among the most destructive of these policies. Huguenots (French Protestants) paid the highest price for his religious intolerance. In 1685, **Revocation of the Edict of Nantes**

aimed at humankind in general rather than at specific ruling regimes.

At court and elsewhere, many members of the elite also read historical romances. Perhaps the most popular of these was *Grand Cyrus* by Madeleine de Scudéry (1608–1701), a writer who rose from an impoverished background. The fact that this book was published under the name of the author's brother, Georges, hints at the difficulties women faced in expressing their cultural talents. Other forms of literature included letters and memoirs. The courtier Madame de Sévigné (1626–1696), for example, wrote almost two thousand letters to her daughter that reported what the king said and did as well as news of marriages, deaths, gossip, fads, and conspiracies that marked life at the court of Louis XIV. The Duke of Saint-Simon (1675–1755), who like many nobles felt slighted and grew to resent the king, chronicled life at Versailles in his forty-volume *Memoirs*.

While the literature of the seventeenth century amused monarchs, the visual arts of the period positively glorified them. Kings and aristocrats still favored the baroque **Visual arts** style of painting and architecture (see Chapter 11). As they saw it, the baroque's swirling forms and massive, ornamental elegance perfectly

Louis revoked the Edict of Nantes, which in 1598 had granted tolerance to the Protestant minority. Then he outlawed Protestantism and ordered Protestant churches demolished. The Duke of Saint-Simon lamented that the "ultimate results [of the reversal] were the depopulation of a fourth part of the kingdom and the ruin of our commerce . . . the country was given over to the authorized ravages of dragoons [armed troops], which caused the death of, literally, thousands of innocent people of all ages and both sexes." Although Huguenots were forbidden to emigrate, perhaps as many as 200,000 did, taking their wealth and skills with them to Protestant-friendly areas in Europe and America, "enriching them and causing their cities to flourish at the expense of France," according to Saint-Simon. Up to a million Huguenots who remained in France went underground.

Nor was Louis content to rule in peace as the leader of Europe's most powerful nation. During the last four decades of his 72-year reign, he fought four wars of aggression. The same old reasons prompted him to lead France into battle: more territory, more glory, and more wealth. He set his sights on the Spanish and Austrian Habsburg lands on France's eastern borders and on the Dutch, France's most powerful commercial rivals on the Continent. He put his war minister, the Marquis of Louvois (1639–1691), in charge of organizing France's huge military establishment on the model of a complex business, replete with supply depots and hospitals. While Louvois introduced strict discipline, uniforms, and promotions based on merit, Sébastien de Vauban (1633–1707) designed sturdy fortifications and brilliant siege operations. It was a common saying that whereas a city defended by Vauban was safe, one besieged by Vauban was doomed.

Louis initiated his foreign adventures in the War of Devolution (1667–1668), waged against Spain for French claims in the Spanish Netherlands and Franche-Comté (Burgundy). When victory seemed within reach, the United Provinces, England, and Sweden joined Spain to prevent France from upsetting the balance of power. The Treaty of Aix-la-Chapelle (1668) brought Louis only minor gains (see **Map 13.1**). In 1672, Louis turned against the Dutch, whom he blamed for organizing the alliance against him and who were France's chief trade competitors. The Dutch stopped the invading French only by opening the dikes and flooding the land. Dutch diplomacy brought Spain, Sweden, Brandenburg, and the Holy Roman Empire into an alliance against the French. Louis fought them to a standstill and gained some valuable territories in the Peace of Nijmegen (1679). In the following

Wars of aggression

FIGURE 13.5 Claude Lorraine, *The Marriage of Isaac and Rebekah (The Mill)*, 1640 This calm, balanced Italian landscape by a leading French artist exemplifies seventeenth-century classicism with its emphasis on control and restraint.

years, Louis made enemies of the Austrians by refusing to help in their war against the Turks, and he alienated Europe's Protestants by turning against the Huguenots. Fearful that he intended to upset the balance of power and dominate the Continent, much of Europe formed the Grand Alliance against him. The eight-year War of the League of Augsburg (1689–1697) gained France little territory at the cost of much bloodshed and misery. Louis' final struggle, the War of the Spanish Succession, was fought over French claims to the Spanish throne and the partition of Spanish holdings in the Netherlands and Italy. The war lasted eleven years (1702–1713), and the Grand Alliance defeated French and Spanish forces in a series of battles. Beaten, impoverished, and facing revolts fueled by despair and opposition to taxation, Louis XIV was forced to accept the Peace of Utrecht (1713), which ended Louis' ambitions to create a partnership of Bourbon monarchs in France and Spain—with France the senior partner. **Map 13.1** depicts France in 1661, when Louis XIV took control of the monarchy, and the territories he eventually acquired. In the end, he possessed little more than what he had started with some fifty years earlier, and he had even fewer holdings in North America.

Louis XIV died only two years after the Peace of Utrecht. He had long outlived his popularity. One widely circulated letter from an aristocratic critic, Archbishop Fénélon, complained that "for thirty years, your principal ministers have . . . overthrown all the ancient maxims of the state in order to increase your authority beyond all bounds. . . . For the sake of

MAP 13.1

France Under Louis XIV, 1661–1715

This map shows France's provinces and the territorial gains the state made during the reign of Louis XIV. In four wars between 1667 and 1713, France fought against various rivals and coalitions of states to the south, north, and east.

Explore the Map

1. Notice that most of Louis' gains came from Spanish lands and German states on France's eastern border. What might this pattern imply about vulnerable areas of Europe and changing power relationships at the time?

2. Consider how small France's gains were despite the almost endless, costly wars the state waged. What were the wars' likely consequences for France's finances and the popularity of its monarch?

getting and keeping vain conquests abroad, you have destroyed half the real strength of your own state." As the coffin carrying Louis XIV's body was drawn through the streets of Paris, some of his abused subjects cursed his name.

The Sun King had built the French state into the envy of Europe, and his glittering court at Versailles outshone all others. His success relied on knowing how to use the old system, modified by preceding state-builders such as Richelieu, to his advantage. He tamed rather than fought the nobility, who at the same time remained the crown's most important ally and potent competitor. Clearly, strong central governments enjoyed advantages, and none were stronger than France's under Louis XIV. For many monarchs, France under Louis XIV became the model of absolutism. However, his expenditures and wars created unprecedented misery for most commoners saddled with relentlessly rising taxes, more military service, and famines. Recognizing that the continued power of the state required some support of the people, Louis' successors would try to avoid his mistakes and ameliorate the worst threats to the lives of French people.

Assessing Louis XIV

THE STRUGGLE FOR SOVEREIGNTY IN EASTERN EUROPE

In eastern Europe, people struggled just as fiercely to survive and to define sovereignty as they did in the west. However, the two regions differed sharply, and those differences affected the outcomes of battles over these issues. States east of the Elbe River (see **Map 13.2**) were less commercially developed than those in western Europe. Instead of farms worked by legally free and mobile peasants, estate agriculture (large landed estates owned by lords and worked by their serfs) dominated those economies. By the sixteenth century, the nobles who owned these estates had reversed the medieval trends toward greater freedom for the peasantry and the growth of towns. Most people who worked the fields sank into serfdom, bound to the land and owing ever-increasing services to their lords. The middle classes in the towns also declined, failing to gain in numbers and wealth like their counterparts in western Europe. Finally, most central governments at the beginning of the seventeenth century proved weaker than those in western European states, as powerful nobles retained much independence. Despite all this, several monarchs decided to change things in their own favor.

Centralizing the State in Brandenburg-Prussia

In Brandenburg-Prussia, the "Great Elector" Frederick William (r. 1640–1688) inherited a scattered patchwork of poorly managed lands weakened by years of war and population decline. He faced a number of other problems as well. His army was tiny—too weak to keep foreign forces out of his lands or to discipline internal opponents. His nobles, or Junkers, had an independent streak and had found ways to avoid most taxes. Finally, his cities remained uncooperative, asserting their long-established political and economic independence.

Frederick William set out to correct the situation. He believed that the key was to strengthen his standing army. Only then could he gain control of his lands and make Brandenburg-Prussia a desired ally in international affairs. During the 1640s, he more than tripled the size of his army. This new strength and effective diplomacy won him several new territories at the end of the Thirty Years' War (see **Map 13.2**). With energy and skill, he next centralized and administered the governments of his fragmented holdings—while continuing to boost the size of his army. He prevailed over the **Estates**—the representative assemblies of the realm—and acquired the crucial authority to collect taxes. He then used his newly powerful army to enforce tax payments and organize state resources. In a pivotal compromise with landed aristocrats, he allowed them complete control over their serfs in return for support and service in his bureaucracy and army. Through mercantilistic policies, he protected industries, improved communications, and promoted agriculture. Though Frederick William could not afford a lavish court like that of Louis XIV, his policies ratcheted up his power. "Hold fast to the eminence of your superior position . . . [and] rely on your own strength," he advised his son. At the Great Elector's death in 1688, Brandenburg-Prussia was well on the road to becoming a major player in European politics. He also left a legacy of military values and reliance on armed might that would influence much of Prussia's subsequent history.

In 1701, his son, Frederick I (r. 1688–1713), increased the dynasty's status by acquiring the title of King of Prussia in return for helping the Holy Roman Emperor in a war against France. He used state revenues to turn his Berlin court into a great social and cultural center. By his death in 1713, Brandenburg-Prussia had become a respected force in eastern Europe.

Austria Confronts the Ottomans and Expands Its Control

Austria's Leopold I (r. 1657–1705), facing extreme local, language, and ethnic differences within his diverse lands, could not hope to acquire the same power as that enjoyed by Louis XIV in France or even Frederick William in Prussia. Localities retained considerable autonomy, especially in matters of taxation. The practical Leopold focused on securing his own Habsburg lands, rather than cementing the minimal control he had over the Holy Roman Empire, and allied himself closely with the Catholic Church. He gained the allegiance of the nobles by making them his chief advisors and granting them rights to

thinking about
GEOGRAPHY

MAP 13.2

Central and Eastern Europe, 1648

This map shows the border between the western and eastern agrarian zones, running from the mouth of the Elbe River south to Trieste on the Adriatic Sea.

Explore the Map

1. Which states lay to the east of this border?

2. What did this dividing line imply about social differences between eastern and western European states at the time?

3. What problems did these differences pose for eastern European states such as Austria and Brandenburg-Prussia, which controlled provinces to the west of this line?

exploit lands and the peasants on them. Some peasants revolted, but as elsewhere in Europe, they did not pose a serious challenge to authorities. With the help of Poland's king, Jan Sobieski (r. 1674–1696), Leopold also fought the Ottoman Turks, who controlled most of Hungary as part of their large and still-powerful empire.

During the fifteenth and first half of the sixteenth century, the Ottomans had enjoyed great power and relative prosperity. The sultans in Istanbul, wielding secular and religious authority, ran a strong autocratic state that could compete with any European power. Increasingly, they struggled to maintain authority in

The Ottomans

the face of competition from bandit armies, mutinous army officers, and squabbling elites, but seventeenth-century Ottoman rulers managed to maintain control. In 1683, Ottoman armies pushed into Austrian lands and laid siege to the capital, Vienna. Leopold and Sobieski's forces saved the city, however, and then brought most of Hungary under Austrian control (see **Map 13.3**). The loss shocked Ottoman elites, and for good reason. From that point on, the empire ceased to expand, and during the following decades, the Ottomans' sources of wealth dried up. Moreover, the military weaponry and tactics of Ottoman armies and navies lagged behind those of their European foes. Ottoman power and imperial leadership would deteriorate further as weakened rulers struggled against political corruption, provincial revolts, and military insubordination.

After his victory in Vienna, the Austrian king tried to install his own nobility in Hungarian lands and ally himself with powerful Hungarian nobles at the expense of the peasantry. He succeeded only partially, and the still-independent Hungarian nobles remained a thorn in the side of the Austrian monarchy. Facing west, Leopold helped build a coalition that stood against Louis XIV. By the Austrian king's death in 1705, the Habsburg state had become one of the most powerful in Europe.

Russia and Its Tsars Gain Prominence

Even farther east, the Russian monarchy slowly rose to prominence. Already in the sixteenth century, Ivan IV ("the Terrible") (r. 1533–1584) had added both to the authority of the Russian tsars (caesars, or emperors) and to the span of territories over which they ruled. He destroyed the remaining power of the Mongols in southeastern Russia and annexed most of their territory. Next, he began Russia's conquest of Siberia. Within his expanding state, Ivan ruled as a ruthless autocrat, creating his own service gentry to bypass powerful nobles and using torture and terror to silence all he saw as his opponents.

A difficult period known as the Time of Troubles (1584–1613) followed Ivan IV's death. Ivan's feeble-minded son Fyodor ruled ineffec-tively and left no successor upon his death in 1598. Great nobles vied for power among themselves and against weak tsars. To end the political chaos, a group of leading nobles in 1613 chose the 17-year-old Michael Romanov (r. 1613–1645) to rule as tsar. He began a dynasty that ruled Russia for over three hundred years.

| The Romanovs |

Despite the political stability Michael and his immediate successors brought, discontent among those below the tsar and the nobility mounted during the century as the authorities increasingly restricted the freedom of the masses. The notorious Law Code of 1649, for example, merged peasants and slaves into a class of serfs and gave the landowning nobility the power to treat them as property. In a spate of uprisings between the late 1640s and early 1670s, the lower classes rebelled against landowners and officials by killing them and looting or burning their estates. The discontent reached a climax in the late 1660s and early 1670s with the revolts of Cossacks (free warriors) in south Russia led by Stenka Razin. A shrewd, seasoned warrior, Razin claimed to "fight only the boyars and the wealthy lords. As for the poor and the plain folk, I shall treat them as brothers." His rebel army marched north, and many towns opened their gates to welcome Razin's forces, now swelling with the addition of discontented peasants and the urban poor. Russian soldiers finally caught, tortured, and executed Razin, and the uprisings tapered off.

By the final decades of the seventeenth century, the Romanov tsars had shored up the government's central administration and extended their authority throughout the country. Lured by visions of wealth from access to Siberian furs, Russians had driven eastward into Asia, establishing fortified settlements, bringing indigenous peoples under their control (in the process decimating them with raids and diseases such as smallpox), and planting their flag on the shores of the Pacific. Moreover, through increased trade and travel, Russia's commercial and cultural contacts with the West expanded, bringing new European goods and ideas into the country. The stage was set for a dynamic tsar to propel Russia more fully into European affairs.

| Russian expansion |

This new, energetic emperor came in the person of Peter I ("the Great") (r. 1689–1725). Standing nearly seven feet tall, Peter seemed born to rule. At the age of 17, he seized the reins of government from his elder sister. He soon concluded that the best way to bolster his own political and military power was to copy Western practices. To this end, he traveled to western Europe and learned as much as he could about Western politics, customs, and technology.

| Peter the Great |

Back home, Peter took decisive steps to solidify his authority. In 1698, he crushed a revolt of his bodyguards and silenced critics with a ruthlessness that cowed all potential troublemakers. "Every day was deemed fit and lawful for torturing," wrote an observer. He also made five years of education away from home and state service requirements for the nobility and allowed movement within the ranks only through merit. Peter applied the bureaucratic system of western European monarchs to both central and local government to secure his rule. He also brought Western technicians to Russia in large numbers and protected new industries with mercantilistic policies. Western social customs were introduced to the upper

MAP 13.3

Central and Eastern Europe, 1640–1725

This map shows the changing political landscape in central and eastern Europe during the seventeenth and early eighteenth centuries.

Explore the Map

1. Notice how Russia's expansion to the west increased its contacts with European commerce and affairs.

How might these widening interactions alter the balance of power in Europe?

2. Consider the gains made by the Austrian Habsburgs against the Ottomans. What did the declining fortunes of the Ottoman Empire imply for the future of this part of the Western world?

3. Locate Poland-Lithuania. What problems did this country face, hemmed in as it was by three growing powers?

and middle classes of Russian society, such as bringing Russian women out of seclusion to appear in Western dresses at official dinners and social gatherings. In addition, Peter banned the long beards and flowing Oriental robes that Russian men traditionally wore. When the patriarch of the Russian Orthodox Church opposed the tsar's authority and some of his Westernizing policies, Peter took control of the church and confiscated much of its wealth. Henceforth, the Orthodox Church served as a powerful instrument of the Russian government.

All these reforms left the peasantry in even worse straits than before. Peasants made up 97 percent of Russia's population during Peter's

> **Russia's military establishments**

reign, and they became tied down in a system of serfdom bordering on slavery. The taxes they were forced to pay ballooned by a whopping 500 percent, and their feudal obligations and military service increased. Nowhere was peasant life harsher than in Russia, and Peter's efforts to Westernize the nobility only widened the gap between the educated elites and the enserfed peasantry. "The peasants are perfect slaves, subject to the arbitrary power of their lords," wrote a British envoy to Peter's court. They are usually "transferred with goods and chattels; they can call nothing their own."

To keep Russia in step with the West and support his ambitions for territorial expansion, Peter devoted particular attention to his military establishment. He built a navy and patterned his expanded and modernized conscript army on the model of Prussia. Recruits were drafted for life and even branded with a cross on their left hand to deter desertion. Officials arbitrarily assigned serfs to work in mines and manufacturing establishments to supply the military with equipment and arms.

Peter meant to use his new military might. **Figure 13.6** depicts the clean-shaven tsar Peter the Great in heroic military pose. Clad in armor and carrying a sword, Peter asserts his authority over all potential rivals, who offer him their swords. Beneath the feet of his horse lies a defeated dragon. Above, an angel crowns Peter with divine authority. The tsar waged numerous military campaigns over his long reign, and he designed many of his great reforms to strengthen and modernize his armed forces. In the background of the painting, his troops surge to victory in a mighty battle.

Lacking warm-water access to the West, Peter tried to seize lands bordering the Black Sea that the Ottoman Turks held. Though they had weakened during the seventeenth century, the Ottoman Turks

FIGURE 13.6 Anonymous, *The Apotheosis of Tsar Peter I the Great* The painter portrayed the Russian tsar as a heroic, all-conquering military figure who is blessed with divine authority.

remained a formidable obstacle, and Peter's armies could not dislodge them. Frustrated, Peter turned northwest toward Sweden, which controlled lands bordering the Baltic Sea. Under King Gustavus Adolphus (r. 1611–1632), this Nordic country had become the dominant military power

> **Conflict with Sweden**

in northeastern Europe in the early seventeenth century (see Chapter 11). At the opening of the eighteenth century, Sweden held large areas east and south of the Baltic in addition to the homeland, and it ranked second only to Russia in size. Much of its success and the power of its monarchs came from the almost constant wars it fought during the seventeenth century. However, it lacked the population and resources to hold its far-flung territories for very long. Though Peter initially lost battle after battle to his brilliant Swedish adversary, Charles XII (r. 1697–1718), his persistence finally paid off. In the Battle of Poltava (1709), the Russians destroyed the Swedish army and managed to wound Charles.

GLOBAL CONNECTIONS

The Rise and Fall of the Mughal Empire in India

While monarchs in Europe struggled to consolidate their authority during the seventeenth century, powerful rulers rose in the Asian states. These emperors would become strong enough to rival the Western powers and control relations with European traders. The Asian leaders had a proud history. During the sixteenth century, the Mughals (Moguls), a fierce Islamic Turkish tribe, had swept into the Indian subcontinent and established a flourishing realm ruled by able emperors such as Babur (1483–1530) and Akbar (1542–1605).

In 1605, the 38-year-old Jahangir succeeded the great Mughal leader Akbar and assumed the title of "the world-subduing emperor." In his memoir, he described the lavish ceremonies accompanying his crowning. During the festivities, the high officials of the empire, "covered from head to foot in gold and jewels, and shoulder to shoulder, stood round in brilliant array, also waiting for the commands of their sovereign."

By that time, the Portuguese had already established a flourishing trading base on the west Indian coast. As the seventeenth century unfolded, the Mughals also allowed the English, French, and Dutch to establish trading bases in India, but without power to be of any concern. The Mughals themselves paid little attention to foreign trade but welcomed the revenues from the commerce into their treasuries.

Though Jahangir wielded power arbitrarily, he also felt compelled to follow certain traditions and laws. In his view, to bring "prompt punishment to the man who violates the laws of his country is an alternative with which no person entrusted with the reins of power is authorized to dispense." Jahangir also struggled to bring unruly sections of his empire more firmly under his control, at one time ordering a bloody campaign against rebellious Afghans. The Mughal emperor recorded how prisoners from one battle were paraded before him "yoked together, with the heads of the seventeen thousand slain in the battle suspended from their necks." Reflecting on the burdens of office, Jahangir lamented, "There is no pain or anxiety equal to that which attends the possession of sovereign power, for to the possessor there is not in this world a moment's rest." Nevertheless, the emperor gave his wife, Nur Jahan, a major role in running the government. He also managed to find time to support and enjoy sports, literature, and art as well as to smoke opium regularly. He completed his *Memoirs* before his death in 1627.

An eventual successor, Aurangzeb, became Mughal emperor in 1658 and held power for almost fifty years. One of his chroniclers, Bakhta'war Khan, claimed it was "a great object with this Emperor that all Muslims should follow the principles of the religion." The biographer also boasted that his emperor "has learned the Qur'an by heart."

But Aurangzeb's reign marked both the apex of Mughal power and the beginning of its end. By the time of his death in 1707, reckless spending, endless military campaigns, and persecution of Hindus and Sikhs had weakened the regime. Widespread rebellions broke out, which Aurangzeb's weaker successors failed to overcome. In the 1720s, one observer, Khafi Khan, reported that many townships "have been so far ruined and devastated that they have become forests infested by tigers and lions, and the villages are so utterly ruined and desolate that there is no sign of habitation on the routes."

As the Mughal empire disintegrated, rivals quickly took power. European traders also gained influence—especially the British and French, who were competing for the Indian trade in textiles, spices, and sugar. By the mid-eighteenth century, the land controlled by Aurangzeb's successors had dwindled to Delhi. Meanwhile, the British and French forged strategic political alliances with Indian states and jockeyed for a dominant position on the subcontinent.

Making Connections

1. What were the similarities between the European and Mughal monarchs, particularly Louis XIV of France and Aurangzeb of India?

2. What policies weakened their respective states?

Through the Treaty of Nystad in 1721, Russia received the Swedish Baltic provinces and some Polish territories (see **Map 13.3**). On the shores of the Baltic Sea, Peter triumphantly built a modern capital, St. Petersburg, that faced west. Reigning from this new court, he emulated the cultured, royal ways of the West to enhance his personal authority. At his death in 1725, Russia had taken its place as a major player on the European stage.

The Victory of the Nobility in Poland

Not all the eastern European states drifted toward monarchical absolutism. In Poland, the competition between the monarchy and the nobility took a different turn—with severe consequences for the nation. In the sixteenth and seventeenth centuries, Poland seemed poised to become a major power. Taking advantage of Russia's Time of Troubles (1584–1613), the Poles had captured Moscow for a few years until the Russians finally drove them out in 1613. In reality, however, the Polish nation, which included Lithuania in a dual kingdom, was far from strong. Sprawling over a large area between Russia and the German states, it had no natural, protective boundaries either to the east or to the west. Ethnic and religious divisions undermined the Polish rulers' hopes for unity, and the economy stumbled. In the late Middle Ages, a sizable overland commerce between the Black and Baltic seas had flowed across Poland. However, with the shifting of commercial routes and centers to the west in the sixteenth century, Poland's commerce withered. Worse, the Polish nobility, protective of its own power and fearful of an alliance between merchants and the king, deliberately penalized merchants by passing legislation to restrict trade. The great mass of the Polish people remained serfs, bound to the estates of the powerful nobility.

In the face of such forces, only a strong central government could have ensured stability for Poland. Yet this was precisely where Poland proved weakest. For many years, Poland's nobles had been gaining the upper hand, and they closely guarded their power to elect the king. When King Sigismund II died in 1572, ending the long-ruling Jagellon dynasty, the nobles saw to it that no strong king ascended the throne. They monopolized the legislative body (the Diet) and, to safeguard their rights, required a unanimous vote to pass any measure. This system guaranteed political anarchy in which, in the words of a mid-seventeenth-century observer, "there is no order in the state," and "everybody who is stronger thinks to have the right to oppress the weaker."

Over the course of the seventeenth century, revolts by Ukrainian Cossack warriors and wars with Russia, Sweden, and Brandenburg-Prussia resulted in the loss of Polish territories. Rivalries among the Polish nobles worsened the chaos. Moreover, Tatar slave raiders carried off many people. Incursions and internal wars destroyed towns, and the once-thriving Jewish populations were pushed from their homes and often slaughtered. Tens of thousands of Jews were murdered in the pogroms (organized persecutions) that swept through Poland between 1648 and 1658. Protestants also suffered at the hands of the Catholic majority. Not surprisingly, Poland's population declined sharply in these years. By the beginning of the eighteenth century, it lay vulnerable to surrounding powers that boasted stronger central governments.

THE TRIUMPH OF CONSTITUTIONALISM

As the tendency toward absolutism intensified in central Europe, another major struggle began to unfold in a small island nation far to the west. Kings desiring absolute power in England faced a situation significantly different from that in France. In France, the nobility had little history of common action between classes and lost their solitary struggle against absolutism. In England, however, there had been a tradition of joint parliamentary action by nobles and commoners who owned land, and this helped contribute to a different outcome in the struggle for sovereignty. Instead of government residing in the person of an absolute monarch, it rested in written law—constitutions, not kings, would come to rule.

The Nobility Loses Respect

For over one thousand years, the English had taken for granted the idea of separate social classes. Peasants and members of the middle classes showed the high nobility an unmistakable deference, turning out to greet them when they emerged, gazing downward and holding their hats respectfully in their hands. Even upwardly mobile landowners with some wealth (the gentry) knew that they ranked well below the peers (the old nobility). In England, there were only about four hundred noble families, and they jealously guarded their exclusive position. Commentators wrote that "nobility is a precious gift" and accepted this privilege as the natural order of things: "Men naturally favor nobility."

At the beginning of the seventeenth century, several disturbing incidents pointed to ominous cracks in the wall of privilege. One member of the gentry actually jostled and swore at an earl as the two passed in a narrow passageway, and some tenant farmers neglected to turn out, hats in hand, to welcome passing noblemen. Later, a Protestant sect, the Quakers, enacted a religious policy that forbad members to take off their hats to men in authority. Something had changed and nobles no longer seemed so essential or so noble.

What explained this apparent loss of respect for the English upper crust? We can find a partial answer in the shifting role of money. In the early modern world, the old wealth of the nobility had declined relative to the "new money" of merchants and other enterprising individuals. Furthermore, the medieval base of noble power, the military, had also declined. No longer were nobles in charge of defending the realm; mercenary armies made up of commoners now took care of these matters. England had a relatively large sector of independent craftsmen compared to other countries, and noblemen depended

New wealth

more on "free labor"—that is, on wage laborers who could enter into contracts for their labor. These differences led commoners increasingly to feel they could control their own lives rather than defer to their "betters." In addition, education had become the key to upward mobility. More and more, knowledge and service, rather than birth, seemed the measure of a man.

The members of the nobility did not relinquish their traditional place easily. Indeed, critics complained that noblemen were becoming more arrogant than ever in exerting their privileges. Sometimes, nobles even exceeded the bounds of propriety. In 1635, the Earl of Arundel lost his temper when the mayor of a city did not turn out to greet him in the traditional way. The earl sought out the mayor, grabbed his staff of office, and proceeded to beat him with it, shouting, "I will teach you to . . . attend Peers of the Realm!"

As early as the sixteenth century, laws throughout Europe had begun to supplement tradition in keeping the social classes separate, and the situation in England was no different. Governments issued **sumptuary laws** to regulate what kinds of clothing were appropriate for members of each social class. For example, an individual could not wear velvet unless he had an independent income of over 100 pounds a year, and laborers could not wear cloth costing more than 2 shillings a yard. These laws were supposed to preserve social distinction, but the newly rich recognized that the path to gaining social respect lay in part in *looking* noble. Thus, men and women insisted on purchasing luxurious clothing to rival that of the highest classes. In 1714, a Sicilian traveler observed: "Nothing makes noble persons despise the gilded costume so much as to see it on the bodies of the lowest men in the world." Now, it seemed, there was no visual marker of a person's noble status.

The nobles had more success in guarding their property rights than their fashion privileges. In 1671, Parliament passed game laws giving the nobility the exclusive prerogative to hunt on their own lands. The new mandates even allowed them to set lethal trapguns to kill poachers. Not surprisingly, these laws only exacerbated the common people's anger, as the poor continued to poach simply to survive in times of hunger. Still, many members of the nobility tried to hang on to their privilege while others pressed to undo them.

The portrait of James Stuart, a member of the royal family, shown in **Figure 13.7** captures the arrogance and complacency of the typical English nobleman of 1630, who was oblivious to the gathering social storm that would soon disrupt his idyllic world. James stands proudly dressed in the opulent clothing of the nobility that the sumptuary laws carefully tried to preserve.

Sumptuary laws

FIGURE 13.7 Anthony Van Dyck, *James Stuart, Duke of Richmond and Lennox,* **ca. 1630** The English nobility worked to set themselves apart from lesser folk in their appearance and privileges. Here, James Stuart is shown in the lavish clothing that only the noble could wear, accompanied by the giant dog that accompanied him in the hunt, another privilege reserved for the nobility.

His stockings are made of the finest silk, and the lace at his throat is expensive and handcrafted. Adorning his jacket sleeve is a sun image embroidered in silver thread—an early forerunner of Louis XIV's trademark symbol. The painting portrays James with his huge hunting dog, again proclaiming his privileged position through his hunting rights. The dog gazes up adoringly at his master with the kind of deference that James had come to expect. Sadly for members of the nobility, they would receive fewer and fewer admiring glances from their fellow humans.

Protestantism Revitalized

A good deal of social criticism also came from Protestants, many of whom believed that the implementation of Reformation ideas in England had not gone far enough. Because many Protestants were involved in the increasingly lucrative commerce, their wealth helped make their concerns more visible. For many, the compromise of Elizabeth I (discussed in Chapter 11) that allowed worshipers of many beliefs to share one Church of England was unacceptable. These critics believed that the Church of England (the Anglican Church) should be "purified"—that is, trimmed of any practice that lacked biblical precedent or smacked of Catholicism. They especially objected to priestly garments and the elaborate rituals of the Anglican Church. Some wanted to eliminate bishops altogether, preferring rule by church elders instead. (This was the practice common in Scotland, where Protestant churches came to be called Presbyterian—"ruled by elders.")

In their zeal, many Protestants became increasingly anti-Catholic, and their political actions were shaped by this prejudice. Other Protestants even wanted to purify daily life, objecting to theater, cockfights, and other seemingly frivolous activities. Although individuals disagreed among themselves on exactly how they wanted the Church of England purified, they all concurred that change was essential. Many members of this loose group of critics, called **Puritans,** became influential members of Parliament.

Puritans in England reconsidered the political relationship between monarchs and their subjects, wondering about competing loyalties between law and conscience, for example. These questions formed the backdrop of a struggle for sovereignty that dominated the seventeenth century. As early as 1561, the Scottish reformer John Knox warned Queen Mary of Scotland that monarchs were responsible to their subjects: "If their princes exceed their bounds, Madam, no doubt they may be resisted, even by power." This was tantamount to a call to revolution. As Puritans gathered to discuss the purification of the church, they could not help but consider the possibility of political action.

James I Invokes the Divine Right of Kings

Because Queen Elizabeth I had died childless, the throne went to her cousin, the king of Scotland, who became King James I of England (r. 1603–1625). As soon as James heard of Elizabeth's death, he rushed to England brimming with great plans. He made promises to many who greeted him on his way south to London, rapidly knighted thousands of gentry, and even ordered an accused thief hanged without a trial—assuming incorrectly that as king he had the right to do so. Many of his subjects turned out to see their affable new monarch, but, unfortunately for him, he would not prove as popular, or as politically shrewd, as Good Queen Bess.

The honeymoon of the new monarch and his people faded rather quickly, for unlike his predecessor, he was unable to mollify the varying religious beliefs of his people. He was a Calvinist, yet he favored Anglicanism, and his most enduring heritage was the translation of the Bible he commissioned, the King James Bible, which remains widely admired as both religion and beautiful literature. However, the king managed to offend his subjects who hoped for his support for religious change. At the beginning of his reign, Calvinists approached the king, hoping to eliminate the Anglican episcopal system and bring it in line with the Presbyterian Scottish practice with which the king was familiar. They were sadly disappointed, for James threatened to "harry them out of the land" if they did not conform to Anglicanism.

Religious problems

James also offended his Catholic subjects, banning Jesuits and seminary priests. In 1605, a conspiracy of Catholics planned to blow up Parliament while it was in session. The plot failed and the conspirators were executed. Yet, the "gunpowder plot," as it came to be known, increased the anti-Catholic feelings in the country, which were exacerbated when James planned a political marriage between his son and a Catholic Spanish princess. Although the marriage negotiations fell through, the attempt alienated Calvinists and Anglicans alike.

Thus by 1610, there was much animosity between the king and many of his subjects. James thought the English ungrateful, and they found him arbitrary and arrogant. Unlike Elizabeth before him, James was disinclined to compromise his theoretical notions of divine right monarchy. Even before he ascended the throne, James had written two treatises in which he asserted the divine right of kings, and in 1610 he presented this position to a skeptical Parliament. As he put it, "Kings have power of . . . life and death; [they are] judges over all their subjects and in all causes, and yet accountable to none but God." This position was consistent with his hasty execution of the accused thief, but it offended many Puritans in the House of Commons, as well as many lords who viewed the king as subject to the law of the land.

Divine right

During James's rule, the English colonies in North America grew. In part, the attention to the New World stemmed from James's financial difficulties: The first permanent English colony, named Jamestown after the monarch, was founded in Virginia in 1607. James hoped to generate new income from the Virginia colonies, which in 1619 had imported slaves from Africa to grow tobacco, an increasingly popular crop. Colonial settlement was also forwarded by James's high-handed attitude toward religious dissidents. When the king threatened to harry nonconformists out of the land, some took him literally and emigrated to North America to establish colonies.

Colonies

They avoided Jamestown, which was sympathetic to the Church of England, and instead landed farther north, founding their first colony in Plymouth, Massachusetts, in 1620. The New World was not to be the solution to either James's religious or fiscal problems. He died leaving a shortage of money and an oversupply of ill will among both Parliament and Protestants.

Charles I Alienates Parliament

James's son, Charles I (r. 1625–1649), inherited both his father's rule and his policies. This sober monarch, continuing to invoke the divine right of kings, considered himself answerable only to God, not Parliament. His relationship with his subjects deteriorated rapidly. He approached Parliament in the same way his father had—calling it when he needed money and disbanding it when the members demanded concessions.

Showing a remarkable insensitivity to his Protestant subjects, Charles married a sister of the Catholic king Louis XIII of France. Soon after his wedding, Charles granted concessions to English Catholics, even allowing the queen and her entourage to practice Catholic rituals in the court itself. English Protestants were horrified at what they saw as outrageous behavior by the family of the titular head of the Church of England. Charles responded to critics by persecuting Puritans, whom he viewed as disloyal. More Puritans fled to North America, settling so many colonies in the northeast that the region came to be called New England. Meanwhile, the situation in old England grew more desperate.

> **Concessions to Catholics**

As we saw in Chapter 11, warfare had become extremely expensive, and Charles's costly and fruitless wars with Spain and France had so strained his finances that he even tried to pawn the crown jewels. The king called Parliament several times in the 1620s, only to disband it repeatedly. Things came to a head in 1640, when the Scots, who also objected to the king's high-handed religious policies, invaded the north of England. To raise the army and funds he needed to fight the Scots, Charles called Parliament again. This time, Parliament forced him to agree that he could not disband it without the members' consent. The first crack in Charles's armor of divine right had appeared. The Long Parliament, as it came to be called, continued to meet from 1640 to 1653. Over time, it acquired a measure of power and established protections for the religious freedom of Anglicans and Puritans alike.

> **Parliament gains power**

However, the temporary compromise between the king and Parliament came to an end when troubles in Ireland caused both to agree to send troops. However, their alliance ended there. The question of who would command the army remained. Parliament did not trust the king to suppress his religious sympathies to fight the Catholic Irish, and the king did not trust Parliament to share control of any army it raised. In the end, Parliament appointed officers to raise an army, and Charles withdrew from London to raise an army of his own. The Irish no longer seemed the immediate enemy for either side.

"God Made Men and the Devil Made Kings": Civil War, 1642–1649

As **Map 13.4** shows, the alignments in the English civil war show some divisions in English life. The rural areas were more likely to support the king, and the Puritan strongholds in the cities followed the forces of Parliament. In response to Charles's call for support, noblemen, cavalry officers, and Irish Catholics rallied to his banner. His royalist supporters were called Cavaliers, or horsemen, as a reference to medieval knights who fought for their kings. Back in London, Parliament recruited an army 13,000 strong, drawn from the commoners, merchants, a few noblemen, Scots, and Puritans. All these generalizations, however, are drawn in broad strokes, and frequently the choice to support one side or another derived from private decisions, based sometimes on religion and sometimes on long-standing personal grudges against neighbors.

The strength of the parliamentary forces, called **Roundheads** for their short haircuts, stemmed mainly from their skilled infantry, the support of major sections of the navy, and their religious conviction. Parliament's forces also benefited from the leadership of Oliver Cromwell, a Puritan who not only forwarded the cause of revolutionary change in Parliament but also took charge of the army and forged it into a formidable force called the New Model Army. The royalists had more experience in battles and more skilled generals. The lines were drawn—the royalist forces led by the king fought a civil war against the forces led by Cromwell.

By 1646, Parliament forces had won a series of victories, and Charles surrendered to the Scots, who later turned him over to Parliament in exchange for their back military pay. While the king was moved from prison to prison as royalists conspired to free him, leaders of Parliament confronted new challenges: a series of social upheavals as more and more people were drawn into the turbulent events of the 1640s.

> **Charles captured**

Women from all social groups participated in unprecedented numbers in the English civil war. In their husbands' absence, a number of noblewomen defended their fortified castles against parliamentary

> **Women in war**

forces, inspiring many accounts of great heroics considered surprising in the "weaker sex." Working women disguised as men also passed themselves off as Roundhead soldiers. In 1643, Charles issued a proclamation intending to prevent women from joining the army: "Let no woman presume to counterfeit her sex by wearing man's apparel under pain of the severest punishment which law shall inflict." However, the king was in no position to enforce this edict, and women continued to serve as soldiers. It is impossible to know exactly how many women fought for their cause, but the fact that Charles tried to legislate their exclusion suggests that at least he and his advisors thought the numbers significant.

Women were well suited as spies, because people expected them to be noncombatants. One such woman, Jane Whorwood, dedicated herself fiercely to the king's cause. The tall redhead repeatedly tried to free Charles during his imprisonment after 1646. She smuggled money to him and once brought in acid to weaken the metal bars so that he could break free. One of Charles's aides described Whorwood as "the most loyal person to King Charles I in his miseries."

Other previously uninvolved members of society also jumped into the fray. After 1646, radicals, both men and women, raised new **Levellers** demands for social justice. Their complaints stemmed mostly from the severe economic problems that had hamstrung England in the 1640s. A series of bad harvests caused food shortages and rising prices, and disabled soldiers returning home discovered they could no longer earn a living. Crime increased as people stole to feed their families, and the social order deteriorated. One contemporary observed: "Necessity dissolves all laws and government, and hunger will break through stone walls." From these difficult circumstances, groups of radical Protestants arose. Known as **Levellers,** they insisted that social justice become part of Parliament's agenda. A pamphlet sympathetic to their cause claimed that "God made men and the Devil made kings."

Levellers were as varied a group as the Puritans, encompassing people with a broad array of agendas. In general, however, they harked back to a tradition of English religious radicals like John Ball (see Chapter 9) and espoused as their goal to level social differences. To that end, they advocated some reforms of Parliament. For example, they believed Parliament should be chosen by the vote of all male heads of households, which would represent a dramatic broadening of the vote. Furthermore, they wanted members of Parliament to be paid, so that even those with no independent income could serve. Although these ideas may seem natural to us, they posed a major threat to those who believed that only property brought privilege.

Controlled by the Parliamentarians, Beginning of 1645

Controlled by the Royalists, Beginning of 1645

Conquered by the Parliamentarians in 1645

★ **Battle Sites**

MAP 13.4

The English Civil War, 1642–1649

This map shows England during the civil war years, identifies the locations of the parliamentarian and royalist supporters, and pinpoints the major battles.

Explore the Map

1. Notice the scale of the map. How did the distances affect the progress of the war?

2. Why might the royalists have drawn from rural rather than urban centers?

3. Based only on the information on the map, does it seem possible for the royalists to have won without help from abroad? Explain.

The King Laid Low

In the midst of these controversies, the civil war broke out again in 1648 as Charles encouraged his supporters to rise up to free him. Cromwell's forces promptly crushed the uprisings, and some army leaders concluded that they would never come to peaceful terms with the king. With Cromwell's support, they demanded that Charles be tried for treason. The majority of Parliament members refused to take this extreme step, but in December 1648 invading soldiers purged Parliament of the cautious. The remaining members, scornfully called the Rump Parliament by opponents and historians, brought the king to trial.

The Rump Parliament tried Charles as a king, rather than deposing him first and then trying him as a private citizen. In other words, they wanted to find the *king*, not just the man, guilty. This bold act represented a direct clash between two theories of government—one claiming that the king stood above Parliament, the other declaring that he must answer to it. This unprecedented, highly public trial became the first in history to receive full press coverage. Newspapers had initially emerged in England in 1641, on the eve of the civil war; by 1649, six licensed newspapers recorded the testimony in the trial and provided differing opinions on the proceedings.

Charles was accused of claiming to rule by divine right: He who had been "trusted with a limited power to govern . . . had conceived a wicked design to . . . uphold in himself an unlimited and tyrannical power to rule according to his will. . . ." Though he genuinely believed in divine right, Charles refused to answer this or any other charge. Instead, he claimed that Parliament had no right to bring charges against him at all. He gained much popular support over the few days of the trial as he consistently reiterated his position, rising above a stutter that had plagued him all his life in order to express his views firmly and with dignity. He challenged Parliament to justify "by what power I am called hither." Both sides clearly understood the magnitude of the trial's central question: Who had sovereignty? Charles claimed that God had sovereignty and had delegated it to the king; the Puritans in Parliament claimed that they had sovereignty. There was no room for compromise, and neither side gave way. Charles was found guilty and sentenced to die.

On January 30, 1649, the condemned king was led to a scaffold erected in front of Whitehall Palace. His public execution inspired a rash of etchings and paintings. **Figure 13.8** depicts the crowds who gathered to watch, including women, whose interest in the execution seemed remarkable to contemporary commentators. Many in the crowd were sympathetic to their king. Jane Whorwood, for example, who had worked tirelessly to free Charles, ran forward to greet the king as he walked to the scaffold. **Figure 13.8** shows some of these sympathizers; note the old man in the foreground, leaning on his cane and crying, and the woman fainting in the center.

==Charles executed==

Charles bravely addressed the few people near him on the scaffold and repeated his views on sovereignty: "I must tell you that the liberty and freedom [of the people] consists in having a government. . . . It is not for having a share in government. Sir, that is nothing pertaining to them. A subject and a sovereign are clear different things." Charles then laid his head on the block, and the executioner severed it cleanly with one blow. The man on the side of the platform in **Figure 13.8** holds the king's head up to show the crowd. The monarchy had ended, and a new form of

FIGURE 13.8 Weesop, *Execution of Charles I,* 1649 During the English civil war, King Charles I was put to death. This image documents the shocking event and shows how the audience was both attracted to and repelled by this act.

government arose to take its place: a republic in which sovereignty rested with representatives of those who owned property. England called its new republic the Commonwealth.

A Puritan Republic Is Born: The Commonwealth, 1649–1660

As the Rump Parliament began to rule the republic, chaos erupted throughout the realm. The new commonwealth faced warfare outside its borders and dissension within. Fortunately, Parliament had an able champion in Oliver Cromwell (1599–1658). While Parliament ruled, Cromwell with his army controlled the policies.

Rebellions broke out in Catholic Ireland and Protestant Scotland, and Cromwell led his army to those lands, putting down the revolts so brutally that the Irish still remember his invasion with anger. However, Cromwell was effective and brought Scotland and Ireland tightly under English rule. Yet Parliament had more to worry about than just these expensive wars.

Within England, Levellers continued to agitate for social reform, and many of their leaders were imprisoned. Then, in 1649, a gathering of women entered the House of Commons bringing a petition asking for "those rights and freedoms of the nation that you promised us." One member of Parliament taunted the women, saying their public stance was "strange," to which a petitioner responded, "It was strange that you cut off the king's head." These were odd times indeed, and many wondered whether Parliament's victory in the civil war had created more disorder than it had resolved.

The 1649 cartoon in **Figure 13.9** expresses the fears of royalists and moderates alike during this difficult era and serves to illustrate the tumultuous times of the Commonwealth. In this complex image, ax-wielding men (representing the Roundheads) chop down the Royal Oak of Britain, England's longtime symbol of authority and tradition. The oak teeters, threatening to fall and take with it the Bible, the Magna Carta, and the traditional rule of law. Soldiers assist the woodsmen in destroying the tree and the order it represents. The pigs in the center symbolize the common people, being "fattened for the slaughter." Oliver Cromwell stands at the left, supervising the destruction. Below his feet is hell, although he is oblivious to how close he is to damnation. While this cartoon clearly vilifies Cromwell and all he embodied, it also reveals the disorder that had torn at England since the civil war began. Could the parliamentary forces under Oliver Cromwell resolve these fears and tensions?

Domestic distress

FIGURE 13.9 *The Royal Oak of Britain,* 1649   Royalists and moderates feared that the civil war would destroy England and its traditions. This cartoon captures these fears as it shows revolutionaries chopping down the oak, symbol of Britain, and bringing down with it religion, the Magna Carta, and other texts hanging from the tree.

Parliament seemed incapable of uniting the various constituents that demanded action after Charles's death. In 1653, when the House of Commons considered a proposal to dismantle Cromwell's large army, the general lost patience. He disbanded Parliament altogether, named himself Lord Protector of the Commonwealth of England, Scotland, and Ireland, and established a military dictatorship—the republic remained only as an ideal. Cromwell faced the same problems that had confronted Parliament and the king—foreign wars and religious struggles. A pious Puritan, Cromwell set out to make England the model of a Protestant land, banning horse races, cockfights, and even theater. He ultimately proved as intolerant of Anglicans as they had been of Puritans, and he alienated most of the population with his intrusive policies. The brief experiment with a rule purely by Parliament had failed, and a military dictatorship could not be popular in a land with such a tradition of participatory government.

Lord Protector

Who Has the Power to Rule?

Charles's trial and execution, and the disorder that followed, did not resolve the issue of who had the ultimate power in England. In 1651, the English philosopher Thomas Hobbes (1588–1679) wrote a political treatise, *The Leviathan,* that offered an answer to this question in the form of a new theory of government.

Thomas Hobbes

Perhaps shaken by the chaos of the civil war, Hobbes harbored a pessimistic view of human nature. He claimed that everyone was driven by a quest for power and that given the chance, people would try to exercise their power at the expense of their neighbors—even if it meant taking their property and their lives. In this state of nature where there was no controlling authority, Hobbes described human life as "solitary, poor, nasty, brutish and short." However, he held out a ray of hope: Humans, he explained, recognized their inability to live peacefully, so they created a social contract by which they erected a ruler above them. By this contract, subjects willingly surrendered their sovereignty to a ruler who, in turn, agreed to rule over them absolutely.

With this explanation, Hobbes reconciled the Protestant views of sovereignty—in which the people held the right to rule—with absolute monarchy, where the ruler (the king or Lord Protector) possessed sole sovereignty. In the famous frontispiece of *The Leviathan*, shown in **Figure 13.10**, Hobbes visually portrayed the benefits of his system. The ruler is shown at the top wielding the sword and scepter of absolute power. Even more significant, he comprises all the people of the land—he is the body politic. The king derives his power from his subjects, without whom he would not exist. However, with this delegated power, he presides over an orderly and peaceful countryside and village. Church, state, the army, and Parliament are all neatly ordered along the sides of the page. This tidy, comforting vision stands in stark contrast to the chaos shown in **Figure 13.9** and reveals Hobbes's hope that absolute monarchy would guarantee peace in the land.

Hobbes omitted a key point in his thesis: Absolute rule is only as effective as the ruler. Although Cromwell preserved order (albeit while offending many), he failed to develop an institution that could maintain the Puritan republic. When he died in 1658, he named his son Richard his successor. However, the young man could not lead with the same energy and fervor that his father had shown. Under pressure from members of Parliament, Richard resigned, and the right to govern again returned to the people's representatives.

The Monarchy Restored, 1660–1688

Sobered by the chaos that had followed Charles's execution, Parliament decided to reinstate the monarchy. It invited Charles II (r. 1660–1685), son of the executed king, to resume the throne. Ships sailed from England to Holland to escort the king home from his place of exile. Among those in attendance when the king returned was Samuel Pepys (see Biography on pages 442–443), an English diarist who became noted

FIGURE 13.10 Thomas Hobbes, Frontispiece of His Work *The Leviathan*, 1651 Thomas Hobbes warned that only an absolute monarchy would save people from violence, a life he famously called "nasty, brutish, and short."

for the detailed accounts he kept of events from 1660 to 1669. According to Pepys, the people of England greeted their new king with much fanfare and excitement. Charles II came home to a restored monarchy that had all the luxury that his father had enjoyed—and all the problems that had plagued this troubled institution.

Samuel Pepys devoted several pages of his diary to Charles's coronation in 1661. "So glorious was the show with gold and silver," he wrote, "that we were not able to look at it, our eyes at last being so much overcome with it." Like most of his countrymen, Pepys drank ale with wild abandon during the celebration—the years of Puritan temperance seemed to melt away in a haze of drunkenness.

Yet, not everyone got caught up in the celebration. Former Cromwell supporters saw the Restoration in a very different light. John Bunyan (1628–1688), for example, who had fought with Cromwell, was imprisoned in 1660 for preaching against the Restoration. His original sentence of three months was extended to twelve years because he refused to stop preaching.

John Bunyan

After his release in 1672, he continued to preach, and he wrote his masterpiece, *Pilgrim's Progress*, in 1678. Probably the most widely read book by an English author, *Pilgrim's Progress* tells of a hero named Christian and his search for salvation through an allegorical world. This tale of hope and confidence in the human power to prevail through times of tribulation was balanced by Bunyan's lesser-known work, *The Life and Death of Mr. Badman* (1680). In this allegory, Bunyan criticized the loose life of Restoration England by describing the journey of a man who goes straight to hell. Bunyan's works strongly suggested that the Restoration had definitely not solved the political struggles of England.

Charles II grappled with the same fiscal problems that had plagued James I and Charles I, but he had to face a Parliament that had proven its strength during the civil wars. The king was **Fiscal problems** bound by law to call Parliament at least every three years, and the members of Parliament had severely curtailed royal power over taxation. Like his predecessors, Charles needed money, and to buttress his revenues without the restrictions Parliament imposed, the new king tried to exert more control over the colonies in North America. He increased the customs duties permitted by the Navigation Acts (imposed in 1651) and fought a war with the Dutch in 1665. This conflict ended in a treaty that gave the English New York in exchange for Dutch control of Surinam in South America.

Charles's international dealings were hampered by disasters at home. In 1665, England **Plague and fire** experienced a plague of frightening intensity—70,000 people died in London alone. The following year, a devastating fire broke out in London, engulfing the city and destroying 13,000 dwellings and 87 churches, including the venerable St. Paul's Cathedral. After the fire had died out, Charles ordered the city rebuilt and hired the skilled architect Sir Christopher Wren to redesign the main buildings. Wren's masterpiece, the new St. Paul's Cathedral, still marks the London skyline.

In addition to these disasters, the issue of religion again came to the fore. Charles had Catholic sympathies, and to circumvent Parliament, he had several times turned to the Catholic king Louis XIV of France for help and money. The Protestant Parliament, wary of Charles's granting concessions to Catholics, passed the Test Act in 1673. The law required an oath of Protestant loyalties to prevent Catholics from holding public offices, but legislation could not affect the king's conscience, or alleviate Parliament's fears of Catholicism. In 1685, Charles died after converting to Roman Catholicism on his deathbed.

Charles's successor, his brother James II (r. 1685–1688), was not able to avoid direct confrontation with the Protestant Parliament. A Catholic, James demanded in vain that Parliament repeal the Test Act, and he proceeded to place Catholics in high office in violation of Parliament's law. Many English feared that James would adopt Louis XIV's policies against Protestants and even try to institute absolute rule. They may well have been right, but the members of Parliament were not going to wait and see. In 1688, when James's Catholic wife produced a Catholic heir to the throne of England, leading members of Parliament took action.

The Glorious Revolution

To preempt James, parliamentary leaders turned to the king's eldest daughter, Mary, a Protestant and the wife of William of Orange of the Netherlands. William staunchly opposed the policies of the Catholic Louis XIV, so both his politics and his religion suited the English Protestants. William gathered a fleet and an army of 14,000 men and landed in England in November 1688. He marched slowly and peacefully toward London, while most of the English population rallied to his side. Recalling Charles I's fate, James decided to flee to France "for the security of my person." Louis XIV received his Catholic counterpart with kindness.

William and Mary

The Irish Catholics did not welcome the new Protestant king. Indeed, they thought of James II as a Catholic hero, and Irish leaders conspired with James to help him retake his throne while the French king helped fund this enterprise. Early in his reign, William led an army into Ireland and ruthlessly suppressed what he saw as Catholic treason. Abandoning both Ireland and his claim to the throne, James lived out his life in lavish exile in France, leaving the Irish to bear the brunt of William's wrath. The new king

KEY DATES

ENGLISH CIVIL WAR

1625	Charles I becomes king
1629	Charles dissolves Parliament
1642	Outbreak of civil war
1649	Charles I executed
1649–1660	Commonwealth in England
1651	Hobbes, *The Leviathan*
1660	Restoration of monarchy with Charles II
1685	James II becomes king
1688	Glorious Revolution
1689	William and Mary become monarchs
1690	Locke, *Second Treatise of Government*

BIOGRAPHY

Samuel Pepys
(1633–1703)

Enterprising

Clerk,

Member of

Parliament,

and Diarist

Samuel Pepys was born in London on February 23, 1633, the fifth of eleven children. Only he and two of his siblings survived childhood. Samuel's father was a relatively modest tailor and his mother was the sister of a butcher. Nevertheless, the family had relatives who included landed gentry, lawyers, and a physician. The Pepyses were Puritans, and although Samuel uncharitably recalled his mother as "quarrelsome and feebleminded" and his father as "always needing some kind of aid," the family did provide him with the educational opportunities he needed to succeed.

As a young boy, Pepys was sent to live with an uncle and attend the same grammar school where the young Oliver Cromwell had been educated. Samuel must have seemed a promising student, for when he was about 13 he returned to London to attend St. Paul's School, a stronghold of Puritanism and classical learning. He won scholarships to attend Cambridge University and received his bachelor's degree in 1654. After graduating, he found a job as secretary to a distant relative who had taken an important position in Cromwell's new Commonwealth.

A year later, Pepys married Elizabeth, the 15-year-old daughter of a French Protestant refugee. She brought no dowry to the marriage, though Samuel was probably drawn to her beauty—throughout his diary, he repeatedly made notes about attractive women. His domestic life proved stormy, but he wrote often about being pleased with his marriage during the more harmonious times in his household. Pepys complained that Elizabeth was untidy and that she mismanaged the household. For his part, Samuel was no model husband; he always kept his wife short of money and was relentlessly unfaithful to her. He recorded the details of his infidelities and of Elizabeth's pained reactions to them. Elizabeth died young and childless in 1669, and Samuel never remarried.

Through the late seventeenth century, Pepys was an active participant and a careful chronicler of the major events of the era. While still at Cambridge, he witnessed the execution of Charles I and supported the Commonwealth as a clerk. However, he must have harbored royalist sympathies, for his political career blossomed in 1660 with the Restoration. Pepys accompanied the fleet that escorted the new monarch back to England, and his contacts on that journey ensured him a position suited to his many talents.

Pepys began his diary in 1660 and for nine years detailed the events of his times, both great and small. In this extraordinary text, we have an eyewitness account of the devastating plague that scourged London in 1665, followed by the great fire the year after. Pepys juxtaposed historical events with the most intimate details of his daily life, from the food he ate

---

reduced Ireland to colonial status and offered new opportunity for English landlords to take possession of Irish Catholic lands. Irish anger toward the English festered and would grow, but William's victory was cheered in England.

William and Parliament turned to the immediate task of establishing the legitimacy of his kingship. Parliament decided that James's flight from England constituted an abdication of the throne. The sovereignty that, according to Hobbes, the people had surrendered to their king had been returned to Parliament, who now had the right to install a new monarch. Parliament determined to clarify its relationship with the king, and in 1689 it passed a Bill of Rights firmly stating that kings were subject to the laws of the land, thus creating a constitutional monarchy—the triumph of **constitutionalism.** Within the Bill of Rights, William agreed to "deliver this kingdom from

England's Bill of Rights

popery [Catholicism] and arbitrary power" and to preserve freedom of speech, election, and the rule of law. The bill secured the position of Protestantism in England by ruling that "no person embracing Catholicism or married to a Catholic is eligible to succeed to the throne." Through this bloodless **Glorious Revolution,** Parliament had finally demonstrated that the power to rule rested with the people through their representatives, rather than absolutely with the king. After this, Parliament began to meet annually, which was a practical way to secure its authority.

Royalism Reconsidered: John Locke

Many English men and women were proud of their bloodless "revolution" that so peacefully changed their monarch, but others were uncertain about the legality of this step. The English philosopher John Locke (1623–1704) wrote an influential political

FIGURE 13.11 J. Hayls, *Samuel Pepys,* 1666

royal patronage under the reigns of Charles II and James II, but the Glorious Revolution of 1688 caused his fortunes to change. He lost the parliamentary election in 1689, and in the following year he was arrested on suspicion that he supported the deposed James II. Pepys had always been more interested in observing political events than in engaging passionately in them, and when he was released from prison he removed himself from political life. He spent the rest of his years reading, playing music, and exchanging letters with friends, including such eminent scholars as Isaac Newton. His last years were devoted to building a substantial library, which he bequeathed at his death to his alma mater, where it still remains intact and unaltered. He died peacefully in 1703.

Pepys wrote his diary in a shorthand that was used by clerks in the seventeenth century; Newton used the same shorthand for taking his notes. The four-volume, handwritten, leatherbound diary written in a forgotten code lay ignored on the library shelves until the nineteenth century. Then, an undergraduate of the college took on the gigantic task of transcribing the diary (omitting the erotic passages) and it became an instant success. Modern editions of the complete diary continue to engage readers with its direct picture of seventeenth-century England. It has ensured that Samuel Pepys will not be forgotten.

Connecting People & Society

1. How does Pepys's life reveal the impact of the Glorious Revolution and the growing power of Parliament on the individual?

2. What does this example show about the importance of educational opportunities in the seventeenth century?

to the arguments he had with his wife. He stopped keeping his diary in 1669 because his eyesight was failing him.

Pepys took an active role in political life by working in the naval office. In 1685, he was even elected to the House of Commons. He continued to receive the benefits of

---

tract—*The Second Treatise of Government* (1690)—to justify "to the world [and] the people of England" the Revolution of 1688 and proclaim the legitimacy of William. Locke did much more—he articulated a new relationship between king and subjects that provided a theoretical framework for constitutional forms of government. Like Hobbes, Locke believed that power originally rested with the people and that citizens themselves established a monarchy to keep order. However, whereas Hobbes had said that the people turned over their sovereignty completely to the monarch, Locke claimed that they retained it but created a contract of mutual obligations with their ruler. Locke argued that if the king broke the contract, the people had the right to depose him and install a new monarch, just as Parliament had done during the Glorious Revolution.

Locke's political theories were not intended to support full democracies—in his time, the "people" meant only those who owned property. He did not intend for individuals, such as the landless Levellers, to threaten property owners. Nor did he view women as sharing in the popular sovereignty of the privileged social order. Locke's highly influential rhetoric, in which he claimed natural rights of life, liberty, and property, actually applied to relatively few people in 1690. However, in time, his theory would broaden to form the basis for democracy as well as constitutional monarchy.

Parliament soon had the opportunity to exert its king-making authority once again. William and Mary died without an heir, so the crown went to James II's Protestant daughter, Anne. Queen Anne (r. 1701–1714) also died without an heir, whereby the Protestant Stuart dynasty evaporated. Parliament then passed the crown to George I (r. 1714–1727), a great-grandson of James I, who ruled the German principality of Hanover, introducing the Hanoverian dynasty

Hanover dynasty

thinking about
GEOGRAPHY

Legend:
- United Provinces in 1609
- Spanish Netherlands
- Linguistic Boundary (French/Flemish)
- Boundary of the Holy Roman Empire

MAP 13.5

The United Provinces and the Spanish Netherlands, 1609

This map shows the location of the Netherlands in Europe and its division into two separate states. Notice the scale of the map and consider how small the United Provinces were.

Explore the Map

1. How did the location of these states contribute to their wealth and importance in the seventeenth century?

2. How might the Catholic Spanish Netherlands have served as a buffer between Catholic France and Protestant United Provinces?

to England. This peaceful transition demonstrated once and for all that the struggle for sovereignty in England was over—Parliament ruled.

The Netherlands Maintain a Republic

The English nobles asserted their rights over the king by exercising their authority through a parliament that ruled over a highly centralized government. This struggle created a strong constitutional monarchy that preserved popular sovereignty while creating a state that would prove highly stable. Another way for people to preserve their sovereignty was to resist a strong central government in order to strengthen local institutions. In the seventeenth century, the Netherlands developed this political structure, which also gave power to the people instead of to absolute rulers. They instituted another form of constitutionalism that structured the government around consent of the propertied.

When the Low Countries split in 1609, the southern Catholic regions remained subject to the absolutist monarch, Philip III of Spain. **Map 13.5** shows the division of the Low Countries in 1609. The Spanish Netherlands of the south (now Belgium) formed a buffer between the United Provinces of the north and the divine right monarchy of France. In the United Provinces, which became largely Calvinist after the wars with Catholic Spain, a Protestant state developed that successfully resisted any attempts at royal absolutism.

The United Provinces—also known as the Dutch Republic—was the only major European power to maintain a republican form of government throughout the seventeenth century. Each province was governed locally by an assembly (called the State) made up of delegates from cities and rural areas. In reality, the States were dominated by an oligarchy of wealthy merchants. The union of the provinces was only a loose confederation, with each province sending deputies to the States General, a national assembly that implemented provincial assembly decisions.

Executive power at the local level was vested in governors (Stadholders) of each province. At the national level, executive power was given to the Council of State, made up of deputies drawn from the provinces.

This remarkable decentralization worked effectively for local issues but had some drawbacks for implementing foreign policy. During the 1650s, Holland—the largest province—began to take an informal lead in directing the state's foreign policy in the first two wars against England. After 1672, William III, a prince of the hereditary house of Orange, became the captain-general of the republic's military forces against France. The House of Orange had a permanent vote in the States General and served as a unifying point. However, William of Orange exercised more power once he became king of England in 1689 than he ever had in the Netherlands. Document 13.3 provides a description of the governmental structure of the Dutch Republic. The 1648 Treaty of Westphalia, which ended the Thirty Years' War (see Chapter 11), formally recognized the Republic of the United Provinces.

The United Provinces

An Ambassador Describes the Dutch Government

Sir William Temple (1628–1699) was an English diplomat who served as ambassador to the Netherlands in 1668 and again in 1674. He negotiated the marriage of William of Orange to Princess Mary of England. This political insider was an acute observer of the government of the United Provinces of the Netherlands as shown in this account.

In the first constitution of this government, after the revolt from Spain, all the power and rights of Prince William of Orange, as Governor of the Provinces, seem to have been carefully reserved. But those which remained inherent in the Sovereign, were devolved upon the assembly of the States-General, so as in them remained the power of making peace and war, and all foreign alliances, and of raising and coining of monies: in the Prince, the command of all land and sea forces, as Captain-general and Admiral, and thereby the disposition of all military commands, the power of pardoning the penalty of crimes, the chusing of magistrates upon the

nomination of the towns; for they presented three to the Prince, who elected one out of that number. Originally the States-General were convoked by the council of State, where the Prince had the greatest influence: nor, since that change, have the States used to resolve any important matter without his advice. Besides all this, as the States-General represented the sovereignty, so did the Prince of Orange the dignity, of this State, by public guards, and the attendance of all military officers; by the application of all foreign ministers, and all pretenders at home; by the splendor of his court and magnificence of his expence; supported not only by the pensions and rights of his several charges and commands, but by a mighty patrimonial revenue in lands and sovereign principalities and lordships, as well in France, Germany, and Burgundy, as in thy several parts of the Seventeen Provinces; so as Prince Henry was used to answer some that would have flattered him into the designs of a more arbitrary

power, that he had as much as any wise Prince would desire in that State; since he wanted none indeed, besides that of punishing men, and raising money; whereas he had rather the envy of the first should lie upon the forms of the government, and he knew the other could never be supported, without the consent of the people, to that degree which was necessary for the defense of so small a State against so mighty Princes as their neighbors.

SOURCE: *The Works of Sir William Temple,* vol. I (London, 1814), pp. 118–119 in *Modern History Sourcebook,* www.fordham.edu/halsall/mod/17dutch.html.

Analyze the Document

1. Which powers remained in the hands of the prince and which in the assembly of the States General?

2. How does this division of rights compare with the governmental forms described in Document 13.1?

3. What might be the strengths and weaknesses of this form of government?

What were the special circumstances that led the Netherlands to develop and maintain this strong sense of local sovereignty when other areas of Europe were moving to centralized governments? In large part, such political independence was facilitated by prosperity. The seventeenth century has been called the golden age of the United Provinces, for this small region was a tremendous European and colonial power. Amsterdam became the commercial and financial center of Europe as ships brought huge quantities of herring from the North Sea, as well as sugar, tobacco, glass, and many other items from around the world, through the bustling port.

In addition to commerce, the Dutch prospered through skilled shipbuilding that was the wonder of Europe. Not only did they design remarkable ships that could sail with fewer crew members than more traditional ships; they also built them quickly and cheaply. They obtained timber, pitch, and rigging from the

nearby Baltic regions, and they used the most modern technology for the assembly: mechanical saws, hoists for masts, and the manufacture of interchangeable parts. Contemporary witnesses were amazed to report that given two months' notice, Dutch shipbuilders could turn out a warship every week for the rest of the year. **Figure 13.12** shows an engraving of a Dutch shipyard that was the envy of the rest of Europe. It is no wonder that silver from the New World found its way into the coffers of Dutch builders.

The Dutch also grew rich from their activities as major slave traders in the New World. The population of Amsterdam grew from about 30,000 people in 1570 to 200,000 by 1660, and the growth was testimony to the wealth and opportunities people saw there. Its financial importance was secured in 1609 by the foundation of the Exchange Bank of Amsterdam, the greatest public bank in northern Europe. Europeans were astonished by the prosperity and enterprise of the Dutch.

FIGURE 13.12 Dutch Shipyard Even small states such as the Netherlands could become rich in the new global marketplace. Dutch shipbuilding was the wonder of Europe, and it was proudly depicted in many images, including this anonymous engraving.

FIGURE 13.13 Rembrandt van Rijn, *Syndics of the Cloth Guild,* **ca. 1661** The painter Rembrandt had good reason to depict these wealthy merchants, for they had given him coal to heat his house when he had fallen on hard times.

The Dutch had other elements that contributed to their resistance of absolutism. The Dutch aristocracy was not as wealthy as that of England or France, for example. Their wealth lay more in commerce than in land, so the aristocracy had more in common with the merchants of their land than they did with the landed gentry in England or with the nobility at the court of Versailles. Furthermore, in the United Provinces, the Protestant faith cultivated an ideology of moderation—rather than the aristocratic excess that marked the nobility of other states. That is not to say that the seventeenth-century United Provinces espoused notions of egalitarian democracy—the nobility were as interested in trying to increase their power as those of other countries. They were just not able to exert much centralized control over the prosperous, Protestant residents that were the wonder of Europe.

Overall, the Dutch exhibited an unusual degree of religious toleration for their time. They even allowed Catholics and Jews to practice their religions, a policy that encouraged religious refugees to flock to the Netherlands from all over Europe. These refugees greatly enriched the cultural and economic life of the republic. Not only did the United Provinces attract intellectuals, such as René Descartes from France and John Locke from England, but the open-minded assemblies stimulated the spread of ideas through the press. The United Provinces became a leading center for book publishing and transmitted ideas, even revolutionary ones, all over Europe. In 1649, for example, an anonymous pamphlet published in the Netherlands attacked Cromwell's government for not supporting the ideas of the Levellers. The pamphlet called for an "equality of goods and lands" and condemned the government that "hangs a poor man if he do steal, when they have wrongfully taken from him all his maintenance."

> Religious toleration

The refugees streaming into the Netherlands included some destitute travelers and in some ways burdened the small country. The Dutch, however, generously assisted the needy, who never sank to the same depths of hardship that faced the poor in many other European cities. In his brief stay in the Netherlands, Samuel Pepys recorded in his diary the provisions the Dutch made for the poor. He observed a guesthouse, "where it was very pleasant to see what neat preparation there is for the poor." He further noted that there were special entertainment taxes to raise money for the needy.

The wealthy middle classes treated themselves well also. For example, they commissioned paintings that depicted their unique way of life. The Dutch artist Jan Vermeer (see Chapter 12) was one of several whose talents flourished in the free Dutch environment. Even more celebrated was the Dutch artist

Rembrandt van Rijn (1606–1669), whose brilliant use of light and forceful expressiveness made him among the greatest of western European painters.

In the painting *Syndics of the Cloth Guild* (**Figure 13.13**), Rembrandt portrays the serious, successful merchants who had been chosen to manage the wealthy guild. The artist captures the proud intensity with which they work over a book on the table. In the uniformity in their clothing, they stand in striking contrast to the man in **Figure 13.7,** on page 434, who boasts luxurious designs and fabrics that set him apart from people precisely like these successful syndics. Rembrandt offered this painting to the cloth guild in thanks for their charity—the painter, who had fallen on hard times, needed coal to heat his house for the winter, and the cloth guild had provided it.

The preeminence of the Dutch began to wane by the beginning of the eighteenth century. The economies of England and France had gathered strength both in Europe and abroad and encroached on the commercial empire forged by the Dutch. Yet the two geographically small countries of England and the Netherlands had contributed much to the political development of the West. Both established the sovereignty of the people through constitutionalism—England through Parliament, and the Netherlands through local autonomy. For all their tremendous impact for the future, at the opening of the eighteenth century both nations seemed hardly whispers in a Europe dominated by strong monarchs proclaiming a divine right to rule.

LOOKING BACK *&* MOVING FORWARD

Summary   For upper-crust members of Western societies, the seventeenth century was a period of both comfort and struggle. The comfort came from these elites' continued dominance. From the beginning to the end of the century, they held most of the riches, status, and power. Those below them sometimes revolted, but the real threats came from competing colleagues and the monarch above. The efforts by monarchs to increase their power, to become "absolute" in both theory and practice, sparked intense struggles within states. In some places, such as France, Prussia, and Russia, strong monarchs offering order and stability won. In other places, such as Poland, England, and the Netherlands, powerful nobles—sometimes allied with commoners—overcame kings.

For the vast majority who toiled in the fields, the period offered struggle without much comfort. In western Europe, demands from expanding central governments for taxes and conscripts only aggravated the hardships wrought by unusually bad harvests and disease. In eastern Europe, landowning nobles added to these problems by burdening peasants under an increasingly heavy yoke of serfdom.

Thus the structure of this hierarchical society may have loosened enough for some people in western Europe to improve their lot. However, that structure only tightened in eastern Europe. For all of Europe, war, revolt, and even revolution shook societies without breaking the traditional hierarchies. Nevertheless, some traditions started to crumble. Important changes in science and thought were already afoot that would soon transform the intellectual foundations of Western society.

KEY TERMS

Great Chain of Being, *p. 416*
royal absolutism, *p. 419*
Fronde, *p. 421*
classical style, *p. 423*
Estates, *p. 427*
sumptuary laws, *p. 434*
Puritans, *p. 435*
Roundheads, *p. 436*
Levellers, *p. 437*
constitutionalism, *p. 442*
Glorious Revolution, *p. 442*

REVIEW, ANALYZE, *&* CONNECT TO TODAY

REVIEW THE PREVIOUS CHAPTERS

Chapter 11—"Alone Before God"—examines the Reformation, which shattered the unity of western Christendom, and the entwined religious and dynastic wars that followed. Chapter 12—"Faith, Fortune, and Fame"—told how several European powers expanded overseas during this same period and grew rich from the commerce developed in their colonies.

1. Analyze how the religious divisions and wars of the sixteenth and seventeenth centuries laid the groundwork for both the growth of absolutism in France and central Europe and the struggle against it in England and the Netherlands.

2. In what ways might the competition for overseas empires and the commerce that resulted have affected the power of central governments and their responsibilities? How might the Netherlands' political structure have contributed to its commercial expansion?

ANALYZE THIS CHAPTER

Chapter 13—"The Struggle for Survival and Sovereignty"—describes how kings and nobles battled for power, the resolutions of those struggles, and their impact on the millions of people outside the elites.

1. Analyze the ways monarchs tried to increase their power.

2. What groups opposed the increase in monarchical power, and what political theories were developed to support their positions?

3. In what ways might the term *absolutism* also apply to the Mughal emperors?

4. How do you explain why in some areas monarchs won the battle for sovereignty, whereas in others they lost?

5. Describe the struggles peasants throughout Europe faced during the seventeenth century. How did their conditions differ in western and eastern Europe?

CONNECT TO TODAY

Think about this chapter's account of the struggles for power between rulers and various groups, and consider the political theories that those in power developed to justify their positions.

1. Why might some people in today's world still find the idea of monarchy appealing?

2. Why would most people in the West today oppose monarchical rule? How might they justify their views?

3. What lessons from this chapter might today's political leaders do well to apply?

BEYOND THE CLASSROOM

STRESSES IN TRADITIONAL SOCIETY

Braudel, Fernand. *Civilization and Capitalism: The Structures of Everyday Life.* New York: Harper & Row, 1981. An excellent survey by an important historian that details the transformations in economic and social history.

Chartier, Roger, ed. *A History of Private Life, Vol. III: Passions of the Renaissance.* Cambridge, MA: Harvard University Press, 1989. Part of a fine series that describes the creation of the sphere of private life.

Gottlieb, Beatrice. *The Family in the Western World from the Black Death to the Industrial Age.* Oxford: Oxford University Press, 1994. A thorough survey of the transformations in family life.

Sturdy, D.J. *Fractured Europe: 1600–1721.* London: Wiley/Blackwell, 2002. A comprehensive introduction, nicely organized around regions.

ROYAL ABSOLUTISM IN FRANCE

Bercé, Yves-Marie. *The Birth of Absolutism.* London: Macmillan, 1996. A solid examination of French absolutism from the reign of Louis XIV to 1789.

Phillips, Henry. *Church and Culture in Seventeenth-Century France.* Cambridge: Cambridge University Press, 2002. Excellent analysis of French culture and its connections with the Catholic Church.

Treasure, Geoffrey. *Louis XIV.* London: Longman, 2001. A well-written study of the king and his times.

THE STRUGGLE FOR SOVEREIGNTY IN EASTERN EUROPE

Goffman, Daniel. *The Ottoman Empire and Early Modern Europe.* Cambridge: Cambridge University Press, 2002. An informative survey of the topic.

Hughes, Lindsey. *Russia in the Age of Peter the Great.* New Haven, CT: Yale University Press, 1998. A recent study of this important figure.

Kirby, David G. *Northern Europe in the Early Modern Period: The Baltic World, 1492–1772.* London: Longman, 1990. A good survey of the region during this period.

Wilson, Peter H. *Absolutism in Central Europe.* London: Routledge, 2000. A good comparative study of absolutism in Prussia and Austria.

GLOBAL CONNECTIONS

Richards, John F. *The Mughal Empire.* Cambridge: Cambridge University Press, 1993. A solid, useful survey of Mughal history.

THE TRIUMPH OF CONSTITUTIONALISM

Braddick, Michael. *God's Fury, England's Fire: A New History of the English Civil Wars.* New York: Penguin Global, 2009. A splendid history of the civil wars that details events and people from the earliest rebellions through the execution of Charles. Gives careful attention to all parts of the United Kingdom.

Cust, Richard. *Charles I.* Harlow, UK: Pearson, 2007. Balanced exploration of this complex man whose reign spawned the civil war.

Fraser, Antonia. *The Weaker Vessel.* New York: Knopf, 1984. A detailed, illustrated, and comprehensive study of women in seventeenth-century England.

Gaunt, Peter. *Oliver Cromwell.* Cambridge, MA: Blackwell, 1995. A good study on the life and career of the Lord Protector.

Geyl, Pieter. *History of the Dutch-Speaking Peoples 1555–1648.* Phoenix, AZ: Phoenix Press, 2001. A fine historical summary that illuminates questions of national identity and the problems of a small country functioning in the shadows of great powers.

Hill, Christopher. *A Nation of Change and Novelty: Radical Politics, Religion, and Literature in Seventeenth-Century England.* London: Routledge, 1990. A history of the revolution by an eminent historian.

Miller, John. *Restoration and the England of Charles II,* 2nd ed. White Plains, NY: Longman, 1997. Clarifies the complex issues of the major political and religious themes surrounding the Restoration.

Purkiss, Diane. *The English Civil War: Papists, Gentlewomen, Soldiers, and Witchfinders in the Birth of Modern Britain.* New York: Basic Books, 2007. Vividly illuminates the details of everyday life and the personalities of the participants in the English civil war.

Sharpe, Kevin. *Culture and Politics in Early Stuart England.* Stanford, CA: Stanford University Press, 1994. A revisionist look at the culture and politics in England at this time.

van Deursen, A.Th. *Plain Lives in a Golden Age: Popular Culture, Religion, and Society in Seventeenth-Century Holland.* Translated by M. Ultree. New York: Cambridge University Press, 1991. A fascinating analysis of how laborers, peasants, and sailors made their living.

FRONTISPIECE TO MARCO VINCENZO CORONELLI'S ATLAS, 1691

In this frontispiece from an atlas, a globe and ship occupy center stage and represent the West's exploration of the world. Just above, the banner of a trumpeting angel reads, "Yet farther"— words that contrast sharply with the traditional medieval expression "No farther." Drawings of the numerous instruments that characterized the new age of exploration and science occupy the periphery of the image.

A New World of Reason and Reform

The Scientific Revolution and the Enlightenment, 1600–1800

In 1655, French scientist Blaise Pascal (1623–1662) retired from his studies and began recording his thoughts in writing. "Man is but a reed, the most feeble thing in nature; but he is a thinking reed," he wrote. "All our dignity consists, then, in thought . . . by thought I comprehend the world." Pascal's words hint at the changes emerging in scholars' thinking about ideas, the world, and the place of humans in it.

We can detect more clues about these changes in the artwork on page 450. The 1691 world atlas itself, published by the accomplished Venetian mapmaker and mathematician Marco Coronelli (1650–1718), echoes the overseas expansion of Europe, already two centuries old. It also reveals the underlying culture of the Renaissance, which stressed learning and exploration through reading and art. Coronelli chose this illustration to open his new atlas. With the images of a ship, the earth, and scientific instruments and the provocative phrasing "Yet farther," he declared the end of limits to the search for knowledge. The entire illustration suggests a people proudly using science to fuel their growing power—over other peoples as well as nature itself.

Buoyed by the accumulation of scientific discoveries, this optimism about the power of thought and the search for knowledge grew and spread throughout the West during the eighteenth century. Widening circles of intellectuals and the reading public learned about the new ways of thinking being applied to all fields, from politics and religion to economics and criminology. Despite resistance from church and state, this dawning of what became known as the Age of Reason would gather strength, filter down through the ranks of society, and form the intellectual foundation for life in the modern West. Certainly the West was not unique in reasoning about the world. In the centuries preceding Europe's Renaissance, the Chinese had made many scholarly and scientific advances. The Arabs not only had prized learning and science but also had provided Europeans with tools such as translations of Greek science and Arabic numerals that were essential for Europe's scientists. On the other hand, by the sixteenth century most European scientists had university educations, whereas non-Western civilizations lacked institutions comparable to the medieval universities in places such as Bologna, Paris, and Oxford. Moreover, during the seventeenth and eighteenth centuries, the Islamic, Chinese, Japanese, and other civilizations of the world declined to question their traditional ways. Only Westerners challenged the standard assumptions of their civilization. The power and attitudes that the West gained from this intellectual exploration helped redefine Western civilization and distinguish it from the non-Western world.

TIMELINE

- Copernicus 1543
- Kepler 1609
- Galileo 1630
- Descartes 1640
- Newton 1687
- Locke 1691

Enlightenment 1733–1789

- Voltaire 1740
- Rousseau 1750

Age of Ideologies

French Revolution and Napoleon 1789–1815

Scientific Revolution 1543–1687

1480   1550   1620   1690   1760   1830

FIGURE 14.1 The Medieval View of the Universe, 1559
This woodcut shows the earth at the center of a stable, finite universe. A band with signs of the zodiac suggests the importance of astrology within this Christian understanding.

QUESTIONING TRUTH AND AUTHORITY

On June 22, 1633, the well-known Italian scientist Galileo Galilei (1564–1642) knelt in a Roman convent before the cardinals who served as judges of the Inquisition. The cardinals informed Galileo that he was "vehemently suspected of heresy." They also showed him the customary instruments of torture, though they did not use them. Next, they ordered him to deny "the false opinion that the sun is the center of the universe and immovable, and that the earth is not the center of the same"—views that Galileo had supported in a book he published the previous year. Threatened with being tried and burned as a heretic, Galileo had to denounce his views as heresy. The court and papacy sentenced Galileo to house arrest in Florence for the rest of his life and forbad him to publish on the topic again. Nevertheless, Galileo would not change his mind. The sequence of events leading to Galileo's trial and conviction is a story of its own, but the conflict lay at the core of a major development of the age: the Scientific Revolution.

The Old View

Until the sixteenth century, most European scholars shared the standard medieval understanding of the physical nature of the earth and the universe. This understanding was based on a long legacy stretching back to the views of the fourth-century B.C.E. Greek philosopher Aristotle. His ideas had been modified in the second century C.E. by Ptolemy of Alexandria and then passed on through Byzantine and Arab scholars to medieval European thinkers. After the thirteenth century, Europeans translated Aristotle's works into Latin and merged his thinking with Christian ideas about the universe.

According to this Christian medieval understanding, illustrated in the woodcut in **Figure 14.1,** the earth rested at the center of an unchanging universe. Around it in ascending order rose the perfect spheres of air, fire, the sun, the planets, and the stars (the firmament), with God (the prime mover) just beyond. The signs of the zodiac are recorded on one band in the illustration, revealing the importance of astrology. Westerners accounted for the succession of day and night by explaining that this finite universe rotated in precise circles around the earth once every twenty-four hours. The heavenly abode of angels consisted of pure matter, and the earthly home of humans was made of changeable, corrupt matter. This universe was clear, finite, and satisfyingly focused on the earthly center of God's concern.

Common sense supported this worldview. A glance at the sky confirmed that the sun and stars indeed circled around the earth each day. Under foot, the earth felt motionless. To careful observers, the motion of planets, whose position often changed, was more perplexing. To explain this mystery, Ptolemy and others had modified their theories, concluding that planets moved in small, individual orbits as they traveled

The earth-centered universe

predictably around the earth. People had lived by the wisdom of the ancients and authoritative interpretations of the Bible for centuries. Accordingly, investigation of the physical universe generally consisted of making deductions from these long-accepted guides.

Undermining the Old View

During the fifteenth and sixteenth centuries, new problems began undermining this traditional view. Authorities of all kinds—including Aristotle—came into question during the Renaissance. Some of this questioning stemmed from the Renaissance search for classical writings, which led scholars to discover and read the works of Greek authorities who contradicted Aristotle. **Neoplatonism,** based on the ideas of Plato, stressed the belief that one should search beyond appearances for true knowledge; truth about both nature and God could be found in abstract reasoning and be best expressed by mathematics. Neoplatonic **Hermetic doctrine** provided especially powerful alternatives to Aristotelian thought.

According to Hermetic doctrine, based on writings mistakenly attributed to Hermes Trismegistus (supposedly an ancient Egyptian priest), all matter contained the divine spirit, which humans ought to seek to understand. Among many scholars, this doctrine stimulated intense interest in botany, chemistry, metallurgy, and other studies that promised to help people unlock the secrets of nature. The Hermetic approach also held that mathematical harmonies helped explain the divine spirit and represented a crucial pathway to understanding God's physical world. This approach encouraged scholars to use mathematics and to measure, map, and quantify nature. Moreover, Hermetic doctrine also held that the sun was the most important agency for transmission of the divine spirit and thus rightly occupied the center of the universe. Finally, these beliefs fostered the idea of the natural magician who could unleash the powers of nature through alchemy (the study of how to purify and transform metals, such as turning common minerals into gold), astrology (the study of how stars affect people), and magic. Scholars often saw no distinction between seeking to understand the harmony, oneness, and spiritual aspects of the natural world and what we would call scientific observation and experimentation. Although Hermetic doctrine often proved not useful, all these ideas encouraged investigators to question traditionally accepted knowledge.

Figure 14.2, an illustration from a book on alchemy by the German Heinrich Khunrath, shows these close connections between spiritual beliefs and

Hermetic doctrine

FIGURE 14.2 Heinrich Khunrath, *The Laboratory and the Chapel,* 1609 Amid the tools of his trade, an alchemist prays in a small chapel. This seventeenth-century illustration reveals the close connections between spiritual beliefs and alchemy.

the "science" or "Hermetic art" of alchemy. At the left, the author prays in a small chapel. Lettering on the drapery of the chapel states, "When we attend strictly to our work, God himself will help us." At the center, musical instruments and a pair of scales rest on a table, representing the links among music, harmony, and numbers so characteristic in alchemy. The inscription on the table reads, "Sacred music disperses sadness in evil spirits." On the floor lie containers and other apparatus used to mix materials, and at the upper right are flasks and other storage containers.

In addition to new ideas and beliefs, geographic exploration during the Renaissance also upset traditional assumptions. The discovery of the New World, for example, disproved Ptolemaic geography. Furthermore, overseas voyages stimulated demand for new instruments and precise measurements for navigation. This demand, in turn, encouraged research, especially in astronomy and mathematics.

Exploration

Finally, the recently invented printing press enabled even out-of-favor scholars to publish their findings, which spread new ideas and discoveries even further. Renaissance rulers supported all these efforts in hopes of gaining prestige as well as practical tools for war, construction, and mining. Church authorities did the same at times, especially backing

The printing press

research in astronomy in the hopes of improving the calendar to date Easter more accurately.

Like the Renaissance, the Reformation unleashed forces that provoked the questioning of long-held views. Most researchers had religious motives for their work, though those motives were not necessarily grounded in tradition. In particular, they yearned for insights into the perfection of God's universe. As we read in Chapter 11, the Reformation shattered confidence in religious authorities. By upsetting hallowed certainties, sixteenth- and seventeenth-century scholars hoped to establish new, even sounder certainties and thereby regain a sense of mastery over nature.

DEVELOPING A MODERN SCIENTIFIC VIEW

Even with these rumblings of change, no sudden breakthrough cleared away the centuries-old understanding of nature. Most scientific work still proceeded slowly, as did scholarly and public acceptance of its findings. Investigators had to demonstrate the effectiveness of their new methods again and again to convince even their colleagues. Indeed, few scholars suggested a wholesale rejection of traditional authorities; most simply chipped away at old notions. By the end of the seventeenth century, however, an entirely new scientific view of reality, initiated by just a handful of scholars, had replaced the traditional view. To understand this startling shift, we need to trace developments in astronomy, physics, and scientific methodology.

Astronomy and Physics: From Copernicus to Newton

During the sixteenth and seventeenth centuries, astronomy and physics attracted the most systematic attention from scholars. Researchers in these fields became particularly dissatisfied with the inability of Aristotelian theory to explain, simply and efficiently, careful observations and mathematical calculations of the stars. The Ptolemaic system for predicting planetary movements seemed overly complex and cumbersome to these scholars. Their findings would dramatically alter Westerners' perceptions of nature and of the earth's place in the universe. As the English poet John Donne complained in 1611, "New philosophy calls all in doubt."

Nicolaus Copernicus (1473–1543), a Polish clergyman with an interest in astronomy, astrology, mathematics, and church law, took the first steps in this intellectual adventure. Like so many other northern European scholars, he crossed the Alps to study in an Italian university. There he became influenced by the rediscovery of Greek scholarship, Neoplatonism, and the Hermetic doctrine.

Nicolaus Copernicus

FIGURE 14.3 Andrea Cellarius, *The Copernican System,* 1661 This page from Cellarius's *Celestian Atlas* shows the "Copernican System of Planets," with the sun at the center of the universe and the planets circling around it.

Copernicus sought a simpler mathematical formulation to explain how the universe operated. His search convinced him that the earth was *not* at the center of the universe. Instead, he believed that the sun "sits upon a royal throne" in that location, "ruling his children, the planets which circle around him." Moreover, Copernicus concluded that the earth was not stationary: "What appears to be a motion of the sun is in truth a motion of the earth." According to Copernicus, the earth moved in perfect, "divine" circles around the sun, as did other bodies in the universe. Day passed into night because the earth turned on its axis. **Figure 14.3** shows this view of the universe. At the center is the sun, circled by the earth (showing night and day) and the other planets, (note Jupiter and its moons on the right). The signs of the zodiac are on the outer band, suggesting continuing beliefs in astrology. The figure on the lower right, holding a globe and a scientific instrument, is Copernicus. This change from an earth-centered (geocentric) to a sun-centered (heliocentric) universe would become known as the **Copernican revolution.**

Copernicus worked on his **heliocentric model** of the universe for almost twenty-five years. However, fearing ridicule and disapproval from the clergy, he waited until 1543—what became the year of his death—to publish it. Few people outside a limited circle of scholars knew of his views, and even fewer accepted them. Nevertheless, Catholic and Protestant authorities who were wedded to the earth-centered system soon recognized the threat to the Christian conception of the universe that these ideas represented. They denounced the Copernican system as illogical, unbiblical, and unsettling to the Christian faith. One Protestant associate of Martin Luther complained that "certain men . . . have concluded that the earth moves. . . . It is want of honesty and decency to assert such notions publicly. . . . It is part of a good mind to accept the truth as revealed by God and to acquiesce in it."

Still, Copernicus's thinking had some supporters. An Italian monk, Giordano Bruno (1548–1600), tested Catholic authorities by openly teaching and extending Copernican thought, arguing that "the universe is entirely infinite because it has neither edge, limit, nor surfaces." Bruno also professed a series of unusual religious notions. Outraged, the Catholic Inquisition burned Bruno at the stake. Nevertheless, Copernicus's views began to influence other scholars who were investigating the physical nature of the universe.

The Danish aristocrat Tycho Brahe (1546–1601) did not share Copernicus's belief in a heliocentric universe, nor did he grasp the sophisticated mathematics of the day. Still, he became the next most important astronomer of the sixteenth century. He persuaded the king of Denmark to build for him the most advanced astronomy laboratory in Europe. There he recorded thousands of unusually accurate, detailed observations about the planets and stars over a period of twenty years—all without a telescope. His discoveries of a new star in 1572 and a comet in 1577 undermined the Aristotelian belief in a sky of fixed, unalterable stars moving in crystalline spheres. Although Brahe mistakenly concluded that some planets revolved around the sun, which itself moved around the earth, other astronomers with better understandings of mathematics would use his observations to draw very different conclusions.

Tycho Brahe's assistant, Johannes Kepler (1571–1630), built on Brahe's observations to support the Copernican heliocentric theory. A German Lutheran from an aristocratic family, Kepler—like other Hermetic scholars—believed in an underlying mathematical harmony of mystical significance to the physical universe. He sought one harmony that would fit with Brahe's observations. Between 1609 and 1619, he announced his most important findings: the three laws of planetary motion. After determining the first law—which stated that the planets moved in ellipses around the sun—he excitedly wrote, "It was as if I had awakened from a sleep." The second law declared that the planets' velocity varied according to their distance from the sun. The third law concluded that the physical relationship between the moving planets could be expressed mathematically. Kepler thus showed "that the celestial machine . . . is the likeness of [a] clock," further undermining the Aristotelian view and extending the Copernican revolution.

Document 14.1 reveals that in 1597, Kepler responded to a letter from Galileo Galilei, the Italian astronomer, physicist, and mathematician discussed at the beginning of this chapter. Although Galileo expressed a reluctance to publicize his beliefs in Copernican ideas, Kepler encouraged him to take the risk. "Be of good cheer, Galileo, and appear in public. If I am not mistaken there are only a few among the distinguished mathematicians of Europe who would dissociate themselves from us. So great is the power of truth."

Galileo already believed that the world could be described in purely mathematical terms. "Philosophy," he wrote, "is written in this grand book, the universe, which stands continually open to our gaze. . . . It is written in the language of mathematics, and its characters are triangles, circles, and other geometric figures without which it is humanly impossible to understand a single word of it. . . ." Galileo also felt that harmonies could be discovered through experimentation and mathematics. By conducting controlled experiments such as rolling balls down inclines, he demonstrated how motion could be described mathematically. He rejected the old view that objects in their natural state were at rest and that all motion needed a purpose. Instead, he formulated the principle of inertia, showing that bodies, once set into motion, will tend to stay in motion. He thus overturned Aristotelian ideas and established rules for experimental physics.

Galileo, hearing about the recent invention of the telescope, then studied the skies through a telescope that he built in 1609 out of a long tube and magnifying lenses. He saw that the moon's surface, instead of being a perfect heavenly body, was rugged (like the earth's), with craters and mountains indicated by lines and shading. The telescope also revealed that Jupiter had moons and that the sun had spots. These observations confirmed the view that other heavenly bodies besides the earth were imperfect and further convinced him of the validity of Copernicus's hypothesis. For years, Galileo had feared the disapproval of the Catholic Church. Now, however, he was ready to publicly argue that "in discussions of physical problems we ought to begin not from the authority of scriptural passages, but from sense-experiences and necessary demonstrations." Galileo published his findings in 1610.

Six years later, the church attacked his proposition that "the earth is not the center of the world nor immovable, but moves as a whole, and also with a daily motion." This statement, the church said, was "foolish and absurd philosophically, and formally heretical." To back up its claim, the church cited the authority of both the Bible and itself. For the next several years, Galileo kept his thoughts to himself. In 1632, believing that the church might be more open, he decided again to present his views. To avoid challenging the church, he submitted his book to the official church censors and agreed to some changes they demanded.

Tycho Brahe

Johannes Kepler

Galileo Galilei

thinking about
DOCUMENTS

DOCUMENT 14.1

Kepler and Galileo Exchange Letters About Science

Many leading European scholars of the Scientific Revolution feared publishing their views, which were often unpopular with religious authorities. Such scholars sometimes turned to each other for support, as the following late-sixteenth-century letters between Kepler and Galileo suggest. Here the two men discuss their beliefs in Copernican theory.

Galileo to Kepler: "Like you, I accepted the Copernican position several years ago. I have written up many reasons on the subject, but have not dared until now to bring them into the open. I would dare publish my thoughts if there were many like you; but, since there are not. I shall forbear."

Kepler's Reply: "I could only have wished that you, who have so profound an insight, would choose another way. You advise us to retreat before the general ignorance and not to expose ourselves to the violent attacks of the mob of scholars. But after a tremendous task has been begun in our time, first by Copernicus and then by many very learned mathematicians, and when the assertion that the Earth moves can no longer be considered something new, would it not be much better to pull the wagon to its goal by our joint efforts, now that we have got it under way, and gradually, with powerful voices, to shout down the common herd? Be of good cheer, Galileo, and come

out publicly! If I judge correctly, there are only a few of the distinguished mathematicians of Europe who would part company with us, so great is the power of truth. If Italy seems a less favorable place for your publication, perhaps Germany will allow us this freedom."

SOURCE: Giorgio de Santillana, *The Crime of Galileo* (Chicago: University of Chicago Press, 1955), pp. 11, 14–15.

Analyze the Document

1. Why is Galileo reluctant to publish his views on the Copernican position?

2. How does Kepler respond to Galileo's concerns?

3. In what ways does Kepler's reply suggest that the Scientific Revolution was already a growing movement by the end of the sixteenth century?

Finally he published his *Dialogue on the Two Chief Systems of the World*—in Italian rather than the less-accessible Latin. This text advocated Copernicanism, portrayed opponents of the Copernican system (such as the Jesuits) as simpletons, and brought Galileo directly into public conflict with conservative forces in the Catholic Church. Because Galileo could show that his book had already been approved by church officials, prosecutors had to use questionable evidence against him. **Figure 14.4,** painted by an anonymous artist, shows Galileo, wearing a black suit and hat, sitting alone facing church officials. Behind him a man records the trial, while surrounding them are observers—some members of the clergy, others laypeople. In the lower left, two men discuss or argue the issues being decided within; above them some members of the audience look out toward the viewers and the greater world. As we saw at the beginning of the chapter, the Roman Inquisition ultimately forced Galileo to renounce his views.

News of Galileo's sensational trial spread throughout Europe, as did fear of publishing other radical views. Soon, however, his book was translated and published elsewhere in Europe, and his views began to win acceptance by other scientists. Even though Galileo admitted that the new science was beyond the grasp of "the shallow minds of the common people," he effectively communicated its ideas to his peers. By the time

FIGURE 14.4 Anonymous, *Trial of Galileo Before the Inquisition* In 1632, Galileo came into conflict with conservative forces in the Catholic Church over his Copernican views. In this painting by an anonymous artist, Galileo sits facing the church officials who will judge him.

DOCUMENT 14.2

Isaac Newton: God in a Scientific Universe

Like Galileo and Descartes, Newton was well aware that his ideas had profound implications for theology. His views, he realized, might even be considered contrary to religious doctrine. Yet Newton was a deeply spiritual man and took pains to distinguish the appropriate realms of science and religion. In the following selection from Opticks (1704), his analysis of light, Newton emphasizes that his ideas and systems still allow room for God in the universe.

All these things being consider'd, it seems probable to me, that God in the Beginning form'd Matter in solid, massy, hard, impenetrable moveable Particles, of such Sizes and Figures, and with such other Properties, and in such Proportion to Space, as most conduced to the End for which he form'd them; and that these primitive Particles being Solids, are incomparably harder than any porous Bodies compounded of them; even so very hard, as never to wear or break in pieces; no ordinary Power being able to divide what God himself made one in the first Creation. . . .

It seems to me farther, that these Particles have not only a *Vis inertiae*, accompanied with such passive Laws of Motion as naturally result from that Force, but also that they are moved by certain active Principles, such as is that of Gravity, and that which cause Fermentation, and the Cohesion of Bodies. These Principles I consider, not as occult Qualities, supposed to result from the specifick Forms of Things, but as general Laws of Nature, by which the Things themselves are form'd; their Truth appearing to us by Phaenomena, though their Causes be not yet discover'd. . . .

Now by the help of these Principles, all material Things seem to have been composed of the hard and solid Particles above-mention'd, variously associated in the first Creation by the Counsel of an intelligent Agent. For it became him who created them to set them in order. And if he did not, it's unphilosophical to seek for any other Origin of the World, or to pretend that it might arise out of a Chaos by the mere Laws of Nature; though being once form'd, it may continue by those Laws for many Ages.

SOURCE: Sir Isaac Newton, *Opticks*, 4th ed. (London, 1730), pp. 400–402.

Analyze the Document

1. What is Newton's view of God's role in the universe?

2. What objections might scientists today have to these ideas?

3. What does Newton mean by "Principles" and "Laws"?

---

of his death in 1642, Europe's intellectual elite had begun to embrace the Copernican outlook.

In England, Isaac Newton (1642–1727) picked up the trail blazed by Copernicus, Brahe, Kepler, and Galileo. Late in life, Newton described his career modestly: "I do not know what I may appear to the world; but to myself I seem to have been only like a boy playing on the sea-shore, and diverting myself in now and then finding a smoother pebble or a prettier shell than ordinary, while the great ocean of truth lay all undiscovered before me." Newton may have held himself in humble regard, but his accomplishments were astonishing.

Isaac Newton

In 1661, Newton entered Cambridge University, where he studied the ideas of Copernicus and Galileo as well as the advantages of scientific investigation. He distinguished himself enough in mathematics to be chosen to stay on as a professor after his graduation. Like most other figures of the Scientific Revolution, Newton was profoundly religious and, as indicated by Document 14.2, hoped to harmonize his Christian beliefs with the principles of science. He also believed in alchemy and elements of Hermeticism.

Starting in his early 20s, Newton made some of the most important discoveries in the history of science. He developed calculus and investigated the nature of light; he also formulated and mathematically described three laws of motion: inertia, acceleration, and action/reaction. Yet he is best known for discovering the law of universal attraction, or gravitation. After working on the concept for years, he finally published it in 1687 in his great work *Principia* (*The Mathematical Principles of Natural Knowledge*). In the book, he stated the law with simplicity and precision: "Every particle of matter in the universe attracts every other particle with a force varying inversely as the square of the distance between them and directly proportional to the product of their masses." In his view, this law applied equally to all objects, from the most massive planet to a small apple falling from a tree.

Newton's *Principia*

Newton had managed to synthesize the new findings in astronomy and physics into a systematic explanation of physical laws that applied to the earth as well as the heavens. This Newtonian universe was infinite and had no center. Uniform and mathematically describable, it was held together by explainable forces and was atomic in nature. Essentially, everything in the universe consisted of only one thing: matter in motion.

The Revolution Spreads: Medicine, Anatomy, and Chemistry

Although astronomy and physics led the way in dramatic scientific findings, researchers in other fields made important discoveries as well. Many of these advances also had roots in the sixteenth century. For example, several scholars developed new ideas in the related fields of medicine, anatomy, and chemistry.

In medicine, a flamboyant Swiss alchemist-physician known as Paracelsus (1493–1541) strongly influenced the healing arts. A believer in Hermetic doctrine, Paracelsus openly opposed **Paracelsus** medical orthodoxy and taught that healers should look for truth not in libraries ("the more learned, the more perverted," he warned) but in the Book of Nature. "I have not been ashamed to learn from tramps, butchers, and barbers," he boasted. As a teacher and wandering practitioner, he treated patients, experimented with chemicals, recorded his observations, and developed new theories. Paracelsus concluded that all matter was composed of salt, sulfur, and mercury—not the traditional earth, water, fire, and air. Rejecting the standard view that an imbalance in the humors of the body caused disease, he instead looked to specific chemical imbalances to explain what caused each illness. He also encouraged research and experimentation to find natural remedies for bodily disorders, such as administering mercury or arsenic at astrologically correct moments. Though rejected by most established physicians, Paracelsus's ideas became particularly popular among common practitioners and would later influence the study of chemistry.

Other researchers founded the modern science of anatomy. In the sixteenth century, Andreas Vesalius (1514–1564), a Fleming living in **Andreas Vesalius** Italy, wrote the first comprehensive textbook on the structure of the human body based on careful observation. **Figure 14.5** shows the 28-year-old Vesalius displaying one of his studies on human anatomy from his 1543 treatise, *On the Fabric of the Human Body*. This figure is one of more than two hundred woodcut illustrations showing the composition of the body, stage by stage. Vesalius himself dissected cadavers, as suggested by the scalpel resting on the table. A notable aspect of this illustration is that Vesalius boldly looks the viewer in the eye, perhaps to challenge directly the old, authoritative assumptions about human anatomy. Nevertheless, his dissections of human bodies brought him into conflict with traditional physicians and scholars. Disgusted, he finally gave up his scientific studies and became the personal physician to Emperor Charles V.

Despite relentless criticism, other scholars continued anatomical research. A line from a poem written for the opening of the Amsterdam Anatomical Theatre

ANDREÆ VESALII.

FIGURE 14.5 Andreas Vesalius, from *On the Fabric of the Human Body,* 1543 Vesalius looks boldly out at the viewer while displaying one of his studies of human anatomy.

in the early seventeenth century reflects the sense that this research needed special justification: "Evil doers who while living **William Harvey** have done damage are of benefit after their death." In other words, the body parts of criminals "afford a lesson to you, the Living." The most important of these researchers was William Harvey (1578–1657), an Englishman who, like Vesalius, studied at the University of Padua in Italy. Harvey dissected hundreds of animals, including dogs, pigs, lobsters, shrimp, and snakes. He discovered that the human heart worked like a pump, with valves that allowed blood to circulate through the body: "The movement of the blood occurs constantly in a circular manner and is the result of the beating of the heart." Yet, despite this mechanistic view, he also considered the heart the physical and spiritual center of life—in his words, "the sovereign of everything."

By the seventeenth century, anatomists and others benefited from several newly invented scientific instruments, such as the microscope. Anton van Leeuwenhoek (1632–1723), a Dutchman, became the chief pioneer in the use of this instrument.

In observations during the 1670s, he described seeing

Anton van Leeuwenhoek

"little animals or animalcules" in water from a lake. "It was wonderful to see: and I judge that some of these little creatures were above a thousand times smaller than the smallest ones I have ever yet seen, upon the rind of cheese, in wheaten flour, mould and the like." Leeuwenhoek discovered what would later be identified as bacteria in his own saliva: "little eels or worms, lying all huddled up together and wriggling. . . . This was for me, among all the marvels that I have discovered in nature, the most marvellous of all."

Around this same time, Robert Boyle (1627–1691), an Irish nobleman particularly interested in medical chemistry, helped lay the foundations for

Robert Boyle

modern chemistry. Drawing inspiration from Paracelsus, Boyle attacked many assumptions inherited from the ancients and began a systematic search for the basic elements of matter. Relying on the experimental method and using new instruments, he argued that all matter was composed of indestructible atoms that behaved in predictable ways. Boyle also discovered a law—which still bears his name—that governs the pressure of gases. His exacting procedures set a standard for the scientific practice of chemistry.

The Methodology of Science Emerges

The scientists who challenged traditional views in their fields also used new methods of discovery—of uncovering how things worked and of determining "truth." Indeed, this innovative methodology lay at the heart of the Scientific Revolution. Earlier techniques for ascertaining the truth—by referring to long-trusted authorities and making deductions from their propositions—became unacceptable to the new scientists. They instead emphasized systematic skepticism, experimentation, and reasoning based solely on observed facts and mathematical laws. The two most important philosophers of this methodology were Francis Bacon and René Descartes.

Francis Bacon (1561–1626), an English politician who was once lord chancellor of England under James I, took a passionate interest

Francis Bacon

in the new science. He rejected reliance on ancient authorities and advocated the collection of data without preconceived notions. From such data, he explained, scientific conclusions could be reached through inductive reasoning—drawing general conclusions from particular concrete observations. "Deriv[ing] axioms from . . . particulars, rising by gradual and unbroken ascent, so that it arrives at the most general axioms of all. This is the true way," he proclaimed. In addition, Bacon argued that scientific knowledge would

be useful knowledge: "I am laboring to lay the foundation not of any sect or doctrine, but of human utility and power." He believed that science would benefit commerce and industry and improve the human condition by giving people unprecedented power over their environment.

Figure 14.6, the title page from Bacon's 1620 book, *New Instrument,* graphically depicts these views. The illustration shows a ship of discovery sailing out from the western end of the Mediterranean Sea into the unknown. Below is the quotation "Many shall venture forth and science shall be increased." Here is an optimistic assertion that knowledge is limitless and that science constitutes a voyage of discovery— a view that would be echoed again and again, as we saw in the picture at the beginning of this chapter. As **Figure 14.6** suggests, Bacon thus became a noted propagandist for the new science as well as a proponent of the **empirical method.**

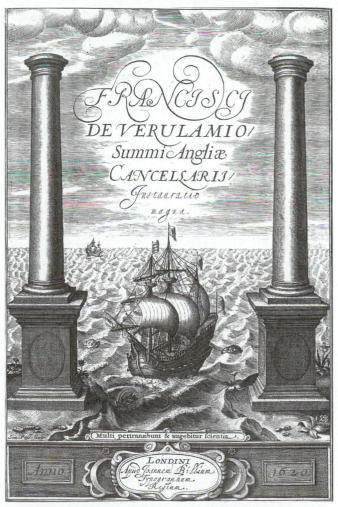

FIGURE 14.6 The New Science The title page of Francis Bacon's book *New Instrument* (1620) asserts optimistically that science is like a voyage of discovery with almost limitless potential.

Despite his brilliance, Bacon did not have a thorough understanding of mathematics and the role it could play in the new science. His contemporary René Descartes (1596–1650) would René Descartes be the one to excel in this arena. Born in France, Descartes received training in scholastic philosophy and mathematics at one of France's best Jesuit schools and took a degree in law. He entered military service and served during the Thirty Years' War. During his travels, he met a Dutch mathematician and became interested in the new science. An ecstatic experience in 1619 convinced him to commit to a life of the mind. He spent his most productive years as a mathematician, physicist, and metaphysical philosopher in Holland. In 1637, he published his philosophy and scientific methodology in the *Discourse on Method*—in French, not Latin. The book presented an eloquent defense of skepticism and of abstract **deductive reasoning**— deriving conclusions that logically flowed from a premise. "Inquiries should be directed, not to what others have thought, nor to what we ourselves conjecture, but to what we can clearly and perspicuously behold and with certainty deduce; for knowledge is not won in any other way."

Descartes questioned all forms of authority, no matter how venerable—be it Aristotle or even the Bible. He tried to remove systematically all assumptions about knowledge and advocated doubting the senses, which he claimed could be deceptive. Taken to its logical conclusion, his argument left him with one God-given experiential fact—that he was thinking. "I think, therefore I am" became his starting point. From there he followed a rigorous process of deductive reasoning to draw a variety of conclusions, including the existence of God and the physical world. He argued that there were two kinds of reality: mind, or subjective thinking and experiencing; and body, or objective physical matter. According to this philosophy, known as **Cartesian dualism,** the objective physical universe could be understood in terms of extension (matter occupying space) and motion (matter in motion). "Give me extension and motion," vowed Descartes, "and I will create the universe." He considered the body nothing more than "an earthen machine." In his opinion, only the mind was exempt from mechanical laws.

Descartes emphasized the power of the detached, reasoning individual mind to discover truths about nature. Unlike Bacon, he put his faith in mathematical reasoning, not in empirical investigation. By challenging all established authority, by accepting as truth only what could be known by reason, and by assuming a purely mechanical physical universe, Descartes established a philosophy and methodology that became the core of the new science.

SUPPORTING AND SPREADING SCIENCE

Only a small group of people actually participated in the **Scientific Revolution.** Of these, a handful of women managed to overcome barriers to take part as patrons for scientists or as scientists themselves. Men ignored or discounted their work, and scientific societies usually excluded them. The few women engaged in science, such as the naturalist Maria Sibylla Merian (see Biography, page 405) and the Germany astronomer Maria Winkelmann (1647–1717), had to rely on their own resources or work in collaboration with their husbands.

Few scientific scholars—whether male or female— got far without calling on a network of peers and soliciting the support of wealthy patrons. To spread their ideas, these scientists needed to publish their works, interact with like-minded colleagues, and gain the backing of prestigious elites. Fortunately for them, these elites were eager to comply.

Courts and Salons

Governments and wealthy aristocrats served as benefactors and employers of scientists. Kepler, for example, received help from the imperial court, serving in Bohemia as Rudolf II's official mathematician. Galileo became court mathematician to Cosimo de' Medici in Tuscany. Vesalius served as physician to Holy Roman Emperor Charles V, and Harvey as royal physician in England.

Queen Christina of Sweden, like several other monarchs, invited scholars and artists to her court. **Figure 14.7** shows her in 1649 with the French philosopher and mathematician René Descartes (on the

KEY DATES

THE SCIENTIFIC REVOLUTION

1543	Copernicus's heliocentric model published
1543	Vesalius, *Fabric of the Human Body*
1609–1619	Kepler, three laws of planetary motion
1620	Bacon, *New Instrument*
1633	Trial of Galileo
1637	Descartes, *Discourse on Method*
1662	English Royal Society founded
1687	Newton, *Principia*
1690	Locke, *Essay Concerning Human Understanding*
1697	Bayle, *Historical and Critical Dictionary*

right, pointing to papers). Books, papers, and instruments attest to the importance of the new science at this meeting. In this Protestant country, the religious figure on the far right seems to indicate that there is little conflict between science and religion. The artist portrays Christina, a deeply religious person (who would later become a Catholic), as an interested and gracious benefactor helping to bring to light scientific findings.

Rulers had their own motives—namely, practicality and prestige—for assisting scholars and scientists. Royals especially hoped that scholarship and scientific inquiry would yield discoveries that would enhance the strength and prosperity of the state. For example, they sought experts in building projects, armaments, mapmaking, navigation, and mining. They also tried to burnish their own reputations as powerful, educated people by patronizing scholarship, science, and the arts. In this way, support of science became a supposed hallmark of good government. Enticed by this assistance, learned people gathered at royal courts, which gradually filled rooms with new tools, machines, exotic plants and animals, and books.

Beyond the court, people formed private salons and local academies where those interested in science could meet. In the 1540s, the first academy for scientific study was established, in Naples. Women ran several important salons where scientists discussed their findings along with literature, art, and politics. Some scientists even found benefactors at these meetings.

FIGURE 14.7 Queen Christina and Descartes The Swedish queen Christina displays her support of science in this depiction of a 1649 meeting with the French philosopher René Descartes.

The Rise of Royal Societies

During the second half of the seventeenth century, central governments stepped up their support of scientific experimentation, publications, and academies. In 1662, for example, Charles II chartered the Royal Society in England; four years later, Louis XIV's finance minister, Jean-Baptiste Colbert, founded the Académie des Sciences in France. These organizations, and others patterned after them, furnished laboratories, granted subsidies, brought scientists together to exchange ideas, published their findings, and honored scientific achievements. This governmental support of science added to the growing prestige of science and the scientific community.

Religion and the New Science

Religious organizations played a mixed role in the spread of the new science. Traditionally, the Catholic Church supported scholarship and learning in general, including, in natural science. Moreover, religious orders staffed most universities, and many key figures of the Scientific Revolution held university positions. Numerous leading scholars also felt a profound sense of spirituality. Copernicus, for example, who dedicated his work to the pope, was a cleric, as were many other natural scientists. Although we may be tempted to assume that the skepticism inherent in the scientific method would lead to atheism, the great scientists attacked neither faith nor established religion. Nor were they dispassionate investigators holding themselves apart from the spiritual nature of their age. They often believed in magic, ghosts, and witchcraft and typically considered alchemy, astrology, and numerology (predicting events from numbers) valuable components of natural science. Galileo, though he later decried his trial as the triumph of "ignorance, impiety, fraud and deceit," remained a believing Catholic. Even Robert Boyle, who like others came to think of the universe as a machine, attributed its origin to God: "God, indeed, gave motion to matter . . . and established those rules of motion, and that order amongst things . . . which we call the laws of nature." Newton agreed: "This most beautiful system of the sun, planets, and comets, could only proceed from the counsel and dominion of an intelligent and powerful Being. . . . He endures forever, and is everywhere present. . . ."

Nevertheless, the new science did challenge certain tenets of faith and the traditional Christian conception of God's place in the ordering of the world. Neither Protestant nor Catholic leaders welcomed Copernican ideas and the implications of the new science. The Catholic Church, itself ordered in a hierarchy that paralleled the old view of the universe, stayed particularly committed to established authorities. Moreover, the church's condemnation of Galileo in 1633 discouraged scientific investigations throughout much of Catholic Europe. Descartes was not alone in deciding not to publish ideas incorporating Copernican assumptions. As he explained in 1634, "It is not my temperament to set sail against the wind. . . . I want to be able to live in peace . . . out of sight." Although the French government would actively promote science, after the mid-seventeenth century most scientific work and publishing took place in Protestant areas—particularly in England and the Netherlands.

The New Worldview

By the end of the seventeenth century, the accumulation of convincing scientific findings and the support for those findings among the educated elites had broken the Aristotelian-medieval worldview and replaced it with the Copernican-Newtonian paradigm. According to the new view, the earth, along with the planets, moved around the sun in an infinite universe of other similar bodies. The natural order consisted of matter in motion, acting according to mathematically expressible laws. Scientific truths came from observing, measuring, experimenting, and making reasoned conclusions through the use of sophisticated mathematics. Religious truths still had their place, and the orderliness of nature reflected God's design (see Document 14.2, on page 457). However, science now claimed precedence in explaining the material world.

The Copernican-Newtonian paradigm

In the sixteenth and early seventeenth centuries, great thinkers such as Copernicus and Galileo had been ridiculed and persecuted for their ideas. By the late seventeenth and early eighteenth centuries, Isaac Newton's fate revealed the acceptance of the new paradigm among educated elites. Famous and popular, Newton became a member of Parliament, served for many years as director of the Royal Mint, and was knighted by Queen Anne.

LAYING THE FOUNDATIONS FOR THE ENLIGHTENMENT

In the course of the eighteenth century, the ideas of the Scientific Revolution spread widely and were applied in stunning new ways. With this broadening, the eighteenth century witnessed the birth of a major cultural movement known as the **Enlightenment.** At the heart of this movement lay the firm conviction— especially among intellectuals—that human reason should determine understanding of the world and the rules of social life. "[H]ave the courage to use your own intelligence," and leave your "self-caused immaturity," exhorted the German philosopher Immanuel Kant (1724–1804). "All that is required for this enlightenment is freedom, and particularly . . . the freedom for man to make public use of his reason in all matters."

The Enlightenment hit its full stride in the middle decades of the eighteenth century, when it particularly influenced literate elites of Europe and North America. Yet, its roots stretched back to the end of the seventeenth century. At that time, the thinking that would characterize the Enlightenment emerged in the writings of people who popularized science, applied a skeptical attitude toward religious standards of truth, and criticized accepted traditions and authorities.

Science Popularized

Unevenly educated and facing challenging findings, members of scientific societies often struggled to understand one another's work. For the nonscientific public, the problem of communicating new, complex ideas was even worse. Late in the seventeenth century, several talented writers, nonscientists themselves but believing that science had established a new standard of truth, began explaining in clear language the meaning of science to the literate public. For example, the French writer Bernard de Fontenelle (1657–1757) enjoyed a long, brilliant career as a popularizer of science. In *Conversations on the Plurality of Worlds* (1686), he presented the Copernican view of the universe in a series of conversations between an aristocratic woman and her lover under starry skies. The English essayist and publisher Joseph Addison (1672–1719), in the March 12, 1711, issue of his newspaper, *The Spectator,* said that he hoped to bring "philosophy out of closets and libraries, schools and colleges, to dwell in clubs and assemblies, at tea-tables and in coffee-houses." He aimed his daily paper not only at men but at women "of a more elevated life and conversation, that move in an exalted sphere of knowledge and virtue, that join all the beauties of the mind to the ornaments of dress, and inspire a kind of awe and respect, as well as love, in their male beholders." Other writers also targeted women. In 1737, for example, *Newtonianism for Women* was published in Naples and was soon translated into English. Writings such as these helped make science fashionable in elite circles.

In the mid-eighteenth century, this popularization of science merged with another foundation of Enlightenment thinking: the belief that

Teaching science

every educated man and woman should be familiar with the nature and methods of science. **Figure 14.8,** an illustration from a British book on the arts and sciences, depicts this connection between science and education. Here a teacher instructs three young men in the principles of astronomy by demonstrating the planetary movements on a new machine—the orrery. The stuffed animals hanging from the ceiling underscore the importance of natural history. Atop the bookcase and on the floor are seminal instruments of science—an air pump, a microscope, a telescope, and a globe. A human skeleton hangs in the closet.

Soon scientific ideas were being taught to children of the middle and upper classes. For example, the year 1761 saw the publication of *The Newtonian System of Philosophy, Adapted to the Capacities of Young Gentlemen and Ladies*, a book engagingly advertised as the "Philosophy of Tops and Balls." In it, a fictional boy named Tom Telescope gave lectures on science topics to children while also teaching the virtues of good manners and citizenship. The book proved immensely popular, going through many editions in Britain and in other countries.

Many of these books emphasized Newton—and for understandable reasons. Enlightenment thinkers saw this brilliant Englishman as the great

Glorifying Newton: reason and nature

synthesizer of the Scientific Revolution, an astute observer who rightly described the universe as ordered, mechanical, material, and set into motion by God. From Newton, they concluded that reason and nature were compatible: Nature functioned logically and discernibly; therefore, what was natural was also reasonable. Many writers of the day agreed with the spirit of a poem written for Newton by the English author Alexander Pope upon the scientist's death in 1727:

Nature and Nature's Laws lay hid in Night.
God said, "Let Newton be," and all was Light.

In simple terms, Newton had become a European cultural hero, as **Figure 14.9** suggests. At the left center of this allegorical painting, a great urn "wherein is supposed to be deposited the Remains of the deceased Hero" is displayed. Above the urn shines a beam

FIGURE 14.8 Science, Education, and Enlightenment, 1759
Surrounded by scientific instruments and objects, a teacher instructs three students. This illustration reveals the growing sense during the Enlightenment that an educated person should be familiar with science.

of light, broken into the colors of the spectrum by a prism—a bow to Newton's famous prism experiments. At the right are pages filled with mathematical calculations; below them, a globe and measuring instruments. Various figures in classical dress admire these objects and perhaps discuss Newton's ideas. The entire painting glorifies not only Newton but all of science.

Enlightenment thinkers also admired the ideas of Newton's compatriot John Locke (1632–1704), who applied scientific thinking to human psychology. This English philosopher did not hold the mind exempt from the mechanical laws of the material universe. In his *Essay Concerning Human Understanding* (1690), Locke pictured the human brain at birth as a blank sheet of paper that sensory perception and reason filled as a person aged.

The psychology of John Locke

FIGURE 14.9 Giovanni Battista Pittori, *Allegorical Monument to Isaac Newton*, 1727–1730 This celebratory painting pays homage to Isaac Newton by glorifying the urn that stores his remains and highlighting his scientific discoveries.

"Our observation, employed either about external sensible objects or about the internal operations of our minds perceived and reflected on by ourselves, is that which supplies our understanding with all the materials of thinking." Locke's empirical psychology rejected the notion that human beings were born with innate ideas or that revelation was a reliable source of truth. What we become, he argued, depends solely on our experiences—on the information received through the senses. Schools and social institutions should therefore play a major role in molding the individual from childhood to adulthood. These

ideas, like those of Newton and the Scientific Revolution, also set the stage for the skeptical questioning of received wisdom.

Skepticism and Religion

Locke's ideas, along with those of Newton and the Scientific Revolution, set the stage for the questioning of established wisdom that came to define the Enlightenment. Among several writers, skepticism—or doubts about religious dogmas—mounted. Pierre Bayle (1647–1706), a French Huguenot forced to flee to the Dutch Republic because of Louis XIV's religious persecutions, became the leading proponent of skepticism in the late seventeenth century. In his *News from the Republic of Letters* (1684), Bayle bitterly attacked the intolerance of the French monarchy and the Catholic Church. In most of Europe, where religious principles shared by ruler and ruled underlay all political systems, nonconformity was a major challenge. Therefore, the book earned him condemnation in Paris and Rome. Eventually, however, Bayle would have the last word. In 1697 he published the *Historical and Critical Dictionary*, which contained a list of religious views and beliefs that Bayle maintained did not stand up to criticism. Bayle cited human reason and common sense as his standard of criticism: "Any particular dogma, whatever it may be, whether it is advanced on the authority of the Scriptures, or whatever else may be its origins, is to be regarded as false if it clashes with the clear and definite conclusions of the natural understanding." Bayle also argued that "morals and religion, far from being inseparable, are completely independent of each other." For Bayle, a person's moral behavior had little to do with any particular religious doctrine or creed. With these stands, Bayle pushed much harder than Galileo in challenging the Catholic Church and other religious beliefs. He became recognized as an international authority on religious toleration and skeptical criticism of the Bible.

New information and arguments added weight to Bayle's criticism of biblical authority. For example, geological discoveries suggested that life on Earth had actually begun earlier than biblical accounts claimed. Investigators also began casting doubt on reports of miracles and prophecies. David Hume (1711–1776), a first-rate Scottish philosopher and historian, carried the skeptical argument even further. In *An Essay Concerning Human Understanding* (1748), he insisted that nothing—not even the existence of God or our own existence—could be known

Pierre Bayle

David Hume

for sure. Reality consisted only of human perceptions. To Hume, established religions were based on nothing but hope and fear. Reason demanded that people live with skeptical uncertainty rather than dogmatic faith.

Broadening Criticism of Authority and Tradition

Travel writing had a long history, and by the eighteenth century many Enlightenment thinkers had read explanations of China's lucid Confucian traditions as well as accounts of customs and beliefs in Islamic, Buddhist, and Hindu lands. Several writers—among them the Baron de Montesquieu (1689–1755), a wealthy judge in a provincial French court, and the French author Voltaire (1694–1778)—used comparisons of place and time to criticize authority and tradition during the early decades of the eighteenth century. Journeying abroad and writing about their experiences gave such people a new perspective on their home societies. Montesquieu and Voltaire, for their part, chastised European customs in general and French institutions in particular for being contrary to reason and good ethics.

> Travel writings of Montesquieu and Voltaire

Both presented the traveler as an objective observer. In his best-selling book *Persian Letters* (1721), Montesquieu bitingly satirized the customs, morals, and practices of Europeans from the point of view of two Persian travelers. Through this comparative perspective, Montesquieu painted the French as lacking in both good morals and effective government. Voltaire, in his widely read *Letters Concerning the English Nation* (1733), similarly criticized French politics and Catholic intolerance. In the island nation, "one thinks freely and nobly without being held back by any servile fear." Like many people, Voltaire idealized England because it allowed greater individual freedom, religious differences, and political reform than most other countries, especially France. England was also enviably prosperous and was the home of Newton and Locke, so admired in France. Many French intellectuals wanted for their own country what the English already seemed to have.

Other writers took a new historical perspective to criticize tradition and trumpet rapid change. For them, the tools of science and reason enabled people to surpass their historical predecessors, even the admired Greeks and Romans of antiquity. History became a story of relentless human progress, and people living in the eighteenth century stood on the brink of unprecedented historical achievements. Some people, such as the American scientist and philosopher Benjamin Franklin (1706–1790), embraced the idea of progress with an almost religious

> History and progress

fervor: "The rapid Progress of *true* Science now occasions my regretting sometimes that I was born so soon. It is impossible to imagine the Height to which may be carried . . . the Power of Man over Matter, . . . all diseases may by sure means be prevented, . . . and our lives lengthened at pleasure."

THE ENLIGHTENMENT IN FULL STRIDE

Building on the foundations of science, skepticism, and criticism, Western intellectuals systematically investigated the ethical, political, social, and economic implications of science after the 1730s. For them, nature—with its laws, order, simplicity, and rationality—served as a guide for human thought and society. "The source of man's unhappiness is his ignorance of Nature," claimed France's influential Baron d'Holbach (1723–1789). The Marquis de Condorcet argued, "The time will therefore come when the sun will shine only on free men who know no other master but their reason" (see Document 14.3). These optimistic intellectuals pushed for reform and change, using critical and empirical reasoning to back up their arguments. Specifically, they urged people to shrug off the shackles of tradition and custom and to participate in the accelerating progress of civilization. The spark of reason would soon dispel ignorance and enlighten all human understanding. Indeed, it was this image that lent the Enlightenment its name.

The *Philosophes*

Although Enlightenment ideas bubbled up throughout Europe and North America, France was the true heart of the movement. There Enlightenment thinkers came to be called *philosophes,* the French term for "philosophers." In a sense, the questions these thinkers grappled with were philosophical: How do we discover truth? How should we live our lives? Yet the *philosophes* were not traditional philosophers. Coming from both noble and middle-class origins, they were intellectuals—though often not formally trained by or associated with a university. They tended to extend, apply, or propagandize others' ideas rather than initiate new concepts themselves. They also wrote more plays, satires, histories, novels, encyclopedia entries, and short pamphlets than formal philosophical treatises. Finally, they considered themselves part of a common intellectual culture, an international "republic of letters" held together by literature, correspondence, and private gatherings. In the eyes of leading *philosophes* such as Jean Le Rond d'Alembert (1717–1783), this republic of letters should "establish the laws of philosophy and taste for the rest of the nation."

DOCUMENT 14.3

Condorcet Lauds the Power of Reason

No one lauded the power of reason and the Enlightenment, or had more hope for the future—thanks to the Enlightenment—than the French mathematician and philosophe the Marquis de Condorcet (1743–1794). The following is an excerpt from his Sketch of the Progress of the Human Mind, *a book tracing human "progress" over time, which he completed in 1794.*

Our hopes for the future condition of the human race can be subsumed under three important heads: the abolition of inequality between nations, the progress of equality within each nation, and the true perfection of mankind. Will all nations one day attain that state of civilization which the most enlightened, the freest and the least burdened by prejudices, such as the French and the Anglo-Americans, have attained already? Will the vast gulf that separates these peoples from the slavery of nations under the rule of monarchs, from the barbarism of African tribes, from the ignorance of savages, little by little disappear? . . .

In answering these three questions we shall find in the experience of the past, in the observation of the progress that the sciences and civilization have already made, in the analysis of the progress of the human mind and of the development of its faculties, the strongest reasons for believing that nature has set no limit to the realization of our hopes.

If we glance at the state of the world today we see first of all that in Europe the principles of the French constitution are already those of all enlightened men. We see them too widely propagated, too seriously professed, for priests and despots to prevent their gradual penetration even into the hovels of their slaves; there they will soon awaken in these slaves the remnants of their common sense and inspire them with that smoldering indignation which not even constant humiliation and fear can smother in the soul of the oppressed. . . .

The time will therefore come when the sun will shine only on free men who know no other master but their reason; when tyrants and slaves, priests and their stupid or hypocritical instruments will exist only in works of history and on the stage; and when we shall think of them only to pity their victims and their dupes; to maintain ourselves in a state of vigilance by thinking on their excesses; and to learn how to recognize and so to destroy, by force of reason, the first seeds of tyranny and superstition, should they ever dare to reappear amongst us.

SOURCE: Jean Antoine Nicholas Caritat, Marquis de Condorcet, *Sketch for a Historical Picture on the Progress of the Human Mind*, trans. June Barraclough (London: Weidenfeld and Nicolson [Orion Books], 1955), pp. 236–237, 244.

Analyze the Document

1. What "hopes" does Condorcet have for the future of humanity?

2. According to Condorcet, what will open the door to such great progress?

3. In Condorcet's opinion, why are the French and the Anglo-Americans the most "enlightened" peoples?

The witty, versatile François Arouet, who took the pen name Voltaire (1694–1778), best represented the philosophes. The son of a Parisian lawyer, Voltaire received a fine classical education from the Jesuits and soon denounced their religious doctrine. He became the idol of French intellectuals while only in his 20s, and the enemy of many others. He soon ran afoul of state authorities, who imprisoned him in the Bastille for writing verses that criticized the crown. Released, he became embroiled in a dangerous conflict with a prominent nobleman and again landed in the Bastille. By promising to leave the country, he gained his freedom. In England, he encountered the ideas of Newton and Locke and came to admire English parliamentary government and the nation's religious tolerance. As we saw, he popularized Newton's and Locke's ideas and extolled the virtues of English society in his writings.

Slipping back into France, Voltaire hid for a time under the protection of Émilie du Châtelet (1706–1749), a wealthy woman who became his lover and match. Châtelet had already shown brilliance as a child. By the age of 12, she could speak four languages and had already translated Greek and Latin texts. Her mother worried that she would not find a mate because she "flaunts her mind, and frightens away the suitors her other excesses have not driven off." In 1733, she insisted on joining a group of male intellectuals who met regularly at a Parisian coffeehouse, donning men's clothes after the management refused to admit her because of her gender. Voltaire lived openly with Châtelet and her husband. In the great hall of their country chateau, she hung rods, pipes, and balls from the ceiling for her experiments in physics. She made her reputation by publishing a three-volume work on the German mathematician and philosopher Leibnitz and translating Newton's *Principles of Mathematics*. A *philosophe*, accomplished scientist, and leading proponent of Newtonian thought in her own right, Châtelet helped Voltaire gain a better understanding of the sciences and their significance. When she died in childbirth in 1749, the despondent Voltaire accepted an invitation from King Frederick II of Prussia to join his court. However, they soon argued, and Voltaire returned to France.

Having made both a fortune in financial speculations and a rich network of friends and acquaintances, Voltaire was not without resources. He wrote poetry, drama, history, essays, letters, and scientific treatises—ninety volumes in all. The novel *Candide* (1759) became his best-known work. In this dark satire, Voltaire created the epitome of the "ivory-tower" intellectual, ridiculed the pretensions of the nobility and clergy, and skewered the naïveté of optimists who believed that "this is the best of all possible worlds and all things turn out for the best." He aimed his cynical wit especially at the Catholic Church and Christian institutions. His *Philosophical Dictionary* became the most famous, wide-ranging attack on supernatural religion and churches. Voltaire mounted several campaigns for religious toleration, coming to the defense of individuals attacked by prejudice. In his *Treatise on Tolerance* (1763), he attacked the mentality that led to the torture and murder of a Protestant merchant, Jean Calas, on the false charges of murdering his son for threatening to convert to Catholicism. "Christians ought to tolerate one another. I will go even further and say that we ought to look upon all men as our brothers. What! call a Turk, a Jew, a Siamese, my brother? Yes, of course, for are we not all children of the same father, and the creatures of the same God?" Voltaire was celebrated as a national hero and lionized internationally, and his popularity reveals the widespread acceptance of Enlightenment thought throughout the West by the late eighteenth century.

The *Encyclopedia*

No work better summarizes the philosophy of the Enlightenment than the *Encyclopedia*, a collaborative effort by many *philosophes* under the editorship of Denis Diderot (1713–1774) and Jean Le Rond d'Alembert. In the preface, the editors stated their aim: "to overturn the barriers that reason never erected" and "contribute to the certitude and progress of human knowledge." The *Encyclopedia* embodied the notion that reason alone could be used to discover, understand, or clarify almost anything. This massive work explored the complete spectrum of knowledge, offering articles on subjects ranging from music to machinery interpreted through the lens of the *philosophes*' criticism and empiricism. The authors wrote with supreme self-importance: "I can assure you," said d'Alembert in a 1752 letter, "that while writing this work I had posterity before my eyes at every line."

The first volume of the *Encyclopedia* was published in 1751. **Figure 14.10** shows one of its many

FIGURE 14.10 The *Encyclopedia*, 1751 This page from the *Encyclopedia* shows a chemical laboratory and a table with symbols for each chemical substance.

illustrations. In this image of a chemical laboratory, two chemists and their assistants work. Each piece of equipment is numbered in the illustration and labeled in the text. At the bottom of the picture is a "table of affinities," a system used to organize and symbolize each chemical substance. The illustration conveys a sense of both the practicality of chemistry and its ordered progress. Although the study of chemistry and the hundreds of other topics covered in the *Encyclopedia* at first glance may appear innocent enough, they were saturated with the philosophy of the Enlightenment. Church authorities and their governmental allies therefore saw the *Encyclopedia* as a direct threat to the status quo. They censored it, halted its publication, and harassed its editors. Thanks in great part to the persistence of Diderot, who fought the authorities and managed a difficult group of contributing authors, the project was finally completed in 1772.

Battling the Church

Diderot's struggle to publish the *Encyclopedia* was part of a wider conflict between the *philosophes* and the church. Both sides spent much time and effort attacking each other. In countries such as France and Italy, where clerics were strongly entrenched in government, officials censored the writings of the *philosophes* and threatened to imprison or exile them. Governmental censorship was usually more nominal than real. However, Diderot and others trying to publish "offensive" books constantly worried about these threats: "How many times did we awake uncertain if . . . we would be torn from our families, our friends, our fellow citizens. . . ." French authors often sent their works to Holland or Switzerland for publication, and private companies then made a business of smuggling the books back into France across Swiss or Dutch borders.

Sometimes the *philosophes'* "crime" was promoting toleration of religious minorities, whether Christian or otherwise. Montesquieu and Voltaire, in France, were among several who attacked discrimination against Jews, for example. These views were particularly controversial because religious tolerance—formal and informal—was not the rule. Most governments maintained a state religion, rooted in law and viewed as the custodian of received views, that discriminated against nonmembers. For example, Denmark barred Catholic priests from entering the country, and the Catholic Inquisition remained active in Spain.

Some *philosophes,* such as the Baron d'Holbach and David Hume, verged on atheism in their attacks on organized religion. "The Christian

Deism religion not only was at first attended by miracles, but even now cannot be believed by any reasonable person without one," Hume claimed. However, few Enlightenment thinkers pushed matters that far. Most believed in some form of deism—that an impersonal, infinite Divine Being created the universe but did not interfere with the world of human affairs. The prominent author and political philosopher Thomas Paine (1737–1809) stated, "I believe in one God, and no more; and I hope for happiness beyond this life. . . . I do not believe in the creed professed by the Jewish church, by the Roman church, by the Greek church, by the Turkish church, by the Protestant church, nor by any church that I know of. My own mind is my own church." These ideas, like other ideas of the Enlightenment, gained momentum over the course of the eighteenth century. In the long run, the church probably lost more supporters among the upper and middle classes than it gained by so ardently attacking the *philosophes* and their ideas.

Reforming Society

The *philosophes* thought long and hard about reforming society. They wrote and argued

Political thought: Montesquieu and Rousseau about the relationship between the individual and society and reevaluated the functioning of traditional social institutions. Applying their critical reasoning to fields from government to education, they generated influential ideas for reform.

The most important political thinkers of the Enlightenment—Montesquieu and the Swiss-born writer Jean-Jacques Rousseau (1712–1778)—built on John Locke's work. Locke had pleaded eloquently for the "natural rights"—life, liberty, and property—of

human beings. In his *Second Treatise on Civil Government* (1690), Locke had argued that to safeguard these rights, individuals agree to surrender a certain amount of their sovereignty to government. However, the powers of the government, whether it be monarchical or popular, were strictly limited. No government was allowed to violate the individual's right to life, liberty, and property. If it did, the people who set it up could and should overthrow it—something the English had done in their Glorious Revolution, according to Locke.

An admirer of Locke and the English system of government, the Baron de Montesquieu analyzed political systems from a relativistic perspective. In his widely acclaimed political masterpiece, *The Spirit of the Laws* (1748), Montesquieu argued that political institutions should conform to the climate, customs, beliefs, and economy of a particular country. For instance, limited monarchy is most appropriate for countries of moderate size, like France; and republics for small states, like Venice or ancient Athens. Each form of government had its virtues and vices.

Not only did Montesquieu approve of Locke's doctrine of limited sovereignty, but he specified how it could best be secured—by a separation of powers and a system of checks and balances. The alternative, he warned, was tyranny and an end to liberty: "There would be an end to everything, were the same man or the same body, whether of the nobles or of the people, to exercise those three powers, that of enacting laws, that of executing the public resolutions, and of trying the causes of individuals." This theory, equally applicable to monarchies and to democracies, became Montesquieu's greatest practical contribution to political thought. In North America, framers of the U.S. Constitution incorporated his ideas into their structuring of the United States government, creating separate executive, judicial, and legislative branches of government.

Rousseau offered a more radical political theory than Montesquieu's (see Biography). In his *Discourse on the Origin of Inequality* (1755), Rousseau argued that people in the "primitive" state of "noble savagery" were free, equal, and relatively happy. Only when some of them began marking off plots of ground, claiming them as their own and thereby founding civil society, did the troubles begin. Private property created inequality and the need for laws and governments to protect people from crime and wars. In *The Social Contract* (1762), Rousseau began by challenging his contemporaries: "Man is born free; and everywhere he is in chains." He then offered a solution to this conflict between individual freedom and social restrictions. In an ideal state, he argued, people entered into a compact with one another, agreeing to surrender their individual liberty, which was driven by self-interest, to the whole society. In return, the individual gained freedom by virtue of being part of the society's "general will," which was driven by the common good. "This means nothing less than that [the individual] will be forced to be free," explained Rousseau. Although Rousseau never made it clear just how the general will operated in practice, he believed that the people themselves—rather than a monarch or a parliamentary body—should make laws. His controversial ideas would powerfully influence the development of democratic theory over the next two centuries. For some, *The Social Contract* would support participatory democracy, whereas for others, Rousseau's emphasis on conforming to the general will would justify authoritarian political systems.

Although critical and combative, neither Rousseau, Montesquieu, nor the other *philosophes* were political or social revolutionaries. They did not champion the lower classes, whom they dismissed as ignorant, prone to violence, and, in Voltaire's words, "inaccessible to the progress of reason and over whom fanaticism maintains its atrocious hold." Diderot, of humble parents, admitted that he wrote "only for those with whom I should enjoy conversing . . . the philosophers; so far as I am concerned, there is no one else in the world." Most *philosophes* hoped for painless change from above rather than a revolutionary transfer of power to the still-unenlightened masses. Many shared Voltaire's belief that enlightened absolutism—rule by a well-educated, enlightened monarch—offered the best chance for the enactment of Enlightenment reforms such as religious toleration, rule subject to impartial laws, and freedom of speech (see Chapter 15).

If the functioning of the universe and politics could be described by understandable, rational laws, why should the same not hold true for economic activity? Several Enlightenment thinkers turned their thoughts to this question and attacked mercantilism, the system of regulated national economics that still operated throughout much of Europe. A group of French thinkers known as Physiocrats, led by François Quesnay, personal physician to Louis XV, began to teach that economics had its own set of natural laws. The Physiocrats believed that the most basic of these laws was that of supply and demand, and that these laws operated best under only minimal governmental regulation of private economic activity. This doctrine, which became known as *laissez-faire* (noninterference), favored free trade and enterprise. In France, the Physiocrats saw land and agriculture as the main source of national wealth. Other economists would build on their ideas and apply them to different settings.

In 1776, Adam Smith (1723–1790), a Scottish professor of philosophy who associated with the Physiocrats while traveling in France, published

Economic ideas: the Physiocrats and Adam Smith

Wealth of Nations. The book became the bible of laissez-faire economics. By nature, Smith argued, individuals who were allowed to pursue rationally their own economic self-interest would benefit society as well as themselves. Focusing on Britain's economy, Smith emphasized commerce, manufacturing, and labor rather than agriculture as the primary sources of national wealth. Anticipating the industrial age that would first emerge in Britain, he concluded that "the greatest improvement in the productive powers of labor . . . have been the effects of the division of labor." For Smith as well as the Physiocrats, laissez-faire economics held the key to national wealth—whether a nation was built on agriculture or industry.

What Smith and the Physiocrats did for economics, the Italian Cesare Beccaria (1738–1794) did for criminology and penology. Beccaria wrote *On Crimes and Punishments* (1764), an international best-seller, to protest "the cruelty of punishments and the irregularities of criminal procedures, . . . to demolish the accumulated errors of centuries." He argued that criminal laws and punishments, like all other aspects of life, should incorporate reason and natural law. Good laws, he explained, promoted "the greatest happiness divided among the greatest number." Criminal law should strive to deter crime and rehabilitate criminals rather than merely punish wrongdoers. In Beccaria's view, torture and capital punishment made no sense; indeed, only new penal institutions that mirrored natural law could transform convicted criminals.

Criminology, penology, and slavery

Other Enlightenment thinkers used similar arguments to denounce slavery. Abbé Guillaume Raynal (1713–1796), an outspoken and widely read critic of slavery, argued that this institution and many other practices of European and American colonists were irrational and inhumane. In the name of natural

THE ENLIGHTENMENT

1733	Voltaire, *Letters Concerning the English Nation*
1748	Montesquieu, *The Spirit of the Laws*
1751	The *Encyclopedia*
1759	Voltaire, *Candide*
1762	Rousseau, *The Social Contract*
1764	Beccaria, *On Crimes and Punishments*
1776	Smith, *Wealth of Nations*
1792	Wollstonecraft, *Vindication of the Rights of Women*

KEY DATES

BIOGRAPHY

Jean-Jacques Rousseau
(1712–1778)

Jean-Jacques Rousseau described himself as a "singular soul, strange, and to say it all, a man of paradoxes." A celebrity both admired and hated in his own time, he wrote more deeply on a wide range of subjects than any of his contemporaries.

"My birth was my first misfortune," Rousseau once stated wryly. His mother died shortly after he was born in 1712 in the Republic of Geneva. His father, a watchmaker, raised him to the age of 10 and then abandoned him to a series of homes where he served unhappily as an apprentice. One day in 1728, returning late from walking in the countryside, he found the gates of Geneva closed. Anticipating punishment from his master for his tardiness, he turned around and set off on the first of a series of wanderings that would mark the rest of his life.

Singular Soul,

Controversial

Thinker

He lived for much of the next ten years as the guest and lover of a baroness, Madame de Warens. In his own words, Rousseau became her "piece of work, student, friend. . . ." Rousseau addressed Madame de Warens as "Momma," and she referred to him as "my little one." This was the first of Rousseau's numerous relationships, many of them with older women. Yet he also lived as a recluse for long stretches of time during which he educated himself.

In 1742 the shy Rousseau arrived in Paris. He would often live there, though he harbored "a secret disgust for life in the capital," with its "dirty stinking little streets, ugly black houses, . . . poverty, [and] beggars." He first gained attention in Paris by writing about music and by joining the cultural circles. He also earned a modest income by serving as secretary to aristocratic patrons and by copying music. In 1745, Thérèse Levasseur, a young laundress, became his lifelong companion and ultimately his wife. The couple would have four children and abandon them all to a foundling hospital for adoption.

In 1749, Rousseau entered an essay contest that abruptly changed his life. He won the competition by arguing that progress in the arts and sciences corrupted rather than improved human conduct. Suddenly he was controversial and famous. "No longer [was I] that timid man, more ashamed than modest. . . . All Paris repeated [my] sharp and biting sarcasms. . . ." Buoyed by his newfound fame, he contributed several articles on music and political economy to the *Encyclopedia*, edited by his close friend Denis Diderot. He came to know and eventually quarrel with most of the leading figures of the Enlightenment.

Rousseau went on to publish several critical and widely circulated books, including *Discourse on the Origin of Inequality* (1755), *Julie, or*

---

rights, he called for a slave rebellion. An article in the authoritative *Encyclopedia* asserted similar views, declaring that all enslaved individuals "have the right to be declared free. . . ." These arguments, like the ideas of Beccaria and, in politics, of Montesquieu and Rousseau, would resound again and again through eighteenth-century Western society.

Becoming enlightened required education. Diderot claimed that the *Encyclopedia* was written so "that our children, by becoming more educated, may at the same time become more virtuous and happier. . . ." Many Enlightenment thinkers based their ideas on the psychological ideas of John Locke, which emphasized the power of education to mold the child into the adult. These thinkers often attacked organized religion in particular for controlling education.

Education

Rousseau became the outstanding critic of traditional education. In *Émile*, he argued that teachers should appeal to children's natural interests and goodness rather than impose discipline and punishment. "Hold childhood in reverence," he counseled. "Give nature time to work." He also pushed for less "artificial" schools, maintaining that nature and experience were better guides to independent thinking and practical knowledge—at least for males. "I hate books," he pointed out. "They only teach us to talk about things we know nothing about." By emphasizing practical education, learning by doing, and motivating rather than requiring the child to learn, Rousseau's *Émile* became one of the most influential works on modern education. His ideas on the education of females, however, were not so modern. Like most men of his time (enlightened or not), he believed that girls should be educated to fulfill their traditional domestic roles as wives and mothers.

In theory at least, the Enlightenment emphasis on individualism opened the door to the idea of equality between men and women. Several intellectuals explored this controversial issue. Early in the period, some challenging books on the "woman question" were published by female authors. In one of the best known of these, *A Serious Proposal to the Ladies* (1694), the English writer Mary Astell (1666–1731) argued that women should be educated

The "woman question"

The New Heloise (1761), Émile (1762), and The Social Contract (1762). These writings inspired not only learned responses but ardent mail from ordinary readers. One reader of The New Heloise, a novel focusing on the conflict between social demands and personal feelings, wrote, "Ever since I read your blessed book I have burned with love of virtue. . . . Feeling has taken over once again." Yet the books also inspired scorn. Peasants once stoned Rousseau's house, for example, after a pastor attacked him from the pulpit. Authorities issued more serious threats. In 1762, Parisian officials ordered The Social Contract burned and Rousseau arrested. He fled to Geneva, only to discover that officials there were also seeking his arrest. Again he escaped, moving from place to place and finding shelter with friends whom he quickly lost after bitter arguments. **Figure 14.11** shows him in the distinctive fur hat and collar he often wore during this period, when he was a guest of the English philosopher David Hume.

In the last fifteen years of his life, Rousseau felt persecuted and

FIGURE 14.11 Allan Ramsay, *Jean-Jacques Rousseau*, 1766

depressed. "I appear," he wrote, "as the enemy of the Nation." He published stunning, often exaggerated self-revelations in his *Confessions*, disclosing his affairs, lies, and quarrels.

A difficult man and a tortured soul, Rousseau was also a superb writer whose *New Heloise* became the most widely read novel of his age. He counts among the most important educational theorists in history and

became an accomplished composer and musical theorist. Author of one of the most striking autobiographical works ever written, he also proved an extremely influential philosopher and political theorist. "I am different," he wrote, "alone on earth. . . . Whether nature did well or ill to break the mould in which she formed me, this is something one can only judge after reading me." Sixteen years after Rousseau's death in 1778, France's revolutionary government moved his body to a place of honor near Voltaire's burial site in Paris.

Connecting People & Society

1. What were Rousseau's early life experiences, and how might they have colored the ideas in his writings?

2. What do authorities' and ordinary people's harsh reactions to Rousseau's socially critical works reveal about eighteenth-century society?

3. How did Rousseau's work and life reflect the ideas and efforts of other Enlightenment thinkers?

according to the ideas of the new science—reason and debate—rather than tradition. Later, she explained that men seem to know more than women because "boys have much time and pains, care and cost bestowed on their education, girls have little or none. The former are early initiated in the sciences" and "have all imaginable encouragement" while "the latter are restrained, frowned upon, and beaten." In other writings, she questioned the inequality of men's and women's roles: "If all Men are born Free, how is it that all Women are born Slaves?" Later in the eighteenth century, the British author Mary Wollstonecraft (1759–1797) published *Vindication of the Rights of Women* (1792), in which she analyzed the condition of women and argued forcefully for equal rights for all human beings. Like Astell, Wollstonecraft stressed the need to educate women: "If she be not prepared by education to become the companion of man, she will stop the progress of knowledge and virtue; for truth must be common to all, or it will be inefficacious with respect to its influence on general practice."

Few male writers went that far. Although some men supported better education for women, most held the

traditional view that women were weaker than men and best suited for domestic rather than public affairs. According to Immanuel Kant, who spoke so optimistically and eloquently about education and enlightenment, "laborious learning or painful pondering, even if a woman should greatly succeed in it, destroy the merits that are proper to her sex." The editors of the *Encyclopedia* also ignored contributions from women, instead praising those who remained at home. Some of Rousseau's writings were particularly influential among women, primarily because they glorified child rearing, maternalism, and emotional life. Rousseau never suggested that women were independent beings equal to men. For him, "Woman is made to please and to be subjugated to man."

The Culture and Spread of the Enlightenment

The Enlightenment glittered especially in Paris, and salon meetings became the chief social setting for this intellectual culture. These meetings were hosted by wealthy Parisian patrons, usually women of the aristocracy or upper-middle class. In an environment lush with art, music, and wealth, the *philosophes,* Salon meetings powerful nobles, diplomats, statesmen, artists, and well-educated conversationalists gathered regularly to read, listen to, and debate the ideas of the Enlightenment. They also discussed—and sometimes influenced—economic policies, wars, and the king's choice of ministers. The German critic Friedrich Grimm (1723–1807), who published a private newsletter on Parisian life, described the salons of Julie de Lespinasse, who lived openly with the *philosophe* d'Alembert: "Her circle met daily from five o'clock until nine in the evening. There we were sure to find choice men of all orders in the State, the Church, the Court—military men, foreigners, and the most distinguished men of letters. Politics, religion, philosophy, anecdotes, news, nothing was excluded from the conversation." These salon meetings became self-conscious forums for arbitrating and molding public opinion through the open use of reason.

As leaders, patrons, and intellectual contributors to these gatherings, women played a particularly important role in the Enlightenment. Independent, witty, powerful women governed the potentially unruly meetings and discussions by enforcing rules of polite conversation. One of the most famous of these patrons was Madame Marie-Thérèse Geoffrin (1699–1777), a rich middle-class widow who served as a model and mentor for other women leaders of salons. **Figure 14.12,** a painting by Anicet Charles Lemonnier, shows a salon meeting at her home in 1755. Madame Geoffrin, wearing a blue dress and looking at the viewer, sits at the left next to Bernard de Fontenelle, 98-year-old popularizer of science. Above is a bust of Voltaire, the Enlightenment hero living in exile at the time. Women with the right intellectual and social qualifications attended this and other salons, but the star invitees were usually men.

Smaller meetings in other French and foreign cities, from Berlin to Philadelphia, paralleled the Parisian salon meetings. Moreover, all these meetings went hand in hand with an extensive international correspondence carried out by participants. For some, letter writing, like good conversation in the salons, was an art. People also read and discussed Enlightenment ideas in local academies, Freemason lodges, societies, libraries, and coffeehouses. In addition, most municipalities had clubs where the social and intellectual elites could mingle.

Even bookstores, where people could purchase books or pay small fees to read recent works, became hotbeds of Enlightenment ideas. **Figure 14.13** shows

FIGURE 14.12 Anicet Charles Lemonnier, *An Evening at Madame Geoffrin's in 1755,* 1812 *Philosophes,* nobles, statesmen, and well-educated conversationalists often gathered in Enlightenment-age salons led by women such as Madame Geoffrin, shown here sitting on the right in a blue dress.

FIGURE 14.13

Léonard Defrance, *At the Shield of Minerva,* 1781

In this painting, French artist Léonard Defrance depicts a street scene in front of a bookstore in France. Notice the reference in the store's name to Minerva, the Roman goddess of poetry and wisdom. Also note the mix of people and the prominence of the clergyman (in white robes) among them.

Connecting Art & Society

1. What might the packages of books bound for, or being delivered from, Spain, Portugal, Rome, and Naples suggest about the spread of Enlightenment ideas throughout Europe?

2. In what ways does this painting imply that people of all classes were being touched by books—and perhaps by Enlightenment ideas?

3. Why do you think the artist included a member of the clergy in such a central place in this painting?

an eighteenth-century bookstore. In the doorway stand two women, reading books. Just outside are packages of books being delivered from or to Spain, Portugal, Rome, and Naples. In the street, apparently drawn to the bookstore, are people of all classes, from a peasant with his scythe at the left to a cleric in his white robes at the center. The name of the bookstore, "The Shield of Minerva," refers to the Roman goddess of wisdom. In a growing number of bookstores such as this, all sorts of works became increasingly available, from religious tracts and chivalric tales to new novels and Enlightenment literature.

Bookstores

These gatherings and interchanges spread the ideas of the Enlightenment throughout society and enhanced the social respectability of intellectuals. They also helped create a common intellectual culture that crossed class lines and political borders and that contributed to an informed body of public opinion. People who participated in these interchanges came to sense that they could freely express ideas as well as debate political and social issues. By the last quarter of the eighteenth century, Enlightenment ideas could be heard even in the camps of the *philosophes'* traditional opponents—the clergy, governmental officials, and monarchs. As we will see, these ideas pushed some monarchs to enact "enlightened" reforms and encouraged many other people to demand revolutionary change.

LOOKING BACK & MOVING FORWARD

Summary   The great intellectual revolution of the seventeenth and eighteenth centuries was fueled by advances in science. Brimming with new scientific ideas and discoveries, Western civilization relinquished its medieval assumptions and embarked on an innovative journey unique among the cultures of the world. This change in direction became one of the main forces behind the power and dynamism that came to characterize the West. Through science, Westerners hoped to gain greater control over the material world and nature.

Enlightenment thinkers carried these daring aspirations further, self-consciously leading a mission of reform and freedom from the shackles of tradition. By striking the match of reason, they believed, people could at last dispel the darkness of the past and liberate themselves as never before. Thus enlightened, humanity as a whole could move from childhood to adulthood. As the *philosophe* Baron d'Holbach proclaimed, "The *enlightened man,* is man in his maturity, in his perfection; who is capable of pursuing his own happiness; because he has learned to examine, to think for himself, and not to take that for truth upon the authority of others."

Many participants in Enlightenment circles have since been criticized as self-concerned dilettantes reluctant to take on the risks of real reform. Most historians, however, see the *philosophes* as thoughtful, sincere, and sometimes brilliant thinkers. The *philosophes* clearly left a mark on Western culture. Their ideas, like those of the seventeenth-century scientists, threatened the traditional order, especially the church. As their primary legacy, they widened the gap between religiously influenced doctrines and accepted scholarly thought. Equally significant, they set the intellectual stage for a series of revolutions that would soon sweep America and Europe. Above all, their way of thinking—stressing reason, individualism, and progress—would form the intellectual foundation of modern Western society and further distinguish this civilization from its non-Western counterparts.

KEY TERMS

Neoplatonism,   *p. 453*
Hermetic doctrine,   *p. 453*
Copernican revolution,   *p. 454*
heliocentric model,   *p. 454*
empirical method,   *p. 459*
deductive reasoning,   *p. 460*
Cartesian dualism,   *p. 460*
Scientific Revolution,   *p. 460*
Enlightenment,   *p. 462*
philosophes,   *p. 465*

REVIEW, ANALYZE, & CONNECT TO TODAY

REVIEW THE PREVIOUS CHAPTERS

Chapter 12—"Faith, Fortune, and Fame"—told how several European powers expanded overseas during the fifteenth, sixteenth, and seventeenth centuries and grew rich from the commerce. Chapter 13—"The Struggle for Survival and Sovereignty"—focused on how kings and nobles battled for power, the resolutions of those struggles, and their impact on the millions of people outside the elite.

1. Analyze how the expansion of Europe might have stimulated scientific research.

2. In what ways did the effort of monarchs to increase their power and create stability relate to the promotion of science and the desire for greater intellectual certainty?

ANALYZE THIS CHAPTER

Chapter 14—"A New World of Reason and Reform"— examines the changing intellectual foundations of the West.

1. List and analyze the differences between the new scientific views of the world and traditional medieval views.

How did standards for ascertaining the "truth" differ between these two perspectives?

2. Analyze the beliefs and motives of three central figures in the Scientific Revolution. What barriers did they have to overcome to present their views?

3. Do you think the Enlightenment merely popularized the Scientific Revolution, or did it accomplish something more?

4. In what ways did the Enlightenment threaten traditional views and authorities?

CONNECT TO TODAY

Think about the meaning of the Scientific Revolution and the values underlying the Enlightenment.

1. In what ways are our present-day assumptions about the physical universe and the workings of nature based on the ideas and discoveries of the Scientific Revolution?

2. What aspects of world politics today reflect Enlightenment values? What aspects of present-day global politics seem to be opposed to those values?

BEYOND THE CLASSROOM

QUESTIONING TRUTH AND AUTHORITY

Kuhn, Thomas S. *The Structure of Scientific Revolutions,* 2nd ed. Chicago: University of Chicago Press, 1970. A landmark analysis of the nature, causes, and consequences of transformations in scientific concepts.

Mandrou, Robert. *From Humanism to Science.* Atlantic Highlands, NJ: Humanities Press, 1979. A description of how the role of intellectuals changed between 1480 and 1700.

Teresi, Dick. *Lost Discoveries: The Ancient Roots of Modern Science—From the Babylonians to the Maya.* New York: Simon & Schuster, 2003. Focuses on discoveries from non-Western societies that predated Europe's Scientific Revolution.

DEVELOPING A MODERN SCIENTIFIC VIEW

Cohen, H.F. *The Scientific Revolution.* Chicago: University of Chicago Press, 1994. An analysis of when and where modern science began.

Dear, Peter. *Revolutionizing the Sciences: European Knowledge and Its Ambitions, 1500–1700.* Princeton, NJ: Princeton University Press, 2001. A survey of the main ideas of science and its new institutions.

Feingold, Mordechai. *The Newtonian Moment: Isaac Newton and the Making of Modern Culture.* New York: Oxford University Press, 2004. A well-illustrated book that focuses on Newton and how his ideas affected eighteenth-century culture.

Hall, Rupert A. *The Revolution in Science, 1500–1750.* London: Longman, 1983. A useful introduction to the developments in science during this period.

Schiebinger, Londa. *The Mind Has No Sex? Women in the Origins of Modern Science.* Cambridge, MA: Harvard University Press, 1990. An examination of the participation of women in science; stresses how science reflected male biases.

Shapin, Steven. *The Scientific Revolution.* Chicago: University of Chicago Press, 1996. A concise, new interpretation questioning whether there was a "scientific revolution."

Westfall, Richard. *The Construction of Modern Science: Mechanisms and Mechanics.* New York: Cambridge University Press, 1977. A good survey of scientific developments during the seventeenth century that emphasizes the importance of mathematics and mechanics.

SUPPORTING AND SPREADING SCIENCE

Jacob, Margaret C. *The Cultural Meaning of the Scientific Revolution.* New York: Knopf, 1988. Examines the evolution of science within its political, social, and cultural context.

Moran, Bruce T., ed. *Patronage and Institutions: Science, Technology and Medicine at the European Court, 1500–1750.* Rochester, NY: Boydell Press, 1991. Examines the role of royal courts in supporting and shaping science during this period.

LAYING THE FOUNDATIONS FOR THE ENLIGHTENMENT

Outram, Dorinda. *The Enlightenment.* Cambridge: Cambridge University Press, 2005. Presents the various interpretations of the Enlightenment.

Porter, Roy. *The Enlightenment,* 2nd ed. London: Palgrave, 2001. A solid, well-written survey of eighteenth-century intellectual life.

Sklar, Judith. *Montesquieu.* Oxford: Oxford University Press, 1987. A concise, well-written study of Montesquieu and his ideas.

THE ENLIGHTENMENT IN FULL STRIDE

Besterman, Theodore. *Voltaire,* 3rd ed. Chicago: University of Chicago Press, 1976. A useful biography of this major Enlightenment figure.

Darton, Robert. *The Business of Enlightenment: A Publishing History of the* Encyclopedia, *1775–1800.* Cambridge, MA: Belknap Press, 1979. A well-written social history and analysis of the publication of the *Encyclopedia.*

Gay, Peter. *The Enlightenment: An Interpretation,* 2 vols. New York: Knopf, 1966–1969. A classic study, exhaustive, but with a strong point of view.

Goodman, Dena. *The Republic of Letters: A Cultural History of the French Enlightenment.* Ithaca, NY: Cornell University Press, 1994. A study of the cultural and intellectual life of eighteenth-century France that concentrates on the role played by the salons.

Lougee, Carolyn. *Le Paradis des Femmes. Women, Salons, and Social Stratification in Seventeenth-Century France.* Princeton, NJ: Princeton University Press, 1976. Analyzes the foundations and importance of the French salons, emphasizing the role played by women in them.

Melton, J.V.H. *The Rise of the Public in Enlightenment Europe.* Cambridge: Cambridge University Press, 2001. Connects publishing and the reading public during the Enlightenment.

PHILIP VAN DIJK, *BRISTOL DOCKS AND QUAY,* ca. 1780

This painting shows the British port of Bristol, one of many European port cities that benefited from the lucrative overseas trade that grew during the eighteenth century. On the left, ships arrive and dock on the well-protected canal, where they are loaded and unloaded. On the quay are workers, merchants, and families—some of the many who directly benefited from the activity. Around them are well-kept shops, homes, and buildings that reflect the prosperity of this commercial center and the wealth drawn from Britain's colonial empire.

Competing for Power and Wealth

The Old Regime, 1715–1789

" **A** reasonable man is always happy if he has what is necessary for him according to his condition [social rank], that is to say, if he has the protection of the laws, and can live as his father lived before him," wrote a French observer in 1747. The political lesson behind these words was clear. "Essential . . . to the good of a nation is being governed in one constant and uniform manner." Most people living in the eighteenth century would have nodded their heads in agreement. Indeed, they actively upheld the social order—ranked, governed, and sanctioned as it was by tradition and Christian teachings.

Despite this affirmation of stability, change was afoot in these years. During the seventeenth century, kings and queens had struggled with nobles in their own countries for control and with other monarchs to increase their nations' sway. In their continuing competition for power and wealth, eighteenth-century kings and queens tried to strengthen their states while gaining status—often through war—in the international arena. Below them, ambitious aristocrats flexed their muscles, sometimes challenging their monarchs, sometimes forging alliances with them, and often reveling in the new wealth and culture that now lay within their reach. They, along with the growing number of commoners, began to see much promise in the new ways to produce food and organize manufacturing, all fueled by accelerating commerce—especially with overseas colonies, as reflected in the painting facing this page. Moreover, many elites—including some monarchs themselves—also recognized the strength of Enlightenment ideas and began to think of ways to institute "enlightened" reforms. At the base of Western society, the mass of peasants and workers toiled, as they always had. However, their numbers were increasing, and their ways of life were slowly adjusting to the pressures of change. This society and its politics would later be known as the Old Regime, but many living at the time detected the quickening pulse of a new era.

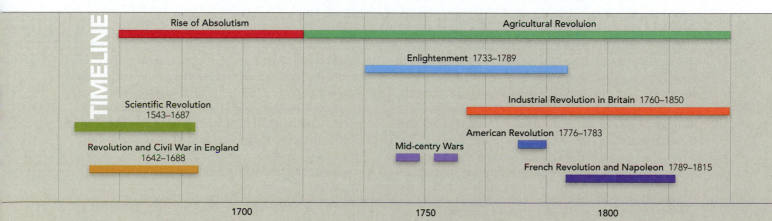

TIMELINE

Rise of Absolutism

Agricultural Revoluion

Enlightenment 1733–1789

Scientific Revolution
1543–1687

Industrial Revolution in Britain 1760–1850

American Revolution 1776–1783

Revolution and Civil War in England
1642–1688

Mid-centry Wars

French Revolution and Napoleon 1789–1815

1700　　　　　1750　　　　　1800

PREVIEW

STATEBUILDING AND WAR

In August 1715, the old and sad Louis XIV fell ill. His legs swelled and turned black as gangrene set in. Remarkably, he had outlived both his son and grandson. On his deathbed, Louis warned his 5-year-old great-grandson, who would succeed him as Louis XV (r. 1715–1774), not to "imitate my love of building nor my liking of war." Neither Louis XV nor many other rulers of the time managed to follow this advice for long. War and building might cost lives and drain royal treasuries, but they made a spectacular show of power in a competitive world. The rulers of Europe clung to their statebuilding ways, straining to secure their central governments and ensure their own position at the top.

During the seventeenth century, this competitiveness had plunged Europe into a series of bloody conflicts—the very battles Louis XIV regretted on his deathbed (see Chapter 13). In western Europe, the violence stopped with the Peace of Utrecht in 1713–1714. Seven years later, the Treaty of Nystad (1721) ended the conflicts in eastern Europe (see **Map 15.1**). For a while, the two treaties held. Monarchs throughout Europe tried to adhere to the principle of a **balance of power** to prevent any one state or alliance from dominating the others. Nevertheless, anyone hoping for an extended period free of war would be sorely disappointed. Up-and-coming states such as

Prussia and Britain bristled with ambition and vied with their established competitors for power, prestige, and wealth. Their struggles spread beyond the borders of Europe to overseas colonies on continents from North America to Asia, in this sense turning European wars into global conflicts. As we will see, this competition subjected millions of people to a fresh round of hardship and irrevocably altered the fate and fortunes of nations throughout the West.

Rising Ambitions in Eastern Europe

Within Europe, the fiercest competition took place in eastern Europe. There, Russia and Brandenburg-Prussia were on the rise. Under Peter the Great, Russia had already defeated Sweden, grabbing much of the northeastern Baltic coast in the process. Russia next hoped to take advantage of the sprawling but weak Polish state farther west (see Chapter 13) and to benefit from the decline of the Ottoman Empire, which controlled the Black Sea to Russia's south. Brandenburg-Prussia also saw opportunities in Poland, which divided and bordered its lands. This militaristic state also coveted some of the holdings of the bloated Austro-Hungarian Empire to the south, which in turn intended to hold its own in the power struggle. Someone would have to pay the price for all these ambitions.

Peter the Great had done much to turn Russia toward the West and make it a great power. By the time of his death in 1725, he had modernized Russia's government and military, established Russia as the dominant power in northeastern Europe, and pressured the Russian nobility into the state bureaucracy and army officer corps. In the process, he made many enemies, from the peasants who paid dearly for Peter's accomplishments to all those who had a stake in the very social, cultural, and religious traditions that Peter attacked. His successors would have to face these enemies and shoulder the task of sustaining Russia's expansion to the south and west.

Six mediocre rulers followed Peter—including an infant, a boy of 12, and a mentally unstable tsar. Despite this shaky leadership, Russia held its ground. From 1725 to 1762, its population increased, and the landowning elite grew wealthier

> New leadership in expanding Russia

than ever. The nobility took back some of the authority it had lost to Peter, diminishing the service it owed to the state; in 1762, nobles freed themselves of all such obligations. Nevertheless, they still staffed the bureaucracy and military officer corps. Moreover, nobles cracked down even more on their serfs, reducing their status to that of mere property. The 1767 Decree on Serfs made the situation crystal clear: "Serfs and peasants . . . owe their landlords proper submission and absolute obedience in all matters."

MAP 15.1

Europe, 1721

This map shows Europe after the Treaties of Utrecht (1714) and Nystad (1721).

Explore the Map

1. Although France and Spain were ruled by Bourbon monarchs, the two nations remained separate. How might a union between the two have altered the balance of power in Europe?

2. Locate the large states in eastern Europe. Which of these states, despite their size, were declining powers?

3. Identify the lands controlled by Austria. Why might this power's holdings have been vulnerable?

The decades of weak leadership ended when a dynamic new leader ascended the Russian throne. Catherine the Great (r. 1762–1796) grew up an obscure princess from one of the little German states. For political reasons, her family married her to young Peter III (r. 1762), the tyrannical and intellectually limited grandson of Peter the Great and heir to the Russian crown. He soon rejected her in all ways, and after he became tsar, he quickly lost most of his supporters as well. Catherine had no intention of languishing in obscurity. "I did not care about Peter," she later wrote, "but I did care about the crown." Less than a year after he took the throne, Catherine conspired with a group of aristocratic army officers, who assassinated him and declared Catherine tsarina of Russia.

Catherine the Great

The new empress used her striking intelligence, charm, and political talent to assert her own power and expand Russian territory and might. Well educated, she thought of herself as attuned to Enlightenment ideas. She often corresponded with French *philosophes* such as Denis Diderot, who spent some time at St. Petersburg as her guest. In 1766, she congratulated Voltaire for triumphing "against the enemies of mankind: superstition, fanaticism, ignorance, quibbling, evil judges, and the power that rests in their hands." Voltaire returned the favor with constant praise for Catherine. She relaxed the traditionally tight constraints on the press in Russia and she confiscated church lands—policies that seemed in line with Enlightenment thinking. Her educational reforms, by which she established new local schools, teachers' colleges, and schools for girls, also suggested a forward-thinking monarch. Most stunningly, Catherine convened a legislative commission, half of whose members were commoners (some even peasants), to reform Russia's legal code. She wrote the *Instruction* (1767) to that commission herself, relying on the works of key Enlightenment figures such as Montesquieu and Beccaria. Her *Instruction* called for equality before the law, the abolition of torture, and other liberal reforms.

These programs promised more than they delivered. The commission members squabbled among themselves, and in the end, the effort yielded only minor reforms before it was finally abandoned. Catherine's early talk of easing the burdens on the peasantry also came to little; in return for the support of noble landowners, she allowed them to subjugate the peasants even further. As Document 15.1 suggests, some observers criticized the treatment of Russia's serfs. For example, Alexander Radischev argued, "What good does it do the country that every year a few thousand more bushels of grain are grown, if those who produce it are valued on a par with the ox whose job it is to break the heavy furrow?" Catherine imprisoned him.

In 1768, Catherine provoked a war against the Ottoman Empire. The event seems to have signaled her turn away from enlightened reform and toward power politics. A massive insurrection by Russian serfs in 1773 under the leadership of a Don Cossack, Yemelyan Pugachev (1726–1775), further soured her on reform. Pugachev claimed to be Catherine's murdered husband, a "redeemer tsar," and promised his followers land and freedom. Thousands of serfs in southwestern Russia turned against their masters—slaughtering hundreds of landlords and officials—and demanded an end to their plight. Catherine's army managed to put down the rebellion, but only with great difficulty. When some disgruntled followers betrayed Pugachev, the army captured him and tortured him to death.

Catherine proved more successful in her ambitious foreign policy. She defeated the Turks in 1774, extending Russia to the Black Sea and the Balkan Peninsula. **Map 15.2** shows Russia's expansion to the south and west during the eighteenth century.

Catherine then turned on Poland. At the beginning of the eighteenth century, Poland was the third-largest country in Europe. Yet, as we saw in Chapter 13, it lacked natural boundaries and a strong central government. Weak and without allies, it became a power vacuum that proved all too tempting to its ambitious neighbors. In 1772, Russia, Prussia, and Austria—having plotted Poland's demise among themselves—annexed slices of Polish territory. This aggression at long last stirred the Polish government to action. The Diet passed sweeping reforms, improved the lot of commoners, and gave the central government power to act effectively. These changes came too late. Poland still could not match the combined armies of its enemies, and in 1795, the three aggressors divided the remainder of the hapless nation among themselves. **Map 15.2** shows the eventual dismemberment of Poland, which left Russia, Prussia, and Austria the dominant powers in eastern Europe. When Catherine died in 1796 after thirty-five years of rule, Russia had grown to an ominous size and had taken its place as a major power in world affairs.

The partition of Poland

Farther south, military defeats at the hands of the Russians marked the Ottoman Empire's continuing decline. Throughout the eighteenth century, the Ottoman economy suffered from falling population growth and a rising inability to compete commercially with Europeans. The English, French, and Venetians took over the trade from the East that used to pass through Ottoman hands. Sultans lost administrative authority to the Muslim clergy. Fearing cultural influences from western Europe, this conservative clergy hindered efforts to introduce European science and even printing presses into Ottoman lands for most of the eighteenth century. Unable to maintain their own armaments industry, moreover, the Ottomans had to rely on European suppliers to outfit the empire's army and navy. At the same time, the Ottomans faced uprisings in their Arabian provinces, where a religious reform movement, **Wahhabism,** challenged the sultans' authority. After mid-century, for good reason, many European elites began calling the Ottoman Empire the "sick man of Europe."

The decline of the Ottoman Empire

DOCUMENT 15.1

Landlords and Serfs in Russia

During the eighteenth century, Russian serfs probably fared worse than peasants elsewhere in Europe. Toward the end of the century, Alexander Radischev published a description of Russian serfs and their treatment by noble landowners. For this daring act, the author was imprisoned by Catherine II.

A certain man left the capital, acquired a small village of one or two hundred souls [i.e., serfs], and determined to make his living by agriculture. . . . To this end he thought it the surest method to make his peasants resemble tools that have neither will nor impulse; and to a certain extent he actually made them like the soldiers of the present time who are commanded in a mass, who move to battle in a mass, and who count for nothing when acting singly. To attain this end he took away from his peasants the small allotment of plough land and the hay meadows which noblemen usually give them

for their bare maintenance, as a recompense for all the forced labor which they demand from them. In a word, this nobleman forced all his peasants and their wives and children to work every day of the year for him. Lest they should starve, he doled out to them a definite quantity of bread. . . . If there was any real meat, it was only in Easter Week.

These serfs also receive clothing befitting their condition. . . . Naturally these serfs had no cows, horses, ewes, or rams. Their master did not withhold from these serfs the permission, but rather the means to have them. Whoever was a little better off and ate sparingly, kept a few chickens, which the master sometimes took for himself, paying for them as he pleased.

In a short time he added to his two hundred souls another two hundred as victims of his greed, and proceeding with them just as with the first, he increased his holdings year after year, thus multiplying the

number of those groaning in his fields. Now he counts them by the thousands and is praised as a famous agriculturalist.

"Barbarian! What good does it do the country that every year a few thousand more bushels of grain are grown, if those who produce it are valued on a par with the ox whose job it is to break the heavy furrow? Or do we think our citizens happy because our granaries are full and their stomachs empty?"

SOURCE: Alexander Radischev, *A Journey from St. Petersburg to Moscow* (1790).

Analyze the Document

1. In what ways does the landowner described in this excerpt treat his serfs?

2. How does the author criticize this treatment of serfs?

3. According to Radischev, is the main problem with this "certain man" or with the system of serfdom in Russia?

In east-central Europe, the small but rising Brandenburg-Prussia set its sights on the Austrian Empire, a large power struggling to maintain control over its far-flung lands. From 1713 to 1740, the vigorous Frederick William I ruled Prussia. The king was obsessed with unquestioned absolutism, centralized bureaucratic administration, and, above all, the military. His martial uniforms and preoccupation with Prussian soldiery earned him the label the Sergeant King.

Forging a military state in Prussia

Frederick William's mental image of the perfect military dominated his policies and Prussian society. While he employed his army for road and canal building as well as traditional military service, some 70 percent of the state's budget went to the armed forces, whose size he more than doubled during his reign. Rather than relying on mercenaries, the king required all men to register for military service in local units commanded by German noble officers. The localities, in turn, had to recruit and support these regiments, and soldiers were billeted among the civilian population.

No other state in Europe could boast such a high proportion of men, from peasant to noble, in the military. Nor could any other state point to such a regimented society. In Prussia, the higher ranks of the military and state bureaucracy were reserved for the nobility; the middle classes were clearly prevented from rising to noble status; and the peasantry was a subordinate, overburdened people, often still serfs living in almost slavelike relationships to their landowning masters.

Despite the martial tenor of life in Prussia, the king left a surprisingly progressive legacy. Frederick William I avoided wars, promoted a strong economy, welcomed Protestant and Jewish refugees, and filled the treasury. In 1740, he passed all that he had built, intact, on to his talented son Frederick II (r. 1740–1786), later known as Frederick the Great. The new king soon used this army—the fourth largest in Europe—and the money his father had accumulated to make a bold bid for Austrian lands.

In the same year that Frederick II ascended the throne in Prussia, Maria Theresa (r. 1740–1780) became empress of the Austrian Habsburg dominions.

Boundary of Poland to 1772
Boundary of the Three Powers at 1795
Russian Gains 1721–1795
Poland 1793–1795

MAP 15.2

The Expansion of Russia and the Partition of Poland, 1721–1795

This map shows eastern Europe during the eighteenth century, identifying the partition of Poland and the expansion of Russia and Prussia.

Explore the Map

1. In what ways did the partition of Poland benefit Russia, Prussia, and Austria?

2. How might Poland's decline change the balance of power?

3. Where might the rising powers of Russia and Prussia look for further expansion?

Austria was not a tightly controlled, militaristic state like Prussia. Rather, it had already lost most of the indirect control it once held over the central German states as head of the Holy Roman Empire. Austria's own lands contained a complex array of language groups and consisted of some semi-autonomous territories. Austria could barely control Hungary, and its nobility fully dominated its serfs, who paid most taxes directly to their lords rather than to the crown.

> **Austria tries to hold on**

As a result, Maria Theresa could afford only a relatively small army.

The empress's father had feared that these weaknesses might prove Austria's undoing when he died. Moreover, there was only weak precedent for a female ruler of Habsburg lands. Therefore, he spent the final twenty years of his life securing agreement among all the European powers (embodied in a document called the Pragmatic Sanction) that his daughter would succeed him without question. In spite of his diligence, when he died in 1740, competitors arose to challenge her authority. As for the principle of balance of power among states implying a desire for peace, Frederick II of Prussia dismissed the idea bluntly: "The fundamental rule of governments is the principle of extending their territories."

As soon as Maria Theresa took the crown, Frederick challenged her authority, a common occurrence when a succession was questionable in any way. Acting on his maxim that "the safety and greater good for the state demands that treaties should be broken under certain circumstances," the Prussian king marched his troops into Silesia (see **Map 15.3**), the richest of the Habsburg provinces. He also shrewdly forged alliances with other German states against Austria. His aggressive scheming plunged most of the major European states into a series of wars for the mastery of central Europe.

The mid-century land wars

The War of the Austrian Succession dragged on for eight years (1740–1748). Maria Theresa rallied Hungarian arms to her defense and repelled Prussia's allies—Bavarians, Saxons, French, and Spanish. The conflict eventually turned into a military stalemate, which led to a 1748 peace treaty that ended the hostilities. Maria Theresa had managed to preserve the Habsburg state as a major power, but she had been unable to dislodge Frederick from Silesia.

Neither she nor her advisors intended to tolerate this robbery of their fair province by the upstart Prussians—even if it meant starting negotiations for an alliance with their traditional rival, France. Frederick grew fearful of being isolated by his enemies and left vulnerable to invasions. In 1756, when he signed an alliance with Great Britain—Prussia's opponent only a few years earlier—Maria Theresa solidified a new alliance with France. Document 15.2 reveals how difficult the change of allies was for Maria Theresa. This astounding shift of alliances—the so-called Diplomatic Revolution—suddenly transformed former enemies into friends. Meanwhile, Maria Theresa shored up Austria's internal resources by honing her government's control over taxation, dimin-

The Diplomatic Revolution

ishing burdens on the peasantry, and reorganizing the bureaucracy. All this strengthened her position as a ruler who could command strong forces and who enjoyed backing from a powerful ally. **Figure 15.1**, a painting by Habsburg court artist Martin Meytens, shows the empress with her husband (seated on the left) and thirteen of her sixteen children. Her son Joseph, heir to the throne, stands in a favored place at the center of the star floor. As this painting suggests, even though she led Austria through wars, Maria Theresa often chose to present herself as a good mother to both her family and her nation.

Not one to wait for his enemies to strike first, Frederick reopened hostilities by overrunning Saxony in 1756, initiating the Seven Years' War (1756–1763). However, Frederick soon found himself at bay as France and Austria—now joined by Russia and Sweden, both of which hoped to gain lands at Prussia's expense—closed in on him from all directions. His only backing came from Britain, which saw an opportunity to weaken its longtime opponent, France. After holding off his enemies for six years, the exhausted Prussian king finally seemed near defeat.

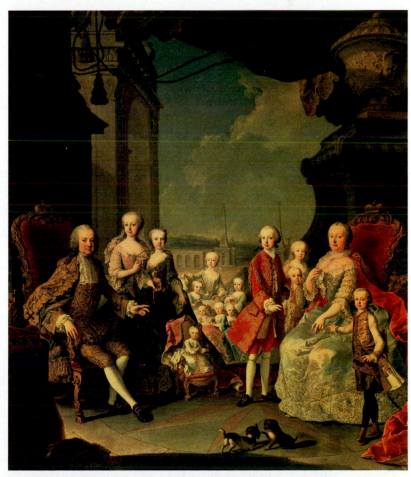

FIGURE 15.1 Martin Meytens, *Maria Theresa and Her Family*, 1750 The artist portrayed the empress with her husband and many children, suggesting that she was a good mother as well as a powerful ruler. To her right stands the heir to her throne, Joseph.

MAP 15.3

Prussia and the Austrian Empire, 1721–1772

This map shows two growing eighteenth-century powers, Prussia and Austria.

Explore the Map

1. Compare the holdings of these two states. Which do you think was stronger? Why?

2. What problems did both face in creating a strong, unified state?

3. To the west lay France, and to the east was Russia—both large and unified states. Where were Austria and Prussia most likely to compete with each other or to expand? Why?

"I believe all is lost," he confessed in private. Then in 1762 his luck revived. The Russian tsarina Elizabeth, one of his most reviled enemies, died. Her successor, the weak Peter III, happened to admire Frederick and suddenly pulled Russia out of the war. The remaining allies soon lost stomach for the fight. The peace in 1763 left matters much as they had been before the war began, but as we will see (pages 494–496), the fighting in Europe spread to India, the Caribbean, and North America.

Having narrowly escaped destruction, Frederick spent the remaining twenty-three years of his life reconstructing his war-ravaged territories. He encouraged agriculture, subsidized and protected industry, and invited immigrants into his well-governed territories. At no time, though, did he neglect his army or lose his sense of practicality. Indeed, in 1772 he joined Austria and Russia in the first partition of Poland. **Map 15.3** shows Prussia's expansion under Frederick, first at the expense of the Austrian Empire when he

DOCUMENT 15.2

Austria's Empress Explains the Diplomatic Revolution

During the eighteenth century, alliances among European states often shifted. They changed most dramatically in the 1756 Diplomatic Revolution preceding the Seven Years' War (1756–1763). In the following excerpt, Empress Maria Theresa of Austria explains why she turned toward her traditional adversary, France, to form a coalition against the newly allied Prussia and Great Britain.

"I have not abandoned the old system, but Great Britain has abandoned me and the system, by concluding the Prussian treaty, the first intelligence of which struck me like a fit of apoplexy. I and the king of Prussia are incompatible; and no consideration on earth will ever induce me to enter into any engagement to which he is a party. Why should you be surprised if, following your example in concluding a treaty with Prussia, I should now enter into an engagement with France?

"I am far from being French in my disposition, and do not deny that the court of Versailles has been my bitterest enemy, but I have little to fear from France, and I have no other recourse than to form such arrangements as will secure what remains to me. My principal aim is to secure my hereditary possessions. I have truly but two enemies whom I really dread, the king of Prussia and the Turks; and while I and Russia continue on the same good terms as now exist between us; we shall, I trust, be able to convince Europe, that we are in a condition to defend ourselves against those adversaries, however formidable."

SOURCE: Maria Theresa, William Coxe, *History of the House of Austria*, vol. 3 (London: Bohn, 1847), pp. 363–364.

Analyze the Document

1. Why does Maria Theresa forge an alliance with France?

2. What problems does she anticipate in allying Austria with France?

3. Why might Maria Theresa have identified the king of Prussia and the Turks as the "two enemies whom I really dread"?

took Silesia, and then at the expense of Poland as he used the territory to unify the main portions of his country. The map also shows Prussia's chief competitor, Austria, with its farther-flung territories. By the time of his death in 1786, Frederick had raised Prussia to the status of a great power and shared the leadership of central Europe with Austria.

Warfare in the Eighteenth Century

The nature of wars fought by these eighteenth-century nations had evolved and changed from earlier times. Now armies consisted primarily of professional forces whose size and elaborate organization mirrored the centralized, bureaucratic governments they served. Officers were paid as full-time servants of the state in both peace and war. However, the troops they commanded were not all so professional. Conscripts, volunteers, mercenaries, and even criminals made up their rank and file. In this sense, armies served as a depository for men without means and for those seen as threats to the social order. Officers tried to tame these motley groups by stressing harsh discipline and incessant drilling.

Weapons and tactics were also changing. Reliable muskets; bayonets that no longer hindered fire; mobile cannons; and skilled coordination of troops, artillery, and cavalry all made warfare potentially more destructive than ever. Still, generals typically avoided all-out battles, preferring to expend their resources judiciously.

"I do not favor pitched battles, especially at the beginning of a war," said Marshall Saxe, a leading French officer and writer on war tactics, in 1732. "I am convinced that a skillful general could make war all his life without being forced into one." Even Frederick the Great—not one to shy away from warfare—expressed this preference in his *Instructions for His Generals* (1747): "The greatest secret of war and the masterpiece of a skillful general is to starve his enemy." Instead of embarking on grand, decisive battles, then, eighteenth-century generals focused on building fortifications, initiating and maintaining sieges, securing supply lines, gaining superior positions, and piling up small advantages. Moreover, most military campaigns lasted only four or five months a year. Meanwhile, life outside the military—commerce, farming, culture, travel, and politics—went on as usual.

Yet, as Frederick the Great recognized, "war is [ultimately] decided only by battles and is not finished except by them." Outright fighting, when it finally occurred, took a heavy toll in human lives. Typically, soldiers arranged themselves in dense rows at least three men deep and fired their muskets, row by row, on command. Each side hurled artillery fire into the opposing troops and sent the cavalry charging in. Casualties mounted, but at the end of the day generals usually pulled their forces back from the battle with enough survivors to fight again.

Maritime battles cost fewer lives than land wars but could be crucial in the overall outcome of war.

FIGURE 15.2 An Eighteenth-Century French Warship This view of a French warship shows some of the weapons, men, animals, stores, and equipment carried by this powerful vessel of war.

The largest ships of war in the eighteenth century carried up to one hundred cannons. **Figure 15.2,** a cutaway view of a French warship, shows cannons poking out of the top three decks. Sailors are depicted at drill and at rest. At the upper right are officers' quarters, and the bottom decks house supplies, including livestock. Often firing at each other at point-blank range, many warships were destroyed or suffered grievous damage in these brutal clashes, and thousands of sailors perished.

A single battle, whether on land or sea, rarely led to a definitive outcome. More likely, the relentless draining away of money and men prompted diplomats to come to the bargaining table and end the war. This hemorrhaging of money and men was not missed by critics of the military, especially Enlightenment thinkers, who denigrated the old warrior culture as irrational and wasteful. Their criticisms, however, could neither prevent nor end wars in a society in which most people still regarded war as a normal—perhaps necessary—part of life.

Western Europe and the Great Colonial Rivalry

Like eastern Europe, western Europe experienced its own brand of statebuilding and rivalry for power. In this region as well as overseas, France and Britain uneasily shared dominance. Their seventeenth-century rivals, Spain and Holland, were declining. On the Continent, Spain—lacking the finances, manpower, and royal leadership that made it such a power in the late sixteenth and early seventeenth centuries—could no longer threaten France. Holland—damaged by three Anglo-Dutch wars and economic warfare with Britain during the seventeenth century—had

gradually lost much of its trade and international position. Overseas, however, Spain and Portugal had managed to hold on to most of their lands. In the Americas, they remained great colonial powers, controlling most of the territory stretching from Mexico to the South American continent. There, they dominated the Amerindians, disrupting their cultures and turning them into laborers on large plantations and in mines, which still produced massive loads of gold and silver for shipment to Europe. Holland also had retained its Pacific colonies, which supported a valuable coffee and spice trade. However, the Dutch had lost some of their empire in Asia and much of their sea power to the British. With Spain and Holland thus occupied, France and Britain became the primary colonial rivals (see **Map 15.4**).

Louis XIV had made France a model of absolutism. However, the French monarchy never again achieved the clout it had enjoyed under his guidance. To be sure, France remained a first-rank power with a large army, a centralized bureaucracy, and a growing economy. Yet, even during the last decades of his reign, Louis XIV's stature diminished. Thoughtful people criticized him for dragging France into what they saw as meaningless foreign conflicts. Louis' expensive wars and unreformed taxation policies also depleted the treasury. As Voltaire reported in 1751, "In the minds of the majority of his subjects, he lost during the last three years of his life all the prestige of the great and memorable things he had accomplished. . . ."

After Louis' death in 1715, French nobles in governmental councils and France's *parlements*—the thirteen judicial courts that had to sign royal decrees before those documents could become

> The French monarchy in decline

MAP 15.4

Overseas Colonies and Trade, 1740

This map shows Europe's colonies and overseas trade patterns during the mid-eighteenth century.

Explore the Map

1. Locate British and French holdings. Where were conflicts most likely to break out between these two powers? Why?

2. Describe the triangular trade across the Atlantic Ocean. What continents did this trade connect? Why was slavery so central to this system?

3. Which goods dominated trade? Which goods were Europeans most interested in selling and buying? Why?

law—angled for a restoration of the powers they had lost to the king. The *parlements* claimed to speak for the nation, though in fact they voiced only the interests of the elites. The nobles bargained with the crown, sometimes to the point of open defiance. They faced a stubborn opponent. The young Louis XV, who had ascended the throne at the age of 5, would rule for almost sixty years. Like Louis XIV, he asserted that "sovereign power resides in my person only . . . my courts [*parlements*] derive their existence and their authority from me alone . . . to me alone belongs legislative power without subordination and undivided."

Despite his longevity and support from some able ministers, Louis XV governed far less effectively than his predecessor had. Ignoring administrative matters, he allowed his royal bureaucracy to weaken. As resistance from the *parlements* ate away at the king's authority, France's fiscal pressures from old debts and continued military expenditures grew. The rising tensions centered on the issue of taxes. Specifically, the crown wanted to tap France's wealth by raising taxes, but the nobility sidestepped this move by using the *parlements* to protect their tax exemptions. Moreover, private tax farmers still controlled the collection of taxes, keeping one-third for themselves. Clearly, the monarchy was missing out on large sources of revenue. In 1716, the crown had tried to change this system. The effort led to the creation of a private bank, promoted by a brilliant Scottish financier, John Law, with the power to produce its own notes as legal tender and to monopolize overseas commerce. Within just a few years, however, overspeculation in his Mississippi Company had brought the bank to ruin the "Mississippi Bubble," leaving France saddled again with its inefficient old system.

Nothing drained money from the treasury more than wars. By avoiding major wars until 1740, the crown achieved relative financial stability. Thereafter the story changed, as France was drawn into a series of costly conflicts with Continental and colonial rivals. Struggling to fund these endeavors and lacking the appropriate financial institutions and taxable resources, France staggered under a relentlessly expanding debt.

In the 1770s, the king and his chancellor finally dissolved the *parlements* and tried to enact an ambitious program of reform. The move came too late. The inept Louis XV had never projected the image of a dynamic, reforming, enlightened monarch. On the contrary, he had a reputation for living lavishly within his opulent court. Underground pamphlets accused him of allowing his mistress and his sexual taste for girls to distract him from attending properly to courtly matters and the demanding business of managing the state. By the end of his reign, he had earned the dislike and even hatred of his subjects. Louis XV's death in 1774 was met with conspicuous silence, and his tardy reform program evaporated.

Hoping to gain popularity, Louis' successor, Louis XVI (r. 1774–1792), quickly restored the *parlements* and their powers. Again, these aristocratic bodies thwarted new plans for financial reform—even those offered by talented ministers. In France, unlike in most other European powers, the crown and the nobility failed to find a satisfactory way of working together. Again and again, reform efforts faltered, annoying those hoping for change. As frustrations intensified, the crown became increasingly isolated from traditional sources of support within the country.

France needed all the strength it could muster to compete for colonies and stature with Great Britain, where a much different situation had evolved. In 1714, a year before Louis XIV's death, Queen Anne had died. The crown passed to George I (r. 1714–1727), the first of the German Hanoverian line. The British monarchy had already sustained damage from the civil war and revolution of the seventeenth century (see Chapter 13). Though the king remained the chief executive of the state, ordained by God and tradition, Parliament now had the upper hand. Divided into the House of Lords (for nobles only) and House of Commons (elected representatives of commoners), Parliament controlled critical functions such as taxation, lawmaking, and the process for bringing grievances to the monarchy. Clearly, king and Parliament had to find a way to work together rather than in opposition.

Making the British system work

The answer came in the form of a new institution: the cabinet system. Under this structure, the king chose members of Parliament, usually from the House of Commons, to serve as his ministers. If he hoped to enact policies, he had to select ministers who could command plenty of votes. These men tended to be the leaders of the major groups, or parties, in the House of Commons. By the eighteenth century, two groups dominated the House. Whigs, favoring commercial interests and a strong Parliament, remained staunchly opposed to any return of the Catholic Stuarts to the crown. Whigs also championed popular rights more than the conservative Tories did. Tories usually favored large landowners and a strong monarchy and had stood less firmly against the Stuarts than the Whigs had.

Differences between the two groups came to a head in 1714. That year, the Tories considered supporting James, a Catholic Stuart raised in France, against George I. An unsuccessful rebellion in favor of James discredited the Tories in the eyes of the monarchy. In 1746, the English army put down another rebellion in Scotland that had attempted to support a Catholic Stuart. This latest fiasco further alienated the Tory leadership from the British crown.

For these reasons, George I and his son George II (r. 1727–1760) selected their ministers from the Whigs rather than the Tories. The two kings' lack of talent and public support made them all the more dependent on Whig leadership for governance. That leadership came in the person of Robert Walpole (1676–1745). Already recognized as a superb speaker and leading Whig in the House of Commons, Walpole became First Lord of the Treasury and the most important minister in George I's Privy Council in 1721. Much of Walpole's prominence derived from his successful handling of a financial crisis after an overseas

KEY DATES

EIGHTEENTH-CENTURY POLITICS AND SOCIETY

1740–1748	War of the Austrian Succession
1740–1780	Reign of Maria Theresa in Austria
1740–1786	Reign of Frederick II in Prussia
1756–1763	Seven Years' War
1762–1796	Reign of Catherine the Great in Russia
1773–1775	Serfs revolt in Russia
1776–1783	American Revolution
1772, 1795	Partitions of Poland

trading company collapsed in 1720 (the South Sea Bubble). After that coup, he brought in other Whigs who could control votes in Parliament. He flattered and "managed" the monarch to remain in favor. Through patronage—control over money, contracts, offices, and honors—and the manipulation of elections, he ensured the dominance of the Whigs and his own leadership for twenty years.

Many complained about this pattern of political corruption, which both Whigs and Tories used. One critic—the British artist William Hogarth (1697–1764)—produced many prints lambasting British political and social life. In **Figure 15.3,** one of a series of works on British elections, Hogarth shows a corrupt political campaign in progress. At the center, a voter emerges drunk from a riotous tavern. He has been bribed and is being instructed how to vote, which at the time was done publicly. At the left, the Tory candidate is purchasing cheap jewelry for a woman on the balcony. He makes his purchase from a Jewish merchant, despite his own anti-Jewish record in Parliament.

FIGURE 15.3 William Hogarth, *Canvassing for Votes—The Election,* **1754**   This satirical scene of what went on during an election campaign shows an irresponsible candidate and his supporters bribing people for their votes.

Walpole's successors continued his strategy of patronage to ensure parliamentary support, and the Whigs held office for another twenty years. By the middle of the eighteenth century, a pattern had emerged. A group of ministers—themselves led by a prime minister, chosen from Parliament, who could command enough votes in the House of Commons to pass legislation—served the monarch and remained responsible to Parliament. Unlike in France, where most political debate took place outside the government, in Britain, debate occurred within Parliament between the party in power and the "loyal opposition." People thus perceived the nation as being governed by the rule of law rather than the whim of a monarch. This system often moved slowly, but it worked.

Although Britain's government may have been more representative than France's, it was far from democratic. Only some 200,000—most of them the wealthiest males—could vote. Rich landowners and powerful local elites staffed the government. Not surprisingly, Parliament listened most carefully to representatives of the 400 families whose massive estates included one-fourth of Britain's arable land. British officials did not seek to exempt themselves from taxation, as did most of their counterparts in France, but instead ruled along with the crown by controlling Parliament.

Prosperity formed the foundation of Britain's strong position in these years. The middle class in particular agreed with the popular British author and observer Daniel Defoe that "the greatness of the British nation is not owing to war and conquests . . . it is all owing to trade, to the increase of our commerce at home, and the extending it abroad." Goods poured into Britain from India and North America. The nation transformed itself into an agricultural exporter and a flourishing manufacturing center. By the middle of the eighteenth century, Great Britain had become Europe's leading economic power. It pursued its interest in European affairs through diplomacy, alliances, and the subsidizing of its allies' arms. Its naval dominance alone made it a formidable opponent. After 1740, Britain used both its economic strength and its military might in the great mid-century wars with France that stretched across three continents. To understand this story, we must shift our attention to the West's overseas colonies and the nature of trade among them.

More than anything else, France and Britain fought over colonies. For both countries, foreign trade quadrupled in the eighteenth century, and a large part of that increase derived from transactions with colonies. The two nations also made their greatest profits from trade across the Atlantic. However, their overseas presence differed crucially. The French had only 56,000 colonists living in North America in 1740—a fraction of the British colonial population. Yet French colonists carried out an extensive, highly profitable fur trade. Further, because of their small numbers and trade arrangements, they experienced limited conflict with Amerindians.

British colonists, clustered along the eastern seaboard, had a different experience. First, they grew rapidly—from 250,000 in 1700 to 1.7 million in 1760.

Colonies, trade, and war

As they occupied and exploited more and more land, they pushed the Amerindians out. Their expansion, combined with resistance from local tribes, led to savage battles. The fighting, in turn, convinced the colonists that removing or even exterminating the Amerindians was justified. As they became more firmly established, the British colonists bought manufactured goods from Britain in return for tobacco, rice, cotton, and indigo dye, much of which Britain re-exported to the European continent.

These North American colonists participated in the even more lucrative triangle of trade that connected Europe, Africa, and the Americas and that centered on the Caribbean (see Map 15.4). The British and French, along with the Dutch and Spanish, held islands there that supported sugar, rum, coffee, and dyestuffs trade produced by slave labor. In particular, the demand for sugar and coffee seemed endless. European craving for these items grew so much that, for many, they became necessities rather than occasional luxuries.

The triangle of trade

At the heart of this thriving colonial commerce was the slave trade (see Chapter 12). Slavery was long common throughout Africa and in other societies. For centuries, Islamic merchants had purchased slaves through well-established African networks and transported them by caravan across the Sahara Desert to the Mediterranean basin or by ship from east African ports across the Indian Ocean to Asia.

The slave trade

In the eighteenth century, the dramatic demand for slaves in the Americas shifted Africa's slave trade westward to the Atlantic coast. Ships from Europe carried manufactured goods (most notably, guns) and gin to western Africa and traded them for slaves—two-thirds of them males, because they best provided heavy labor. Usually captured by African middlemen, slaves languished in pens in towns or forts on the African coast. European trading ships then carried them across the Atlantic in a perilous two-month sea voyage known as the **Middle Passage.**

Figure 15.4, an 1846 watercolor, suggests what conditions were like belowdecks on a slave ship. Typically, slaves were packed like cargo into the holds of ships "where the light of day does not penetrate." As many as 700 slaves—naked, branded, and shackled—might be crammed into one ship. A French writer describing these voyages told of a "continuous state of alarm on the part of the white men, who fear a revolt, and . . . a cruel state of uncertainty on the part of the Negroes, who do not know the fate awaiting them." In Document 15.3, Olaudah Equiano, a captured African, describes how this Middle Passage experience soon made him "so sick and low" that he "wished for the last friend, death."

Traders took most of their slaves to the West Indies and Brazil; less than 10 percent went to North American destinations. After unloading their human cargo, the ships filled up with sugar, rum, and other goods—sometimes stopping farther north in the American colonies to take on additional products such as cotton, tobacco, timber, and furs. From there, the ships returned to Europe. Merchants then re-exported many of these products to other European nations.

Disease, abuse, and suicide took the lives of many slaves. In addition, African women often suffered the horror of rape by their captors. Those who survived the Middle Passage were then sold for profit and put to work on a plantation or in the mines or households of colonists. **Figure 15.5** depicts slaves harvesting sugarcane on a West Indies plantation. Men, women, and children share the difficult work. In the foreground, a manager on horseback gives orders to a slave, who looks up deferentially to his master. On the right, sugarcane is being loaded into a cart, to be carried to the mill in the distant background. Slaves suffered from poor diets, inadequate housing, broken families, and stiff corporal punishment. The uprooting, the trauma of transportation, and the harsh conditions in the colonies stripped much away from these people. Still, slaves often resisted their masters by working slowly, sabotaging equipment, running away, and revolting. Despite their lack of freedom, slaves built hybrid cultural traditions from African, American, and European sources.

Within the slave societies of Brazil, the West Indies, and North America, the notion of race was becoming tied to slavery, adding to earlier notions of racial prejudice. The unprecedented

FIGURE 15.4 A Transatlantic Slave Ship, 1846 This mid-nineteenth-century watercolor depicts a slave ship where the human cargo is packed tightly belowdecks.

DOCUMENT 15.3

Olaudah Equiano Describes the Middle Passage

The slave trade between Africa and the Americas involved the horrors of capture and the Middle Passage, a harrowing two-month voyage across the Atlantic. In the account below, Olaudah Equiano (1745–1797)—a west African who was captured by slave raiders when he was 10 years old—describes the ocean journey. He survived the voyage and twenty-one years of slavery before purchasing his freedom.

The first object which saluted my eyes when I arrived on the coast was the sea, and a slave ship which was then riding at anchor and waiting for its cargo. These filled me with astonishment, which was soon converted into terror when I was carried on board. I was immediately handled and tossed up to see if I were sound by some of the crew, and I was now persuaded that I had gotten into a world of bad spirits and that they were going to kill me. . . .

I was not long suffered to indulge my grief; I was soon put down under the decks, and there I received such a salutation in my nostrils as I had never experienced in my life; so that with the loathsomeness of the stench and crying together, I became so sick and low that I was not able to eat, nor had I the least desire to taste anything. I now wished for the last friend, death, to relieve me; but soon, to my grief, two of the white men offered me eatables, and on my refusing to eat, one of them held me fast by the hands and laid me across I think the windlass and tied my feet while the other flogged me severely. I had never experienced anything of this kind before, and although not being used to the water I naturally feared that element the first time I saw it, yet nevertheless if I could have gotten over the nettings I would have jumped over the side, but I could not; and besides, the crew used to watch very closely over those of us who were not chained down to the decks, lest we should leap into the water, and I have seen some of these poor African prisoners most severely cut for attempting to do so, and hourly whipped for not eating. This indeed was often the case with myself. . . .

One day when we had a smooth sea and moderate wind, two of my wearied countrymen who were chained together (I was near them at the time), preferring death to such a life of misery, somehow made through the nettings and jumped into the sea; immediately another quite dejected fellow, who on account of his illness was suffered to be out of irons, also followed their example; and I believe many more would very soon have done the same if they had not been prevented by the ship's crew, who were instantly alarmed. Those of us that were the most active were in a moment put down under the deck, and there was such a noise and confusion amongst the people of the ship as I never heard before, to stop her and get the boat to go after the slaves. However, two of the wretches were drowned, but they got the other and afterwards flogged him unmercifully for thus attempting to prefer death to slavery. In this manner we continued to undergo more hardships than I can now relate, hardships which are inseparable from this accursed trade.

SOURCE: Olaudah Equiano, *The Interesting Narrative of the Life of Olaudah Equiano, or Gustavus Vassa, the African, Written by Himself,* 2 vols. (London, 1789).

Analyze the Document

1. How are captured Africans treated on the slave ship?

2. In what ways do they try to resist?

3. Notice the date and place of publication. Why might a London firm have been interested in publishing this account by Equiano?

---

dependence on slavery and the associated development of racism would stain these societies in ways that persist to this day.

The consequences of the slave trade also rippled through sub-Saharan Africa. Traditional trade routes north to the Mediterranean and east to the Indian Ocean disintegrated as more lucrative commerce shifted west to the Atlantic coast of Africa. To supply more human cargo to the Europeans, west African kingdoms raided inland tribes. Bloody internal wars erupted—more deadly than ever thanks to the guns supplied by Europeans to the Africans.

Because many slaves perished in the Americas, and the plantations that depended on them kept expanding, the demand for fresh supplies of slaves increased relentlessly. This rising need perpetuated the triangular commerce among Europe, Africa, and the Americas. European traders took 50,000 to 100,000 slaves across the Atlantic each year during most of the eighteenth century. By the time slave trafficking abated in the mid-nineteenth century, more than 11 million Africans had been ripped from their homes, transported across the Atlantic, and sold into slavery. Another 4 million died resisting seizure or while in transport.

Planters and merchants on both sides of the Atlantic profited from this trade, and European cities serving as slave-trade ports flourished, particularly in England. The coastal town of Liverpool, for example, grew from a small town to a major city in

FIGURE 15.5 A West Indies Sugar Plantation, 1823 This painting shows slaves cutting the sugarcane and loading it onto carts under the watchful eye of a manager, who is on horseback giving instructions.

the eighteenth century. In 1750, its slave merchants and fleet of almost two hundred ships carried almost half of Europe's slave trade. Thousands of men from Liverpool worked on both merchant and naval ships, and more than a dozen banks and several insurance companies served slave-trade merchants. The wealth spread outward from Liverpool, helping to finance Britain's burgeoning industry as well as its rising position on the world stage. "Our West-Indies and African Trades are the most nationally beneficial of any we carry on. . . . The Trade to Africa is the branch which renders our American Colonies and Plantations so advantageous to Great Britain," argued one British defender of the slave system in 1746. "The daily bread of the most considerable part of our British Manufacturers are owing primarily to the labor of Negroes." Although the statement may be an exaggeration, slavery generated much commerce and wealth in this eighteenth-century Atlantic economy, whether by direct or indirect means.

As Europeans' commercial activities, profits, and presence increased in the Americas, so did competition and friction, especially between the French and the British. In North America, British colonists along the eastern seaboard pushed inland, beyond the Appalachian Mountains into the Ohio Valley. The French strengthened their holdings by building forts along the Great Lakes and the large rivers of the St. Lawrence and Mississippi valleys. When the War of the Austrian Succession broke out in Europe in 1740, Britain and France soon locked horns on the Continent as well as overseas. Most of the fighting took place in the Americas, however.

Fighting on three continents

Wins and losses on each side balanced out, and by the time the conflict ended in 1748, each side had settled for what it had held in the beginning.

The peace would not last long. In 1755, war—sometimes known as the French and Indian War—erupted again, this time initiated by a British offensive against a French stronghold near Pittsburgh in North America. At the same time, the two powers were also competing in India, each trying to take advantage of the declining power of the Mughals (India's Muslim rulers—see Global Connections in Chapter 13). After 1715, the subcontinent had split apart into bickering, independent kingdoms. India became fertile ground for the British and French, working through their chartered trading companies and backed by their superior weapons of war, to make deals, gain influence, and line up allies among India's opposing princes and political factions. In 1759, British colonialist and soldier Robert Clive (1725–1774), representing Britain's East India Company, explained how a combination of force and bribery could gain the company and England "absolute possession of these rich kingdoms" in India that would provide "an income yearly of upwards of two million sterling." Moreover, he added, Britain would gain advantages over "the several European nations engaged in the commerce here," especially "against the French." This competition between the British and French for trade and imperial power developed into an undeclared war that, after 1756, coalesced with the hostilities breaking out across Europe (the Seven Years' War), the Caribbean, and North America.

In this widespread war, which involved Asians and Amerindians as well as Europeans, France invested most of its energy and resources in the European arena, whereas Britain focused on the battle overseas. Initially, the French, assisted by the Amerindian allies they had gained, held their own in North America. Then the British, with their superior navy and more extensive population, began capturing French strongholds one by one. The fall of Quebec in 1759 opened all of Canada to British forces. British naval power overwhelmed the French and their Spanish allies in the Caribbean as well. In India, the British also prevailed, crushing the French and subduing several resisting Indian states. During the succeeding decades, as **Map 15.5** reveals, the British increasingly took direct control over areas around their bases of power.

Figure 15.6 also attests to this British success. This late-eighteenth-century painting shows William Kirkpatric, a British officer, with his attendants—a group of Indian princes and merchants. Kirkpatric's prominence reflects his authority over those around him and his sword reveals the source of his power.

Western Africa, Brazil, and the Atlantic Slave Trade

Drawn by commercial opportunities, European vessels flocked to the west coast of Africa during the seventeenth and eighteenth centuries. The new trade, especially the lucrative and rapidly expanding commerce in slaves, turned west Africans' attention toward the Atlantic Ocean as well. European textiles, metal goods, and firearms poured into west Africa off the European ships. From Brazil and other lands in the Americas came new crops, such as manioc and maize, to supplement the yams, millet, and bananas that served as staples for sub-Saharan Africans. Prosperous port cities emerged, and west African states such as Dahomey and Asante gained power.

Other African societies weakened, and once-powerful kingdoms fell in the turmoil and wars provoked by slaving. In 1730, an officer of the Dutch West India Company involved in the slave trade concluded, "The great quantity of guns and powder which the Europeans have from time to time brought" to west Africa have caused "terrible wars among the kings, princes . . . of those lands, who made their prisoners of war slaves." Moreover, the profits from slaving made many Africans "forget all labor." Consequently, there was now "very little trade among the coast Negroes except in slaves." Other methods of obtaining slaves only worsened the turmoil and dislocations that were tearing African societies apart. According to Alexander Falconbridge, a British surgeon who served on slaving ships during the 1780s, "There is great reason to believe that most of the negroes shipped off from the coast of Africa are *kidnapped*." As a result, "continual enmity is thus fostered among the negroes of Africa, and all social intercourse between them destroyed."

The slave trade shaped the Portuguese colony Brazil, as well. During the eighteenth century, Europeans shipped millions of slaves across the Atlantic; more than a third of them went to Brazil. Although most slaves worked on large plantations producing crops such as sugar and tobacco for export, many also served as domestics and manual laborers. The English navigator Captain William Dampier, stopping in Brazil, reported that everyone kept slaves in their houses except "people of the lowest degree of all." Tradesmen, he continued, "buy Negroes, and train them up to their several Employments," and "Many of the Portugueze, who are Batchelors, keep these black Women for Misses."

Another British traveler to Brazil, Henry Koster, reported that all slaves in Brazil "follow the religion of their master." Many were "baptized in lots before they left their own shores," whereas others were converted upon arrival in Brazil. "The system of baptizing the newly imported negroes," he reported, rendered the slaves "more tractable." Over time, these slaves learned to speak Portuguese, while "their own dialects are allowed to lie dormant until they are, by many of them, quite forgotten." Many slaves died from diseases such as yellow fever or from brutal working conditions and poor nutrition. However, Koster claimed that slaves adapted to "the habits of their masters." At the same time, their masters "imbibe[d] some of the customs of their slaves; and thus the superior and his dependent are brought nearer to each other."

The trans-Atlantic slaving connection between west Africa and Brazil continued into the nineteenth century. In 1888, Brazil—by then an independent nation—became the last state in the Americas to abolish slavery.

Making Connections

1. What were the consequences of the slave trade for the societies of western Africa and Brazil?

2. How did Brazilian masters deal with their slaves?

The British had to conquer native forces as well as the French to increase their holdings in the Indian subcontinent. The papers on the table represent the taxes collected by British authorities and suggest the imposition of British law over local states. In the background stands a magnificent estate, suggesting how colonial holdings and commerce created great wealth in the officer's homeland.

Maps 15.6 and 15.7 show the changing fortunes of France and Britain in North America between 1755 and 1763. The Treaty of Paris, which ended the fighting in 1763, gave Britain control of Canada and of France's holdings east of the Mississippi. Britain also received France's West Indian possessions, except for Guadeloupe and Martinique, and most of France's holdings in India. British control over most of India

Bombay

Ganges R.

Indus R.

Bay of Bengal

Kandy

INDIAN

OCEAN

British Acquisitions
- 1756–1767
- 1772–1785
- 1786–1793
- 1798–1805

Enclaves
- ● French
- ● Portuguese

MAP 15.5

India, 1756–1805

This map shows British acquisitions in India between 1756 and 1805.

Explore the Map

1. Notice where the British concentrated their holdings in the subcontinent. What connections might these holdings have had to trade and transportation?

2. Locate where the French and Portuguese maintained a presence. Why might that limited presence have been important to the French and Portuguese?

3. How might the British have maintained and extended their control over such large areas in India with a limited number of "settlers"?

THE TWILIGHT OF MONARCHIES? THE QUESTION OF ENLIGHTENED ABSOLUTISM

In both Britain and France, the eighteenth-century monarchies were in decline, but for different reasons. In Britain, the monarchs ruled in partnership with Parliament. However, the kings were undistinguished, and Parliament continued to gain the upper hand. In France, the successors to Louis XIV lacked the interest, talent, and support to make the monarchy dynamic or popular. The twin threats to the crown in these nations—the growing complexity of effective governance, and demands from elites to share power—arose elsewhere as well.

However, in several other nations, monarchs managed to maintain their authority—often by justifying their rule in innovative ways and instituting new policies. In the second half of the eighteenth century, some of these monarchs styled themselves as "enlightened," or attuned to Enlightenment beliefs and willing to initiate reforms for the good of the state and its people. Some historians have distinguished these rulers from their predecessors, calling them "enlightened absolutists" or simply "enlightened." Yet, how valid is this characterization? Several historians claim that these

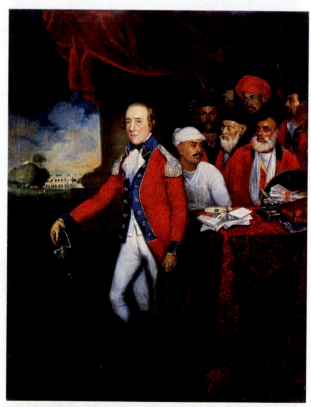

FIGURE 15.6 The English School, *Dixton Harvesters*, ca. 1725 This late-eighteenth-century painting shows a British officer in India and his Indian attendants. It suggests the power and wealth gained by the British as they increased their presence on the Indian subcontinent.

dates from this period. France and several other nations still retained important overseas colonies, but Britain now reigned as the top colonial and commercial power. This "great war for empire" paved the way for the British to establish their worldwide empire in the nineteenth century.

thinking about GEOGRAPHY

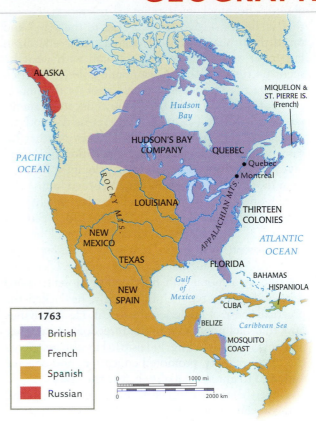

MAPS 15.6 and 15.7

North America, 1755 and 1763

These maps show North America before and after the Seven Years' War.

Explore the Maps

1. Notice France's large holdings in 1755. What advantages helped the British defeat France in this part of the world?

2. What new problems did Britain face as a result of its victory?

3. Identify what other competitors to the British remained in North America after 1763. How would you assess their relative strength?

---

monarchs primarily followed the long tradition of trying to buttress the central government's power and efficiency. Other historians argue that they genuinely initiated reforms in line with Enlightenment thinking.

The most sensational of the self-described enlightened monarchs was Frederick the Great (Frederick II) of Prussia. Even as a boy, Frederick loved music, poetry, and philosophy. After ascending to the throne, he still found time to perform in concerts as an accomplished flutist in his Palace of San Souci. There he also hobnobbed with towering cultural figures such as Voltaire, savored books in his library, and carried on a lively correspondence with leading French intellectuals. He knew and spoke the

Frederick the Great

phrases of the Enlightenment. Like several other monarchs, he also wanted to display his awareness of culture and intellectual life to help justify his position as monarch. He described "the good monarch" as one who behaved "as if he were each moment liable to render an account of his administration to his fellow citizens." He claimed to act only in the common interest of the people, declaring himself to be "the first servant of the state" rather than a divinely appointed ruler.

At the end of the Seven Years' War (1756–1763), the second of his two wars of aggression, Frederick made some attempts at "enlightened" reforms. For example, he initiated codification of the laws, abolished torture, and ended most capital punishment.

The Twilight of Monarchies? The Question of Enlightened Absolutism   497

Believing that "all religions, if one examines them, are founded on superstitious systems, more or less absurd," he proclaimed religious toleration. Nevertheless, he considered Jews "useless to the state" and taxed them heavily. He advocated public education but spent very little on it compared with what he spent on his army. In his economic policy, Frederick did share the Physiocrats' appreciation of the importance of agriculture and tried to introduce new methods of cultivation (see page 468). Yet he did nothing to free the serfs or lessen their burdens. Neither his wars nor his involvement in the partition of Poland revealed any hint of enlightened principles different from those of the monarchs who preceded him.

No one tried more sincerely to be enlightened than Joseph II of Austria (r. 1780–1790). "Since I have ascended the throne," he said **Joseph II** in 1781, "I have made *philosophy* the legislator of my empire." Viewing his rule as a moral and holy calling, Joseph issued thousands of decrees. Unfortunately, he lacked the practical sense of Frederick the Great. He did change laws that had previously limited freedom of the press and religion (including Judaism). He also restricted the death penalty, promoted education, and enacted and tried to enforce equality before the law.

Nevertheless, Joseph still ruled as an autocrat, antagonizing most of the powerful groups in his lands. Even peasants, unable to understand exactly what all the decrees meant, failed to support him. His well-meaning but ill-conceived efforts—to centralize the administration of the widely dispersed Habsburg territories, to replace the numerous languages of his subjects with German, to subordinate the strongly entrenched Roman Catholic Church, and to free the serfs in a society still based on feudalism—all backfired. Opposition and even open revolt swelled in his lands. In 1787, Joseph lamented, "[I] hope that when I am no more, posterity will examine, and judge more equitably . . . all that I have done for my people." His vision would not come to pass. Within a few years of his death in 1790, most of his reforms were abolished and the Habsburg lands reacquired their old, conservative ways.

Other monarchs, such as those of Sweden, Sardinia, Spain, and Portugal, attempted or enacted reforms that could be seen as enlightened. In Russia, Catherine the Great certainly prided herself on being enlightened (see page 482). She once described the true aim of monarchy as "not to deprive People of their natural Liberty; but to correct their Actions, in order to attain the supreme good." Ultimately, however, Catherine failed to put most of her reforms into practice. Instead, she resorted to the tried-and-true tactic of appeasing elites at a price paid by the peasantry.

Certainly these monarchs found it easier to manifest their "enlightenment" in style rather than substance.

Moreover, they rarely lost sight of traditional goals: to increase their own military and economic power. Few attempted to enact fundamental social, political, or economic reforms dictated by Enlightenment thought. Even those who tried, such as Joseph II in Austria, generally failed to overcome opposition to those reforms from tradition-minded people.

Style, substance, or survival?

Nevertheless, thoughtful observers of the eighteenth century—looking for tendencies and possibilities for reform rather than revolutionary change—believed that several rulers displayed the enlightened spirit of the times. Despite great obstacles to reform within the traditional order, some of these rulers made progress toward fulfilling the *philosophes'* agenda of promoting more religious tolerance, humane social institutions, and rational administration. In the eyes of contemporaries, they earned the label "enlightened".

Finally, from another perspective, **enlightened absolutism** also may have reflected a growing sense that, in the long run, monarchs could no longer *claim* to embody the state. The need for governmental efficiency had grown too much to be entrusted to a poorly qualified individual who happened to be a king or queen. Moreover, governments increasingly had to recognize the emergence of a public sphere within their lands where individuals and groups exchanged information, voiced ideas, and engaged in criticism. Public opinion became a potential tool that monarchs might use to their advantage—or a force they might ignore to their detriment. If the institution of monarchy were to survive, kings and queens had to justify their position in these new, ostensibly enlightened ways.

CHANGES IN COUNTRY AND CITY LIFE

Eighteenth-century European monarchs and officials faced not only the risky politics and wars of their times but also the changes unfolding in their very societies. Especially in western Europe, new economic and social forces began to upset old traditions (see Chapter 13). For some, these changes created a sense that life was improving and would continue to do so. For others, the changes only deepened their misery. The greatest shifts emerged in the countryside, where the vast majority of the population (some 80 percent) lived and depended on agriculture for their livelihood and very survival.

Historically, toiling in the fields within Europe's traditional subsistence economies produced little more than enough food to survive. During the late seventeenth and eighteenth centuries, new methods of agricultural production that had originated in

Holland spread to England and then to other areas of western Europe. These innovative methods allowed fewer people to work the fields and still produce far more food than they needed. The new techniques and the changes flowing from them became so important that they are known as the agricultural revolution.

The Agricultural Revolution

Most early-eighteenth-century farmers used methods that differed only marginally from those employed in previous centuries. They grew the same crops year after year, left one-third to one-half of the land fallow (unplanted) to allow the soil to replenish itself with nutrients for the next planting, and saved only enough fodder to feed small numbers of domestic animals during the winters. Individual families worked small strips of land, and large, uncultivated fields, brushlands, and forests (the commons) were reserved for general use by the community. Traditional community practices usually determined decisions about crops, animals, and land use. Overall, only a small minority of people made their living outside of agriculture, and an even smaller percentage had the good fortune to afford luxuries.

This traditional, agricultural economy had the potential to support a limited measure of population growth. In the eighteenth century, population increases stepped up the demand for food, and hence for hands to clear fields, drain swamps, terrace hillsides, carry water, and till the soil. Most of these efforts were simply an intensification of old methods for increasing agricultural yields, and the growing population consumed most of the extra food they produced. Something had to change if large numbers of Europeans hoped to increase their standard of living and provide enough food for people living in the cities as well as the countryside.

At the heart of the **agricultural revolution** lay two developments: first, the introduction of new crops and the use of new farming techniques that dramatically boosted agricultural yields; and second, the transformation of rural lands farmed for subsistence into large, controlled properties that produced crops for commerce. The primary agricultural advances came first in Holland and Britain, where farmers began experimenting with new crops such as clover, turnips, and legumes, as well as the potato from America. These crops replenished the soil rather than depleting it and therefore could be grown on lands that farmers periodically had to leave fallow. Farmers now used the new crops to feed livestock during the hard winters. More cattle meant more protein-rich dairy products; more horses and oxen eased the workload for humans and provided transportation; and more sheep produced more wool.

New crops and techniques

All this livestock, improving with new crossbreeding practices, yielded more meat, leather, and soap as well as manure with which to fertilize fields. Other new foods, such as nutrient-rich potatoes, also made the land more productive than ever before. Some landowners became renowned for their farming innovations. In England, for example, Charles "Turnip" Townshend (1674–1738) experimented with crop rotation and growing turnips. His compatriot Jethro Tull (1674–1741) advocated the use of a seed drill and manure, which made planting more efficient and productive.

Not all farmers adopted the new agricultural methods. For many, traditional ways were comfortably familiar. Even those who realized how much profit they might make by selling their surpluses in the cities and other distant markets needed money to fund the new farming methods. They also required control over larger tracts of land to introduce the new crops, apply the innovative methods, and specialize in certain products—whether sheep for wool, grain for flour, or cattle for meat and dairy.

By all means, fair and foul, these market-oriented landowners dispossessed individuals of their small plots and communities of their commons to enclose land with fences, hedges, and walls as their own. **Figure 15.7,** a mid-eighteenth-century English painting, shows a large, rich estate in Gloucestershire, England. The fields are consolidated and enclosed. In the center, organized groups of men and women workers toil on the harvest while wagons haul away the produce, destined for commerce rather than local consumption. Other fields are carefully planned and managed for the marketplace. Gone are the small farms, subsistence crops, and open fields that used to dominate the English countryside. After 1750, Britain's Parliament furthered this trend by authorizing a wave of these **enclosures.** Over the decades, wealthy landowners created large, controlled tracts that yielded products for the market. They reserved only a small part of their land for their own needs or bought their food elsewhere. Through this process, thousands of small, independent landowners, sharecroppers, and tenant farmers lost their land—and the status and security that had come with it. Rural communities disintegrated, eroding the support and human interactions that had so characterized life in the country.

Enclosures

Manufacturing Spreads in the Countryside: Cottage Industry

The spreading agricultural revolution became one force pushing, forcing, or freeing people to work more in nonagricultural jobs. When families lost their self-sufficient farms, they had to find new sources of

FIGURE 15.7 Enclosed Fields in England, mid-eighteenth century Large, rich estates such as this one in Gloucestershire, England, consolidated and enclosed separate fields, transforming the countryside. This shift in agricultural practice enabled large landowners to raise crops more effectively for commerce.

income to supplement the meager day-labor wages their landowning employers paid them. Manufacturing seemed to offer a solution. Growing commerce, particularly overseas trade, had heightened demand for manufactured goods—and thus workers to produce them. Traditionally, well-paid urban artisans had done this sort of work. Now, with demand high and rural workers available by the thousands, merchants turned to the countryside to increase production and take advantage of the cheap labor. Moreover, by shifting more production itself to the countryside, merchants avoided urban guild regulations that historically had controlled wages and the quantity and quality of goods.

All these changes stimulated the growth of **cottage industry,** also known as the putting-out system. This system, which had already existed in the sixteenth and seventeenth centuries but to a much smaller degree, worked in a specific way. An entrepreneur provided raw materials (usually for production of textiles such as wool or linen) and sometimes equipment (such as a handloom or a spinning wheel) to peasants. The entrepreneur might be anyone—from a city merchant to a rural landowner—who managed to amass enough money to make an initial investment in raw materials and perhaps equipment. Peasants, who sought employment during times of the year when there was less need for agricultural labor, worked in their homes (hence the term *cottage industry*) to turn these raw materials into finished products. Mainly, they spun wool into yarn and wove the yarn into cloth. Sometimes enterprising peasants contracted out raw material to other spinners to keep weavers busy, since weavers depended on spinners to provide a steady supply of yarn. Women and children often worked while men were off performing day labor for large landowners. The entrepreneur periodically returned, paid for the peasants' labor by the piece, and distributed the finished products to distant markets.

As **Figure 15.8** shows, whole families participated in cottage-industry work. Women and children usually washed, combed, and spun the raw material into thread, while men often wove the yarn on looms. In this print, members of a rural household in Ireland beat and comb flax into linen, which will later be spun and woven. The light streaming in from the open window, the smiling laborers, and the little girl playing

FIGURE 15.8 Cottage Industry, eighteenth century This illustration shows a rural family working together to produce textiles that will be collected for commerce.

with a dog all distract our attention from the realities of the work: the dark, cramped quarters of single-room cottages and the tedious nature of this labor.

Cottage industry spread rapidly during the eighteenth century, particularly in Great Britain and parts of France and Germany. In addition to textiles, all sorts of goods—from buttons and housewares to knives, nails, and clocks—were produced through this system. The quality of these products varied, and relations between merchants and laborers often broke down over accusations of theft and disputes over wages. Still, more and more people came to depend on the system. For many of these workers, cottage-industry labor changed from a part-time to a full-time occupation.

The primary appeal of the work was its availability. Cottage industry allowed many people to remain in rural areas in a time of shrinking demand for farm workers. It also helped large families keep up and enabled young people to get an earlier start on marriage. On the other hand, the pay rarely rose above starvation wages, and the labor was drudgery.

Wherever it spread, cottage industry extended the money economy and the web of the commercial marketplace. Along with the agricultural revolution, the growth of cottage industry helped set the stage for an even greater economic transformation that would eventually sweep from Britain throughout the West and into the non-Western world: the industrial revolution.

More People, Longer Lives

As these new economic and social forces began to alter traditional ways of life, Europe's population jumped from approximately 110 million in 1700 to 190 million in 1800. **Figure 15.9** reveals the population growth throughout most of Europe during the eighteenth century. Relatively large populations help explain the strength of three major powers—England (along with Ireland), France, and Russia (note that much of Russia's increased population came from territorial expansion). Earlier marriages, more and better food, and fewer plagues raised the birthrate and lowered the death rate. Agricultural and commercial prosperity, along with improvements in the transportation of food, reduced the number and severity of famines in many areas. In particular, the widespread cultivation of the potato during the second half of the eighteenth century made this cheap, nutritious food available to millions. A spate of good weather helped to improve harvests. In some areas, new urban sanitation practices—cleaning wells, draining swampy areas, and burying refuse—probably improved health as well.

Surprisingly, medical practices rarely contributed to better health. Certainly the medical field saw some

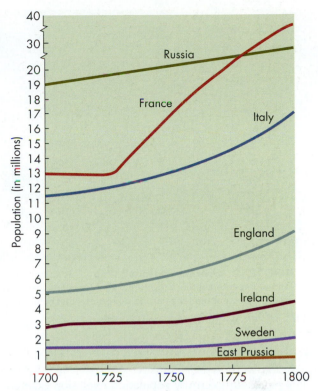

FIGURE 15.9 Population Growth in Europe, 1700–1800

advances. Inoculation against smallpox, for example, spread to Europe from the Middle East during the eighteenth century, although it was not used widely until the last decades of the century. Surgeons also made some improvements in the treatment of battlefield injuries. For instance, they learned to treat soldiers for shock before operating, and to clean wounds around the trauma.

Despite these signs of progress, eighteenth-century medicine was still dangerous. **Figure 15.10** provides a glimpse into a German hospital. In just one room, a bewildering array of medical procedures takes place. At the center, a surgeon saws off the leg of a patient. At the right lies a woman with a grotesquely swollen leg; just behind her, a woman prepares to give birth. At the far left, a priest administers last rites to a dying patient. In the background, women distribute food, men haul a body away, and sufferers lie crowded together in beds. French hospitals were no better. The French encyclopedist Denis Diderot described the Hôtel-Dieu in Paris, considered one of France's finest hospitals at the time: "Imagine a long series of communicating wards filled with sufferers of every kind of disease who are sometimes packed three, four, five or even six into a bed, the living alongside the dead and dying, the air polluted by this mass of unhealthy bodies, passing the pestilence of their afflictions from one to the other, and the spectacle of suffering and agony on every hand. That is the Hôtel-Dieu."

FIGURE 15.10 A German Hospital, 1746 This illustration from the mid-eighteenth century shows a hospital room and the kinds of activities—from amputations to food deliveries—that commonly took place there.

Deepening Misery for the Poor

The eighteenth-century population explosion exacted an ironic price. Stiffening competition for food drove prices up, while competition for jobs kept wages down. As a result, more and more people fell into poverty. A governmental commission in Austria reported to Empress Maria Theresa that "the peasants live in a condition of real slavery. . . . In their ruinous huts, the parents sleep on straw, the children naked on the wide shelves of earthenware stoves . . . all the charges of the Kingdom are born by the peasants, who are the sole taxpayers." Despite a widespread sense that people were better off than ever and that things would improve, in truth more people meant more misery.

In a desperate attempt to survive, poor people fled to the cities, hoping to find work in trade and manufacturing or as day laborers and domestics. Only some of them managed to find jobs; the rest were left to fend for themselves. A large percentage of urban dwellers missed out on the new wealth and opportunities of the cities. They eked out a living at little more than a subsistence level, and their lot worsened as more and more of them crowded in from the countryside.

Indeed, the surplus of workers; inflation; and disasters such as war, disease, and failed harvests hit the poor in cities and countryside alike. In France, economist Jacques Turgot (1727–1781) described the disastrous harvest of 1769: "The people could exist only by exhausting their resources, by selling at a miserable price their articles of furniture and even their clothes. Many of the inhabitants have been obliged to disperse themselves through other provinces to seek work or to beg, leaving their wives and children to the charity of the parishes. . . ." One Spanish official described how "wives and children are without work, and all, piled together in cities or large towns, live at the expense of charity. . . ." Even for those who found steady employment, wages simply did not keep pace with escalating prices.

In bad times, food riots and tax revolts broke out in cities and rural areas across Europe. A rise in the price of grain often sparked attacks on merchants, granaries, and convoys of grain slated for armies. People turned on officials as well, blaming them for not keeping grain prices affordable or for allowing food to be shipped out to higher bidders elsewhere. Crime increased and more people slept along the sides of rural roads and city streets. Crowds of mothers pushed into foundling hospitals, desperate to leave children they could not care for. Some foundling hospitals established lotteries to determine which children they could afford to take in.

This deepening of poverty put a huge strain on traditional systems for aiding the poor, such as through the church or private charity. Some people were reduced to begging and to teaching their children this dubious art. Some authorities sympathized; others turned a blind eye. As one French official put it, "Beggary is the apprenticeship of crime; it begins by creating a love of idleness . . . in this state the beggar does not long resist the temptation to steal." A few countries devised legislation, such as the English Poor Laws, that required the impoverished to work on public projects or in workhouses. Officials used these sorts of laws more to control and discipline the poor than to help them. Often the same institution served as a workshop for the unfortunate, a hospital, and a prison. True, the poor had always suffered. Now, however, the population boom pushed their numbers to overwhelming new heights.

Prosperity and the Bourgeoisie

Like the agricultural revolution, urban growth made life worse for some and better for others. Those who gained most during this era were the middle and aristocratic classes, particularly those who seized opportunities in commerce and industry and in the expanding governmental bureaucracies. The urban middle class—in French, the *bourgeoisie*—expanded and found itself in a particularly odd situation. Wealthier than most, the bourgeoisie lived off their investments in trade, manufacturing, or land rather than working with their hands like their fellow commoners. They also found ways to avoid the restrictions of the guild system of production. While those laboring below them envied and resented their success, the bourgeoisie tried to distance themselves from "less respectable" commoners.

Middle-class people also had difficult relationships with those above them—the aristocracy. Successful members of the bourgeoisie resented the privileges enjoyed by the aristocracy, but—even more strongly—they wanted those privileges for themselves. They longed to join the aristocracy, and they were willing to spend money to do it. Money got them titles and offices, large estates, and judicious marriages—the trappings of success that they hoped would earn them acceptance into the ranks of the aristocracy. The aristocrats, for their part, viewed this method of social climbing—and the people who attempted it—with disdain. As they saw it, true nobility derived from birth, not wealth.

Nevertheless, the bourgeoisie persisted and thrived. These merchants, manufacturers, and professionals made money, expanded their businesses, invested in government bonds, and took chances on shaky financial schemes. They valued hard work and the accumulation of money. Moreover, they had the means to purchase a vast variety of luxuries, from coffee and chocolate to wallpaper, cotton clothing, and watch chains—goods produced outside the home, often even outside the country. For them, the market—rather than the household—supplied staples as well as conveniences and luxuries.

Over time, the richest among the bourgeoisie might manage to gain entrance into the aristocracy. Yet even if they could not get into the courts, estates, and homes of the aristocracy, the bourgeoisie developed a public culture of their own. They educated their children at universities and attended public theaters, music halls, and galleries. They filled tea rooms, coffeehouses, literary societies, and clubs and devoured newspapers, journals, and books written especially for them. Over time, they acquired their own sense of identity, as well as an impatience when further opportunities to rise in society were denied them.

THE CULTURE OF THE ELITE: COMBINING THE OLD AND THE NEW

The culture of the bourgeoisie and the aristocracy reflected the continuance of old trends along with the new developments that characterized the eighteenth century. For example, the courts of Europe still sponsored painters, composers, and musicians. In their private halls, aristocrats savored these artists' paintings, concerts, and operas. The prevailing spirit remained classical, inspired by the Greek and Roman appreciation for formal symmetry, proportion, and reason. On the other hand, artistic styles were changing. Several artists and authors put a new emphasis on emotion and nature in their works, an artistic trend

sometimes referred to as the **cult of sensibility.** Audiences for these new cultural forms expanded, and the stream of literature being published for the growing numbers of literate Westerners swelled.

The Advent of the Modern Novel

Much of the reading public consisted of members of the middle class, and, not surprisingly, the modern novel reflected middle-class tastes. A compelling story, complex and varied characters, and realistic social situations formed the core of this new literary form. Novels also conveyed current ideas, manners, news, and information in witty and dramatic ways. In several popular novels, the English writer Daniel Defoe (1660–1731) wrote about individuals who planned ahead and used their entrepreneurial skills to meet challenges. The adventures of a character in a Defoe novel might take place at home in England or on exotic islands, as in *Robinson Crusoe* (1719). Similarly, Defoe's book *Moll Flanders* (1722) tells of a woman of lower-class origins who manages to navigate through all sorts of difficult situations, from prisons to a position in high society, in England and America.

Samuel Richardson (1689–1761) and Henry Fielding (1707–1754), also British, used the novel to analyze human personality, emotions, and psychology. In *Pamela, or Virtue Rewarded* (1740), Richardson recounts the story of a servant girl who tries to retain her virtue in the face of her wealthy employer's sexual advances. The book's characters and circumstances powerfully reflected contemporary realities, and the novel inspired a wave of similar works. Henry Fielding, for one, expanded on Richardson's effort, weaving a rich tapestry of English society in his novel *Tom Jones* (1749).

Many novels appealed particularly to women readers. British writer Fanny Burney (1752–1840) gained fame with the publication of her novel *Evelina or A Young Lady's Entrance into the World* (1778). The book portrays a provincial girl who makes a life for herself in London. Although the story ends with a marriage, it also reveals the social restrictions and dangers facing eighteenth-century women who tried to live an independent life. Burney would go on to publish several other popular novels.

During the second half of the century, novels and works of poetry by authors such as Jean-Jacques Rousseau in France and Johann Wolfgang von Goethe (1749–1832) in the German states emphasized emotion, relationships, and social problems. These authors presented the emotions as natural virtues, rejecting the artificiality of formal manners. Their style, which would become known as romanticism, grew in popularity during the last quarter of the century.

FIGURE 15.11 Antoine Watteau, *A Pilgrimage to Cythera,* 1717 Many of Watteau's popular paintings depicted aristocrats at play. In this scene, they wander through nature on a mythical island of love.

Pride and Sentiment in Art and Architecture

Unlike literature, the fine arts still typically reflected the tastes of the dominant aristocracy. Artists vied with one another for commissions to paint the portraits of royals and aristocrats, depicting their proud subjects adorned with plumes, buckles, silks, brocades, and laces. The scenes might include children and dogs and, in the background, lavish estate grounds. The distinctive clothing, haughty poses, and elaborate settings marked subjects as members of the landowning elite.

Many paintings showed intimate scenes of aristocratic private life—meetings, picnics, flirtations, and conversations among the upper classes. In Antoine Watteau's (1684–1721) popular paintings, for example, the context might be classical mythology, but the figures were eighteenth-century aristocrats. In *A Pilgrimage to Cythera* (a mythical island of love), shown in **Figure 15.11,** aristocrats wander leisurely through an idyllic garden of nature. Cupids at the left and Venus at the right bless the scene. The line between life, mythology, and the social roles played by the subjects blurs in this lush scene. The painting also has an underlying seriousness, as the lovers, reluctantly preparing to depart to the everyday world, enjoy a moment of life that will pass too quickly.

Whereas the aristocracy tended to populate Watteau's works, other artists painted well-received, sentimental scenes of ordinary people experiencing dramatic moments. **Figure 15.12,** a painting by the French artist Jean-Baptiste Greuze (1725–1805), shows one of these works. Here, the father at the left curses his departing son, who is determined to find his own way through life by joining the army. The young man's mother and other members of the family try in vain to reconcile the two men and to prevent

the breakup of the family on such a painful note. In an accompanying painting, the grief-stricken son returns to find his father on his deathbed. William Hogarth's works (see **Figures 15.3** and **15.14**) also explored everyday experiences in the lives of ordinary people, but usually from a satirical or moralistic perspective.

Eighteenth-century architecture could not portray sentiments in the same detail as paintings, but buildings in the baroque style still expressed well the gaudy splendor of the eighteenth-century monarchs and their courts. At the same time, architects began deemphasizing size and instead relied on multiple curves and lacy, shell-like ornamentation to convey a sense of pleasing luxury. This style is usually referred to as **rococo.** Some new government buildings and urban residences followed a more neoclassical style, which stressed clarity of line and form modeled on Greek and Roman ideals.

Gardens complemented the buildings they accompanied, extending them and reflecting the mix of old and new tastes. As we saw in Louis XIV's Versailles palace (see Chapter 13), the French garden in particular emphasized rational, geometric forms marked off by hedges. Here, nature was shown completely tamed by human power and reason. By contrast, the eighteenth-century English garden looked freer and more natural. In fact, these gardens were not natural at all. Landscape architects designed them to imitate a vision of nature or to turn the grounds of an estate into an idealized version of nature. This managing of nature in English gardens was a compromise between old and new ideas about human beings' place in the natural world.

Reaching New Heights in Music

Of all the eighteenth-century arts, music left the most profound legacy. Much of it reflected the tastes of its royal, aristocratic, and ecclesiastical patrons. Composers and musicians, therefore, usually stuck to established forms, and music was typically heard as a pleasing background to conversations, balls, and other social occasions in the bastions of the aristocracy. Increasingly, however, music was played in public concert halls to a larger audience. Opera houses opened everywhere, and composers could now hope to make money from paying audiences as well as from court and aristocratic patronage. Several cities became well-known musical centers, but Vienna topped them all. This Austrian city became the musical heart of Europe, drawing hundreds of musicians who competed for favor there.

The first half of the eighteenth century saw the high point of baroque music, a style that had originated in the seventeenth century and that was still favored in royal courts and aristocratic homes.

The greatest practitioners of the baroque style were Johann Sebastian Bach (1685–1750) and George Frideric Handel (1685–1759). Bach was a member of a German family long distinguished

Baroque music by its musical talent. Noted in his own lifetime chiefly as an organist rather than a composer, he created a vast array of great music for organ, harpsichord, clavichord (forerunner of the piano), orchestra, and chorus. Sadly, much of Bach's work has been lost. Much of his music was religiously inspired, but he also wrote a large amount of secular music. Handel was born in central Germany in the same year and same region as Bach. He studied Italian opera in Germany and Italy and wrote forty-six operas himself. He also became court musician in Hanover. Later, he made his home in England, as did the elector, who became King George I of England. Handel wrote an enormous quantity of music—both instrumental and vocal—all of it marked by dignity, formal elegance, and harmony.

During the last decades of the century, the restrained baroque style gave way to the more melodic "classical"

The classical style style, with its striking depth, structure, and emotion. Franz Joseph Haydn (1732–1809) and Wolfgang Amadeus Mozart (1756–1791) led the way. Their most stunning work was the symphony; by the end of their careers, they had created symphonies of rich harmonic complexity and emotional depth within the restrained classical form. During his long career in Vienna, Haydn wrote more than a hundred symphonies in addition to scores of compositions for other forms, particularly chamber music. Toward the end of his career, he became so popular that he left noble patrons and signed a lucrative contract with his music publisher.

Haydn became a friend and a source of inspiration for the young Mozart (see Biography). **Figure 15.13** shows the 7-year-old Wolfgang playing the piano. Accompanying him are his father on the violin and his sister, who is singing. Here the performers are exquisitely dressed for their aristocratic audience. Ultimately, Mozart composed more than six hundred works and excelled in all forms, but he became most appreciated for his symphonies, piano concertos, and operas. His music was stunningly clear, melodic, elegant, and graceful. In his hands, the classical style reached its peak.

The Grand Tour

The music, art, and literature of the elites were part of a broader, cosmopolitan culture that spilled across national boundaries. This culture manifested itself in elaborate styles of dress, polished manners, and highly structured conversation. French was its international language. The growing popularity of travel and travel literature added to the sense of a common European cultural identity, at least among elites. Indeed, the

thinking about

ART

FIGURE 15.12

Jean-Baptiste Greuze, *The Father's Curse,* ca. 1778

In this eighteenth-century painting, French artist Jean-Baptiste Greuze depicts a dramatic family conflict between a father, issuing a curse, and his son, who is departing for the army. Hoping to hold the family together, the women and children plead with the father, on the left, and especially with the son, on the right. On the far right, a shadowy figure—perhaps an army recruiter who has influenced the son's decision—waits.

Connecting Art & Society

1. What does this depiction reveal about the roles of men, women, and children in this family?

2. Why might viewers of this scene be touched and fascinated?

3. Why might the father have been so disturbed by his son's departure?

4. How do the structure and lighting of the painting reflect the drama of its content?

wealthy often considered the **grand tour** a necessary part of education. Travelers on the tour stopped in main cities to indulge in coffeehouses, storefront window displays, public gardens, theaters, opera houses, and galleries. They might also visit art dealers or public auctions to purchase quality paintings. Family connections

The Culture of the Elite: Combining the Old and the New   505

BIOGRAPHY

Wolfgang Amadeus Mozart
(1756–1791)

Child Prodigy, Musical Genius

Musicians quickly recognized the young Wolfgang Amadeus Mozart as a unique genius. His father, Leopold, a well-known Austrian composer and violinist, called him the "miracle which God let be born in Salzburg." Born in 1756, Wolfgang wrote his first compositions when he was just 5 years old. He embarked on the first of many tours throughout Europe as a 6-year-old child prodigy, playing the clavier with his elder sister, Nannerl, also a child prodigy, and his father (see **Figure 15.13**). They played at several royal courts for monarchs such as Louis XV of France, Maria Theresa of Austria, and George III of Britain. They also performed at the homes of leading nobles as well as in public theaters. Wolfgang's father, always eager to promote his young son, wrote that "our great and mighty Wolfgang seems to know everything at the age of seven that a man acquires at the age of forty."

By the time he had reached 14, Mozart had composed several concertos, sonatas, and an opera. Announcements for his performances stressed his virtuosity. For example, for a concert in Italy, the 14-year-old would play "A Symphony of his own composition; a harpsichord concerto which will be handed to him, and which he will play on first sight; a sonata handed him in like manner, which he will provide with variations, and afterwards repeat in another key. . . ." The boy could play the organ and violin almost as well. After hearing Mozart in 1771, one well-known composer said, "This boy will cause us all to be forgotten."

FIGURE 15.13 The Mozarts

The prestigious Haydn, who strongly influenced Mozart's music, would later tell Mozart's father that "your son is the greatest composer known to me. . . ."

In 1781, Mozart settled in Vienna as a teacher and composer. Short, slim, with engaging blue eyes and a full head of fine hair, the young man enjoyed an active social life, including billiards and dancing. Yet music preoccupied him. He wrote, "You know that I am, so to speak, swallowed up in music, that I am busy with it all day—speculating, studying, considering." Keenly aware of his own talents, he at times arrogantly criticized other musicians' limitations. He felt certain that he could outshine any rival.

In 1782, despite the doubts of his father and sister, Mozart married Constanze Weber, a singer. Mozart wrote that "as soon as we were married, my wife and I both began to weep" for joy. Their marriage seems to have been happy. They would have six children, of whom only two survived. Neither parent managed the family finances well. Even though Mozart became brilliantly successful as a composer, a virtuoso pianist, and a teacher; received numerous commissions and fees; and attained appointment as royal chamber composer to Emperor Joseph II of Austria, he continually borrowed money to support his growing family.

Mozart could never quite satisfy his demanding and increasingly distant father. Hearing that Leopold had fallen seriously ill in 1787, Mozart wrote a letter of consolation that included his own views on death: "As death . . . is the true goal of our existence, I have formed during the last few years such close relations with this best and truest friend of mankind that his image is no longer terrifying to me but rather very soothing and consoling." Leopold died a month later. In July 1791, a stranger appeared at Mozart's door with a commission to write a requiem in secrecy. Mozart was still working on the project in December when he died in relative poverty. He was just 35. Although he probably had succumbed to an infection and fever, unsubstantiated rumors circulated for years that a competitor had poisoned him.

Connecting People & Society

1. How did Mozart's career reflect eighteenth-century society—still dominated by the aristocracy but with a growing middle class interested in the culture of the day?

2. In what ways did Mozart's family life influence his career as a musician?

3. What image of young Mozart do you think is projected in **Figure 15.13?**

offered them accommodations and introduced them to local society, Enlightenment salons, or potential candidates for marriage. The tour usually continued to historical ruins, which featured revered models of Greek and Roman antiquity that further strengthened the viewers' sense of a common cultural identity.

CULTURE FOR THE LOWER CLASSES

The lower classes were not without cultural outlets that fit their lives and provided a sense of common identity. For peasants, artisans, and the urban poor, culture typically came in the form of shared recreation, songs, tales, and the passing down of wisdom at gatherings and celebrations. Many of these activities also coincided with religious gatherings and celebrations.

Festivals and Popular Literature

Villagers worked together and celebrated together—at fairs, harvests, plowings, weddings, and religious holidays. Numerous festivals and public ceremonies had seasonal themes that were of particular importance and interest to people so dependent on agriculture. Other celebratory events related to the Christian calendar and centered on holidays, such as Christmas and Easter. Traditional weddings involved a community procession and festivities as well as a religious ceremony, and they featured music, dancing, feasts, games, and play. In the cities, artisans participated in their own organizations that combined recreational activities with mutual aid and religious celebrations.

Certain forms of literature also became popular among ordinary people. Literacy was growing, thanks to the printing press, the demands of business, and an increase in the number of primary schools. By the end of the eighteenth century, some 40 to 60 percent of the population in England and France could read (more men than women). With the rise in literacy, popular literature also expanded. Stirring religious tracts, almanacs, and tales of chivalric valor—typically, small, cheap booklets—circulated widely. More often, however, the "literature" of ordinary people was passed on orally. At night, people might gather to share folktales and songs that told of traditional wisdom, the hardships of everyday life, the hopes of common people, the dangers of life in the forests or of strangers who could be monsters or princes, and the ways to get along in life.

In the past, elites had fully participated in this popular culture, but during the eighteenth century they increasingly abandoned it to the lower classes. The "respectable" classes now often considered the leisure activities of ordinary people too disorderly and crude. Nevertheless, the middle and upper classes read some of the same popular literature enjoyed by the lower classes. Moreover, everyone—aristocrats and peasants alike—might be found at village festivals, fairs, and sporting events or enjoying jugglers, acrobats, magic lantern shows, and touring troupes of actors. Men of all classes watched and wagered on cockfights and dogfights. Other sports, such as soccer and cricket, gained popularity and drew large, animated crowds.

Gin and Beer

All the social classes also engaged in drinking—whether wine or brandy in the privacy of a wealthy home, or gin and beer in popular taverns. Especially in England, the ravages of drinking gin seemed to grow to alarming proportions. **Figure 15.14,** another moralistic work by William Hogarth, graphically depicts the evils of gin drinking in England. At the center a pox-ridden, impoverished, and drunken woman lets her baby fall over a wooden rail. Near her, a man slowly starves to death. In the background, workers haul bodies away, a man hangs himself in an upstairs tenement, children drink glasses of gin, and buildings collapse for want of repair. The scene is one of physical, social, and moral decay from excessive alcohol

FIGURE 15.14 William Hogarth, *Gin Lane*, 1750 In this disturbing scene, the British artist William Hogarth documented the physical, social, and moral decay that could result from excessive alcohol consumption.

consumption. Though this image is an exaggeration, the actual problems caused by drinking were so extensive that in 1751 the British government passed a heavy tax on cheap gin to curtail its consumption.

Religious Revivals

Popular culture also merged with deeply felt spiritual beliefs and religious activities. Despite the many secular trends of the period, Christianity still stood at the center of Western culture and life. Churches rather than the state ran the schools and hospitals. The poor, aged, and crippled relied on churches for social services. Church bells announced the time of day everywhere, and religious holidays marked the year.

Within this Western religious culture, popular piety persisted. Indeed, especially among Protestants, a sense grew among ordinary churchgoers that official churches were becoming bureaucratized, complacent, and unresponsive to peoples' spiritual needs. In response, religious revivals spread from community to community and across national borders. In the German and Scandinavian states, **pietism**—which minimized dogma and formal ritual in favor of inner piety, holy living, and the private emotional experience of worshiping—gained strength. Revival movements in Britain and its North American colonies attracted thousands to huge gatherings.

Pietism

The greatest of these revival movements was Methodism, founded in England by John Wesley (1703–1791). While studying for the Anglican ministry at Oxford, Wesley and a band of fellow students became disillusioned with the spiritual emptiness that had fallen upon the Anglican Church as well as its subservience to the government and the aristocracy. The group's lives became such examples of piety and moderate regularity that their fellow students branded them "Methodists" in derision. Methodism stressed humble faith, abstinence, and hard work. Barred from preaching in the Anglican churches, Wesley rode horseback from one end of England to the other until well into his 80s, preaching the "glad tidings" of salvation in thousands of sermons in streets, fields, and anywhere else he could find even a small audience. He claimed "to lower religion to the level of the lowest people's capacities."

Among Catholics, similar movements—such as Jansenism in France and Italy and Quietism in Spain—spread among elites and others. East European Jews had their own revivalist movement with the founding of the Hasidic sect in the 1740s. Hasidim (meaning "most pious") spread throughout Poland, rejecting formalism, stressing simplicity, and engaging in loud, joyful singing prayers. These religious movements revealed the power with which spiritual matters still influenced people in the West. Nevertheless, like the broader cultural forms of the time, religious revivals left the overall social order intact.

FORESHADOWING UPHEAVAL: THE AMERICAN REVOLUTION

For most of the eighteenth century, neither wars, colonial rivalries, nor changes in country and city life upset the fundamental social and political stability of Western societies. In the last quarter of the eighteenth century, however, new forces erupted that would ultimately transform the West. The first of these disturbances occurred in Britain's thirteen North American colonies. This upheaval shifted the tide of events in North America and foreshadowed a far deeper and broader revolution that would strike at the heart of Europe itself.

Insults, Interests, and Principles: The Seeds of Revolt

By the mid-eighteenth century, more than two million people lived in the colonies. The seaboard cities in particular flourished, benefiting from a thriving commerce with Europe, Africa, and the West Indies. The colonists thought of themselves as British. Furthermore, the thirteen colonies in theory were part of Great Britain, governed in the same way and therefore subject to British trade regulations. In practice, however, the colonists often acted as they pleased, even if that meant quietly ignoring those regulations. They developed their own patterns of local government, manipulated British governors, and worked around British mercantilist policies.

Tensions between the island nation and these prospering colonies arose just after the Seven Years' War ended in 1763. Feeling that they had helped defend the American colonists against the hostile French and Indians, the British expected the colonists to help pay off the huge debt incurred in the fighting. To tighten their control over the colonial empire for which Britain had just fought so long and hard, British officials enacted new commercial regulations and taxes. Perhaps the most irritating of these was the Stamp Act of 1765, which taxed printed documents such as newspapers, pamphlets, and wills.

New commercial regulations and taxes

The colonists reacted to the new policies with complaints, boycotts, protest meetings, outrage, and sometimes riots. Because colonists were not represented in Britain's Parliament, headlines in newspapers and pamphlets screamed, "No taxation without representation!" In their Stamp Act Congress of 1765, colonists announced that they were "entitled to all the inherent rights and liberties of his [the king's] natural born subjects within the kingdom of Great Britain." Local circumstances and the distance from Britain meant that "the only representatives of these colonies are persons chosen therein by themselves, and that no taxes ever have been, or can be constitutionally imposed on them, but by their respective legislatures." The British compromised, repealing most of the taxes, but many colonists were still not satisfied.

Both sides translated their disagreements into ideological terms. American newspapers, propagandists, and political groups, echoing Enlightenment ideas, argued that violation of their fundamental rights justified a fight for independence. Most people in Britain stood against rebellion and for parliamentary sovereignty as a matter of principle. They argued that they were making only reasonable and minimal demands on the colonies.

In the end, each side felt backed into a corner. The notion of full independence gained appeal among the colonists. American political leaders who were critical of British policies organized the First Continental Congress in 1774, hoping to persuade Parliament to abandon its efforts to directly control colonial affairs. In response, King George III increased British armed forces in America, convinced that "blows must decide whether they are to be subject to the Country or Independent."

A War for Independence

The first blows were exchanged in 1775 between British troops and American militiamen in New England. The Second Continental Congress appointed George Washington (1732–1799) its military commander, setting the course for armed rebellion and independence. On July 4, 1776, that Congress issued the Declaration of Independence, written primarily by Thomas Jefferson (1743–1826) and based on the ideas of John Locke and other Enlightenment thinkers. Citing "self-evident" truths; "inalienable" natural rights such as "Life, Liberty, and the pursuit of Happiness"; and "a long train of abuses" to reduce the people under "absolute Despotism," the Declaration passionately justified rebellion.

Odds favored the stronger British forces, and at first they had the upper hand. Indeed, many British leaders viewed the rebel troops with disdain, one official calling the rebels a "rude rabble without a plan." Nevertheless, despite much internal division, an American victory at Saratoga in 1777 persuaded the French to help the Americans with money, ships, and troops against France's longtime enemy. The Dutch and Spanish eventually declared war on Britain, increasing the stakes for the British. Now British possessions in the West Indies, the Mediterranean, and perhaps even India hung in the balance. In 1781, the victory of the French fleet off Virginia forced a large British army to surrender at Yorktown. This indignity convinced the British that the effort to keep the American colonies was not worth the costs. After two years of negotiations, the combatants drew up the Treaty of Paris in 1783. Britain agreed to recognize American independence

and ceded to the United States the lands between the Mississippi River to the west, Canada to the north, and Spanish Florida to the south.

Creating the New Nation

In 1787, a new American constitution established a central government balanced by a separation of powers and strong states' rights. A Bill of Rights was soon enacted, protecting individual liberties and separating church and state. These principles, though lofty, did not apply to everyone. Although the Declaration of Independence had proclaimed that "all men are created equal" as a "self-evident" truth, one-fifth of the people remained slaves, and only property owners and men could vote. Nevertheless, the new nation had instituted—to an unprecedented degree—popular control, personal freedom, and formal toleration.

Some historians deem the American rebellion a war for independence, and others call it a revolution. At the time, people throughout the West—not just in America and Great Britain—viewed the events as dramatic and significant. A growing body of European readers avidly followed the action in newspaper accounts. Many of these readers saw the American Revolution as a victory for Enlightenment ideas. As revealed by **Figure 15.15**, a 1786 print, the French in particular celebrated the Revolution as a triumph in their own competition with their British rivals. In the center of the print, titled *Independence of the United States*, stands a monument topped by a rooster, symbolizing the French nation, and an image of French king Louis XVI. Below him are

> War for independence or revolution?

FIGURE 15.15 *Independence of the United States* This eighteenth-century French print celebrates the "partnership" of the French and North American colonists against the British during the war for independence.

images of other heroes of the American Revolution, Franklin and Washington. To the right stands a noble savage, representing America and standing with a foot on the defeated British lion. To the left are ships, suggesting the aid France gave Americans in their fight against the British. Neither the anonymous artist, the king, nor the French people realized at the time that the debts incurred by France and the ideas promoted by the American Revolution would soon come back to haunt the French monarchy.

LOOKING BACK & MOVING FORWARD

Summary

On the surface, life between 1715 and 1789 seemed to change only incrementally for most Westerners. The vast majority still lived in the countryside and worked the fields. Moreover, society and politics in the so-called Old Regime remained dominated by the aristocracy and, in most places, the monarchy. As in the seventeenth century, cultural forms still reflected elite tastes and the traditional values of commoners below them.

Below the surface, however, the West changed in crucial ways during this period. The political balance of power shifted as Russia and Prussia rose in the east while Britain gained prominence in the west. Success in the international arena often reflected how well central governments conducted their internal affairs. Some monarchs managed to dominate or work with the nobility, enact reforms, and even take on the trappings of "enlightened" rulers, whereas others—such as the French kings—failed in these ways. More important, mushrooming commerce, the agricultural revolution, and the spreading of cottage industry altered the ways by which millions of people earned a living, and these changes generated enormous new wealth. Finally, across the Atlantic in Britain's North American colonies, the American Revolution posed a challenge to the status quo that the French would soon take up in a much more fundamental way. These developments, combined with the spread of Enlightenment ideas, mark the eighteenth century as a period in which Westerners—knowingly or not—laid foundations for the great transformations to come.

KEY TERMS

balance of power, *p. 480*
Wahhabism, *p. 482*
parlements, *p. 488*
Middle Passage, *p. 492*
enlightened absolutism, *p. 498*
agricultural revolution, *p. 499*
enclosures, *p. 499*
cottage industry, *p. 500*
cult of sensibility, *p. 503*
rococo, *p. 504*
grand tour, *p. 505*
pietism, *p. 508*

REVIEW, ANALYZE, & CONNECT TO TODAY

REVIEW THE PREVIOUS CHAPTERS

Chapter 13—"The Struggle for Survival and Sovereignty"—told the story of kings and nobles battling for power, the results of those struggles, and their impact on millions of people throughout the West. Chapter 14—"A New World of Reason and Reform"—shifted focus to the changing intellectual foundations of the West.

1. In what ways was the eighteenth century a continuation of the struggle between monarchs and elites that had marked the seventeenth century?

2. Analyze how Enlightenment ideas—themselves stemming from the Scientific Revolution—affected Western society and especially politics during the eighteenth century.

ANALYZE THIS CHAPTER

Chapter 15—"Competing for Power and Wealth"—examines the battles of Western powers over land, position, and commerce, as well as the economic and social changes affecting eighteenth-century life in the West.

1. Which nations do you think were the biggest winners and which the biggest losers in this period? How do you explain their varying fortunes?

2. How did eighteenth-century rulers try to shore up and justify their own powers and those of their central governments?

3. Analyze the impact of slavery on Africa, the Americas, and Europe.

4. Analyze the benefits and costs of the growing commerce, the agricultural revolution, and cottage industry.

5. Why might this period be considered one of both growing prosperity and deepening social misery?

6. Delineate the differences between elite and popular culture during this period. How do you explain those differences?

CONNECT TO TODAY

Think about the ways in which Western powers competed during the eighteenth century.

1. How are states in today's world competing politically and economically with one another, both in the West and in the world as a whole?

2. What connections are there in the world today between statebuilding and warfare—such as efforts to create a politically strong state, and policies that promote military buildup and willingness to go to war—that are similar to or different from those connections during the eighteenth century?

BEYOND THE CLASSROOM

STATEBUILDING AND WAR

Blanning, Tim. *The Pursuit of Glory: Europe: 1648–1815.* New York: Viking, 2007. A respected, topically organized survey.

Davis, Ralph. *The Rise of the Atlantic Economies.* Ithaca, NY: Cornell University Press, 1973. A survey of the early modern economic history of the countries on the western fringe of Europe and their colonies in North and South America.

de Madariaga, Isabel. *Catherine the Great: A Short History.* New Haven, CT: Yale University Press, 1990. A solid, useful study.

Jasanoff, Maya. *Edge of Empire: Lives, Culture, and Conquest in the East, 1750–1850.* New York: Knopf, 2005. A well-written reinterpretation of British imperialism and its consequences.

MacDonagh, G. *Frederick the Great.* New York: St. Martin's Press, 2001. A fine, comprehensive biography.

Manning, Patrick. *Slavery and African Life: Occidental, Oriental and African Slave Trades.* Cambridge: Cambridge University Press, 1990. A wide-ranging study that demonstrates how the external slave trade affected African societies.

Weigley, R.F. *The Age of Battles: The Quest for Decisive Warfare from Breitenfeld to Waterloo.* Bloomington: Indiana University Press, 1991. A study of the period between 1631 and 1815, when economic, social, and technological circumstances enabled governments to concentrate large forces in the field.

GLOBAL CONNECTIONS

Conniff, Michael, and Davis, Thomas. *Africans in the Americas: A History of the Black Diaspora.* New York: St. Martin's Press, 1998. Excellent coverage of the slave trade and the African diaspora.

THE TWILIGHT OF MONARCHIES? THE QUESTION OF ENLIGHTENED ABSOLUTISM

Gagliardo, John G. *Enlightened Despotism.* Arlington Heights, IL: AHM Publishing, 1967. A respected examination of the topic in its European context.

Scott, H.M., ed. *Enlightened Despotism.* Ann Arbor: University of Michigan Press, 1990. A book of essays by leading historians analyzing Europe's rulers and nobility.

CHANGES IN COUNTRY AND CITY LIFE

Blum, Jerome. *The End of the Old Order in Rural Europe.* Princeton, NJ: Princeton University Press, 1978. A comprehensive study of life in rural Europe from the early eighteenth to the mid-nineteenth century; especially good on the abolition of serfdom.

Clarkson, Leslie A. *Proto-Industrialization: The First Phase of Industrialization?* London: Macmillan, 1985. Stresses the importance of cottage industry for the beginning of industrialization.

Overton, Mark. *Agricultural Revolution in England.* Cambridge: Cambridge University Press, 1996. A survey of the transformation of England's agricultural economy between 1500 and 1850.

THE CULTURE OF THE ELITE: COMBINING THE OLD AND THE NEW

Black, Jeremy. *Eighteenth-Century Europe.* London: Macmillan, 1990. A thorough survey of the period.

Richetti, John. *The Cambridge Companion to the Eighteenth-Century Novel.* Cambridge: Cambridge University Press, 1996. Useful views on the origins of the novel and its cultural context.

CULTURE FOR THE LOWER CLASSES

Burke, Peter. *Popular Culture in Early Modern Europe.* New York: Harper & Row, 1978. A survey of popular culture from the Renaissance to the French Revolution.

Muchembled, Robert. *Popular Culture and Elite Culture in France, 1400–1750.* Baton Rouge: Louisiana State University Press, 1985. An examination of popular culture and the means higher authorities used to destroy it.

FORESHADOWING UPHEAVAL: THE AMERICAN REVOLUTION

Weintraub, Stanley. *Iron Tears: America's Battle for Freedom, Britain's Quagmire: 1775–1783.* New York: Free Press, 2005. A fresh look at the war from various perspectives.

Wood, Gordon. *The American Revolution: A History.* New York: Random House, 2002. A fine survey and important interpretation.

Moving into the Modern World

The world had changed dramatically since Europe began its "expansion" in the fifteenth century. By the mid-eighteenth century, the West had been sending out explorers, making new commercial contacts, establishing links, and racking up conquests in the non-Western world for almost three centuries. Had Europe's expansion changed the meaning of the West?

During the eighteenth century, the actual "boundaries" of the West did begin to shift. Russia brought under its direct control lands to the east in Siberia. By the second half of the century, Russians easily outnumbered those regions' indigenous inhabitants. It also pushed its borders south, particularly in the Caspian Sea region. Russia's growing empire blurred any line between the West and the non-Western world on the Eurasian landmass. Across the Atlantic, Europeans had colonized parts of the Americas so thoroughly that large sections of the Western Hemisphere were much more than mere outposts. Though thousands of miles away from Europe, they were becoming part of the West itself.

If not in control of other major regions of the world, people from the West were certainly in increasing contact with other cultures and civilizations across the globe. From the broadest perspective, Westerners shared important similarities with several of these civilizations. For example, all had economies based on agriculture and handicrafts; the factories, railroads, and steamships that would mark the industrial era in the West were yet to come. Moreover, several Asian civilizations had enough wealth and military might to put them in the same league as the European nations.

China, for instance, remained the dominant power in east Asia. By 1750, Qing emperors (1644–1911) had extended their control far into central Asia and the south. In those regions, they made Vietnam, Burma, and Nepal their vassal states. The long rule of the talented emperor Qianolong (Chi'en Lung) (1736–1795) marked the height of the Qing (Chi'ing) dynasty. Wealthy, sophisticated, well-organized, and powerful, Qing China controlled the degree of contact it had with the West and supported its own trading networks throughout east and southeast Asian lands. China and other east Asian societies benefited from the West's growing thirst for their unique products as well as from crops that originated in the Americas. Farther east, Tokugawa shoguns had unified the Japanese islands and secured their rule. Like the Chinese, they managed to keep Western people at arm's length while promoting their own conservative values, such as adherence to a carefully ranked society and Confucian principles.

By the dawn of the eighteenth century, three powerful Islamic empires governed by Turkish dynasties had come to dominate southern and southwestern Asia. The Mughals ruled most of the Indian subcontinent and commanded a formidable, cosmopolitan society. The Safavid dynasty reigned in Persia, prospering as a trade link between the East and West. The powerful Ottomans had expanded from their base in Anatolia into eastern Europe, southwestern Asia, and north Africa. As recently as 1683, they had mustered enough force to lay siege to Vienna, the capital of the Habsburgs' Austrian Empire. But the days of all three Islamic empires were already numbered. By 1750, the Safavid Empire had disappeared entirely, much of Mughal India was disintegrating and falling under British rule, and the Ottomans were losing control over various provinces.

Meanwhile, in the Western Hemisphere, the Spanish and Portuguese ruled most of Latin America. A varied mix of Europeans, Africans, and Amerindians populated those lands. In the Caribbean, Western administrators governed societies populated predominantly by African slaves. Farther north, firmly established British and French colonies were spreading west at the expense of indigenous peoples. The twin disasters of disease and violence had already reduced these natives to a fraction of their numbers from 250 years earlier.

In Africa, states and societies based on kinship groups continued to develop as they had for centuries. Societies in west Africa and on the east African coast maintained long-established trade with Muslims from the north and east. By the eighteenth century, Islam had spread through these African societies. But the growing slave trade to the west generated wealth in Atlantic port cities and power in west Africa's coastal kingdoms, while creating great turmoil and human loss throughout much of sub-Saharan Africa.

Most of Oceania remained scarcely touched by the West during this time. Only toward the end of the eighteenth century did Europeans begin settling in Australia and initiating substantial contact with that land's aboriginal peoples. During that same period, a number of Western explorers, merchants,

Legend:
- China
- Japan
- Mughal Empire
- Safavid Empire
- West's Colonial Holdings in the Americas
- Ottoman Empire
- Russian Empire

The World, ca. 1700

missionaries, and settlers arrived on islands throughout the Pacific.

In the mid-eighteenth century, European ships carried goods and people overseas in astounding numbers and with great regularity. Some sailed to Western ports; others, to lands beyond Europeans' control. Demand in the West for goods such as sugar, tea, coffee, and tobacco, along with demand in China for silver, fueled this long-distance commerce. As the same time, a burgeoning hunger for slave labor forced millions of enslaved Africans across the Atlantic into the Americas.

In some areas, Western nations were chipping away at holdings of competitors such as the Ottomans in southeastern Europe and western Asia and the Mughals in southern Asia. In other areas, such as North America beyond the Atlantic colonies and Oceania, Western societies were starting to overwhelm indigenous

peoples. But in vast regions of the world, eighteenth-century Europeans gained access only on coastlines. East Asian societies easily kept them at bay, remaining in control of their own affairs. Western newcomers had only recently made inroads into lands of the once-powerful Mughal and Safavid empires. The Ottomans, though declining economically and politically, nevertheless managed to retain control over most of their lands. And in Africa, much of the continent remained too difficult for the West to penetrate.

Western explorers still sailed and marched off in search of new opportunities. However, they were limited to the most remote regions—Oceania, the frozen stretches of the far north and south, jungle-choked lands in South America and sub-Saharan Africa. In many ways, the mid-eighteenth-century world was growing

more tightly interconnected. At the same time, that world was becoming a stage for widespread competition and conflict between states and civilizations.

Thinking Globally

1. In what ways had the meaning of the West changed by the eighteenth century?

2. How did the civilizations of the West compare to civilizations in the wider world?

3. In what regards might people of the times have looked at the Atlantic world (that is, areas with easy access to the Atlantic Ocean) as an interactive whole?

4. What geographic considerations might have helped to account for the West's lack of control over various areas of the globe outside the Atlantic world?

JEAN-PIERRE HOUEL, *THE STORMING OF THE BASTILLE,* ca. 1789

On July 14, 1789, a crowd of Parisians stormed the Bastille, a castle-prison that stood as a symbol of all that was oppressive under the Old Regime. For most people, this event marked the beginning of the French Revolution.

Overturning the Political and Social Order

The French Revolution and Napoleon, 1789–1815

France was beginning to stir. On October 17, 1787, Arthur Young, a British farmer and diarist traveling through France, described "a great ferment amongst all ranks of men, who are eager for some change, without knowing what to look to, or to hope for." People whom Young talked with in Paris concluded that "they are on the eve of some great revolution in the government."

Two years later, the French Revolution brought the French monarchy to its knees. During the following ten years, revolutionaries eliminated the monarchy, overturned the social system of France's Old Regime, and transformed France's institutions. Moreover, the Revolution, with its compelling banner of "Liberty, Equality, Fraternity," proved so potent that its impact spread far beyond the borders of France. It soon spawned wars that engulfed most of Europe for more than two decades. Riding the twin forces of revolutionary turmoil and war, one individual—Napoleon Bonaparte—would rise to a legendary pinnacle of power. He would rule over a new French empire and a nearly conquered continent. In the process, Napoleon spread the ideals of the French Revolution well beyond France. This tide of change, turmoil, and war mounted by the French Revolution and Napoleon would eventually subside, but for France—and for much of Western civilization—the course of history had shifted permanently.

TIMELINE

American Revolution 1776–1783

The French Revolution and Napoleon 1789–1815

Early Phases 1789–1793

The Terror 1793–1794

The Thermidorian Reaction 1794–1795

The Directory 1795–1799

Napoleon in Power 1799–1815

Restoration 1815–1830

Age of Ideologies

Enlightenment

Industrial Revolution in Britain

1787   1794   1801   1808   1815

"A GREAT FERMENT": TROUBLE BREWING IN FRANCE

Arthur Young recognized discontent percolating among the French population, but there was good reason for people everywhere to assume that any crises would pass without a fundamental change in the monarchy or social order. The French monarchy had remained intact for centuries. Both Louis XVI and his predecessor, Louis XV, ruled over the leading nation on the Continent—a country more populous, wealthy, and educated than ever. Although neither king could claim much popularity, Louis XVI could at least bask in the glory of supporting the American revolutionaries in their victory over the British, France's chief competitor.

Then what caused the "great ferment" in France described by our British traveler? Below the surface bubbled growing complaints within France's social orders. Members of the aristocracy and middle classes, many influenced by the ideas of the Enlightenment, wanted more rights and power from the monarchy. Peasants suffered hardships that could, as in the past, create disorder and uprisings. However, the immediate, visible problem came from a conflict over France's finances.

The Financial Crisis Weakens the Monarchy

When Louis XVI ascended the throne in 1774, he inherited a large—and constantly growing—national debt. Much of that debt had been incurred financing wars and maintaining the military (see Chapter 15). Yet this debt should not have broken a nation as rich as France. Great Britain and the Netherlands had higher per-capita debts than France, but these countries also boasted taxation systems and banks to support their debts. France lacked an adequate

The taxation system

banking system, and most of the national debt was short term and privately held. Moreover, France's taxation system offered little help. The French nobility, clergy, and much of the bourgeoisie controlled the bulk of France's wealth and had long been exempt from most taxes. Nearly all direct taxes fell on the struggling peasantry. There was no consistent set of rules or method for collecting taxes throughout the country, and private tax collectors diverted much revenue from the treasury into their own pockets. Unless something was done, royal bankruptcy loomed ahead.

To stave off financial ruin, Louis XVI appointed the Physiocrat Jacques Turgot (1727–1781), a friend of Voltaire, as his minister of finance in 1774. Turgot proposed to abolish guilds, eliminate restriction on the commerce in grain, institute a small new tax on landowners, and cut down on expenses at court. However, people who benefited from the old system soon engineered his dismissal, and his modest reform measures were rescinded. A succession of ministers tried all kinds of temporary solutions, but to no avail. Costs incurred to support the Americans in their war of independence against England made matters worse. Now interest payments on the debt ate up half of all government expenditures. Bankers began refusing to lend the government money.

Reform efforts

Desperate, Louis called an Assembly of Notables in 1787 and pleaded with these selected nobles, clergy, and officials to consent to new taxes and financial reforms. Still they refused, as did the judges (all members of the nobility) in the *parlement*, or law court, of Paris when Louis turned to them. Instead, leading nobles and officials demanded a meeting of an old representative institution, the Estates General. They fully expected to control these proceedings and thereby assert their own interests. With bankruptcy imminent and nowhere else to turn for help, the king gave in. No one knew it at the time, but Louis' decision set the stage for turning France's financial crisis into a political and social movement of epic proportions.

The Underlying Causes of the Revolution

Louis' financial woes were just the most visible part of France's problems. When these tensions combined with the conflicts tugging at the fabric of French society, a dangerous blend resulted. One of the most troubling conflicts stemmed from the relationship between the monarchy and the nobility. For centuries, the French nobility, less than 2 percent of the population, had been the foundation on which the monarchy established its rule. However, the nobility was also the monarchy's chief rival for power, and it had grown increasingly assertive during

Revolt of the nobility

the eighteenth century (see Chapter 15). Through institutions such as the *parlements* that they controlled, nobles resisted ministerial efforts to tax them. More and more, nobles claimed to be protecting their rights as well as France itself from "ministerial despotism." So, when the monarchy turned to this group for financial help, the nobles refused for two reasons. First, they wanted to protect their own financial interests. Second, they used the crisis to assert their independence. Indeed, they argued that they represented the nation. They established a price for their cooperation: a greater share of power. Understandably, France's kings refused to pay that price. Thus, when the Assembly of Notables turned a deaf ear to Louis' pleas in 1787 and instead demanded a meeting of the Estates General, the king faced a financial crisis that was linked to a virtual revolt of his own nobility.

Louis might have thought he could find allies within the middle class in his standoff with the nobility. After all, French and other European kings had occasionally turned to wealthy members of this class for support in the past. Nevertheless, as events would prove in the tumultuous months of 1789, the middle class had changed—it now nursed its own set of grievances. This growing social sector—having almost tripled during the century to some 9 percent of the population—had benefited greatly from France's general prosperity and population boom after 1715. Many talented, wealthy, and ambitious members of the middle class managed to gain the high offices, titles, and privileges enjoyed by the nobility. Others rubbed shoulders and shared ideas with the nobility in salons and did their best to copy the nobles' style of life. Moreover, most had found ways to avoid paying heavy taxes.

Middle-class demands

However, numerous members of the bourgeoisie—particularly younger administrators, lawyers, journalists, and intellectuals—had encountered frustrating barriers to the offices and prestige enjoyed by the nobility. They also had grown impatient with the monarchy's failure to enact reforms that would benefit them specifically. By 1789, many applauded broad attacks on the privileged orders and the status quo. An example of such an attack was Abbé Emmanuel-Joseph Sieyès' widely circulated pamphlet *What Is the Third Estate?* According to Sieyès, "If the privileged order should be abolished, the nation would be nothing less, but something more." The sorts of reforms that these middle-class critics had in mind were no more palatable to the monarchy than those of the nobility.

People from both the middle class and the nobility had begun expressing ideas and using highly charged political terms that profoundly threatened the monarchy. In the decades before 1789, salon meetings and new publications had spread key ideas of the

Enlightenment ideas and language

Enlightenment to an increasingly literate public, particularly the aristocratic and middle-class elite in Paris and other French cities (see Chapter 14). These ideas emphasized the validity of reason and natural rights and questioned long-established institutions. They also undermined notions of the divine rights of kings and traditional ways of life—all while intensifying expectations of rapid reforms. In addition, terms such as *nation, citizen,* and *general will* had increasingly cropped up in the political discourse and reflected a growing sense that politics should include more than the concerns of the monarch and a tiny elite. So, when nobles asserted their own interests against the king, they often used language and ideas that attacked monarchical absolutists as unjustified tyrants and that accused the king's minister of "despotism." Middle-class men and women shared these sentiments and later extended them to demands for legal equality.

Thus, given all the resentments brewing among the nobility and the middle class, Louis and his often unpopular ministers risked much after they exposed themselves to discussions of reform within the Estates General. Three other developments—all beyond the powers of the king, nobility, and middle class—added an underlying sense of disappointment, desperation, and disorder among the French people in these decades.

First, a gap opened between rosy expectations and frightening realities. Before 1770, France had enjoyed a long period of prosperity. This growing wealth engendered a sense of rising expectations—that economically, things would keep getting better and better. After 1770, a series of economic depressions struck, turning these high expectations into bitter disappointment and frustration. Worse, in 1788 the countryside suffered unusually bad harvests. In May and July of that year, hailstorms wiped out crops throughout France. Drought and then the most severe winter in decades followed. The price of bread soared, and with it came hunger, desperation, and even starvation. Droves of peasants crowded into the cities in search of jobs and help, but the agricultural depression had already spread there and had thrown thousands of artisans and laborers out of work. In the spring of 1789, peasants and urban poor looking for food turned to violence in France's cities and villages. Women led groups demanding grain and lower prices for flour. Desperate people attacked bakeries and stores of grain wherever they could find them. Arthur Young wrote, "the want of bread is terrible: accounts arrive every moment from the provinces of riots and disturbances, and calling in the military, to preserve the peace of the markets." The populace angrily blamed governmental figures and "parasitical agents" of the Old Regime for their plight.

Disappointed expectations

By 1789, many pamphlets and cartoons portraying the connection between suffering and France's privileged orders circulated throughout France. **Figure 16.1** is an apt example of these publications. This illustration shows the thin "common man," who represents the vast majority of the people, carrying three heavy figures from the privileged classes on his back. In front, wielding a whip and claiming feudal rights, is the king, representing oppressive royal power. Just above him is a clergyman in robes, brandishing papers representing the threat of an inquisition and clerical privileges. In back rides a judge with a list of the jealously guarded rights of the noble-controlled *parlements*. The illustration depicts the common man as a naked beast kept under control by reins, chains, and a blindfold. He crawls pitifully across barren fields, bleeding from the hands, knees, and loins, while his tormentors spur him on.

The second unsettling development came with the increasing demands for political participation and

governmental reform throughout the West in the years before 1789. These movements, arising in various countries, were led by ambitious elites. In Poland, agitation for independence from Russian influence surfaced between 1772 and 1792. Across the Atlantic, what started as a tax revolt in Britain's North American colonies turned into the American Revolution and war for independence that directly involved French aristocrats and common soldiers alike and led to government without a king (see Chapter 15). In the Dutch Republic, demands for reform in the 1780s erupted into open revolt in 1787. In the Austrian Netherlands (Belgium and Luxembourg), elites rose against the reforms initiated by Emperor Joseph II in 1787. Well-informed French elites, keeping abreast of these disturbances, began to surmise that they, too, might successfully challenge the political status quo.

The economic hardship and political uprisings across Europe were damaging enough. A third problem—the French people's disrespect for their own king—made matters worse. For much of the eigh- Unpopular kings teenth century, France had been ruled by the unremarkable, unpopular, and long-lived King Louis XV. Unlike some of his European counterparts, neither he nor his successor, Louis XVI, managed to forge an effective alliance with the nobility or consistently assert their authority over it. Nor did they succeed in enacting reforms or even give the impression of being "enlightened" monarchs. Louis XVI had little particular taste or talent for rule, and his unpopular Austrian wife, Queen Marie Antoinette, increasingly drew fire for her supposed extravagance and indifference to those below her. According to a widely circulated story, she dismissed reports that the poor could not buy bread with the phrase "Let them eat cake!" Though the story was untrue, it reflected the growing anger against the king and queen.

Desperate to stave off the immediate threat of bankruptcy, the relatively weak Louis XVI looked for support. Instead of able allies, he found a jealous nobility, a disgruntled middle class, a bitter and frustrated peasantry, and an urban poor made desperate by hunger.

The Tennis Court Oath

In this ominous atmosphere, Louis XVI summoned the Estates General in 1788. This representative body, which had not met since 1614, was divided into France's three traditional orders, or estates: the first estate, the clergy, The Estates General owned over 10 percent of France's best land; the second estate, the nobility, owned more than 20 percent of the land; and the third estate, the so-called commoners, included the bourgeoisie, the peasantry, and the urban populace. During the early months of 1789, elections of representatives to the Estates General were held. All men who had reached the age of 25 and who paid taxes could vote. In thousands of meetings to draw up lists of grievances to present to the king, people found

FIGURE 16.1 France's Privileged Orders, ca. 1789 This French cartoon shows an enslaved "common man" as a beast of burden carrying the merciless, privileged monarchy, clergy, and aristocracy on his back. Cartoons such as this example not only captured popular opinion but also served as propaganda that helped to fuel the revolution.

their political voices and connected their dissatisfactions with inflating expectations of reform. Hundreds of pamphlets appeared and public debate spread widely. Each of the three estates elected its own representatives. Because the third estate made up more than nine-tenths of the total population, Louis XVI agreed to grant it as many seats as the other two estates combined. However, by tradition, the three estates sat separately, and each group had one vote.

In April 1789, delegates began streaming into Versailles armed only with *cahiers*, or the lists of grievances from all classes of people, that had been called for by the king. Of the 600 representatives of the third estate, not one came from the peasantry. Except for a handful of liberal clergy and nobles elected to the third estate, these delegates—mostly ambitious lawyers, petty officials, administrators, and other professionals—were all members of the bourgeoisie. They fully expected to solve the financial crisis quickly and then move on to addressing the long lists of complaints that they had been accumulating for years. Most bourgeois representatives, like many liberal nobles, wanted to create a constitutional government with a national assembly that would meet regularly to pass taxes and laws.

After religious services and a solemn procession in Paris, the delegates met in Versailles on May 5. Immediately they debated the voting system. The two privileged estates demanded that, according to custom, the three estates meet separately and vote by order—that is, each estate cast one vote. This procedure would place power squarely in the hands of the nobility, which controlled most of the first estate as well as its own order. The third estate demanded that all the orders meet jointly and that delegates vote by head. This method would favor the third estate, for not only did this order boast as many members as the other two combined, but a number of liberal clergy and nobles in the first and second estates sympathized with the reforms called for by the third estate. All sides realized that the outcome of this voting issue would be decisive.

The delegates haggled for six weeks. Louis waffled from one side to the other. Finally, the third estate, backed by some clergy from the first estate, took action and declared itself the National Assembly of France on June 17 and invited the other two estates to join it in enacting legislation. Three days later, when the third-estate deputies arrived at their meeting hall, they found it locked. Adjourning to a nearby building that served as an indoor tennis court, they took the **Tennis Court Oath,** vowing not to disband until France had a constitution.

Figure 16.2 dramatizes and glorifies this act of defiance. The painting is based on a pen and ink drawing by Jacques-Louis David (1748–1825),

> The National Assembly

a talented contemporary painter and active supporter of the Revolution. In the center of the picture, the presiding officer, Jean-Sylvain Bailly (1736–1793) (soon to become mayor of Paris), raises his arm in a pledge and reads the oath aloud. Below him, from left to right, a white-robed Carthusian monk represents the second estate, a black-robed Catholic curate the first estate, and the brown-clad Protestant minister the third estate. These same three figures also stand for France's main religious groups: the secular clergy, the regular clergy, and Protestantism. All three figures join, symbolizing the transformation of the meeting into the newly formed National Assembly. Around these figures, representatives also take the oath. From above, light streams through billowing curtains as if blessing the heroic activities below, and members of the populace approvingly watch the scene.

On June 23, the king met with the three estates in a royal session. He offered many reforms but also commanded the estates to meet separately and vote by order. Then the king, his ministers, and members of the first two estates regally filed out. The third-estate representatives, however, defiantly remained seated. When the royal master of ceremonies returned to remind them of the king's orders, Count Mirabeau (1749–1791), a liberal nobleman elected by the third estate, jumped to his feet. "Go and tell those who sent you," he shouted, "that we are here by the will of the people and will not leave this place except at the point of the bayonet!" When the startled courtier dutifully repeated these words to his master, Louis XVI, with characteristic weakness, replied, "They mean to stay. Well, damn it, let them stay." A few days later, the king reversed himself and ordered the three estates to meet jointly and vote by head. The third estate had won the first round.

Storming the Bastille

The monarchy might have been able to reassert control had not the new National Assembly received unexpected support from two sources: the Parisian populace and the French peasantry. Both groups had been suffering from the unusually poor economic conditions initiated by bad harvests. Revolutionary events raised expectations in hard times, making these people in the city and countryside particularly volatile. The first important disturbances broke out in Paris, whose population of 600,000 made it one of the largest cities in Europe. In early July, rumors that the king was calling the professional troops of the frontier garrison to Versailles raced through the streets of Paris. Alarmed, residents concluded that the king meant to use force against them. Then Louis dismissed his popular finance minister, Jacques Necker (1732–1804). This move seemed to confirm the fears of the third estate, who saw Necker as an ally.

FIGURE 16.2 School of Jacques-Louis David, *The Tennis Court Oath*, ca. 1792 On June 17, 1789, the third estate, dramatically declaring itself the National Assembly, took an oath to create a constitution for France.

At this critical juncture, the common people of Paris acted on their own. On July 14, riotous crowds of men and women searching for arms marched on the **Bastille,** a gloomy old fortress-prison in a working-class quarter. Few people were actually in the weakly guarded Bastille, but it symbolized the old order. Many died in the confused battle. With the help of mutinous troops, however, the crowd eventually took the Bastille, hacked its governor to death, and paraded around Paris with his head on a pike. "This glorious day must amaze our enemies, and finally usher in for us the triumph of justice and liberty," proclaimed a Paris newspaper.

The scene on page 514, one of many paintings and drawings made to celebrate this event, reveals the importance of this famous battle. The Bastille is portrayed as a massive castle that, against all odds, has come under attack by commoners and troops who have rallied to the side of the people. Only a few cannons seem necessary, for the people supposedly have heroic revolutionary spirit and numbers enough to surge forward and somehow storm across the bridge toward the Bastille entrance. The picture poignantly captures the symbolism of the act—the Bastille, representing the old feudal regime of the past, falls because of corruption within and the heroic power of an outraged people fighting under the revolutionary banner of "Liberty, Equality, and Fraternity." In fact, this show of force by the artisans, shop owners, and laborers of Paris stayed the king's hand and sparked uprisings in other cities across France. Under pressure, royal authority began to crumble.

Uprisings in the countryside echoed events in Paris. That July and August, peasants throughout France revolted against their lords. Burning tax rolls, the peasantry attacked manors, reoccupied enclosed lands, and rejected the traditional rights of **Peasant revolts** noble landowners—dues on land, flour mills, wine presses, and law courts, and the tithes (taxes) landlords charged their tenants. These revolts intensified with the spreading of unfounded rumors that bands of brigands, perhaps assembled by nobles, were on the loose in the countryside. Panicked by this "Great **The "Great Fear"** Fear," many nobles—including one of the king's brothers—fled France and became known as the *émigrés* (exiles).

The End of the Old Order

Now the nobility as well as the monarchy was in retreat. The National Assembly—dominated by the middle-class deputies from the third estate but now including many deputies from the clergy and nobility—tried to pacify the aroused peasantry. On

thinking about DOCUMENTS

New Laws End the Feudal System in France

During the summer of 1789, revolutionary activities swept France. On July 14, a mob stormed the Bastille, symbolizing a violent tearing down of the ancien régime. In the countryside, the peasantry rose against the nobility. Cracking under these pressures, nobles in the National Assembly moved on August 4 and 5 to abolish their own feudal rights and privileges. The following excerpts describe some of the laws passed to end the feudal system.

ARTICLE I. The National Assembly hereby completely abolishes the feudal system. It decrees that, among the existing rights and dues, . . . all those originating in or representing real or personal serfdom or personal servitude, shall be abolished without indemnification.

IV. All manorial courts are hereby suppressed without indemnification. . . .

V. Tithes of every description, as well as the dues which have been substituted for them . . . are abolished, on condition, however, that some other method be devised to provide for the expenses of divine worship, the support of the officiating clergy, for the assistance of the poor, for repairs and rebuilding of churches and parsonages, and for the maintenance of all institutions, seminaries, schools, academies, asylums, and organizations to which the present funds are devoted.

VII. The sale of judicial and municipal offices shall be suppressed forthwith. Justice shall be dispensed *gratis*.

IX. Pecuniary privileges, personal or real, in the payment of taxes are abolished forever. Taxes shall be collected from all the citizens, and from all property, in the same manner and in the same form. . . .

X. . . . All the peculiar privileges, pecuniary or otherwise, of the provinces, principalities, districts, cantons, cities and communes, are once for all abolished and are absorbed into the law common to all Frenchmen.

XI. All citizens, without distinction of birth, are eligible to any office or dignity, whether ecclesiastical, civil or military; and no profession shall imply any derogation.

SOURCE: James Harvey Robinson, ed., *Translations and Reprints from the Original Sources of European History*, vol. I, no. 5 (Philadelphia: University of Pennsylvania Press, 1898), pp. 2–5.

Analyze the Document

1. What conclusions about the grievances underlying the French Revolution might this document support?

2. What does this document reveal about the rapidly declining position of the aristocracy?

3. In what ways did these laws transform the *ancien régime*?

4. How did these laws change the relationship between commoners and nobility, as well as between citizens and the king?

August 4, during a night session of the National Assembly, one nobleman after another stood up and renounced his traditional rights and privileges in an effort to make the best of a bad situation. A leader of the Assembly hailed the "end of feudalism." As Document 16.1 shows, the National Assembly quickly decreed the end of serfdom, traditional dues owed to landlords, special taxation rights, and privileged access to official posts. The peasantry seemed pacified for the time being.

Success spurred the National Assembly to take further steps. The most important of these actions occurred on August 26, when the Assembly proclaimed the **Declaration of Rights of Man and Citizen.** Enlightenment ideas and phrases similar to those in the American Declaration of Independence filled this document. "Men are born and remain free and equal in rights," it stated. The natural rights included "liberty, property, security, and resistance to oppression." Sovereignty—supreme authority—rested with the nation as a whole,

Declaration of Rights of Man and Citizen

not the monarchy. Enacted laws should express the "general will"—a term and idea made popular by Jean-Jacques Rousseau (see Chapter 14). The document proclaimed freedom of opinion "even in religion," freedom of the press, and freedom from arbitrary arrest. In 1791, this spirit would lead to the liberation of France's Jews from old legal disabilities.

Some of these rights, such as freedom of the press, applied to women as well as men, but only men gained the full measure of new social and political rights. In the months and years that followed, many women objected to this limitation. Organizing groups and writing petitions and pamphlets, these women demanded to be included. In 1791, Olympe de Gouges (1748–1793), a writer and strong supporter of the Revolution, wrote one of the best-known and more challenging pamphlets, the *Declaration of the Rights of Women*. She argued that women should have the same political and social rights as men: "The only limits on the exercise of the natural rights of woman are perpetual male tyranny; these limits are to be reformed by the laws of nature and reason." Some members of the government, such as the Marquis de Condorcet (1743–1794), voiced similar demands. However, their arguments fell on deaf ears.

Despite this rising tide of defiance, Louis refused to sign the August decrees. Instead, he once more assembled troops around Versailles and Paris. In answer to this new threat of force, on October 5 and 6, a huge crowd of Parisian women, already infuriated by high bread prices and food **March to Versailles** shortages, marched 11 miles through the rain to Versailles. The contemporary print shown in **Figure 16.3** depicts the marchers, armed with pikes, axes, swords, and cannon. With the exception of the well-dressed, reluctant figure at the left, their faces express a striking determination and authority. (Notice the woman riding in the cart with the cannon and the woman at the front to the far right).

At Versailles, the marchers surrounded the palace. With the help of members of the recently formed National Guard—units of armed civilians under Lafayette—they forced the king and his family to accompany them back to Paris, bringing him closer to the people and away from the protected isolation of Versailles and the king's aristocratic advisors. As the carriage bearing the royal family rolled toward the capital, where the royal family would be virtually imprisoned in the Tuileries Palace, the surrounding crowd of women and men shouted jubilantly, "We have the baker [the king], the baker's wife, and the little cook boy! Now we shall have bread!" Although this image of women taking political action into their own hands made them heroines of the Revolution in some eyes, others would nervously look back on the women's behavior as something inappropriate and even frightening. Most men were not ready to accept such a change in women's traditional roles.

A few days later, the National Assembly moved its sessions to Paris. The third estate, building on the anger and hunger of the peasantry and the urban poor, had triumphed. The old order had disintegrated.

THE CONSTITUTIONAL MONARCHY: ESTABLISHING A NEW ORDER

Flushed with success, the National Assembly now turned to the task of transforming French institutions. Guiding principles were represented by the revolutionary banner "Liberty, Equality, and Fraternity."

FIGURE 16.3 The March to Versailles In this spirited scene from the times, determined Parisian women, carrying weapons and hauling a cannon, march to Versailles to confront the king with their demands and to force the royal family back to Paris.

At that time, the idea of liberty meant freedom from arbitrary authority and freedom of speech, press, conscience, assembly, and profession. Equality meant equal treatment under the law and equality of economic opportunity—at least **Liberty, Equality, Fraternity** for men. Fraternity meant comradeship as citizens of the nation. During the next two years, the Assembly passed a series of sweeping reforms that altered almost all aspects of life in France.

The central government, now based on national sovereignty, was transformed into what amounted to a constitutional monarchy. The National Assembly served as its legislature, and the king (still an important symbol of author- **Constitutional monarchy** ity for many) remained its chief executive officer. Because only tax-paying males could vote and win election to office, the bourgeoisie firmly held the reins of power. For the time being, the governance of France was decentralized. To undermine old loyalties and the power of the provincial nobility, the National Assembly created eighty-three newly named departments, each almost equal in size and administered by locally elected assemblies and officials (**Maps 16.1** and **16.2**). Similarly, the National Assembly took France's judicial system out of the hands of the nobility and clergy. It created new civil and criminal courts, with elected judges. France's complex, unequal system of taxation was also swept away, replaced by uniform taxes on land and the profits of trade and industry.

The new government linked reform of the Catholic Church with the financial problems it faced. Repudiating France's debt was out of the question because part of it was owed to members of the bourgeoisie. To pay for its expenditures, the National Assembly issued what amounted to paper money called *assignats*. To back up the *assignats*, pay off the debt, and at the

thinking about GEOGRAPHY

MAPS 16.1 AND 16.2

Reorganizing France in 1789

These maps show France's historic provinces, each with its own political identity (Map 16.1, left), and the nation's revolutionary departments after 1789 (Map 16.2, right).

Explore the Maps

1. Why do you think France's Assembly reorganized the nation so that the old provinces were different sizes, while the newly created departments were almost equal in size?

2. Why do you think the Assembly eliminated the historic names of the provinces and renamed most of the new departments for geographic features (mountains, such as the Alps; rivers, such as the Seine)?

3. Would this sort of political and administrative reorganization inspire local resistance or undermine it? Why?

same time bring the church under governmental control, government officials confiscated and sold church property.

This seizure of property constituted a major step toward the nationalization of the church. Next the Assembly dissolved all convents and monasteries and prohibited the taking of religious vows. People would elect the clergy, including non–Roman Catholics, and the state would pay their salaries. These measures were incorporated in the **Civil Constitution of the Clergy,** to which all members of the clergy were required to take an oath of allegiance in order to perform their functions and

Civil Constitution of the Clergy

draw their salaries. This last step proved too much for many religious officials, for it threatened the very independence of the clergy. Pope Pius VI called the oath of allegiance "the poisoned fountainhead and source of all errors." Approximately half the clergy of France, including nearly all the bishops, refused to take the oath. This defection of the nonjuring clergy created a long-lasting division among France's Catholic population. Many, especially rural women, fought against this disturbance of their religious life, vowing to defend their faith "with the last drop" of blood. The Revolution would lose the support of many French citizens who felt loyal to the old church and their local priests.

The King Discredited

Louis XVI must have bitterly resented these changes, for they diluted his power and put Paris under the control of his former subjects. Nonetheless, he managed to make things even worse for himself. On June 20, 1791, the royal family, in disguise, escaped from Paris and headed by coach to France's northeastern frontier, where Louis hoped to find supporters and perhaps reverse the tide of events. Unfortunately for him and his family, a postmaster recognized them just before they could reach safety. Officials arrested the royal family in Varennes and returned them to Paris. To save face, the government concocted a thin story about the royal family being kidnapped, but in many eyes the king and queen had now become traitors.

Flight of the royal family

In October 1791, the National Assembly gave way to the Legislative Assembly, with all new representatives elected under the new rules. In only two years, and with relatively little bloodshed, France had been made over. A written constitution ruled supreme over the diminished monarchy. The church lost its independence from the state. The nobility forfeited its special rights and privileges. Men gained individual rights and liberties and legal equality. Though excluded by the reformers, women would nevertheless continue to voice demands for political and social rights and play important roles as the Revolution evolved. France now boasted a more democratic electoral system than England or the United States. Events had already gone well beyond anything our British traveler, Arthur Young, might have imagined two years earlier.

Reactions Outside France

Outside France, writers and reformers in Europe and the United States hailed the French Revolution or the principles underlying it. In elegant salons, elites spiritedly discussed these dramatic events, and in newspapers and pamphlets, writers dissected and debated their meaning. Supporters established societies in Britain and in states along France's eastern borders. Some activists, such as the American writer Tom Paine, traveled to Paris to participate directly. In Britain, Charles Fox, a leader of the Whigs, called the Revolution "much the greatest event that ever happened, and much the best." Others argued against the French Revolution. The most famous attack was launched by Edmund Burke in his *Reflections on the Revolution in France* (1790). This British statesman argued that France moved too quickly in the name of abstract notions of natural rights and justice. As a result, revolutionaries replaced a despotic monarchy with anarchy. In his view, societies should evolve slowly, drawing reforms from the long historical experience of a national culture. Good government came from good habits. Reforms worked well when based on a nation's best traditions.

Most governments opposed the Revolution when they realized the threat it posed to their own security. If a revolution could rise in France, end aristocratic privileges, and undermine the monarchy, the same might happen elsewhere. Officials welcomed and listened to the aristocratic émigrés who fled France. They suppressed pro-revolutionary groups within their borders. Within a few years, most states joined coalitions to fight against the revolutionary armies.

TO THE RADICAL REPUBLIC AND BACK

The new government, launched with such optimism in October 1791, lasted less than a year. Up to that point, the bourgeoisie and the peasants had been the primary beneficiaries of the Revolution. The bourgeoisie had gained political control over the country and social mobility. The peasantry had won freedom from feudal obligations. To the many peasant landowners who owned their land before the Revolution were now added others who had seized the lands of émigré nobles or had purchased confiscated church lands (though many of these lands went to middle-class buyers).

However, other groups remained quite dissatisfied. The royal family and much of the aristocracy and high clergy yearned for the restoration of their traditional positions. On the other hand, many Parisians urged a more radical approach to the Revolution. These shopkeepers, artisans, bakers, innkeepers, and workers had won little beyond theoretical rights and legal equality. Those who owned no property still could not vote, yet they had supplied much of the physical force and anger that had saved the third estate and made the reforms possible. Increasingly, these men and women formed organizations, held meetings, and intently discussed the numerous pamphlets, petitions, and newspapers printed daily in Paris. Some of these clubs became egalitarian meeting places for women and men; others, such as the Society of Revolutionary Republican Women, insisted that women should participate more fully in the Revolution. Many of the most politically active came to be known as the *sans-culottes* because they wore long pants instead of the fashionable knee breeches of the elites. A pamphlet described a *sans-culotte* as "a man who has no mansions, no lackeys to wait on him, and who lives quite simply. . . . He is useful, because he knows how to plough a field, handle a forge, a saw, or a file, how to cover a roof or how to make shoes and to

Sans-culottes

shed his blood to the last drop to save the Republic." Typically the *sans-culottes* carried pikes and addressed people as "Citizen" or "Citizeness." Eventually they and their supporters gained control over the municipal government of Paris—the Commune.

Leadership for this urban populace fell into the hands of radical members of the bourgeoisie, who allied themselves with the *sans-culottes* and favored overthrow of the monarchy and extension of the Revolution. Well organized and ably led, these radicals came together in numerous clubs that formed to debate and plan political matters. The **Jacobin** Club, which had hundreds of affiliated clubs outside of Paris, became the most important of these political organizations. Its membership included more than 200 deputies, and over time, militant radicals gained strength within the organization.

The Jacobin Club

War and the Breakdown of Order

Events—particularly the rumors of war that had begun circulating throughout France—soon played into the hands of the Parisian radicals. The monarchs of Austria and Prussia, fearing the spread of revolutionary ideas to their own lands and urged on by French émigrés, began to make threatening moves and to issue meddlesome warnings to the French revolutionaries. In France, many groups welcomed the prospect of war, though for different reasons. The royal family and its supporters believed a French victory would enhance the prestige and power of the throne; even a French defeat could help by restoring the Old Regime and royal power. Radicals, who wanted to turn France into a republic, believed that war would expose the inefficiency and disloyalty of the king and topple the monarchy.

The war that broke out in April 1792 became the first of a series of conflicts that would span twenty-three years and ultimately embroil most of the Western world. At first, inflation, food shortages, and breakdowns of order hampered France's war effort. The French armies suffered from lack of experienced leadership; nearly all the high-ranking officers were members of the nobility and had either fled or been deposed. The Austrian and Prussian armies badly defeated the French and advanced toward Paris. Panic broke out in the city. "Everywhere you hear the cry that the king is betraying us, the generals are betraying us, that nobody is to be trusted . . . that Paris will be taken," exclaimed an observer. When the Prussian commander, the Duke of Brunswick, announced that he would deliver the royal family "from their captivity," French radicals rightly accused Louis XVI and Marie Antoinette of being in treasonable communication with the enemy. On August 10, local leaders in Paris organized a huge Parisian crowd of men and women, who then attacked the king's palace. The royal family fled for their lives to the Legislative Assembly. The invading crowd wrecked the interior of the palace and slaughtered hundreds of the king's guards. The Legislative Assembly suspended and imprisoned the hapless Louis XVI. Under pressure from the people of Paris, it called elections—this time with almost all men enjoying the right to vote—for a National Convention to draw up a new, more radical constitution.

Meanwhile, one of the Jacobin leaders, Georges-Jacques Danton (1759–1794), used his great skills as an orator and organizer to gather recruits for the army and rush them to the front. As the recruits prepared to leave Paris to meet the invading Prussians, rumors—spurred by the propaganda of radical journalists like Jean-Paul Marat (1743–1793)—spread that reactionary clergy and nobles planned to murder their wives and children. Frightened and enraged people began murdering members of the nonjuring clergy (who would not swear allegiance to the new order) and nobles being held in the prisons of Paris. During the first three weeks of September 1792, more than a thousand fell victim to these massacres.

Panic and massacres

In the elections for the National Convention, held amid this hysteria, republicans—favoring elimination of the monarchy altogether and the creation of a French republic—won a sweeping victory. Document 16.2

National Convention

THE FRENCH REVOLUTION (1789–1799)

1787	Assembly of Notables
May 5, 1789	Meeting of the Estates General
June 20, 1789	Tennis Court Oath
July 14, 1789	Fall of the Bastille
August 4, 1789	Renunciation of noble privileges
August 26, 1789	Declaration of Rights of Man and Citizen
October 5–6, 1789	March to Versailles
June 20, 1791	Flight to Varennes
October 1791	Legislative Assembly
April 1792	War breaks out
September 1792	France declared a republic
January 1793	Louis XVI executed
1793–1794	The Terror
1795–1799	The Directory

KEY DATES

thinking about

DOCUMENTS

DOCUMENT 16.2

The Jacobins' Revolutionary Politics

In the years following 1789, the Jacobin Club of Paris became the most influential political club in the city and, with many affiliated clubs outside of Paris, the most important in France. The Jacobins pushed politics in an increasingly more radical direction. The following document, which they circulated on September 12, 1792, reveals some of the club's evolving goals and tactics.

Since the 10th of August conspirators have expiated their offences; the public spirit has risen again; the sovereign, recovered possession of its rights, triumphs at length over the scoundrels leagued against its liberty and its welfare. Nevertheless, the people of Paris have felt the necessity of preserving an imposing attitude and of exercising a strict surveillance over the Minions and agents of the traitor, Louis the Last. Be apprehensive, brothers and friends, lest new intrigues shall follow the baffled intrigues. The head, the cause and the pretext of the machinations still lives! Despotism moves in the darkness; let us be ready to engage in a combat to the death with it, under whatever form it presents itself. . . .

Let us impress our minds then with the spirit of the orders of the electoral body of Paris; they alone can save us from all sorts of despotism and the dangers of convulsions too long a time prolonged, etc.

These orders are in substance:

The purgatorial examination of the National Convention, in order to reject from its midst the suspected members who may have escaped the sagacity of the primary assemblies;

The revocability of the deputies to the National Convention who have attacked or who attack by any motions the rights of the sovereign;

The sanction, or the popular revision of all the constitutional decrees of the National Convention;

The entire abolition of royalty and the penalty of death against those who may propose to reestablish it;

The form of a republican government.

These, friends and brothers, are the important matters which the electors, the Commune, and the Primary Assemblies of Paris, invite us to discuss earnestly in order to fortify and encompass the National Convention with your opinion upon these matters.

SOURCE: F.M. Anderson, ed., *The Constitution and Other Select Documents Illustrative of the History of France 1789–1901* (Minneapolis: H.W. Wilson Co., 1904), pp. 127–128.

Analyze the Document

1. What is the Jacobin Club's vision of the monarchy and its supporters?

2. What does the club stand for?

3. What tensions within France does this document expose?

---

reveals how the Jacobin Club of Paris, branding the king "Louis the Last," pushed for a republic and legislators who favored Jacobin views. Most of the conservative elements fearfully stayed away from the polls. This Convention ruled France for the next three years, taking the Revolution down a new, more radical road.

Radical Republicans Struggle for Power

The struggle for political dominance among the different Jacobin factions intensified after the election. The Girondins, so called because many of their leaders came from the vicinity of Bordeaux in the department of the Gironde, had once been the most powerful and radical faction of the Legislative Assembly. Because they had sat on the speaker's left, they had come to be known as "the Left." In the new National Convention, the Girondins found themselves on the Right as the more conservative faction. Now the Left consisted mostly of members of the Jacobin political club from Paris. These Jacobins came to be called "the Mountain" because they occupied the highest seats in the convention hall.

Girondins and Jacobins

On September 22, 1792, the National Convention declared France a republic. The government then disposed of the king, who had squandered most of his support since his flight to Varennes in 1791. The Convention tried Louis and found him guilty of treasonable communication with the enemy. An extended debate ensued over whether to execute the king, with most of the Girondins opposed and the Mountain in favor. On January 21, 1793, the Convention voted by a narrow margin to execute Louis.

The Republic

Figure 16.4 depicts the scene of Louis' execution. On the platform, Louis addressed the crowd for the last time: "I die innocent." An eyewitness described how the executioners "dragged him under the axe of the guillotine, which with one stroke severed his head from his body." The revolutionary government adopted the newly invented guillotine as its instrument of choice because it considered the device more efficient and therefore humane than other methods of execution, such as hanging and the ax. In the painting an executioner holds up the head of the king for the troops and crowd to view. An observer reported that a few seconds later, "cries of 'Vive la

Execution of the king

Répub'" [long live the Republic] were heard . . . and in less than ten minutes this cry, a thousand times repeated, became the universal shout of the multitude, and every hat was in the air." The troops, with their backs to the crowd, are there to witness what is presented as a patriotic event. Although other executions would not have the same significance or draw the same crowds, this scene would be repeated thousands of times over the next two years. Beheadings not only served as affirmations of revolutionary justice but also provided entertainment—people often rented chairs and purchased food, drinks, and souvenirs, including miniature guillotines. Those who could not attend might purchase widely sold prints such as the one pictured.

FIGURE 16.4 Execution of Louis XVI, ca. 1794 In this depiction, an executioner holds up the head of Louis XIV, who has just been guillotined before a crowd of troops and other onlookers in central Paris.

Ten months later the queen, Marie Antoinette, followed Louis XVI to the guillotine. These executions sent a shudder of horror through the royal courts of Europe, as did the new French army recruits' surprising success against the Austrian and Prussian coalition. The hastily assembled revolutionary armies, swelling with numbers and enthusiasm, had checked the advancing Austrian and Prussian armies at Valmy in September 1792. France now went on the offensive. Alarmed, Britain, the Dutch Netherlands, Spain, Portugal, Sardinia, and Naples joined Austria and Prussia in a great coalition against France.

Internal and external enemies

This new external threat was compounded by internal threats to the revolutionary government. The peasants of the Vendée region in western France, stirred up by the nonjuring clergy and others, rebelled against the republican government. "We want our king, our priests and the Old Regime," cried the rebels. **Figure 16.5** shows a young aristocratic general leading the rebels in the midst of one of the close-quarter battles that often occurred in the Vendée revolt. Standing in tall boots and yellow pants, a white sash around his waist, and his wounded right arm in a sling, Rochejaquelein fires a gun at the enemy, so close in front of him that we see to the right the opposing bayonet just inches away. Behind Rochejaquelein stand his equally determined but more modestly dressed peasant guerrilla followers, one with a rifle, another with only a pitchfork to stress the popularity of this rebellion. Above flies the white flag of the rebel royalist cause that is echoed by the sacred heart pinned to the hero's chest. Rochejaquelein would survive this battle only to be killed in 1794. However, the uprising he helped lead spread until some sixty of the eighty-three departments suffered revolts. Lyons, France's second-largest

FIGURE 16.5 Pierre Narcisse Guérin, *Henri Duverger, earl of the Rochejaquelein* This painting portrays a heroic royalist leader during a bloody rebellion against the republican government in France's Vendée region.

BIOGRAPHY

Manon Roland
(1754–1793)

Manon Roland, describing herself as a "friend of humanity" and "lover of liberty," welcomed the French Revolution "with rapture." Born in 1754 into the family of a Parisian engraver, she learned to read by the age of 4. By her early 20s, she was fluent in two foreign languages, had mastered the Greek and Roman classics, and embraced the ideas of Rousseau. She also rejected her Catholic faith and formed a lasting hatred for the pretensions of the aristocracy—and of the royal family in particular. She married a lawyer twenty years her senior who gained a position as inspector of manufacturers in Lyons. At the outbreak of the Revolution in 1789, she was at the center of a group of idealistic intellectuals and admirers who met regularly in Lyons. She argued for a republic rather than a constitutional monarchy and demanded that the royal family be put on trial.

The turmoil of revolutionary events created opportunities for the couple. In 1791, the city government of Lyons sent Manon's husband to Paris as a negotiator. Manon accompanied him, thrilled to be at the political center of France. They attended meetings of the Jacobin Club, and Manon quickly gathered around her a social circle of men, including Robespierre, whom she would later describe as "ardent, jealous, avid for popularity." The Rolands also associated with Girondins.

Manon's husband often attended gatherings of this circle, and Manon let him do all the public speaking for both of them. Upholding the traditional, formal role of a proper wife, mother, and homemaker, she mostly listened. "I knew the role that suited my sex, and I never abandoned it," she noted.

Similarly, she did not argue for the rights of women or even invite other women to these gatherings, but she often resented men's attitudes toward women: It takes "a great deal of patience or vanity to hear with cool head, from men's own mouths, the value they attach to their superiority over us." Yet she was more politically and intellectually ambitious than her husband. Often, she was the force behind her husband's words and the author of writings that came out under his name. **Figure 16.6** shows this strong woman looking directly at the viewer, pen in hand.

In 1792, with the rise to power of the Girondins, Manon's husband was offered the high post of minister of the interior. She talked him into accepting it and, from behind the scenes, shared his new position of power and prominence. It was she who did most of the necessary writing—the instructions, circulars, and public announcements—and who accepted visitors eager to get an audience with the busy minister.

Events, however, moved too rapidly for Manon Roland as her life and the city, rose against the government in May. Toulon, the chief French naval base on the Mediterranean, invited in the British fleet to help in the fight against France's radical government. All-too-real enemies outside and within France's borders surged forward to fight against the Revolution.

The Terror

Faced with a seemingly inevitable demise of their cause and threatened by radical demands from the *sans-culottes*, the leaders of the Mountain decided to take drastic action. For support they turned to the Paris Commune, as the city government was called, which radicals and the *sans-culottes* controlled. The *sans-culottes* wanted to carry the Revolution even further, toward more direct democracy and governmental controls over the price of bread. Although the Mountain's leaders did not fully agree with the *sans-culottes*, they were willing to work with them to gain supremacy.

The National Convention, now dominated by the Mountain and surrounded by a threatening Parisian crowd of women and men urged on by *sans-culotte* leaders, voted the expulsion and arrest of their chief competitors, the Girondin leaders, on June 2, 1793. To pacify the *sans-culottes*, the National Convention also agreed to enact the Law of the Maximum to control the price of bread, flour, and other essentials. Finally, the Convention drafted a democratic constitution based on universal male suffrage that promised rights to education and even subsistence (a job or poor relief). However, the Convention soon suspended the constitution and formed the 12-member **Committee of Public Safety** to guide the country. The committee had two main tasks: to secure the Republic against its enemies—both internal and external—and to carry out a radical republican program. With the vast authority granted by the Convention, it enjoyed dictatorial powers. The committee came under the ideological leadership of the gifted and feared Maximilien Robespierre (1758–1794). A lawyer from the provinces when elected to the Estates General in 1789, he quickly rose to head the Jacobin Club in Paris. This stern, determined

> **Committee of Public Safety**

FIGURE 16.6 Manon Roland

Revolution took more radical turns. She fell in love with Buzot, a young Girondin in her circle. She told her husband of her feelings, and although the two honored the form of their marriage out of a sense of propriety and discipline, they were miserable together. Manon made new political enemies, particularly Danton and the more radical Jacobins. The radical press called her a whore and her salon a hotbed of intrigue. Then the Girondins began to lose power, and Manon's husband's career stumbled as well. He resigned from office two days after the execution of the king in early 1793. The Revolution had gone too far even for Manon Roland, who wrote that she was "ashamed of it. It has been dishonored by scoundrels." Over the next few months, both Rolands drew criticism from the press and their political enemies. Threatening groups of *sans-culottes* lurked in front of their apartment.

Too late, the Rolands tried to flee Paris. On May 31, 1793, Manon's husband, like many other Girondins, was arrested. He soon escaped, but then Manon suffered the same fate. After languishing in jail for months and writing her memoirs (modeled on Rousseau's *Memoirs*), she was tried on November 8, 1793, and found guilty of crimes against the Republic. That same day, she was escorted to the very guillotine where her longtime enemies Louis XVI and Marie Antoinette had perished. On the platform, she raised her eyes to David's statue representing liberty and lamented, "O Liberty, what crimes are committed in thy name." Upon hearing of her death, her husband committed suicide. Just weeks later, her lover, Buzot, facing arrest himself, also committed suicide.

Revolutionary events that had drawn Manon to Paris and initially fulfilled her hopes quickly spun out of control. At the forefront of change in 1789, she found herself left behind and labeled an enemy of the Revolution just four years later. For Manon Roland and so many like her who rose with the Revolution, the wry statement of a moderate observer held true: "The Revolution . . . devours its children."

Connecting People & Society

1. What does Manon Roland's life reveal about the attitudes underlying the Revolution?

2. What does her biography reveal about the rapidly changing events that disrupted people's lives?

3. What does she mean by the words "O Liberty, what crimes are committed in thy name"?

---

idealist was influenced by Rousseau and was bent on the creation of a virtuous republic. In pursuit of this dream, Robespierre and his fellow committee members struggled both to appease and to control the unpredictable, threatening *sans-culottes*.

To protect the Republic from its internal enemies and to satisfy demands from the *sans-culottes* for immediate action, the Committee of Public Safety instituted a Reign of Terror. "We must annihilate the enemies of the Republic at home and abroad, or else we shall perish," Robespierre warned. He justified the Terror by arguing that in this time of revolution, "the first maxim of our politics ought to be to lead the people by means of reason and the enemies of the people by terror." Accordingly, agents of the committee searched out and summarily tried anyone suspected of being counterrevolutionaries. Even those who had once supported the Revolution—such as the Girondins, whose views had fallen out of favor—were arrested and executed. Jean-Sylvain Bailly, shown leading the 1789 Tennis Court Oath in **Figure 16.2;** Manon Roland (see Biography); and Olympe de Gouges, the woman who argued so strongly for revolutionary principles in the beginning, fell to the guillotine. Though many people became victims of arbitrary justice, officials used the Terror most often where real threats arose—regions in revolt and vulnerable areas near France's borders. During this violent phase of the Revolution, probably between 200,000 and 400,000 victims of the Terror went to prison. Some 25,000 to 50,000 died in jail or at the hands of executioners.

To secure the Republic against external enemies, the government ordered a ***levée en masse,*** or general call-up of all men, women, and children to serve the nation. As able-bodied young men were rapidly trained and rushed to the front, the army swelled to 850,000 men—a number that far exceeded the forces of France's opponents. Everyone else was supposed to contribute to the war effort by collecting or manufacturing supplies for the troops and by bolstering spirits. Women stitched clothing and served as nurses, children made bandages, and old men delivered stirring, patriotic speeches. This united activity for defense of

Reign of Terror

Levée en masse

the country produced an intense national patriotism. One soldier wrote home from the front to explain his feelings: "When *la patrie* calls us to her defense, we ought to fly there.... Our life, our wealth, and our talents do not belong to us. It is to the nation, *la patrie*, that all that belongs." With the officer corps now open to talent and the massive mobilization of men, materials, and spirit, the citizen armies turned back coalition forces by the end of 1793. By the summer of the following year, they had carried the war beyond France's borders.

The Republic of Virtue

While fighting this war, Robespierre and the Committee of Public Safety carried out their radical republican program. They attempted to reform institutions and infuse all aspects of French life with revolutionary politics. They intended to create a Republic of Virtue based on Rousseauian ideas of reason and natural law.

First, they targeted those institutions that, in their view, represented the worst of the Old Regime. Many officials saw the Catholic Church in this negative light and sold church buildings, turned them into warehouses, or rededicated them as "temples of reason." Angry radicals disfigured religious statues, even sending some wooden figures of saints to the guillotine and melting down church treasures. The most enthusiastic radicals searched out nonjuring clergy for prosecution and pressured even the clergy who had sworn to uphold the Revolution to leave their vocations. Some radical leaders hoped that the new festivals established to celebrate the Revolution would provide a sufficient substitute for Christian rituals. Other revolutionaries tried to create new beliefs, such as the Cult of Reason, to replace Christianity. Robespierre tried in vain to institute his own deistic Cult of the Supreme Being.

`Attacking the Catholic Church`

The National Convention also enacted legislation that took the rules governing family life and education away from the church and placed them in state hands. Marriage became a civil rather than a religiously ordained act. New rules for divorce allowed thousands of couples to end marriages they would have been bound to under church rules. Births were registered at city halls rather than local churches. Women could sue for equal inheritance for the first time. Education became a responsibility of the state. New legislation mandated free primary schooling for all girls and boys and state-run secondary schooling, though in fact the government had neither the funds nor enough trained teachers to support such a system.

`Family life and education`

Women—especially those living in the cities—welcomed the new marriage, divorce, inheritance, and education laws, for they increased women's rights.

However, the Jacobins had no desire to free women from their traditional role in the private sphere. Rather, they rejected women's participation in politics and outlawed female associations such as the Society of Revolutionary Republican Women. Jacobins declared that women's primary duties lay in nurturing children. They concluded that women had no proper role as active citizens and that women's political groups only disrupted the republican order. As one member of the government explained, "It is horrible, it is contrary to all laws of nature for a woman to want to make herself a man."

The new government went far beyond simply rooting out opponents of the Revolution and attacking institutions tied to the Old Regime. It also tried to create support for the Republic by infusing the objects and activities of everyday life with revolutionary symbols. The figure of Liberty replaced royal symbols on everything from coins and statues to plates and posters. Patriotic groups planted liberty trees throughout France. Women adopted the flowing robes and hairstyles of ancient Greece that reflected rejection of the traditional social order. People sported revolutionary ribbons on their hats. Songs such as the "Marseillaise," rallying the "children of the nation . . . against . . . the bloody standard of tyranny!" rang out among crowds and troops. Plays and paintings that supported the Revolution were encouraged. Officials promoted festivals that featured revolutionary symbols, mass loyalty oaths, and patriotic celebrations. Titles of all kinds were discarded and replaced with the terms "citizen" and "citizeness."

`Revolutionary symbols`

Pamphlets and posters spread throughout France, proclaiming what the Republic stood for. The 1792 poster shown in **Figure 16.7,** printed in 1794 (Year 2 of the French Republic), is a typical example. The poster announces principles at the core of the Republic: "Unity, indivisibility of the Republic. Liberty, equality, fraternity, or death." Above, the eye of God shines its blessings on these principles. Two female figures representing liberty and equality hold up laurel crowns of victory. On the two pillars are pikes, topped by red liberty caps and bound by fasces (rods) symbolizing the strong union of revolutionaries. Below is the new revolutionary calendar.

In the name of reason and revolutionary principles, the government revamped the calendar, making the months equal in length and naming them after the seasons. Weeks were made ten days long, with one day of rest. (This change eliminated Sunday, a day of traditional Christian importance.) September 22, 1792—the date of the declaration of the Republic—became the first day of Year I. The new metric system of weights and measures, based on units of 10, was introduced and eventually would spread beyond France's borders to countries throughout the world.

FIGURE 16.7 A Republican Poster, ca. 1794 Many pamphlets and posters such as this example, announcing principles such as liberty, equality, and fraternity and displaying symbols of the Republic, spread throughout France during the early years of the French Revolution.

The Revolution Spreads Outside of France

Since 1792, France had fended off various coalitions of European powers. After initial defeats, France's citizen armies had gone on the offensive.

Sister republics During the struggles that ensued, France incorporated lands on its northern and eastern borders, claiming that these additions conformed to France's "natural boundaries" of the Rhine and the Alps. By 1799, more victories on the battlefield enabled France to set up "sister" republics in Holland, Switzerland, and Italy. To these areas, the French brought their own Enlightenment-inspired revolutionary principles and legislation. However, the gains carried a tremendous price tag: Hundreds of thousands died in the fighting, and the constant warfare disrupted trade and created shortages of essential goods.

The Revolution also powerfully influenced opinion outside France. Initially, many groups in nearby countries supported the Revolution

Outside opinion and its principles. However, part of that support rested on seeing France, a powerful rival, weakened. As people began to understand the seriousness of the attacks on monarchy and aristocracy and the threat to their own political independence, support waned. Still, many intellectuals and liberal political groups continued to uphold the ideals of the Revolution, at least until 1793, when the Revolution took a more radical turn.

The Revolution helped promote other developments farther away. In Poland, patriots tried to use inspiration from France to assert independence from Russia. Despite some initial successes, however, their efforts failed. In Ireland, the revolutionary doctrines of liberty, equality, and natural rights touched many, encouraging them to rise against their British **Uprisings** lords and make Ireland a republic. Irish patriots even anticipated a French invasion to help their own rebellion, although the invasion never took place.

In the Caribbean, slaves in France's lucrative colony of St. Domingue (Haiti) took heart from revolutionary principles and revolted. As **Figure 16.8,** a French print, reveals, the 1791 slave uprising struck fear in the hearts of white settlers. Slaves, outnumbering white settlers, attack a plantation. Women and men fall under the knives, swords, and cannon of the slaves, while plantation buildings go up in flames. Reports from French settlers, such as the wealthy Madame de Rouvray, described how the slaves "slaughtered and torched much of the countryside hereabouts" and warned, "how can we stay in a country where slaves have raised their hands against their masters?"

After much maneuvering and the abolishing of slavery by the National Convention in February 1794, the rebel leader Toussaint L'Ouverture and his black generals gained control of St. Domingue. The determined group would go on to successfully oppose English, Spanish, and French armies, turning the island into the independent republic of Haiti in 1804.

Resistance to the Republic Rises

Despite the Reign of Terror and efforts to establish a Republic of Virtue, violent resistance to the Republic persisted and in some cases grew. Its leadership consisted primarily of local aristocrats and notables, officials who had fallen out of favor with the Jacobins, Girondin sympathizers, and members of the nonjuring clergy who had gone underground. They gathered additional support from remaining royalists, conservative peasants who had already gained most of what they wanted, opponents of military conscription, and the many citizens who remained loyal to Catholicism and their nonjuring priests. Of the many armed revolts that broke out across France, the most important occurred in the Vendée, a region in western France (see pages 527–528). In what amounted to a regional civil war that raged for most of 1793 and dragged on for years thereafter, both sides committed atrocities

FIGURE 16.8 Slave Rebellion in St. Domingue (Haiti) This French illustration depicts the 1791 slave rebellion in France's Caribbean colony as a bloody affair that cost white settlers their plantations and their lives.

FIGURE 16.9 Jacques-Louis David, *The Death of Marat,* 1793 In this scene vividly capturing the French revolutionary conflict and resistance, radical journalist and deputy Jean-Paul Marat lies mortally wounded by an assassin while in a bath.

and thousands lost their lives before republican soldiers gained the upper hand.

Figure 16.9 reveals another form of resistance and the symbols of conflict during the radical phase of the Revolution. The painting, by the politically active artist Jacques-Louis David, depicts the death of Jean-Paul Marat, a journalist and leading radical deputy, in July 1793. Marat, ironically already suffering from a terminal skin condition, was working in his bathtub when Charlotte Corday, a supporter of the Girondins, assassinated him. Corday felt that it was her duty to kill Marat because of his persistent demands for more executions. This painting shows the mortally wounded Marat with pen and paper still in his hands and Corday's knife on the floor. David and others eulogized Marat as a martyr for the Revolution. On the side of his writing stand are the words "Not having been able to corrupt me, they assassinated me." Corday, widely denounced but convinced that she had "avenged many innocent victims," was soon guillotined.

Meanwhile, discontent with Robespierre and his policies increased. With the defeat of the invading coalition armies and the suppression of internal rebellion, most people no longer saw any need for the Terror—yet the Terror only intensified. When the influential Danton counseled moderation, Robespierre sent him and his most prominent followers to the guillotine. No one, not even the members of the National Convention, felt safe. Finally, on July 27, 1794 (9 Thermidor on the Revolutionary calendar, and thus referred to as the **Thermidorian reaction**), the Convention overthrew Robespierre. In an ironic ending, the Jacobin leader died by the guillotine: the same device to which he had sent so many others to their deaths.

> Thermidorian reaction

Reaction: The "White" Terror and the Directory

With the leader of the Terror now dead, the propertied bourgeoisie quickly gained control of the government. Eliminating the "Red" Terror of the Committee of Public Safety, they replaced it with the "White" Terror of reaction. They executed the former terrorists and imprisoned many supporters of Robespierre, including the painter, Jacques-Louis David. Armed bands of bourgeois hirelings roved around beating and killing Jacobins. Restrictive measures of Robespierre's regime were repealed, and many individuals, weary of the Republic's code of discipline and restraint, reveled in an outburst of licentious living. Middle- and upper-class women wore more revealing clothing; mistresses appeared more publicly, even in the political arena. On the other hand, women of the poor in the small towns and countryside often turned back to the Catholic Church. They hoped that a return to God would end the turmoil of the revolutionary years.

A new constitution in 1795 reflected conservative reaction. The right to vote for members of the legislative bodies was limited to the wealthier property owners. Executive functions were placed in the hands of five directors—the **Directory.**

Men of reasonable competence staffed the Directory (1795–1799), but they failed to restore tranquillity. War dragged on, governmental finances unraveled further, and brigands terrorized the countryside and the cities. The five directors tried to balance threats from the royalists on the Right and the Jacobins on the Left. They turned against the *sans-culottes* by removing price controls and had to be saved by governmental forces when the *sans-culottes* stormed the Convention in May 1795. Five months later, the government barely put down a royalist uprising, thanks to a quick-acting artillery officer named Napoleon Bonaparte. The directors finally resorted to purges to control the legislature and increasingly relied on the army for support. All in all, the situation was ripe for the arrival of a strongman who could bring both order at home and peace abroad.

NAPOLEON BONAPARTE

Within France, the Revolution provided unprecedented opportunities for ambitious soldiers of talent. Most prerevolutionary army officers had come from the nobility and had fled the country or lost their commands as the Revolution gathered momentum. This leadership drain, as well as the need to expand the army, created a huge demand for skilled officers. Napoleon Bonaparte, a talented artillery officer, stepped in to take full advantage of these opportunities.

Napoleon's Rise to Power

Born into a poor but well-known family on Corsica in 1769, just a few months after the Mediterranean island was transferred from the Republic of Genoa to France, Napoleon was hardworking, assertive, independent, and even arrogant as a youth. These qualities would stay with him for the rest of his life. The young Napoleon attended French military school (where he proved particularly strong in mathematics) and received his commission as second lieutenant when he was just 16. When the Revolution broke out in 1789, Napoleon was already familiar with Enlightenment ideas and resented the aristocratic pretensions of those around him. He quickly sided with the revolutionaries. In 1793, he attracted attention during the recapture of Toulon. Two years later, when he happened to be in Paris, the National Convention called on him to quell a threatening Parisian crowd.

Using artillery—his legendary "whiff of grape-shot"—Napoleon quickly dispersed the crowd and became the hero of the Convention. He fell in love with and married the politically well-connected Josephine de Beauharnais (1763–1814), a 32-year-old widow eager to provide security for her children.

Napoleon then used his growing prominence to secure command of the French army still fighting in northern Italy. Calling his forces "soldiers of liberty" and announcing to the people of Italy that "the French army comes to break your chains," he skillfully galvanized the lethargic French forces into defeating the Austrians and Sardinians. Along with loads of Italian art, Napoleon sent home glowing reports of his exploits. In 1797, he personally negotiated the favorable Treaty of Campo Formio with Austria, which recognized French expansion and the creation of the Cisalpine Republic in northern Italy (**Map 16.3**). Over the next two years, French armies moved south, helping to set up more French-controlled republics throughout the Italian peninsula. Napoleon's successes in Italy established his reputation as a brilliant military leader and able statesman.

Turning toward the British, Napoleon and the Directory concluded that an expedition to Egypt would deal a telling blow to British commerce with its colonies in Asia. Egypt could also serve as the foundation for a new French colony. Moreover, a conquest there might enhance Napoleon's image as a daring, heroic conqueror. Yet, despite some spectacular battlefield successes, the expedition failed; Admiral Nelson (1758–1805), who became one of Britain's most admired naval commanders, destroyed the French fleet at the Battle of the Nile on August 1, 1798. The French land campaign in Egypt and Syria persisted for a while, but it was doomed by a lack of supplies and reinforcements. Napoleon avoided personal disaster by slipping back to France with a few chosen followers, cleverly controlling the reports from Egypt and emphasizing the expedition's scientific explorations and exotic discoveries (he sent 165 scholars to Egypt in hopes that they might help him control the country) as well as its few victories.

Meanwhile, matters took a bad turn for France's government, the Directory. The expedition to Egypt prompted Great Britain, Austria, and Russia to join in a new coalition. These allies inflicted defeats on French armies and threatened to invade France itself. Eyeing this foreign threat, as well as bankruptcy, insubordinate army commanders, and disruptions in the countryside, rival factions within France vied for power. One conservative faction, led by a member of the Directory, Abbé Sieyès, concluded that a coup d'état would gain them needed control over the government.

Italian campaign

Expedition to Egypt

Coup d'état

ENGLAND

North Sea

BATAVIAN REPUBLIC **1798**
Amsterdam

PRUSSIA

AUSTRIAN NETHERLANDS (BELGIUM) AND RHINELAND PROVINCES **1795**

Paris

ATLANTIC OCEAN

FRANCE

BAVARIA

Bordeaux

Geneva

HELVETIC REPUBLIC **1798**

AUSTRIAN EMPIRE

SAVOY **1792**

Turin

Milan

Campoformio

Lyons

PIEDMONT

VENICE

Venice

Marseilles

Genoa

CISALPINE REPUBLIC **1797**

OTTOMAN EMPIRE

SPAIN

NICE **1792**

TUSCANY

ROMAN REPUBLIC **1798**

Adriatic Sea

NAPOLEON'S INVASION OF EGYPT 1798

CORSICA

Rome

PARTHENOPIAN REPUBLIC **1799**

SARDINIA

Naples

French Republic at 1792

Annexed to France 1792–1795

Sister Republics

0   200 mi
0   400 km

Mediterranean Sea

SICILY

MAP 16.3

France and Its Sister Republics

This map shows the expansion of France and the creation of its sister republics between 1792 and 1798.

Explore the Map

1. Notice the dates of annexation and of the creation of sister republics. Who do you think was most threatened by these developments? Why?

2. The arrow indicates Napoleon's invasion of Egypt in 1798. Why might Napoleon have moved against British interests in Egypt rather than against Great Britain itself?

This situation provided Napoleon with another opportunity to advance his career. Sieyès and others conspired with him to overthrow the Directory on November 9, 1799 (18 Brumaire). The conspirators expected that the 30-year-old military hero would make a popular figurehead representing authority, and they would actually govern the country. As events would prove, they were very mistaken.

Napoleon Consolidates Control

Napoleon quickly outmaneuvered his partners. He had a new "short and obscure" constitution drawn up and accepted by members of the old legislature. In a national **plebiscite** where people could vote to accept or reject the new constitution, the French overwhelmingly approved it (though the government falsified the results to give it a more lopsided victory). As one observer explained, people "believed quite sincerely that Bonaparte . . . would save us from the perils of anarchy." Napoleon named himself "first consul" and assumed the powers necessary to rule— all with the ready support of the Senate. The remaining two consuls, as well as voters and the handpicked legislative bodies they thought they were electing, had only minimal powers. Next, Napoleon placed each of France's eighty-three departments under the control of a powerful agent of the central government— the *prefect*. Thus, at both the local and the national levels, Napoleon ended meaningful democracy in France.

> First consul

With the touch of a skilled authoritarian politician, Napoleon proceeded to gather support. He welcomed former Old Regime officials as well as moderate Jacobins into his service. By approving the end of serfdom and feudal privileges as well as all transfers of property that had occurred during the Revolution, he won favor with the peasantry. He gained the backing of the middle class by affirming the property rights and formal equality before the law that adult males had secured during the Revolution. He welcomed back to France all but the most reactionary émigrés, most of whom had come from France's old aristocracy. The educated elite admired Napoleon for patronizing science and inviting leading scientists to join him in his government. To deter opposition, he created a secret police force, suppressed independent political organizations, and censored newspapers and artistic works. Finally, for those who displayed the highest loyalty and the most spectacular achievements (particularly in the military), he created the prestigious Legion of Honor.

Keenly aware of the political and social importance of religion—once calling religion "excellent stuff for keeping the common people quiet"—Napoleon made peace with the pope and ended the ten-year struggle between the French revolutionary governments and the Roman Catholic church. Their Concordat (formal agreement) of 1801 declared the Catholic religion the religion of the majority of the French people but ensured freedom for Protestants. Later, Napoleon granted new rights to Jews, as well. Under his rule, the clergy was paid by the state and required to take an oath of allegiance to the state. Confiscated Catholic Church property was not returned.

> The Concordat

Reforming France

Napoleon followed up this pattern of blending compromise and authoritarian control with a remaking of France's legal, financial, and educational systems. The Civil Code of 1804 (the **Napoleonic Code**), for example, generally affirmed the Enlightenment-inspired legal reforms that the early French revolutionaries had sought. Progressives throughout Europe and even overseas would embrace this law code. For men, the code guaranteed legal equality, careers open to talent, and paternal authority over women, children, and property. In particular, it catered to middle-class employers by forbidding strikes and trade unions. At the same time, the code rejected many of the rights and liberties gained in 1789 as well as the more radical measures enacted after 1792. For women, the code represented a clear defeat. Rather than granting them legal or political equality, it gave power over property and the family to men and left married women legally and economically dependent on their husbands. The code also severely restricted the right to divorce, particularly for women. These measures reflected Napoleon's belief that women belonged in the home and that their concerns should center on domestic life.

> Napoleonic Code

To stabilize France financially, Napoleon established the Bank of France to handle governmental funds and issue money. To promote economic health, he involved the state in a huge program of public works, supported certain industries, and established price controls. To restructure educational institutions, he created a long-lasting system of secondary schools tied to the University of France and infused it with patriotic trappings. Napoleon also actively supported scientific research and rewarded surgeons, chemists, mathematicians, and other scientists with governmental posts and honors.

> Finance and education

Creating the Empire

Napoleon's rise to power hinged on his ability to remove external military threats as well as internal disruptions. This he managed by crossing the Alps in

FIGURE 16.10 Jacques-Louis David, _Napoleon's Coronation_ In this richly detailed canvas that took several years to complete, David, France's leading painter at the time, shows the newly crowned emperor Napoleon wearing a laurel wreath. Standing in front of Pope Pius VII, the new emperor prepares to place a crown on his kneeling wife, Josephine, to make her his empress.

THE AGE OF NAPOLEON

1796–1797	The Italian campaign
1798	The Egyptian campaign
1799	Napoleon's coup d'état
1801	Concordat with the Roman Catholic Church
1802	Peace of Amiens
1804	Napoleonic Code
	Napoleon crowned emperor
1805	Battle of Austerlitz
1807	Treaty with Russia
	Napoleon's Continental System imposed
1812	Invasion of Russia
1814	Napoleon exiled to Elba
1815	Battle of Waterloo

KEY DATES

1800 with a French army to crush the Austrian forces in northern Italy and knock Austria out of the coalition of powers opposing France. Next, he made peace with Russia and persuaded Great Britain to sign the Peace of Amiens in 1802.

In the first five years of his rule, Napoleon scored spectacular successes. Law and order reigned at home, and he secured peace abroad. Public morale was high. Napoleon's vision of a centralized, paternalistic state that would make France the model of a modern nation through reason, authority, and science seemed almost real.

However, two problems lurked beneath this promising exterior. First, Napoleon had an insatiable craving for public recognition and legitimacy. He satisfied this need at least partially with a bold move in 1804. That year, with the approval of the Senate and the French people in a lopsided plebiscite, Napoleon formally established France as an empire—and then crowned himself emperor.

> Emperor Napoleon

As Jacques-Louis David's painting in **Figure 16.10** reveals, Napoleon controlled all aspects of the coronation. Although he invited Pope Pius VII (seated behind him) to preside over the ceremony, it is Napoleon—ever the self-made man—who takes matters into his own hands. As splendidly dressed spectators look on, Napoleon raises a crown, preparing to place it on the kneeling Josephine's head to make her his empress. He has already boldly crowned himself emperor with a laurel wreath that alludes back to Roman emperors and Charlemagne, crowned emperor by the pope in the year 800. Aware of the importance of details, Napoleon had shrewdly instructed his ardent supporter David to paint the reluctant pope raising his hand in blessing.

The new emperor then elevated members of his family to princely status and granted new titles and honors to his wealthy supporters who had proved themselves, usually as officers on the battlefield. Later, he divorced Empress Josephine, whose relationship with Napoleon became more formal than intimate, and who failed to produce a male heir. He married Princess Marie-Louise of Austria, giving him a stronger image as legitimate royalty.

In addition to his hunger for formal recognition, Napoleon had a second problem. He had risen to prominence and power through his military conquests. "I am an upstart soldier," he admitted. "My domination will not survive the day when I cease to be strong, and therefore feared." These martial ties would push Napoleon to seek still greater conquests on the battlefield. "Conquest has made me what I am; only conquest can maintain me." Yet even when battle after battle brought him victory, war also came at great cost and risk.

> Need for conquests

War and Conquest

The interests of Great Britain and Napoleon clashed too often for their peace to last long. By the end of 1803, the two countries were again at war, and by 1805, the ambitious Napoleon had to battle a new coalition of European powers. That year, he marched to the English Channel with a huge army and seemed poised to invade England. Before him stretched 24 miles of water and British sea power. To overcome those barriers, Napoleon amassed a combined French and Spanish fleet and plotted his next move. Alert for any opportunity, he suddenly turned his army eastward, surrounded an exposed Austrian army, and on October 20, forced it to surrender. The next day, however, England's Admiral Nelson sighted the combined French and Spanish fleets off Cape Trafalgar on the southwest point of Spain and annihilated them. Although Nelson perished early in the battle, his navy's victory saved Great Britain from the menace of an invasion and limited Napoleon's conquests to the European continent.

Battle of Trafalgar

On land, Napoleon fared much better—in fact, he seemed invincible. His success stemmed in part from his independent units that could move quickly and then join in a mass attack. Equally important, he possessed an unusually talented officer corps and enjoyed the loyalty of a large number of nationalistic citizen-soldiers. The strategy of sending a mass of spirited soldiers in a column of attack aimed at dividing opposing forces served Napoleon well. Fighting alongside his troops, he cleverly used these military strengths to crush the combined forces of Austria and Russia at Austerlitz in December 1805. Prussia made the mistake of declaring war on France after it was too late to join the Austrians and Russians. As the French troops moved east through villages and cities, people reported how "the dreadful cry was heard in the streets, 'the French are coming!'" Napoleon virtually obliterated the Prussian forces. When the Russian troops began massing again, Napoleon moved eastward and decisively defeated them in the great Battle of Friedland (1807). Although the resulting Treaties of Tilsit (July 1807) were technically between equals, they actually left Russia only a junior partner to France. France commanded the greater resources, and Napoleon expected to have his way on the European continent.

Military strengths

Despite all these triumphs, Napoleon still could not find a way to get his troops across the Channel to attack England directly. He finally hit on an alternative plan—the **Continental System**—that he hoped would destroy his rival's commercial economy by preventing the importation of British

The Continental System

goods into continental Europe. To implement the plan, he ordered a continent-wide blockade against British ships, confiscated all British goods, and set French privateers upon British merchant ships. Britain responded with new regulations that amounted to its own blockade on shipping to continental ports. Now the naval war between France and Britain affected even neutral states, including the United States.

By 1810, Napoleon had redrawn the map of Europe (**Map 16.4**) and the political balance of power. He had dismembered Prussia and abolished the Holy Roman Empire. Now most German states were unified into the Confederation of the Rhine. Holland and the Italian peninsula had come under French control. Spain was a dependent state, and Austria, Russia, and a diminished Prussia had become reluctant allies of France. Only Great Britain and still-defiant parts of Spain and Portugal remained active opponents.

The new European order

In those areas annexed to France, Napoleon ruled directly and imposed all of France's laws and institutions. In dependent states, he installed French-controlled governments to rule with the help of local elites. He usually made members of his family monarchs in these areas—his brother Louis, king of Holland, his brother Jérôme, king of Westphalia, and his brother Joseph, king of Spain. As Document 16.3 suggests, some of France's "enlightened" institutions and policies were introduced. These usually included constitutional government, equality before the law, careers open to talent, the Napoleonic Code, civil rights to Jews and other religious minorities, and the creation of similar public works improvements—schools, roads, bridges—that Napoleon supported in France. Wherever Napoleon conquered, except Russia, he abolished serfdom. At the same time, the reforms included tax increases and conscription quotas to help finance and provide soldiers for Napoleon's armies.

The Impact Overseas

Naturally, Napoleon's policies exerted their greatest impact in Europe, but other areas—particularly in the Western Hemisphere and the British Empire—also felt the effects of his rule and expansion. In the Caribbean, Napoleon failed to put down the black population's struggle for independence and freedom in St. Domingue (Haiti) (see page 531). He also cut his losses in North America and sold Louisiana to the United States.

The Napoleonic Wars had dramatic consequences in the colonies of Spain and Portugal in the Americas. Discontent with colonial rule had been mounting

Revolt in Latin America

MAP 16.4

Europe, 1810

This map shows Europe at the height of Napoleon's empire.

Explore the Map

1. What was the extent of the area Napoleon controlled—directly and indirectly?

2. Where would you expect Napoleon's rule to have exerted the greatest impact?

3. What geographic problems did Napoleon face in trying to control his empire?

4. Locate the areas that remained hostile to Napoleon. How might geography help to explain why those areas retained their independence?

during the eighteenth century. In particular, the colonists resented the economic and political restrictions imposed by the mother country. As the native-born Creoles began to outnumber the Spanish and Portuguese-born settlers, the ties of loyalty to home countries weakened. The successful revolt of the English colonies to the north and the birth of the United States also impressed colonial liberals and intellectuals.

DOCUMENT 16.3

Napoleon Issues an Imperial Decree at Madrid

When Napoleon scored military successes outside of France, he demanded more from the conquered peoples than subservience to French rule. Typically, he applied some of the same reforms and institutions of the French Revolution to the conquered lands. This policy is shown in the following decree, issued from Napoleon's imperial camp at Madrid on December 4, 1808.

To date from the publication of the present decree, feudal rights are abolished in Spain.

All personal obligations, all exclusive fishing rights and other rights of similar nature on the coast or on rivers and streams, all feudal monopolies (*banalités*) of ovens, mills, and inns are suppressed. It shall be free to every one who shall conform to the laws to develop his industry without restraint.

The tribunal of the Inquisition is abolished, as inconsistent with the civil sovereignty and authority.

The property of the Inquisition shall be sequestered and fall to the Spanish state, to serve as security for the bonded debt.

Considering that the members of the various monastic orders have increased to an undue degree and that, although a certain number of them are useful in assisting the ministers of the altar in the administration of the sacraments, the existence of too great a number interferes with the prosperity of the state, we have decreed and do decree as follows:

The number of convents now in existence in Spain shall be reduced to a third of their present number. This reduction shall be accomplished by uniting the members of several convents of the same order into one.

All regular ecclesiastics who desire to renounce the monastic life and live as secular ecclesiastics are at liberty to leave their monasteries. . . .

In view of the fact that the institution which stands most in the way of the internal prosperity of Spain is that of the customs lines separating the provinces, we have decreed and do decree what follows:

To date from January 1 next, the barriers existing between the provinces shall be suppressed. The custom houses shall be removed to the frontiers and there established.

SOURCE: James Harvey Robinson, ed., *Readings in European History*, vol. II (Boston: Ginn, 1904), p. 512.

Analyze the Document

1. What benefits might Napoleon have been hoping for by issuing this decree?

2. In what regards are these measures consistent with the spirit of the French Revolution?

3. In what ways might this decree have inspired resistance within Spain?

Spanish colonists' attachment to Spain faltered further when Napoleon overthrew the Spanish king and placed his own brother, Joseph Bonaparte, on the throne. By 1810, many colonists were in open revolt.

Over the next ten years, Spain struggled to regain its colonies. In 1814, Argentina drove off a Spanish army and won its independence. Elsewhere, Simón Bolívar (1783–1830), known as The Liberator, led the fight for independence against Spanish forces. **Figure 16.11** shows him in heroic pose, probably to symbolize his military campaigns in Venezuela, Colombia, Ecuador, and Peru. The painting is modeled on a well-known work by David that portrays Napoleon leading his troops across the Alps. Bolívar points upward while a wind blows at his back—a traditional posture of victory.

As **Map 16.5** shows, by 1822 almost all of Spain's colonies, as well as Portugal's huge colony of Brazil, had gained their independence. Nevertheless, Bolívar's and others' hopes for unity within Spain's old colonies soon faded as various South American regions began dividing into separate states. Most of these new states would adopt the Napoleonic Code as their basis of civil law, and oppressive white minorities would rule them for many years.

FIGURE 16.11 Simón Bolívar Using a famous portrait of Napoleon as a model, an unknown artist portrayed The Liberator in a heroic military pose.

MAP 16.5

Latin America After Independence

This map shows that within a twelve-year period, Spain and Portugal lost most of their possessions in the Americas.

Explore the Map

1. In several areas there are differences between the date of independence from the colonial power and the date of separation from other states. What might these differences mean?

2. What territories were still held by European nations after 1830?

3. What might differentiate the territories that remained under European control from those that gained their independence?

Remaining Colonial Possessions

- Spanish Possessions
- Former Borders of Spanish Viceroyalties
- LA PLATA   Former Names of Spanish Viceroyalties
- British Possessions
- French Possessions
- Dutch Possessions

Date of independence from colonial power / Date of separation from other states
1821/1823

Islas Malvinas/ Falkland Islands
British 1765–1770; Spanish 1770–1820

Napoleon's dominance over the European continent inspired England to step up its overseas expansion and tighten control over its own colonies and areas of influence. Sea power enabled it to capture and take over French and Dutch colonies in

England's overseas expansion

Africa, Asia, and America. In addition, England began trading more briskly with South America. However, one of England's strategies—its counterblockade of Napoleonic Europe—had a major, unintended drawback. By enforcing the blockade, England ended up embroiled in the War of 1812 with the United States. That war, in turn, spread farther north when the United States attempted to invade Britain's loyal colonies in Canada.

In Egypt, Napoleon's invasion failed, but in its wake local elites rebelled against Ottoman overlords. In 1805, the Egyptian general Muhammad Ali was victorious, and he set himself up as effective ruler of Egypt for the next three decades. Using European models, he strengthened and modernized Egypt's army, which eventually became the most powerful force in the Islamic world.

In the decades that followed, states from Asia to the Americas that reformed their own governments

and laws would look to the Napoleonic Code and adopt parts of it. In this way, some of the ideals of the Enlightenment and the French Revolution would be translated through the Napoleonic Code to many areas around the globe.

Adopting the Napoleonic Code

Decline and Fall

Napoleon had an even more ambitious vision—to rule Europe as the head of a single imperial administration. Before he could make his vision real, new problems plagued him. Even at the height of his power, Napoleon and his empire suffered from dangerous weaknesses. Between 1808 and 1812, three crucial vulnerabilities—flawed policies, resistance to his rule, and overextension of his military reach—would intensify and erode Napoleon's power.

The Continental System that Napoleon devised to cripple England economically was not working well enough. With control of the sea, Great Britain applied an effective counterblockade against the

FIGURE 16.12

Francisco de Goya, *The Executions of the Third of May, 1808*

This 1814 painting by the great Spanish artist Francisco de Goya shows French soldiers executing Spanish citizens in retaliation for riots against French troops who had occupied Madrid. On the left, Spanish victims meet their end. On the right, French soldiers fire at terrifyingly close range. In the background, shrouded under a black sky, stands the monastery.

Connecting Art & Society

1. What message might Goya have been trying to convey to Spanish viewers by means of this painting?

2. What does this message suggest about the French occupation of Spain?

3. What associations might viewers of Goya's day have made to the central figure in white?

4. Why might Goya have decided to paint the sky over the monastery ink black?

Napoleon-dominated Continent. Port cities and industries relying on external commerce suffered. Smuggling further weakened the system. In some areas, such as Holland and Russia, the restrictions of the system

Flawed policies

became a constant source of irritation and resentment against the French. In the long run, the Continental System stiffened opposition to Napoleon on the Continent and failed to weaken England. Again and again, that island nation would finance Napoleon's enemies.

People across Europe had other reasons besides the Continental System to resist Napoleon's rule. In the wake of France's conquering armies, a new national spirit developed among many subject peoples. In Spain, for example, Napoleon had no sooner placed his brother Joseph on the Spanish throne than his unwilling subjects rose up against him. The painting in **Figure 16.12** by the influential Spanish artist Francisco de Goya depicts the popular resistance in Spain to the Napoleonic occupation and the reprisals that resulted. Here, in a night scene of May 3, 1808, a firing squad of anonymous French soldiers brutally executes citizens in retaliation for riots against French troops in Madrid. The magnitude of the French atrocity is emphasized by the central figure, who resembles a crucified Christ about to be shot. Monks and commoners, selected at random for execution, surround the man at the center, and the bodies of those already executed lie scattered on the bloody earth around him. Goya, who painted this scene six years after the actual event, intended the work as a statement against the evils of war.

Growing resistance

The Madrid rebellion and reprisals by Napoleon's soldiers inspired other Spanish uprisings and organized resistance against French troops in the years to come. Larger French armies, even when led by Napoleon himself, managed only limited success against the hit-and-run guerrilla tactics used by the Spanish. England took advantage of the situation by sending supplies and troops to Spain under the Duke of Wellington (1769–1852), the British commander who would plague Napoleon's forces to the end. Spain became a running abscess that drained Napoleon's military strength.

In Prussia, similar national sentiments encouraged the government—partly in secret—to modernize its army and civil institutions in preparation for liberation from France. In Austria, the government again declared war on Napoleon in a premature effort to free itself from subservience to the French emperor. In Holland, opposition to Napoleon's policies ran so strong that in 1810 he had to annex the country to France to bring it under control. All this resistance drained French forces and raised the specter of open revolt at the least opportunity.

Napoleon himself created that opportunity by overextending his imperial reach. Successes on the battlefield added to his growing dreams of creating an empire ruled from Paris that would encompass all of Europe. Russia, already chafing against the commercial restrictions of the Continental System and harboring its own ambitions for expansion in eastern Europe, stood as the main barrier to Napoleon's dreams. In 1812, these conflicting ambitions soured

Overextension

Invasion of Russia

the alliance between Russia and France. Against the advice of his closest associates, Napoleon decided to invade Russia. Amassing an immense army of more than 600,000, he plunged into the vastness of Russia. Half of his troops, however, were unenthusiastic conscripts from dependent states. The Russian army retreated into the interior of their huge country, following a scorched-earth policy and luring Napoleon ever farther from his base of supplies. "We believed that once in Russia, we need do nothing but forage—which, however, proved to be an illusion. . . . All the villages were already stripped before we could enter," wrote Jakob Walter, a German conscript in Napoleon's army. One of Napoleon's aides explained the deepening problem: "We were in the heart of inhabited Russia and yet we were like a vessel without a compass in the midst of a vast ocean, knowing nothing of what was happening around us." At Borodino, the Russians turned and made a stand. In one of the bloodiest battles of the nineteenth century—taking a toll of more than 80,000 casualties—the two armies fought until the Russians withdrew.

The French army may have won the battle, but it failed to destroy Russia's forces. In September, Napoleon's Grand Army, weakened by battlefield losses and even more so by hunger, fatigue, and disease, finally entered Moscow. Tsar Alexander I, however, refused to capitulate. The future looked even worse for the French when a fire destroyed much of Moscow, leaving the invaders without enough shelter or supplies to ride out the notorious Russian winter. "Here in the white country we'll all have to die of hunger," wrote Hohann Wärncke, a German soldier in Napoleon's army. Napoleon began his retreat, but too late. The winter caught his forces overburdened with loot. Tens of thousands of them froze, starved, or succumbed to disease. Russian Cossacks, riding out of the blizzards, cut down or captured thousands more. Many of Napoleon's men surrendered to Russian forces. Of the original 600,000 who marched into Russia, fewer than 100,000 struggled home.

Napoleon himself was able to dash back to France. Behind him, one nation after another, aided by British money, joined the Russians in a war of liberation. Back home, Napoleon raised new conscripts for his army and again rushed them eastward. At Leipzig in central Germany, in October 1813, allied armies at last decisively defeated Napoleon. The next year, the allies entered Paris and exiled Napoleon to the island of Elba, off the coast of Italy.

Defeat at Leipzig

Napoleon still had some fight left in him. While the allies squabbled over the peace settlement and discontent weakened France's new government under Louis XVIII, Napoleon escaped back to France. "Soldiers! In exile I heard your voice," he announced. "Now I have landed

Waterloo

[in France]." He quickly raised yet another army from the remains of his old, still loyal supporters. However, he was finally defeated in June 1815 by British and Prussian forces at Waterloo in Belgium. This time his captors imprisoned him on the bleak island of St. Helena in the South Atlantic. "Posterity will do me justice," he wrote while in exile. "The truth will be known; and the good I have done will be compared with the faults I have committed." Six years later, Napoleon died, probably of stomach cancer.

LOOKING BACK & MOVING FORWARD

Summary   In 1815, a king from the old house of Bourbon again ruled France. Many aristocrats and royalists hoped to turn back the clock to the days before 1789, when they enjoyed unchallenged power and prestige. However, too much had changed. The Revolution had destroyed a French monarchy based on the divine right of kings. French aristocrats might still boast impressive titles, but the revolutionaries and Napoleon had secured legal equality for French men, if not women. Members of the middle class, though no longer enjoying the control they had exercised during the revolutionary years, would not relinquish the opportunities for position and prestige that they had gained. The peasantry, which had played such an important role during the early months of the Revolution, would never again be burdened by the traditional dues and services they once owed to lords. Finally, the Catholic Church had forever lost the lands and position it had possessed before the Revolution.

Napoleon's connection to the Revolution was contradictory. He subverted key elements of the Revolution by removing the substance from representative institutions and eliminating freedom of speech and press. On the other hand, he preserved other elements of the Revolution by affirming the end of feudalism, protecting the rights of property, and ensuring equality before the law for men; through his conquests, he spread the ideas and institutions of the Revolution beyond France's borders. When he maximized the political and military power of the state by rationalizing the government, he acted like an eighteenth-century enlightened despot.

Finally, the French Revolution and Napoleon created two potent, long-lasting images. First, people had learned that a popular revolution could topple the government and social order of even the most powerful country. This image would inspire revolutionaries and unnerve those representing the status quo for decades to come. Second, Westerners also saw in Napoleon a nationalistic, charismatic leader who could suddenly seize power and exert his will with ease. This compelling image would inspire other individuals who envisioned themselves as potential Napoleons. Perhaps even more important, it would seduce people who yearned for easy, decisive solutions to complex problems.

After 1815, the old forces of order tried desperately to reassert their control. Although they scored some temporary successes, the ideas and institutions of the Revolution, spread by the armies of the French Republic and Napoleon, had taken root permanently in France and beyond its borders. The French Revolution had become a watershed event, and those who ignored it did so at peril.

KEY TERMS

Tennis Court Oath, *p. 519*

Bastille, *p. 520*

Declaration of Rights of Man and Citizen, *p. 521*

Civil Constitution of the Clergy, *p. 523*

sans-culottes, *p. 524*

Jacobins, *p. 525*

Committee of Public Safety, *p. 528*

levée en masse, *p. 529*

Thermidorian reaction, *p. 532*

Directory, *p. 533*

plebiscite, *p. 535*

Napoleonic Code, *p. 535*

Continental System, *p. 537*

REVIEW, ANALYZE, & CONNECT TO TODAY

REVIEW THE PREVIOUS CHAPTERS

Chapter 14—"A New World of Reason and Reform"—revealed how Enlightenment ideas challenged traditional values and institutions in the West. Chapter 15—"Competing for Power and Wealth"—followed the battles of Western powers over land, position, and commerce as well as the economic and social changes affecting eighteenth-century life in the West.

1. In what ways were Enlightenment ideas reflected in the values and reforms of the French Revolution?

2. Do you think the French Revolution conformed to or contradicted the main political trends of the eighteenth century?

3. In what ways did Napoleon embody the eighteenth-century trend toward enlightened absolutism?

ANALYZE THIS CHAPTER

Chapter 16—"Overturning the Political and Social Order"—examines the great upheaval in France that shocked and transformed the West.

1. Analyze the roles of France's aristocracy, bourgeoisie, peasantry, and urban workers in causing the French Revolution.

2. What might Louis XVI have done to keep his throne?

3. Why do you think the Revolution turned more radical, resulting in the establishment of a republic and leading to the Reign of Terror?

4. How do you explain Napoleon's rise? Was his rise a logical consequence of revolutionary events?

5. Analyze Napoleon's accomplishments. Do you think they were worth the costs?

CONNECT TO TODAY

Think about the causes of the French Revolution, the events of 1789–1815, and the Revolution's consequences.

1. From the example of the French Revolution, what signs that a revolution is possible might we look for today?

2. How might the example of Napoleon and the circumstances that enabled his rise to power help to explain the appeal of other strong leaders in more recent revolutionary situations?

BEYOND THE CLASSROOM

"A GREAT FERMENT": TROUBLE BREWING IN FRANCE

Chartier, Roger. *The Cultural Origins of the French Revolution*. Translated by Lydia G. Cochrane. Durham, NC: Duke University Press, 1991. Examines the developments that contributed to the cultural destabilization of the Old Regime.

Doyle, William. *The Oxford History of the French Revolution*. Oxford: Oxford University Press, 2003. A thorough, highly respected survey.

Furet, François. *Interpreting the French Revolution*. Cambridge: Cambridge University Press, 1981. An important book that refutes the traditional theory of the French Revolution as a bourgeois revolution.

Landes, Joan. *Women and the Public Sphere in the Age of the French Revolution*. Ithaca, NY: Cornell University Press, 1988. Explores the historical evolution of the male-oriented public sphere and the consignment of women to the private realm of domesticity.

Lefebvre, Georges. *The Coming of the French Revolution*. Translated by R.R. Palmer. Princeton, NJ: Princeton University Press, 1947. A landmark analysis of the social structure of prerevolutionary France and the opening phase of the Revolution.

Schama, Simon. *Citizens: A Chronicle of the French Revolution*. New York: Random House, 1990. A popular, well-written narrative of events.

THE CONSTITUTIONAL MONARCHY: ESTABLISHING A NEW ORDER

Andress, David. *The French Revolution and the People*. New York: Continuum, 2004. A book that focuses on the impact of the Revolution on ordinary people.

Hunt, Lynn. *Politics, Culture and Class in the French Revolution*. Berkeley: University of California Press, 1984. Focuses on the political culture of language, dress, and festivals created by the revolutionaries.

Jones, P. *The Peasantry in the French Revolution*. New York: Cambridge University Press, 1988. Examines the role of the peasantry in the revolutionary events from 1789 to 1799.

TO THE RADICAL REPUBLIC AND BACK

Higonnet, Patrice. *Goodness Beyond Virtue: Jacobins During the French Revolution*. Cambridge, MA: Harvard University Press, 1998. A study of the Jacobins, their ideas, and the Terror.

Hufton, Olwen. *Women and the Limits of Citizenship in the French Revolution*. Toronto: University of Toronto Press, 1992. Analyzes attitudes toward women during the French Revolution that led to female exclusion from the rights of citizenship.

Kennedy, Emmet. *A Cultural History of the French Revolution*. New Haven, CT: Yale University Press, 1989. Examines the role of the arts, clubs, and intellectual institutions during the Revolution.

Lyons, Martyn. *France Under the Directory*. New York: Cambridge University Press, 1975. A brief yet wide-ranging survey of the Directory period.

Palmer, Robert R. *Twelve Who Ruled: The Committee of Public Safety During the Terror*. Princeton, NJ: Princeton University Press, 1970. A well-written account of the Terror and its leaders.

NAPOLEON BONAPARTE

Broers, Michael. *Europe Under Napoleon, 1799–1815*. London: Edward Arnold, 2002. Examines how Napoleon's rule affected people in conquered nations.

Connelly, Owen. *Blundering to Glory: Napoleon's Military Campaigns*. Wilmington, DE: Scholarly Resources, 1987. An assessment of Napoleon's military strategy and achievements.

Lyons, Martyn. *Napoleon Bonaparte and the Legacy of the French Revolution*. New York: St. Martin's Press, 1994. A solid reevaluation of Napoleon and his legacy.

Schom, Alan. *Napoleon Bonaparte: A Life*. New York: HarperCollins, 1998. An up-to-date, critical biography of Napoleon.

J. M. W. TURNER, *DUDLEY, WORCESTERSHIRE,* 1832

In his 1832 watercolor of Dudley, Worcestershire, a city of about 23,000 in 1831 in the heart of
Britain's industrial Black Country, British painter J. M. W. Turner shows the transformation of
old towns and traditional landscapes wrought by the industrial revolution. In the foreground on
one of the canals that crisscrossed this region, barges laden with cargo—typically coal for fuel,
iron ore for smelting, and lime for flux, all plentiful in the region and used in the production of
iron—dock for unloading and wait to receive goods from factories along the banks. The vessel at
the right carries hoops of sheet iron destined for one of Dudley's finishing shops. The numerous
mills' chimneys and coal-fired hearths produce dense clouds of polluting smoke that dim the
city and encrust it with soot. On the right, a white and orange glow bursts from iron furnaces.
In the background, the church steeples and battlements of a ruined castle rise into the moonlit
sky, indicating how the old town has had to adapt to the new realities of modern industry, where
work never seems to stop. Charles Dickens (1812–1870), who visited the region during the 1830s,
would describe it as "cheerless," a "mournful place" filled with "tall chimneys, crowding on each
other and presenting that endless repetition of the same dull, ugly form," chimneys that "pour
out their plague of smoke, obscured the light, and made foul the melancholy air."

Factories, Cities, and Families in the Industrial Age

17

The Industrial Revolution, 1780–1850

In 1828, a German visitor described Britain as a land where the "new creations springing into life every year bordered on the fabulous." These creations were the machines and factories of the **industrial revolution** that were replacing agriculture and handicrafts as the basis of the traditional economy. They turned industrial cities like Manchester into what the French writer Alexis de Tocqueville called "the greatest stream of human industry" that "flows out to fertilize the whole world."

However, this wave of industrial developments, which made Britain wealthy and envied, brought disturbing consequences in its wake: great swings of economic prosperity and depression and a new working class harnessed to the rhythm of machines. A British journal in 1826 spoke of a growing "accumulation of misery endured by thousands" in industrial areas. A few years later, the French consul in Edinburgh argued, "Who would want the prosperity of Liverpool and Manchester in France . . . beside these base miseries offered by manufacturing establishments?"

These "miseries" haunted not only the new factories and mines. Workers hoping for jobs crowded into unprepared cities. There, life for them, as well as for middle-class employers, professionals, and shopkeepers, was rapidly changing. In bad times, unemployment and business failures made urban life particularly harsh. In prosperous times, filth and disease still marked these cities. Here even the family, which for so long labored together as a cooperating unit of economic life, was shifting under the weight of new ideas and pressures. Western societies were entering the industrial age.

TIMELINE

Nationalism and Statebuilding

The "Old Regime"

Spread of Industrial Revolution

Industrial Revolution in Great Britain 1760–1850

French Revolution and Napoleon 1789–1815

Restoration 1815–1830

Age of Ideologies 1815–1850

• Revolutions 1830

• Revolutions 1848

1780   1790   1800   1810   1820   1830   1840   1850   1860

THE INDUSTRIAL REVOLUTION BEGINS

In this new era, Britain led the way. There a middle-class couple such as Richard and Elizabeth Cadbury (see Biography on pages 572–573) might expect to work hard and see the cloth and dry goods store they opened in 1794 support them and their several children. Thirty-five years later their sons, Benjamin and John, had become wealthy retailers and manufacturers.

Others did not consider the industrial age such a boon. One railroad worker told of a day when two thousand of his coworkers lost their jobs: "They were all starving, the heap of them, or next door to it." This worker had recently injured his leg at work and was laid up for one month, living "all that time on charity; on what the chaps would come and give me. When I could get about again, the work was all stopped, and I couldn't get none to do. . . . I went to a lodginghouse in the Borough, and I sold all my things—shovel and grafting-tool and all, to have a meal of food. When all my things was gone, I didn't know where to go. . . . Now I'm dead beat, though I'm only twenty-eight next August."

Stories about successful merchants like the Cadburys and less-fortunate laborers like this railroad worker give us a glimpse at the two faces of Britain's industrial revolution. Year by year, the work and home lives of these people and others changed only gradually. However, between the 1780s and 1850s—little

more than a single lifetime—astonishing developments transformed economic and social life in Britain.

The scene pictured in **Figure 17.1** captures some of what that transformation meant to people. In the foreground of this 1851 painting is a romanticized vision of nature and the countryside, featuring trees, bushes, rock formations, hills, and a road winding around a lake. On the left, a couple, perhaps enjoying a picnic, relax with their dog—all apparently at one with nature. In the distance looms Manchester, which between 1780 and 1851 grew from a small country town to a large, industrialized city. Manchester's numerous factory chimneys belch clouds of smoke into the air. The sense of contrast is striking: In the city, people grind out the new wealth of this civilization, all while enduring crowds and filth away from the imagined delights of nature and the rural life they once knew.

In the mid-eighteenth century, most British people had lived in the countryside. Women and men who laboriously spun fibers into thread and yarn and then wove it into cloth with the aid of only simple tools and handlooms barely noticed the few new machines that could quickly spin American cotton into thread and weave it into cloth by the thousands of yards. At the edges of forests where wood was available for smelting iron, most ironmasters still forged metal using slow methods inherited from their ancestors. To transport their goods to markets, these people, like their predecessors from centuries back, relied on coaches drawn by horses over rutted dirt roads, and on wooden ships pushed by currents and winds across the seas. Steam engines, already present for several decades, were inefficient and rare outside of coal mines.

By 1850, things had changed dramatically. Over half of Britain's population, which had more than doubled during the period, now lived in cities. Cotton factories churned out hundreds of millions of yards of cloth that were sold throughout the world every year and were driving those who still made cloth the old way out of business. New mines, machines, and production techniques made vast quantities of iron cheap to produce, easy to work, and available everywhere. Railroads carried people and merchandise to their destinations quickly, inexpensively, and reliably. Recent generations of efficient coal-burning steam engines powered these factories, foundries, and railroads. Waves of inventions and innovations built on earlier breakthroughs cheapened production while improving quality. Entrepreneurs and business organizations applied these machines and production methods to other industries in Britain and elsewhere in the West. Although marked by periodic crises and downturns, a self-sustaining process of economic growth and technological change had been achieved and would continue through the decades after 1850.

FIGURE 17.1 William Wyld, *View of Manchester*, 1851   In this hazy vista, smokestacks in Manchester, England, stand in sharp contrast to the surrounding unspoiled rural landscape. By the time of this painting, the city had grown to become one of England's leading industrial centers.

What created this phenomenon—which French observers in the 1820s termed an industrial revolution—and why did it happen first in the West and particularly in Britain?

A Booming Commercial Economy in the West

Why the industrial revolution emerged first in the West rather than in other civilizations such as China or India is difficult to say. Before 1500, Europeans enjoyed no fundamental advantages in how they produced goods over their Asian counterparts; in some areas, such as iron and steel production, they even lagged behind. Many qualities, such as intellectual traditions and politics, differentiated Eastern civilizations from the West and may help explain the early appearance of the industrial revolution in the West. However, the rise of commerce during the sixteenth, seventeenth, and eighteenth centuries distinguished the West economically. Civilizations elsewhere usually participated in this growing commerce only reluctantly. China, for example, may have produced luxury goods dearly desired by Westerners, but, except for gold and silver, the Chinese wanted little in trade from the West (see Global Connections on page 550). Moreover, the occupation of merchant

The Western and non-Western worlds

had a low social status in China, further discouraging any potential bloom of commerce in that part of the world. In the West, however, the growth of commerce encouraged people to produce more agricultural and manufactured goods and sell them for a profit in the marketplace. Merchants and entrepreneurs became devoted to buying low and selling high, thereby amassing more and more wealth. The growth of commerce helped create the potential markets, producers, entrepreneurs, and capitalists that would fuel the industrial revolution in the West.

Britain's Unique Set of Advantages

Commerce also helps explain why Britain industrialized first. During the sixteenth and seventeenth centuries, commercial activity in England intensified along with English sea power and overseas holdings. In the eighteenth century, Britain became Europe's leading commercial and colonial power (see Chapter 15). Britain's economy efficiently turned out goods for export, and the island nation enjoyed considerable access to expanding markets—both internal, from its rapidly growing and relatively wealthy population, and external, from its colonies and established commercial connections.

Commercial vigor

Cross-Cultural Misunderstandings: China and Great Britain

As industrialization spread in England during the last decades of the eighteenth century, British merchants sought new markets across the globe for their manufactured goods. China constituted a huge potential market for trade. In 1776, the British economist Adam Smith concluded that China's home market was "perhaps in extent not much inferior to the market of all the different countries of Europe put together." Indeed, during the eighteenth century, China under the Qing (Ch'ing) dynasty enjoyed considerable peace, prosperity, and population growth. But the emperors had always limited European merchants' access to China. Moreover, the Qing, determined to minimize foreign influences on their society, imposed strict restrictions on Western commerce within China.

Eager to widen the opening to China, the East India Company persuaded the British government to send an experienced diplomat, Lord George Macartney, to China in 1792. There, Macartney presented a formal request from King George III for a lessening of trade restrictions. But Emperor Qianlong (Ch'ien Lung) (r. 1736–1796), a capable and humane ruler, rejected the request. In a letter to King George III, he stressed that China "possesses all things in prolific abundance and lacks no product within its own borders." Therefore, China had "no need to import manufactures

of outside barbarians [Europeans] in exchange for our own produce." Clearly, in the emperor's mind, it was the British who "yearned after the blessings of our civilization" and not the reverse. Indeed, Qianlong expressed sympathy for the British, condemned as they were to "the lonely remoteness of your island, cut off from the world by intervening wastes of sea." He went on to lament the persistent desire of Christian missionaries for greater access to China. The Chinese had no need for these missionaries, he argued. "Ever since the beginning of history, sage Emperors and wise rulers have bestowed on China a moral system [Confucianism] and inculcated a code, which from time immemorial has been religiously observed by the myriads of my subjects." The emperor ended his letter by denying all British requests for greater access to China. He also threatened to treat any future violations of his rules harshly: "Do not say that you were not warned in due time!"

Lord Macartney, in turn, criticized the Chinese. "Morality is a mere pretense in their practice, though a common topic of their discourse." As for science, the Chinese, he claimed, considered it a mere "intruder." However, Macartney admitted that China was "an old first-rate man of war, which a succession of vigilant officers has continued to keep afloat." And in the government as well as the family, he observed, authority was

"usually exercised with kindness and indulgence."

In 1816, the British tried again, sending Lord Amherst on a similar mission to China. This effort, too, met with failure. However, British observers had even more positive things to say about China than Lord Macartney had. One official under Lord Amherst noted that the "lower orders of Chinese seem to me more neat and clean than any Europeans of the same class." Many other Western observers who traveled in China during the first half of the nineteenth century agreed with Robert Fortune's conclusion: "In no country in the world is there less real misery and want than in China."

By this time, however, China's population growth was outstripping its economic growth. The government struggled to cope with its people's needs, but poverty worsened. Local banditry rose and rebellions broke out with alarming frequency. The weakening Qing empire was losing its ability to meet the growing challenges from the British and the West.

Making Connections

1. In what ways did British and Chinese views about China differ?

2. How did China try to defend itself?

3. How did Britain respond to China's isolation?

Commercial vigor, however, is not enough to answer the question of why Britain led the industrial revolution. Other areas of Europe enjoyed advantages that would be important for industrialization. For example, during the first half of the eighteenth century, Holland's agriculture and financial institutions were second to none. France was the wealthiest nation in the West. Britain, however, boasted a unique combination of advantages that, when added to its commercial leadership, laid a solid foundation for the birth of the industrial revolution.

Water transportation—far cheaper and quicker than overland shipping—played a crucial role in moving the coal, iron, cloth, and machines pumped out

MAP 17.1

Eighteenth-Century England

This map shows England's system of navigable waterways, as well as areas of coal and iron production in the eighteenth century.

Explore the Map

1. What were the advantages of England's natural resources for industrialization?

2. How did England add to those advantages during the second half of the eighteenth century?

3. Why were rivers and canals becoming so important during the eighteenth century?

Transportation by Britain's new factories and mines. Already crisscrossed with countless navigable rivers (see **Map 17.1**), Britain enhanced its natural internal transportation system even more by building an extensive network of canals after 1760.

Certain raw materials—especially coal, iron, and cotton—also had an essential part in the island's industrialization. Britain's American colonies harvested large quantities of cotton. Not only did **Raw materials** the British countryside contain plentiful deposits of coal, but they were often conveniently located near iron deposits where foundry workers used the two materials in the newer processes of smelting to make iron products.

An expanding population and a particularly large and mobile force of both skilled and unskilled workers gave Britain another advantage. **Labor** Already less tied to villages than others in many parts of the continent, this class of rural laborers grew as waves of enclosures in the eighteenth century made many small farmers landless (see Chapter 15). These men and women could fill the rising demand for cheap industrial labor in the cities.

Britain had the capital to invest in industry for several reasons. First, its growing agricultural and commercial prosperity made it one of the wealthiest countries—per capita—in Europe. Second, it gained an unusual ability **Capital** to amass and mobilize that wealth into capital for potential investment, thanks to the development of a national banking system. Third, unlike most of its continental competitors, Britain was long free of internal tariff barriers, had a uniform and stable monetary system, and—since the Glorious Revolution of 1688 (see Chapter 13)—had a government that sympathized with business interests. All this encouraged wealthy individuals and families to risk money on commerce and industry. Therefore, inventors, innovators, and those who saw an opportunity could more easily find the means to start an industrial enterprise in Britain than elsewhere in Europe.

Finally, and according to some analysts, most important, entrepreneurship—at the heart of industrialization—was more socially acceptable in England than elsewhere. "In

England commerce is not looked down upon as being derogatory, as it is in France and Germany," concluded an eighteenth-century Swiss observer. Members of England's aristocratic families—especially younger sons left without inherited lands—often sought careers in commerce and manufacturing. Social barriers between them and the business-minded middle class were lower than elsewhere. More than in most European nations, British merchants and **entrepreneurs** occupied a strong, respected place in society. On the other hand, in France, for example, most elites looked on commerce and industry as a means—often regrettable—to gain money to purchase office, estates, and aristocratic status; as soon as possible, French aristocrats usually left commerce or distanced themselves from their businesses.

`Entrepreneurship`

In short, Britain had the most potential both to nurture and to take advantage of Europe's first industrial stirrings. Yet, what was it that finally transformed this potential into reality? Oddly, the crucial development came with advances in agriculture.

A Revolution in Agriculture

The agricultural revolution, with its new crops, methods of rotating crops, breeding of animals, and enclosures of open fields, spread in Britain during the late seventeenth and eighteenth centuries (see Chapter 15). Production increased, as did profits for the large landowners who shipped their crops to markets near and far. Declining food prices enabled more British families to purchase manufactured goods such as shoes, knives, and cloth. As the agricultural revolution picked up speed, fewer and fewer people produced more and more food. The new, large-scale farmers grew crops and livestock to feed the growing number of people working in factories, digging in the mines, and building their lives in the cities. Moreover, these well-to-do, enterprising landowners could use their profits to invest in the many business and commercial opportunities becoming available.

By 1850, the majority of Britain's population no longer raised food or lived in the countryside. Most lived and worked in cities and factory towns. Whether people were better off in these urban centers is a question we will turn to later. For now, the stage was set for Britain's industrial revolution.

NEW MARKETS, MACHINES, AND POWER

As wealth increased and people moved away from subsistence farming toward the burgeoning urban centers, the demand for manufactured goods reached unheard-of levels. Inventors and entrepreneurs rushed to fill this demand, dreaming up new machines and designing novel manufacturing methods. The machines, gaining complexity almost every year, seemed like mechanical wonders. The methods of production transformed the workplace. Coal and steam provided all the power necessary to make these machines and production methods work. Manufactured goods poured forth, available to all with the money to purchase them.

The Rising Demand for Goods

The old methods of production—slow, unreliable, and costly—could not satisfy the rising clamor for manufactured goods (see pages 498–500). In fact, the population growth in Britain and Europe alone created an ever-expanding pool of potential customers for low-cost clothing, nails, pottery, knives, and so forth. Eager overseas buyers, particularly in the colonies, offered raw materials in return for Britain's manufactured goods. At home, Britain's own successful farmers and merchants added to the demand.

Between the middle decades of the eighteenth century and 1850, inventors and entrepreneurs introduced new machines and methods that began to satisfy these hungry markets. Most inventors were practical men who embodied the widespread British interest in devices, gadgets, and machines of all kinds and had more talent as curious tinkerers than as scientific thinkers. Industrial entrepreneurs were also practical. Sometimes inventors themselves, they more often used the new devices and processes invented by others. Entrepreneurs purchased machines, employed workers, ran factories and mines, and found the necessary capital and markets.

`Inventors and entrepreneurs`

Some entrepreneurs were landowning aristocrats; others rose from rags to riches. Many were Protestant dissenters, such as Calvinists and Quakers, who had been discriminated against by the dominant Anglican Church. Denied careers in government, they jumped at the opportunities presented by commerce and industry. Most, however, came from the middle classes. They took advantage of journals that promoted new techniques and ideas, divided and redivided the processes of production, and trained a work force unaccustomed to working with machines in factory conditions. Buying raw materials from both local and distant suppliers, they promoted their products to the public. Through their resourcefulness and sometimes outright greed, they pursued profits. Navigating a risky competitive environment, they often reinvested their profits in their shops and factories, buying new machines and boosting production. The story of how they took advantage of new markets in the early decades of the industrial revolution is a narrative of new developments in cotton, iron, and steam.

Cotton Leads the Way

Changes in cotton production came first and with dramatic results. Before 1750, most thread and yarn was spun by women and woven into cloth by men who worked in rural cottages or small urban shops. Using only simple spinning wheels and handlooms, these laborers produced thread, yarn, and cloth of uneven quality. How much they produced was limited by many things—the supply of fiber, farmwork that took them away from their spinning and weaving, the wages paid by the entrepreneurs who organized much of this work, and, above all, the tools and methods they used.

In 1733, John Kay (1704–1764) invented a device called the flying shuttle, which doubled the speed at which cloth could be woven on a loom. The shuttle, in turn, intensified the demand for thread. In the 1760s, James Hargreaves (d. 1778) invented the spinning jenny, which revolutionized thread production. By 1812, one spinner could produce as much cotton thread as 200 spinners had in 1760. Other inventions, such as Richard Arkwright's (1732–1792) water frame and Edmund Cartwright's (1743–1823) power loom, allowed weavers to turn cotton into cloth in tremendous quantities. Two American developments added to the acceleration in textile production: Eli Whitney's (1765–1825) cotton gin (1793), which efficiently removed seeds from raw cotton; and the expanding slave plantation system in the South. Indeed, British manufacturers' growing demand for cotton became an important force perpetuating slavery in the cotton-growing areas of the United States.

By 1850, British cotton manufacturers had boosted cloth production from less than 40 million yards per year during the 1780s to more than 2,000 million yards per year. Cotton had become hugely popular and, alone, accounted for some 40 percent of British exports.

Weaving and spinning

Iron: New Processes Transform Production

Machines for the new cotton industry were just one source of a growing demand for iron. Armies needed guns and cannons; civilians needed nails and pans. Until the eighteenth century, British iron makers were limited by the island nation's dwindling forests, for they knew how to smelt iron ore only with charcoal, which came from wood. Even during the days of plentiful charcoal, ironworkers had only their own and their animals' muscle power with which to work the iron into usable

forms. Most of this iron production came out of small family firms or homes of artisans.

In 1708, Abraham Darby discovered an efficient way to smelt iron with coal in a blast furnace. This innovation would make the iron industry a key driver of the industrial revolution. By the end of the century, other new processes enabled iron makers to double production again and again. As suggested by **Figure 17.2,** foundry workers began using steam engines to operate smelting furnaces, drive forge hammers to shape the iron, and roll the iron into sheets. The Coalbrookdale ironworks became one of England's most important industrial centers, renowned for its production of pig iron and casting of cylinders for steam engines. In the center of Loutherbourg's painting, blistering flames and sulfurous clouds of smoke billow out from the coke hearth. To the right stand an engine house and a casting building. In the foreground, two dray horses haul a loaded cart along a road leading out from the ironworks. People standing along the road and to the left are dwarfed by the larger scene as well as the derelict industrial artifacts lying along the road. The painting suggests that the town—located in the rolling, wooded hills of central England—is being transformed into an industrial inferno. Ironworks such as these, with their tall, smoke-belching furnaces, were joining cotton factories as symbols of the industrial revolution.

Smelting with coal

The Steam Engine and the Factory System

Both the cotton and the iron industries created ever-higher demands for power. At the beginning of the

FIGURE 17.2 Philip James de Loutherbourg, *The Coalbrookdale Ironworks at Night,* 1801 Flames and smoke light up the night at Coalbrookdale, one of England's iron-producing centers.

eighteenth century, people had to rely on muscle, wind, and water to supply the energy to do their work. Early mills used water power, which meant that their owners had to build them near waterfalls. A drought in the summer or a cold snap in the winter could threaten to dry up or freeze this essential power source.

The steam engine, first used in the early eighteenth century to pump water out of deepening coal mines, provided a solution and would become the industrial revolution's most important technological advance. Portable and easily controlled, the earliest models were nevertheless not yet efficient enough for widespread application. Over the course of the eighteenth century, inventors such as Thomas Newcomen (1663–1729) and James Watt (1736–1819) improved the power and efficiency of these engines. Watt, a skilled craftsman backed by the daring entrepreneur Matthew Boulton (1728–1809), worked for years on the engine, making several design changes and eventually converting the reciprocal motion of the piston into a rotary motion. Now steam engines could be used not only to pump coal mines but also to drive the other new machines of the day, such as powering bellows for iron forges, mills for grains, and looms for textiles. The steam engine came to symbolize the new industrial age.

Reliable power from steam engines also made it possible for entrepreneurs to locate factories away from water power sites and build even larger cotton, iron, and other factories. In huge buildings, entrepreneurs hoped to guard their industrial secrets and mold a new labor force. Hundreds of workers, who produced goods in a repetitive series of steps and specialized tasks, tended rows of machines. The **factory system** had emerged. "The principle of the factory system . . . is to substitute mechanical science for hand skill, and the partition of a process into its essential constituents, for the division or graduation of labor," explained Andrew Ure, a professor of applied science, in 1835 (see Document 17.1). As we will see, factories generated unprecedented wealth for their owners and investors but brought new hardships for the people who toiled in them.

Figure 17.3 reveals the nature of the factory system. This realistic 1859 painting of a factory interior in France shows the mixture of raw materials (zinc ore), machines, and division of labor that epitomized factories in the industrial age. In the upper left and center, workers bring ore from the mines and dump it into machines for initial washing and processing. After the ore is split and sorted, workers shovel it into large ovens to be melted down. Men, women, and children work together in this hot, noisy building; the men have

FIGURE 17.3 François Bonhomme, *Workshop with Mechanical Sieves*, 1859   This interior view of a French zinc factory reveals the processing of raw materials, rows of machines, and division of labor that characterize the factory system.

DOCUMENT 17.1

Andrew Ure Defends Industrial Capitalism

From the beginning, industrialization had its critics and defenders. Andrew Ure, a British doctor, was one of the most effective public advocates of industrial capitalism. In the following excerpt from his 1835 book, The Philosophy of Manufacturers, *Ure focuses on the factory system and its consequences for workers.*

In my recent tour, continued during several months, through the manufacturing districts, I have seen tens of thousands of old, young, and middle-aged of both sexes, many of them too feeble to get their daily bread by any of the former modes of industry, earning abundant food, raiment, and domestic accommodation, without perspiring at a single pore, screened meanwhile from the summer's sun and the winter's frost, in apartments more airy and salubrious than those of the metropolis, in which our legislative and fashionable aristocracies assemble. In those spacious halls the benignant power of steam summons around him his myriads of willing menials, and assigns to each the regulated task, substituting for painful muscular effort on their part, the energies of his own gigantic arm, and demanding in return only attention and dexterity to correct such little aberrations as casually occur in his workmanship. The gentle docility of this moving force qualifies it for impelling the tiny bobbins of the lace-machine with a precision and speed inimitable by the most dexterous hands, directed by the sharpest eyes. Hence, under its auspices, and in obedience to Arkwright's polity, magnificent edifices, surpassing far in number, value, usefulness, and ingenuity of construction, the boasted monuments of Asiatic, Egyptian, and Roman despotism, have, within the short period of fifty years, risen up in this kingdom, to show to what extent, capital, industry, and science may augment the resources of a state, while they meliorate the condition of its citizens. Such is the factory system, replete with prodigies in mechanics and political economy.

The principle of the factory system then is, to substitute mechanical science for hand skill, and the partition of a process into its essential constituents, for the division or graduation of labour among artisans. On the handicraft plan, labour more or less skilled, was usually the most expensive element of production—*Materiam superaba opus;* but on the automatic plan, skilled labour gets progressively superseded, and will, eventually, be replaced by mere overlookers of machines.

By the infirmity of human nature it happens that the more skilful the workman, the more self willed and intractable he is apt to become, and, of course, the less fit a component of a mechanical system, in which, by occasional irregularities, he may do great damage to the whole. The grand object therefore of the modern manufacturer is through the union of capital and science, to reduce the task of his workpeople to the exercise of vigilance and dexterity,—faculties, when concentred to one process, speedily brought to perfection in the young. In the infancy of mechanical engineering, a machine-factory displayed the division of labour in manifold gradations—the file, the drill, the lathe, having each its different workmen in the order of skill: but the dexterous hands of the filer and driller are now superseded by the planing, the key-groove cutting, and the drilling machines; and those of the iron and brass turners by the self-acting slide-lathe.

SOURCE: Andrew Ure, *The Philosophy of Manufacturers* (Charles Knight, 1835).

Analyze the Document

1. What is the essence of the factory system?
2. How, according to Ure, does this system affect workers?
3. How might you argue that Ure's views are unfair?

the more authoritative and skilled jobs (a foreman sits in the rear to the left), while the women and children are assigned to sorting and splitting chunks of ore.

Coal: Fueling the Revolution

As the industrial revolution hit its stride, the demand for coal also intensified. Steam engines devoured coal as fuel. Iron makers required more and more coal to run their furnaces. Britain's doubling population needed coal to heat their homes.

People poured huge amounts of money and labor into digging mines, extracting the coal, and developing the roads, canals, and rails necessary to transport the mineral to waiting customers. Not only did coal fuel the industrial revolution; mining and manufacturing became so entwined that it was hard for people to think of one without the other.

Railroads: Carrying Industrialization Across the Land

The advent of the railroad age brought everything together. In the eighteenth century, horses had pulled carts along rails radiating out from mines, hauled barges along the growing network of canals, and pulled carriages along roads. Only wind in the sails of ships could move heavy cargoes and passengers across the seas.

During the 1820s, as steam engines began to power ships, the British inventor George Stephenson

FIGURE 17.4

William Powell Frith, *The Railway Station*, 1862

William Powell Frith's 1862 painting *The Railway Station* was viewed by thousands and helped make him one of England's most popular painters. It depicts the crowd in London's Paddington Station just before the departure of the Great Continental Express.

Connecting Art & Society

1. In what ways does this painting celebrate the connection between railroads and modern urban life?

2. What stands out about the various people in this depiction?

3. Why might viewers of the times have found this scene so interesting?

4. In what ways does the building enshrine the railroad and people in this scene?

(1781–1848) developed the practical modern railroad. In 1830 his new train, the Rocket, initiated the Liverpool-to-Manchester railway line. The Rocket's speed (16 miles per hour) and reliability excited the imaginations of everyone. People eagerly invested in railway companies, rode the new lines out of curiosity, and traveled by rail to vacation spots.

The railway carried heavy freight with unprecedented ease and speed. By 1850, trains were chugging over 2,000 miles of track in Britain, reaching astonishing speeds of up to 50 miles an hour. Steaming across bridges and through tunnels to the railway stations dotting the land, the new locomotives embodied the power and the promise that seemed to characterize the industrial age. Optimistic observers such as the British politician Edward Stanley argued that "of all the promoters of civilization, the Railway System of communication will be amongst the foremost in its effects, for it cannot fail to produce many and mighty changes in manufactures, in commerce, in trade, and in science."

Figure 17.4, by the popular British artist William Powell Frith, captures the drama and excitement of the railroad age. The Great Continental Express is about to depart from Paddington Station in London. At the center is a middle-class family. The mother kisses her son, who is holding a cricket bat and is being sent away to school with his brother. Farther right, a bearded foreigner whose dress suggests wealth haggles over the fare with a cab driver. A wedding party bids adieu to a bride and groom. Behind them, a boy sells newspapers to departing passengers, and a soldier in a red uniform kisses his plump baby good-bye. On the far right, two well-known London detectives arrest a criminal as he steps into the train. Behind them, workers load luggage onto carriage roofs. On the far left, working-class people hurry toward the third-class cars, and porters push luggage toward the train. Above the bustling platform and trains, the wrought-iron-ribbed ceiling and numerous hanging lamps mark the train station as one of London's appealing industrial wonders.

The railroad seemed to pull together all the trends that emerged during the industrial revolution. It ignited demand for an array of related products—coal-thirsty steam engines to power the trains, iron to build the rails and cars, cloth and leather to make furnishings, and bricks and glass to erect the new stations. Like the cotton factories, iron foundries, and coal mines, the railroad industry created new jobs while destroying old ones. In addition, it left its own permanent mark on the land and neighborhoods it affected. As Charles Dickens (1812–1870) described in *Dombey and Son* (1846), a new rail line meant that "houses were knocked down; streets broken through and stopped; deep pits and trenches dug in the ground; enormous heaps of earth and clay thrown up . . . everywhere carcasses of ragged tenements, and fragments of unfinished walls and arches, and piles of scaffolding, and wilderness of bricks, . . . mounds of ashes blocked up rights of way." All this "wholly changed the law and custom of the neighborhood," before the railroad "trailed smoothly away, upon its mighty course of civilization and improvement."

Finally, like the other new industries, the railroads could be a risky investment opportunity. Some owners and investors grew fabulously wealthy; others suffered devastating financial losses. Just as the cotton and iron industries continued to face competition from older methods such as the putting-out system (cottage industry), handicrafts, small family firms, and agriculture, the railroads had to fight to steal business from the roads and canal systems that were expanding across Britain at the same time. Those who had thrown their lot in with the railroads need not have worried too long about the wisdom of their investment, however. Like the cotton and iron factories, the railways were the wave of the future, and they rolled inexorably across the British landscape.

> **Effects of the railroad**

Britain's Triumph: The Crystal Palace Exhibition

In 1851, that shining future was put on display for all the world to admire. That year, London hosted the first international industrial fair at the glass and iron Crystal Palace. At this dazzling exhibit, millions of visitors came to gaze reverently at the British miracle.

Figure 17.5 shows the interior of the Crystal Palace—its arching glass roof like a cathedral, its steel framing a testament to modern engineering. Matthew

FIGURE 17.5 The Crystal Palace Exhibition Under a majestic glass and iron roof, visitors from around the world viewed commercial and industrial displays. This 1851 international fair marked Britain's new industrial might.

Wyatt, one of the directors of the exhibition, proudly described the construction of the palace as an industrial triumph: "But for the perfect system of discipline, which frequent practice in directing the labour of masses of workmen has now made general throughout England, it would have been impossible to have fashioned, in so short a time, so novel and so vast a structure . . . the gates of which may . . . be thrown open to the world at large, for many years to come." To Wyatt and many others in 1851, the Crystal Palace was at once an architectural masterpiece and a jewel of mass production that could not help but appeal to popular taste. In addition to admiring the building itself, visitors could view displays from various nations.

The awe-inspiring palace confirmed economic realities. Britain produced more than half the world's cotton cloth and iron, and, despite periodic downturns, the nation enjoyed sustained economic growth. Britain had become the world's first industrialized nation.

INDUSTRIALIZATION SPREADS TO THE CONTINENT

It was not until after 1830 that industrialization spread with much force outside Britain (see **Figure 17.6**). Before then, people from France, the German states, and elsewhere were interested in Britain's economic wonders. Some traveled to Britain to copy machines, and others enticed British technicians and capital to their own countries. A few modern industrial shops and machines sprang up on the Continent, but overall, agriculture and tradition still dominated economic life there.

After 1830, industrialization spread to certain regions, especially Belgium, northeastern France, the northern German states, and northwestern Italy (see **Figure 17.6**). These areas had plenty of urban laborers, deposits of iron and coal, and developed transportation facilities. Envious of British wealth, pressured by British competition, and recognizing the military potential of cheap iron and rail transportation,

Governmental aid

FIGURE 17.6 Industrial Production in Europe, 1831–1850

continental governments took a more active role in supporting industrialization than British rulers had. They enacted tariffs to protect their manufacturers from British goods, and they subsidized new industries. Railroads, partially financed by governments and foreign capital, led rather than followed the advent of other industries, widening markets and creating demand for coal and iron. These countries could not yet hope to catch up to Britain. At mid-century, a

Railroads Completed, ca. 1850
Major Exposed Coalfields
Scattered Ironworks
Emerging Industrial Areas
Industrial Areas

MAP 17.2

The Industrial Revolution in Europe, 1850

This map illustrates the spread of industrialization in Europe by 1850.

Explore the Map

1. Locate the industrial areas. What connections are there among these areas, their resources—such as coalfields—and access to transportation by water or rail?

2. How does the extent of industrialization in England compare to that in the nations of continental Europe?

3. What does the location of railways suggest about the kinds of areas that early railways were intended to serve?

German official complained that Germany would never "be able to reach the level of production of coal and iron currently attained in England." But soon Germany and other nations would manage to industrialize more selectively and quickly, thanks to the groundwork that Britain had laid.

As **Map 17.2** indicates, by 1850 large industrial centers had arisen in Belgium, France, and those areas of northern Germany bounded by the 1834 Zollverein (a customs union that eliminated tariffs between independent German states). Other regions, particularly around Milan in northern Italy and in the northeastern United States, had also begun to industrialize.

Most of southern, central, and eastern Europe, however, remained virtually untouched by industrial

Industrialization Spreads to the Continent 559

development. Lacking well-placed resources, efficient transportation, mobile workforces, commercialized agriculture, and capital for investment, these regions retained their traditional and rural character. The vast majority of people in these areas remained in the countryside tied to subsistence farms or, especially in the east, large agricultural estates. Small villages rather than booming cities were the rule. Wealthy urban elites might purchase manufactured goods from industrial regions to the west, but their own countries could not produce them in the same way. Governments and perhaps a few ambitious and wealthy individuals sometimes imported the latest machines and built a few railroad lines, but these signs of industrialization primarily had symbolic or military value. Relying on old methods of production, merchants in these lands had trouble selling their manufactured goods in international markets. Nations, such as Spain and Russia, that once exported cloth saw their sales dry up in the face of British textiles.

Remaining traditional economies

There were a few exceptions in these traditional economies. For example, Austria's Bohemian lands developed a spinning industry, and a few factories sprang up around St. Petersburg and Moscow in Russia. Even so, British technicians and industrialists were often needed to support these limited efforts. On the whole, all these countries would have to wait before experiencing both the benefits and the burdens of the industrial revolution.

BALANCING THE BENEFITS AND BURDENS OF INDUSTRIALIZATION

How did industrialization affect everyday life for Europeans? To answer this complex question, we might first explore the impact of the new machines, factories, and railroads on people's work conditions, home lives, and social relationships. It is also important to ask who received the lion's share of the new wealth.

New wealth

Foreign observers marveled at Britain's wealth; indeed, to this day many of us associate machines, factories, and railroads with prosperity. Statistics seem to confirm this impression: Britain's national product increased more than threefold between 1780 and 1850. The population in Europe also surged during the same period and absorbed some of the new wealth. Probably thanks to better food supplies (especially cultivation of the potato), earlier marriages, and declining mortality rates, Europe's population ballooned from fewer than 175 million in 1780 to 266 million in 1850. During this same period, Britain's population more than doubled.

Population growth

These startling numbers suggest a sense of economic well-being on the part of Europeans, but they also frightened some contemporaries. In his influential *Essay on the Principle of Population* (1798), British economist Thomas Malthus (1766–1834) warned that population growth would inevitably outstrip food supplies. A few years later, another well-known economist, David Ricardo (1772–1823), argued that overpopulation would restrict wages to no more than subsistence levels.

Nevertheless, industrialization generated new wealth so rapidly that personal income rose faster than population growth in these years. Between 1800 and 1850, per-capita income skyrocketed by a whopping 75 percent in Britain. As other countries—such as Belgium, Germany, and France—industrialized, they too enjoyed similar gains. But who exactly was receiving these new riches?

The Middle Class

The middle classes (bourgeoisie), still a minority of the population even in Britain, prospered. The newest, most dynamic group within the middle classes was the industrial entrepreneurs—the factory and mine owners. They gained the most, some amassing enormous fortunes. Many bankers, smaller factory owners, professionals, merchants, and shopkeepers enjoyed more modest gains, as did those who earned interest and profits from investing their savings in industrial and commercial ventures. All investments, however, did not pay off. Some loans were not repaid. People took financial risks, and some lost their bets. Firms failed all the time, and periodic economic downturns spawned a string of losses and bankruptcies.

Still, over the long haul, the middle class as a whole benefited the most from industrialization. As their wealth and numbers grew, so did their prestige, political power, and cultural influence. The Scottish philosopher and scholar James Mill (1773–1836) claimed that the "heads that invent . . . the hands that execute, the enterprise that projects, and the capital by which these projects are carried into operation" all came from the middle class. Marked by their modest, sober clothing, the middle class gradually displaced the once-glittering aristocracy who were still tied by tradition to the land. This process unfolded slowly, and some aristocrats and landowners managed to adjust quite well to the change.

The Working Classes

The picture is far less clear for the working classes—those who labored in the factories, tended the machines, and toiled in the mines. For people who shifted from the agricultural life or jobs as artisans to work as factory laborers, industrialization may have hurt more than it helped, especially in its earlier decades. These people worked six days a week, twelve to sixteen hours a day, earning only subsistence-level wages. William Harter, a British silk manufacturer, justified the long hours to a parliamentary commission: Reducing the hours of labor "would instantly much reduce the value of my mill and machines . . . every machine is valuable in proportion to the quantity of work which it will turn off in a given time." In textile factories, whole families typically labored together. Women's earnings were between one-third and two-thirds of men's, and children's wages were a mere fraction of that. As a result, factory owners employed women and children whenever possible to save money, and they even contracted with orphanages to provide cheap child laborers.

Figure 17.7, an 1853 woodcut, shows the interior of a cotton factory. Here the supervisor of an English cotton factory whips a boy as a woman in tattered clothing looks on. Whipping was one way in which supervisors disciplined child workers to the rhythms of the machinery. In the scene's background, women and men tend the spinning machines while three other men talk, apparently unconcerned by the violence. Middle-class reformers such as Frances Trollope (1780–1863) used pictures like these to decry the harsh treatment of children in the cotton mills. One governmental investigation of child labor described how children "were rendered pale, weak and unhealthy" from "labouring for hours like little slaves." Employers, anxious to keep their machines running and wages low, replied that "it was absolutely necessary that the children should be employed within the mills from six o'clock in the morning till seven in the evening, summer and winter." Document 17.2 reveals some of the typical factory rules that employers insisted were necessary to keep their machines running smoothly and profitably.

After the 1820s, factory workers' wages started to climb. By the 1840s or 1850s, they were earning more than their agricultural counterparts. This change did not make them rich, however, for most of them had to spend some two-thirds of their income on food alone. In 1842, Flora Tristan reported that most workers in English factories "lack clothing, bed, furniture, fuel, wholesome food—even potatoes!" and that their bodies were "thin and frail, their limbs feeble, their complexions pale, their eyes dead."

Money was only one variable in the quality-of-life equation. Industrial workers faced job insecurity, physical dangers, and painful changes unique to their way of life. The worst insecurity centered on employment itself. Even in good times, some firms failed. During economic downturns and crises, such as the "Great Hunger" of the 1840s, wages plummeted below subsistence levels, and many workers lost their jobs.

Factory labor

Insecurity

FIGURE 17.7 Child Labor, 1853 New factories typically employed women and children. As this woodcut of a cotton factory interior suggests, supervisors sometimes used harsh methods of discipline.

For these industrial laborers there was no unemployment insurance to turn to, and no foraging, cottage industry, or gardening that people living in the countryside could resort to in hard times.

The work itself carried a high risk of severe physical injury. Factory owners made no provisions for safety. In cotton factories, children regularly climbed under and on top of the equipment to free jammed machines, collect cotton, and tie broken threads; many young workers suffered terrible injuries to their hands and even lost fingers. Long hours and exposure to chemicals, dust, smoke, and industrial residue all led to ill health. Indeed, industrial populations had a far shorter life expectancy and higher incidence of disease and deformity than rural populations. In the 1840s, the military turned down 90 percent of volunteers from some urban areas for health reasons—double the rate of rejection for rural volunteers.

Risks of injury

Besides job insecurity, injury, and ill health, the new industrial age brought lifestyle changes that are harder to evaluate. Industrial workers experienced

DOCUMENTS

DOCUMENT 17.2

Factory Owners Establish Discipline for Workers

Employers and overseers in the new factories needed workers who would labor in rhythm with the machines and according to the demands of industrial capitalism. To these ends, they instituted rules and disciplinary measures. The following document discusses such measures, which went into effect at a Berlin factory in 1844.

In every large works, and in the co-ordination of any large number of workmen, good order and harmony must be looked upon as the fundamentals of success and therefore the following rules shall be strictly observed.

1. The normal working day begins at all seasons at 6 A.M. precisely and ends, after the usual break of half an hour for breakfast, an hour for dinner and half an hour for tea at 7 P.M., and it shall be strictly observed. . . .

   Workers arriving 2 minutes late shall lose half an hour's wages; whoever is more than 2 minutes late may not start work until after the next break; or at least shall lose his wages until then.

4. Repeated irregular arrival at work shall lead to dismissal. This shall also apply to those who are found idling by an official or overseer, and refused to obey their order to resume work.

6. No worker may leave his place of work otherwise than for reasons connected with his work.

7. All conversation with fellow-workers is prohibited; if any worker requires information about his work, he must turn to the overseer or to the particular fellow-worker designated for the purpose. . . .

SOURCE: Sidney Pollard and Colin Holmes, *Documents of European Economic History*, vol. 1 (St. Martin's Press, 1968).

Analyze the Document

1. What problems do employers face, as suggested by these rules?

2. How might a labor union argue against some of these rules?

3. What do *you* think of these rules?

---

a new rhythm of labor that no longer bore any resemblance to the natural rhythms of daylight and seasonal changes.

Lifestyle changes

Now, workers toiled unrelentingly to keep pace with the machines and schedules of the factory owner. Employers and their stewards maintained workplace discipline with fines, curses, and whippings. Children who could not keep up were beaten at times (see **Figure 17.7**); some were even chained to their machines. There were no slack days, like the traditional Monday of preindustrial times. Wages took the form of cash, which workers had to save and apportion carefully over the week for food and housing despite the temptations of alcohol and other leisure activities. At the end of the long workday, laborers trudged home to poor housing clustered around noisy mills or mine entrances or to cheap, overcrowded rooms and cellars of industrial cities.

The question remains: Did the overall quality of life improve for the working classes in the early decades of the industrial revolution? One way to judge is to ask what would have happened to these people without industrialization. Communal villages and agricultural labor had their advantages. In a widely popular poem, "The Deserted Village" (1770), Oliver Goldsmith lamented the loss of rural life:

> *Ill fares the land, to hastening ills a prey*
> *Where wealth accumulated . . .*
> *But a bold peasantry, their country's pride*
> *When once destroyed, can never be supplied.*

People growing up on farms and in small villages at least had traditions they could rely on. But this traditional life also had its own harsh side. Poverty was no stranger to the countryside, nor was child labor, cold, uncertainty, and squalor in windowless hovels. One contemporary, Frederick Eden, argued that the difficulties experienced by small farmers and villagers were only "temporary" and a small price to pay for "the greater good which may be expected from the improvement." However we evaluate all this, life in the city did give the working class something no one could have foreseen: a new sense of class consciousness, an awareness of their own unique burdens and hardships that emboldened them into action and alarmed the onlooking middle classes.

Developing Working-Class Consciousness

Because industrial workers lived in the same areas, labored in the same oppressive buildings, grappled with similar problems, socialized and commiserated together, and joined the same trade or civic organizations, they began to see themselves as a separate class. This sense of solidarity came partly from a tradition among artisans and craftsmen of membership in guilds. Although guilds were made illegal after 1791 and were opposed by middle-class people committed to gaining control over the workplace, other workers' organizations such as fraternal societies, trade organizations, and mutual aid societies

Workers' organizations

persisted. These groups laid the foundation for the emergence of trade unions, made legal (though severely restricted) in England in 1824 and elsewhere after 1850.

Figure 17.8, a nineteenth-century trade union membership certificate, reveals the pride and values in union labor during this industrial age. Like most unions of the period, the Associated Shipwright's Society—a British shipbuilders' union—was made up of skilled workers. Toward the top of this membership certificate is a blue shield; above it are two hands clasped in brotherhood, and below it are the words "WE ARE AS ONE." In the center is a construction site where ships are being built. Just above are pictures of ships, particularly the steamships that carried people and commerce throughout the world. On the bottom of the certificate are pictures of some of the typical benefits of union membership, including accident insurance, retirement income, and death payments. By mid-century, labor leaders had formed the beginnings of national unions, such as the Grand National Consolidated Trades Union in Britain in 1834, the National Trades Union in the United States in 1834, and the General Workers' Brotherhood in Germany in 1848.

FIGURE 17.8 A Trade Union Membership Certificate, nineteenth century This union certificate from Britain's Associated Shipwright's Society reveals the benefits and pride that labor union membership conferred during this industrial age.

Sometimes workers turned to violence against what they saw as threats from industrialization by destroying the new machines. After 1811, English hand weavers, losing their work to the new power looms, went on rampages, smashing the machines to pieces or campaigning to get rid of them. Glove makers destroyed the new stocking frames that threatened their jobs. These forms of protest came to be known as **Luddism** in honor of a legendary (and perhaps fictitious) leader, Ned Ludd. The British Parliament quickly named industrial sabotage a capital offense and heavily suppressed the violence. Nevertheless, sporadic episodes of violence continued to erupt for several years, not only in Britain but elsewhere as the industrial revolution spread. In the 1830s, silk workers in Lyons, France, rose up against attempts to lower their pay. In 1836, Spanish workers burned a textile factory in Barcelona. During the 1840s, several governments had to call out troops against strikers.

`Luddism`

Most of these efforts brought few concrete results in the period before 1850. In addition to the power wielded by wealthier classes and governments, many internally divisive forces chipped away at the fledgling working-class solidarity. Labor leaders, for example, who usually came from the more skilled trades—the cabinetmakers, printers, tailors, masons, and blacksmiths—tended to look down on unskilled industrial workers. Most women were not invited to join worker organizations, though they forged some of their own trade associations. Other loyalties based on religion, region, trade, or even neighborhood undermined worker unity. Sometimes the only connection holding laborers together was a sense of shared problems, the belief that workers had a right to a just wage, and the impression that their employers were exploiters rather than economic partners.

Despite the forces dividing workers, their sense of themselves as a separate, unique class strengthened over time. Increasingly, members of the middle class began to see them as dangerous and even savage. As we will see in following chapters, with the sharpening of working-class consciousness, the power of the traditional artisan groups and the peasantry would decline—quickly in the decades after 1850, especially in highly industrialized places such as Britain, Belgium, and parts of Germany. The process would unfold more gradually in moderately industrialized places, such as France, and slowly in most of southern and eastern Europe.

For good or ill, industrialization was transforming everyday life across Europe. The economic and human balance shifted from the countryside to the city. Now the dramatic social transformations took place in the growing urban centers where, as one young worker described London in the 1820s, "a wilderness of human beings" lived.

LIFE IN THE GROWING CITIES

The unprecedented growth of cities from 1780 to 1850 stemmed from a combination of forces. Population was increasing in both urban

Urban growth

and rural areas. Enclosures of land by market-oriented landowners that dispossessed individuals of their small farms and communities of their commons further uprooted rural families. These pressures pushed people from the land. At the same time, the cities, with their promise of jobs and the lure of beer halls and theaters, attracted people in droves. Industrial towns sprang up where none had existed before. Towns ballooned into cities, and already large cities grew even more imposing. Some of the most spectacular urban growth happened in industrial cities, such as Manchester, which expanded from 25,000 in 1772 to 367,000 in 1850; and Birmingham, Leeds, and Saint-Étienne in France, which more than tripled in size. Other already substantial cities, such as London and Paris, became increasingly crowded and sprouted new suburbs.

Most cities flourished through industrial activity, such as mining and manufacturing. Other areas scarcely touched by industrialization, such as Naples, St. Petersburg, and Vienna, also grew dramatically through the expansion of governmental bureaucracies and traditional commerce.

The Promise and Pitfalls of Work in the Cities

Industry, however, had the strongest pull. It inevitably attracted new commerce and gave rise to a broad range of consumer and service needs. Women flocked to the textile factories, but even more women living in the cities worked as domestics. Many young women came for what jobs they could find, perhaps hoping to send home part of their pay and still save enough to start a new life. The building trades drew growing numbers of men, who sometimes left their wives and children in the countryside to survive on a patch of land and dwindling cottage-industry employment. Many men periodically returned to the countryside, particularly in winter, when construction slowed, or during planting and harvest times.

Living with Urban Growth

Industrialization and urbanization also altered the landscape that people traveled through to reach the cities. Forests shrank as people cut down more and more trees for construction of cities, mines, factories, and railroads. The same mines and railroads cut scars into the land, and the cities and factories ate up rural landscapes. Rivers once fit for fish or drinking became polluted with industrial and human wastes.

Approaching the cities, travelers saw smoke in the air from the dirty coal fires used to heat buildings and from the engines of industry. In the city, and particularly in the poor working-class areas, the air smelled foul, for there were no modern sewers, sorely inadequate toilet facilities, and not

Environmental changes

enough clean water. Garbage and animal waste collected in the streets until heavy rains washed them away. In Manchester, only two-thirds of the houses had toilets, and many of those flushed into inadequate cesspools. Human and animal waste mixed in rivers that people used for drinking water. Charles Dickens's description of the fictionalized Coketown in his novel *Hard Times* (1854) would have struck a familiar chord for nineteenth-century travelers to Britain's industrial cities: "It was a town of machinery and tall chimneys, out of which interminable serpents of smoke trailed themselves for ever and ever. . . . It had a black canal in it, and a river that ran purple with ill-smelling dye, and vast piles of buildings full of windows where there was a rattling and a trembling all day long, and where the piston of the steam-engine worked monotonously up and down."

Overwhelmed by these surroundings, newcomers to the cities tended to settle in areas where they knew someone else. Whole neighborhoods grew up populated by people who had come from the same rural region. This tendency led to a sense of segregation and separate identities within the cities, as people familiar with one another clustered together.

Few neighborhoods were planned. Indeed, the expansion of most cities became increasingly uncontrolled. The rampant growth created far more problems for the working class than for anyone else. The middle classes, for example,

Different neighborhoods

most likely lived in lower-floor apartments in the more desirable sections of town and had the benefit of some running water. They also could afford to employ servants. It was in the working-class sections and poverty-stricken areas that the social ills and squalor of the age reached their worst levels. As the manufacturer and socialist Friedrich Engels (1820–1895) described, "The houses are packed from cellar to attic and they are as dirty inside as outside." In the Irish quarter of London, as many as 38 people crowded into small buildings down narrow alleys where the walls were crumbling, and "piles of refuse and ashes lie all over the place and the slops thrown out into the street collect in pools which emit a foul stench." In the bad quarters lived "the poorest of the poor. Here the worst-paid workers rub shoulders with thieves, rogues and prostitutes."

Document 17.3 describes conditions where poor workers lived. **Figure 17.9,** a mid-nineteenth-century woodcut by the French artist Gustave Doré (1832–1883), also portrays the squalor and crowding of a London slum. In the center, a young child carries a

DOCUMENT 17.3

A Middle-Class Reformer Describes Workers' Housing

During the first half of the nineteenth century, most urban workers gained little more than just enough to get by. Their dwellings reflected their precarious existence. The following is a description of housing in Nantes, France, during the 1830s.

If you want to know how he [the poorer worker] lives, go—for example—to the Rue des Fumiers which is almost entirely inhabited by this class of worker. Pass through one of the drain-like openings, below street-level, that lead to these filthy dwellings, but remember to stoop as you enter. One must have gone down into these alleys where the atmosphere is as damp and cold as a cellar; one must have known what it is like to feel one's foot slip on the polluted ground and to fear a stumble into the filth: to realise the painful impression that one receives on entering the homes of these unfortunate workers. Below street-level on each side of the passage there is a large gloomy cold room. Foul water oozes out of the walls. Air reaches the room through a sort of semi-circular window which is two feet high at its greatest elevation. Go in—if the fetid smell that assails you does not make you recoil. Take care, for the floor is uneven, unpaved and untiled—or if there are tiles, they are covered with so much dirt that they cannot be seen. And then you will see two or three rickety beds fitted to one side because the cords that bind them to the worm-eaten legs have themselves decayed. Look at the contents of the bed—a mattress; a tattered blanket of rags (seldom washed since there is only one); sheets sometimes; and a pillow sometimes. No wardrobes are needed in these homes. Often a weaver's loom and a spinning wheel complete the furniture. There is no fire in the winter. No sunlight penetrates [by day], while at night a tallow candle is lit. Here men work for fourteen hours [a day].

SOURCE: Sidney Pollard and Colin Holmes, *Documents of European Economic History,* vol. 1 (New York: St. Martin's Press, 1968), pp. 494–495.

Analyze the Document

1. What most bothers the author about workers' housing?

2. In what ways were housing conditions connected to public health problems?

3. How do you think a middle-class person might have responded to this account during the 1830s?

baby, perhaps because her mother is working. Around her in the alley, dejected men, women, and children stand listlessly. Dark tenements tower over them, and laundry sags from clotheslines. Though criticized for overdramatizing the plight of the poor, Doré effectively conveys the anguish of unemployment, poverty, and crowding marring this rich city. As this and works by novelists such as Charles Dickens, Elizabeth Gaskell, Frances Trollope, and Honoré de Balzac showed, the burgeoning cities were fostering a whole set of social concerns.

Worrying About Urban Society: Rising Crime

One of those social concerns centered on patterns of criminal behavior. People in the upper classes complained about crime and the social disorder it implied. Had cities become hotbeds of crime, as some middle-class observers claimed, or were these critics simply overly worried about their own safety and well-being?

Crime certainly plagued people in the West long before the industrial revolution. In rural areas, along highways, and in the preindustrial cities of Europe, crimes ranging from pickpocketing to murder occurred all too frequently. Professional thieves had reportedly run rampant in Germany, England, and France in past centuries.

In the early stages of industrialization, theft and robbery in particular did rise in the cities. Crowds provided prime opportunities for pickpockets. In urban taverns and dance halls, men sometimes fell into violent brawling, sometimes over women. In these establishments, alcohol flowed freely and almost certainly played a role in outbreaks of fighting. The widening gaps between rich and poor and the desperation of living in hard times also made tempers short. Finally, the anonymity of life in the city and the tempting array of luxury items to steal made crime harder to resist.

Whether justified by the realities of more crime or not, the specter of urban crime and fear of disorder prompted new efforts to improve law enforcement. In 1829, under the leadership of Robert Peel, Parliament passed a law establishing the first modern police force in London. Peel's new police, called "Bobbies" in his honor, emphasized regular patrols by uniformed officers as a way to deter crime and present a visual image of security. Both the middle and the working classes accepted the Bobbies, in part because the police were not allowed to be engaged for political purposes such as domestic espionage, and in part because people saw them as the first line of defense against all disorder. By the early 1830s, there were some 3,000 uniformed officers in the force.

Crime and law enforcement

they drew even more people eager to take advantage of the available work and other opportunities. Contemporaries associated the cities with overcrowding, filth, crime, moral degeneracy, and an unruly working class. "They [the working class] live precisely like brutes . . . they eat, drink, breed, work and die," complained a middle-class British observer in 1850. "The richer and more intelligent classes are obliged to guard them with police." Perhaps most disturbing, however, were the disease and death that haunted urban centers.

PUBLIC HEALTH AND MEDICINE IN THE INDUSTRIAL AGE

People had good reason to fear for their health and safety in the growing cities, especially in the poorer sections of town. On average, city dwellers fell ill more often and died at a far earlier age than their rural counterparts. Within the cities, the poor lived half as long as the rich.

Industrialization itself was dangerous. The new machines maimed factory workers, and cave-ins, floods, and explosions killed miners. Various diseases stemmed directly from mining and manufacturing. Coal miners became ill and died from black-lung disease. Cotton workers developed brown-lung disease. In textile factories, women suffered particularly high mortality rates. Metalworkers, especially grinders, developed lung diseases from inhaling shavings. Poisonings from mercury, lead, and phosphorus used in industrial processes also increased.

The Danger of Disease

The greatest danger came from infectious diseases. They were the great causes of sickness and death before the nineteenth century, and the rapid growth of crowded cities that lacked sanitation facilities made matters worse. People living in working-class quarters and urban slums were most vulnerable. Tuberculosis and diphtheria thrived in the most heavily populated areas and killed millions during the nineteenth century.

Worse, plagues periodically swept through cities. Cholera epidemics struck Europe several times, causing great panic as people in city after city awaited the arrival of the illness (see **Map 17.3**). Suggested remedies included taking several measures to restore warmth to the body, giving laudanum (opium dissolved in alcohol), and seeking medical aid. In 1831 alone, cholera killed some 100,000 in France and 50,000 in England.

People disagreed about the causes of diseases. Some observers blamed illnesses on physical weakness and immorality of individuals. In these

FIGURE 17.9 Gustave Doré, *A London Slum,* mid-nineteenth century Dark, crowded urban areas such as the district shown in this woodcut were home to innumerable poor workers and other impoverished individuals.

The frightening consequences of rapid urbanization were becoming all too apparent. Year by year, the cities grew more densely packed and seemingly more dangerous. In bad times, they teemed with desperate people hoping to find jobs; in good times,

thinking about
GEOGRAPHY

MAP 17.3

The Spread of a Cholera Epidemic

This map shows the spread of the cholera epidemic that originally broke out in eastern India in 1817.

Explore the Map

1. In what direction did the epidemic mainly spread over time?

2. What does this pattern reveal about growing connections between the Western and non-Western worlds?

critics' view, disease was rooted in

[Causes of disease] inferior genetic background, overindulgence, degenerate lifestyle, poor hygiene, and irresponsibility. Only self-help could solve the problem, they argued.

Other commentators and some doctors theorized that disease spread through contagion—that people caught diseases from one another. This theory had more to do with magic, belief in the devil, or a desire to keep the ill out of sight than any notion of modern germ theory. It seemed to explain sexually transmitted diseases like syphilis but could not answer the question of why some people contracted various diseases while others did not. In these commentators' minds, quarantine offered the best solution to fighting contagious diseases.

Most doctors eventually concluded that disease stemmed less from personal contact than from environmental forces. They believed in miasma, the centuries-old notion that people caught diseases by breathing fumes given off by human waste, rotting vegetables, decaying flesh, marshes, or stagnant ponds. They also blamed poor diets for weakening resistance to these sources of disease. In a widely respected 1840 study, the French physician Louis Villermé attributed the prevalence of disease in the working-class slums of Lille to the cellars and crowded rooms where "the air is never renewed," where "everywhere are piles of garbage, of ashes, of debris from vegetables picked up from the streets, of rotten straw," where "one is exhausted in these hovels by a stale, nauseating, . . . odor of filth, odor of garbage." This helped him and others explain why people living in barracks, workhouses, and the worst parts of cities more often fell ill and died.

Seeking Medical Care

None of these theories about disease aided individuals seeking medical care. Doctors may have been well-meaning, but in 1850, anyone visiting a doctor was more likely to be [Doctors] hurt than helped. Most people consulted physicians reluctantly and had little trust in the power of treatments or medicine. To our twentieth-century sensibilities, medicine in the early 1800s can indeed seem quite alarming. To alleviate a fever, for example, doctors often turned to traditional cures such as initiating bloodletting by opening a vein or applying leeches to the skin, or they recommended laxatives to purge the bad humors and fluids from the body. Physicians routinely prescribed pills that at best did nothing and more likely contained toxic substances such as mercury. Frequently, the addictive drug laudanum was suggested for the treatment of pain, sleeping problems, difficulties with children, and a variety of other complaints. Such treatments more often led to fluid depletion, poisoning, and addiction than any improvement of the patient's condition.

More benignly, doctors might recommend fresh-air cures or taking the waters at health spas. Many of the wealthy traveled to coastal resorts and centers in Caldas da Rainha in Portugal, Bath in England, and Baden-Baden in Germany for these health cures. They may have gained some temporary relief from conditions such as arthritis, but they more likely

Public Health and Medicine in the Industrial Age   567

FIGURE 17.10 Caroline Naudet, *Journey of a Dying Man to the Other World,* **1820** In this grim scene, doctors lead a dying man, a death-dealing surgeon, a sinister apothecary, and an undertaker. A harsh commentary on patients' fate under the care of early-nineteenth-century doctors, the work captures popular attitudes toward physicians.

enjoyed the lively social events and casinos that also attracted them to these spas.

Figure 17.10, an 1820 print by the French artist Caroline Naudet (1775–1839), reveals popular attitudes toward physicians. Titled *Journey of a Dying Man to the Other World,* the print depicts a wealthy doctor in black robes leading a procession that includes a dying man, a clergyman pointing up, a surgeon with a fluttering bat over his head, a sinister-looking apothecary carrying an enema device, and an undertaker. The solemn physician carries a banner that describes the traditional treatment for diseases: "To give a clyster [enema], after that to bleed, finally to purge."

Many sufferers looked for treatments opposed by ordinary doctors to cure their ailments. Homeopathy, which emphasized the use of herbal drugs and natural remedies, gained in popularity during the period. Other options—from vegetable laxatives, claimed to be effective for all ills, to faith healers—saw wide use. These alternatives at least gave sufferers a sense of controlling their own health.

Alternative medicine

As for surgery, people turned to this option only as a last resort. Surgical methods became safer in the first half of the nineteenth century, but anesthesia and antiseptics still lay in the future. Those who managed to survive the pain of an operation faced a likelihood of dying from an infection afterward.

Surgery

Promising Developments for Public Health

Despite all the dangers, the period had a few bright spots for the future of public health. Improvements in diet

probably held the most promise. Many nutritious foods had become more available than ever, especially potatoes, which were an affordable, rich source of vitamin C and minerals; dairy products, which helped newborns survive infancy and childhood; and meat, which contained high-grade proteins. Inexpensive cotton underwear, thanks to the new cotton mills, kept people warmer and cleaner than before. The smallpox vaccine, developed during the eighteenth century and made into a safe form in 1796 by Edward Jenner in England, would virtually erase a disease that had once afflicted almost 80 percent of Europeans and killed millions. The discovery of anesthetics—nitrous oxide and, after 1846, ether and chloroform—began to make surgical trauma bearable.

Other developments showed some potential as well. Following the lead of a small group of influential French physicians, European doctors applied scientific methods to medicine and made great strides in pathology and physiology. Hospitals proliferated and increasingly became places to observe the sick and gather information. New laboratories allowed doctors to conduct more experiments. Professional organizations and educational institutions for doctors and nurses formed, and governments, particularly in France, began taking some responsibility for medical education and licensing.

New developments in medicine

Many doctors no longer relied solely on a patient's description of the problem. Physical examinations became common—feeling the pulse, sounding the chest, taking the blood pressure, looking down the throat. Some doctors used the new stethoscope, which became a crucial tool for diagnosing bronchitis, pneumonia, and pulmonary tuberculosis (commonly called consumption). Among the upper classes, the family physician was even gaining some favor as a respected social contact and confidant.

In England, Edwin Chadwick (1800–1890) initiated a campaign to improve public health. In his 1842 report for a parliamentary commission, *The Sanitary Condition of the Laboring Population of Britain,* he emphasized that the accumulation of human and animal waste near people's dwellings was a crucial cause of disease. He proposed a system of underground tunnels that would allow constantly running water to carry waste out of the city.

Nevertheless, the gains from these promising new developments would not come until the second half of the nineteenth century. In Britain, one of every three people still died of contagious diseases in the decades surrounding 1850. Health, therefore, remained a great public and private concern. It was not the only concern that crossed the lines between public and private life, however. The day-to-day events in everybody's lives, whether in illness or health, unfolded within a crucial setting: the family. In this period of industrialization and urbanization, the family as an institution and the roles within it began to shift in the face of enormous economic and social pressures.

FAMILY IDEALS AND REALITIES

The ways that people come together into families and the roles they play in their families usually evolve slowly, if at all. During this period, however, the middle class redefined accepted notions of the family, and working-class families struggled under the new pressures beleaguering them. In subtle but important ways, family ideals and realities were changing.

Middle-Class Ideals: Affection, Children, and Privacy

With their numbers, wealth, and status in urban societies rising, the middle class not only developed its own ideas about what the proper family should be but also propagated those ideas as the norm for everyone else. The result was an evolution of, rather than a break from, old notions about the family. Compared with families of earlier times, the ideal middle-class family emphasized emotional bonds, attention to children, and privacy.

People were supposed to marry because of affection, love, and emotional compatibility. Social rank and wealth remained important, but these values exerted less influence than they had in the past. Love could bridge social and economic gaps. Indeed, one of the great themes in the flood of new novels that appeared during the nineteenth century centered on this very conflict: the tension between love and money in marriage. In stories that ended happily, love won out—though most characters in these plots never were relegated to a life of poverty as a consequence of their choice.

The new middle-class family was smaller and more child centered than before. Europeans were choosing to limit the size of their families, and by mid-century this preference led to declining rates of population growth. Women gave birth to fewer children—two or

three rather than the five or six of an earlier era—and more infants than ever survived the first, riskiest years of life. Unlike workers and peasants, middle-class parents did not have to view their children as economic assets—as hands to work the fields, help with the crafts, or labor in the factories. Wealthier urban parents could afford to raise perhaps just two or three children as fulfilling products of a good home. More than ever, children came to be seen as innocent, impressionable, vulnerable persons who should be separated from the corrupting influences of adult society. Mothers and fathers began investing more time, effort, and other resources in child rearing. Boys, especially, needed training and education designed to ensure their success as adults in the changing urban world. To arm them with these essentials, parents extended the time period of childhood and economic dependence. All this required planning and intensified emotional ties between parents and children. Parents increasingly centered their attention and family activities on children.

More than ever, mothers and fathers idealized their home as a private "haven in a heartless world," separate from and above the world of paid work. The home represented the reward for competing on the job—a protected, glorified place for a satisfying personal life. There husband and wife could enjoy the delights of material possessions and, hopefully, the rewarding intimacy of family life. As indicated by the growing number of popular books by authors such as Jane Austen (1775–1817), Mary Ann Evans (1819–1880) (writing under the pen name George Eliot), and Charlotte Brontë (1816–1855), home was a setting of many appealing, moralizing dramas where the virtues of prudence, love, sacrifice, self-reliance, and persistence could usually overcome all obstacles.

Separate Spheres: Changing Roles for Middle-Class Women and Men

With the rise of industrialization and urban life, the roles of middle-class husbands and wives grew more and more separate. In the seventeenth and eighteenth centuries, most middle-class families had worked together as one economic unit—sharing the responsibilities of running a shop or business and living near their place of work in back rooms, upstairs, or next door. During the nineteenth century, the tasks assigned to men and women, and the private world of home and the public place of paid work, became increasingly distinct. As the locus of work shifted from the home to the factory, store, or office, women lost their traditional employments that contributed to

Family size

Children

The home

Marriage

FIGURE 17.11 Carolus Duran, *The Merrymakers* Children became the center of domestic life for middle-class families of the industrial age.

Women faced a very different set of cultural expectations. A host of marriage manuals, medical tracts, advice books, and religious dictates reminded women that their place was within the domestic sphere. A woman should provide emotional The woman's domestic sphere support for her husband and cultivate a virtuous home environment to counteract the amoral, competitive marketplace. She should care for the children, make sure the house was clean and the meals served, supervise domestic servants (a requirement for any middle-class home), and manage other domestic tasks, from sewing to administering household accounts.

In the mid-nineteenth-century painting shown in **Figure 17.11,** Carolus Duran depicts two middle-class women at home. The center of the women's attention, and the painting, is a playful child sitting on her mother's lap and reaching for a pet bird or figurine. Across the table from the two well-dressed women, a maid or house servant leans toward the child with a folded paper figurine, perhaps in mock play with the bird. On the lower right are more petlike figurines. Indeed, middle-class families often considered pets as much a part of domestic life as the food and drink on the table.

In some ways, a middle-class woman's domestic sphere extended outside the home. She might manage the family's social life, for example, or lead in religious matters. If she had the time and means, she might also participate in philanthropic activities, social movements such as temperance or the abolition of slavery, and certain cultural events—but only as long as these activities added to her image as virtuous, dutiful, maternal, supportive, and sensitive. These activities put women in a position of power as representatives of the family in religious, social, and cultural matters and often gave them the last word on such matters within the family.

Involvement in politics was out of the question for most women. A few middle-class women joined movements to gain political and legal rights, but their efforts did not lead to real reforms during this period. Nor did paid work fit the domestic image. Although a woman might serve without wages as a clerk or secretary in her husband's store or office, paid work outside the home was considered inappropriate and generally not available to married women. Even for unmarried women, only occupations directly connected to the domestic role, such as governess, elementary school teacher, lady's companion, or seller of women's clothing, were deemed acceptable. There were exceptions, especially in cultural fields such as painting and writing, but most people raised a skeptical, disapproving eyebrow at women who had such careers.

At home, a wife was expected to be the counterpart to her controlled, strong husband. "In every

the family economy. Paid employees working outside the home now occupied the role previously played by women who had run thriving family businesses. The new economic growth also allowed middle-class families to afford the homes, servants, and leisure previously reserved for the elite. Eventually, the ability of middle-class women to devote more time to their homes and families without having to do paid work, and to hire servants to lighten domestic burdens, became symbols of social success. The home became women's sphere, and within the home, child rearing began requiring far more maternal attention than ever. As the task of raising children and socializing them with the values and training needed for success expanded, so did the responsibilities of motherhood. Becoming "rational mothers," fully able to meet the new demands of child rearing, turned into a revered duty.

The man was supposed to be the respected economic provider who operated primarily in his sphere: the competitive world of work outside the home. He was expected to behave in an authoritative, competent, and controlled manner. These qualities reflected the legal and economic realities of the time. Under British common law and the Napoleonic Code on the Continent, for example, a man had legal authority over his wife and children. He also had control over his wife's personal property as well as over any money earned by her. Furthermore, only men could vote. Most positions in the middle-class world of work were reserved for men. Those jobs usually required specialized skills in planning and information managing—abilities that came primarily from formal schooling. Young men were more likely than women to receive a formal education in areas of study such as accounting or law. Through apprenticeships and clerkships in commerce, industry, or finance, men also found many opportunities to equip themselves for success in the growing industrial-urban economy.

The man's sphere

thing . . . that women attempt, they should show their consciousness of dependence" on men, explained Elizabeth Poole Sandford in her widely read book, *Woman in Her Social and Domestic Character* (1842). Law hindered most married women from acquiring economic independence and generally placed them, as well as children, under the formal power and protection of men. Women were to be emotional and even frail, and therefore capable of only domestic tasks. The training of young women reinforced these qualities. Instead of a secondary schooling or professional education, women's formal training focused on religion, music, and perhaps languages. Any other skills a young woman might need, she picked up at home.

Educators and scientists generally agreed that women were ill suited for occupations outside the home and that they lacked the emotional control, mental acuity, and assertiveness of men. Doctors usually held the same views, and even believed that menstruation incapacitated women and that women had no interest in sex. Clothing, too, emphasized this vision of women's proper role. Middle-class husbands wore prudent and practical clothing for the world of work—trousers and jackets in modest black or gray. Their wives endured tight corsets and full decorative skirts more suited for display than action.

In short, the middle-class ideal was a small, private family bonded by love and authority. In such a family, the wife and husband willingly fulfilled the expected roles of their separate spheres. Families measured their success in achieving this ideal by the luxury items they bought, collected, and self-consciously displayed; by the accomplishments of their children; by how well their lives matched the uplifting dramas that the novels and paintings of the day depicted; and by their participation in appropriate social, religious, and philanthropic activities.

Middle-class success is well illustrated by the economic and social rise of wealthy commercial and industrial families such as the Cadburys (see Biography on pages 572–573). The 1824 drawing by E. Wall Cousins in **Figure 17.12** shows the still-modest Cadbury shops on Bull Street in Birmingham. To the right is Richard's original dry-goods (linens) store; to the left, his son John's tea and coffee shop. The plate-glass windows and the dress of people on the street indicate the store's intention to appeal to middle-class and wealthy clients. Above are the family's apartments, which include plants and pets. When the business expanded, the Cadburys moved away from this store to a suburban house, with separate nursery and schoolrooms for the children. The idea of separate rooms for children, and for eating, cooking, reading, and socializing, was new and reflected the growing wealth of the middle class and how the idea of differentiation—separate areas for

Middle-class success

different tasks and the division of labor—already spreading in the industrial world affected the domestic sphere as well.

Working-Class Realities

The middle class assumed that its vision of the proper family served as the standard for all. However, this vision did not fit the urban and industrial realities facing the far more numerous working classes.

Industrialization pulled many working-class women away from their homes and into factory jobs. Employers preferred to hire women because they worked for lower salaries and seemed more pliable than men. In the early decades, young children often accompanied their mothers, providing even cheaper labor and falling victim to the harsh, disciplined factory environment. During the 1830s and 1840s, public outcry against child labor (led by middle-class reformers, not the working class) prompted women to leave their younger children at home in the care of an older child or neglectful "babyfarmers," women who took in far too many children. Many mothers resorted to drugging their children with laudanum to keep them out of harm's way while the adults were at work.

Women workers

Middle-class critics demanded reforms that would limit women's ability to work away from home, although working-class women objected that they had no better alternatives. As one group of women factory workers from Manchester pointed out, "Hand loom has been almost totally superseded by power loom weaving, and no inconsiderable number of females, who must depend on their own exertions, . . . have been forced . . . into the manufactories, from their total inability to earn a livelihood at home." During recessions, women's plight worsened. Employers laid off the more highly paid men first, leaving women with the overwhelming burden of managing both a paid job and all the domestic tasks at home.

Working-class and peasant families were being pulled apart in other ways as well. Adolescent boys left home to seek work in the mines or cities. Daughters, too, sought jobs as factory laborers or as domestics in middle- or upper-class homes. In the cities, women were all the more vulnerable during economic downturns when low-paying jobs disappeared.

Prostitution

Hard times left unmarried and married women alike in particularly desperate straits. To survive, some women turned to prostitution, which grew along with Europe's mushrooming cities. In 1850, there were probably some 30,000 prostitutes in Paris and 50,000 in London. Unemployment and the dangers of solitude were probably the main forces driving women

BIOGRAPHY

The Cadburys

A Rising

Middle-Class

Family

By the late eighteenth century, the Cadburys were a well-established Quaker family of shopkeepers in western England. Young Richard Tapper Cadbury used his father's connections to find positions as an apprentice and journeyman to drapers (selling retail cloth and dry goods) in Gloucester and London. In 1794, his father helped him again, giving him money to start his own cloth and dry goods store on a main street in Birmingham, one of Britain's leading industrial cities.

In 1800, Richard, his wife, Elizabeth, and their growing family moved into an apartment above their shop on Bull Street. Middle-class families such as the Cadburys typically lived in the same building as their business until they could afford to buy a separate home. Elizabeth Cadbury, like most middle-class women of moderate means, worked in the family enterprise but had received no professional training. She picked up skills on the job, helping rather than leading, and taking over for her husband when he was away. As a married woman, Elizabeth had no independent legal identity and could not have owned a business on her own. Formally, their family business belonged to Richard, but like many businesses during the period, it also functioned as an informal partnership between the couple. In addition to working in the business, Elizabeth was also responsible for running the household, which included eight children and young apprentices.

Draper retailers such as the Cadbury family played a major role in the revolution of Britain's textile industries. Like producers, retailers benefited from the new sources of supply and expanding demand for cloth. The Cadbury shop expanded and brought in enough income for Richard and Elizabeth to rent a house and land for a garden on the outskirts of Birmingham in 1812. The younger children, their nurse, and their pets moved there. Elizabeth and her older daughters traveled back and forth, managing the two households.

Richard and Elizabeth's sons eventually apprenticed in retail businesses in different cities—Benjamin as a draper, John as a tea and coffee dealer. The daughters had no such training. Instead, they learned what they could from their mother as they helped in the shop, house, and garden.

John (1801–1889) opened a tea and coffee store next door to his parents' shop (see **Figure 17.12**). He and his first wife, who died in 1828, lived over the shop. When John accumulated enough money, he also opened a plant to manufacture the cocoa and chocolate for which the family name would become so famous. In 1834, John and his second wife, Candia, moved their home away from the city, with its filth and crowds, to a new, planned

to prostitution. Many prostitutes had come from outside the cities and had no family to help them. Others were out-of-work domestics, seamstresses in need of income during a slow season, daughters of unemployed workers, or women abandoned after being impregnated by masters or lovers. Low wages also led to prostitution; a woman earned as much money in one night prostituting herself as she could acquire in an entire week of work at the factory.

Many of these women worked as prostitutes for relatively short periods, and only part-time. While the work helped them financially, it also exposed them to venereal disease, which ran rampant during this period. Finally, in some people's minds, prostitution linked working-class women to images of urban crime and immorality. To middle-class moralists, prostitutes embodied unrestrained sexuality and therefore were the ultimate outcasts. However, despite its dangers, prostitution would persist as a sign of the difficulties that many working families faced in Europe's growing cities.

Stress and Survival in the Working Classes

The new tensions swirling through working-class family life had severe consequences for some. Peasant, artisan, and working-class families had worked together as economic units for longer than the middle class had, and industrialization and urbanization corroded this unity. The stresses proved so great that some families broke apart, leaving a growing number of women to work and manage households on their own.

However, the picture was not all bleak. As a rule, the family survived, providing a haven for workers and a home for children. Like peasants' and artisans' families, many working-class families clung to the old putting-out system or the newer piecework system, in which entrepreneurs distributed jobs, such as tailoring or decorating, to workers at their homes. Unions, better wages, and new social policies would ease the burdens on workers in the decades after 1850. In the end, most families adjusted and found ways to meet the many challenges of the industrial age.

middle-class suburb just outside of Birmingham. Candia generally stayed at home, busy with her domestic tasks and gardening, while John rode to town every day to take care of business and political affairs. Candia could not look after the family business as her mother-in-law, Elizabeth, had, for the demands of child rearing had grown and the training necessary for John's more complex business had increased. John's and Candia's spheres were much more distinct than the elder Cadburys' had been.

In 1861, John's sons, Richard and George, took over their father's failing business. They visited a chocolate factory in Holland that was using a new process to transform cocoa beans into cocoa and chocolate. In 1866, they successfully introduced that process into their own factory. This new technique helped them to break the near monopoly that French chocolate products had previously enjoyed in the British market. In the decades that followed, the brothers built Cadbury into a prosperous cocoa and chocolate manufacturing firm. Richard painted the designs for

FIGURE 17.12 E. Wall Cousins, *The Cadbury Shops,* 1824

fancy Cadbury chocolate boxes that idealized children and their innocence, using his own children as models.

In 1879, the brothers moved their firm from industrialized Birmingham to a rural site they called Bournville. There they introduced improved conditions for their workers and a private social security program, reforms well ahead of their time. George, holding firmly to the Quaker

views of his parents and grandparents, had long taught in a Birmingham "adult school" for workingmen. Concluding that poor housing lay at the root of many social evils, he began building high-quality working-class housing that featured gardens. By 1900, that community included 313 houses and served as a model for British "garden cities" and "garden suburbs."

In 1901, George and members of his family acquired the *London Daily News* and other newspapers, which they used to express their Liberal Party views. By this time, Cadbury, which had grown unevenly from the seeds planted by Richard and Elizabeth in 1794, had become a vast, worldwide company.

Connecting People & Society

1. Why did the Cadburys benefit so greatly from the industrial revolution?

2. In what ways did members of the family exhibit typical nineteenth-century middle-class values?

3. In what ways did the roles played by Elizabeth and Candia differ?

LOOKING BACK & MOVING FORWARD

Summary   Industrialization meant unprecedented, sustained economic growth, and it soon became a measure of whether people considered a society "modern" or "traditional." Carrying in its wake fundamental changes in literally all aspects of life, industrialization altered the ways people worked, what they could buy, how they lived their lives, and where they stood on the social ladder. Its railroads, dams, bridges, factories, and mines transformed the land, the rivers, and the air. Nations that industrialized left others behind in the competition for wealth. That wealth was all too easily translated into power, leaving traditional agrarian societies in the West vulnerable to their industrialized neighbors.

The new riches pumped out by the machines of industry also propelled the West into an even stronger position to dominate over unindustrialized, non-Western societies throughout the world. Decade after decade, a widening gap of wealth and power opened up between the industrializing regions of the West and nonindustrializing regions of Asia, Africa, and Latin America.

KEY TERMS

industrial revolution,   *p. 547*

entrepreneurs,   *p. 552*

factory system,   *p. 554*

Luddism,   *p. 563*

At the same time, the cities grew. There, old ties to traditional communities and beliefs loosened; long-established religions even lost some of their influence. Despite a host of social problems, the cities had a vibrancy and an image of opportunity that continued to attract people. While some people lost when they migrated to the cities, others gained, whether by hard work, luck, or the advantages of birth. Perhaps life in the countryside, with its slower pace and simpler pleasures, simply could not compete with what the city promised.

Through these decades, most families found ways to adapt to new circumstances. Middle-class families responded to their improving positions by developing a compelling new set of ideals about how men and women should behave. Working-class families did their best to hold themselves together in the face of divisive forces; looking to the future, workers began seeing themselves as a new class of people who just might have the power to determine their own fate.

This growing awareness by both classes added to the fundamental changes being wrought by industrialism. Conflict—whether in an intellectual realm, at the work site, in the courts, or on the barricades—would often be the result. These conflicts, along with those stemming from the French Revolution, would profoundly shape social and political life in the West in the decades to come.

REVIEW, ANALYZE, & CONNECT TO TODAY

REVIEW THE PREVIOUS CHAPTER

Chapter 16—"Overturning the Political and Social Order"—examined the revolution that transformed France and whose consequences were felt throughout the West. The chapter also focused on the role Napoleon played during that period and the battles he waged throughout Europe until his final defeat in 1815.

1. Who do you think were the main beneficiaries of the French Revolution and the industrial revolution? Were they the same groups?

2. In what ways might the French Revolution and the industrial revolution be related?

ANALYZE THIS CHAPTER

Chapter 17—"Factories, Cities, and Families in the Industrial Age"—analyzes the industrial revolution and urbanization.

1. How do you explain why Britain industrialized before other European nations and non-Western societies such as China?

2. Compare the consequences of industrialization for the middle class and the working class.

3. In what ways did moving from the countryside to the city change people's lives during this period?

4. Analyze how the family and ideas about women's and men's roles altered within the middle class. In what ways were circumstances different for working-class families?

CONNECT TO TODAY

Think about the economic changes that industrialization brought, as well as the social consequences that followed in its wake.

1. Why might some people living in nonindustrialized countries today fear the prospect that their country might be industrialized—or have regrets when industrialization begins?

2. How might the changes involved in industrialization—such as the shift to factory production, technological advancement, and improved transportation—have influenced the globalization that we are experiencing today?

BEYOND THE CLASSROOM

THE INDUSTRIAL REVOLUTION BEGINS

Allen, Robert C. *The British Industrial Revolution in Global Perspective.* Cambridge: Cambridge University Press, 2009. An analysis of why the industrial revolution originated in Britain and not elsewhere.

Bayly, C.A. *The Birth of the Modern World, 1780–1914: Global Connections and Comparisons.* London: Blackwell, 2004. A highly regarded comparative approach to the period.

Landes, David. *The Wealth and Poverty of Nations.* New York: W.W. Norton, 1999. Connects cultures to economic development in a broad international context.

GLOBAL CONNECTIONS

Pomeranz, Kenneth. *The Great Divergence: China, Europe, and the Making of the Modern World Economy.* Princeton, NJ: Princeton University Press, 2000. A bold comparison of economic development in Europe and Asia.

NEW MARKETS, MACHINES, AND POWER

Deane, Phyllis. *The First Industrial Revolution*, 2nd ed. Cambridge: Cambridge University Press, 1979. A respected account of British industrialization and its consequences.

Landes, David S. *The Unbound Prometheus: Technological Change and Industrial Development in Western Europe from 1750 to the Present.* London: Cambridge University Press, 1969. A classic treatment of technological development in a broad social and economic context.

Mokyr, Joel. *The Lever of Riches: Technological Creativity and Economic Progress.* New York: Oxford University Press, 1992. An attempt to explain why technological creativity occurred in some places and not in others.

INDUSTRIALIZATION SPREADS TO THE CONTINENT

Pollard, Sidney. *Peaceful Conquest: The Industrialization of Europe, 1760–1970.* Oxford: Oxford University Press, 1981. Charts the process of industrialization as it spread from Britain to the European continent.

Stearns, Peter. *The Industrial Revolution in World History.* New York: Westview Press, 1998. A wide-ranging interpretation.

BALANCING THE BENEFITS AND BURDENS OF INDUSTRIALIZATION

Chinn, Carl. *Poverty Amidst Prosperity: The Urban Poor in England, 1834–1914.* Manchester: Manchester University Press, 1995. Focuses on the poverty created by the industrial revolution.

Gray, Robert. *The Factory Question and Industrial England, 1830–1860.* Cambridge: Cambridge University Press, 2002. An examination of the controversy over industrialization.

Thompson, E.P. *The Making of the English Working Class.* New York: Random House, 1966. A remarkable book of sympathy and insight that has been hugely controversial and influential.

LIFE IN THE GROWING CITIES

Lawton, Richard, and Robert Lee, eds. *Urban Population Development in Western Europe from the Late Eighteenth to the Early Twentieth Century.* Liverpool: Liverpool University Press, 1989. Examines urban growth throughout western Europe.

Traugott, Mark, ed. *The French Worker: Autobiographies from the Early Industrial Era.* Berkeley: University of California Press, 1993. Presents a working-class perspective on the effects of industrialization.

PUBLIC HEALTH AND MEDICINE IN THE INDUSTRIAL AGE

Porter, Roy. *A Medical History of Humanity.* New York: W.W. Norton, 1998. A wide-ranging and interesting survey that covers the period well.

FAMILY IDEALS AND REALITIES

Honeyman, Katrina. *Women, Gender and Industrialization in England, 1700–1850.* New York: St. Martin's Press, 2000. Analyzes connections between work and gender roles.

Maynes, Mary Jo. *Taking the Hard Road.* Chapel Hill: University of North Carolina Press, 1995. Examines German and French workers' lives during the industrial revolution.

Tilly, Louise, and Joan Scott. *Women, Work and Family.* New York: Holt, Rinehart and Winston, 1978. A classic study of the family as an economic unit, especially during the first half of the nineteenth century.

ANTON ZIEGLER, *THE BARRICADE IN MICHAELER SQUARE*
ON THE NIGHT OF MAY 26TH, 1848
This painting by the Austrian artist Anton Ziegler depicts the "glory days" of the 1848
revolutions. In the image, men and women of various classes in Vienna guard a revolutionary
barricade made of paving stones, timbers, and carts. Behind the barricade, a community of
people stands ready to help one another politely in the common effort (notice the man aiding a
woman across a wooden footbridge). The atmosphere has an almost festive quality, and nothing
in the picture hints at the violence and loss of life that came with this turbulent year.

Coping with Change

18

Ideology, Politics, and Revolution, 1815–1850

Prince Clemens von Metternich (1773–1859), Austria's conservative and powerful minister of foreign affairs, discussed ideas in candlelit salons as easily as he wielded power in somber cabinet meetings. Like other cosmopolitan aristocrats born into traditional eighteenth-century societies, he spoke French as well as the German of his birthplace. In 1820, five years after the fall of Napoleon, he wrote to his ally Tsar Alexander I (r. 1801–1825) of Russia. "Kings have to calculate the chances of their very existence in the immediate future," he complained. "Passions are let loose and league together to overthrow everything which society respects as the basis of its existence; religion, public morality, laws, customs, rights, and duties, all are attacked, confounded, overthrown, or called to question."

Metternich, Alexander I, and people everywhere were struggling to adjust to the political and social forces unleashed by the French Revolution and Napoleon's domination of Europe. The industrial revolution, wherever it set its roots, spawned another set of problems along with the wealth it created. Together, these waves of change were undermining traditional political, social, and economic orders.

Some, such as Metternich, fought to maintain the old order; others, displaying the "passions" Metternich complained about, fought for all-encompassing reforms. People on all sides turned to ideologies—sets of ideas, attitudes, and beliefs about how the world is and should be—to try to cope with the new realities of Western life in the nineteenth century. One of those realities was the possibility of revolution again raising its unpredictable head. The outcomes of these struggles of ideologies and politics would profoundly shape much of nineteenth-century history.

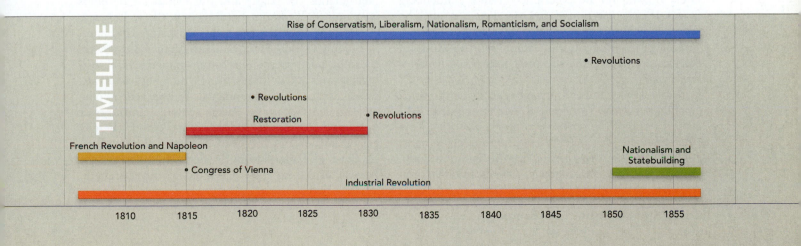

TIMELINE

Rise of Conservatism, Liberalism, Nationalism, Romanticism, and Socialism

• Revolutions

• Revolutions

Restoration

• Revolutions

French Revolution and Napoleon

Nationalism and Statebuilding

• Congress of Vienna

Industrial Revolution

1810   1815   1820   1825   1830   1835   1840   1845   1850   1855

THE CONGRESS OF VIENNA: A GATHERING OF VICTORS

In the autumn of 1814, the leaders of the powers who had finally vanquished Napoleon gathered to redraw territorial boundaries and fashion a lasting peace. The conference also attracted representatives of every state in Europe, hundreds of dispossessed princes, agents of every interest, and adventurers. Nearly everyone who thought he or she was somebody of importance in high circles attended. The representatives reveled in the glittering gatherings and entertainments. In addition to the public conferences, many private meetings took place—though just how private remains uncertain, for Austrian spies regularly opened letters and searched wastebaskets. Elsewhere, in newspapers from St. Petersburg, Rome, and Paris to London and even Boston, people closely followed the daily events in the beautiful Austrian capital. Something immensely important and exciting seemed to be unfolding there.

The four major victors over Napoleon—Great Britain, Prussia, Russia, and Austria—set peace terms with France around the time of Napoleon's overthrow in April, and these four dominated the congress. The able Lord Castlereagh (1769–1822) represented Great Britain and the experienced Baron Hardenberg (1750–1822) represented Prussia. Russia's tsar, the unsteady Alexander I, headed his own delegation. The elegant, arrogant Metternich led the Austrian delegation and became the most influential figure of the congress.

Jean-Baptiste Isabey's formal portrait of the principal figures at the Congress of Vienna (**Figure 18.1**) gives a sense of the seriousness of this event and the ideals that the victors represented. From left to right, Austria's polished Metternich stands before a chair, Great Britain's Castlereagh sits with crossed legs, and

The victors

the elderly Talleyrand (1754–1838) of France rests with his right arm on the table. In a fine but business-like eighteenth-century salon, these powerful men are gathered around a table to participate in the reading and signing of crucial documents. Their clothing marks them as members of the aristocracy: Almost all the men sport gold trim and knee breeches with high stockings; some wear military coats and carry swords reflecting victory in the field over Napoleon. Most display medals symbolizing their achievements and position. Yet these clothes also hint at change: Most of the figures in the painting lack the more elegant clothing and wigs of the eighteenth century. Above the men, as if approving of what they are doing, hangs a symbol of the restoration of the old regime: a portrait of a king draped in regal robes.

As guiding principles in the negotiations, the conferees decided on legitimacy and stability. By *legitimacy* they meant that territories should once more be placed under the control of the old ruling houses of the traditional order. By *stability* they meant establishing and maintaining a balance of power within Europe, with particular focus on restraining France. The main powers agreed that the settlement should apply to all of Europe.

Legitimacy and stability

Yet the conferees proved lenient in their settlement toward France. Thanks to the victors' desire to turn France into an ally rather than a resentful enemy and to Talleyrand's diplomatic skills, France, the original force behind all the turmoil, escaped the proceedings with only light penalties. Having already restored the French throne to the Bourbons, the powers merely reduced France roughly to its 1789 boundaries. Because of Napoleon's 100-day return (see page 542), they also required France to pay an indemnity of 700 million francs, return stolen art treasures, and submit to occupation by allied forces until the indemnity was paid.

To confine France within its frontiers and discourage future French aggression, the powers established strong buffer states along France's borders. As **Map 18.1** shows, Prussia received a sizable block of territory along the Rhine; the Austrian Netherlands (Belgium) and the Dutch Netherlands were unified; Piedmont-Sardinia in northern Italy was enlarged; and the old monarchy was restored in Spain.

Territorial arrangements

Trading among themselves, the four main powers took new territories. Great Britain gained several strategic islands and colonies, all of which boosted its sea power and overseas dominance. Prussia added some areas in central Europe. Russia acquired control over a reduced, nominally independent Poland, thereby edging farther into the heart of central Europe. Russia also took Finland from Sweden, which in turn got Norway at the expense of Napoleon's ally Denmark.

FIGURE 18.1 Jean-Baptiste Isabey, *The Congress of Vienna,* 1815 Isabey's painting shows the main diplomats and governmental officials who negotiated the peace settlement after the Napoleonic Wars and suggests the principles that guided their decisions.

Austria gained Lombardy and Venetia in northern Italy as well as the permanent presidency over the weak German Confederation—the thirty-nine German states that remained after Napoleon's destruction of the Holy Roman Empire.

Although they displayed little concern for the wishes of the peoples being placed under the control of one power or the other, the conferees did produce a settlement that contributed to a century of freedom from Europewide war. Moreover, thanks to the persistent efforts of the British, the powers agreed in principle to abolish the slave trade. They also achieved—at least temporarily—their conservative goals of promoting legitimacy and stability that meant so much to them.

The Concert of Europe: Securing the Vienna Settlement

Metternich and his colleagues, pleased with their handiwork, set up the political machinery for perpetuating the Vienna settlement. Conveniently at hand was the Holy Alliance, conceived by Alexander I to

establish and safeguard the principles of Christianity. Russia, Austria, and Prussia—the three bastions of conservatism—formed the nucleus of this alliance.

> **The Holy Alliance**

Though Metternich and professional diplomats put little faith in it, the Holy Alliance did symbolize a commitment to preserving the Vienna settlement. Perhaps more important, it suggested a possible willingness to intervene in other countries in support of its conservative principles.

The Quadruple Alliance, also known as the **Concert of Europe,** proved a much more earthly agency for perpetuating the Vienna settlement. Austria, Russia, Prussia, and Great Britain created this military alliance in November 1815 to

> **The Concert of Europe**

guarantee the Vienna settlement. The powers agreed to hold periodic meetings to discuss common problems. In 1818, France completed its payment of indemnities and joined the Alliance.

Soon this conservative partnership showed its strength. In 1821 it authorized an Austrian army to put down an insurrection in Naples against King

MAP 18.1

Europe, 1815

This map shows Europe after the Congress of Vienna in 1815.

Explore the Map

1. Compare this map with Map 16.4, on Napoleon's empire. What are the main changes that occurred in these years?

2. Locate the enlarged states—the Netherlands, Prussia, and Piedmont-Sardinia. Why did the Congress of Vienna strengthen these states?

3. Consider the effects of the settlement on the major European powers. Do you think the settlement severely punished France? Explain.

Ferdinand I. The Neapolitan liberal rebels, no match for the Austrian troops, were soon defeated and their leaders executed, imprisoned, or exiled. In 1822 the Alliance, despite Britain's withdrawal, authorized France to intervene against a liberal revolt in Spain. A French army streamed across the Pyrenees and easily crushed the rebellion. That same year, the conservative powers supported Alexander's proposal to send a Russian fleet to help put down the revolt of Spain's Latin American colonies (see Chapter 16).

The great strength of the Alliance, however, remained bound within the European continent. Across the Atlantic Ocean, President Monroe of the United States announced what would come to be called the Monroe Doctrine: The United States would regard any interference on the part of European powers in the affairs of the Western Hemisphere as an "unfriendly act." British support of the doctrine—stemming from Britain's own economic interests in Latin America—killed any further thought of Holy Alliance intervention in the Western Hemisphere, for Great Britain enjoyed unchallenged dominance of the seas.

IDEOLOGIES: HOW THE WORLD SHOULD BE

The principles underlying the settlement at Vienna and the international cooperation to enforce it reflected the deep conservatism of Metternich and many others during these years. Their conservatism was more than just a whim or political mood. Under the impact of the French Revolution and the industrial revolution, the centuries-old aristocratic order and agriculturally based society had started to crumble. Intellectuals in particular tried to grasp these changes by exploring ideologies, or sets of beliefs about the world and how it should be. These ideologies exerted immense power. People wrote, marched, fought, and died for them. Indeed, they fueled many of the struggles that would erupt in the years to come and ultimately would shape our very definition of the modern world.

Conservatism: Restoring the Traditional Order

The changes initiated during the French Revolution and supported by Enlightenment ideas threatened and even terrified conservatives. They wanted desperately to preserve the traditional way of life. **Conservatism** provided the ideas to refute Enlightenment and revolutionary principles and all those who stood behind them. At the heart of conservatism lay a belief in order and hierarchy. The social and political order, conservatives believed, should be based on a hierarchy of authoritative institutions whose legitimacy rested on God and tradition. As conservatives saw it, the revolutionary notion of equality was wrong. The elite were equipped to rule; the rest were not. The most formidable enemy was the bourgeoisie, "this intermediary class" ready to "abandon itself with a blind fury and animosity . . . to all the means which seem proper to assuage its thirst for power," according to Metternich. Conservatives also warned that the idea of individualism promoted by the Enlightenment and favored by the rising middle class would fragment society and lead to anarchy. In the mind of a conservative, all change was suspect. If change did come, it should take the form of slow evolution of social and political institutions.

In 1790, the influential Anglo-Irish writer and statesman Edmund Burke (1729–1797), horrified with the outbreak of the French Revolution, outlined some of the principles of conservatism (see page 524). He argued that the revolutionaries' radical reforms based on abstract reason and notions of equality unraveled hard-won victories against savagery: "[I]t is with infinite caution that any man ought to venture upon pulling down an edifice which has answered . . . for ages the common purposes of society." The monarchy and nobility should be preserved because they, like the church, were established links to an organic past and the best hopes for preserving the order necessary for societies to thrive.

The French writers Joseph de Maistre (1753–1821) and Louis de Bonald (1754–1840) represented a later generation of conservative thinkers who proved more rigid and ultraroyalist than Burke. As Document 18.1 suggests, they attacked everything about the French Revolution and Enlightenment as contrary to religion, order, and civilization. De Maistre called the French Revolution an "insurrection against God." Both writers argued that authority rightly rests in the monarchy and the church, both of which derive that authority from God. "When monarchy and Christianity are both attacked, society returns to savagery," declared de Bonald. These conservatives felt that deep down, humans were more wicked than good, more irrational than rational. Only the time-tested traditions and institutions could hold the bad impulses of humans in check. All means, including fear and violence, should be used to roll back the changes from the French revolutionary and Napoleonic periods and return to societies dominated by monarchs, aristocrats, and clergy.

Not surprisingly, people from these same three groups found conservatism most appealing. Conservatism also attracted many who believed in a Christian view of society, particularly members of the established churches rather than religious minorities. Some even

thinking about

DOCUMENTS

DOCUMENT 18.1

A Conservative Theorist Attacks Political Reform

Many conservatives resented the reforms sparked by the French Revolution. The extremely conservative theorist Joseph de Maistre was no exception. In the following excerpt from his Essay on the Generative Principle of Political Constitutions, *published in Russia in 1810 and then Paris in 1814, de Maistre attacks written constitutions and the reform of political institutions.*

Every thing brings us back to the general rule—*man cannot create a constitution; and no legitimate constitution can be written.* The collection of fundamental laws, which must essentially constitute a civil or religious society, never has been written, and never will be, *a priori.* It is only when society finds itself already constituted, without being able to say how, that it is possible to make known, or explain, in writing, certain special articles; but in almost every case these declarations or explanations are the effect of very great evils, and always cost the people more than they are worth.

. . . Not only does it not belong to man to create institutions, but it does not appear that his power, *unassisted,* extends even to change for the better institutions already established. . . . *Nothing* [says the philosopher, Origen] . . . *can be changed for the better among men, without God.* All men have a consciousness of this truth, without being in a state to explain it to themselves. Hence that instinctive aversion, in every good mind, to innovations. The word *reform,* in itself, and previous to all examinations, will be always suspected by wisdom, and the experience of every age justifies this sort of instinct.

. . . To apply these maxims to a particular case . . . the great question of parliamentary reform, which has agitated minds in England so powerfully, and for so long a time, I still find myself constrained to believe, that this idea is pernicious, and that if the English yield themselves too readily to it, they will have occasion to repent.

SOURCE: Scholars' Facsimiles & Reprints (New York: Delmar, 1977), reprinting of the edition of Joseph de Maistre, *Essay on the Generative Principle of Political Constitutions* (Boston: Little and Brown, 1847).

Analyze the Document

1. On what basis does de Maistre object to written constitutions?

2. Would any political reforms have merit, according to de Maistre?

3. Why might de Maistre be so concerned about "parliamentary reform"?

saw the revolutionary and Napoleonic periods as divine retribution for the presumption and evil that had long marred human beings. In the international field, conservatism was epitomized by Metternich's policies, the Holy Alliance, and the Concert of Europe. In domestic policies, this conservatism was characterized by the restoration of power to the traditional monarchs and aristocrats, the renewed influence of Christianity, and the suppression of liberal and nationalistic movements.

Appeal of conservatism

However, conservatives faced formidable opponents, even during the early years after the fall of Napoleon. The French Revolution had turned the ideas of liberalism into a powerful, persistent force. The clash between conservatism and liberalism had just begun and would endure into the twentieth century.

Liberalism: Individual Freedom and Political Reform

In contrast to conservatism, **liberalism** drew on the promises of the French Revolution and the Enlightenment. Conservatives sought to maintain traditional society; liberals fought to change it. Liberals wanted a society that promoted individual freedom, or liberty.

However, many laws, customs, and conditions of the traditional order stood in their way. Liberals therefore opposed the dominance of politics and society by monarchs, aristocrats, and clergy, and governments' arbitrary interference with individual liberty. To the extent that these elements of the traditional order remained in place, liberals demanded reform and fought resisting conservatives.

From the Enlightenment and the theories of John Locke, liberals adopted ideas about natural laws, natural rights, toleration, and the application of reason to human affairs (see Chapter 14). From political thinkers such as Montesquieu, they took the idea that governmental powers should be separated and restricted by checks and balances. From the French and American revolutions, they drew on the principles of freedom, equality before the law, popular sovereignty, and the sanctity of property.

Sources of liberalism

Liberalism reflected the aspirations of the middle class, which was gaining wealth but lacked political and social power in the traditional order. Not surprisingly, then, liberals advocated government limited by written constitutions, the elimination of political and social privileges, and extension of voting rights to men of some property and education (most liberals stopped short of suggesting universal male suffrage or extension of the vote to women.) In addition, liberals desired representative institutions where none existed and an extension of the right to participate in representative institutions that remained the preserve of the aristocratic and wealthy elite. They demanded that governments guarantee the sanctity of property and individual rights, such as freedom of the press, speech, assembly, and religion.

Certain economic policies also had great importance to liberals and reflected the stake that the middle class had in commerce and industry. The Scottish economist Adam Smith (1723–1790) formulated the ideas that guided economic liberalism (see page 469). In *The Wealth of Nations* (1776), Smith argued that economics, like the physical world, had its own natural laws. The most basic economic law was of supply and demand, he explained. When left to operate alone, economic laws, like an "invisible hand," would keep the economy in balance and, in the long run, create the most wealth. According to Smith, self-interest—even greed—was the engine that motivated people to work hard and produce wealth: "It is not from the benevolence of the butcher, the brewer, or the baker that we expect our dinner, but from their regard to their own interest." Governments should therefore follow a policy of laissez-faire (hands-off), limiting their involvement in the economy to little more than maintaining law and order so that an unfettered marketplace could flourish.

Other liberal economic thinkers extended Smith's ideas. The British economist Thomas Malthus (1766–1834) cast gloom on hopes for progress among workers. He argued that population would always increase more than food supplies, resulting in poverty and death by "the whole train of common disease, and epidemics, wars, plague and famine." Malthus concluded that workers themselves were "the cause of their own poverty," because they lacked the moral discipline to avoid sexual activity. The politically influential Englishman David Ricardo (1772–1823) refined Malthus's arguments into the "iron law of wages," explaining that wages would always sink to subsistence levels or below because higher salaries just caused workers to multiply, thereby glutting the labor market and lowering wages. He emphasized that the economy was controlled by objective laws. The lessons for these "classical" liberals (to distinguish them from modern American liberals, who usually favor government programs to regulate certain economic and social affairs) were clear: no intervention in economic matters by government, no tariffs or unions that artificially raise prices or wages, and no restrictions on individual enterprise.

Over time, liberalism evolved and developed several variations. The English philosopher Jeremy Bentham (1748–1832) and his followers advocated a kind of liberalism that became particularly influential in Britain. Known as utilitarianism, it held that all activities and policies should be judged by the standard of usefulness. "Nature has placed mankind under the governance of two sovereign masters, *pain* and *pleasure*," explained Bentham. What was useful, the utilitarians decreed, was what created more pleasure than pain; the best laws and policies were therefore those that promoted "the greatest good for the greatest number" of people. Bentham's utilitarians fought for more governmental intervention in economic and social affairs than other liberals. For example, they supported reforms to protect women and children workers in factories and to improve urban sanitation. Democracy was implicit in utilitarianism, for the best way for the greatest number to maximize their own happiness was for each person to vote. Nevertheless, most liberals during this period actually opposed democracy. They feared the supposedly unruly "masses" and hoped to keep government in the hands of the propertied and well educated. They would not start to embrace democratic reforms until the middle of the nineteenth century. At that time, some of them, such as John Stuart Mill (1806–1873) (see Biography), would also begin arguing for major social programs to protect workers and even the right to vote for women.

As we saw earlier, liberalism appealed especially to the rising middle classes, who were prospering from commerce and industry and wanted political power along with their growing wealth and confidence. Liberals had faith that history was on their side, that liberalism, like progress, was inevitable and that the forces they opposed were of the past. That optimism gave them strength to fight against the conservative forces of tradition and rally to protect their gains.

Nationalism: A Common Identity and National Liberation

Like the liberals, nationalists harbored a spirit of optimism. They, too, were aroused by the French Revolution, for it promoted the idea that sovereignty rested not in a monarch or a church but in the people, and that they, banded together, constituted the nation. **Nationalism** promised to unify nations, liberate subject peoples from foreign rule, create a sense of fraternity among members of a national community, and lead that community to a common destiny. At its core was a feeling of cultural identity among distinct groups of people who shared a common language and traditions and who belonged in a nation-state of their own.

France became an early source of nationalist sentiments. There a sense of membership in the state

BIOGRAPHY

John Stuart Mill & Harriet Taylor
(1806–1873)   (1807–1858)

John Stuart Mill and Harriet Taylor were one of the most famous and extraordinary couples of the nineteenth century. Born in 1806, John described his own childhood as "remarkable." His father, the well-known liberal philosopher James Mill (1773–1836), raised John according to the cut-and-dried principles of Jeremy Bentham's utilitarianism. John learned Greek at the age of 3, Latin when he was 7, logic at 12, and economics at 13.

On their daily walks, James encouraged little John to summarize assigned readings for him. He wanted to turn John's mind into a logical machine for radical thought and utilitarian reform.

Extraordinary

Victorians

In 1822, John and several other young men founded the liberal Utilitarian Society. John, like other liberals, had great faith in the power of knowledge and reason to right human errors: "Knowledge has triumphed. It has worked the downfall of much that is mischievous." For the young Mill, utilitarianism was virtually "a religion." In 1823, John took his first job with the East India Company, the vehicle of British rule in India. He would remain with that company for thirty-five years, reading dispatches from the company's agents in India and drafting replies.

In 1826 he suffered a "crisis." Recoiling from his sterile, intellectualized upbringing, John came to doubt the value of his education and ambition, concluding that neither of these qualities led to happiness. He turned to romanticism—a movement that featured the lush music and especially the writings of Wordsworth, Goethe, and other cultural icons of the day. In time, he came to believe that "poetry is higher than logic, and . . . the union of the two is philosophy."

During these same years, 19-year-old Harriet Hardy had married John Taylor, a wealthy partner in a wholesale drug firm. Taylor adored his intellectual wife, who was bolder and more brilliant than he. However, after giving birth to two children, Harriet began to lose interest in John. She increasingly found sex with him an unpleasant imposition and criticized marriage as a sexual contract that was unfair to women.

In 1830 Harriet Taylor and John Stuart Mill met. They became "intimate and confidential friends." Mill was a constant visitor to the Taylor household and a frequent companion to Harriet in London. Although their relationship created a scandal in London society, John Taylor, unwilling to see his wife unhappy, acquiesced in it.

In 1843, Mill published *A System of Logic,* the first of several major works that marked him as one of the leading thinkers of the nineteenth century. In 1851, Harriet published anonymously *The Enfranchisement of Women,* which argued for universal suffrage and more equal companionship between men and women. Mill would go on to publish *On Liberty* (1859), his most famous political work, in which he argued for freedom of thought and warned against the tyranny of the majority. In 1869, he published *The Subjection of Women,* which made him one of the leading feminists of the century. It is fundamentally wrong, he said, for society to "ordain that to be born a girl instead of a boy, any more than to be born black instead of white, or a commoner instead of a nobleman, shall decide the person's position through all life."

Mill was happy to describe most of his works as jointly produced by himself and Harriet. But Mill may have been too generous in his praise of her role.

---

became especially important when the Revolution transformed the kingdom into a nation. Popular sovereignty, wider political participation, and the abolition of old provincial boundary lines gave the French a feeling of solidarity among themselves and with the national government. Universal conscription into the revolutionary armies added to feelings of fraternity in a righteous cause and helped make those armies strong. Powerful new symbols, such as the tricolor flag, stood for national unity and willingness to sacrifice for the sake of the nation.

> **The French Revolution**

Nationalism also moved people who did not yet share a state. In the German-speaking areas, for example, scholars and intellectuals developed a cultural basis for nationalism. Writers such as Johann Gottfried von Herder (1744–1803) fostered a sense of common national identity arising from German folk culture and oral traditions. Georg Wilhelm Friedrich Hegel (1770–1831) provided philosophical and historical bases for German nationalism and the importance of the national state. Romantics such as Ernst Moritz Arndt (1769–1860) urged Prussians, Austrians, Bavarians, and others with common roots to "be Germans, be one, will to be one by love and loyalty, and no devil will vanquish you." Groups and secret societies such as Young Germany—usually composed of students, intellectuals, and members of the middle class—promoted a sense of national identity and unity.

> **Cultural nationalism**

In Italy, Poland, and elsewhere, nationalists formed similar organizations and intellectuals created interest in national languages and folk culture.

FIGURE 18.2 John Stuart Mill

Just how much she contributed has long been a matter of heated debate. In 1849, two discreet years after John Taylor's death, Mill and Harriet Taylor married. They were proud that their relationship was based on rationality, intellectual companionship, affection, and intimacy, but not sex. They imagined their marriage as a utopian union of equals. It lasted until 1858, when Harriet died.

In the years before his death in 1873, Mill was elected to the House of Commons, where he argued for liberal reforms such as the abolition of capital punishment, feminist reforms such as the extension of suffrage to women, and socialist reforms such as poor relief. **Figure 18.2** shows a caricature drawing of Mill that was published in the widely read journal *Punch* in 1867. Readers could easily recognize the famous liberal intellectual (depicted with an unusually large head). The illustration shows him leading women, who are demanding the right to vote, by pushing aside resisting men with his arm and his logical arguments. He concluded that "the social problem of the future" would center on "how to unite the greatest individual liberty of action with a common ownership in the raw material of the globe."

Thus Harriet and John embodied many nineteenth-century trends. Liberalism, romanticism, and socialism all played a role in their lives. In addition, what brought them together was the middle-class ideal—affection, companionship, the shared life at home. In other ways, however, they did not reflect the times at all. Their views on marriage and relations between men and women, for example, the long triangular relationship with John Taylor, and the intensity of their intellectual collaboration all alarmed many of their contemporaries. Only in the decades to come would these unusual views gain more favor.

Connecting People & Society

1. Why was Mill labeled a leading proponent of liberalism?

2. In what ways might the Mill family and the Cadbury family discussed in Chapter 17 (see Biography, pages 572–573) be compared?

3. In his life, writings, and politics, why is Mill considered a leading feminist of the nineteenth century?

Scholars resurrected and developed languages from previous eras and elevated myths to national histories. Schoolteachers taught these languages and histories to their students and thereby spread a sense of ethnic unity. Nationalists used this growing interest in language and history to proclaim their nation's special mission—for example, of the Czechs to become leaders of the Slavs, or the Italians to lead Europe again as it had during Roman times.

Nationalism promised a new sense of community as the old order with its traditional allegiances declined. **Sense of community** It offered a sense of strength and unity that appealed to many peoples: to those threatened with foreign domination, such as the Spaniards and Italians under the French during the Napoleonic era; to those dissatisfied with the dominance of one ethnic group, such as Czechs, Magyars, or Serbs under the Germans within the Habsburg Empire; and to those feeling suppressed by what they considered foreign domination, such as the Greeks under the Ottomans, the Poles under the Russians, and the Italians under the Austrians.

From such sources, it was a short step to calls for national liberation and political unification. Nationalism soon acquired attributes of a religion and became a powerful political force. **National liberation and unification** For example, the Italian nationalist Giuseppe Mazzini (1805–1872), who founded the revolutionary Young Italy movement in 1831, called Italy "the purpose, the soul, the consolation of our thoughts, the country chosen of God and oppressed by men." Some nationalist leaders, such as Mazzini, began demanding loyalty and solidarity from members of their organizations.

Before 1848, most nationalists supported liberal causes, for liberals also struggled for national rights. Both liberals and nationalists typically believed that sovereignty should rest with the people, united by common loyalties and language. They also had faith that change would bring political, social, and economic progress. Campaigns by liberals to promote agricultural improvement and industrial development often merged into German, Italian, and Hungarian calls for national unity.

Later, nationalists would ally themselves with conservatives, for both believed in the value of historical traditions and in an organic society over the rights of the individual. Nationalism would also become more entwined with notions of national superiority and special national missions that so often appealed to conservatives. All nationalists, however, insisted that each nation of people, unified into a self-governing state, should be the primary focus of political loyalty and that the political boundaries of the state should be the same as ethnic boundaries of the people. The widespread political and emotional appeal of nationalism made it an increasingly powerful ideology over the course of the century.

Romanticism: Freedom, Instinct, and Spontaneity

The origins of nationalism in literature and history also made it attractive to believers in **romanticism.** This ideology became the dominant spirit in literature and art during the first half of the nineteenth century. Its significance stretched beyond culture, however. Romanticism reflected a new recognition that human beings were complex, emotional, and only sometimes rational creatures. In a civilization that was growing ever more scientific, materialistic, industrial, and urban, romanticism became a counterweight for the human experience. It stood against eighteenth-century classicism and the Enlightenment and the ideals of reason and order that so characterized those eras. Instead, romanticism emphasized individual freedom and spontaneity.

The origins of romanticism can be traced back to Jean-Jacques Rousseau, the acclaimed writer and philosopher we met in Chapter 14. Though a central figure of the Enlightenment, Rousseau had stressed feeling, instinct, emotions, and love of nature. He described walking away from the city into the fields and woods, stretching himself out on the ground, digging his fingers and toes into the dirt, kissing the earth, and weeping for joy. In several of his most widely read writings, he seemed to idealize love, childhood, and "the noble savage."

Rousseau

Other strands of romanticism came from the German "Storm and Stress" (Sturm und Drang) literature of the late eighteenth century. German writers gave much weight to inner feelings fully experienced and expressed by sensitive individuals. Johann Wolfgang von Goethe provided a model of the emotional individual searching for love and self-understanding in his novel *The Sorrows of the Young Werther* (1774). Like Rousseau, Goethe had many interests. He delved into philosophy, science, and public affairs as well as literature. His masterpiece, the philosophical drama *Faust*, featured a medieval scholar who, dissatisfied with the fruits of knowledge, sells his soul to the devil in return for earthly pleasure and wisdom. In Goethe's medieval interests, his emotional spontaneity, and his love of nature and of individual personality, this renowned writer exemplified the heart of romanticism.

"Storm and Stress" literature

All these qualities explored by Rousseau and Goethe came to characterize the work of succeeding romantic writers and artists. Many romantics expressed a new interest in the Middle Ages. They revived the popularity of medieval tales, Gothic architecture, the Knights of the Round Table, and heroic figures, thereby turning the medieval era from the Dark Ages into the Age of Faith.

Reviving the Middle Ages

This fascination with the Middle Ages reflected romanticism's passionate concern with the drama of history. Written by scholars such as Thomas Babington Macaulay (1800–1859) in Great Britain, history was literary and exciting, featuring heroic individuals, great accomplishments, and national struggles. These same themes were explored by the Prussian philosopher Hegel. In Hegel's view, history was a great spiritual drama of heroic individuals that would lead to a new sense of national identity and freedom.

History

Romanticism also stressed the emotion of Christianity and the mystical presence of God in nature. According to romantic theologians, the important part of religion was the feeling of dependence on an infinite God rather than religious dogma or institutions. In his widely read book *The Genius of Christianity*, the French writer François Auguste-René de Chateaubriand (1768–1848) described in lush words how "every thing in a Gothic church reminds you of the labyrinths of a forest; every thing excites a feeling of religious awe, of mystery, and of the Divinity." In part, religious revivals during the late eighteenth and early nineteenth centuries, with their stress on piety and emotional outpourings, reflected these spiritual qualities of romanticism.

Christianity

The connections among the love of nature, the spiritual presence of God, and the power of emotions were most striking in the romantic literature, art, and music of the period. In the literary realm, the English poets William Wordsworth (1770–1850) and Samuel Taylor Coleridge (1772–1834) became closely associated with the beautiful lake country of northwest England—Wordsworth by birth and Coleridge by adoption. Together the two men traveled to Germany, where they fell under the influence of German romanticists. They collaborated on *Lyrical Ballads* (1798), which included Wordsworth's "Lines Composed a Few Miles Above Tintern Abbey" and Coleridge's "Rime of the Ancient Mariner." Both writers glorified nature and sensed a brooding, mystical presence of the divine. Wordsworth saw in nature a higher wisdom than what scholars might offer:

> One impulse from a vernal wood
> May teach you more of man,
> Of moral evil and of good
> Than all the sages can.

Wordsworth's and Coleridge's ardent appreciation of nature, their introspective concern for the individual, and their preoccupation with the spiritual rather than the material made them leaders among Britain's many romantic poets.

In France, Germaine de Staël (1766–1817) led the romantic movement in literature. Although she admired the passionate Rousseau, she attacked most Enlightenment thinkers for not being free enough. She turned to writing in order to grapple with her own emotional experiences with several lovers and to argue for living the passionate life. Often writing about female heroes and genius in works such as *Corinne*, de Staël also looked to history for a vision of another, better world. She and other romantics created an image of the ideal romantic heroine who followed her emotions rather than tradition or reason—a model that some tried to follow in life. Also in France, George Sand (Amandine Dupin Dudevant) (1804–1876) became an extraordinarily creative writer and an unconventional, even threatening woman. Abandoning her tyrannical husband for an independent life in Paris, Sand became an intellectual leader whose private life included several love affairs with well-known people. At her own convenience, she dressed as a man or a woman. Like several other women writers, she also took a male pseudonym to add legitimacy to her writings. Several of her novels explored romantic love and featured strong, intensely emotional heroines.

Leading romantic painters also stressed emotional images. **Figure 18.3,** an oil painting by the German artist Karl Friedrich Schinkel, shows an idealized image of a medieval town at twilight. In the center stands a magnificent Gothic cathedral, its spires stretching toward the heavens above. The parting clouds and setting sun seem to bless this church and town. Below, humble workers bring abundant supplies from the river. They are dwarfed by the cathedral, the central stairs leading up to the cathedral, the high-arching bridge that echoes the arches of the cathedral, their finely built town on the right, and nature above. The painting contains the key elements of romanticism: glorification of nature, religious mysticism, adoration of an idealized medieval era, and expression of emotion.

The romantic love of magnificent landscapes can be found in **Figure 18.4.** This 1817 painting emphasizes the theme of the poet both immersed in nature and conjuring up a majestic natural setting like a god. Here the robed poet with his harp stands on a cliff, his arm stretched out to the swirling heavens above. Below him, waters rage and a knight on a white horse (lower left) gallops off into the distance. In the background stands a medieval castle built into the mountains.

In music, a number of romantic composers followed in the footsteps of Ludwig van Beethoven (1770–1827). The music of this famed German composer overflowed the bounds of classic forms, becoming freer, more individualistic, and more emotional than anything that had come before. Beethoven composed his *Pastoral Symphony* as a musical link to nature. "How happy I am," he wrote in 1810, "to be able to stroll in the woods, among the trees, bushes, wild flowers and rocks. No one can love the country as much as I do." The lyrics to one of his choral works explain his feelings about music:

> When the magic of sound holds sway
> and works bring inspiration,
> glorious things must appear,
> darkness and turmoil become light.

One critic explained that romantic music should "paint to the eyes of the soul the splendors of nature, the delights of contemplation, the character of nations, the tumult of their passions, and the languor of their sufferings. . . ."

The painting by the Austrian artist Josef Danhauser shown in **Figure 18.5** brings together leading figures of romantic art and literature. At the center, the Hungarian virtuoso and composer Franz Liszt plays the piano for his friends. Standing, from left to right, are the French writer Victor Hugo, the Italian violinist Niccolò Paganini, and the composer Antonio Rossini. Sitting are the French writers Alexandre Dumas, George Sand (characteristically in men's clothing), and Daniel Stern (Marie d'Agoult, who had a long-term liaison with Liszt). Above the group are a portrait of Lord Byron and a bust of Beethoven, the deceased "saints" of romantic poetry and music.

FIGURE 18.3

Karl Friedrich Schinkel, *Medieval Town on a River, 1815*

In this 1815 painting, Karl Friedrich Schinkel depicts an imaginary medieval town. A stunning Gothic cathedral, blessed by the setting sun, dominates the people below as well as the scene itself. The town in the background appears well ordered, as do the town's citizens, working calmly and enjoying the fruits of this civilization.

Connecting Art & Society

1. What impression of medieval life do you think the artist intended to convey to viewers?

2. In what ways does this painting represent romanticism?

3. Why do you think Schinkel chose to make the cathedral so prominent?

4. How might the scene in this painting contrast with a realistic urban scene of the nineteenth century?

Through much of romanticism, strands from all the ideologies combined and recombined in a variety of ways. Nationalism, for example, played a prominent role in some romantics' lives. In the 1820s, England's romantic poet Lord Byron (1788–1824) fought for Greek national independence against the Turks (see **Figure 18.7**). Some of Frederic Chopin's (1810–1849) dramatic music

Connections to nationalism

self-consciously evoked nationalistic sentiments for his native Poland, which was still under Russian rule. The Italian Giuseppe Verdi (1813–1901) and the German Richard Wagner (1813–1883), who developed the opera into a fully integrated art form of music, theater, ballet, and special effects, were among many other composers whose works brought together romantic and openly nationalistic themes.

Liberals, too, found comfort in various aspects of romanticism, which helps explain the movement's wide appeal. By breaking sharply with past forms,

Connections to liberalism romanticism attracted liberal and revolutionary spirits. Indeed, many romantic writers and artists sided with liberal causes. Germaine de Staël, for example, in her own life as well as in her novels, histories, and political tracts, fostered romanticism and liberalism in France. Few liberal romantics, however, were more popular than the French writer Victor Hugo (1802–1885), who idealized the masses of underprivileged humanity and preached redemption and purification through suffering.

At the same time, certain dimensions of romanticism appealed to conservatives as well—especially

Connections to conservatism the return to the past, the emphasis on Christianity, and the stand against the rationalism of the Enlightenment. Sir Walter Scott (1771–1832), who in novel and verse glorified the Middle Ages and his native Scotland, was a conservative. So was the French writer François Auguste-René de Chateaubriand, who advocated a return to mystic Catholicism and dreamed of noble Indians in tropical America.

Romanticism found expression in many cultural forms—in the new English gardens that imitated nature rather than confining it to geometric forms, in the image of the artist as a nonconforming genius, in the glorification of walks down wooded lanes, in the popularity of the Grimm fairy tales that evoked images of medieval life, and in the sentimentalization of love in life and literature. In its qualities, its popularity, and its persistence, romanticism proved to be more than a casual change of taste or a mood. It reflected the revolutionary social, political, and intellectual developments of the era.

Early Socialism: Ending Competition and Inequities

Romantics questioned the existing system from cultural and emotional perspectives. **Socialists** questioned it from social and economic perspectives. As socialists saw it, the common people—the workers—were missing out on the astounding power and wealth generated by the industrial revolution. Socialists called for a reordering of society so as to end the competition and class divisions that caused inequalities and suffering. Such calls made the socialists enemies of both the conservative and liberal camps.

During the early decades of the nineteenth century, a few intellectuals—some of whom came to be

FIGURE 18.4 John Martin, *The Bard,* 1817   This vision of a poet immersed in nature in a dramatic medieval landscape exemplifies the romantic impulse in art.

FIGURE 18.5 Josef Danhauser, *Liszt at the Piano,* 1840   This painting, rich with symbolism, brings together images and portraits of leading writers, musicians, and composers of the romantic era.

called Utopian Socialists—contended that society should be based on cooperation rather than competitive individualism and that property should be owned communally. One of the first of these early socialists was the French nobleman Henri de Saint-Simon

(1760–1825). During the French Revolution, Saint-Simon abandoned his noble title. Turning to land speculation, he made and lost a fortune. He and his followers believed that society should be reorganized on the basis of a "religion of humanity," that all people should work, and that the inheritance of private property should be abolished. In Saint-Simon's ideal world, women would be elevated from their inferior social positions. Superior artists, scientists, engineers, and businesspeople would be rewarded according to the formula "from each according to his capacity, to each according to his deserts." Saint-Simon's influential followers became convinced that the best scientists and managers could use their expertise to plan and run prosperous societies for the benefit of everyone.

Utopian Socialists

Saint-Simon

Charles Fourier (1772–1837) was also an early Utopian Socialist who, like Saint-Simon, gathered a following. A Frenchman who had been a traveling salesman, he advocated doing away with economic competition, which he saw as the very source of evil. In his utopian society, agriculture and industry would be carried on by voluntary cooperatives whose members would pool their resources and live in communal apartment houses (*phalansteries*). Housework and child care would be a shared responsibility of the community. Women, like men, would have the right to work and to control their own money. Fourier also considered traditional marriage too restrictive sexually. Work and pleasure would merge as people did as they pleased while still carrying out the tasks their society required to survive. People would be paid according to the labor, capital, and talent that each contributed.

Fourier

In fact, the communities that Fourier's followers established in the United States and Europe rarely lasted for long. Fourier's ideas, however, inspired many people looking for a more joyful, communal alternative to the competitive industrial societies spreading in the West.

Robert Owen (1771–1858) had different ideas. Born in Wales, Owen quickly made an industrial fortune in Manchester and bought large cotton mills in New Lanark, Scotland. Early in the nineteenth century, he set out to make New Lanark a model community. He raised wages, shortened work hours, improved working conditions, abolished child labor, provided educational and recreational facilities for employees, and established sickness and old-age insurance. Productivity in his mills soared, and profits rose. Owen spent years drawing up plans for model socialist communities, which he envisioned as being located in rural settings and as mostly self-sufficient.

Owen

The plans called for community members to raise children together and for women to share in governing. Like Fourier, Owen advocated loosening the bounds of marriage to create greater sexual freedom for women and men. Several such communities were established in America, most notably New Harmony, Indiana. However, all soon succumbed to internal disagreements and economic difficulties. The efforts cost Owen most of his fortune. He retained his fame, especially within the labor movement and among those establishing modest workers' cooperatives. However, he died in 1858 without having created a lasting alternative to the harsh industrial capitalism he deplored.

In the 1830s, several Frenchwomen began linking socialist demands with calls for the emancipation of women. The most famous of these women was Flora Tristan (1801–1844), who was influenced by Fourier's ideas. French law discriminated against women in many ways, including automatically awarding custody of children to fathers after a marital separation. When Tristan's abusive husband was awarded their children, she fought back. Eventually she turned this dispute into a campaign to end discrimination against women within marriage, in the law, and on the job. She traveled throughout Europe and Latin America, speaking passionately for unions and the creation of centers for the care and education of workers. In her *Worker's Union* (1843), she argued that equality between women and men could free the whole working class and transform civilization.

Tristan

These and other early socialists recognized both the significance of the industrial revolution and its possibilities. They attacked the unbridled pursuit of profits in an unregulated, industrial economy. Only a well-organized society, they explained, could eliminate the misery of industrial capitalism and promote happiness. Most also attacked middle-class restrictions on women, emphasized the importance of sensual pleasure, and questioned traditional Christianity. The wave of socialist thought that these leaders unleashed became profoundly influential by the middle decades of the nineteenth century. As it evolved, it took on a more revolutionary quality, and it bore the distinctive stamp of one of the most authoritative thinkers of the nineteenth century: Karl Marx.

"Scientific Socialism": Karl Marx and *The Communist Manifesto*

"A specter is haunting Europe—the specter of Communism," announced Karl Marx (1818–1883) in 1848. "Let the ruling classes tremble at a Communist revolution." Born into a German middle-class family, his father was a Jewish lawyer who had converted to Christianity. A brilliant student, Marx attained his doctorate in philosophy and history, but he was denied an academic position because of his radical views. After embarking on a career in journalism, he was exiled from Germany for his attacks on censorship and his economic views; later, France exiled him because of his revolutionary socialist ideas. He spent the last thirty-four years of his life in London researching, writing, and trying to build organizations to put his ideas into action. Marx collaborated with his friend Friedrich Engels (1820–1895), son of a wealthy German manufacturer, in writing the seminal work *The Communist Manifesto* (1848). This treatise, along with the later *Das Kapital*, contained the fundamentals of what Marx called "scientific socialism."

Marx argued that economic interest, more than anything else, drove human behavior. He also

| Economic interest |

thought that the dominant characteristic of each historical epoch was its prevailing system of economic production—how people made a living. In his view, politics, religion, and culture were all shaped mainly by economic and social realities.

Marx also described how human societies in each historical era became divided into the "haves" and the "have-nots." The haves owned

| Class struggle |

the means of economic production—in nineteenth-century Britain, for example, the industrial capitalists who owned the machines and factories. They also controlled the state and the ideas that dominated their societies. The have-nots were the exploited laborers—for example, Britain's industrial working class. Each side consisted of classes of people with opposing interests. As Marx wrote, "[T]he history of all hitherto existing society is the history of class struggle." At a certain point, economic and social change would bring these class struggles to a revolutionary crisis. The French Revolution, he explained, was an example of one of those conflicts coming to a violent head, as the bourgeoisie (the middle-class capitalists) overcame the aristocracy (the feudal landlords.)

Marx focused much of his analysis on his own industrial society of the nineteenth century. In this

| Industrial capitalism |

society, he explained, the bourgeoisie (capitalists) exploited workers by paying them only subsistence wages rather than compensating them for the true value created by their work. "These labourers, who must sell themselves piecemeal, are a commodity, like every other article of commerce," Marx lamented. At the same time, Marx saw capitalists as locked in a competitive struggle with one another. This contest forced them continually to introduce new, costly machines and build larger factories: "Constant revolutionizing of production, uninterrupted disturbance of all social conditions, ever-lasting

uncertainty and agitation distinguish the bourgeois epoch from all earlier ones." Soon, Marx warned, greater and greater quantities of goods would be produced by a system running out of control. Eventually, the relentless competition and the periodic economic crises that plague industrial societies would thin the ranks of the bourgeoisie. At the same time, the working class would grow stronger as its numbers and consciousness increased. Inevitably, the workers—with "nothing to lose but their chains" and with "a world to win"—would revolt, seize the factories, destroy the capitalist system, abolish private property, and establish a classless socialist society.

Marx only hinted at the general nature of this new socialist society. His writings suggest that the elimination of capitalism would end the division of society into classes of

| Socialist society |

haves (capitalists) and have-nots (workers). The state itself would eventually wither away, for its only purpose was to protect the interests of the haves against the have-nots. Freed from exploitation and the pressures of capitalist competition, all people would lead more varied, cooperative, creative lives—in this sense, free and truly human.

Marx's socialism gained immense appeal. Because he based much of his analysis on evidence and logic, it attracted intellectuals and students. Because his socialism reflected the social and emotional turmoil being produced

| Appeal of socialism |

by the industrial revolution, especially the suffering of the working poor, it spoke convincingly to workers and their leaders. During the second half of the nineteenth century, Marx's socialism would become a major force in the West.

RESTORATION AND REPRESSION

Socialism as well as the other ideologies reflected the political and social realities of their era, particularly the efforts of people to understand and cope with changes that either threatened them or offered promise. In the three decades following 1815, however, socialism played only a limited part in the great struggles for policies and power. During these years, it was the forces representing conservatism, liberalism, and nationalism that instead took center stage.

The struggles for influence and power among believers of these ideologies took place in pamphlets and newspapers, in courts and parliaments, in universities and police barracks, and in streets and fields throughout Europe. In the first years after the defeat of Napoleon, conservatism held sway in international and diplomatic affairs. The Vienna agreements and the cooperative arrangements to repress the threat of revolution in Europe epitomized this ideology. Conservatism also prevailed in domestic politics across most of Europe.

The Return of the Bourbons in France

When the victorious armies of the coalition powers entered France and deposed Napoleon in the spring of 1814, they brought "in their baggage" the members of the Bourbon royal family who had fled the Revolution. In their wake trooped the émigré nobility. The brother of the guillotined Louis XVI was placed on the throne as Louis XVIII (r. 1814–1824). (The son of Louis XVI, who had died in prison without having ruled, was considered Louis XVII.)

> Louis XVIII

The "restored" king ruled with an odd mixture of conservatism and moderation. He issued a charter that retained Napoleon's administrative and legal system as well as civil and religious liberties. He also placed lawmaking in the hands of a two-chamber legislature. However, only a small, wealthy elite could vote, and the king kept most of the power.

Nevertheless, Louis XVIII used his authority with moderation, thinking that a mild leadership style would help ensure his hold on the crown and tranquillity in France. Most of the returned émigrés, however, had little appreciation for his relaxed rule—they were more conservative and angry than he was and wanted action. Led by the king's younger brother, the comte d'Artois, these ultraroyalists controlled the legislature. Through the rest of Louis XVIII's reign, they agitated for a return of their privileges and indemnification for their lost lands.

After Louis XVIII's death in 1824, d'Artois was crowned King Charles X (r. 1824–1830); he followed more conservative policies that favored the old aristocracy and the Catholic Church. He offered money to indemnify those who had lost land in the Revolution and gave the church greater control over education. Those policies provoked growing opposition to his rule. When elections increased the size of the opposition, he dissolved the Chamber of Deputies. In the face of still-increasing opposition, he abolished freedom of the press and drastically restricted the right to vote.

> Charles X

Reaction and Repression in the German States

The German states in 1815 consisted of thirty-seven little states and two large ones—Prussia and Austria. All belonged to the German Confederation, which lacked an army, a treasury, and even a flag. Austria and Prussia politically dominated the German lands. Both states were firmly conservative, if not reactionary.

In multilingual Austria, the Habsburg emperor and Metternich, the conservative diplomat we met at the beginning of the chapter, held sway. The Austrian leaders had good reason to fear liberalism and nationalism like the plague, for the empire included many ethnic groups—including Hungarians, Czechs, Serbs, and Italians—with their own languages and customs. In the wake of the French Revolution, they began to stir with national consciousness. Metternich used all means—police, spies, censorship, and travel restrictions—to ensure the status quo. The only possible threats to conservative control came from within some of the small states in the weak German Confederation, and Austria enjoyed permanent presidency over that organization.

> Metternich

When students and professors formed organizations and staged festivals that supported liberal and nationalistic principles, conservative officials became alarmed. "We want a constitution for the people that fits in with the spirit of the times and with people's own level of enlightenment," explained one student. "[A]bove all, we want Germany to be considered *one* land and the people *one* people."

The murder of a conservative dramatist by a member of a student organization, Karl Sand, gave Metternich his opportunity to strike. After Sand's trial and public execution, Metternich called the princes of the leading German states to Carlsbad and had them draw up a set of harsh decrees outlawing the organizations. He also issued an ominous warning: "The duty of especial watchfulness in this matter should be impressed upon the special agents of the government." The Carlsbad Decrees established strict censorship and supervision of classrooms and libraries. Spies and police terrorized liberal students and professors. Although Sand became a political martyr in the eyes of many young nationalists, the crackdown worked: The small liberal and nationalistic movements evaporated.

> Carlsbad Decrees

In Prussia, the conservative, militaristic Hohenzollern kings reigned. Behind them stood the equally conservative landed aristocracy, the Junkers. The Junkers served as officers in the Prussian army and filled the key posts in the civil service and administration. They had no sympathy for any reforms that seemed even faintly liberal or nationalistic, and they reversed many of the changes of the Napoleonic era. However, to better connect its separated territories, Prussia began making commercial treaties with its smaller German neighbors, providing for the free flow of trade among them. By 1834, nearly all the states of the German Confederation except Austria had joined the Prussian-sponsored **Zollverein** (customs union), which would prove of great importance in the march toward national unity.

> Prussia

Restoration in Italy

Austria dominated Italy even more completely than Germany. Metternich described Italy as only a "geographical expression." Austria annexed the northern states of Lombardy and Venetia outright. Most other states were ruled by Austrian princes or under Austria's protection and guidance. Piedmont-Sardinia in the northwest was free from Austrian control, but its ruling House of Savoy was no less conservative than Metternich.

In 1815, the deposed aristocracy and clericals trooped back to the Italian states intent on regaining their old positions. They and their Austrian masters soon sent nearly all the Italian intelligentsia to prison or exile. When revolts in Naples, Sicily, and Piedmont flared up in 1820, the forces of order quickly used overwhelming force to put them down.

The Papal States in central Italy were no exception in this period of restoration. Pope Pius VII revived the Inquisition, reconstituted the *Index* of prohibited books, annulled Napoleonic laws of religious toleration, and even did away with French innovations such as street lighting. His successor, Pius VIII, followed equally conservative ideas. In 1829, he condemned almost everything even faintly liberal, including secular education and civil marriage.

Conservatism in Russia

Russia remained a vast agricultural nation with a feudal social structure and a tiny urban bourgeoisie. The Orthodox Christian Church, dominated by an upper clergy drawn from the aristocracy, served as an arm of the government. After fighting against the French, suffering a ravaging invasion in 1812, and playing a major role in Napoleon's defeat, Russia commanded considerable respect and power in Europe. Russia's tsar was the unstable Alexander I—at first a man open to reform, such as granting the Poles a constitution and proclaiming religious toleration, and later more of a reactionary mystic who resumed religious repression. He fell under the influence of Metternich in international affairs and his own aristocratic magnates at home. At his death in 1825, Russia remained a champion of autocracy and conservatism.

His successor, Nicholas I (r. 1825–1855), was an austere autocrat whose military career wedded him to the concepts of discipline and authority. When he assumed the throne in December 1825, a group of his young liberal military officers—hoping to write a constitution and free the serfs—revolted. Nicholas immediately crushed these "Decembrists" and bitterly turned against any hints of liberalism. He followed a policy of demanding submission of everyone to the autocracy and to the Orthodox Church. Although the Decembrists would later gain a reputation as liberal political martyrs, Russia's government now stood as a bastion of conservatism and would remain so for many decades.

Holding the Line in Great Britain

Although Great Britain had for years been a home of representative government, conservatives dominated its government in 1815. Property qualifications so severely restricted the suffrage that only about 5 percent of adult males could vote. The distribution of seats in Parliament was so distorted that a relatively small number of families dominated the House of Commons. Furthermore, the emerging industrial cities of the north were scarcely represented at all. The conservative landed aristocracy and the Tory Party, which had seen the country through the Napoleonic Wars, had a firm grip on power.

Things became even more restricted when an economic depression left thousands of returning veterans jobless. Luddite riots (see page 563) and the specter of revolutionary activity prompted the government to take strong measures against the restless workers. The climax came in 1819 when troops charged on a crowd that had assembled in St. Peter's Fields, outside Manchester, to listen to reform speeches. A number were killed and hundreds injured in this Peterloo Massacre.

Figure 18.6, a print by George Cruikshank, shows the troops of the conservative British government breaking up this rally for liberal and radical political reform. On the platform, women and men

FIGURE 18.6 George Cruikshank, *The Peterloo Massacre*, 1819 Cruikshank's print shows Britain's conservative forces violently breaking up a rally for liberal and radical reform.

wave banners demanding universal suffrage, religious freedom, and liberty; a banner is topped with liberty caps, a radical symbol from the French Revolution. This depiction of the violence that erupted at St. Peter's Fields near Manchester seeks to evoke sympathy for the reformers. It portrays merciless troops on horseback striking down and trampling nonresisting women, men, and children. An army officer on horseback repeats orders from a higher authority: "Cut them down." A participant confirmed this depiction: "Women, white-vested maids, and tender youths, were indiscriminately sabred or trampled. . . . In ten minutes from the commencement of the havoc the field was an open and almost deserted space." Parliament would not back down. It soon passed the Six Acts of 1819, which further restricted public meetings and facilitated prosecution of radicals.

The government treated the Irish no less harshly. The Irish had long been ruled and exploited as a conquered people. In the 1801 Act of Union, Britain formally absorbed Ireland into the United Kingdom. In this predominantly Catholic land, the Protestant minority controlled most of the land and political power. The Catholic peasantry suffered from such acute poverty that the threat of famine was not uncommon. Irish nationalists organized to agitate for the right to send elected Catholic representatives to Parliament. In 1829, fearing a civil war in Ireland, the conservative British government reluctantly passed the Catholic Emancipation Act, which allowed Roman Catholics to become members of Parliament.

Ireland

A WAVE OF REVOLUTION AND REFORM

Despite conservative efforts to maintain order and halt change during the years after 1815, liberal and nationalistic causes simmered just under the surface. The demands for greater political participation and recognition of national identity strengthened and spread. Moreover, Europeans could no longer ignore the changes stemming from early industrialization and urbanization. In some cases, revolts and revolutions broke out. In other cases, people clamored for and gained major reforms.

The Greek War for Independence

A hint of the problems to come occurred during the 1820s, when Greeks mounted a national liberation movement against their Ottoman Turk overlords. The Ottoman Empire still sprawled over vast territories, from the north African coast and southwest Asia to southeastern Europe, but it had been weakened

by internal dissension and external threats. By 1815, revolts had enabled Serbia to gain virtual independence, and in Egypt, Mehemet Ali ruled with only nominal subordination to the Ottomans. The Greek revolt began in 1821, which resulted in the death of many defenseless Turks. After the Turks met Greek insurrections with force and atrocities, romantic and liberal idealists formed an international movement to support Greek independence. Britain's well-known romantic poet Lord Byron was one of several who traveled to Greece to contribute to the cause. He brought money and enlisted in a regiment but lost his life to malaria at Missolonghi.

Figure 18.7, by the romantic French artist Eugène Delacroix (1798–1863), captures Greece's struggle for independence. The year is 1826, during the months when the Turks laid siege to the Greek stronghold of Missolonghi and the garrison of 4,000 finally succumbed to 35,000 attackers and the Ottoman fleet. The remaining defenders blew up the city and

FIGURE 18.7 Eugène Delacroix, *Greece Expiring on the Ruins of Missolonghi*, 1827 In this canvas capturing Greece's struggle for independence, a woman symbolizing Greek liberty kneels in the ruins of a Greek city in a plea for help against Turkish overlords.

themselves rather than surrender to the Turks. Greece is represented as a beautiful, defenseless peasant woman and a classical symbol of liberty. Under a dark, foreboding sky, she kneels on what are both the ruins of Missolonghi's city walls and the stone remains of Greek culture in a desperate, mute appeal for aid. But it is already too late for the martyred freedom fighter (perhaps evoking the memory of the fallen Byron), whose arm is thrust forward toward the viewer. Behind the woman, a Turkish soldier strikes a victorious pose. The painting, like the Greek cause in Europe, blends the themes of romanticism, liberalism, and nationalism that so characterized the era.

In the end, intervention by Great Britain, France, and Russia finally secured Greek independence. Although Europeans thought of Greece sympathetically as Christian and as the birthplace of European civilization, these countries' motives had more to do with their own greedy hopes of gains at the expense of the Turks than with genuine support for the Greek revolutionaries. They achieved their objective, but this dramatic chapter in Greek history still revealed the strength of nationalistic movements and the power of liberal and romantic ideals to fuel these movements.

FIGURE 18.8 Horace Vernet, *The Duc d'Orléans Proceeds to the Hôtel de Ville, July 31, 1830,* 1833   In this high-energy scene portraying the July Revolution in France, Louis-Philippe, carrying the hopes of the revolutionaries, rides victoriously to Paris's city hall.

Liberal Triumphs in Western Europe

In 1830, a new series of revolutions tested and sometimes overwhelmed established governments. In

> The July Revolution in France

France, a struggle arose for liberal reforms against the reactionary King Charles X. Since ascending the throne in 1824, Charles had tried to reverse the moderate policies of his predecessor, Louis XVIII, and return France to the days before the French Revolution. He aligned himself with the most extreme ultraroyalists and the Catholic Church, angering the wealthy bourgeoisie and even the peasantry with his reactionary policies. Support for his regime weakened and he lost control over the Chamber of Deputies, the most representative of France's two-chamber legislature. His efforts to dissolve the Chamber, censor the press, and narrow the electoral laws only stiffened liberal opposition. In July 1830, things came to a head. Liberals in Paris joined with workers outraged by rising food prices. Workers took to the streets of Paris and set up barriers against the king's unenthusiastic troops. Uprisings—fueled by hunger, suspicions of hoarding, and resentment against taxes—spread throughout France. After three days of haphazard fighting, the insurgents gained the upper hand. Charles X, the last Bourbon king of France, fled to Great Britain.

Figure 18.8, a painting by Horace Vernet, reveals how the victors in France's revolution of 1830 interpreted the dramatic events of that year. In the center of the painting, the new constitutional monarch, Louis-Philippe, rides victoriously to the Hôtel de Ville (city hall), the seat of power in Paris. Before him a man carries the French revolutionary tricolor flag, replacing the old Bourbon flag of Charles X. Louis-Philippe's horse picks its way through the paving stones, which the people of Paris had used to construct barricades and hurl at the royal troops. In the foreground, rich and poor walk arm in arm with regular and irregular soldiers in victory; a wealthy man stops to drop alms into a basket for the poor or fallen. Women and men of all classes hail the new king and the revolutionary cause.

While many in France had hoped for a republic to replace the Bourbon monarchy, more conservative liberals took control and created a constitutional "bourgeois monarchy" under Charles X's cousin, Louis-Philippe (r. 1830–1848). Recognizing that a new, more liberal era had dawned in France, Louis-Philippe assumed the role of "citizen king," casting aside the clothes and ornaments of royalty and dressing in the style of his Parisian upper-middle-class supporters. He reduced property qualifications for voting, thereby doubling the electorate (though still only the property-owning elite could vote).

The year 1830 also brought revolutionary trouble in the Belgian provinces of the kingdom of the Netherlands. The union forced on

Revolution in Belgium

Belgium (predominantly Catholic) and the Netherlands (mainly Calvinist) at Vienna had never been a happy one. Although numerically a minority, the Dutch staffed most of the country's political institutions. As one Belgian nationalist put it in 1830, "By what right do two million Dutchmen command four million Belgians?" Desires for national liberation combined with tensions over high food prices to fuel a revolt in August 1830. When the halfhearted efforts of the Dutch government failed to suppress the revolt, Austria and Russia threatened to intervene. Britain and France resisted the intervention and secured Belgian independence. Belgium soon adopted a liberal constitution.

By that time, liberal reformers had also scored successes in Switzerland, making that

Switzerland and Spain

country the first to grant universal male suffrage. In 1834, a new constitution introduced at least the form of liberal institutions to Spain as well.

Testing Authority in Eastern and Southern Europe

As **Map 18.2** shows, revolutionaries also tested regimes in eastern and southern Europe. In November

Poland

1830, a Polish nationalistic movement led by students and army cadets tried to end Russian rule. They managed to establish a provisional government in Warsaw, but conflict within different social groups and among reformers weakened that government. Russian troops soon defeated the revolutionaries. Nicholas sent thousands of Poles to Siberia in chains and began a harsh program of Russification to crush any hint of Polish independence.

In Italy, nationalists began gathering in secret societies called *Carbonari*. (The word means "charcoal

Italy

burners," suggesting an image of common people meeting around charcoal fires.) The Carbonari had long plotted for political freedom and national unification. In 1831, liberal and nationalist revolutions broke out in central Italy, but Austrian forces promptly suppressed them. The movement again went underground but was kept alive under the leadership of the romantic nationalist Giuseppe Mazzini.

Liberal Demands in Great Britain

In Britain, conservatives had to contend not only with demands for liberal reforms but also with pressures rising from early industrialization and urbanization.

Despite the Peterloo Massacre and the restrictive Six Acts, Britain had already shown signs of political flexibility in response to public opinion in the 1820s. By 1822, it had deserted the conservative Concert of Europe. The government repealed laws preventing laborers from organizing unions and removed civil restrictions against nonconforming Protestants and Catholics. Yet these measures, however encouraging to liberals, did not get at the fundamental issue that had raised reform demands for decades: broadening popular participation in the government.

Now the industrial middle class, gaining in wealth and number, added weight to radicals' demands to extend the right to vote and relocate political strength from the countryside to the underrepresented

Reform Bill of 1832

industrial cities. However, the conservative Tories, who controlled Parliament, remained unwilling or unable to effect electoral reform. In 1830, elections brought the more liberal Whigs to power. These Whigs believed that moderate reform rather than reactionary intransigence was the best way to preserve elite institutions from revolutionary change. Worried that the July Revolution in France might spread to Britain, and facing increasing public demonstrations for reform as well as violent acts of protest, the Whigs decided to bend rather than break. They introduced the Reform Bill of 1832, which answered some of the demands. Speaking in favor of the bill, the English historian and politician Thomas Babington Macaulay warned that "now, while the crash of the proudest throne of the Continent [France] is still resounding in our ears . . . now, while the heart of England is still sound," the Reform Bill must be passed. After considerable effort, the Whigs finally enacted the new law.

The Reform Bill did not grant the universal manhood suffrage called for by radicals, but it lowered property qualifications so that most upper-middle-class men (still a small minority) could vote. More important, the bill redistributed electoral districts, taking power away from the "rotten boroughs" (no-longer-important towns and rural areas) and giving it to the underrepresented cities where commercial and industrial elites dominated. The political struggle to pass the bill enabled the House of Commons to gain power over the House of Lords, which had opposed the law. The long era of dominance by the conservative landed aristocracy was ending. More liberal property owners, including the commercial and industrial bourgeoisie, rose to power. From that point on, Britain's leading political groups realigned themselves into the modern Conservative and Liberal parties.

Britain's government soon turned to other reforms. Britain had for several decades led in the antislavery movement, abolishing its own slave trade in 1807 and pushing the Congress of Vienna to declare against the trade in 1815. Europeans, however, often violated principled declarations against slavery and shipped hundreds of thousands more African slaves to the Americas—especially to the Carib-

Antislavery bean and Brazil. In 1833, Parliament bowed to humanitarian radicals and Protestant reformers and abolished slavery in Britain's colonies. Fifteen years later, France would follow suit by abolishing slavery in its colonies, and in 1888, Brazil joined the list, ending slavery in the Americas.

Britain's Parliament and reformers also tried to cope with growing pressures exerted by the indus-

Economic and social reforms trial revolution. Several new laws aimed to ease some of the disturbing harshness of industrial employment. Between 1833 and 1847, Parliament forbad the employment of women and children in underground mines, prohibited the employment of children under 9 in textile mills, and limited children 9 or older and women to ten hours a day in those factories. Other legislation also reflected the British economy's shift from agriculture to industry. In the name of free trade and lower bread prices, liberals mounted a major attack on the Corn Laws, which imposed tariffs on grain imports. An anti–Corn

Corn Laws Law movement spread throughout the country, accusing the aristocratic landowners who benefited from the Corn Laws of being enemies of the middle and working classes. Victory for the movement came in 1846 with the repeal of the Corn Laws. The repeal reduced the price of bread, but it also opened up the possibility that employers—knowing that workers could afford the cheaper bread—would slash wages.

These liberal principles and reforms, however, only added to the suffering of millions facing the horrible potato famine in Ireland. This

Irish famine mostly rural and impoverished population relied on the potato for food. In 1845, a new, unknown fungus attacked potato plants, ruining the crop. Famine spread as the crops failed year after year. Despite some charitable assistance, Britain's liberal government concluded that the state should not meddle in the economy. More than a million died in Ireland and another million fled overseas while Britain's liberals—often sympathetic and believing that the free market would alleviate the distress—held fast to their principles and did little.

Nor were liberal reforms enough for the hard-pressed urban workers. They were bitterly aware that they had been bypassed by the

Chartism Reform Bill of 1832: "The Reform Act has effected a transfer of power from one domineering faction to another, and left the people as helpless as before," explained one of their leaders. They also complained that Britain's

★ Sites of Revolts, 1820–1831
— Boundary of German Confederation

MAP 18.2

European Revolts, 1820–1831

This map shows the locations of revolts in Europe between 1820 and 1831.

Explore the Map

1. What was the geographic extent of these revolts?

2. What problems might the scope of the uprisings have posed for the efforts of the Concert of Europe to maintain the status quo through international cooperation?

3. Which of these revolts do you think had the most lasting consequences? Why?

unprecedented national prosperity had not benefited workers: "With all these elements of national prosperity, and with every disposition and capacity to take advantage of them, we find ourselves overwhelmed with public and private suffering." In 1838, working-class leaders took action and drew up The People's Charter. The document called for several democratic reforms, including universal male suffrage, election by secret ballot, and the removal of property qualifications for office. "We perform the duties of freemen; we must have the privileges of freemen," announced the charter.

The so-called **Chartists** presented their demands twice to Parliament, which summarily rejected them. Nevertheless, the movement persisted within the working class for years. Women aided the cause by raising money and passing petitions for signatures. They also, unsuccessfully, demanded that the charter include provisions for female suffrage. Finally, in April 1848, the Chartists planned a huge demonstration in London to back up their petition. The frightened government and middle classes prepared to use force to control the gathering, as they had several times against strikes and workers' protests. However, when the reforms were refused once more, only a few mild protests arose, and the Chartist movement sputtered out. Nevertheless, Britain's political parties were becoming aware of the growing influence of the working classes and began considering ways to win their favor.

In Britain, then, reforms designed to meet demands for broader representation and manage the social consequences of industrialization and urbanization were under way by the 1840s. Under pressure, Britain's government bent enough to satisfy much of the middle class. The discontented working classes were not yet powerful enough to force their views on the resisting government. Liberalism, the strongest ideology challenging Britain's traditional order, remained a force for reform rather than revolution.

On the Continent, however, nations followed a different path. Throughout western Europe, liberal and nationalistic movements gained stunning successes in these same years. In eastern and southern Europe, these two ideologies also rose and served notice, but, with the exception of Greece, the conservative forces of order beat them down. In 1848, however, the complicated interplay among all these movements finally reached a volatile turning point.

THE DAM BURSTS, 1848

On New Year's Day, 1848, one could look back to 1830 and conclude that the forces that had opened the gates to a wave of revolutions and reforms had since been held under control. In February 1848, everything would change.

Trouble had already been brewing across Europe. In 1846 and 1847, poor harvests had driven up food prices and even brought famine. These disasters, along with financial crises, undermined markets for manufactured goods, created business failures, and left thousands of workers jobless. Governments tried to maintain order, but the growing resentments of liberals, nationalists, and now socialists, who blamed governments for failing to enact overdue reforms, made things even more difficult.

Antigovernment groups had also begun taking on a disturbing complexity and variety. Some protesters wanted only to widen political participation and institute accepted liberal reforms; others demanded full democracy. Several ethnic groups desired national autonomy; workers wanted jobs and rights. Together, the potential opposition to established governments not only loomed large but also cut across class and ideological lines. Intense, shared opposition to the status quo masked any differences these groups might have had. As the pressure of their frustration mounted, the economic crisis threatened to unlock the floodgates.

The "Glory Days"

The dam broke first in France. Louis-Philippe's constitutional monarchy had allied moderate conservatives and moderate liberals into a regime of wealthy property owners. France Presenting itself as the bearer of national patriotism and political caution, the government managed to quiet both conservative and radical opponents during the 1830s. However, beneath the surface of this apparently stable regime, discontent grew. The king and his chief minister during the

1840s—the moderately liberal historian François Guizot (1787–1874)—opposed any further extension of the suffrage. Workers, who had not shared in the relative prosperity of the period, clamored for the right to vote and the right to organize unions but got neither. The poor harvests and financial crises in 1846 and 1847 heightened frustration with the regime. In Paris, more than 40 percent of the workforce was without a job. One Parisian radical complained, "While half of the population of Paris dies of starvation, the other half eats for two."

The parliamentary opposition and bourgeois reformers began holding banquets to rally support for widening the right to vote. When a banquet to be held in Paris on February 22 in honor of George Washington's birthday (the United States served as a symbol of democracy in this period) promised to attract thousands of sympathetic workers, the government tried to prohibit the event. Opposition erupted in the Parisian streets. King Louis-Philippe tried to quiet people by dismissing his unpopular prime minister, François Guizot. Long in office, Guizot's response to those not rich enough to have the right to vote was "Get rich, then you can vote." The king's effort at appeasement failed. A shot fired during a brawl between a crowd and troops guarding government houses unnerved the troops, who fired a murderous volley into the mob and set off a full-scale insurrection. Barricades against governmental troops flew up all over Paris, and when the king's citizen militia, the National Guard, began taking the rebels' side, Louis-Philippe followed Guizot into exile.

Figure 18.9 depicts the triumph of the revolutionaries and the already simmering political battles to come. In the center, the well-dressed liberal and romantic poet Alphonse de Lamartine (1790–1869) stands with his arm raised in front of the Paris city hall. He persuades the crowd to keep the tricolor flag to represent the new republic rather than the more radical red flag, carried by a woman in plain dress riding a white horse on the left. On the right, troops and ordinary citizens march under the flag in unity. On the left, citizens bring objects of wealth gathered to support the new republic. At the bottom are the paving stones used in the battle and a fallen victim of the struggle.

Lamartine and a group of bourgeois liberals proclaimed the Second Republic and hastily set up a provisional government. The new ruling body was republican in sentiment, but, tellingly, it had only one prominent radical member: the socialist writer Louis Blanc (1811–1882). The provisional government immediately called for the election by universal male suffrage of an assembly to draw up a new constitution. Yet that government turned down demands for political and economic rights by the new woman's newspaper, *The Voice of Women*, and by women's political clubs. Under pressure from the Paris populace, the provisional government did admit workers to the National Guard, there by giving them access to arms.

Document 18.2 reveals that the government, in response to popular demand for the right to work, also set up national workshops. The workshops—an idea once proposed by Louis Blanc—however, were a parody of Blanc's socialist vision. Blanc lamented that they were deliberately planned so as to ensure failure. In this ill-designed undertaking,

National workshops

FIGURE 18.9 Henri-Félix Emmanuel Philippoteaux, Revolutionary Triumph in Paris This vibrant painting shows the poet and liberal leader Alphonse de Lamartine triumphantly saluting a Parisian crowd in 1848.

thinking about

DOCUMENTS

DOCUMENT 18.2

France's Provisional Government Issues Decrees

Shortly after the 1848 revolution that ended the July Monarchy in France, the victors established a new provisional government. They issued the following decrees relating to workers on February 25, 1848—the day after creating the provisional government.

The provisional government of the French republic decrees that the Tuileries shall serve hereafter as a home for the veterans of labor.

The provisional government of the French republic pledges itself to guarantee the means of subsistence of the workingman by labor.

It pledges itself to guarantee labor to all citizens.

It recognizes that workingmen ought to enter into associations among themselves in order to enjoy the advantage of their labor. . . .

The provisional government of the French republic decrees that all articles pledged at the pawn shops since the first of February, consisting of linen, garments, or clothes, etc., upon which the loan does not exceed ten francs, shall be given back to those who pledged them.

The provisional government of the republic decrees the immediate

establishment of national workshops. The minister of public works is charged with the execution of the present decree.

SOURCE: James Harvey Robinson, ed., *Readings in European History*, vol. II (Boston: Ginn, 1904), pp. 560–561.

Analyze the Document

1. What do these decrees suggest about the possible causes of the 1848 revolution?

2. What might have been the advantages and disadvantages of issuing these decrees?

3. How do you think French businessmen reacted to these decrees?

---

laborers were assigned to hastily arranged projects. When more laborers enrolled than could be used, the surplus workers were paid almost as much as the employed ones to remain idle. To make matters worse, tens of thousands of job-hungry laborers rushed to Paris to join the workshops. The resulting demoralization of labor and the cost to the taxpayers frightened peasant and bourgeois property owners alike. Elections held in April 1848 swept conservative republicans and monarchists back into office.

As **Map 18.3** reveals, the February explosion in Paris set central Europe aflame with revolt. One core **Austria** of the revolutions settled in Vienna, the seat of the Habsburg government. After news of the Paris events arrived in Vienna, Austrian students, middle-class reformers, and workers charged into the streets, clamoring for an end to Metternich's system. There, as elsewhere in the streets of Europe's cities, women joined men in the effort, building the barricades, taking care of the wounded, supplying the fighters with meals, and sometimes taking part in battles against armed forces. The painting on page 599 captures the flavor of this revolutionary activity. As the uprising gained momentum, Metternich fled for his life. The Habsburg emperor, Ferdinand I, hastily abolished the country's most repressive laws, ended serfdom, and promised constitutional reform.

In Hungary, the Magyars, under the leadership of the eloquent Louis Kossuth (1802–1894), rose and demanded national autonomy from Austria. The Czechs followed suit in Bohemia and called for a Pan-Slavic congress to meet at Prague. In Austria's Italian

provinces of Lombardy and Venetia, the rebellious populace drove the Austrian forces into defensive fortresses and declared their independence. By June 1848, it appeared **Hungary** that the Habsburg Empire was splintering along ethnic lines and that its German core would commit to liberal reforms.

When the Hohenzollern ruler of Prussia, Frederick William IV (r. 1840–1861), heard of events in Austria, he granted some reforms and promised a liberal constitution. Nevertheless, as Document 18.3 suggests, the **Prussia** news from Paris and Vienna sent middle-class liberals and artisans demonstrating in the streets of Berlin, the capital of Prussia. Frederick William sent in the troops, but their brutality stiffened support for the revolutionary cause. A few days later, he withdrew his troops and promised more reforms and support for German national unity. Hohenzollern Prussia, like Habsburg Austria, appeared on the road to liberal government.

In several other German states, rulers quickly gave in to revolutionary demands. Then a self-appointed group of liberal leaders made a bold move: They called for a popularly **Frankfurt Assembly** elected assembly representing all German states to meet at Frankfurt to construct a liberal German nation. "[A]t last the great opportunity had arrived for giving to the German people the liberty which was their birthright and to the German fatherland its unity and greatness," explained a participant. Three crucial questions confronted the Frankfurt Assembly: (1) whether German-speaking portions of the multilingual Habsburg Empire and other states should be included in the projected German nation, (2) what should be done with non-German ethnic groups living within German states, and (3) who should head the new nation. After almost a year of debate, the assembly decided on a smaller Germany and offered the crown to the king of Prussia.

Meanwhile, in Italy several states established new constitutions. The movement for national unification

Italy kept alive by the idealist Giuseppe Mazzini found additional strength. He backed up his ideas with action: "Insurrection—by means of guerrilla bands—is the true method of warfare for all nations desirous of emancipating themselves from a foreign yoke," he explained. Just one year after the first revolt broke out in France, popular demonstrations brought down the papal government and forced Pius IX to flee Rome. Mazzini soon gained a foothold as head of the newly formed Republic of Rome.

The Return to Order

For the revolutionaries of 1848, a new, victorious age seemed to have dawned. Within a few months, the old governments almost everywhere had been swept from power or seriously weakened. The upheavals were so widespread that at one point Tsar Nicholas I of Russia exclaimed to Britain's Queen Victoria, "What remains standing in Europe? Great Britain and Russia." Unfortunately for the revolutionaries, however, the forces of order showed resiliency and even new strength when events took more radical turns.

In France, divisions rose among those once unified against the monarchy. The more conservative peas-

June Days in France antry and landowners in the countryside stepped back from the radical reforms demanded by Parisian artisans, shop owners, and intellectuals. The gap also widened between the middle class, which felt that reforms had gone far enough or even too far, and workers, who agitated for more social programs. These divisions reached a boiling point when the Constitutional Assembly, which had been elected in the late spring of 1848, abolished the national workshops. Officials told the workers to join the army or go look for work in the provinces. The desperate men and women of the Paris working class resorted to arms and barricades. For four days, war raged in the streets of Paris between the working class, armed with National Guard rifles, and the regular army. The French liberal writer and politician Alexis de Tocqueville (1805–1859), an observer of the events, described the "June Days" as "the revolt of one whole section of the population against another. Women took part in it as well as men . . . and when at last the time had come to surrender, the women were the last to yield."

★ Sites of Revolts, 1848–1849
— Boundary of German Confederation

MAP 18.3

European Revolts, 1848–1849

This map shows the locations of the 1848–1849 revolutions.

Explore the Map

1. What possible reasons might there have been for the eruption of so many revolutions over this wide geographic area?

2. Compare this map with **Map 18.2.** What do the two maps reveal about the breadth of revolutionary activity between 1820 and 1849 and the challenges faced by the conservative forces of order?

Figure 18.10 depicts the fate of the revolutionary workers of Paris during the June Days of 1848. Here the paving stones used so successfully for the barricades in February 1848 are scattered in the rout of the revolutionaries. The revolutionaries and the radical demands they represent—symbolized by the red, white, and blue of a fallen fighter's clothing—lie crushed by army troops, who this time have willingly fired on the people. The artist, Meissonier (1815–1891), witnessed these defenders "slain, shot down,

DOCUMENT 18.3

German Liberals and Nationalists Rally for Reform

The February 1848 revolution ending Louis-Philippe's regime and establishing a republic in France inspired many others throughout Europe who thirsted for reform. In Germany, liberals and nationalists rallied in hopes of uniting the German states and initiating liberal reforms. In the following selection, the journalist Carl Schurz (1829–1906) describes his participation in those events and the feelings he shared with others.

One morning, toward the end of February, 1848, I sat quietly in my attic-chamber, working hard at my tragedy of "Ulrich von Hutten" [a sixteenth-century German knight], when suddenly a friend rushed breathlessly into the room, exclaiming, "What, you sitting here! Do you not know what has happened?"

"No; what?"

"The French have driven away Louis Philippe and proclaimed the republic."

I threw down my pen—and that was the end of "Ulrich von Hutten." I never touched the manuscript again. We tore down the stairs, into the street, to the market-square, the accustomed meeting-place for all the student societies after their midday dinner. Although it was still forenoon, the market was already crowded with young men talking excitedly. There was no shouting, no noise, only agitated conversation. What did we want there? This probably no one knew. But since the French had driven away Louis Philippe and proclaimed the republic, something of course must happen here, too. . . . We were dominated by a vague feeling as if a great outbreak of elemental forces had begun, as if an earthquake was impending of which we had felt the first shock, and we instinctively crowded together. . . .

The next morning there were the usual lectures to be attended. But how profitless! At last we closed with a sigh the notebook and went away, impelled by a feeling that now we had something more important to do—to devote ourselves to the affairs of the fatherland. And this we did by seeking as quickly as possible again the company of our friends, in order to discuss what had happened and what was to come. In these conversations, excited as they were, certain ideas and catchwords worked themselves to the surface, which expressed more or less the feelings of the people. Now had arrived in Germany the day for the establishment of "German Unity," and the founding of a great, powerful national German Empire. In the first line the convocation of a national parliament. Then the demands for civil rights and liberties, free speech, free press, the right of free assembly, equality before the law, a freely elected representation of the people with legislative power, responsibility of ministers, self-government of the communes, the right of the people to carry arms, the formation of a civic guard with elective officers, and so on—in short, that which was called a "constitutional form of government on a broad democratic basis." Republican ideas were at first only sparingly expressed. But the word democracy was soon on all tongues, and many, too, thought it a matter of course that if the princes should try to withhold from the people the rights and liberties demanded, force would take the place of mere petition. Of course, the regeneration of the fatherland must, if possible, be accomplished by peaceable means. . . . Like many of my friends, I was dominated by the feeling that at last the great opportunity had arrived for giving to the German people the liberty which was their birthright and to the German fatherland its unity and greatness, and that it was now the first duty of every German to do and to sacrifice everything for this sacred object.

SOURCE: Carl Schurz, *The Reminiscences of Carl Schurz* (New York: The McClure Co., 1907), vol. 1, pp. 112–113.

Analyze the Document

1. Why did the fall of Louis-Philippe in France have such a strong effect on Schurz?

2. What reforms does Schurz long for?

3. What does Schurz mean by a "constitutional form of government on a broad democratic basis"?

thrown from the windows, covering the ground with their corpses, the earth not yet having drunk up all the blood." Meissonier intended his painting to serve as "a sober warning to the rebels of the future." When the last barricade had fallen during the bloody June Days, some 1,500, mostly workingmen, had perished. Several hundred were sent overseas to French colonial prisons. Louis Blanc fled to Great Britain. The events widened the cleavage between radical urban Paris and conservative rural France—a cleavage that would long complicate France's public life. As a final insult to the revolutionaries, the December presidential elections swept Louis-Napoleon Bonaparte (1808–1873), nephew of Napoleon Bonaparte, to victory. Promising something for everyone and projecting an image of order and authority, Louis-Napoleon held office for three years and then destroyed the republic in 1851 by taking power for himself in a coup d'état.

In Austria, the revolutionaries' inexperience and the rivalries among various ethnic groups gave the Habsburgs the upper hand. Playing one group against another and using their still-formidable military force, the Austrian rulers beat down the liberal and national revolts one after the other. In Hungary, they had the help of the reactionary

Austria and Hungary

Nicholas I of Russia, whose army overwhelmed the Magyar rebels. In Italy, Austrian might (and in Rome, French arms) eventually prevailed.

In Prussia, Frederick William IV fell under the influence of his militaristic and reactionary Junker advisors. Heartened by the news from Vienna

<mark>Prussia</mark> that the Habsburgs had regained their position, he spurned the German crown offered him by the Frankfurt Assembly, contemptuously calling it "a crown from the gutter." His rejection of the crown blasted the Frankfurt Assembly's hopes for a united, liberal Germany. He accused liberals in the Frankfurt Assembly of "fighting the battle of godlessness, perjury, and robbery, and kindling a war against monarchy," and his Prussian troops drove the point home by ousting the few remaining liberals determined to keep the assembly alive.

Figure 18.11 reveals much of what happened in Prussia and elsewhere. The painting by Adolph Menzel shows a funeral that the city of Berlin staged for the fallen on Sunday, March 22, 1848. More than 300 people had lost their lives in the fighting that raged during the early days of the revolution. Caskets are piled in a monumental pyramid. To the left of the church, the black, red, and gold flags of a (hopefully) united Germany flutter outside the optimistic townspeople's houses. To the left, university students, who played a vital role in the revolution, stand at attention. To the right, people energized by the revolution watch the procession, discuss recent events, and read announcements. Groups of the newly armed militia and mourners who supported the revolutionary cause move across the square. Victory once seemed to be in the revolutionaries' grasp. As the only sketched-in figures on the far left suggest, when the revolutionaries suffered reversals a few months later, Menzel lost the heart to finish the painting. His canvas stands as a testament to this "unfinished" revolution.

What Happened?

By 1850, the conservative forces of order had regained control. What happened? How could so many victories by liberals, nationalists, workers, and students be turned into defeats so quickly?

There are several explanations. First, the alliances among middle-class liberals, radicals, socialists, artisans, and workers was one of convenience

<mark>Internal divisions</mark> (based on their shared opposition to the status quo) rather than genuine fellowship. After revolutionary forces gained power, the interests of the various groups proved too divergent for the alliances to endure. These divisions emerged most clearly in France, where the frightened middle class and conservative peasantry broke with the Parisian working classes. Lamartine, a poet and leading politician at the time, explained how the revolutionaries

FIGURE 18.10 Jean-Louis-Ernest Meissonier, *Memory of Civil War (The Barricade),* 1849 Revolutionary workers lie mortally wounded in the streets of Paris after the forces of order crushed the uprising in June 1848.

were divided into two groups: the republicans "were inspired by the hatred of royalty," while the socialists "were inspired . . . by the progress of humanity. The republic and equality was the aim of the one; social renovation and fraternity the aim of the other. They had nothing in common but impatience . . . and hope. . . ."

Second, liberal and nationalistic forces worked best together when out of power; in power, they often stood at cross-purposes. This lack of harmony between liberals and nationalists was particularly pronounced in central Europe, where <mark>Holding power: liberalism vs. nationalism</mark> the nationalist aspirations of German, Polish, Magyar, Croatian, Serbian, and other groups conflicted with efforts to form new governments with liberal institutions. For example, liberals in the Frankfurt Assembly who sought to unify Germany turned against other nationalities who rose up against German rule in Austria and Prussia.

Third, the strength of conservatism should not be underestimated. With industrialization just beginning to emerge in central Europe, the middle and working classes—both discontented with the conservative status quo—were still weak. Revolutionary leaders were inexperienced as well. In Germany, for example,

FIGURE 18.11 Adolph Menzel, *The March Casualties Lying in State,* **1848** On March 22, 1848, Berliners gathered in a somber funeral procession to honor those who died in the early days of the revolution against the Prussian government.

the journalist Carl Schurz explained the failure of the Frankfurt parliament: "That parliament was laboring under an overabundance of learning and virtue and under a want of . . . political experience."

> Conservatism

Finally, once the shock of initial defeat at the hands of revolutionaries had faded, the seasoned leaders of the forces of order marshaled their resources, drew on their own armies and those

> Force

of allies, and overcame the divided revolutionary forces. After they reestablished control, conservative leaders tore up most of the reforms and imprisoned, executed, or exiled revolutionaries. In December 1848, Pope Pius IX summarized the views of angry conservatives: "We . . . declare null and of no effect, and altogether illegal, every act" of reform during 1848. In fact, a few liberal reforms, such as the abolition of serfdom in Austria and Hungary and the limited constitutions in Piedmont and Prussia, would survive, but the great changes and power that for a few months seemed within the grasp of revolutionaries were gone.

LOOKING BACK *&* MOVING FORWARD

Summary In 1815, the conservative forces of order tried to secure their own survival by repressing all those heartened by the principles and reforms of the French Revolution and the Enlightenment. Change became the enemy of conservatives, but the industrial revolution and the growing strength of ideologies such as liberalism, nationalism, and socialism strengthened demands for change.

In the early 1820s, a cycle of revolution and reform timidly emerged. In 1830, revolutionary forces posed a broader challenge, gaining some important victories in western Europe. The cycle returned in full force in 1848, as revolutions broke out through Europe and scored victory after victory. Those victories proved short-lived. By 1850, conservatives were back in power. This quick reversal of fortunes has led many historians to call the revolutions of 1848 "the turning point at which modern history failed to turn."

Yet the revolutions of 1848 left several important legacies. In a few cases, some liberal reforms were retained; in other cases, reforms in modified forms would be passed in succeeding years. Moreover, the overall failure of 1848 did not necessarily ensure a permanent victory for conservatism. As industrialization

KEY TERMS

Concert of Europe, *p. 579*
conservatism, *p. 581*
liberalism, *p. 582*
nationalism, *p. 583*
romanticism, *p. 586*
Socialists, *p. 589*
The Communist Manifesto, *p. 591*
Zollverein, *p. 592*
Chartists, *p. 598*

and urbanization spread year by year, traditional life and the old order it represented kept crumbling. Perhaps most significant, participants and observers had witnessed the power of ideologies, as well as economic and social realities, to galvanize people into political action.

However, the reestablished governments had learned important lessons from 1848, too, and would try to secure their positions with new vigor. They repaired the dam that broke in February 1848. For the time being, at least, everything seemed under control.

REVIEW, ANALYZE, & CONNECT TO TODAY

REVIEW THE PREVIOUS CHAPTERS

Chapter 17—"Factories, Cities, and Families in the Industrial Age"—analyzed the industrial revolution and urbanization. Chapter 16—"Overturning the Political and Social Order"—examined the revolution whose consequences were felt throughout the West.

1. In what ways might the developments described in Chapter 18 be considered a reaction to the French Revolution and industrial revolution discussed in the previous two chapters?

2. What forces stemming from the French Revolution and industrial revolution did conservatives try to repress or contain? To what extent do you think conservatives succeeded?

ANALYZE THIS CHAPTER

Chapter 18—"Coping with Change"—analyzes the struggles between competing ideologies and political forces during the period between Napoleon's fall and the revolutions of 1848.

1. Analyze the ideas of conservatism and policies of the forces of order in the years between 1815 and 1830.

2. In what ways did the ideas and actions of liberals, nationalists, and socialists challenge conservatives between 1815 and 1850?

3. In what ways did romanticism become a new cultural movement and an important ideology?

4. Analyze the commonalities in the several revolutions and movements for reform that developed between 1820 and 1848.

CONNECT TO TODAY

Think about the ideologies and revolutions discussed in this chapter.

1. What struggles in recent times—within Western countries or elsewhere in the world—might be comparable to those that occurred between competing ideologies and political forces in the first half of the nineteenth century?

2. What lessons from the revolutions of 1848 might apply to today's world?

BEYOND THE CLASSROOM

THE CONGRESS OF VIENNA: A GATHERING OF VICTORS

Bridge, F.R. *The Great Powers and the European States System, 1815–1914*. London: Longman, 1980. A thorough diplomatic history of the period.

Chapman, Tim. *Congress of Vienna: Origins, Processes, and Results*. London: Taylor & Francis, 1998. A well-written study that covers the topic well.

IDEOLOGIES: HOW THE WORLD SHOULD BE

Arblaster, Anthony. *The Rise and Decline of Western Liberalism*. Oxford: B. Blackwell, 1984. An analysis of the evolution and key components of liberalism.

Beecher, Jonathan. *Charles Fourier: The Visionary and His World*. Berkeley: University of California Press, 1986. Traces the development of Fourier's ideas through his early years to his emergence as a political prophet and founder of one of the most significant early socialist movements.

Breckman, Warren. *European Romanticism*. London: Bedford/St. Martin's, 2007. A useful, brief history of romanticism, with documents.

Smith, Denis Mack. *Mazzini*. New Haven, CT: Yale University Press, 1999. A biography of this important figure by a well-known historian.

RESTORATION AND REPRESSION

Jardin, André, and André-Jean Tudesq. *Restoration and Reaction, 1815–1848*. Cambridge: Cambridge University Press, 1988. A solid survey of France during this period.

Sheehan, James J. *German History, 1770–1866*. New York: Oxford University Press, 1989. A comprehensive, exhaustive examination of the changes in German social, political, and economic history.

Sked, Alan. *The Decline and Fall of the Habsburg Empire, 1815–1918*. London: Longman, 1989. Studies the growing problems facing the Habsburg Empire during the nineteenth century.

A WAVE OF REVOLUTION AND REFORM

Church, Clive. *Europe in 1830: Revolution and Political Change*. London: Allen & Unwin, 1983. Examines the revolutions that swept across Europe in a comparative context.

Fortescue, William. *Revolution and Counter-Revolution in France, 1815–1852*. London: Blackwell, 2002. A useful survey of the topic and France during this period.

THE DAM BURSTS, 1848

Rapport, Michael. *1848: Year of Revolution*. New York: Basic Books, 2009. A well-written narrative.

Sperber, Jonathan. *The European Revolutions, 1848–1851*, 2nd ed. Cambridge: Cambridge University Press, 2005. A brief yet thorough account that covers the tumultuous events throughout Europe.

ADOLPH MENZEL, *THE DEPARTURE OF WILLIAM I FOR THE ARMY ON JULY 31, 1870,* 1871

This 1871 painting by German artist Adolph Menzel suggests that the inhabitants of Prussia's capital, Berlin, greeted a statebuilding war against France with an outburst of Prussian patriotism and broader German nationalism. Menzel depicts King William I's departure on July 31, 1870, from Berlin to his military headquarters in Mainz to help lead the war against France. On the left, in a white satin-lined coach, the king and his wife pass under cast-iron and glass street lamps along the fashionable tree-lined avenue Unter den Linden. The monarch salutes the crowd, while the tearful queen covers her face with a handkerchief. The crowds are celebrating not only the king but also their own success and anticipated victory. Flags billow in the breeze—both the Prussian and the black, white, and red German flags, signaling a moment of growing national unification. In the distance stands Berlin's new redbrick city hall, evidence of Prussia's growing political and economic power that supports the bold military effort.

Nationalism and Statebuilding

19

Unifying Nations, 1850–1870

On May 31, 1860, just three weeks after landing in Sicily, the Italian nationalist leader Giuseppe Garibaldi toured Palermo, Sicily's main city. He entered the city at the head of a band of one thousand volunteer soldiers to begin the liberation of southern Italy from the old, Austrian-supported Bourbon king. He called for "Italians" to "put an end, once and for all, to the miseries of so many centuries," and "prove to the world that it is no lie that Roman generations inhabited this land." An eyewitness described how "the popular idol, Garibaldi, in his red flannel shirt, with a loose colored handkerchief round his neck . . . was walking on foot among those cheering, laughing, crying, mad thousands." As he moved through the streets, "the people threw themselves forward to kiss his hands, or, at least, to touch the hem of his garment, as if it contained the panacea for all their past and perhaps coming suffering."

In the decades between 1850 and 1870, millions of others in the Italian states—and in regions ranging from the Americas in the west to the Ottoman Empire in the east—would rally, fight, and die in the name of national unity. In Europe, maps had to be redrawn as new nation-states emerged. In the United States, a wrenching battle was entered into in the name of preserving the Union. Political leaders would use nationalistic appeals to build stronger states as well as to tear apart multinational empires. Nationalism was evolving from the ideals of earlier decades to the realities of power politics.

TIMELINE

Drive for Italian Unification

Drive for German Unification

Second Empire in France

Crimean War 1854–1856

U.S. Civil War 1861–1865

New Imperialism

Age of Ideologies

Spread of Industrial Revolution

• Franco-Prussian War

1850   1855   1860   1865   1870

PREVIEW

BUILDING UNIFIED NATION-STATES

"Every German heart hoped for it," wrote the Baroness Spitzemberg in Berlin in 1871. "United into one Reich, the greatest, the most powerful, the most feared in Europe; great by reason of its physical power, greater still by reason of its education and the intelligence which permeates it!" So the baroness expressed her longing for national unification, a passion felt by many others in the West.

In the two decades after 1850, no political force was stronger than nationalism. It pushed people toward national unity in Italy and | Nationalism | Germany and threatened to tear the Habsburg and Ottoman empires apart. In the United States, the principle of national unity helped spark a brutal civil war. In France and elsewhere, rulers enacted major reforms designed to bolster national unity and their authority as leaders of a nation of citizens. All these efforts were intended to build strong, unified nation-states led by central governments that could enjoy the support of their citizens.

Unlike in 1848, however, the nationalist political figures were neither revolutionaries nor idealists. As one advocate of Italian unification | Political realism | observed, "To defeat cannons and soldiers, cannons and soldiers are needed." From positions of established power, this new generation of leaders molded nationalism to fit harsh political realities. They focused their eyes on practical policies, not ideals. They gambled, compromised, manipulated, and fought to achieve their goals. Few struggled more persistently and cleverly than Count Camillo di Cavour (1810–1861).

THE DRIVE FOR ITALIAN UNIFICATION

Cavour was born into a well-to-do, noble family living in Piedmont-Sardinia, a small but relatively powerful independent state in northern Italy that also included the island of | Cavour | Sardinia. As a young man, he gambled, played the stock market, experimented with agricultural techniques, and succeeded in business—a pattern of taking calculated risks he would later try to follow in politics. By the 1840s, he had become committed to Italian unification. Shortly before the revolution of 1848, he founded the newspaper *Il Risorgimento (The Resurgence)*, which passionately argued for a unified Italy. In 1850, Piedmont-Sardinia's King Victor Emmanuel II (r. 1849–1878) made Cavour his minister of commerce and agriculture and, two years later, prime minister.

Cavour's goals were clear. First, he wanted to modernize Piedmont economically and thereby win strength and respect for his homeland. Second, he sought to make | Cavour's leadership | Piedmont the central engine of the drive for national unification. Third, he advocated forming a new Italian state as a constitutional monarchy under Piedmont's king rather than a democratic republic or a confederation under the pope. To achieve all these ends, Cavour lowered tariffs, built railroads, and balanced Piedmont's budget. He supported the nationalistic Italian National Society and its Feminine Committee, which worked toward national unification with Piedmont at the helm. Finally, he employed diplomacy and Piedmont's relatively small army to gain international support for the struggle against the primary obstacle to unification—Austria.

When the Crimean War broke out between Russia and the Ottoman Empire in 1854, Cavour saw an opportunity. He brought Piedmont in on the side of Great Britain and France, countries that had joined the Ottoman Turks against Russia. Cavour hoped to gain the friendship and support of France and Britain and thereby elevate Piedmont-Sardinia's status among the European powers. "I believe that the principal condition for the improvement of Italy's fate," he explained to the Parliament of Piedmont in 1855, "is to lift up her reputation once more . . . to prove that Italy's sons can fight valiantly on battlefields where glory is to be won." Victory in the east, he claimed, "will help the future state of Italy more than all that has been done by those people who hoped to regenerate her by rhetorical speeches and writings."

His risky plan may have paid off. At the Paris Peace Conference in 1856, which ended the war, he pleaded Piedmont's case against Austria so skillfully that he captured the attention of the international community. Two years later, Cavour and France's Emperor Napoleon III met at a French resort to discuss ways to move against Austria, a competitor of France on the Continent and the chief barrier to Cavour's hopes for Italian unity. The two decided to provoke Austria into a war against Piedmont and thereby bring France into the fray. "Together we began to . . . search of those grounds for war which were so difficult to find," explained Cavour in a note to his king. Then "we discovered what we had been trying so hard to find," a way to manipulate Austria into a war that "would not alarm the other continental powers." After Austria declared war, France would help Piedmont drive the Austrians out of Lombardy and Venetia, and these two states would then be annexed to Piedmont-Sardinia. In return, Piedmont would cede the two small, French-speaking provinces of Savoy and Nice to France and allow a kingdom of Central Italy to be created for Napoleon III's cousin.

In 1859, after Cavour mobilized the Piedmontese army and refused an Austrian demand to reverse the act, the unsuspecting Austrians declared war on Piedmont. French armies, using new railroad lines, poured across the Alps to fight alongside the Piedmontese. In the bloody battles of Magenta and Solferino, the French and Piedmontese ousted the Austrians from Lombardy. But to the dismay of Cavour, Napoleon III suddenly made a separate peace at Villafranca with Austria that gave Piedmont Lombardy and left Venetia in Austrian hands. Cavour's side now had momentum, however. Nationalists in other Italian states, inspired by Piedmont's success, rose to the cause of national unity. By early 1860, most of northern and central Italy had joined Piedmont voluntarily.

At this pivotal point in the action, the rawboned nationalist Giuseppe Garibaldi (1807–1882) made a daring exploit. Garibaldi had long struggled to create a unified and republican Italy—organizing people, conducting campaigns of guerrilla warfare, and leading insurrections. Often in exile, he had become a well-known figure in Europe and the Americas. In May 1860, accompanied by a thousand civilian warriors dressed in red shirts, he sailed for Sicily in southern Italy, where many peasants had already launched a revolt. "It is the duty of every Italian to succor them [the Sicilians in revolt] with words, money, arms, and above all, in person," he announced (see Document 19.1). Garibaldi's goal was nothing less than the conquest of the Kingdom of Naples, the largest and most populous of the Italian states, and then Rome itself. Cavour officially condemned the seemingly foolhardy expedition but secretly assisted it.

As **Figure 19.1** suggests, Garibaldi's exploits read like an adventure novel. He heroically lands at the island of Sicily to fight for Italian unification. In the background, his band of volunteer soldiers (the "Red Shirts") pours from three ships and marches in rough formation. Carrying a sword and a flag representing Italian unity, Garibaldi is welcomed by admiring children, women, men, and a priest. In rapid succession, Garibaldi conquered Sicily, crossed the Strait of Messina, and triumphantly entered Naples (see **Map 19.1**, on page 614). The opposing troops had little heart for their own cause. Many, along with civilian women and men by the thousands, joined Garibaldi after his first victories. Made ever bolder by his conquests, the confident Garibaldi advanced north toward Rome.

Not wanting to lose control of the rapidly changing situation and fearing that an attack on Rome by Garibaldi might lead France and Austria to come to the aid of the pope, Cavour sent troops southward in September 1860, gained control over the Papal States, and then skirted the area around Rome. King Victor Emmanuel, marching at the head of his army, met Garibaldi's forces south of Rome. Garibaldi yielded to Victor Emmanuel and his Piedmontese troops. Two years later, Garibaldi, hoping to annex Rome as the capital of Italy, fomented an unsuccessful uprising. The gallant patriot soon retired to his farm on the rocky island of Caprera.

The Kingdom of Italy was formally declared in March 1861, with Victor Emmanuel II as monarch and the Piedmontese Constitution of 1848 as the national charter. The king, along with a parliamentary government elected by limited suffrage, would rule. The red, white, and green Piedmontese flag now flew over all of Italy, from the Alps to Sicily, except in Venetia and Rome (see **Map 19.1**). These two provinces (with the exception of the Vatican palace) joined the Italian state in 1866 and 1870, respectively.

Sadly, Cavour did not live to enjoy the fruits of his labors. Less than three months after the birth of his beloved Italian nation, he died. Paunchy, with ill-fitting glasses, he had never cut an impressive figure. Nor had he made a particularly powerful orator. "I cannot make a speech," he once said, "but I can make Italy."

> War with Austria

> Garibaldi

> Kingdom of Italy

thinking about

DOCUMENTS

DOCUMENT 19.1

Garibaldi Appeals to Italians for Support

The campaign that resulted in the unification of Italy required not just idealism but also a realistic outlook and daring action. With his political manipulations, Cavour provided the realism. With his invasion of Sicily in 1860, Giuseppe Garibaldi provided the daring action. To support the invasion, Garibaldi issued his Proclamation for the Liberation of Sicily.

Italians!—The Sicilians are fighting against the enemies of Italy, and for Italy. It is the duty of every Italian to succour them with words, money, and arms, and, above all, in person.

The misfortunes of Italy arise from the indifference of one province to the fate of the others.

The redemption of Italy began from the moment that men of the same land ran to help their distressed brothers.

Left to themselves, the brave Sicilians will have to fight, not only the mercenaries of the Bourbon, but also those of Austria and the Priest of Rome.

Let the inhabitants of the free provinces lift their voices in behalf of their struggling brethren, and impel their brave youth to the conflict.

Let the Marches, Umbria, Sabina, Rome, the Neapolitan, rise to divide the forces of our enemies.

Where the cities suffice not for the insurrection, let them send bands of their bravest into the country.

The brave man finds an arm everywhere. Listen not to the voice of cowards, but arm, and let us fight for our brethren, who will fight for us tomorrow.

A band of those who fought with me the country's battles marches with me to the fight. Good and generous,

they will fight for their country to the last drop of their blood, nor ask for other reward than a clear conscience.

"Italy and Victor Emmanuel!" they cried, on passing the Ticino. "Italy and Victor Emmanuel!" shall re-echo in the blazing caves of Mongibello.

At this cry, thundering from the great rock of Italy to the Tarpeian, the rotten Throne of tyranny shall crumble, and, as one man, the brave descendants of Vespro shall rise.

To Arms! Let me put an end, once and for all, to the miseries of so many centuries. Prove to the world that it is no lie that Roman generations inhabited this land.

SOURCE: Public Documents, *The Annual Register,* 1860 (London, 1861), pp. 281–282.

Analyze the Document

1. How does Garibaldi appeal to Italians outside Sicily for support?

2. In what ways does this proclamation echo the appeal of nationalism?

3. Who does Garibaldi identify as his enemies? Why?

GERMANY "BY BLOOD AND IRON"

Like Italy, Germany as we understand it did not exist in 1850, except in the hearts of nationalists. Most of the many German states belonged to the loose Germanic Confederation, but this organization, under the dominance of Austria, did not function as a unified nation. Would someone like Piedmont's Count Cavour rise to overcome the obstacles to German unification? By 1860, no one of this caliber had yet stepped forward.

Prussian leadership

The best hope for German unity rested with Prussia, which had achieved a position of strength thanks to its economic expansion and leadership over the Zollverein, a German customs union that fostered industrialization in Prussia and the Rhineland (see page 592). By 1853, every German state except Austria had joined the Zollverein. However, Prussia was torn by the political struggle between liberals in the legislature and the conservative aristocracy. The two sides fought over plans to strengthen Prussia's military. When Prussia's new king, William I, and his military advisors proposed to double the size of the

army, the liberals, who distrusted Prussian militarism and hoped to gain a stronger role for the legislature in the Prussian government, defeated the measure. Faced with a deadlock between these uncompromising forces and convinced that his royal authority was being threatened, William I called on Otto von Bismarck (1815–1898).

"I was born and raised as an aristocrat," Bismarck once explained. He would remain loyal to Prussia's landowning aristocracy his whole life. As a young man, Bismarck showed little promise of future greatness. While attending university, he spent more time gambling than studying. A religious conversion in 1846 and marriage seemed to give him more of a sense of purpose. He entered politics in 1847 and came to believe that only an alliance of conservatism and nationalism could preserve the aristocracy and strengthen Prussia. His enemies were the liberals, who had failed in 1848, and Austria, Prussia's chief competitor and supposed senior partner within the German states.

Bismarck

Bismarck assumed the office of prime minister of Prussia in 1862. With the backing of the king, the aristocracy, and the army, he promptly defied the

FIGURE 19.1

Garibaldi Landing in Sicily

This painting illustrates Giuseppe Garibaldi and his band of soldiers landing in Sicily in May 1860. This event and the campaign that followed it played an important role in the unification of Italy. Notice the spirit and mood captured by the artist.

Connecting Art & Society

1. How has the artist depicted Garibaldi, who stands in the center of the picture, and the "Red Shirt" soldiers behind him?

2. In what ways does this depiction glorify Garibaldi's exploits and the unification movement?

3. How has the artist presented the people surrounding Garibaldi?

liberals in the legislature, violated the constitution, and ordered taxes collected for military reform. "Necessity alone is authoritative," he argued. He would pursue a policy of realism—**Realpolitik**—to achieve his goals. "Not by speeches and majority resolutions," Bismarck rumbled, "are the great questions of the time decided—that was the mistake of 1848 and 1849—but by blood and iron." As the prime minister argued, Germans looked to Prussia for leadership not because of its liberalism but because of its power.

Like Cavour in Italy, Bismarck sought out political opportunities, created them when they failed to materialize, and did not hesitate to take calculated risks, including war. In 1864, Denmark provided his first opportunity when it tried to incorporate Schleswig and Holstein, two small provinces lying between Prussia and Denmark. The provinces' legal status had been disputed for decades. Posing as a defender of German nationalism, Prussia promptly declared war on Denmark, pulling Austria—anxious to retain leadership of the German Confederation—in as Prussia's reluctant ally. In the complicated settlement—Schleswig and Holstein were to be ruled jointly by Prussia and Austria—Bismarck shrewdly planted the seeds for a future conflict with Austria.

Bismarck soon used this unworkable arrangement to stir up trouble with Austria. He obtained the

Wars for unification

MAP 19.1

The Unification of Italy

This map shows the unification of Italy in the years after 1859.

Explore the Map

1. Locate Lombardy and Nice. Do you think Piedmont gave up too much for what it gained in its bargain for French support? Explain.

2. Find the route of Garibaldi's campaign. Why were Garibaldi's exploits so important—and threatening—to Piedmont's plans to unify Italy?

3. How important were the territories still outside the Italian state in 1860? Explain.

■	Piedmont-Sardinia Before 1859
■	Areas Annexed in 1859
■	Areas Annexed in 1860
■	Areas Annexed in 1866
■	Areas Annexed in 1870
■	Areas Annexed from 1919 to 1924
—	Italian Boundary at 1924
■	Fortress
→	Garibaldi's Route

support of Italy by promising Austria's province of Venetia as a prize. He gained Russia's sympathy by supporting its intervention against rebellious subjects in Poland. He neutralized Napoleon III by personal persuasion and deception. Finally, as Document 19.2 suggests, he manipulated domestic politics to achieve his ends. In 1866, Bismarck took a risk by using threats and maneuvers to provoke Austria into declaring war on Prussia. Austria was twice the size of Prussia, with double the population, and had long dominated central Europe. Nevertheless, Prussia's modern and mobile armies managed to overwhelm the surprised Austrian forces in just seven weeks. Austria suffered four times as many casualties as Prussia, in great part because of the fast-firing needle-guns used by Prussian troops and the army's use of railroads to move forces quickly to battlefields. Bismarck boldly expelled Austria from the German Confederation and even annexed several German states that had sided with Austria. Nevertheless, hoping for Austrian support in the future, Bismarck refused the desires of Prussia's king and army leaders to annex Austrian territories.

> **Austro-Prussian War**

Prussia now controlled the newly created North German Confederation. Despite some democratic forms, such as a legislative body (the Reichstag) elected by universal male suffrage, the government was fundamentally an **autocracy.** The legislature had no control over the chancellor—appointed by and responsible only to the king or his cabinet—and little control over the budget or armed forces. However, some of the southern German states, with larger Catholic populations than Prussia had, still lay outside Bismarck's grasp (see **Map 19.2**). He wisely recognized that these remaining, reluctant states might join the fold if German nationalism could be rallied against a common, foreign threat. France, Bismarck decided, might just fit the bill.

> **Franco-Prussian War**

Bismarck's opportunity to confront France came in 1870 when the Spanish crown was offered to a Hohenzollern prince—a relative of Prussia's William I. When Bismarck persuaded the reluctant prince to accept the Spanish offer, the French immediately

DOCUMENT 19.2

Bismarck Masters Politics in Prussia

Like Cavour in Italy, Otto von Bismarck became a master of both politics and war in his effort to unify Germany under Prussia. Just before Prussia's war with Austria in 1866, Bismarck, despite his conservatism, instituted a constitution that included universal male suffrage. In the following excerpt from his Memoirs, Bismarck describes his support for universal suffrage.

Looking to the necessity, in a fight against an overwhelming foreign Power, of being able, in extreme need, to use even revolutionary means, I had had no hesitation whatever in throwing into the frying-pan, by means of the circular dispatch of June 10, 1866, the most powerful ingredient known at that time to liberty-mongers, namely, universal suffrage, so as to frighten off foreign monarchies from trying to stick a finger into our national omelette. . . .

The acceptance of universal suffrage was a weapon in the war against Austria and other foreign countries, in the war for German Unity, as well as a threat to use the last weapons in a struggle against coalitions. In a war of this sort, when it becomes a matter of life and death, one does not look at the weapons that one seizes, nor the value of what one destroys in using them: one is guided at the moment by no other thought than the issue of the war, and the preservation of one's external independence; the settling of affairs and reparation of the damage has to take place after the peace. Moreover, I still hold that the principle of universal suffrage is a just one, not only in theory but also in practice, provided always that voting be not secret, for secrecy is a quality that is indeed incompatible with the best characteristics of German blood. . . .

The counterpoise to this lies in the influence of the educated classes, which would be greatly strengthened if voting were public, as for the Prussian Diet. It may be that the greater discretion of the more intelligent classes rests on the material basis of the preservation of their possessions. . . . Every great state-commonwealth that loses the prudent and restraining influence of the propertied class, whether that influence rests on material or moral grounds, will always end by being rushed along at a speed which must shatter the coach of state, as happened in the development of the French Revolution.

SOURCE: Otto von Bismarck, *The Memoirs*, trans. A.J. Butler (Howard Fertig, 1890).

Analyze the Document

1. What exactly does Bismarck mean by "universal suffrage"?

2. Why might he support this apparently democratic institution?

3. To what groups of people does he particularly appeal? Why?

took alarm at the prospect of being surrounded by Hohenzollerns. The French exerted heavy pressure on Prussia, and both the prince and King William yielded. However, the unsatisfied French ministers demanded more. After a meeting at Ems between the French ambassador and the Prussian king, the chancellor saw an opportunity to provoke the French into war. Cleverly editing the Ems telegraph dispatch so as to make it appear that the French ambassador and the Prussian king had insulted each other, he published it to the world. The French government was offended and walked into Bismarck's trap. Buoyed by public demands for action, France declared war.

The chancellor had taken his greatest risk, for France seemed to possess enough military might and economic resources to humble Prussia. As France's confident prime minister stated, "We go to war with a light heart." Again, however, the able Prussian troops quickly scored resounding successes. One French army was surrounded at the fortress city of Metz. The Prussians encircled another French army at Sedan, forcing it to surrender. Napoleon III himself was one of the captives. When this news reached Paris, the liberals overthrew the government of the Second Empire and declared the Third French Republic. Paris held out for a few more months, surrounded by the Germans, but finally surrendered in January 1871.

On January 18, 1871, Bismarck called the heads of all the German states to Versailles in France. Gathering in the Hall of Mirrors, the dignitaries proclaimed Prussia's King William I emperor of the new German Empire; he would rule until 1888. **Figure 19.2** celebrates that moment. In this well-known painting by Anton von Werner, who witnessed the event, Prussian officers hail William, who stands at the left. But the center of the painting belongs to Bismarck, dressed in white, the architect of this historical moment. He alone holds the document proclaiming the new empire that he, more than anyone else, had built. The dramatic scene is set in France's historic symbol of monarchical power, the Versailles palace. By choosing this location, Bismarck drove home the point that Prussia had achieved German unity by defeating France in war. He also wanted to make it crystal clear that Germany, now in possession of France's rich provinces of Alsace and Lorraine and owed a war indemnity of 5 billion francs in gold from the French, had replaced the humiliated France as Europe's leading continental power.

MAP 19.2

The Unification of Germany

This map shows the steps taken to achieve German unification in 1871.

Explore the Map

1. Notice the changes in 1866 and 1867. How do you explain this expansion of Prussian control?

2. How do you explain Prussia's ability to add more territory to the south and west in 1871?

3. Who might have been most threatened by a powerful Germany after 1871? Why?

The constitution that Bismarck had drafted for the North German Confederation became the constitution for the new German Empire. Its twenty-five states retained control over many domestic matters, but Prussia dominated the union. Known as the Second Reich (Germans honored the old Holy Roman Empire as the First Reich), the powerful nation included a large and rapidly growing population, a vibrant industrial economy, and a feared military. Bismarck, of course, remained chancellor and lived to rule over his creation for the next nineteen years. In Germany, as in Italy, a clever, realistic political leader had employed diplomacy and war to transform the unruly forces of nationalism into German unification.

FIGURE 19.2 Anton von Werner, *Proclamation of the German Empire,* **1885** After defeating France on the battlefield, Bismarck and other dignitaries salute Prussia's King William I, now the emperor of the new German Empire, in this scene celebrating German unification.

THE FIGHT FOR NATIONAL UNITY IN NORTH AMERICA

The struggle for unification flared up in other parts of the West besides Italy and Germany. Between 1800 and 1861, the United States' political institutions had evolved along democratic and nationalistic lines. Almost all white men had gained the right to vote. A modern, broad-based political party system had formed and wrestled political power from the elite circles of the old colonial well-to-do. The nation had expanded westward to the Pacific Ocean, conquering the Amerindians and displacing them to reservations. When Mexico stood in the way of expansion, it also lost its lands to the United States armed forces. Commercial interests led the United States across the Pacific to Japan. Finally, American culture began to free itself from strictly European influence. Citizens proudly thought of themselves and their institutions as having a distinct flavor within Western civilization.

The United States

However, as the nineteenth century progressed, the nation labored under growing regional differences. The North was an expanding, urban, industrial society based on free labor. **Figure 19.3,** a lithograph of the Stillman, Allen & Co. Novelty Iron Works of New York City, illustrates one of the many manufacturing facilities growing up in

North-South divisions

the North's cities in the middle decades of the nineteenth century. The South remained agricultural, dependent on plantation crops such as cotton, and based on slave labor. **Figure 19.4,** a painting by Charles Giroux, portrays this rural society with its large population of slaves. The North enjoyed a growing population and generally favored federal over state power. The South, worried that its influence over national policies was slipping away, emphasized states' rights over federal power. In the decades before 1861, these two regions, with their increasingly different societies and interests, clashed politically on several occasions.

It was the issue of slavery, though, that gave these clashes a dangerous emotional intensity and tied together the other problems dividing the North and the South. By the early 1800s, the northern states had eliminated slavery. However, the institution persisted in the South, where

Slavery

agriculture, and especially cotton plantations, reigned supreme. There, slaveholders viewed slaves as the very basis of their wealth, power, and status. Meanwhile, in the free-labor North, antislavery sentiment grew. "[T]his government cannot endure permanently half slave and half free," declared Abraham Lincoln (1809–1865) in 1858, just two years before the nation elected him president.

In 1861, all these regional differences, fueled by the question of whether to abolish slavery, ignited a bloody war between the North, led by Lincoln, and the South, under Jefferson Davis (1808–1889). The

The Civil War

conflict raged for four years until the North finally defeated the Southern armies. Ultimately the war took more than 600,000 lives, making it the bloodiest conflict in the Western world since the end of the Napoleonic Wars. Lincoln had achieved his primary goal: to reestablish national unity and affirm the power of the national government. In the aftermath, slavery was abolished in the United States.

Farther north, a different struggle for national independence and unity had been unfolding in Canada. William Lyon Mackenzie (1795–1861), a nationalist politician, called for Canadians to "put down the villains [the British] who oppress and

Canada

enslave our country" and gain "freedom from British tribute." Britain responded to a rebellion in 1837 by

FIGURE 19.3 A Northern Factory The smokestacks and busy harbor activity in this print illustrate the U.S. North's industrial might, which played a crucial role in the Civil War.

FIGURE 19.4 Charles Giroux, a Southern Plantation, ca. 1850s The economic strength and social structure of the U.S. South were represented by cotton plantations such as the one immortalized in this painting.

granting Canada some control over its own domestic affairs. Nevertheless, the Canadian territories were not yet joined into a single nation, and Canadians feared the growing power of the United States. Demands for union and complete nationhood increased. Finally, in 1867, the British North American Act united Canada into a single nation with its own constitution.

DIVIDED AUTHORITY IN THE AUSTRIAN AND OTTOMAN EMPIRES

Nationalism pulled Austria's multiethnic empire apart rather than bringing it together (see **Map 19.3**). Czechs, Serbs, Romanians, Magyars

<mark>Austria</mark>

(Hungarians), and other ethnic groups wanted to form their own, independent nations rather than rally behind Austria, which was predominantly German.

Austria's emperor, Francis Joseph (r. 1848–1916), was no reformer or politician in the mold of Bismarck, Cavour, or Lincoln. Under pressure from liberals and nationalists, he agreed in 1860 to a moderate decen-

tralization of the empire and the creation of a parliament. After Austria's defeat by Prussia in 1866, the dominant German minority in Austria compromised with the assertive Magyars rather than fight them over issues of nationality. Their agreement, the Compromise of 1867, set up the **Dual Monarchy** of Austria-Hungary. Each country had its

<mark>Austria-Hungary, 1867</mark>

own separate parliament, but the two were united under a common ruler, the head of the House of Habsburg. This arrangement was essentially an alliance between the Germans of Austria and the Magyars of Hungary against other competing ethnic groups. The empire therefore divided authority in an effort to control even more threatening movements for national independence. This arrangement did not please other national groups, especially the Czechs, who would persistently demand equality with the Hungarians.

Like the Austrians, Ottoman rulers also had to struggle with the divisive forces of nationalism. In 1850, at least nominally, the Ottoman Empire was still extensive.

<mark>The Ottoman Empire</mark>

From its base in Anatolia, it maintained varying degrees of control over much of southeastern Europe, as well as over provinces stretching from North Africa to the Persian Gulf. However, the empire was already in decline. Its North African provinces—Egypt, Libya, Tunisia, and Algeria—were virtually autonomous. Egyptian rulers in particular tried to modernize the army, bureaucracy, and economy using western European models; Mehemet Ali (r. 1805–1848) at one point had become strong enough to threaten Ottoman control in Syria and Anatolia. To the north, powerful, ambitious neighbors—especially the Russians, who attacked the Turks in 1853 and again in 1877—maneuvered to take advantage of the Ottomans' weaknesses: lack of economic development, declining finances, internal dissension, and difficulties instituting reforms. But the greatest threats to the empire's integrity came from its restless Balkan provinces in southeastern Europe. In this area, nationalism rose, producing the same sorts of movements for independence that had weakened the Austrian Empire.

By 1830, the Ottoman Empire had already lost Serbia and Greece to independence movements (see **Map 19.4**). Nationalism had fueled an unsuccessful revolt by the Romanians in 1848 as well. In 1856, the

<mark>Balkan nationalism</mark>

Romanians gained international support as part of the settlement of the Crimean War. Over the next twenty years, they pressed the Ottomans for their freedom, finally winning full independence in 1878.

Nationalist movements also cropped up among the Bulgars. Encouraged by Serbia and Russia, the Bulgars revolted in 1876. Each side in the conflict

MAP 19.3

Language Groups of Austria-Hungary

This map shows the concentrations of language groups in Austria-Hungary at the end of the nineteenth century.

Explore the Map

1. What does this map reveal about the difficulties facing the Austro-Hungarian Empire in an age of growing nationalism?

2. In what areas was the empire most vulnerable? Why?

3. Notice the surrounding states. What language groups might have found support from outside the empire's borders?

committed atrocities, but those committed by the Turks especially shocked Europeans. That year, Bosnia and Herzegovina also rose against the Turks. Serbia and Russia then joined forces against the Ottoman Empire. By 1878, international agreements, most notably the Treaty of Berlin, had secured the independence of Bulgaria and placed Bosnia and Herzegovina under Austro-Hungarian rule. Movements for national independence, with the aid of powers eager to take advantage of the empire's declining strength, had ended Turkish control throughout most of the Balkans. However, these developments also left a jumble of dissatisfied groups and nationalities—a few who had their own states, some who longed for political independence, and others who did not like being annexed by Austria-Hungary.

USING NATIONALISM IN FRANCE AND RUSSIA

The power of nationalism to motivate people to join revolutionary organizations, form new political allegiances, follow powerful politicians, and go to war in the name of national unity made itself clear in Italy and Germany. Under different conditions, nationalism weakened and dismembered long-established multinational states such as the Austrian and Ottoman empires.

Nationalism also pushed governments in well-established states to reach out to citizens for support. These governments tried to justify and sustain their authority by performing public services, and they bolstered their power by promoting the idea of national greatness. They paid more attention to everyday life

MAP 19.4

The Decline of the Ottoman Empire, 1683–1914

This map shows the loss of territory from the Ottoman Empire between 1683 and 1914.

Explore the Map

1. Who were the Ottomans' main European rivals in this region?

2. What areas in particular were lost during the nineteenth and early twentieth centuries?

3. Why did the growth of nationalism become such a threat to the empire?

Map legend:
- Ottoman Empire Boundary in 1683
- Areas Lost 1683–1815
- Areas Lost 1815–1878
- Areas Lost 1878–1912
- Areas of Ottoman Empire Lost in Balkan Wars 1912–1913
- Ottoman Empire in 1914
- Anglo-French Interventions, 1853 and 1854

so as to maintain social peace and cultivate loyalty to the nation—and especially to its leaders. These efforts to channel nationalism into statebuilding are especially well illustrated by the paths that France and Russia took after 1850.

Napoleon III and the Second Empire

In France, Louis-Napoleon Bonaparte, nephew of Napoleon Bonaparte, promised reform while creating a regime based on authoritarian nationalism. Louis-Napoleon was originally elected president of France's Second Republic in 1848 (see page 602). He benefited from his illustrious name, his appeal to property owners longing for order, and his well-publicized promises to link democracy from below with reforming leadership from above. When the National Assembly refused to change the constitution so that he could run for a second term, he organized a coup d'état and seized power on December 2, 1851. Resistance was limited, although hundreds were killed and thousands were arrested and deported. He quickly granted universal male suffrage, and during the following year, he held two plebiscites in which more than 90 percent of the voters supported him, establishing the Second Empire and making him hereditary emperor—Napoleon III. "I believe," he

confidently wrote, "that there are certain men who are born to serve as the means for the march of the human race. . . . I consider myself to be one of these."

Building on his uncle's legend, Napoleon III tried to convince citizens that he would lead the nation to new heights in domestic as well as foreign affairs. Napoleon III kept the elected legislature firmly under his thumb by minimizing its authority over his ministers and manipulating the electoral machinery. When it served his purposes, he encouraged industrialization and economic growth by promoting railroad construction, public works, and financial institutions—policies that appealed to the middle and working classes. His prefect of Paris, Georges Haussmann (1809–1891), rebuilt Paris into an envied model of a modern, wealthy, powerful capital (see Chapter 20). To project a progressive image, Napoleon also directed the building of hospitals, nurseries, and homes for the aged. To gain support from workers, he kept bread prices low, instituted a system of voluntary social insurance, encouraged cooperatives, and partially legalized labor unions.

The French emperor's foreign adventures gained him prestige at first but lost him everything in the end. He brought France into the Crimean War and played the glorious host to the peace conference that ended that conflict. In addition, he tried to increase French influence on the Italian peninsula by joining Piedmont in a war against Austria, but he underestimated the strength of Italian nationalism; that nation unified without becoming beholden to France. In 1862, his armies marched into Mexico City and set up a Habsburg prince, Maximilian, as puppet emperor for France. A few years later, problems at home and a threatening army from the United States forced Napoleon to withdraw his troops, leaving the doomed Maximilian to the mercy of Mexican forces. French artist Edouard Manet (1832–1883) depicts the scene on June 19, 1867 (**Figure 19.5**). In an arena with spectators looking over the brick wall, as if this were a ritual killing at the end of a bullfight, a Mexican firing squad aims and fires at point-blank range, executing Maximilian and two of his generals. However Maximilian did not die immediately; the soldier on the far right is casually reloading his rifle as if anticipating that the emperor would have to be given a final degrading coup de grâce. The soldiers are in uniforms similar to those of the French army to emphasize France's role in this affair. The Mexican fiasco added to the growing unpopularity of Napoleon III with the French people.

FIGURE 19.5 Edouard Manet, *The Execution of Emperor Maximilian*, 1868 In this violent scene, Mexican troops execute Maximilian, the emperor set up by France in their failed Mexican adventure during the 1860s.

Meanwhile, declining prosperity further weakened Napoleon's position within France. Trying to allay the mounting discontent of liberals and workers, he made one concession after another. By 1870, the liberal parliament had begun gaining the upper hand. That year, the ailing and discouraged Napoleon III blundered into a war with Prussia. Defeated and captured, he and his government fell.

Fall of Napoleon III

Alexander II and Russia

Napoleon III had stood for order, reform from above, and national grandeur. Until he faltered, the French gave up their liberal sentiments for those ends. In Russia, Tsar Alexander II made similar appeals in an effort to overcome that country's troubles.

By 1850, Russia had earned a reputation as the most conservative of European powers. Its government remained autocratic under the tsar, its feudalistic society still bound serfs to the land and their lords, and its large army enjoyed an aura of near invincibility. After the Crimean War, it became clear that things would have to change.

Russia's autocracy

In 1853, war broke out between Russia and the Ottoman Turks. Although the causes for this outbreak of hostilities were complex, Russia hoped to snatch territory from the weakening Ottoman Empire. In addition, Russia sought to gain shipping access to the world from the Black Sea through the Turkish Straits and gain influence in the Near East. Early the next year, after the Russian navy sank the Ottoman fleet in a single devastating battle, France, Britain, and Piedmont-Sardinia, driven by their own ambitions rather than principles, joined the Ottoman Turks and poured their military forces into the Black

Crimean War

NATIONALISM AND STATEBUILDING

1851	Louis-Napoleon becomes emperor of France
1854–1856	Crimean War
1860	Italian unification
1861	Russia frees the serfs
1861–1865	U.S. Civil War
1866	Austro-Prussian War
1867	Canadian independence and unification
	Creation of Austro-Hungarian Dual Monarchy
1868	Meiji Restoration in Japan
1870	Franco-Prussian War
1871	German unification

KEY DATES

BIOGRAPHY

Florence Nightingale
(1820–1910)

In October 1854, a British journalist in Constantinople reported the successes enjoyed by the British army in the Crimean War. He also described in dramatic detail the horrendous condition of the army's medical facilities where the wounded and sick languished and died.

One of the many readers outraged by the report was Florence Nightingale. Just three years earlier, in a private note, she had written, "What am I that their [other women's] life is not good enough for me? . . . why, oh my God, cannot I be satisfied with the life that satisfied so many people?" The war, which was causing so much suffering on and off the battlefield, suddenly created an opportunity for Nightingale to take control of her own life, gain fame as "the Lady with the Lamp," and be hailed as a national heroine.

Born in 1820 into an upper-class family, she received an unusual classical education—including several languages, philosophy, history, and science—from her father. Her mother tried to train her to conform to the domestic responsibilities of her class—the domestic rituals, long meals, and formal sociability Florence resisted. She complained that "daughters are now their mothers' slaves . . . they are considered their parents' property, they are to have no other pursuit, nor power, nor independent life, unless they marry." She rejected suitors, explaining, "I have a moral and active nature which requires satisfaction, and that would not find it in his [a husband's] life."

Instead, she pleaded with her family to allow her to train as a nurse. They responded with rage, for at the time nursing was considered a menial occupation reserved for the lowest classes. Her society offered few opportunities for "respectable" women to gain independence, and Florence described the suffering caused by these restrictions: "I see the numbers of my kind who have gone mad for want of something to do."

Her frustration and torment with family life became entwined with her anguished spiritual life. She first reported hearing God speak to her when she was 16. The depth of her despair is revealed by her petitions to God: "Forgive me, God & let me die—this day let me die." But she also looked to God for purpose: "God has something for me to do for him—or he would have let me die some time ago."

Her chance for a purposeful life came in 1854 when reports of the lack of proper medical care for sick and wounded British soldiers in the Crimean War appeared in the newspaper. Despite her family's opposition, Nightingale had managed to gain some training as a nurse in Germany, France, and Ireland. Now she was serving as superintendent of the Hospital for Invalid Gentlewomen in London. Using her family's wealth and political connections, she obtained from the British government a commission to lead a team of 38 nurses to Turkey.

On November 4, 1854, they arrived at the barrack hospital at Scutari—a suburb outside Constantinople near the Black Sea (see **Map 19.4**). In a November 14 letter, she described conditions at Scutari: "We have no room for corpses in the wards. . . . Not

"Angel of the Crimea" and Medical Reformer

Sea. They laid siege to Russia's naval base Sebastopol, on the Crimean peninsula.

The war dragged on until 1856, and both sides fought with gross incompetence. The flavor of this war, and in particular one suicidal charge by the British light cavalry, would be immortalized in a poem by Alfred, Lord Tennyson:

'Forward, the Light Brigade!'
Was there a man dismay'd?
Not tho' the soldier knew
Some one had blunder'd:
Their's not to make reply,
Their's not to reason why,
Their's but to do and die:
Into the valley of Death
Rode the six hundred

Thanks to new telegraph lines and expanded press coverage, the public in the West could follow the conflict closely. People learned almost immediately, in graphic detail, about the horrific loss of life both on the Crimean battlefield and in the pitifully inadequate medical facilities (see Biography). More than 250,000 soldiers died, most of them from disease caused by poor sanitation, starvation, and lack of medical assistance. In the end, no one could claim much of a victory, but Russia, whose massive military no longer looked so formidable, was humbled.

Even before the Crimean disaster, peasant revolts and workers' protests had plagued Russia. In all of Europe, only Russia still allowed serfdom, which left millions tied to the land. Russia's serfs deeply resented the labor and dues they owed for the right to farm lands, and protests and insurrections broke out with

FIGURE 19.6 J. A. Benwell, *Florence Nightingale in the Military Hospital*, 1856

on *Nursing* (1859) became a primary text for nurses, and the nursing school she established in London (1860) became a model for similar institutions in Europe, Australia, and North America. Suffering from what she called "nervous fever," she spent much of the rest of her life in her own sickbed battling the sense of despair that had risen during her youth. Nevertheless, she used her prestige, political connections, and writings to campaign for reform of military health care, public sanitation, and social policy. In 1907, three years before her death, she was honored as the first woman to be awarded the British National Order of Merit. The Angel of the Crimea had revolutionized nursing and transformed military and public health care in the West.

a sponge, nor a rag of linen, not anything have I left. . . . These poor fellows have not had a clean shirt nor been washed for two months before they came here. . . . I hope in a few days we shall establish a little cleanliness." She advocated fresh air, sunshine, hygiene, and diet.

Figure 19.6, a lithograph of a ward at Scutari, shows Nightingale holding up her lamp and organizing care for the patients. Images such as this gave her the label "Lady with the Lamp."

Within six months and despite opposition, incompetence, and corruption within the British army, she transformed the medical facility, and the death rate fell from 40 percent to 2 percent. Her fame quickly spread. The *London Times* declared, "There is not one of England's proudest and purest daughters who at the moment stands on as high a pinnacle as Florence Nightingale."

The end of the war in 1856 did not end her efforts. Her best-selling *Notes*

Connecting People & Society

1. How does Nightingale's experience reveal the different ways in which war can alter people's lives?

2. How does her life illustrate the problems caused by the social limitations on women during this period (see Chapter 17)?

3. What impressions does **Figure 19.6** convey about the hospital and Florence Nightingale?

alarming frequency. Between 1825 and 1855, more than five hundred serf rebellions occurred in Russia. Food shortages struck all too often, yet most aristocrats took little responsibility for the suffering of their serfs. Many within the privileged class feared rebellion.

The peasants' low standard of living is revealed in **Figure 19.7,** a photograph of peasants in a Russian village during the second half of the nineteenth century. The man on the left wears tattered clothes. He and all the others stand barefoot in the mud street and beside the simple houses. This image contrasts sharply with **Figure 19.8,** an 1861 photograph that shows a noble landowner standing on the front steps of his mansion and reading a decree to some of his assembled serfs. Well-dressed members of his family watch from the stairs and the second-floor balcony, while household servants stand by attentively.

Not surprisingly, serfs conscripted into Russia's armies showed a distinct lack of enthusiasm. Their sullenness finally helped make Russia's leaders see that their country was being left behind by the other powers. The country simply lacked the social support, armaments, and railroads (it took Russia months instead of weeks to move troops and supplies to the Crimean front) to win a modern war. Moreover, because serfs were bound to the land, Russia lacked a large mobile labor force to support industrialization and thereby keep up with nations to the west.

The new tsar, Alexander II (r. 1855–1881), was a complex, well-educated individual who recognized Russia's problems from the moment he took office. He was determined to introduce reforms to strengthen and modernize Russia and prop up his own rule. Like Napoleon III's policies, Alexander's **"Great Reforms"**

FIGURE 19.7 Peasants in a Russian Village   The mud streets, rude housing, and worn clothing in evidence in this photo from the second half of the nineteenth century suggest the low living standard of Russia's peasants.

FIGURE 19.8 A Noble's Estate in Russia, 1861   In this mid-century photograph, a Russian landowner reads a decree to his assembled serfs.

came from above but proved much more far-reaching and dramatic. In 1861, Alexander freed Russia's 22 million serfs and, a few years later, 25 million state-owned peasants. "It is better to abolish serfdom from above than to wait until the serfs begin to liberate themselves from below," he told a group of his nobles. This bold move, occurring at almost the same time that millions of slaves were emancipated in the United States, put an end to a notorious form of human bondage and transferred land to the freed peasantry. In **Figure 19.8,** the noble landowner is reading the decree that abolished serfdom. Document 19.3 reveals one serf's reactions to this decree. However, emancipation did not make the peasants fully independent and self-sufficient. In general, they received the poorest land, owed payments for their land and freedom, and were tied by collective ownership to their village commune, the *mir,* whose elected officials assigned parcels of land and determined what could be planted.

Other reforms made the judicial system more independent, created local political assemblies (*zemstva*) with elected officials, encouraged primary and secondary education by opening thousands of new schools, and reduced military service. However, expectations for further reform rose too fast for Alexander and

> **Alexander II's "Great Reforms"**

came to haunt him. His efforts to relax control over Poland and grant amnesty to thousands of Poland's political prisoners seemed only to provoke a major Polish revolution in 1863, leading Alexander to repress the divisive nationalistic uprisings there and elsewhere within Russia's empire. To counter budding nationalism among minorities, he tried to force them to adopt the Russian language and culture. The universities he reopened became centers of intellectual discontent. Nor did his emancipation of the serfs end peasant rebellions.

Alexander intended to transform Russia into a modern authoritarian state that could command the allegiance of its citizens and wield power through a reformed, supported military. At best, he succeeded only partially. Certainly some of his reforms created important, long-lasting changes, but he did not turn his nation into a modern, national monarchy. Alexander himself, though called the "tsar liberator," was never popular. After an assassination attempt in 1866, he became more close-minded and increasingly turned Russia into a police state. Unrest still simmered among Russia's different nationalities. In addition, dissatisfaction among the peasantry and growing dissent among Russia's intellectuals, middle classes, and workers spelled trouble for the years ahead.

DOCUMENT 19.3

A Serf Reacts to the Russian Emancipation Proclamation

In 1861, Tsar Alexander II issued a dramatic proclamation emancipating Russia's serfs. Many people anticipated great changes stemming from this proclamation. The following excerpt depicts the reaction of Aleksandr Nikitenko, a former serf.

5 March. A great day. The emancipation manifesto! I received a copy around noon. I cannot express my joy at reading this precious act which scarcely has its equal in the thousand-year history of the Russian people. I read it aloud to my wife, my children and a friend of ours in my study, under Alexander II's portrait, as we gazed at it with deep reverence and gratitude. I tried to explain to my ten-year-old son as simply as possible the essence of the manifesto and bid him to keep inscribed in his heart forever the date of March 5 and the name of Alexander II, the Liberator.

I couldn't stay at home. I had to wander about the streets and mingle, so to say, with my regenerated fellow citizens. Announcements from the governor-general were posted at all crossways, and knots of people were gathered around them. One would read while the others listened. I encountered happy, but calm faces everywhere. Here and there people were reading the proclamation aloud, and, as I walked, I continually caught phrases like "decree on liberty," "freedom." One fellow who was reading the announcement and reached the place where it said that manor serfs were obligated to their masters for another two years, exclaimed indignantly, "The hell with this paper! Two years? I'll do nothing of the sort." The others remained silent. I ran into my friend, Galakhov. "Christ has risen!" I said to him. "He has indeed!" he answered, and we expressed our great joy to each other.

Then I went to see Rebinder. He ordered champagne and we drank a toast to Alexander II.

SOURCE: Aleksandr Nikitenko, *The Diary of a Russian Censor* (1893).

Analyze the Document

1. How did various people react to the tsar's proclamation, according to Nikitenko?

2. In what ways does their response reveal aspects of Russian culture?

3. How might members of Russia's aristocracy have reacted to this proclamation?

LOOKING BACK & MOVING FORWARD

Summary   By the 1870s, the most successful political leaders had learned new lessons about the power of nationalistic sentiment. Nationalism was a mighty force more easily used than opposed. It could fuel successful movements for national unification, disintegrate multinational empires, enhance existing unity in already established nations, and strengthen central governments.

Shrewd political realists, rather than the idealists of earlier times, led successful nationalist struggles. These leaders relied on power politics, war, and diplomacy to achieve their aims. But such politicians, sometimes viewed as heroes who gamely shouldered the burden of unification, stood on ground that idealists and revolutionaries had broken in the years before 1850. Moreover, the hardest work was often carried out by nationalist groups, students, soldiers, intellectuals, journalists, and others who rose to the call of national unity. The costs for everyone were high. Many Italians, for example, lost their lives in the struggle for independence. Also tragic, those Italians who survived these turbulent years were left with a new nation that was far from rich and that still suffered from regional and political differences. Germany bought its unification with arms. From that point on, German nationalism remained linked with military prowess rather than liberal ideals. In the United States, Lincoln had preserved the Union—but only after a four-year nightmare that would mar American society for generations and cost Lincoln his life.

KEY TERMS

Realpolitik, *p. 613*
autocracy, *p. 614*
Dual Monarchy, *p. 618*
"Great Reforms," *p. 623*

Other leaders, such as Napoleon III and Tsar Alexander II, recognized that reforms initiated from above could foster needed national unity and win them greater power. Moreover, Napoleon saw that real power flowed upward from a nation of citizens who deeply identified with their state and government. Increasingly, however, the cry "for the good of the nation" served as the only rationale for such leaders' policies and whims. As the era unfolded, even war could be presented to an unwary public as an act of national will and politics.

REVIEW, ANALYZE, & CONNECT TO TODAY

REVIEW THE PREVIOUS CHAPTER

Chapter 18—"Coping with Change"—analyzed the struggles between competing ideologies and political forces during the period between Napoleon's fall and the revolutions of 1848.

1. In what ways do you think the politics of this era reflect the efforts of governments to adjust to the changes initiated by the French Revolution and the industrial revolution?

2. How did the ideological struggles initiated during the first half of the century continue during the following decades?

ANALYZE THIS CHAPTER

Chapter 19—"Nationalism and Statebuilding"—examines the efforts to build national unity and strength between 1850 and 1870.

1. Analyze the methods used by leaders such as Cavour and Bismarck to achieve national unity. How do they compare with efforts during the revolutions of 1848?

2. How did leaders such as Napoleon III in France and Alexander II in Russia try to link nationalism and statebuilding?

3. In what ways was nationalism divisive in the Austrian and Ottoman empires?

CONNECT TO TODAY

Think about the force of nationalism and problems related to it.

1. In what ways is nationalism still a potent force in today's world?

2. What do you think are nationalism's benefits in our times? What are its drawbacks?

BEYOND THE CLASSROOM

THE DRIVE FOR ITALIAN UNIFICATION

Clark, Martin. *The Italian Risorgimento.* New York: Pearson, 1998. A well-written, succinct summary.

Coppa, Frank J. *The Wars of Italian Independence.* New York: Longman, 1992. A thorough discussion of the subject.

Mack Smith, Denis. *Cavour.* London: Weidenfeld and Nicolson, 1985. An excellent biography of this important figure in Italian unification.

GERMANY "BY BLOOD AND IRON"

Blackbourn, David. *A History of Germany, 1780–1918.* London: Blackwell, 2002. An excellent political history and a fine analysis.

Carr, William. *The Wars of German Unification.* London: Longman, 1991. Analyzes the three wars that led to the unification of Germany.

Pflanze, Otto. *Bismarck and the Development of Germany. I: The Period of Unification, 1815–1871.* Princeton, NJ: Princeton University Press, 1990. An exhaustive biography and history of Germany during the period.

THE FIGHT FOR NATIONAL UNITY IN NORTH AMERICA

Bensel, Richard Franklin. *Yankee Leviathan: The Origins of Central State Authority in America, 1859–1877.* Cambridge: Cambridge University Press, 1990. A discussion of state formation and the extension of central state authority during the Civil War and Reconstruction.

McPherson, James. *Battle Cry of Freedom.* New York: Oxford University Press, 2003. A well-written one-volume history of the American Civil War.

DIVIDED AUTHORITY IN THE AUSTRIAN AND OTTOMAN EMPIRES

Shaw, Stanford J. *History of the Ottoman Empire and Modern Turkey. II: Reform, Revolution and Republic: The Rise of Modern Turkey, 1808–1875.* Cambridge: Cambridge University Press, 1983. An effective analysis of the causes for the Ottoman decline during the nineteenth century.

Sked, Alan. *The Decline and Fall of the Habsburg Empire, 1815–1918.* London: Longman, 2001. A particularly strong analysis of the Habsburg Empire during this period.

USING NATIONALISM IN FRANCE AND RUSSIA

Edgerton, Robert. *Death or Glory: The Legacy of the Crimean War.* New York: Perseus, 1999. Covers the war and its significance.

Kolchin, Peter. *Unfree Labor: American Slavery and Russian Serfdom.* Cambridge, MA: Harvard University Press, 1987. A comparative study of the two experiences.

Lincoln, W. Bruce. *The Great Reforms: Autocracy, Bureaucracy, and the Politics of Change in Imperial Russia.* DeKalb: Northern Illinois University Press, 1990. Puts the social reforms during the reign of Alexander II in a broad political, social, and intellectual context.

Price, Roger. *People and Politics in France, 1848–1870.* Cambridge: Cambridge University Press, 2004. Clearly surveys the politics of the Second Empire in France.

OPENING OF THE SUEZ CANAL, 1869

In 1869, after ten years of construction, the Suez Canal—linking the Mediterranean and Red seas—opened. This drawing of the opening ceremony shows a crowd of traditionally dressed local inhabitants on the banks watching the line of new European boats, powered by steam as well as sails. European dignitaries, separated from this crowd, also attended the ceremonies. The canal, built by the French and later acquired by the British, shortened the sea route from Europe to India and the Far East by thousands of miles, and the new, large, smoke-belching steamboats carried cargo more rapidly and reliably than ever, facilitating the West's imperial expansion.

Mass Politics and Imperial Domination

Democracy and the New Imperialism, 1870–1914

"We have conquered for ourselves a place in the sun," announced Germany's Kaiser William II (r. 1888–1919) in 1901. Addressing an audience from Hamburg's business community, he boasted that "it will now be my task to see to it that this place in the sun shall remain our undisputed possession, in order that the sun's rays may fall fruitfully upon our activity and trade in foreign parts, that our industry and agriculture may develop within the state." William was referring to Germany's territories, gained in the scramble for overseas conquests that had been going on over the previous two decades. His audience and many others in the industrialized Western world expected to gain wealth from this recent imperial expansion.

He also may have been reminding his listeners that the German nation had been unified in the 1860s through war and conquest (see Chapter 19). Indeed, underlying his words was an appeal to pride in the growing power of this new nation. Like other political leaders in the West, William had learned to use nationalism to gain support from listeners and readers.

Politicians such as William could no longer ignore public opinion, for democracy was on the rise. Between 1870 and 1914, demands for democracy, or political participation by common people, spread as more and more people struggled to gain access to politics. Now the new politics of nationalism combined with industrialism to multiply the power of the West and push it outward into Africa and Asia in a great imperial expansion. The West was rising to a new level of world dominance.

TIMELINE

The "Second Industrial Revolution"

World War I

The New Imperialism

Democratic Reforms

Growth of Nationalism

Italian and German Unification

1870   1880   1890   1900   1910   1914

PREVIEW

DEMANDS FOR DEMOCRACY

In 1896, the Russian statesman Konstantin Pobedonostsev (1827–1907) published what would become a widely read attack on democracy. "What is this freedom by which so many minds are agitated, which inspires so many insensate actions, so many wild speeches . . . ?" His answer was democracy, "the right to participate in the government of the State." He complained that "the new Democracy now aspires to universal suffrage—a fatal error, and one of the more remarkable in the history of mankind."

However, between 1870 and 1914, it became increasingly clear to those who had long enjoyed political power in the West that, sooner or later, the beliefs of the masses would count in politics. Since the French Revolution in 1789, a widening pool of Europeans had tasted political power, a trend that ruling elites feared. Some politicians, such as Pobedonostsev, tried to turn their backs on democracy. Others tried to tame it, and still others flourished with it.

During the 1870s and 1880s, three developments became entwined with demands for democracy. First, many governments established national systems of free and compulsory public education at the primary-school level. With this policy, they hoped to create more patriotic citizens. They also wanted to provide citizens with the skills and discipline needed by modernizing economies and military establishments. Moreover, they wanted their voting electorate to be educated. To liberals especially, access to the schoolhouse and democracy went hand in hand.

Public education

Second, educated, voting citizens could read newspapers, and popular journalism responded to the call. Before 1850, newspapers were few, small, expensive, and written for a limited readership. By the end of the century, a new kind of newspaper had popped up everywhere—one that was cheap, sensational,

Popular journalism

and wildly popular. In the United States, publishers such as Joseph Pulitzer (1847–1911) and William Randolph Hearst (1863–1951) built influential newspapers featuring screaming headlines, flag-waving patriotism, an easy style, sensational news, and attention-getting columns. Other newspapers throughout Europe, especially in the capital cities, followed the same pattern. They catered to the newly educated public's hunger for news and, in turn, powerfully molded public opinion.

Third, politicians realized they had to appeal to the new voters. They devised innovative campaign strategies, such as crisscrossing the country by railroad and delivering stirring campaign speeches to cheering crowds in large halls and outdoor forums. They listened to newly formed interest groups—whether business organizations, reformers, or labor unions. These interest groups held rallies on their own, to gather support and gain influence through newspaper coverage of their meetings. Finally, politicians began creating all sorts of state institutions, from census bureaus to social security administrations, to satisfy the demands of their politically aroused societies and persuade new voters to support them. All these changes vastly reshaped parliamentary politics.

Political campaigns

Such developments put pressure on politicians to adjust the way they conducted themselves, for democratic reform meant more than widening the right to vote and bringing new faces into government. To succeed in the new world of mass politics, politicians had to learn to monitor—and navigate—the shifting tides of public opinion. More and more, rising to and staying in political office meant pleasing interest groups, journalists, educated readers, and newly enfranchised voters.

Liberal Democracy in Western Europe

Would European societies ease toward a liberal democratic consensus? Many people hoped so, particularly in western Europe, where Great Britain and France had experimented with democratic reforms, but in different ways.

Great Britain started the second half of the nineteenth century in a strong, stable position. It had avoided the revolutionary turmoil that swept over the European continent between 1848 and 1850, largely because the British adapted just enough to contain the pressures for radical change (see Chapter 18). Liberalism—stressing little governmental involvement in economic and social affairs, low taxes, and free trade—seemed to work well in Britain, and the island nation boasted the most modern economy in the world.

For most of the 1850s and 1860s, liberals controlled the British government. But they were more willing to call on national pride, sympathize with move-ments for national liberation abroad, and parade British naval might than to accommo-date those who demanded entry into the political system. It was the Con-servative Party, under Benjamin Disraeli (1804–1881), that finally decided to bend and take the credit for democratic reform before the Liberals themselves could grab it. The Conservatives passed a new measure—the Reform Bill of 1867—which doubled the electorate and gave the vote to the lower-middle class for the first time. In addition, they gathered support from the working class by passing laws that limited working hours, established sanitary codes, cre-ated housing standards, and aided labor unions. In 1884, the Liberal Party, under William Gladstone (1809–1898), countered by pushing through another reform bill that gave two-thirds of adult males the vote. To sweeten the deal even further, the Liberals opened the army and civil service to talent and made primary education available to all.

Reform bills of 1867 and 1884

FIGURE 20.1 Alfred Morgan, *An Omnibus Ride to Piccadilly Circus, Mr. Gladstone Travelling with Ordinary Passengers*, 1885 In the scene illustrating the politics of democracy, British political leader William Gladstone joins middle-class riders in a bus, thus presenting himself as a man allied with the people.

Having both jumped on the reform bandwagon, British Conservatives and Liberals now had to compete for power in new ways. For the first time, politicians such as Gladstone used the railways to campaign throughout the nation, speaking before crowds of thousands. A growing corps of journalists followed the campaigns, shaping public opinion by reporting speeches and scandals daily in cheap news-papers with mass circulation. New interest groups, mostly from the middle class, bent the ears of politi-cians who wanted their support in return.

Figure 20.1, a painting by Alfred Morgan, reveals some of these trends in British politics. The artist depicts the political leader William Glad-stone (wearing a tall hat, sitting stiffly, and staring straight ahead) riding in an omnibus. This form of transportation, which carried more than two dozen passengers at a time, was relatively inexpensive and available to all classes of people. The man (hold-ing a newspaper), women, and children who share the bus with Gladstone are dressed well but are not members of Britain's wealthy elite (who still rode in small carriages such as the one seen through the rear window). As this image indicates, Gladstone tried to appeal to the growing electorate by portraying himself as an upright, hardworking individual who allied himself with the people. Britain was moving toward democracy, but in ways that worried tradi-tional politicians used to deciding things among their "own kind."

France's path toward democracy took more violent turns than Britain's. A birthplace of democracy, France nevertheless started the 1870s on a turbulent note. The Franco-Prussian War of 1870 spelled the end of Napoleon III's Second Empire and the emer-gence of the Third French Republic (see Chapter 19). The first elections, held in February 1871 after Napoleon III's fall and the surrender of Paris, resulted in a victory for the monarchists, who hoped to limit democracy and open the door for the restoration of a monarchy. Still the city of Paris refused to submit to the domination of conservative, rural France. It demanded home rule and set up its own city government, or commune.

France's Third Republic

The **Paris Commune** would gain a reputation as a democracy out of control or as an experiment in Marxist socialism. In reality, the Commune stood for decentralizing power in France, self-governance, support of working-class organiza-tions, and greater equality for women. Its roots lay in the city's resistance to the Germans between Septem-ber 1870 and January 1871. During those horrific months, Parisians had braved starvation and isolation in the face of the German siege. Most of the rich fled the city. The lower classes not only resented this exo-dus but also took over positions of power that the wealthy had abandoned. The February 1871 elections ended the German siege, but not the division between Paris and the rest of the nation. Parisians felt betrayed by France's new conservative government when it concluded the peace with Germany. When govern-ment troops tried to disarm them, they rebelled and fighting erupted. The government troops withdrew, and again Paris was put under siege, this time by

The Paris Commune

FIGURE 20.2 The Paris Commune, ca. 1871 This altered photo portrays executions during the Paris Commune period. It was used by government troops as propaganda against Communards.

French troops. Two months later, the government troops attacked, killing some 25,000 Parisians, arresting thousands more, and deporting more than 5,000 to distant penal colonies.

Both sides in the Paris conflict committed bitter reprisals. The "photograph" shown in **Figure 20.2** purports to show Communards—including women and nonuniformed men—executing 62 hostages. In fact, the "photograph" is a photomontage—a composite photograph—used by government troops to justify retaliation against Communards.

The fall of the Paris Commune ended the immediate threat to the integrity of France, but not the political and social uncertainties that still lurked below the surface. A period of restless political struggle followed. At first, monarchists almost regained power, but they failed to agree on which of three possible royal houses (the Bourbon, the Orleanist, or the Bonaparte) they should rally around. By the end of the 1870s, liberals, elected by universal male suffrage, controlled the French Republic. Conservatives, however, refused to give up. In the late 1880s, they joined nationalists, supporters of the military, and opponents of parliament to rally around a handsome man on horseback, General Georges Boulanger, who became so popular that he might have overthrown the Republic had he been bolder and more skillful or had the republican leaders been less courageous. As it turned out, when he was summoned to answer charges of treason against the Republic, he fled to Belgium and eventually committed suicide on the grave of his late mistress.

Meanwhile, several forces reoriented politics toward the wider voting public. First, public schooling spread throughout France. Republican teachers replaced Catholic teachers, bringing in a common secular curriculum and promoting patriotism and republican virtues. Second, military service became compulsory and

Spread of democratic institutions

helped turn young, rural men into French citizens with new political awareness. Third, a popular national press took root in Paris and attracted readers throughout the nation. These papers reported all the political scandals, especially the sensational and far-reaching **Dreyfus affair** (see page 637), and soon readers in the provinces began avidly following national politics. In France, as in Britain, democratic institutions were spreading throughout the nation and redefining the nature of politics.

For and Against Democracy in Central and Eastern Europe

In contrast to the western European governments, national leaders in central and eastern Europe were more autocratic. Monarchs and their ministers in these regions had the last word in political decision making. Like nations in western Europe, those in central and eastern Europe struggled with pressure to institute democratic reforms. In some cases, these nations took reluctant steps toward democracy; in others, they declined to change. In addition, the tensions between autocratic and democratic forces in central and eastern Europe became particularly entwined with aggressive nationalism. The cases of Germany, Austria, and Russia provide apt examples of the various ways in which this struggle manifested itself.

In Germany, the constitution stipulated universal suffrage, but real power rested with the king and his ministers. Bismarck, who dominated as Germany's chancellor between 1870 and 1890, supported universal male suffrage from the beginning only because "in a country with monarchical traditions and loyal sentiments" such as Germany, "universal suffrage would lead to . . . eliminating the influence of the liberal bourgeois classes." Bismarck believed that most workers and peasants would vote for his conservative policies.

Germany under Bismarck

Bismarck solidified the German states and people under Prussia. He also brought the law codes, currencies, and military forces of the lesser states into conformity with those of Prussia. He then turned to issues of ethnic divisions and cultural unity. Laws and schools pressured non-German language groups to give up their languages and traditions. In 1872, Bismarck struck out against Roman Catholics for being insufficiently nationalistic. Known as the *Kulturkampf* (the struggle for civilization), the roots of Bismarck's attack lay in Germany's Protestant-Catholic religious divisions and the newly vigorous papacy of Pius IX, who declared papal infallibility in 1870, opposed cooperation with Protestantism, and attacked the growth of state power. With support from

Conflict with Catholic Church

liberals, Bismarck passed laws asserting the state's right to restrict religious orders, require civil marriage,

Conflict with Socialists

and bring all education (including schools run by the Catholic Church) under state control. When the Roman Catholic clergy resisted, authorities arrested hundreds of priests and six bishops. Many of these measures backfired, however: They made the Roman Catholic Center Party stronger. In 1878, Bismarck repealed the most severe of the anti-Catholic laws, but only because he wanted support for a more important struggle—the fight against the democratically minded and socially radical Socialists.

In a twelve-year crusade against the Socialists, who attacked the autocratic nature of Germany's government and were gaining popularity in elections, Bismarck outlawed the Social Democratic Party's publications, organizations, and meetings and set the German police force on them. When his repressive tactics did little to diminish Socialist votes, Bismarck tried to undercut the party's appeal to the working class by removing "the causes for socialism." Borrowing some of the Socialists' programs, between 1883 and 1889 he established a comprehensive system of social insurance that provided accident, sickness, and old-age benefits.

Ironically, in fighting against the Social Democrats, the conservative Bismarck made Germany a leader in enacting progressive social policies. Nevertheless, Bismarck's campaign against the Social Democratic Party would fail. The Socialists had built a solid following and continued to gain public support. In 1890, two years after the death of Kaiser William I, the new monarch, Kaiser William II, dismissed the aging chancellor. William II, eager to rule himself, "dropped the pilot" of the German ship of state and ended an era in German history.

In Austria, liberalism spread during the 1870s along with the rise of the bourgeoisie in that country. Liberals supported the constitutional monarchy, parliamentary government, and restricted suffrage. They also believed that it was possible to hold a multinational empire together. In the

Nationalistic discontent in Austria

1880s, nationalistic demands from different language groups began to overwhelm liberals and play into the hands of conservatives. Parliamentary sessions in Austria frequently degenerated into shouting matches, in which representatives from different language groups hurled inkstands at one another. This nationalistic discontent proved even more intense in Hungary than in Austria. Moreover, the partnership between Austria and Hungary threatened to disintegrate altogether (see page 618). The introduction of universal male suffrage in 1907 only made the empire more difficult to govern. More often than not, the emperor and his advisors bypassed parliament and ruled by decree.

In Russia, Alexander II's "Great Reforms" did little to open the doors to democracy beyond the local level (see pages 623–624). Indeed, they may have sparked more dissatisfaction than celebration. For serfs, liberals, and intellectuals, the reforms

Radical action in Russia

did not go far enough. A group of sons and daughters of the aristocracy and middle classes decided to take action. In a well-intentioned but ill-fated movement, they traveled to rural areas in an effort to uplift the lives of country dwellers. They received a rude welcome in several ways: Rural people resented what they saw as condescending attention from inexperienced urban intellectuals, and the tsar's police promptly repressed them.

Some of the young idealists fled; others remained and turned to terrorism. One group, The People's Will, defined terrorism as "the destruction of the most harmful persons in the Government, the protection of the party from spies, and the punishment of official lawlessness and violence." Vera Zasulich became an early heroine in this movement when she attempted to assassinate the St. Petersburg chief of police in 1878. Her action initiated a series of violent eruptions and assassinations, in which terrorists killed numerous bureaucrats and police officials, and the government brutally suppressed the rebels. The cycle of terrorism and repression turned Alexander II to a more conservative course, and he halted all further reforms. In 1881, members of The People's Will retaliated by murdering Alexander II with a bomb.

The new tsar, Alexander III (r. 1881–1894), blamed his father's death on softness and set out to erase every trace of liberalism and democracy in Russia. His secret police arrested thousands of suspects, and the tsar himself initiated

Reaction under Alexander III

a sweeping program of Russianization. Authorities forced minority groups to use the Russian language and persecuted followers of non-Orthodox religions, especially Jews. Russia, much more so than Austria, would not yet bend to the democratic winds blowing from the west.

INSIDERS AND OUTSIDERS: POLITICS OF THE EXTREMES

During the late nineteenth century, those democratic winds in the West spread beyond what had been the mainstream of politics. New groups and causes emerged to challenge the established center of liberal and conservative politics. These new groups gained strength and complicated the trend toward democracy. To the political left of liberals stood the unions, socialists, and anarchists. To the political right of conservatives were anti-Semites and ultranationalists. Still outside, without the vote, were women, who increasingly demanded a voice in national politics.

These groups and causes appealed to large numbers of people, particularly those who had previously been left out of politics. They became so prominent that established political leaders could not ignore them. With the political spectrum widening, it seemed less and less likely that Europe's nations would find some consensus or social peace.

The Spread of Unions

Until the 1880s, labor unions were limited chiefly to skilled workers, organized by crafts, who proved moderate in their aims and methods. **Strikes** In the 1880s, unionization spread rapidly to unskilled workers. These new union members adopted more radical methods and turned toward socialist programs. Seeking more than mutual aid, they demanded a say in working conditions and wages. They went on strike and flexed their political muscle through the vote. One worker described an 1890 strike of textile workers in Bradford, England, that dragged on for six months. "Twice and sometimes three times a week we had processions of the workpeople marching from near the millgates by several routes to the center of Bradford. The women strikers established a well-conducted soup kitchen, and the sympathy of the shopkeepers was very broad and the butchers gave their bones and greengrocers and grocers and bakers gave peas, lentils and loaves, and thus children were fed." As a man who employed thousands of dockers in Marseilles, France, explained, "The days of the employer's arbitrary power are past, unfortunately. . . . For long we

could hope to subdue these trade unions that rose against our authority. . . . That too is finished, over."

Figure 20.3 captures some of the ideals of the new unions. This strike at Saint-Ouen, near Paris, France, is sympathetically portrayed by the artist, Paul Louis Delance. Workers, young and old, stream from smoke-belching factories carrying red flags, the symbol of their cause and of socialism. Their faces convey suffering and grim determination. The welfare of a woman and child—the core of the typical working-class family—represents the strikers' goal. The strikers are supported by humble people, heads bowed, upon whom a few rays of sunshine fall as if in blessing for the nobility of their cause.

As the end of the century approached, organized labor became a formidable force. Labor unions in Great Britain formed the National Trades Union Congress and became identified with the new Labour Party. In Germany, unions, especially among the unskilled workers, grew dramatically and coalesced into a national Marxist organization. In France, various unions banded together into the giant General Confederation of Labor, with a radical political program. In the United States, the abundance of cheap immigrant labor and the determined resistance by industrial capitalists hindered the emergence of unions. In 1886, however, Samuel Gompers founded the American Federation of Labor—the first successful national labor organization in America. By 1914, unions had become sufficiently large and organized to make them a major power, both in the workplace and at the polls.

Socialism Gains Strength

Like the labor unions, socialism also became a major force within the working class and in politics during the late nineteenth century. Most socialists looked to the ideas of Karl Marx for inspiration (see Chapter 18). Marx **The First International** had argued that modern industrial society was splitting into two opposing classes: the capitalists, or owners of the means of production, and the workers. Capitalism, he explained, was bound to be replaced by a socialist system through revolution by the working class. Marx helped union organizers to form the International Working Men's Association (the First International) in 1864. The organization fell apart in the 1870s, but in 1889, socialists formed the Second International. These organizations helped socialists unify and spread their cause. A sense of shared struggle and beliefs inspired them to form unions, create political parties, and fight powerful employers and strong politicians.

Yet, the strength of socialism varied in each country. In Britain, established politicians

FIGURE 20.3 Paul Louis Delance, *Strike*, 1908 Under red flags symbolizing their cause, striking French union members stream out of distant factories.

excluded the working classes or socialist thinkers from politics until the 1880s. Then a The Fabians group of well-known intellectuals formed the **Fabian Society,** which advocated the adoption of socialist policies through politics rather than revolution. Beatrice Webb (1858–1943), one of the founders of the Fabians, explained that she became a socialist because of "the physical misery and moral debasement following in the tracks of the rack-renting landlord and capitalist profit maker in the swarming populations of the great centres of nineteenth century commerce and industry." Webb could see no way out of "the recurrent periods of inflation and depression—meaning for the vast majority of the nation, alternate spells of overwork and unemployment."

During the 1890s, both unions and socialists in Britain developed enough political muscle to form the Labour Party and elect members to Parliament. Britain's Labour Party By 1906, Labour had pressured the Liberals, led by David Lloyd George (1863–1945), to adopt new policies providing accident, sickness, old-age, and unemployment insurance for workers. As Labour members of Parliament argued, these old men and women were "the veterans of industry, people of almost endless toil, who have fought for and won the industrial and commercial supremacy of Great Britain. Is their lot and end to be the everlasting slur of pauperism?" To pay for the new policies, the Liberals shifted the "heaviest burden to the broadest backs." A steeply graduated income tax and high taxes on inheritances landed on the rich. When Conservatives in the House of Lords resisted, the Liberal and Labour parties passed a bill that stripped the House of Lords of most of its former power.

In France, socialism gained strength during the 1890s. During the following decade, socialist parties France and Jaurès helped push France's republican government to enact a limited program of unemployment, old-age, accident, and sickness insurance for workers. By this time, the different wings of the French socialists had joined to form the United Socialist Party under the leadership of scholar-orator Jean Jaurès (see Biography). By 1914, the United Socialist Party numbered 1.5 million voters and had 110 seats in the Chamber of Deputies.

Socialism enjoyed its greatest success in Germany. In 1890, Germany's main socialist party, the Social Democrats, won the vote of 20 percent of the electorate. Officially the party adhered to the idea that revolution was historically inevitable. A German Social Democrats party leader, August Bebel, expressed the optimism of this view: "Every night I go to sleep with the thought that the last hour of bourgeois society strikes soon." In practice, however, the party usually followed the ideas of the "revisionist" socialist Eduard Bernstein (1850–1932). This German writer and politician urged socialists to cooperate with the capitalist classes to obtain immediate benefits for labor and advocated a gradual approach to socialism. By 1914, the Social Democrats polled some 4.5 million votes, making it the largest political party in Germany.

Even in conservative Austria, socialists gained strength in industrial areas for the same reasons they did elsewhere in the West. The plight of workers was their top priority. Anna Maier, who started a life of work in a tobacco factory when she was 13, captured this concern when she explained that "young girls were often abused or even beaten" on the job. One day Maier read a copy of the *Women Workers'* newspaper smuggled into the factory by one of the older women. Eventually, she managed to join the Social Democratic Party. After she had taken part in demonstrations, her factory manager took her "off a good job" and put her "in a poorer one," but as she later reported, "nothing stopped me." When the tobacco workers union formed in 1899, she joined them and became "a class-conscious fighter." Maier's story was repeated by many other workers throughout the West in the decades before 1914.

Anarchism: Freedom from All Authority

While sometimes associated with socialists, **anarchists** made more radical demands. Drawing on the ideas of leaders such as the Russian activist Mikhail Bakunin (1814–1876) and Russian theoretician Pyotr Kropotkin (1842–1921), Bakunin they stressed the elimination of any form of authority that impinged on human freedom. "So long as there exist States, there will be no humanity," Bakunin argued. "The masses of the people will be de facto slaves even in the most democratic republics." Anarchists believed that human beings, once freed from the corrupting institutions that oppressed them, would naturally cooperate with one another. "Life will be open to all," an anarchist leader explained. "Everyone will take what he needs—this is the anarchist ideal."

Anarchism became particularly influential in Spain, Italy, and France, where it appealed to trade unionists, artisans, agricultural laborers, and shopkeepers suffering from unemployment and declining wages. Its supporters favored direct action through unions and cooperatives rather than parliamentary politics. After the turn of the century, many anarchists hoped the grand solution to their problems would come with a "general strike," as described by the popular French writer Georges Sorel (1847–1922). Such a strike, they believed, would force the capitalist system to grind to a sudden halt. A small wing of the anarchist movement went beyond hoping

BIOGRAPHY

Jean Jaurès
(1859–1914)

Orator and

Socialist

Politician

One observer described the French politician Jean Jaurès as such a spellbinding orator that "he could raise the masses and enchant the elite at the same time." **Figure 20.4** shows Jaurès standing beneath the red flag of socialism, addressing a crowd in 1913. Jaurès's speeches in France's Chamber of Deputies sometimes lasted for hours. He also wrote so prolifically that it would take ninety volumes, four hundred pages each, to amass all his writing. Some called him an obvious genius. He called himself "a cultured peasant." Certainly an intellectual, he wore the typical middle-class long, black overcoat. However, the coat was usually dirty, his pants always too short, and his pockets forever stuffed with books and papers. Between the 1880s and 1914, he became one of France's most respected politicians.

Born in 1859 to a rural, middle-class family of little wealth, Jean excelled at school, winning a series of prizes and scholarships. He became a teacher in 1881 and then a professor of philosophy at the University of Toulouse in southern France in 1883. In 1885 he was elected to the Chamber of Deputies as an unaffiliated republican. Just 25, he was France's youngest deputy. That year he met Louise Bois, the daughter of a merchant, and a year later the couple married. Attracted to Paris by the political activity there, the couple settled in an apartment and eventually had two children.

FIGURE 20.4 Jean Jaurès

Defeated in his 1889 bid for reelection to parliament, Jean became interested in socialism and made it the subject of his doctoral dissertation. He won fame for his support of striking miners at Carmaux in 1892. After this event, he was reelected to the Chamber of Deputies, this time as a socialist. He accepted the possibility of socialism by evolution rather than revolution: Class struggle might properly be replaced by democratic political struggle. To Jaurès and a growing number of other socialists, the forces of history suggested that socialism was inevitable. He rose in the Socialist Party, becoming a leader by 1900. In 1904, he helped found a newspaper, *L'Humanité*, which became France's chief socialist periodical. By 1908, he had solidified the party.

Jaurès became increasingly concerned with the problem of war. He argued that France wasted its resources on military preparations. "What will the future be like when the billions now thrown away in war preparations are spent on useful production to increase the well-being of the people?" he asked. He saw the West's recent imperial expansion into the non-Western world as a primary cause for wars. "The fever of imperialism has become a sickness. It is the affliction of a badly organized society which cannot utilize its energies and productive forces at home." More and more, Jaurès championed pacifism and Franco-German reconciliation, but his stand won him and his followers ridicule and accusations of treason, particularly by right-wing nationalists.

During the evening of July 31, 1914, Jaurès began composing an antiwar appeal. At 9:00 P.M., he and a group of other socialist journalists met and decided to dine at a crowded café on the rue Montmartre. At 9:40 a young man who was affiliated with a nationalist group burst in and fired two shots, killing Jaurès. The French socialist leader was murdered on the very eve of the war he warned against.

Connecting People & Society

1. In what ways does Jaurès's life reflect the promises of democracy?

2. How is it representative of the political problems faced by people in this era?

3. What does his life suggest about the nature and strength of socialism during this period?

for a general strike and turned to violence. Among its victims were President Sadi Carot of France in 1894, King Umberto I of Italy in 1900, and President William McKinley of the United States in 1901.

Anti-Semitism and Ultranationalism

Usually at the opposite end of the political spectrum from socialism and anarchism, **anti-Semitism** often appealed to conservative nationalists. Followers of Judaism had long suffered from anti-Semitism—hostility toward or hatred of Jews. Since the Middle Ages, Jews had been accused of murdering Christ, segregated into special quarters known as ghettos, and persecuted. However, between 1789 and the 1870s, the spreading ideals of the Enlightenment and the French Revolution had enabled Jews to gain new rights and a degree of legal equality, though rarely full acceptance. At least in western and central Europe, this progress led many Jews to believe that finally they could join their nation-states as full citizens.

During the last decades of the nineteenth century, however, nationalism took on militant and authoritarian tones. All too easily, this spreading strain of nationalism strengthened racist and anti-Semitic thought. Comte de Gobineau (1816–1882), a Frenchman, and Houston Stewart Chamberlain (1855–1927), an Englishman who became a German citizen, wrote widely read tracts arguing that race determined much of history. The two men helped formulate the Aryan myth, which held that Germans belonged to a special race and therefore possessed superior qualities: "[T]he Germanic races belong to the most highly gifted group, the group usually termed Aryan. . . . Physically and mentally the Aryans are pre-eminent among all people; for that reason they are by right . . . the lords of the world." Chamberlain's ideas veered off into anti-Semitism, as did the thinking of other well-known racist writers. Their pseudoscientific thought—which labeled Jews as a separate, inferior race—became increasingly popular, as indicated by this excerpt from a speech delivered by an anti-Semitic member of the German parliament: "A Jew who was born in Germany does not thereby become a German; he is still a Jew. Therefore it is imperative that we realize that Jewish racial characteristics differ so greatly from ours that a common life of Jews and Germans under the same laws is quite impossible."

During the same period, anti-Semitic politics gained force, especially among artisans, small shopkeepers, rural workers, and others who felt threatened by liberalism and capitalism and saw Jews as being linked to both. These people scornfully called Jews outsiders and capitalists and blamed them for their own economic ills and fears. Ultranationalist politicians used anti-Semitism to rally crowds, shift the blame for failed policies away from themselves, and win votes.

Right-wing newspapers such as *La Libre Parole* popularized scandals as well as anti-Semitic stories that coalesced most dramatically in the Dreyfus affair. People throughout France followed every development of "the affair" day after day and year after year. In 1894, a group of bigoted army officers falsely accused and convicted a Jewish captain, Alfred Dreyfus, of treason and sent him to solitary imprisonment on Devil's Island in South America. Three years later, evidence of Dreyfus's innocence appeared. Nevertheless, high-ranking officers refused to reopen the case. Newspaper articles, sensational trials, accusations, and huge public demonstrations divided the nation between the political Left and Right. Republicans, socialists, and intellectuals, inspired by the famous French writer Émile Zola, who attacked the judgment of the military and judiciary in the case, rallied for Dreyfus. Nationalist, conservative, monarchist, and anti-Semitic forces supported the army. In 1899, a second court-martial again convicted Dreyfus, despite evidence of another officer's guilt in the affair. The president of the Republic pardoned Dreyfus, but it took seven more years to get Dreyfus fully acquitted.

> The Dreyfus affair

The Dreyfus affair marked not only the battle over anti-Semitism but the evolution of French politics. The victory for Dreyfus became a victory for republicanism and anticlericalism. Electoral victories made republicans strong enough to separate church and state in 1905 and initiate a program of social legislation. Socialists, who had joined republicans in the Dreyfus case, gained greater legitimacy and popularity. The political power of monarchists and the Catholic Church had been dealt a debilitating blow.

For Jews, persecution was worse in central and eastern Europe. These regions had the highest Jewish population and the most aggressive strain of nationalism. Nationalistic anti-Semitic organizations, such as the Pan-German Association and the Christian Social Workers' Party, emerged in Germany. Anti-Semitic journals warned of the dangers to "the native-born Christian population" as Jews gained access to the press, to state offices, and to professions such as teaching and law. One anti-Semitic deputy in Germany's parliament explained in an 1895 speech that "every Jew who at this moment had not done anything bad may nevertheless under the proper conditions do precisely that, because his racial qualities drive him to do it."

> Central and eastern Europe

In Austria, the Christian Socialist Party and the German National Party took a decidedly anti-Semitic stand. By the 1890s, a new breed of politics based on symbols, charisma, nationalism, racism, anticapitalism, and anti-Semitism had arisen. The election of Karl Lueger in 1897 as mayor of Vienna symbolized this political trend; Lueger campaigned

FIGURE 20.5 Samuel Hirszenberg, *The Black Banner*, 1905 Horrified and grief-stricken Jewish people, bearing their dead, flee anti-Semitic attacks (pogroms) in Russia-dominated Poland.

on an anti-Semitic platform and triumphed even in this bastion of Austrian liberalism.

Some of the most violent anti-Semitic acts occurred in Russia. Tsars Alexander III and Nicholas II (r. 1894–1917) sanctioned the persecution of Jews and required them to live in designated areas. Officials labeled Jews as outsiders and excluded them from mainstream society. Whenever anyone wanted to assign blame for their problems, they could point to the Jews. This hostility culminated in a series of pogroms, or organized mass attacks on Jews, led by anti-Semitic groups and government officials. **Figure 20.5** shows a procession of Hasidic Jews in Russian-dominated Poland carrying a coffin, which contains one of the victims of an anti-Semitic pogrom. The faces of people in the procession reflect shock, horror, and desperation as well as mourning, and the sky echoes the ominous dangers still facing these people. The title of Hirszenberg's 1905 painting refers to "The

Black Hundreds," who were the armed gangs of the "Union of the Russian People"—a right-wing, anti-Semitic political movement founded in 1905—and to *The Russian Banner*, the newspaper of this organization, which also received "black money" from Russia's tsar. Between 1870 and 1914, these persecutions helped push more than 2 million eastern European Jews out of their homes and to the west, particularly to the United States (see **Map 20.1**).

Concerns about persecutions in eastern Europe as well as the weakening of Jewish identity through assimilation in western Europe gave rise to **Zionism,** a Jewish nationalist movement to create an independent state for Jews in Palestine—the ancient homeland `Zionism and Herzl` of the Jews. The Hungarian writer Theodor Herzl (1860–1904) became the leading figure in the Zionist movement. While in Paris covering the Dreyfus affair for an Austrian newspaper, he gained a greater sense of the strength of anti-Semitism and his own identity as a Jew. In 1896, he published an influential pamphlet, *The Jewish State: An Attempt at a Modern Solution of the Jewish Question*, urging formation of an international movement to make Palestine a Jewish homeland. He envisioned the homeland transformed into a socialist community of hardworking cooperatives. The following year he led the new World Zionist Organization to prominence. He gained a large following in eastern Europe, found financial support from several sources, and won cautious political support from British governmental officials. "It might be many years before the founding of the State is under way," Herzl warned. "In the meantime, Jews will be ridiculed, offended, abused, whipped, plundered, and slain in a thousand different localities." After Herzl's death in 1904, other leaders advanced his aims and secured more support—including the financial aid of donors such as the French banker Baron de Rothschild, and the cooperation of Arthur Balfour (1848–1930),

KEY DATES

POLITICAL AND SOCIAL DEVELOPMENTS

1864	First International Working Men's Association
1867	Britain's Second Reform Bill
1871	Paris Commune
1872–1878	Bismarck's *Kulturkampf*
1878	Romanian independence
1884	Britain's Third Reform Bill
1889	Second International
1897	World Zionist Organization founded
1897–1899	Dreyfus affair
1908	Hyde Park rally for women's suffrage
1914	World War I

MAP 20.1

Jewish Migration, 1870–1914

This map shows areas and cities with large Jewish populations and traces typical migration routes to the west and south.

Explore the Map

1. In what cities and areas of eastern Europe were Jews most heavily concentrated?

2. What was the significance of the particularly harsh anti-Semitic policies in these areas?

3. Why might Jews have migrated primarily to the west and south?

Legend:
- The Pale: Area Where Russian Jews Were Allowed to Live
- Other Areas of Large Jewish Population
- • Cities with Large Jewish Population
- → Typical Migration Routes

Britain's prime minister. By 1914, some 85,000 Jews had immigrated to Palestine, primarily from eastern Europe.

Still Outsiders: Women, Feminism, and the Right to Vote

By 1914, most of the political groups that had been outside the mainstream of politics had gained a political voice. In the majority of Western countries, universal male suffrage had become the rule by 1914. However, women still remained on the political sidelines, hampered by an ideology that left them unequal economically, trapped in their own "separate sphere" by laws that declared them legally inferior, and excluded by political institutions that deprived them of the vote. Few men in any of the political parties, movements, or unions offered their support for women's suffrage.

During the last decades of the nineteenth century, many women finally turned to political activism. Numerous women—whether as individuals or as activist group members—were already calling themselves "feminist." Groups of feminists organized several movements to promote women's issues, demand legal equality of the sexes, and advocate social and political change. In 1878, representatives of these groups from twelve nations came together in Paris at the International Congress of the Rights of Women and initiated a period of increased activism and international cooperation. Although feminists were still a minority

among women, their strength grew dramatically. In Britain and the United States, women with middle-class and aristocratic backgrounds fought especially hard for the right to vote. They argued that without the vote, women would continue to suffer from a range of inequalities. "The idea that the possession of political rights will destroy 'womanliness,' absurd as it may seem to us, is very deeply rooted in the minds of men," British writer Frances Power Cobbe (1822–1904) pointed out in 1884. Men, Cobbe explained, "really prize what women now are in the home and in society so highly that they cannot bear to risk losing it by any serious change in their condition." A few years later, Elizabeth Cady Stanton (1815–1902) expressed the views of many Americans in the women's suffrage movement: "If we are to consider [a woman] as a citizen, as a member of a great nation, she must have the same rights as all other members."

Another group of feminists tried to gain equality through social reform—focusing on the needs of the working class and often voicing socialist sympathies. Led by women such as Louise Michel (1830–1905) in France and Clara Zetkin (1857–1933) in Germany, they argued that only when workers as a whole gained freedom from economic and social oppression would women achieve justice. In 1885, Michel looked forward to a transforming revolution that would introduce a new era "when men and women will move through life together as good companions, and they will no more argue about which sex is superior than races will argue about which race is foremost in the world." Ten years later, Zetkin explained that proletarian women could attain "salvation only through the fight for the emancipation of labor."

The strongest women's suffrage movements arose in Great Britain. The movement was exemplified by organizations such as the National Union of Women's Suffrage Societies, led by Millicent Fawcett (1847–1929), and the more radical Women's Social and Political Union, led by Emmeline Pankhurst (1858–1928) and her two daughters. The leaders of these movements had reached a crucial conclusion: Being polite was not going to win them the right to vote. They worked as other political groups did, forming organizations, presenting petitions, pressuring politicians, forging alliances, holding demonstrations, publishing newspapers, and marching for the franchise. They continued despite scorn from men, ridicule by newspapers, rejection by politicians, cold shoulders from labor unions and socialists, and force

> Suffrage
> movements

by the police. **Figure 20.6** shows a policeman arresting Emmeline Pankhurst. "We have tried every way," explained Pankhurst. "We have presented larger petitions than were ever presented for any other reform, we have succeeded in holding greater public meetings than men have ever had for any reform . . . we have faced hostile mobs at street corners . . . we have been ridiculed, we have had contempt poured upon us . . . we know that we need the protection of the vote even more than men have needed it."

In 1908, a rally for female suffrage drew some 250,000 women to Hyde Park in London. After 1910, feminism in Britain took a more public and violent turn as women resorted to window smashing, arson, assaults, bombing of railway stations, and chaining themselves to the gates of Parliament. Police arrested them, judges imprisoned them, and, when they went on hunger strikes, authorities force-fed them.

Still the British government as well as most other Western authorities refused to give in to the feminists' demands. Finland granted women the right to vote in 1906—the first victory for the women's suffrage movement—but other victories would take years. Women would not gain the vote until after 1918 in Britain, Germany, and the United States; until the 1940s in France; and until the 1970s in Switzerland.

EMIGRATION: OVERSEAS AND ACROSS CONTINENTS

By 1914, most Western societies had taken great, often reluctant, steps toward democracy. A swirl of forces—the growing pressures of nationalism, the spread of industry and commerce, and the competition for military might—fueled those steps and molded the politics that resulted. Some of those same forces also pushed a new wave of Europeans and their governments across the globe.

After the mid-nineteenth century, a great migration of people from Europe gained momentum. Europeans streamed overseas and across continents, hoping to start new and better lives. As they fanned across the globe, they brought money and great quantities of manufactured goods to nonindustrialized areas. Their governments did the same: Imperial powers raced to carve up Africa and establish control in Asia. With their new presence, wealth, and power, Europeans dominated the world as never before.

Leaving Europe

Ever since the first sixteenth-century settlements, Europe had sent a sizable trickle of emigrants to the Americas. The trickle became a flowing stream in the mid-nineteenth century. Great numbers of British, Irish, and then German immigrants landed in the United States during the 1840s, 1850s, and 1860s.

FIGURE 20.6 The Women's Suffrage Movement in Great Britain, 1914 Police arrest suffrage leader Emmeline Pankhurst during a demonstration for the franchise.

FIGURE 20.7

Eugène Laermans,
The Emigrants, 1896

This triptych (three-paneled painting) by Eugène Laermans shows stages in the process of emigration that many Europeans experienced. In the right-hand panel (*The Exordium*), a parish priest addresses the crowd of departing villagers for the last time. For the priest, the news seems bad; this departure of his flock may mark the decline and possibly death of his village. In the background lies the village under dark clouds. The central panel (*The Exodus*) shows a seemingly endless line of humble men, women, and children carrying their meager belongings and dragging their pets. They march along the road and, for the last time, look back at their homeland and village in the distance. In the left-hand panel (*The Exile*), they crowd into the port. The darkening clouds to the west warn of a difficult voyage across the Atlantic and their unknown fate in new lands.

Connecting Art & Society

1. What is the apparent mood of the emigrants in each panel?

2. According to what you see in this painting, why do you think these people might be emigrating?

3. In what ways might this painting be considered a realistic rather than an idealistic depiction of emigration across the Atlantic?

After 1870, the stream swelled to a rushing torrent, as peoples from southern and eastern Europe joined the flow. Between 1870 and 1914, some 30 million Europeans left their homelands and emigrated, mostly to the Americas and Australia.

What explains this immense movement? As suggested in **Figure 20.7** by Belgian artist Eugène Laermans (1864–1940), many of the vast numbers of peasants and workers who emigrated overseas left Europe reluctantly. They felt pushed by the difficulties of their lives on the land and in the villages more than pulled by the apparent opportunities in foreign lands. In several parts of Europe, such as Scandinavia, the British Isles, and southern Italy, the land could no longer support the expanding population. Moreover, the shift to commercial agriculture throughout Europe had left a flood of small farmers landless or unable to com-

> Causes for the migration

pete. Natural catastrophes also played a part. A deadly potato famine in Ireland in the late 1840s forced many Irish to flee their homeland to escape starvation. These hardships impelled people—even in relatively rich western European countries such as Laermans's Belgium—to head for more promising shores. Many emigrated to the Americas, especially between 1880 and 1892.

Many opportunities, both real and imagined, also beckoned from across the oceans. Visions of free or cheap land, already taken away from native peoples, attracted Europeans to the Americas, Australia, and New Zealand. People heard news of plentiful jobs in America's growing cities. Steamships and railroads made the trip faster and cheaper than ever, though not pleasant for the crowds who traveled in ships' bottom compartments with baggage and supplies.

Unfortunately for these hopeful travelers, reality often proved far less appealing than their dreams.

thinking about
DOCUMENTS

DOCUMENT 20.1

Kaiser William II Links Nationalism and Imperialism

For many people, the distance between the increasingly assertive nationalism of the late nineteenth century and the new imperialism of the period was short. The following speech at Hamburg in 1901, delivered by Kaiser William II of Germany, exemplifies this view.

In spite of the fact that we have no such fleet as we should have, we have conquered for ourselves a place in the sun. It will now be my task to see to it that this place in the sun shall remain our undisputed possession, in order that the sun's rays may fall fruitfully upon our activity and trade in foreign parts, that our industry and agriculture may develop within the state and our sailing sports upon the water, for our future lies upon the water. The more Germans go out upon the waters, whether it be in the races of regattas, whether

it be in journeys across the ocean, or in the service of the battleflag, so much the better will it be for us. For when the German has once learned to direct his glance upon what is distant and great, the pettiness which surrounds him in daily life on all sides will disappear. Whoever wishes to have this larger and freer outlook can find no better place than one of the Hanseatic cities.[1] What we have learned out of the previous history of our development amounts really to what I already pointed out when I sent my brother to the East Asiatic station (Dec. 15, 1897). We have merely drawn the logical conclusions from the work which was left us by Emperor William the Great, my memorable grandfather, and the great man whose monument we have recently unveiled. These consequences lie in the fact that we are now making our

efforts to do what, in the old time, the Hanseatic cities could not accomplish, because they lacked the vivifying and protecting power of the empire. May it be the function of my Hansa during many years of peace to protect and advance commerce and trade! . . .

As head of the empire I therefore rejoice over every citizen, whether from Hamburg, Bremen, or Lübeck, who goes forth with this large outlook and seeks new points where we can drive in the nail on which to hang our armour.

SOURCE: C. Gauss, *The German Kaiser as Shown in His Public Utterances* (New York: Charles Scribner's Sons, 1915), pp. 181–183.
[1]*The Hanseatic cities formed a league in the late Middle Ages to facilitate trade.*

Analyze the Document

1. How does William II connect nationalism and imperialism?

2. By what means does he hope to spread German influence throughout the world?

3. In what ways might this speech appeal to both liberals and conservatives?

New arrivals usually got only the most remote or poorest lands and the lowest-paying jobs. Lonely or adrift in their new world, they sent letters and money back home, maintaining ties to old communities for a while or asking others to join them. Millions gave up the search for a better life or found reason to turn back; about one-third of those emigrating overseas from Europe eventually returned home.

THE NEW IMPERIALISM: THE RACE FOR AFRICA AND ASIA

In the 1880s, this mass migration of individuals was paralleled by an expansion of Western power into non-Western parts of the world. European nations raced to gain control over Africa and Asia especially. They subdued local opposition and reshaped the existing societies to fit their own purposes. They brought Western culture and institutions to Africa and Asia whether those peoples wanted them or not. By 1914, imperial powers had seized most of Africa and much of Asia, taking direct or indirect control over almost half a billion people.

Imperialism was not new. Since the fifteenth century, Europeans had been extending their influence over the globe. Increasingly during the eighteenth and nineteenth centuries, Western nations developed and mobilized the ships, weapons, and finances that gave them advantages over other civilizations. Spurred on by competitive rivalries among themselves for power and wealth, European states used these advantages to impose their will again and again in Asia and Africa. But the burst of expansion between about 1880 and 1914 was so rapid and extensive that historians call it the **new imperialism.**

Money and Glory

There were many forces driving this wave of imperialism. For one thing, as Document 20.1 indicates, people thought they could make money from it. "It is in order to foster the growth of the trade of this country, and to find | Economic causes | an outlet for our manufacturers and our surplus energy, that our far-seeing statesmen and our commercial men advocate colonial expansion," concluded a British colonial administrator. Industrial nations hungered for new markets, cheap raw materials, and juicy investment opportunities. Western manufacturers, merchants, financiers, shippers, investors, adventurers, and settlers thought they would find all these things in Africa and Asia, and European workers believed that the guaranteed markets would keep them employed. Political leaders, egged on by other pressures as well, usually agreed.

Yet the race for riches often proved more difficult than people expected. Many colonies cost European governments far more to acquire and maintain than riches received. The colonizing process got complicated politically as well. Imperial powers took some colonies not because they saw them as money-makers but because they wanted to protect the borders of other, more lucrative colonies. In many such buffer colonies, loans were never paid off, mines never yielded enough minerals to cover their expenses, and markets proved not worth the cost of building railroads to reach them. But in the beginning, people hoped for great profits or at least security for money-making ventures in distant lands. Competition and the optimistic taking on of risks were at the heart of capitalism, and this led many Westerners and their nations into Africa and Asia.

Politics of imperialism

A different, probably more powerful competition—the drive for international prestige—also drove governments, cheered on by millions of their citizens, to snap up colonies. The renewed burst of imperialism came at precisely the time when nationalism was on the rise in Europe. As Document 20.2 suggests, nationalistic sentiment easily translated into a new struggle for imperial conquest—for remote islands, barren deserts, and impenetrable jungles as well as for more lucrative prizes. Governments used such conquests to display their muscle, especially when such a display was lacking at home. France's expansion, for example, helped French citizens feel compensated for losses suffered in the Franco-Prussian War. Italian conquests overseas promised to make up for Italy's failure to acquire first-rate power status on the Continent. Gaining colonies became a measure of status, proof of a nation's political and economic prowess. To be left behind in the imperial race marked a nation as second class. "[A]ll great nations in the fullness of their strength have desired to set their mark upon barbarian lands, and those who fail to participate in this great rivalry will play a pitiable role in the time to come," the nationalist German historian Heinrich von Treitschke announced. People in the West avidly followed the race for colonies. Newspapers reporting on incidents and conquests in Asia and Africa framed these developments as adventures and patriotic causes. Thrilling stories about action overseas sold countless papers. In books and classrooms, people could see their national colors spreading across oceans and continents.

Nationalism and imperialism

This competition for economic gain and international prestige gained a life of its own, a momentum that became hard to curb. When one nation moved into a new area, others followed, for fear of being left with nothing. To protect established colonies, imperial powers seized adjoining territories. To ensure supply lines to distant colonies, nations grabbed up islands, ports, and bases. To form alliances and collect bargaining chips for when disputes arose, imperial powers made colonial claims.

Finally, people found ways to justify imperialism. Westerners saw themselves as bringing "blessings" of their civilization to "backward" peoples. The British writer Rudyard Kipling (1865–1936) expressed the belief of many Westerners when he wrote of the "white man's burden" to civilize the "lesser breeds" of the earth. Missionaries took to heart the injunction to "Go ye into all the world and preach the gospel to every creature."

Justification

Figure 20.8, a cover illustration from a French Catholic magazine, *The Pilgrim,* reveals Westerners' idealized views of imperialism. Here a member of the White Sisters, a Catholic order, teaches already converted Ugandan girls how to use a sewing machine. The image plainly contrasts the devoted, beautiful

FIGURE 20.8 A European Vision of Imperialism This pro-imperialism publication depicts a member of a Catholic order teaching Ugandan girls how to improve their lives.

DOCUMENT 20.2

Economics and Imperialism in Africa

With new conquests made in the scramble for Africa, many people expected commerce to accelerate and new markets for manufactured goods to emerge. This attitude shows up in Lord Lugard's account of his experiences in colonial service. A British soldier and administrator, Lugard helped bring large parts of Africa into the British Empire.

The Chambers of Commerce of the United Kingdom have unanimously urged the retention of East Africa on the grounds of commercial advantage. The Presidents of the London and Liverpool chambers attended a deputation to her Majesty's Minister for Foreign Affairs to urge "the absolute necessity, for the prosperity of this country, that new avenues for commerce such as that in East Equatorial Africa should be opened up, in view of the hostile tariffs with which British manufacturers are being everywhere confronted." Manchester followed with a similar declaration; Glasgow, Birmingham, Edinburgh, and other commercial centres gave it as their opinion that "there is practically no middle course for this country, between a reversal of the free-trade policy to which it is pledged, on the one hand, and a prudent but continuous territorial extension for the creation of new markets, on the other hand." . . .

This view has been strongly endorsed by some of our leading statesmen. Space forbids me to quote extracts from speeches by our greatest politicians, which I might else adduce as proof that they held the opinions of the Chambers of Commerce, which

I have quoted, to be sound and weighty. . . .

The "Scramble for Africa" by the nations of Europe—an incident without parallel in the history of the world—was due to the growing commercial rivalry, which brought home to civilised nations the vital necessity of securing the only remaining fields for industrial enterprise and expansion. It is well, then, to realise that it is for our *advantage*—and not alone at the dictates of duty—that we have undertaken responsibilities in East Africa. It is in order to foster the growth of the trade of this country, and to find an outlet for our manufactures and our surplus energy, that our far-seeing statesmen and our commercial men advocate colonial expansion. . . .

There are some who say we have no *right* in Africa at all, that "it belongs to the natives." I hold that our right is the necessity that is upon us to provide for our ever-growing population—either by opening new fields for emigration, or by providing work and employment which the development of over-sea extension entails—and to stimulate trade by finding new markets, since we know what misery trade depression brings at home.

While thus serving our own interests as a nation, we may, by selecting men of the right stamp for the control of new territories, bring at the same time many advantages to Africa. Nor do we deprive the natives of their birthright of freedom, to place them under a foreign yoke. It has ever been the key-note of British colonial method to rule through and by the natives, and it is this method, in contrast to the arbitrary

and uncompromising rule of Germany, France, Portugal, and Spain, which has been the secret of our success as a colonising nation, and has made us welcomed by tribes and peoples in Africa, who ever rose in revolt against the other nations named. In Africa, moreover, there is among the people a natural inclination to submit to a higher authority. That intense detestation of control which animates our Teutonic races does not exist among the tribes of Africa, and if there is any authority that we replace, it is the authority of the Slavers and Arabs, or the intolerable tyranny of the "dominant tribe." . . .

***

So far, therefore, as my personal experience goes, I have formed the following estimate: (1) No kind of men I have ever met with—including British soldiers, Afghans, Burmese, and many tribes of India—are more amenable to discipline, more ready to fall into the prescribed groove willingly and quickly, more easy to handle, or require so little compulsion as the African. (2) To obtain satisfactory results a great deal of system, division of labour, supervision, etc., is required. (3) On the whole, the African is very quick at learning, and those who prove themselves good at the superior class of work take a pride in the results, and are very amenable to a word of praise, blame, or sarcasm.

SOURCE: Captain F.D. Lugard, *The Rise of Our East African Empire*, vol. I (London: William Blackwood and Sons, 1893), pp. 379–382, 473.

Analyze the Document

1. How does Lugard connect nationalistic and economic motives for imperialism?

2. How does he respond to arguments against imperialism?

3. What are Lugard's perceptions of Africans?

European woman and the humble, well-behaved children. The implied promise is that the West will bring the benefits of its technology, faith, and civilization to a new generation of thankful Africans.

Some people put imperialism in a less rosy context. These observers described colonial competition and conquest as part of an unavoidable, Darwinian struggle

for survival of the fittest (see Document 20.3). In such a struggle, the white "race" would surely prevail, they believed. France's prime minister even claimed that "the superior races have rights over the inferior races," a view supported by many.

There were people who opposed imperialism. Intellectuals, reform clubs, and politicians such as

Progress and the Struggle of Race with Race

During the late nineteenth century, ideas about social Darwinism and eugenics—the study of hereditary "improvement" by selective breeding—spread in the West and were used to justify competition, war, and imperialism. Karl Pearson (1857–1936), trained as a mathematician, became an outspoken proponent of eugenics, claiming the best scientific thinking backed it. The following is an excerpt from his 1901 book, National Life from the Standpoint of Science.

History shows me one way, and one way only, in which a high state of civilization has been produced, namely, the struggle of race with race, and the survival of the physically and mentally fitter race. . . . The struggle means suffering, intense suffering, while it is in progress; but that struggle and that suffering have been the stages by which the white man has reached his present stage of development, and they account for the fact that he no longer lives in caves and feeds on roots and nuts. This dependence of progress on the survival of the fitter race, terribly black as it may seem to some of you, gives the struggle for existence its redeeming features; it is the fiery crucible out of which comes the finer metal. You may hope for a time when the sword shall be returned into the plowshare, when American and German and English traders shall no longer compete in the markets of the world for their raw material and for their food supply, when the white man and the dark shall share the soil between them, and each till it as he lists. But, believe me, when that day comes mankind will no longer progress; there will be nothing to check the fertility of inferior stock; the relentless law of heredity will not be controlled and guided by natural selection. Man will stagnate; and unless he ceases to multiply, the catastrophe will come again; famine and pestilence, as we see them in the East, physical selection instead of the struggle of race against race, will do the work more relentlessly, and, to judge from India and China, far less efficiently than of old.

SOURCE: Karl Pearson, *National Life from the Standpoint of Science* (London: A & C Black, 1901).

Analyze the Document

1. In what ways might Pearson's ideas justify imperialism?

2. How should competition and struggle take place, according to Pearson?

3. In what ways might Pearson's ideas be considered racist today?

Jean Jaurès called it an unjustifiably cruel and costly exploitation. However, such voices did not carry enough weight. Powerful economic interests and politicians had found imperial expansion irresistible, and most citizens were all too willing to support the adventure. Moreover, imperial conquest became so easy it seemed foolish not to take advantage of it.

Opposition to imperialism

The Tools of Conquest

Before 1850, it was either too difficult or not worth the effort for Westerners to penetrate into Africa's interior or extensively expand colonial holdings in Asia. After 1850, science and technology gave the industrialized nations the tools they needed to conquer and control nonindustrialized lands.

Steam-powered iron ships conveyed messages, materials, and people across oceans quickly and cheaply. Smaller steamboats took travelers up rivers. Railroads carried them across vast stretches of land. The Suez Canal cut thousands of miles off journeys to Asia, and the Panama Canal promised much the same (see the drawing on page 628). In 1800, mail took as long as one year to get from London to India. In 1880, a telegram took just hours.

Transportation facilities

Innovations in weaponry also gave the West new clout. Europeans had long possessed more firepower than non-Western peoples. The new breech-loading rifles and machine guns multiplied that advantage. Local societies resisted, but with the destructive power of these new weapons, European soldiers numbering only a few hundred annihilated local forces in the thousands. Winston Churchill, Britain's future prime minister and an observer of the 1898 Battle of Omdurman in the Sudan, described the effects of the machine gun on natives: "It was not a battle but an execution. . . . The bodies were . . . spread evenly over acres and acres." In that particular battle, 11,000 Muslim tribesmen died, whereas only 28 British soldiers lost their lives. Many other battles, large and small, took place in the series of open and guerrilla wars over the years. Imperial powers usually prevailed, but conquest and control came with much bloodshed and brutality. As the British novelist Joseph Conrad wrote in his 1902 classic, *Heart of Darkness*, "The conquest of the earth, which mostly means the taking it away from those who have a different complexion

Force

or slightly flatter noses than ourselves, is not a pretty thing when you look into it much."

Disease, more than distance or resistance, had also kept Europeans out of most of Africa. But by 1830, the French had discovered the power of quinine to protect their soldiers from deadly malaria long enough to take Algeria in North Africa. After 1850, explorers, missionaries, traders, soldiers, and officials came into sub-Saharan Africa armed with the new medicine.

Medicine

Various Europeans used these tools of conquest at different times. Sometimes missionaries and explorers entered new lands first; at other times, traders or even military officers made decisions on their own to move in. Once there, they called on home governments to provide support, enforce contracts, and protect private interests. Newspapers reported "atrocities" committed against the unwelcome intruders and stirred up European cries for revenge and protection of national honor. Western governments that had requested the cooperation of local political leaders and had been refused turned to force. Indirect control could quickly turn into direct control as problems arose. Control expanded even more as neighboring areas attracted the interest of the intruders.

Patterns of conquest

The Scramble for Africa

Imperial control spread most dramatically in Africa. In the early nineteenth century, Africa was the seat of several vital civilizations. In the north were the long-established Islamic societies. In sub-Saharan Africa—particularly in the western and central Sudan, where the Sahara Desert gave way to grasslands and trade flourished—a rich array of societies and states had developed over the centuries. In most kingdoms of the Sudan and western Africa, Islam had become a major cultural influence. Trade and contact with Europeans affected Africa, but except for coastal and certain other limited areas, such as South Africa, most of Africa remained free from European control.

By the middle decades of the nineteenth century, however, the French had conquered and annexed Algeria in North Africa and had pushed their way up the Senegal River in the west. The British had taken the Cape Colony in South Africa from the Dutch during the Napoleonic Wars, and the Dutch settlers had moved northward into the interior (see **Map 20.2**). In the late 1870s, two developments initiated an international scramble to carve up Africa.

North Africa

The first occurred in Egypt. This North African state had long interested France and Britain as a market for European goods and investments and as a bridge to Asia. European bankers financed the construction of port facilities, railroads, and telegraph lines in Egypt, granting high-interest loans to Egypt's government. In 1869 the Suez Canal, built by a French company, opened and became the vital link from the Mediterranean Sea through Egypt to the Red Sea and the Indian Ocean (see the drawing on page 628). The British desired control over the canal so as to secure their lucrative position in India. In 1875, Great Britain took advantage of the Egyptian government's financial distress and purchased the Egyptian ruler's, or khedive's, controlling portion of the canal stock. Four years later, France and Britain seized Egypt's treasury to secure their investments. When nationalist groups in Egypt revolted, British troops occupied Egypt. Formally, the khedive remained in office, but after 1882, Britain held most of the real power. By then, 3,000 ships a year passed through the Suez Canal.

The British reshaped Egypt's economy so that it produced cotton, silk, and wheat for export in return for manufactured goods. They also disrupted local work life by hiring Egyptian laborers for their own projects—whether as railroad builders or servants. Worse, they insulted unfavored groups—such as Muslims and Arabs—by paying them less than favored groups.

The French reluctantly acquiesced to British control in Egypt in return for Britain's support of French ambitions in northwestern Africa. In the following years, Britain expanded south to secure Egypt and east to maintain its position in India and China. For similar reasons, France expanded from its stake in Algeria to Tunisia, Morocco, and most of northwestern Africa.

At the same time, King Leopold II of Belgium (r. 1865–1909), set out to get "a slice of this magnificent African cake." Hungry for ivory, rubber, hardwoods, palm oil, and glory, he initiated a new competition for acquisitions in sub-Saharan Africa by devouring the Congo. He had claimed that his purpose was "to open to civilization" central Africa, "to pierce the darkness which envelopes whole populations." In fact, his troops killed and mutilated thousands of local peoples in the process of conquest. An American missionary described the brutality with which Leopold's officials forced people into the forest to collect rubber: "The soldiers drive the people into the bush. If they will not go they are shot down, and their left hands cut off and taken as trophies."

Worried about missing out on the land grab, the other European powers voiced their own claims. The French centered their efforts in western Africa, the Germans in eastern Africa, and the British up and down the center, "from Cairo to Capetown." The Berlin Conference of 1885 formalized this scramble for Africa, setting ground rules for territorial acquisition on that continent. According to the conference, colonizers were supposed to have enough physical

Sub-Saharan Africa

MAP 20.2

Imperialism in Africa, ca. 1885

Comparing **Map 20.2**, which shows European holdings in Africa in 1885, with **Map 20.3** on page 648, which shows European holdings in 1914, reveals the results of the Europeans' grab for African lands.

Explore the Maps

1. Which European nations became the main imperial powers in Africa?

2. Notice the dates of acquisition by the European powers. What do these dates reveal about the timing of the scramble for African lands?

3. Locate Britain's possessions. How do these holdings reflect Britain's concern to protect its routes to India?

presence to control and develop an area before they could claim it. They also agreed to treat Africans according to humane standards, although they often used that declaration to disguise the exploitation and abuse they continued to commit.

By 1914, most of the huge continent had been carved up by the various European powers (see **Map 20.3**). The main exception was Ethiopia. There, Emperor Menelik II (r. 1889–1913) cleverly played one European power off another. In the process, he

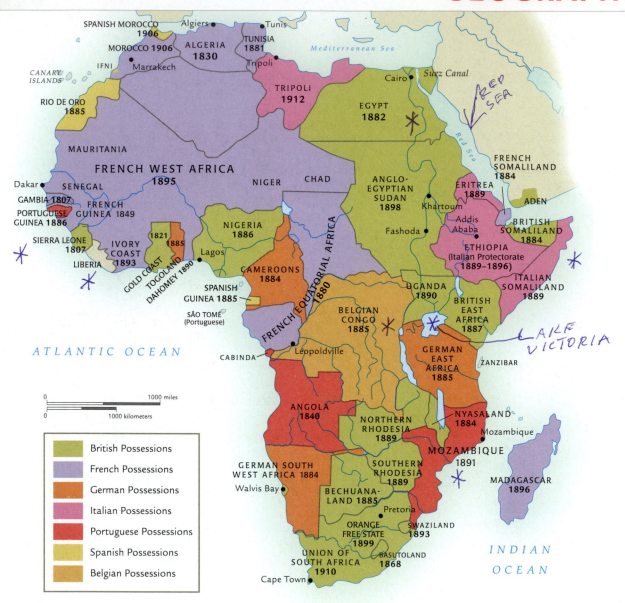

MAP 20.3

Imperialism in Africa, 1914

manipulated the Europeans into supplying his country with modern arms, which he then used to defeat the invading Italians in 1896.

For the Europeans, the costliest struggles occurred among themselves. The imperial powers averted most conflicts by diplomacy. In South Africa, however, even the most skilled diplomacy failed to keep the peace. British settlers began to move into the South African Cape Colony early in the nineteenth century. The Dutch Boers (Afrikaners), who had settled there in the seventeenth century and resented Brit-

ain's abolition of slavery, trekked northward far into the interior, slaughtering the resisting Zulus in their way. Eventually, the British recognized the independence of the two Boer states, Transvaal and the Orange Free State.

However, when rich gold mines were discovered in Transvaal in the 1880s, British immigrants flooded in. The British entrepreneur and empire builder Cecil Rhodes (1853–1902), backed by powerful interest groups concerned about the growing German presence

    Boer War

MAP 20.4

The Middle East and Central Asia, 1850–1914

This map shows the Middle East and parts of Central Asia where Russia and Britain expanded their areas of control and influence during the second half of the nineteenth century.

Explore the Map

1. Where were Russia and Britain most likely to come into conflict? Why?

2. Where were the Ottomans and Persians put on the defensive?

3. Why might the Russians and British have been so concerned about Afghanistan that they nearly went to war over it in 1884–1887?

in southwestern Africa, decided to brush aside the two little Boer republics. But what the British thought would be an easy victory took three years (1899–1902) of military effort and involved severe casualties and enormous costs. Backed by 300,000 troops from India and the homeland, Britain finally won the brutal contest and in the end treated the defeated Boers leniently. The British took them into partnership in the Union of South Africa, and the Boer hero General Louis Botha (1862–1919) was elected the Union's first prime minister. Botha's government announced that it would "permit no equality between colored people and the white inhabitants," a policy that South Africa would hold on to for the next eighty years.

Europeans usually ruled directly over African societies so they could create the economic conditions they wanted. Colonial administrators trained cooperative tribes as their clerks, soldiers, and favored workers. These preferences often sparked bitter tribal jealousies and rivalries. Throughout Africa, Europeans made it clear by their words and actions that they considered themselves, their civilization, and their "race" superior to the Africans. Their dominance established, Europeans prided themselves on bringing Christianity and civilization to the "dark" continent. They had scant appreciation for the qualities of African societies and dismissed the Africans as inferior peoples useful only for manual labor. Often they treated them little better than slaves. They also established new political boundaries that ignored the long-standing

> Dominance, conflict, and consequences

social, cultural, and political realities of local peoples. Some officials even worked to "submerge" Africans from different societies "into a single colored working class," a policy that prevented Africans from maintaining kinship and community ties. Those Africans who resisted might be decimated in armed battle or dispossessed and forced onto reservations. Yet resentment and desperation led many Africans to rebel against their conquerors, despite the hopelessness of their situation. A warrior in South Africa explained the reasons for one of these rebellions: "Our King gone, we had submitted to the white people and they ill-treated us until we became desperate and tried to make an end of it all. We knew that we had very little chance because their weapons were so much superior to ours. But we meant to fight to the last, feeling that even if we could not beat them we might at least kill a few of them and so have some sort of revenge."

Establishing Control in Asia

In Asia, Western powers usually got what they wanted by ruling through local elites. In these large, well-organized societies, where the potential for effective resistance remained great, Westerners' tampering with the established power structure was risky.

India was as linguistically and regionally diverse as Europe. Nevertheless, by the nineteenth century, the British had brought together a variety of states, territories, and tribal groups to create an Indian state under British control. The Indian subcontinent became Britain's richest imperial prize. Nearly twenty times larger than Great Britain and more than seven times as populous, India bought and sold more goods than any other British colony. Britain directed much of its imperial policy toward preserving this lucrative colony. Part of the reason Britain annexed new colonies in Africa and widened its sphere of influence in the Middle East was to protect India from other European states. One of these was Russia, which was expanding its control in areas near India (**Map 20.4**). Competition for power and influence in these lands brought Russia and Britain to the brink of war in 1881 and again in 1884–1887.

Until 1858, the British East India Company, a private-stock company, governed much of India. However, the great Sepoy Mutiny of 1857, the first large-scale uprising of Indians against British rule, almost drove the British out of India. This prompted the British government to take direct control. Instead of meddling with the structure of Indian society, the British used India's elites to support their rule. They employed a half-million Indians to administer the huge country and built railroads, canals, ports, schools,

The Middle East and India

and medical facilities. In one sense, India benefited in that population increased rapidly. On the other hand, living standards for most fell as population increases outstripped economic growth. The British paid low wages and labeled Indians as inferior—at best, in the words of the British historian and politician Thomas Macaulay, "a great people sunk in the lowest depth of slavery and superstition." Through use of tariffs, they forced India to collapse its own cotton industry and accept British imports of cotton cloth instead. They restructured India's economy to specialize in products the British wanted, such as jute, raw cotton, opium, tea, and wheat. As one Indian nationalist explained, "*Pax Britannica* [Britain's peace] has been established in this country in order that a foreign government may exploit the country."

Britain permanently altered this ancient civilization by creating a national unity, whether the Indians desired it or not. Moreover, British men and women in India imported their own cultural standards, lived separately from the "inferior" native societies, and expected the Indians they dealt with—from elites to servants—to adjust to British ways. For example, in her book *The Complete Indian Housekeeper and Cook* (1898), British author Flora Annie Steel boasted that "to show what absolute children Indian servants are," she has "for years adopted castor oil as an ultimatum," adding that this is "considered a great joke, and exposes the offender to much ridicule from his fellow-servants." **Figure 20.9,** a photo of Indian servants catering to a British gentleman, indicates the gulf between the British ruling class and the Indians they governed. It also reveals the appeal of foreign service to the British, who at home may have enjoyed only modest social positions.

The British showed no inclination to grant India self-government. As a result, nationalism—already a potent force in Europe—rose in Asia. Indian dissatisfaction with British rule mounted steadily. In 1885, the nationalist Indian elite formed the Indian National Congress, which would launch a long struggle for Indian independence.

France followed the same pattern as Britain in its southeast Asia colonies. By the 1860s, open resistance to the intruding French had become hopeless. As one of Vietnam's leading statesmen explained in 1867, "The French have come, with their powerful weapons of war . . . no one can resist them. They go where they want, the strongest ramparts fall before them." During the 1880s and early 1890s, France took what would become Vietnam, Cambodia, and Laos and grouped them into the Union of Indochina under French control. As in India, medicine, sanitation, canals, roads, and other projects financed by the French led to population growth in Indochina. French rule also spawned economic

Southeast Asia

dependence and resentment against the European assumption of superiority. A southeast Asian elite arose that, as in India, would struggle to expel Western rule.

China, with its highly structured society, strong central government, and large armed forces, had long kept Western-**China** ers at arm's length. Although the Chinese admitted some European traders and Christian missionaries in the sixteenth and seventeenth centuries, they closed their doors rather tightly thereafter. At the beginning of the eighteenth century, China ranked among the world's most prosperous and powerful societies. The Chinese still considered their huge, populous country the center of civilization surrounded by lesser civilizations. As late as 1793, China's emperor could easily dismiss a proposed trade agreement with Britain: "Our Celestial Empire possesses all things in abundance. We have no need of barbarian products."

However, during the nineteenth century, population explosion, famine, rebellions, and poor leadership under the declining Qing (Ch'ing) dynasty weakened the ancient civilization. The country became a power vacuum that proved all too tempting to the Western powers. Armed with their guns and goods, Westerners streamed into China.

First, the British forced themselves on the Chinese. During the 1830s, Britain began trading Indian opium in China for tea, silver, silk, **Opium Wars** and other products. Soon opium became one of Britain's most important commodities (see Global Connections). Chinese officials tried to stop the economic drain, addiction, and criminal activities stemming from the opium trade by making the drug illegal. As the Chinese official in charge exclaimed to the British, "You do not wish opium to harm your own country, but you choose to bring that harm to other countries such as China. Why?" In response, Britain sent gunboats and troops armed with modern weapons. They easily defeated the Chinese in a series of clashes known as the Opium Wars. By the terms of the Treaty of Nanking (1842), which ended the conflict, the Chinese ceded Hong Kong to the British, opened several tariff-free ports to foreign trade, exempted foreigners from Chinese law, and paid Britain a large indemnity.

At mid-century, disaster struck. China suffered a devastating civil war—the Taiping Rebellion (1850–1864). Subsequent rebel-**Taiping Rebellion** lions extended the internal conflict another ten years. In the end, these wars took perhaps fifty million lives, and the famines that followed cost the lives of millions

FIGURE 20.9 The British in India This period photo showing Indian servants attending to a British man suggests both the gulf between these peoples and the appeal to the British of going overseas to imperial holdings.

more. All this strife weakened the Qing dynasty and revealed the government's inability to control a nation threatened by external enemies and internal upheaval.

In the years that followed, China fought a series of wars against foreigners. It lost them all, and each defeat chipped away at its sovereignty and racked up

Opium and the West in China

Opium, a narcotic derived from the opium poppy, was known and used—especially for medical purposes—in China for centuries. However, not until the nineteenth century did its use become so widespread that millions of Chinese became addicted to the drug. The West was not free from opium, either, for Europeans and Americans increasingly resorted to opium-based products such as morphine and laudanum to calm their nerves, ease aches and pains, and control their noisy children. During the nineteenth century, most of China's opium supply was imported by British merchants from colonial holdings in India.

Chinese officials made only halfhearted attempts to restrict the opium trade until 1838, when Emperor Daoguang finally banned importation of the drug. In 1839, an imperial official, Lin Zexu, wrote a letter to Britain's Queen Victoria complaining about the destructive impact of opium on China. "Unscrupulous" merchants, Lin wrote, were "so obsessed with material gain that they have no concern whatever for the harm they can cause to others." These merchants had flooded China with so much opium "that this poison has spread far and wide in all the provinces." Lin asked the queen to stop the trade and "destroy and plow under all of these opium plants." When Lin began confiscating and destroying imported opium, the British responded with force. As one of China's discouraged commissioners reported, "The ships of the barbarians are sturdy and their cannons fierce." By 1842, British firepower had

overwhelmed the Chinese, and the Treaty of Nanjing legalized the opium trade and granted concessions to Britain and other Western powers.

The struggle against the British over opium was only the beginning of the wars and other upheavals China suffered during the nineteenth and twentieth centuries. Internal problems also increasingly plagued the vast country, weakening the government's ability to resist the West. In 1852, Zeng Guofan, a perceptive scholar and high official in Emperor Xianfeng's government, commented on the situation. Taxes, Zeng claimed, were overwhelming the people. Therefore, "people are complaining and angry, and often the resistance to tax payment bursts forth and mushrooms into full-fledged riot." More and more impoverished people were resorting to banditry to survive. Yet attempts to stop the lawlessness were useless because governmental soldiers "have always been in collusion with the bandits," Zeng maintained, and would soon release the bandits "in return for a handsome bribe." Moreover, people had lost faith in the justice system because so many "innocent men are condemned" and the people "[are unable] to have a wrong redressed." The next year, a series of disastrous uprisings struck China, the worst of which came with the Taiping Rebellion. Over the following ten years, the conflicts devastated large parts of the country. While the government eventually crushed the rebels, the country soon began losing lands and control to imperial powers.

Meanwhile, the destructive consequences of the opium trade

mounted. Isabella Bird Bishop, a British traveler in China during the 1890s, reported on the situation. In addition to noting the continuing importation of opium into China by the British, Bishop observed that "The area devoted to the [opium-producing] poppy in Sze Chuan [province] is enormous." Moreover, its culture was "encroaching on the rice and arable lands" so much that "there was no longer a margin left on which to feed the population in years of a poor harvest." Even though the Chinese regarded the opium habit as a disease, Bishop continued, in that province "opium houses are as common as gin shops in our London slums." In the large cities of that province, she noted, 80 percent of men and 40 percent of women were opium smokers. "It is obvious," she concluded, "that opium has come to stay."

To other observers throughout China and the West, it seemed equally clear that China was caught in the tightening grip of Western and Japanese imperialists as well as a powerful and addictive narcotic.

Making Connections

1. How did Chinese officials try to restrict the opium trade?

2. What do you think of the British response?

3. In what ways did British merchants' selling of opium help to undermine the authority of China's government?

yet more indemnities. The Western powers grabbed up spheres of influence and semi-independent treaty ports where all foreigners were exempt from Chinese jurisdiction. In addition, they built railroads to penetrate farther into China's heartland. As shown on Map 20.5, they also took lands on the huge country's periphery. By all these means, the French and British added to their possessions in south Asia, Russia gained territory in the north, and Japan snapped up Korea and Taiwan in the east.

CRITICAL AREA, 1895–1905

MAP 20.5

Imperialism in Asia, 1840–1914

This map shows the expansion of imperialism in Asia by the Western powers and Japan.

Explore the Map

1. Which powers had gained the largest territorial interests in Asia by 1914?

2. Which lands in particular were controlled by Russia, Britain, and Japan?

3. Where do you think conflicts were likely to break out among Russia, Britain, and Japan? Why?

The United States joined in the frenzy, grabbing the Philippine Islands after a war with Spain in 1898 and a long struggle against Filipino nationalist forces that cost the lives of perhaps 200,000 Filipinos. President William McKinley explained that the United States had the duty "to educate the Filipinos and uplift and Christianize them." To protect its commercial interests in Asia, the United States called for an "Open Door" policy that would avoid further territorial annexations by the imperial powers. Rivalry among the great powers themselves, as much as Chinese resistance, saved China from complete loss of its independence.

Meanwhile, Chinese nationalism rose in response to foreign aggression. In 1899–1900, the Boxer

The Philippines

FIGURE 20.10 John Clymer, *The Boxer Rebellion*, 1900 This dramatic painting shows U.S. marines firing on the Boxers, who in 1899 staged a rebellion against foreign influence in China.

Rebellion, a serious uprising against Western influences, erupted. Furious at those who had betrayed Chinese religion and customs, the

<mark>Boxer Rebellion</mark>

Boxers, a secret organization that believed in the spiritual power of the martial arts, killed thousands of Chinese Christians and a number of foreigners—all with the encouragement of China's dowager empress. **Figure 20.10,** a painting by American artist John Clymer, depicts a battle between the Boxers—in the center, with swords and spears—and U.S. marines—in the lower right, with modern machine guns, rifles with bayonets, and revolvers. The Boxers, represented as wild and bloodthirsty, seem to burst out of the heavily populated Chinese society, while the steadfast U.S. marines fire from the outside into that society. Combined forces from the imperial powers brutally suppressed this nationalist movement and forced China to pay large indemnities.

Even propped up by imperial powers, the corrupt Chinese central government could not last. In 1911, reformers led by Sun Yat-sen (1866–1925), a Western-educated doctor, launched a revolution aimed at freeing China from foreign exploitation and modernizing its society. Rebellions swept most of China and pushed the corrupt, inept, disintegrating dynasty to its final collapse. Sun proclaimed a republic, but power soon dispersed among imperial generals, who became warlords. China's struggles to cope with the encroaching world and its internal problems were far from over.

Japan, even more than China, had long refused direct contact with the West. At the beginning of the nineteenth century, the island nation remained in great part a feudal society ruled by the shogun—a strong military governor—and his military chieftains.

The Japanese emperor had only limited powers. Though long influenced by Chinese culture, Japan also had a sharply defined sense of identity: "[O]ur country is the source and fountainhead of all other countries, and in all matters it excels all the others," explained one Japanese writer.

<mark>Japan</mark>

In 1853, however, the Japanese witnessed an imposing sight: a squadron of well-armed, steam-powered American ships under Admiral Matthew Perry (1794–1858) sailing uninvited into Edo (Tokyo) Bay. Perry's instructions from the American government stressed the United States' desire to "establish commercial intercourse with a country whose large population and reputed wealth hold out great temptations to mercantile enterprise." If friendly negotiations should fail, the instructions continued, Perry should "change his tone" and threaten force. Perry took the charge to heart: "The World has assigned this duty to us," he asserted.

Japan's efforts to resist Perry's encroachment proved futile. Soon the well-armed Western ships intimidated the Tokugawa government into signing unequal treaties with the United States. Japan also inked agreements with Britain, Russia, France, and the Netherlands that opened the country to trade and foreign presences.

Fifteen years after Perry's arrival, the 250-year-old Tokugawa shogunate collapsed in a revolution led by powerful aristocrats who ushered into power the boy emperor Meiji (Enlightened Rule). Weakened by decades of population growth, declining agricultural productivity, popular revolts, and failed efforts at reform, the shogunate gave way.

<mark>The Meiji Restoration</mark>

According to Count Ito, a leader of the **Meiji Restoration,** members of the new government "set themselves to the task of introducing Western civilization into Japan." These leaders quickly dismantled the country's traditional military and social order. Using French, German, British, and American ways, they created a new conscript army, introduced universal education, established a written constitution, and began industrializing the economy. In 1889, Ito declared success: "If we . . . compare the present state of affairs with that which existed some twenty years ago, we shall not exaggerate if we say that the country has undergone a complete metamorphosis."

Within a few decades, Japan had transformed itself on its own terms. Once a feudal society with a preindustrial economy, it was now a modern industrialized nation. **Figure 20.11,** a photograph of a Japanese silk-working factory, reveals how intensively—in form and substance—Japan adopted Western industrial methods: Men dressed in formal Western attire

FIGURE 20.11 Japanese Silk Factory, 1905 This photograph features a Western-clad man supervising women in a large Japanese silk factory.

supervise women who work on row after row of tightly spaced machines.

The industrialized nation soon began flexing its new muscle in Asia. Japan viewed China no longer as a source of culture to be respected but as a weakened land open to conquest and exploitation. In 1894, the Japanese invaded China, forcing it to pay a large indemnity and give up Korea and Taiwan. In 1904, after Russia angered Japan by increasing its presence in China's northern province of Manchuria, the Japanese attacked the tsar's troops. To the world's surprise, Japan defeated the inept Russian forces both on land and at sea and became the dominant power in Manchuria. Industrialized, militaristic, and imperialistic, Japan had taken its place alongside other world powers by 1914.

Russo-Japanese War

The Legacy of Imperialism

With its technology, its industrial capitalism, and above all its aggressive nationalism, the West had subjected most of Africa and Asia to its domination between 1870 and 1914. In Australia and New Zealand, European powers had already established large settler colonies. As in North America, contact and clashes with the incoming settlers proved disastrous for the indigenous populations. In the Pacific, the pattern of imperial conquest that the West had established in Africa and Asia held true. Western adventurers, missionaries, traders, gunboats, troops, and businesses came, took over, and destroyed the world that native peoples had long known. Worse, the Westerners carried diseases that decimated Pacific populations.

Certainly, life in non-Western lands had not been idyllic before the intrusion of the West. As one Ndebele warrior in South Africa put it, "Even in

our own time there were troubles, there was much fighting and many innocent people were killed." Many from the West in these lands may have been well meaning, and they may have brought elements of Western civilization that were of some benefit to people in the non-Western world. In 1900 Lord Curzon, the celebrated British viceroy of India, wrote about the consequences of British rule over India: "I do not see how any Englishmen, contrasting India as it now is with what it was . . . can fail to see that we came and have stayed . . . in obedience to . . . the decree of Providence, ... for the lasting benefit of millions of the human race." In India, British rule probably prevented internal wars and promoted order. In Africa, Europeans did abolish slavery. Imperial powers built ports, railway lines, hospitals, schools, and sanitation facilities. Colonized peoples also learned about Western politics, economics, and education, eventually making use of them to assert their own liberation from imperial powers.

Yet, rather than striving to understand and appreciate non-Western societies, most people in the West viewed them from a condescending, arrogant, or downright racist perspective. The colonized peoples had to endure being treated as menials and subordinates by men and women whose only necessary qualification was being Western. The insults to local peoples' self-respect and their relentless humiliation fueled resistance to Western control.

Western powers not only forcibly drew non-Western lands into a world economy but also exploited the natural and human resources of the conquered lands and profoundly undermined the cultural, social, and religious traditions of the African and Asian peoples. In addition, they distorted non-Western economies to serve the demands of their own commerce. They imposed what one observer called "the European system of monotonous, uninterrupted labour," in which industries such as mining and railroad building subjected native laborers to inhumane and dangerous working conditions. Forced to migrate to find jobs in the alien economy, local workers left behind shattered families and communities. Political structures that had long functioned effectively in these lands broke down in just a few years.

By 1914, tens of thousands of colonial administrators, soldiers, and settlers relied directly on imperialism for their careers, status, and livelihood. They, along with Western tourists, enjoyed a sense of privilege and superiority over Africans and Asians. Many also enjoyed, though less often discussed, sexual contact with their colonized peoples. Indeed, most Westerners had come to view imperialism as normal and harmless. In their home countries, some people in the West visited the proliferating zoos with "exotic" animals, studied anthropology, viewed new works of art, and read literature that reflected interaction with non-Western lands. But few recognized how destructive it could be—not only to colonial peoples but also to themselves. In Asia, for example, Russia's expansion south brought it to the borders of British India and nearly ignited a war with that nation. Farther east, Russia pushed to the Sea of Japan and Manchuria; the action sparked hostilities with Japan. More than once, Britain, France, and Germany narrowly avoided war in Africa. Imperialism extended the already intense economic and political competition among the European states, heightening the potential for major conflict among these powers.

LOOKING BACK & MOVING FORWARD

Summary   In the years 1870–1914, more and more Westerners gained access to the political process. Nationalism opened these doors for them, as did the movement toward democracy. But the combination of nationalism and democracy had its dangers. In Britain, J. S. Mill warned that "the sentiment of nationality so far outweighs the love of liberty that the people are willing to abet their rulers in crushing the liberty and independence of any people not of their race or language." Many political leaders recognized nationalism and democracy as forces that they could use to their advantage. Others simply adjusted to them. Those who resisted did so at their own peril.

Europeans were also moving, not only to their own cities but out of Europe by the millions. Industrialization and the promise of wealth in new places combined with nationalism and mass politics to push the imperial West throughout the world as never before. As a result, Western power—economic, political, military, and imperial—expanded in an environment of intense international competition.

In the years just before 1914, the strain of this competition on Western societies grew obvious. Labor unrest, the movement for women's suffrage, politics of the extremes, civil violence, diplomatic crises, military threats, and a growing sense of uncertainty all pointed to trouble in the making. Yet this was a complex era. During this same period, the civilization that produced such uncertainty also created new engines of wealth, transformed its cities, and supported an explosion of creative thought and culture.

KEY TERMS

Paris Commune, *p. 631*
Dreyfus affair, *p. 632*
Kulturkampf, *p. 632*
Fabian Society, *p. 635*
anarchists, *p. 635*
anti-Semitism, *p. 637*
Zionism, *p. 638*
new imperialism, *p. 642*
Meiji Restoration, *p. 654*

REVIEW, ANALYZE, & CONNECT TO TODAY

REVIEW THE PREVIOUS CHAPTER

Chapter 19—"Nationalism and Statebuilding"—analyzed the efforts to build national unity and strength between 1850 and 1870.

1. In what ways did nationalism remain a powerful force in the decades after 1870?

2. Analyze how nationalism evolved during these later decades, comparing it with the nationalism of 1850–1870 as well as the ideology of nationalism of the early nineteenth century.

ANALYZE THIS CHAPTER

Chapter 20—"Mass Politics and Imperial Domination"—examines the spreading demands for democracy and the West's imperial expansion between 1870 and 1914.

1. In what ways were large numbers of people incorporated into politics during this period?

2. Why were some areas and groups still left out of the political arena in 1914?

3. Analyze the various causes for the rise of imperialism during this period.

4. For both Western and non-Western peoples, what consequences flowed from imperialism?

CONNECT TO TODAY

Think about the development of democratic institutions throughout the West, and consider the many political and economic consequences of imperialism in the non-Western world discussed in this chapter.

1. What difficulties might nondemocratic societies encounter while trying to institute democracy in today's world?

2. What consequences of imperialism might still be influencing world affairs today?

BEYOND THE CLASSROOM

DEMANDS FOR DEMOCRACY

Mayeur, Jean-Marie, and Madeleine Réberioux. *The Third Republic—From Its Origins to the Great War, 1871–1914.* Cambridge: Cambridge University Press, 1987. A solid survey of France during this period, stressing the politics of the republican government.

Rapport, Michael. *Nineteenth-Century Europe.* London: Palgrave, 2005. A reliable, recent survey with much information and analysis.

Wehler, Hans-Ulrich. *The German Empire, 1871–1918.* Leamington Spa, England: Berg Publishers, 1985. An important and controversial work that argues for continuity between the Second and Third reichs.

INSIDERS AND OUTSIDERS: POLITICS OF THE EXTREMES

Hause, Steven C., and Anne R. Kenney. *Women's Suffrage and Social Politics in the French Third Republic.* Princeton, NJ: Princeton University Press, 1984. Examines all aspects of the women's suffrage movement in France from its origins to the years after the end of World War I.

Lindemann, Albert S. *A History of European Socialism.* New Haven, CT: Yale University Press, 1983. An overview of the European socialist tradition from the Enlightenment to the 1980s.

Offen, Karen. *European Feminisms, 1700–1950.* Stanford, CA: Stanford University Press, 2000. A survey of European feminism with good coverage of the late nineteenth and early twentieth centuries.

Pulzer, P. *The Rise of Political Anti-Semitism in Germany and Austria.* Cambridge, MA: Harvard University Press, 1988. Studies the role of anti-Semitism in the world of central European politics.

Schorske, Carl E. *Fin-de-Siècle Vienna: Politics and Culture.* New York: Knopf, 1980. A classic study of the creative intellectual climate of Vienna that emphasizes the connections between culture and politics.

EMIGRATION: OVERSEAS AND ACROSS CONTINENTS

Hoerder, Dirk, and Leslie Page Moch, eds. *European Migrants—Global and Local Perspectives.* Boston: Northeastern University Press, 1996. A collection of articles by several scholars on the migrations of Europeans across the land and overseas.

Wolf, Eric. *Europe and the People Without History.* Berkeley: University of California Press, 1983. An important cross-cultural perspective on the process and consequences of imperialism.

THE NEW IMPERIALISM: THE RACE FOR AFRICA AND ASIA

Doyle, Michael W. *Empires.* Ithaca, NY: Cornell University Press, 1986. A comparative examination of imperialism.

Headrick, Daniel R. *The Tentacles of Progress: Technology Transfer in the Age of Imperialism, 1850–1940.* New York: Oxford University Press, 1988. Argues that the poorer countries failed to develop under imperial rule despite the transfers of Western capital and technology.

Hochschild, Adam. *King Leopold's Ghost: A Study of Greed, Terror, and Heroism in Colonial Africa.* Boston: Houghton Mifflin, 1999. A chilling story of imperial brutality.

Wesseling, H.L. *Divide and Rule: The Partition of Africa, 1880–1914.* New York: Greenwood, 1996. A solid, well-written survey of this imperial conquest.

GLOBAL CONNECTIONS

Gelber, Harry. *Opium, Soldiers and Evangelicals.* London: Palgrave Macmillan, 2004. Revises standard views of the Opium Wars.

WILLIAM P. FRITH, *MANY HAPPY RETURNS OF THE DAY,* 1856

In this painting, a family gathers for a birthday. The rich clothing, carpeting, paintings on the wall, heavy curtains, solid bricks showing through the window, and attentive servant on the left all mark this as an urban middle-class home. In the center, haloed by a wreath, is the innocent "angel" birthday girl. Here is the ideal of the happy home, the center of private life where men, women, and children celebrate together. Yet the scene also reflects the contrasting gender spheres: The women and children gather comfortably. But the father and grandfather—reading a newspaper—sit close to the window and to the outside, public world of the modern city.

Modern Life and the Culture of Progress

Western Society, 1850–1914

In 1864, an observer described Milan in northern Italy as vibrant "without being feverish like Paris or London." Though Milan had become one of the great cultural centers in the newly unified Italian state, workers still lived along narrow, winding streets in the heart of this city. Everyone knew each other and spoke the local Milanese dialect. Citizens "huddled around the cathedral, like a family warming itself at the hearth."

This quaint image would not last long. Over the next thirty years, wide avenues and expensive "great white houses, all straight," replaced Milan's narrow streets and old dwellings. Each year thousands of immigrants—mostly peasants and artisans—streamed into the city looking for jobs and all kinds of other opportunities. In just one decade, the city's population grew by almost a third. By the 1890s, the center of Milan teemed with people from the city's outlying quarters and suburbs who traveled there to work, shop, or amuse themselves. They spoke the common Italian language and shoved "on and off the trams . . . day and night." More people purchased goods in the huge new department store near the cathedral than prayed in that Gothic church. Nearby, in the newly built Gallery, musicians, singers, businesspeople, shoppers, and diners congregated in the shops and cafés under a magnificent glass roof. Milan—like Paris, London, and other great cities in the West—had become a center of industry, growth, and culture—a thriving embodiment of modern life.

In the decades after 1850, industrialization pulled masses of Westerners to new jobs in cities like Milan. Urban growth began to overwhelm the West's centuries-old land-based society. In cities, the continuing spread of liberal ideas and the optimism of wealthy urban leaders created a culture of progress. Dominated by science, which seemed to promise so much, and by competitive values that served the up-and-coming middle class so well, this urban culture altered the ways people thought about the world and their place in it. Those who recognized these engines of change saw their civilization being pushed to modernity. In 1850, however, few understood what modernity meant or even how difficult the ride there could be.

TIMELINE

- Romanticism
- Italian and German Unification
- "Second Industrial Revolution"
- Industrial Revolution
- The New Imperialism
- Spread of Democratic Reforms
- Realism and Naturalism
- Impressionism
- World War I
- Expressionism

1850   1860   1870   1880   1890   1900   1910   1914

PREVIEW

THE SECOND INDUSTRIAL REVOLUTION

"Steam and electricity have conquered time and space to a greater extent during the last sixty years than all the preceding six hundred years," gushed a special issue of *The Illustrated London News* in 1897. Yet in 1850, most people knew little about the industrial revolution. Outside Britain and a few limited areas in the West, more people still lived in the countryside than in the cities, and more worked at home or in home workshops than in factories. Most had never set foot in a railway car. Even in the cities, people probably made their living much as their parents had—as helpers in shops, domestics, artisans, merchants, and day laborers.

By 1914, this scenario had changed so drastically that even Britain had been left behind. Between 1850 and 1870, the coal mines, iron foundries, textile factories, steam engines, and railroads that had made Britain an industrial giant spread broadly into western and central Europe and North America. After 1870, new inventions, manufacturing processes, and methods for getting products to market and selling them rendered the earlier milestones of industrialization out-of-date. Science, technology, and industry marched hand in hand. Large-scale factories dwarfed the textile mills and iron foundries of the early industrial era, and huge department stores displayed endless goods to entice consumers. For the first time in history, people began to expect continuing economic growth. According to some historians, these developments created a "second industrial revolution."

Steel Leads the Way

Steel led the way in this new wave of industrialization. The Bessemer processes for removing impurities from molten iron speeded up and cheapened steel production, transforming it from an expensive luxury product into a strong, affordable improvement over iron. **Figure 21.1,** an 1880 photograph of the Krupp Steelworks, reveals the new technology and massive factories that produced steel and enabled countries such as Germany to become industrial leaders. On the left are the huge converters that turned iron into steel. Dwarfed in comparison, workers (in the foreground and around the converters) toil to keep the process going. By 1914, the annual production of steel had risen more than fiftyfold since 1850. **Figure 21.2** charts the growth of steel production between 1882 and 1912 and the countries that led in the creation of this crucial industrial material. Out of this steel, manufacturers made efficient tools and machines to fabricate metal, textile, leather, and wood products.

With advances in chemistry, textile manufacturers could now use inexpensive synthetic dyes to color their cloth, and paper manufacturers could process wood pulp more efficiently than ever. By 1914, [Chemicals] new chemical-based fabrics and processes had spawned a host of infant industries. Germany's chemical laboratories and their development of industrial uses for chemicals helped propel that nation ahead of Great Britain as an industrial leader.

FIGURE 21.1 The Krupp Steelworks, 1880 This photograph of a German steel factory shows the powerful new machines that helped make Germany an industrial leader.

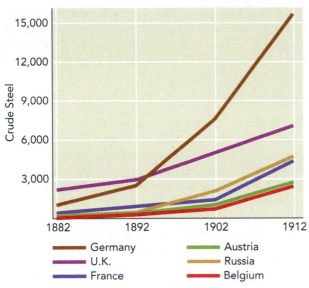

FIGURE 21.2 Steel Production (thousands of metric tons)

Germany	Austria
U.K.	Russia
France	Belgium

Electricity and petroleum became practical sources of power, thanks to the invention of the electrical dynamo, the steam turbine, and the internal combustion engine. By the end of the century, electric lamps glowed in city streets, large stores, and wealthy neighborhoods throughout Europe. Electricity powered factories and workshops and was the magic behind the refrigerators and vacuum cleaners starting to appear in middle-class homes.

Electricity and petroleum

New Transportation and Communication Networks

Getting around, moving things, and communicating became dramatically easier as well. Before 1850, few people had seen more of the world than they could view on foot or by cart or horseback. By 1914, millions traveled enormous distances each year. Even in China, Turkey, and Brazil, trains chugged along, hauling people for astonishing stretches. This was the greatest era of railroad building in history, and with the railroads came hundreds of bridges and long tunnels. At the same time, huge steamships with steel hulls, turbine engines, and screw propellers replaced sailing ships. The opening of the Suez Canal (between the Mediterranean Sea and the Indian Ocean) in 1869 and the Panama Canal (between the Atlantic and Pacific oceans) in 1914 cut thousands of miles off long sea voyages and brought the Western and non-Western worlds into closer contact.

Railroad building

However, the future lay with yet another revolutionary invention: the internal combustion engine. In 1887 the German inventor Gottlieb Daimler (1834–1900) attached his little combustion engine to a wagon—and the automobile was born. Two decades

later in the United States, former bicycle mechanic Henry Ford (1863–1947) introduced the assembly line to the automobile industry. By 1914, cars, taxis, and trucks jammed city streets in Europe and America and created new demand for oil, rubber, and concrete.

Internal combustion engine

Just as these new means of transportation linked millions of people physically, the telegraph and telephone connected them in a giant communication network. In 1844, Samuel Morse sent a message by wire 40 miles from Baltimore to Washington. In 1866, ships laid telegraph cable across the Atlantic, enabling news to travel from London to New York as quickly as it had moved from one side of London to the other. Ten years later, Alexander Graham Bell (1847–1922), an American born in Scotland, invented the telephone.

Telegraph and telephone

The Birth of Big Business

These telephone companies, railroads, shipping lines, steel mills, chemical plants, and new factories became too large for all but a very few individuals to finance. Capitalists now raised money by organizing corporations and selling shares of stock—partial ownership—to investors. Governments helped out by passing laws that limited stockholders' risk to only the money they invested. Luck helped, too, for the discovery of gold in California and Australia in the 1850s and 1860s, and in Alaska and South Africa later in the century, increased the supply of money. This was big business, and it was controlled by large banks and wealthy executives. These executives functioned much as heads of state, conferring with boards of directors and lesser executives. Under them were layers of managers who specialized in areas such as sales, finance, and production and who hired, fired, and supervised employees.

In this new world of business, the big and strong often destroyed the small and weak. Corporations combined into gigantic, monopolistic trusts (called "cartels" in Germany) that commanded markets, prices, and wages. Rockefeller's Standard Oil trust in the United States and the I. G. Farben chemical cartel in Germany are examples of the spectacular business successes of the age. By 1914, big business controlled a large share of industrial production in the West. In Japan, too, which adapted quickly to Western industrialization, five giant corporations dominated three-quarters of that nation's industry.

Monopolies

The Lure of Shopping

With all the new technology, manufacturers habitually churned out more products than they could sell.

So, merchants found new ways to create customer demand. Grandiose department stores, such as the

Bon Marché in Paris and Bocconi's in Milan, rose up in major cities across the West. The stores displayed a dazzling array of enticing goods—ready-made clothes, furniture, rugs, umbrellas, stationery, toilet paper—a cornucopia of foreign and domestic temptations. Prices were fixed and aimed at the middle classes, but even members of the working class might afford some items. Posters announced "sales" to draw more people to their stores' massive glass and iron emporiums. Glossy catalogues mailed to potential customers in other cities and the countryside encouraged people to order the practical goods and the luxuries of modern urban life for delivery by the new national postal services.

As **Figure 21.3** suggests, the stores become tourist attractions, places to spend leisure time, and leading promoters of consumption. This Parisian department store, with its dramatic central staircase, was designed like a theater for visitors as well as a building where a huge variety of goods could be purchased. Men, women, and children—themselves on display as much as the goods for sale—stroll through this monument to prosperity. By 1900, more than 15,000 people passed through the doors of the Bon Marché in Paris every

FIGURE 21.3 A Paris Department Store New stores in large cities, such as the Bon Marché in Paris, offered shoppers a huge choice of products from around the world.

day. Equally amazing, this shoppers' mecca was only one of twelve Parisian department stores that together employed almost 10,000 people. Department stores had come to represent the materialism of the cities.

Winners and Losers in the Race for Wealth

In this intense economic struggle, some people flourished, others fell behind, and many worried about their future. Cycles of prosperity and recession made economic life precarious. New economic powers such as Germany and the United States

rose to challenge and sometimes surpass mighty Great Britain, which failed to invest sufficiently in new processes and marketing techniques. Industrialization spread unevenly east to Russia—St. Petersburg alone would sprout more than nine hundred factories by 1914. Areas in southern and eastern Europe that held on to old ways of making a living fell further behind, although even in these poorer regions industrialization gained some footholds. Overseas, Australia and Canada began to industrialize, and Japan—with its new machines, factories, and railroads—became a major industrial power.

However, most of Latin America, Africa, and mainland Asia scarcely entered the industrial race before 1914. Although Latin American nations boasted some railway lines and substantial foreign trade, they lacked the machinery and manufacturing that marked industrial economies (see Global Connections). A similar pattern held in mainland Asia and most of Africa, which produced cash crops and raw materials to trade to the industrialized West for manufactured goods but were unable to develop industrial economies.

Did this second industrial revolution make life better overall for Westerners? As we saw with our discussion of the first industrial revolution in Chapter 17, this question is difficult to answer. Statistically, the

answer is yes. It certainly paid to be living in the industrializing nations of the West. In these thriving regions, most people benefited from the new wealth—even those living outside the cities. Food prices came down, and larger farms, chemical fertilizers, and threshing machines boosted harvests and lowered costs. Agricultural producers in North America, Argentina, and Australia sent inexpensive grains and meat in new, refrigerated ships. Prices for manufactured products also dropped as the new machines and processes made production more efficient. With declining prices came a rise in real wages for workers, which almost doubled in Britain between 1850 and 1914. Meat, dairy products, sugar, tea, and coffee were no longer luxuries. People snapped up previously out-of-reach manufactured goods. With care and luck, they even saved a bit of money for hard times.

Economic Transformation in Latin America

In 1855, the Yankee speculator and entrepreneur Henry Meiggs arrived in Santiago, Chile, with ambitious plans to introduce railroads into that South American nation. By 1867, his company had built more than 200 miles of railroad lines, many of them across Chile's difficult coastal mountain range. A year later, Meiggs moved north to Peru, which had only 60 miles of track under operation. At a banquet attended by the social elite of Lima, Peru's capital, he promised that his railroads would lead to "a great social revolution." He described the locomotive as "that irresistible battering ram of modern civilization" whose "whistle will awaken the native race from . . . lethargy. . . ." By the time of Meiggs's death in 1877, this man whom Peruvians called the Messiah of the Railway had built more than 700 miles of track, most of them up into the steep Andes and along 2-mile-high plateaus. The entrepreneur had enlisted the help of capital and experts from Europe; machinery from the United States; and more than 20,000 workers from Peru, Chile, Bolivia, and China.

Chile's and Peru's experience with Meiggs and his railroads mirrors similar developments unfolding throughout Latin America between 1850 and 1914. People, money, and machinery flowed from western Europe across the Atlantic to the Americas, and international trade mushroomed. Latin America's subsistence economies blossomed into market economies that exported crops and raw materials to Europe—such as bananas, coffee, sugar, tobacco, nitrates, copper, rubber, cocoa, wheat, and beef. In exchange, Europeans sent industrial goods. This transformation required new railroads, steamships, utilities, communications, harbors, refrigeration facilities, and banks. However, Latin American countries lacked the capital to finance these investments. Spotting a hot opportunity, British, French, German, Belgian, and North American investors sent their money (sometimes in the hands of men such as Meiggs) to fill the voids.

Some larger Latin American countries flourished, thanks to all this trade and economic development. Argentina's economy, for example, expanded at about 5 percent per year between 1880 and 1914. And the population of major Latin American cities such as Montevideo, Uruguay; Buenos Aires, Argentina; São Paulo, Brazil; and Rio de Janeiro, Brazil, more than tripled during the generation that preceded World War I. Not surprisingly, the large landowners and elites in these cities benefited the most from the new economic activity. So did foreigners. British companies owned most of Argentina's meat-processing plants, railways, and telegraph lines as well as many of its banks and merchant houses. This pattern showed up elsewhere in Latin America as well. In Mexico, for example, Belgian, Yankee, and English investors put up much of the money for that nation's railroads. The French controlled the large Mexican department stores; the Germans, the hardware business. North Americans dominated the cement industry, and the Spanish and French ran the textile industry.

Not everyone applauded these developments. "No one can deny the benefits that the railroads, the gas plants, the street cars, and the telegraph and telephone lines have brought to us," admitted the Argentine socialist Juan Bautista Justo in 1896. But "our country is tributary to England. Every year millions of gold pesos leave here and go to the stockholders of English enterprises that are established in Argentina." Others voiced the same sentiments elsewhere. Francisco García Calderón, a Peruvian diplomat and writer, complained, "South America cannot dispense with the influence of the Anglo-Saxon North, with its exuberant wealth and its industries."

Despite such lamentations, there was no turning back. During the decade that followed World War I, Rudyard Kipling described São Paulo as "a metropolis" where "cars and trucks move everywhere, like electrons in the physics texts, across grids of streetcar lines." Outside the city, coffee plantations stretched "as far as the eye could reach, the evenly-spaced twelve-foot trees and their reddening berries covered the rolling hills." The wave of economic transformation that began in western Europe had swept through Latin America and was headed for the rest of the world.

Making Connections

1. What effects did the "second industrial revolution" have on Latin American nations?

2. What problems did this economic transformation create for Latin America?

Those hard times visited some more than others, and here the old pattern held true. The middle classes benefited more than the working classes, skilled workers more than unskilled, and owners of large farms more than agricultural laborers. Nor did the new wealth end misery for those at the bottom of the socioeconomic ladder. Many people remained mired in poverty. Among workers, few could expect to retire without sinking into dependence or impoverishment, let alone ease into the dream of a comfortable cottage with a small garden. The gaps between rich and poor were all too apparent. The upper 20 percent of the population generally received more of a nation's income than the remaining 80 percent. Every day the urban poor could see but not afford the fine apartments, carriages, and clothes of the wealthy.

THE NEW URBAN LANDSCAPE

City life became the new norm for masses of people in the West. Many rural villages declined or died, slowly in some areas, quickly in others. People from outside the local community moved in, bought the land, and hired migrant laborers to work it. Residents flocked to the cities, and those who had established themselves there stayed. An observer in 1899 reflected the experience of millions: "[T]he most remarkable social phenomenon of the present century is the concentration of population in cities." Europe's population ballooned from 270 million in 1850 to 450 million in 1914, and well over half of western Europeans lived in cities. In Britain, only 8 percent of the workforce remained in the countryside. London, Europe's greatest urban center, grew from 2.5 million in 1850 to more than 4.5 million in 1914.

Rebuilding Cities

As these numbers multiplied everywhere, even the physical foundations of cities changed. Urban centers grew out, up, and belowground. Milan, the thriving Italian center described at the beginning of this chapter, was not the only city to rebuild. Governments, entrepreneurs, and speculators tore apart centuries-old housing and winding streets in Paris, Vienna, Brussels, Stockholm, Barcelona, Cologne, and Mexico City. In place of these older features, they constructed broad, tree-lined avenues, parks, fashionable apartment houses, department stores, fancy cafés, government buildings, museums, hospitals, opera houses, schools, and libraries. New neighborhoods, open spaces, transportation systems, and underground water and sewer systems transformed the face and substance of city life.

Paris led the way in this wave of reconstruction. In the French capital, Emperor Napoleon III and his technocratic administrator, Baron Haussmann, initiated the most ambitious plans for demolishing some of the oldest and poorest neighborhoods. According to Napoleon, Haussmann, and their advisors, these reconstruction efforts offered several important benefits. Doctors and reformers argued that filth from overcrowding caused the diseases that often swept through Paris. Wide streets and open spaces, they explained, would let in much-needed fresh air. But those wide streets also gave governments a political advantage: They deterred people from again throwing up revolutionary barricades to fight the forces of order, as they had in 1848, and afforded troops ready access to working-class areas. Finally, reconstruction projects generated untold wealth for investors, speculators, influence brokers, schemers, architects, engineers, and workers from all over France.

As in Milan, the new construction drove the poor out of the center of Paris to the east end or into working-class suburbs. Wealthier Parisians felt little sympathy. After all, they reasoned, the capital city represented the nation in the eyes of citizens and visitors alike. As Haussman explained, "The splendor of this city reflects on the whole country." The power, wealth, beauty, and modernity of Paris must not be marred by images of poverty and misfortune.

Sewers and Subways

Below Europe's city streets, less glamorous but no less important projects hummed along. In 1850, most houses in Europe's major cities did not have running water. Sewage in cities such as Berlin still ran in open gutters, creating an atmosphere of filth and tremendous stench. During the following decades, these standards began to change. First in London and then elsewhere, engineers and workers built water and sewer systems. Doctors, reformers, and planners led the drive to bring in freshwater in aqueducts or pipes from sources upstream and to create hundreds of miles of underground sewers to carry waste downstream. These measures made urban life healthier and more comfortable than before.

More than water and waste moved below the city, however. In 1863, London's underground railway opened. Over the next fifty years, Paris and New York built subways of their own. Along with carriages, trams, and railroads, the efficient, predictable subways enabled people to shop and work in places farther from home than ever. People moved their residences out of crowded urban centers to city fringes and suburbs—whether upscale neighborhoods for the middle class or less expensive areas for workers.

CITY PEOPLE

Who were these people filling the cities of the West? How did they make their way in life, so far away from the land and surrounded by industrial advances and new wealth? Part of the answer is revealed in **Figure 21.4,** a mid-century engraving of a typical Parisian apartment house. At this time, the city's various social classes still lived in close proximity but in different conditions. The drawing portrays the wealthy bourgeoisie living on the first (American second) floor in luxurious comfort; above them lives a bourgeois family of lesser means. The lower classes and aspiring artists—dancing and drinking instead of working, having too many children, and being unable to pay their bills—live on the bottom and upper floors in increasing poverty, thanks to their imprudence.

On Top of It All: The Urban Elite

At the top of the urban social order was a small, elite class of wealthy aristocrats and the richest of the bourgeoisie—the millionaire factory owners, merchants, and bankers. Amounting to less than 1 percent of the population, these people socialized together, turned to each other for help, and intermarried. Through strategic matchmaking, new wealth from the daughter or son of an American captain of industry or banker might enable an aristocratic family to maintain its position. More often, however, aristocrats kept their positions by making shrewd investments, serving governments, holding on to top spots in the military and diplomatic corps, and wisely managing their lands and businesses. They, along with members entering their ranks, had prestige but not the formal privileges that their eighteenth-century predecessors had enjoyed.

Those who had been born into aristocratic families clung to what was left of the old lifestyle. Those aspiring to the aristocratic life used their money to copy that lifestyle. These newly rich bought estate houses in the country and opulent townhouses along the best avenues and parks, attended fancy balls, took hunting trips to Africa, and supported large staffs of servants. They also kept up with the latest fashions and made grand gestures toward cultural and philanthropic activities. However, a few rules of the aristocratic game had changed. Obvious arrogance was frowned upon, as this elite made an effort to comply with middle-class morality. At the very least, they strove to appear responsible, domestic, and religious. Of course, their children got the best of everything. In every way, these elites were truly the upper crust, on top and intent on staying there.

PARIS COMIQUE.   Paris le 1er Janvier.

FIGURE 21.4 The Urban Classes, mid-nineteenth century   In a typical Parisian apartment house such as this, people from various social classes lived in different circumstances but in close proximity.

Pride and Success: The "Solid" Middle Class

Well below this upper crust, the "solid" bourgeoisie held the better jobs, lived in the finer apartments, dined at fashionable restaurants, and commanded at least one good servant. These were the families of small factory owners, merchants, managers, doctors, druggists, local bankers, lawyers, professors, and architects who earned and spent more money than most.

Worried about competitors from below, many middle-class men established "professional" associations designed to keep standards up and rivals down. Nor did they open their professions to women (see Document 21.1). Wives and daughters, they intoned, "best" not work for pay. Beliefs that women and men belonged in "separate spheres"—women at home, men in the public world of work—persisted. "Of all those acquirements, which more particularly belong to the feminine character," explained Isabella Mary

`Women and work`

DOCUMENTS

DOCUMENT 21.1

John Stuart Mill Argues for Women's Rights

During the last decades of the nineteenth century, a number of observers commented on the position of women in Western societies and argued for women's rights. One of the most prominent and influential was John Stuart Mill, who published his essay "The Subjection of Women" in 1869. In the following excerpt from that work, Mill places the question of women's subordination within the context of human progress and morality.

The principle which regulates the existing social relations between the two sexes—the legal subordination of one sex to the other—is wrong in itself, and now one of the chief hindrances to human improvement; and that it ought to be replaced by a principle of perfect equality, admitting no power or privilege on the one side, nor disability on the other.

. . . The masters of all other slaves rely, for maintaining obedience, on fear; either fear of themselves, or religious fears. The masters of women wanted more than simple obedience, and they turned the whole force of education to effect their purpose. All women are brought up from the very earliest years in the belief that their ideal of character is the very opposite to that of men; not self-will, and government by self-control, but submission, and yielding to the control of others. All the moralities tell them that it is the duty of women, and all the current sentimentalities that it is their nature, to live for others; to make complete abnegation of themselves, and to have no life but in their affections. . . .

For what is the peculiar character of the modern world—the difference which chiefly distinguishes modern institutions, modern social ideas, modern life itself, from those of times long past? It is, that human beings are no longer born to their place in life, and chained down by an inexorable bond to the place they are born to, but are free to employ their faculties, and such favourable chances as offer, to achieve the lot which may appear to them most desirable.

If this general principle of social and economical sciences is . . . true, we ought to act as if we believed it, and not to ordain that to be born a girl instead of a boy, any more than to be born black instead of white, or a commoner instead of a nobleman, shall decide the person's position through all life. . . .

SOURCE: John Stuart Mill, "The Subjection of Women," *Three Essays* (Oxford: Oxford University Press, 1975).

Analyze the Document

1. In Mill's view, why is the legal subordination of one sex to the other sex wrong?

2. Other than laws, what means are used to subordinate women, according to Mill?

3. In what ways is the liberation of women related to "the peculiar character of the modern world"?

Mayson Beeton in her best-selling advice book for women, "there are none which take a higher rank . . . than such as enter into a knowledge of household duties; for on these are perpetually dependent the happiness, comfort, and well-being of a family."

Some women managed to swim against the current, however. They engaged in philanthropic activities—in support of the poor and uneducated, or against alcohol and prostitution. British philanthropist Angela Burdette-Coutts (1814–1906), for example, gave away a fortune to schools and housing for the poor. In France, many wealthy women followed the example of Empress Eugénie (consort of Napoleon III), who supported societies that provided assistance to new mothers. In the United States, educated middle-class women staffed hundreds of settlement houses in urban centers that helped immigrants adjust to the customs and language of their new country as well as middle-class values. Only a few women managed to carve out careers in business, teaching, writing, or painting. Exclusion from universities kept most ambitious upper-middle-class women from pursuing lucrative professions, though schools such as Queens College in Britain and the Female Medical College of Pennsylvania promised some professional opportunities to women.

If not arrogant, this bourgeoisie was proud. Who else better represented their civilization? As they saw it, success flowed from character, ability, and effort; in a world open to talent, rewards came from achievement. These people praised discipline, control, and respectability, while attacking public drunkenness, emotional outbursts, and—especially in **Victorian** Britain—open displays of sexual affection. In addition, they respected Christian morality and marital fidelity. Cleanliness went hand in hand with purity and modernity, as did running water for regular baths and several changes of clothes. Certainly, they argued, all good people should live up to these standards, at least in appearance.

Values

Hardworking and Hopeful: The Lower Middle Class

Those just below the solid bourgeoisie probably tried as hard as any group to succeed in modern society. These lower-middle-class people performed skilled services as tellers in banks, sorters in mailrooms, and salespeople in department stores. Reading, writing, and mathematical skills (and for more and more, the new typewriter) enabled thousands to become schoolteachers, postal workers, and clerks in places from government agencies and insurance firms to accounting offices and train stations. Some of these lower-paying "white-collar jobs" became open to educated women, particularly if they were unmarried.

Lower-middle-class people made their living in settings that sometimes resembled factories. **Figure 21.5** shows clerks working in the offices of Cadbury's, the chocolate firm described in Chapter 17. In this huge room, all the chairs, desks, and tasks seem the same. All the clerks are men, and even their clothes look almost identical. **Figure 21.6** shows a French telephone exchange, also set in a large room in which the chairs, fixtures, and activities are similar. Here the employees are all middle-class women, with the exception of male supervisors and a boy who delivers messages. As this image shows, even when jobs opened for middle-class women, they were often separate from men's work and of lower status.

With the heightening tempo of industrialization, these lower-middle-class occupations multiplied. People might move up the economic ladder, and better-off workers could hope to see their educated children rising into this class. In turn, a few children from lower-middle ranks might move into the also-expanding solid middle class. Although moving up remained more the exception than the rule, the possibilities were far greater than before 1850. By 1914, the middle classes overall had grown from between 3 and 10 percent of the population to more than 20 percent in much of the West.

Social mobility

FIGURE 21.5 **Modern Office Work for Men** Many lower-middle-class clerks worked in large offices featuring row after row of desks, as in this photo of Cadbury's chocolate firm in England.

FIGURE 21.6 **French Telephone Exchange, late nineteenth century** In this large telephone office, almost all the employees are middle-class women.

The "Other Half": The Working Classes

Unlike the elites and the middle classes, the working classes lived on crowded side streets, the poorer east side of cities such as London or Paris, or the edge of town where land and rents were cheaper. Though better off than before 1850, they still faced the threat of job loss, which could send them into poverty in an instant.

Even employed workers struggled to make ends meet. A new demand for certain skilled work helped some. Those who could read directions; could build or repair machines; or were printers, plumbers, or cabinetmakers earned respectable wages. They might also join unions and demand reforms. Other skilled workers lost out, for factory owners fit laborers to jobs that had become nothing more than mindless, repetitive tasks. Automaker Henry Ford expressed the views of many industrial managers toward this kind of labor: "I could not possibly do the same thing day in and day out, but . . . to the majority of minds, repetition holds no terrors. . . . The average worker, I am sorry to say, . . . wants a job in which he does not have to think." Whether former artisans with obsolete skills or migrants from the countryside, these workers earned paltry wages and worked at an exhausting pace. They and their children tended to remain low-paid industrial laborers for the rest of their lives.

Despite legislation restricting women from certain jobs, many labored outside and inside the home. Jeanne Bouvier, a Frenchwoman born in 1865, worked as millions of other working-class women did. When she was 11 years old, she took her first job in a silk factory near Lyons. Three years later, she

FIGURE 21.7

Léon Frédéric, *The Stages of a Worker's Life,* 1895–1897

In 1897, Belgian artist Léon Frédéric completed these three panels depicting urban workers. In the left panel, he focused on men. In the right, he depicted the woman's world. Children and families occupy the central panel.

Connecting Art & Society

1. In what ways does the content of this work fit with its title, *The Stages of a Worker's Life*?

2. What are the differences among the roles played by men, women, and children in this painting?

3. What impression of working-class life do you think the painter intended to convey to viewers?

4. What is your own reaction to this painting?

moved to Paris, where she worked as a domestic and then in the hatmaking industry. Later, she worked a twelve-hour day as a seamstress and did piecework on her own.

In addition to their jobs in factories and small shops, many women took in work at home finishing clothes, polishing items for sale, wrapping chocolates, or decorating toys. Some of the new machines of industry even added to the demand for this older piecework. For example, Singer's sewing machine, invented in the 1850s, enabled entrepreneurs to hire women for low wages to work at home or in small "sweatshops." Such women proved especially appealing to these employers because they were easy to fire and posed little threat of forming a union or going on strike.

Still more women worked in traditional urban jobs. Domestic servants could count on meals and housing and perhaps even some savings from their salaries. On the other hand, they suffered from the whims of their employers and the threat of sexual abuse. Women in laundries labored at drudgery for low wages, although some of them enjoyed the sense of comradeship that came with the job at times.

The growth of cities may have increased the work available to these women, but the machinery of the industrial revolution did not yet ease job conditions for them.

Léon Frédéric (1856–1940), for a time Belgium's most famous painter, tried to encompass all stages of a worker's life in a large triptych (**Figure 21.7**). In the foreground of the central panel, children on the right play cards, while on the left they carry and nibble on bread. Their parents and young couples stand just behind them, and in the background are the aged members of the working class whose ultimate fate is marked by the distant but approaching funeral coach. The left panel depicts the man's work world, where men of all ages, from adolescence to old age, engage in manual labor or observe it. In the foreground they are digging, and in the middle ground they struggle with heavy beams. Behind them are the factories where they work. The right panel shows the women's world, all mothering and nurturing with babies in their arms and at their breasts. Behind them are market stalls where they shop. Here is a vision of workers' lives in a nutshell: hard manual labor for men, child rearing and food preparation for women, and at the end, old age and death for all.

What to Do About "Them"

Members of the middle classes looked upon their working-class counterparts with a mixture of fear and sympathy: fear that these were dangerous people who might rise in revolt, commit crimes, or create disorder, and sympathy for the harshness of working-class life. Most middle-class people agreed with the popular writer Samuel Smiles that the working classes suffered from their own faults rather than injustices in the social system: "no laws . . . can make the idle industrious, the thriftless provident, or the drunken sober. Such reforms can only be effected by means of individual action, economy, and self-denial."

However, other members of the middle class—especially younger, college-educated people who were also connected to religious causes—joined organizations to ease the plight of the urban poor. With high optimism and idealism, they established clinics, settlement houses, and maternal-wellness societies. Thousands of middle- and upper-class women visited the poor; ran schools; and inspected asylums, workhouses, and prisons. One Spanish charity worker wrote a guide for visitors to the poor: "In viewing their faults, vices, and crimes, we must ask ourselves this question: Would the poor be what they are, if we were what we ought to be?" Some of these workers spread birth-control information; others touted the benefits of religion. Women's groups in particular distributed prayer books to the poor or sold Bibles to raise money to aid the needy—a reflection of the still-close link between the churches and charitable work. Still others tried to help the poor through political activism, joining socialist organizations such as the Fabian Society in London, which decried the capitalist system as unjust and inefficient.

SPORTS AND LEISURE IN THE CITIES

Building Character Through Athletics

For turn-of-the-century Europeans who had the time and money, city life could be fun. New forms of recreation and sports not only offered entertaining diversions but also built character values important for industry and war. Soccer, rugby, and cricket, once games only for schoolchildren, became extremely popular, competitive team sports for adults. In 1901, more than 100,000 attended a championship game of soccer in Britain. The emphasis on teamwork, competition, and discipline in the sports world reflected the qualities of industrial work and military service so prized during the era. Other new sports, such as

bicycle and auto racing, stressed the speed and power of machines; by no coincidence, industrial firms sponsored some of these contests. Even the growth of scouting and, in Germany, the "wandering youth" clubs revealed the belief that good character required physical vigor and outdoor living. Accordingly, the modern Olympic games—stressing competition and nationalism—were established during this period, with the first games held in Athens in 1896.

Women's sports were less professional and less competitive than men's. Even scouting for girls was designed to instill homemaking values. But women did take to bicycles, despite warnings from the old guard that the loose clothing necessary for bicycling was unfeminine, that the activity would damage enthusiasts' ability to have children, and that women might inappropriately experience sexual pleasure from riding.

The New Tourist

Increasingly, people vacationed away from the cities. More and more, people left town. Those who had the means might imitate the eighteenth-century aristocratic habit of visiting the great cities, museums, and monuments of Europe. Others traveled to resorts on the Mediterranean coast, the Alps, or the shores of the Baltic Sea. By 1890, some 100,000 people visited the resort town of Vichy in central France to "take the waters" (cure their ills), relax, and socialize. Tourism became so popular that special books appeared, and professionally organized tours formed to guide people on their travels.

Workers usually lacked the time or money for such luxuries. Some managed short trips on trains that left cities every day for the coast, perhaps to Dieppe in France or Brighton in England, where piers and amusement parks beckoned. Most, however, stayed in the cities. There, some went to café concerts to see singers, comedians, jugglers, and acrobats. Others attended theaters featuring fast dancing or enjoyed boxing matches, vaudeville shows, and (after the turn of the century) movies.

PRIVATE LIFE: TOGETHER AND ALONE AT HOME

As the tempo of life in factories, stores, government offices, and streets increased, private life grew more precious. The individualism trumpeted by the liberal bourgeoisie accentuated the longing to withdraw from the public arena into the family, the home, and the self. The personal—one's body, sexuality, and internal life—became a subject of intense fascination. The home—the realm of the family protected by walls and locked doors—was the center of private life.

Family: The Promise of Happiness

People believed in the family. Like a religion, the family promised happiness in a difficult world, a meaning that would extend beyond death, and a sacred place free from intrusion by the outside world. As much as their means permitted, people celebrated the family through daily gatherings at meals and special occasions such as weddings, vacations, and birthdays (see the painting on page 658). For individuals, these occasions marked points in their own life cycles. At more private moments, the family home served as a place where individuals shared emotions, or perhaps confessed silently to themselves or in a diary in the solitude of a bedroom.

More than ever, people recorded moments of private life in letters, diaries, and photographs. Families exchanged thousands of letters over a lifetime that told of children, deaths, visits, and health. Such correspondence held the family together when travel and migration to different cities threatened to pull it apart. Diaries of the day reveal much self-concern and introspection. One Frenchwoman explained, "When I am alone, I have plenty to do in following the movement of my ideas and impressions, in exploring myself, in examining my dispositions and my various ways of being, in drawing the best out of myself, in registering the ideas that come to me by chance or that are suggested to me by my reading." People took photographs to capture family occasions—from baptisms to Sunday meals and partings—especially after the invention of the small Kodak camera in the 1880s. They carefully enshrined these photographs in frames and collected them in well-organized albums.

Recording private life

A Home of One's Own

The dream of family life and privacy required having a home of one's own—a private kingdom apart from city and society. But home had another purpose as well: It announced the material success of the bourgeoisie and the pleasures of private life.

As revealed in the 1877 painting of a Paris interior shown in **Figure 21.8,** the typical bourgeois apartment resembled an antique shop, overdecorated in no particular style and bulging with possessions. Heavy drapes hang over the walls and windows, multiple carpets cover the floors, fabrics ornament the mantelpieces and furniture, and tassels dangle everywhere. In such a home, family members could gaze at the many prints and paintings, enjoy music played by an elder daughter on the piano, read a novel in the library, and stay informed by subscribing to journals. Small, private gardens or potted plants and painted landscapes completed the picture by offering a way to appreciate nature.

Servants shared middle-class homes but remained on the fringes of the family's private life. Relegated to their own small quarters in the attic or basement, servants had little freedom to move about the house at their leisure or take part in their employers' lives. Indeed, with the era's emphasis on both individualism and privacy, employers increasingly saw servants as potential intruders into private life. The bedroom and bathroom became off-limits, and people complained about how hard it was to find "good," affordable servants. By the turn of the century, many middle-class families managed with just a single female domestic, or none at all.

Servants

For the typical middle-class man, home was a retreat from public life, to be savored at the end of the workday or on weekends. For the middle-class woman, it was much more. Society glorified her domestic role more than ever. No longer would she be praised for doing "productive" work such as managing a husband's shop. Instead, she orchestrated every aspect of the family's home life, managing the meals, chores, visits, and guests. Her highest duty, however, was to bear and raise children. No longer was reproduction regarded as simply a natural function: It had become a complex, demanding activity. Most likely, a middle-class woman had fewer children than her

Women's roles

FIGURE 21.8 Mihaly Munkacsy, *Paris Interior,* 1877 Middle-class apartments in large cities typically bulged with possessions.

DOCUMENTS

DOCUMENT 21.2

Beeton's Guide for Women

Mrs. Beeton's Book of Household Management became the most popular "guidebook" for the proper middle-class woman in Victorian England. It covered topics from account keeping and the importance of cleanliness to strategies for hiring domestics. In the following selection, Isabella Beeton describes the overall role of the "mistress of a house," proper dress, and the correct treatment of servants.

1. As with the Commander of an Army, or the leader of any enterprise, so is it with the mistress of a house. Her spirit will be seen through the whole establishment; and just in proportion as she performs her duties intelligently and thoroughly, so will her domestics follow in her path. Of all those acquirements, which more particularly belong to the feminine character, there are none which take a higher rank, in our estimation, than such as enter into a knowledge of household duties; for on these are perpetually dependent the happiness, comfort, and well-being of a family.

***

13. The Dress of the Mistress should always be adapted to her circumstances, and be varied with different occasions. Thus, at breakfast she should be attired in a very neat and simple manner, wearing no ornaments. If this dress should decidedly pertain only to the breakfast-hour, and be specially suited for such domestic occupations as usually follow that meal, then it would be well to exchange it before the time for receiving visitors, if the mistress be in the habit of doing so.

***

19. The Treatment of Servants is of the highest possible moment, as well to the mistress as to the domestics themselves. On the head of the house the latter will naturally fix their attention, and if they perceive that the mistress's conduct is regulated by high and correct principles, they will not fail to respect her. If, also, a benevolent desire is shown to promote their comfort, at the same time that a steady performance of their duty is exacted, then their respect will not be unmingled with affection, and they will be still more solicitous to continue to deserve her favour.

SOURCE: Isabella Beeton, *Mrs. Beeton's Book of Household Management* (London: Chancellor Press, 1982).

Analyze the Document

1. What does Beeton mean when she compares the mistress of a house to "the Commander of an Army"?

2. What qualities does Beeton stress?

3. What attitudes toward women does this selection reflect?

---

mother, but she was expected to lavish greater attention on them. Her children would probably remain at home through adolescence, though many families sent their offspring to boarding schools. To help women meet all these expectations, books, magazines, pamphlets, and advice columns offered tips on how to attract a man and marry well; manage a household; sharpen "home economics" skills; and cultivate an appropriate social life that included teas, afternoon visits, and dinner parties.

At the same time, disturbing crosscurrents started to undermine this picture of the home and women's role in it. As Document 21.2 indicates, prominent people circulated new ideas about the restrictions imposed on women. Many women demanded more independent lives, even choosing to live outside the confines of the middle-class home. The British reformer Florence Nightingale (1820–1910) complained of "the petty grinding tyranny of a good English family," refused to marry, and helped found the modern profession of nursing (see Biography in Chapter 19). A few occupations outside the home were gradually opened to middle-class women, and some women entered universities and professions. Growing numbers of "new women" lived in women's clubs or apartments, dressed more practically, and did more "daring" things such as traveling alone and entering the public space as activists.

Poor Housing

Workers could not afford to draw such sharp lines between public and private life. Their homes, typically only one or two rooms in deteriorating buildings, rarely fulfilled all their needs. Often they relocated from one residence to another, carrying what they could. In some cases, they moved so as to search for something slightly better; in others, they sought to avoid a landlord demanding back rent.

The loss of a job might well doom a family to homelessness. With little hope of saving enough to pay for decent housing, workers tended to spend their extra money on clothes to "cut a good figure" and thereby present a well-groomed image in their public lives. For them, the city streets held far more promise than the buildings in which they lived. While the bourgeoisie retreated into homes or private clubs, workers used the public buildings, streets, and spaces of the city for their social and even private lives.

Working-class women enjoyed neither the space, furnishings, nor servants that graced the typical middle-class home. They usually worked at a factory or did poorly paid piecework at home, where they could care for their children. If their children seemed more unruly

Working-class women

and independent than those of the middle classes, moralists condemned these mothers for failing to create a proper home life. Such critics ignored the fact that working-class women lacked the money needed to cultivate the "ideal" family life. Worse, this disapproval helped employers justify paying these women less than men and treating them poorly.

Intimacy and Morality

Private life for working-class families was burdened by tensions involving basic survival. Middle-class families experienced tensions, too, but of a different sort. Founded on love, companionship, and intimacy, the middle-class family could become a pressure cooker of conflicting feelings and desires, of guilt and shame, of misunderstood communication and resentment. Family members often fought over money, but the confining expectations of intimacy could be worse. "Do not admit anyone else into our private life, into our thoughts," counseled a French man to his prospective wife in 1873. People understood such warnings. The home was a center of secrecy. More often than not, at the heart of that secrecy was sex.

For Britain's middle classes in particular, this era witnessed the height of Victorian sexual morality. Sex

Victorian morality

was supposed to be little discussed and limited to the marriage bed, enclosed in a separate "master" bedroom with locked doors. Sexual problems "shouldn't arise," but if they did, "enlightened" sufferers might turn to their doctor—the expert on sex, hygiene, and morality all rolled into one. Mixing moralisms with an image of scientific authority, most doctors confirmed the standard views of other commentators: Healthy and prudent sexuality could take place only within the marriage. Affairs risked scandal (especially for the woman) and illegitimacy. Sex with prostitutes was unhygienic and somehow dangerous to the race. Doctors vaguely connected prostitution, syphilis, tuberculosis, and alcoholism as physical and social "scourges," all resulting from "venereal excesses." Most often, they blamed women for being prostitutes, for forcing their husbands to visit prostitutes, or for having inappropriate sexual appetites.

Masturbation also caught the attention of doctors, priests, and parents. Physicians warned men that masturbation would drain their strength. They condemned masturbation by females even more strongly. To prevent youths from "abusing themselves," they prescribed orthopedic devices, special bandages, and belts.

As for homosexuality, people viewed it in an even worse light. Doctors labeled it a sickness or psychological disorder. Newspapers added to the public condemnation of homosexuality by reporting "scandalous" affairs among public figures and "uncovering" homosexual subcultures. The trial and imprisonment for gross indecency of the famed British author Oscar Wilde (1854–1900) in 1895 promoted a new awareness of homosexuality while revealing how far officials and the public would go to denounce it.

Sexual Realities

Despite these idealized, restrictive notions about proper sexual conduct, reality was quite different. Somehow people, especially the middle classes, discussed sex enough

Birth control

to limit births. While many used the old methods—abstinence and withdrawal—new information and methods also became available. Men began using condoms, and women douched or used diaphragms and sponges soaked in disinfectants. Many resorted to abortion as a method of birth control, particularly in cases of illegitimacy.

These methods seem to have worked. The birthrate declined in these years. In France, for example, it dropped from 33 per 1,000 in 1800 to 19 per 1,000 in 1910. Many people chose to limit births for economic reasons. As people moved from farms to the cities, they no longer needed so many children to help with the work. In the cities, the increasing costs of raising children deterred couples from having large families. Yet successful birth control among the middle classes caused concern, for many worried that the "best" of society were not reproducing themselves as quickly as the "poor" and "uncompetitive." Commentators argued that "good" families needed more children. Nationalists complained that competing states or "alien peoples" would overwhelm their nation or "race" if "the fittest" did not increase their fertility.

Certainly actual sexual behavior failed to live up to the standards of Victorian moralists. The "best" people had affairs, and illegitimacy remained high. Deadly sexually transmitted diseases rose and spread widely among all classes. In addition, prostitution thrived in many urban areas. Tens of thousands of prostitutes in the largest cities displayed themselves on streets and in city parks and in windows and doorways. Some worked in bars or elegant brothels for a more select clientele. Working-class women who lost jobs, domestic servants dismissed because of pregnancy, or young women on their own might turn to prostitution to survive. Men of all classes patronized prostitutes. Governments tried to control prostitution, requiring medical exams of prostitutes and limiting its practice to certain districts. Worse than these inconveniences were the risks of this life. Prostitutes were often subjected to violence, the most famous example of which was the serial killings committed by Jack the Ripper in London in the late 1880s.

By the end of the century, new attitudes, or perhaps the weight of reality, had broken down some of the more restrictive notions of Victorian sexual propriety. More people accepted and expected mutual sexual enjoyment within marriage, and people became educated about the physical facts of sexual contact. Books, pamphlets, and talks about sex enabled women and men to read about the subject and sometimes even discuss it openly. Doctors, psychologists, and intellectuals began to study sex and see that it played a major role in individuals' sense of identity.

New attitudes

Psychic Stress and Alcoholism

Growing concern with sex and private life in this period reflected a broader preoccupation with psychological well-being. Anxieties and emotional disorders seemed all too common. Women especially suffered from fits, paralysis, convulsions, numbness, headaches, oversensitivity to light, digestive disorders, and fatigue. Doctors listened, prescribed pills, and suggested expensive cures such as surgery and health-spa retreats. They sometimes blamed the complexities of city life or the noise and speed of modern life for these disturbing health problems. Other commentators suggested different causes. Within the confines of middle-class life, perhaps people worried too much about being judged by others. Or maybe the rapid changes of the era led to insecurity. Whatever the causes, the evidence of psychic stress was growing in diaries, in the rise of psychoanalysis, in the new descriptions of proliferating "mental illnesses," in the spread of psychiatric clinics, and in the mounting number of chronic patients in insane asylums.

Was widespread alcoholism a sign of psychic stress? **Figure 21.9,** an 1876 painting by Edgar Degas (1834–1917) of a woman drinking absinthe (a strong alcoholic beverage) in a Parisian café, seems to indicate a link between drinking and stress. Although a man sits nearby, the woman's face suggests that she is alone and gloomy. In this evocative image, lines separating social drinking, addiction, and psychic stress blur. Drinkers now seemed more depressed than jovial, and drunkenness appeared to be everywhere—in the streets, at work, in bars, and, increasingly, behind closed doors. New temperance movements attacked the "scourge" of alcohol, and with legitimate reason. In France, the average person consumed more than 60 gallons of wine a year, not including brandy, beer, and the more addictive absinthe shown in this painting. Even drugs such as opium, morphine, heroine, cocaine, and hashish gained footholds, especially among artists. Fear of drug-induced suicides led France to ban such drugs in 1908.

By no coincidence, the practice of **psychoanalysis** emerged during this period (see pages 683–684). Vari-

FIGURE 21.9 Edgar Degas, *Absinthe*, 1876–1877 This painting of a woman drinking a strong alcoholic beverage in a Paris café suggests links between drinking and stress.

ous other movements also focused on psychic stress. One of the best known and popular of these was Christian Science, founded in America by Mary Baker Eddy (1821–1910). Having suffered interminable ailments and nervous disorders as a youth, Eddy turned to a spiritual approach to healing in her adult years. As she explained in her best-selling book *Science and Health* (1875), "mind healing" could dispel sickness and pain. Whatever the causes and supposed cures, stress and emotional pain seemed too widespread to ignore, and many observers connected them to the pressures of modern life.

SCIENCE IN AN AGE OF OPTIMISM

Despite these concerns about the pressures of modern life, most observers embraced the new age enthusiastically. "I see no limit to the extent to which intelligence and will, guided by sound principles of investigation, and organized in common effort, may modify the conditions of existence, for a period longer than that now covered by history," announced British biologist T. H. Huxley (1825–1895) in 1893. "And much may be done to change the nature of man himself," he added.

The eighteenth-century optimism about science spread during the second half of the nineteenth century. Many people—especially members of the rising middle classes—felt certain that their generation would find solutions to the problems that had plagued human beings from the beginning. Scientists confirmed this optimism by making discoveries that answered fundamental questions and that could be translated into practical products, such as industrial goods and medicines. Intellectuals proffered new ways to explain the world and human beings' place in it. Writers and artists found answers to similar questions by looking hard at the lives of people in their changing world. These scientists, intellectuals, and artists thrived in big cities such as London, Paris, Berlin, Milan, and Vienna. In these cultural hubs, some taught in universities or conducted experiments in laboratories. Others might debate in learned societies, do research in libraries, or paint in studios. Still others chatted in cafés or simply wrote in back rooms. Their work generated provocative ideas and added to the sense that life could be understood more fully than ever before.

Science, Evolution, and Religion

The best news came from science. After 1850, word of scientific advances spread from elite circles to the broader public (see Thinking About Science & Technology). Stunning discoveries emerged and directly affected people's lives. However, certain conclusions that appealed to some provoked outrage in others.

No one became a greater hero, or villain, than Charles Darwin (1809–1882). Born into a distinguished British family, Darwin studied medicine and theology. Yet these disciplines failed to challenge him. Instead, the world of plants and animals became his consuming passion. His answer to a single question— how have all living species come to be as they are today?—caused an intense controversy that still continues in some circles.

| Darwin |

In 1831, Darwin, despite frail health, began a voyage around the world as a ship's naturalist on the *Beagle*. He observed and collected fossils and specimens in different environments. He made his most important finds in South America and the Galápagos Islands off the coast of that continent. Gradually he developed his theory of evolution, which, for him, answered his question. In *On the Origin of Species by Natural Selection* (1859), he described the slow evolution of present plant and animal species from earlier, simpler forms through a process of natural selection. Survival, he explained, came from struggle. In the competition for survival, those that possessed the most useful characteristics in a given environment— for example, the horse with the longer legs—survived to produce the most offspring. Through this process, they transmitted their successful qualities to future generations.

These ideas were not completely new. By the mid-nineteenth century, many intellectuals had accepted the concept of a slow and gradual development of the earth's crust and its inhabitants. Liberalism included ideas about the competitive struggle among human beings for food and survival, something that Thomas Malthus had written about at the beginning of the century (see Chapter 17). In addition, Enlightenment thinkers had already popularized the notion of "progress." Many in the mid-nineteenth century already embraced the sense that the present had evolved in progressive stages from a lower past. But no one had ever before supplied an all-encompassing explanation, supported by convincing evidence, for the origin of plants and animals.

What about human beings? Most people believed that humans remained a species apart from all others. At first Darwin avoided the delicate question. In his 1871 work, *The Descent of Man*, he finally took the bold step of arguing that humans evolved from more primitive species by the same process as plants and animals. "Man still bears in his bodily frame the indelible stamp of his lowly origin," he proclaimed. No longer could people "believe that man is the work of a separate act of creation." **Figure 21.11,** one of many satirical cartoons on this topic, ridicules Darwin's idea that humans descended from other species by showing Darwin holding up a mirror to his close relative—a monkey—and depicting Darwin with the body of a monkey.

Though many people already believed in evolution, Darwin's claims became front-page news. Few ideas have provoked such widespread controversy. To some people, his ideas made sense. Much of the scientific world, for example, quickly accepted Darwin's theory of evolution. Dominant social groups everywhere also derived comfort from it. The rising bourgeoisie, for instance, seized upon evolution as a way to explain and justify its own success. Scientists, including Darwin, also found confirmation for their views that women were inferior to men and destined to play a dependent domestic role in the male-dominated family.

| Controversy |

As Document 21.3 suggests, philosophers and scholars also expanded Darwin's thesis and applied it to all human behavior, a doctrine known as **Social Darwinism.** British philosopher Herbert Spencer (1820–1903) built a whole system of influential ideas around the concept of evolution; he and other Social Darwinists extended Darwin's theory far beyond its scientific foundations by making it the key to truth and progress. Spencer even saw the notion of survival of the fittest as justification for the harsh competitiveness of human society: "Under the natural order of things society is constantly excreting its unhealthy, imbecile, slow, vacillating, faithless members," he explained. Helping such people "encourages the multiplication of the reckless and incompetent . . . and discourages the multiplication of the competent and provident. . . ." Other Social Darwinists, such as British criminologist Francis Galton (1822–1911),

| Social Darwinists |

thinking about
SCIENCE & TECHNOLOGY

Universities and the Professionalization of Science

Were science and universities always as closely connected as they are today? Several European universities had been established during the Middle Ages, well before the Scientific Revolution. Some of the early giants of science, among them Copernicus and Kepler, worked primarily outside universities. During the seventeenth and eighteenth centuries, many individuals who investigated the natural world may have been associated with a university or learned society. But the professionalization of science—as an organized program of university study or as a career—lay in the future.

In the closing years of the eighteenth century, institutions such as the École Polytechnique in France and the Royal Institution in England started teaching science in a formal way. After the first decade of the nineteenth century, German universities began offering the study of natural science. **Figure 21.10** shows one such institution, the University of Halle-Wittenberg, in 1836. These schools advanced scientific knowledge in two main ways. First, they promoted scientific research; that is, instead of teaching only established knowledge, professors also conducted research and encouraged their students to do the same. Second, universities helped train future teachers, physicians, and other professionals, who in turn would spread scientific thinking and the fruits of science throughout society.

During the second half of the nineteenth century, the model of the German research university was adopted in the United States and elsewhere. At the same time, polytechnic schools were founded in several Western nations to train students in the application of science to technology and industry. With the advent of the polytechnics, universities could focus more on pure science— that is, science that is concerned not with practical applications but with the development and testing of new theories—and advanced research.

The connections among schools, universities, and science strengthened during the twentieth and twenty-first centuries, particularly with the development of "big science," which we will examine in Chapters 25 and 26.

Connecting Science & Society

1. In what ways did universities and polytechnic institutions help to develop a professional identity for scientists?

2. Generally speaking, why might government and industry support universities and the professionalization of science? How would government and industry benefit?

3. How have societies benefited from universities' training of teachers, scientists, and other professionals?

FIGURE 21.10 The University of Halle-Wittenberg, 1836

suggested that the human race could be improved through selective breeding, or eugenics.

Darwin's ideas threatened many people wedded to traditional Christian beliefs. He tried to reassure his alarmed readers: "I see no good reason why the views given in this volume should shock the religious feelings of anyone." Though many Christians accepted some of Darwin's ideas, his views offended numerous others. Specifically, the notion of a long and mechanistic evolution of all present species, including human beings, from simpler forms seemed to contradict the account of divine creation given in the Bible: "If the Darwinian theory is true," complained one theologian, "Genesis is a lie, the whole framework of the book of life falls to pieces,

Darwinism and religion

FIGURE 21.11 Darwin and a Monkey This satirical cartoon reveals the controversy over Darwin's theories after the publication of his books.

Darwin's allies rushed to his defense. Thomas Huxley, a biologist, surgeon in the British navy, and president of a leading scientific society, popularized Darwin's work in dozens of vigorous and lucid books and pamphlets. Heaping withering scorn on opponents, Huxley called himself "Darwin's bull-dog." Alfred Russel Wallace (1823–1913), a British naturalist, claimed that Darwin "is the Newton of natural history" who "established a firm foundation for all future study of nature."

Over time, many of Darwin's critics moderated their hostility to Darwin's findings. Toward the end of the century the Catholic Church, under Pope Leo XIII (1878–1903), even began taking the position that natural science was not the province of the church, that evolution could be taught as a hypothesis, and that parts of the Bible should be taken figuratively.

Mysteries of the Material and Human World

Research multiplied in many fields besides natural science. Scientists focused especially on the nature of matter. Discovery after discovery in chemistry and physics led them to conclude that all matter was composed of atoms, that each atom was **[Physics and chemistry]** in turn made up of smaller particles that moved in circles like a miniature solar system, and that each chemical element of matter had a specific atomic weight. In 1870, the Russian chemist Dmitri Mendeleev (1834–1907) compiled a new chart showing the atomic weight of all the known elements and indicating by gaps the other elements that remained to be discovered. Chemists and physicists proved him right. Year after year, researchers discovered new elements that fit into the periodic table. In the 1870s, James Clerk Maxwell (1831–1879) analyzed the relationship between light, magnetism, and electricity. His ideas led to a greater sense of physical unity in the universe and practical developments such as the development of the electronics industry.

The successes of Darwin and of chemists, physicists, and others in the natural sciences encouraged scholars to apply the same scientific techniques and principles to psy- **[Psychology]** chology, or the study of human behavior. One of the first to bring this discipline into the laboratory was Wilhelm Wundt (1832–1920). In his laboratory at Leipzig, Wundt and his enthusiastic students tested human reactions and carried out carefully controlled and measured experiments on cats and dogs, assuming that the findings would also apply to human beings.

The Russian scientist Ivan Pavlov (1849–1936), pursuing Wundt's line of inquiry, discovered the conditioned reflex. Pavlov showed meat to a hungry dog

and the revelation of God to man, as we Christians know it, is a delusion and a snare." Evolution, Darwin's critics cried, left God out of the world and diminished the uniqueness of human beings in it.

Some of Darwin's opponents suppressed his books and the teaching of evolution in schools. The Catholic Church angrily rejected Darwin's theory along with many other ideas of the time. In 1864, Pope Pius IX (1846–1878) issued a *Syllabus of Errors* attacking the idea of evolution and secular education. He also railed against religious toleration, free speech, and much else: It is "an error to believe that the Roman Pontiff can and ought to reconcile himself to, and agree with, progress, liberalism, and modern civilization." In 1870, the First Vatican Council bolstered the pope's authority by declaring that, under certain circumstances, the pope's statements on issues of morality and faith should be considered divinely sanctioned truths.

DOCUMENT 21.3

Walter Bagehot on Natural Selection and Human History

Social Darwinism and related doctrines spread, especially among liberals, during the second half of the nineteenth century. The Englishman Walter Bagehot (1826–1877) won notice for presenting views shared by his liberal, middle-class contemporaries. The following is a selection from his 1873 work, Physics and Politics.

. . . Three laws, or approximate laws, may, I think, be laid down. . . .

First. In every particular state of the world, those nations which are strongest tend to prevail over the others; and in certain marked peculiarities the strongest tend to be the best.

Secondly. Within every particular nation the type or types of character then and there most attractive tend to prevail; and the most attractive, though with exceptions, is what we call the best character.

Thirdly. Neither of these competitions is in most historic conditions intensified by extrinsic forces, but in some conditions, such as those now prevailing in the most influential part of the world, both are so intensified.

These are the sort of doctrines with which, under the name of "natural selection" in physical science, we have become familiar; and as every great scientific conception tends to advance its boundaries and to be of use in solving problems not thought of when it was started, so here, what was put forward for mere animal history may, with a change of form but an identical essence, be applied to human history. . . .

The strongest nation has always been conquering the weaker; sometimes even subduing it, but always prevailing over it. Every intellectual gain, so to speak, that a nation possessed was in the earliest times made use of—was invested and taken out—in war; all else perished. Each nation tried constantly to be the stronger, and so made or copied the best weapons, by conscious and unconscious imitation each nation formed a type of character suitable to war and conquest.

Conquest improved mankind by the intermixture of strengths; the armed truce, which was then called peace, improved them by the competition of training and the consequent creation of new power. Since the long-headed men first drove the short-headed men out of the best land in Europe, all European history has been the history of the superposition of the more military races over the less military—of the efforts, sometimes successful, sometimes unsuccessful, of each race to get more military; and so the art of war has constantly improved. . . .

SOURCE: Walter Bagehot, *Physics and Politics* (New York, 1873), pp. 44–46.

Analyze the Document

1. How does Bagehot connect natural selection and human history?

2. In what ways might someone use Bagehot's argument to justify war or imperialism?

3. In what respects do Bagehot's views reflect nineteenth-century liberalism?

---

until the dog's mouth watered. Then Pavlov rang a bell while showing the meat. Eventually, the dog's mouth would water when only the bell was rung. The implication was that many of our human responses are purely mechanical reflexes prompted by stimuli of which we are often unaware.

The field of sociology also acquired status as a social science. Auguste Comte (1798–1857) named the new discipline. He argued that | Sociology | humankind was entering a stage of history in which truths would be discovered by the scientific gathering of factual data. Humans and society, he said, are as susceptible to scientific investigation as minerals, plants, and the lower animals are. He believed that his philosophy, which he called **positivism,** would reveal the laws of human relations and allow social scientists to engineer harmonious societies. Comte's followers, eager and numerous during the second half of the nineteenth century, placed great faith in statistics and amassed copious statistical data on numerous social problems.

Like Comte, most of them believed that sure social knowledge would enable people to remake society for the better.

Historians such as the German Leopold von Ranke (1795–1886) strove to turn history into a social science. Ranke rejected history based on tradition or legend. He also | History | attacked the notion that history could come in the form of a purposeful story about the progress of humanity, the working out of God's will, or other such themes. He argued that historical accounts should be based on an exhaustive accumulation and analysis of documentary evidence. Conclusions could be drawn only from facts, he insisted. In this way, Ranke believed, history would become coldly scientific and morally neutral. His attitude and methodology spread widely, particularly in Germany and the United States.

These scholars believed that individual and social behavior could best be studied by careful, objective observation, experimentation, and analysis.

Like scientists, they considered themselves professionals with specialties rather than amateurs. They also formed societies and published their findings in their own journals. Part of what drove them was their faith that these findings would point the way to improving the quality of human life, and they conveyed that faith to a wider public. In this sense, these scholars and scientists shared and promoted the optimism of the period.

Germs, Cures, and Health Care

No field of science promised more new understanding and dramatic applications than medicine. At mid-century, medicine entered a golden age. The most important discovery came not from a doctor but from a chemist. Louis Pasteur (1822–1895), the son of a French tanner, became interested in what happened to wine and beer during the fermentation process. In the 1860s, he discovered the airborne microorganisms responsible for fermentation and showed that bacteria caused milk to sour. He demonstrated that heating milk—"pasteurizing" it—destroyed the bacteria that caused diseases. His long years of work eventually enabled him to identify disease-producing organisms in humans and create vaccines to prevent diseases such as rabies. Here, finally, was the explanation for how people caught infectious diseases: germ theory.

Many doctors and scientists, still wedded to old ideas and practices, dismissed Pasteur's findings. The German scientist Robert Koch (1843–1910) confirmed the French chemist's conclusions, convincing doctors that bacteria indeed caused diseases. In the early 1880s, Koch discovered the bacteria responsible for two of the most deadly diseases of the time: tuberculosis and cholera. His students used the same research methods to find microbes that caused a list of other diseases from pneumonia and meningitis to syphilis.

Modern doctors of the late nineteenth century now understood that specific microorganisms (germs) caused specific infectious diseases. In addition to this realization, new tools increased physicians' stature as scientists and improved their ability to diagnose ailments. The thermometer, for example, allowed them to measure body temperature, and the stethoscope let them hear what was going on inside the body. The microscope permitted examination of tissue samples, the X-ray (1896) revealed the body's internal structures, and the electrocardiograph (1901) recorded the workings of the heart.

The most advanced doctors realized that although they may have known more about illnesses and the inner workings of the body, they still could do little to cure diseases. Aspirin (1899) reduced fever, inflammation, and minor pain; morphine controlled more serious pain; and barbiturates might induce sleep—but none of these constituted a medical cure. The first great exception was an antitoxin against diphtheria developed in Robert Koch's Berlin laboratory in 1891. For most diseases, however, cures lay in the future. The best that doctors could do was to stop prescribing poisonous pills and dangerous procedures such as bloodletting and purges.

Within medicine, the field of surgery saw especially remarkable progress. During the 1860s and 1870s, the British surgeon Joseph Lister (1827–1912) developed procedures that included the use of antiseptics during operations. These procedures dramatically lowered the risk of infection from the operation itself. Over the following decades, surgeons applied Lister's methods with great success. No longer did they operate in dirty, blood-splattered back rooms, wearing black coats or street clothes. Increasingly, they washed their hands, worked in relatively sterile environments, and wore white surgical gowns, face masks, and rubber gloves to lessen the risks of infection.

In **Figure 21.12,** an 1890 painting of an operating room in a Vienna hospital, a patient is being prepared for surgery. The doctors wear white coats rather than street clothes, and the patient is being anesthetized. However, old practices died slowly. Even though Joseph Lister had developed antiseptic procedures more than twenty years earlier, the surgeon and his assistants in the painting do not wear masks or gloves, and the surgical instruments have not been sterilized. Everyone in the scene is male; most medical schools still denied access to women. The picture also lacks religious symbols. All in all, it conveys a sense of solid confidence in modern science.

**Marginal labels:**
Pasteur and germ theory
Remedies
Surgery

KEY DATES

WESTERN SOCIETY, 1850–1914

1853	Beginning of the rebuilding of Paris
1857	Flaubert, *Madame Bovary*
1859	Darwin, *On the Origin of Species*
1860s	Pasteur's germ theory
1864	*Syllabus of Errors*
1870	Periodic table developed
1876	Telephone invented
1896	Modern Olympic games
1905	Einstein's theory of relativity
1913	Stravinsky, *Rite of Spring*

FIGURE 21.12 Albert Seligmann, *Operation by German Surgeon Theodor Billroth,* 1890 This painting of a Viennese operating room reveals a growing confidence in modern science but the persistence of old patterns in medical practice, including the absence of surgical masks and gloves, the use of unsterilized instruments, and males' dominance of the profession.

Medical advances also made a huge difference in the field of nursing. In hospitals, emergencies, and war, nurses often had the most direct contact with sufferers and the wounded. During the Crimean War (1853–1856), Florence Nightingale transformed nursing into a modern profession (see Biography in Chapter 19). Her reforms stressed cleanliness, fresh air, and discipline and helped make nursing an attractive path to independence and service. A few years later, the philanthropist Dorothea Dix (1802–1887) led similar reform efforts in the United States during the Civil War, and in Switzerland a banker established the International Red Cross, creating new demand for professional nurses.

`Nursing`

By the turn of the century, much in medicine had gained the authority of science and was "professionalized." Better nursing gave the wounded a fighting chance at survival. Doctors who understood diseases and surgeons who performed operations safely now helped more than hurt their patients. Even so, many doctors insisted on practicing traditional medicine, and most remained too expensive for working-class families to afford except when they were in dire need. Many working-class women were forced to prescribe their own curative regime or find some inexpensive "cure."

CULTURE: ACCEPTING THE MODERN WORLD

Faith in science and technology reflected a growing sense that people could observe the facts of everyday life carefully, understand them, and use that understanding to control the world more successfully than ever before. Writers and artists also closely observed contemporary life in their books and paintings. During the second half of the nineteenth century, their focus included the methods of science and the realities of urban life. The romanticism of early-nineteenth-century culture—which had idealized love, religion, and the exotic—gave way to a gritty sense of realism (see Chapter 18). Realists felt free to look modern life full in the face and both praise its successes and criticize its failings.

Realism and Naturalism: The Details of Social Life

The age witnessed the rise of realistic and naturalistic literature, which explored the social dislocation brought about by the industrial revolution, commercial values, and city life. Eugène de Vogüé (1848–1910), a nineteenth-century French writer, `Literature` explained that a realist "observes life as it is in its wholeness and complexity with the least possible prejudice on the part of the artist. It takes men under ordinary conditions, shows characters in the course of their everyday existence." Authors, often focusing on the unpleasant, sordid side of human nature and society, examined how environment and heredity together shaped people's lives. With scientific thoroughness, these writers examined people's public and private lives, their individual and social failings, and the hypocrisy of their religious and moral values.

The French novelist Gustave Flaubert (1821–1880), for example, deftly captured the full flavor of **realism.** His *Madame Bovary* (1857) related the illicit sex life of the wife of a small-town French physician in such full and unblushing detail that it scandalized a public not yet accustomed to such unrestrained revelations. *Madame Bovary* became a model for other novelists. Few writers, however, were as popular as Charles Dickens (1812–1870). As we saw in Chapter 17, Dickens's novels presented realistic descriptions of the middle and lower classes in Britain's urban, industrial society. For example, in *The Old Curiosity Shop*, he refused to shy away from the realities of nighttime in impoverished sections of cities, "when bands of unemployed labourers paraded in the roads . . . when carts came rumbling by, filled with rude coffins . . . or when orphans cried, and distracted women shrieked and followed in their wake, . . . when some called for bread, and some for drink to drown their cares. . . ."

Mary Ann Evans (1819–1880), writing under the pen name George Eliot, also wrote popular novels examining the realities of British social life. In *Middlemarch,* for instance, she linked psychological conflict to the determining social realities surrounding her characters. The Norwegian playwright Henrik Ibsen (1828–1906) presented another perspective on such realities. Ibsen ridiculed bourgeois society in his popular dramas. In *A Doll's House,* probably his best-known play, the heroine, Nora, rebels against her expected role in the "doll's house" that her stodgy, hypocritical, middle-class husband, Helmer, has created for her:

NORA: What do you consider my holiest duties?
HELMER: Need I tell you that? Your duties to your
  husband and children.
NORA: I have other duties equally sacred.
HELMER: Impossible! What do you mean!
NORA: My duties toward myself.
HELMER: Before all else you are a wife and a mother.
NORA: That I no longer believe. Before all else I
  believe I am a human being just as much as you are.

The French writer Émile Zola (1840–1902) explained that the naturalist novel, having evolved from the realistic novel, "substitutes for the study of the abstract man . . . the study of the natural man, governed by physical and chemical laws, and modified by the influences of his surroundings; it is in one word the literature of our scientific age. . . ." He wrote in almost clinical detail about the social problems spawned by industrialism. In one series of novels, he portrayed several generations of a working-class family battered by the forces of heredity and the environment. They struggle to survive, fighting poverty, strikes, alcoholism, and conflict among themselves.

Russia produced some especially talented writers who created stunning realistic literature. An example is Leo Tolstoy (1828–1910) and his masterpiece *War and Peace* (1865–1869). This sweeping novel about Russia during the Napoleonic Wars features scores of characters who battle impersonal social forces and the overwhelming details of everyday life. Even the strongest individuals in the story become ensnared in forces beyond their control. In other writings that reflected the social realities of his own times, Tolstoy attacked capitalism and materialism: "Money is a new form of slavery, and distinguishable from the old simply by the fact that it is impersonal. . . ."

Fyodor Dostoyevski (1821–1881), another legendary Russian author, focused more on psychological and moral realities in his novels. His characters—such as the anguished student Raskolnikov in *Crime and Punishment* (1866), who murders an old woman—struggle with moral conflicts in an age marked by spiritual bankruptcy. Like other realistic writers, Dostoyevski shone a spotlight on the harshness of modern life, particularly its power to overwhelm individuals.

Innovative painters turned to realistic depictions of life on their canvases. The French artist Gustave Courbet (1819–1877), who believed that an artist should "never permit <mark>Art</mark> sentiment to overthrow logic," led the attack on romantic art by painting sober scenes of urban life and rural labor. In *The Stone Breakers* (**Figure 21.13**), he portrays rural laborers as a passerby might see them. Courbet claimed he "saw these people every day on my walk." Here an old worker—with patches on his pants and holes in his socks—breaks up stones, probably for use in building a road. His young assistant, who is "suffering from scurvy" according to Courbet, carries the stones away in a basket. The two men's tattered clothing and averted faces make them seem anonymous and therefore representative of many other workers. While there is dignity in their work, Courbet does not glorify either the stone breakers or nature. The scene, like the men's lives, is harsh. The image suggests that the

FIGURE 21.13 Gustave Courbet, *The Stone Breakers,* 1849 A man and his young assistant break up stones for a road in this realistic painting of rural life.

young assistant is likely to end up the same as his old companion. Courbet and other realistic artists depicted everyday life on large canvases and thereby earned the wrath of those artists and critics who believed that only paintings of historical, mythological, religious, or exotic scenes should be considered great art.

Impressionism: Celebrating Modern Life

Like the realists and naturalists, impressionist painters embraced modern life—but in a different way. Specifically, they applied a new understanding of color, light, and optics to their work. Their paintings—with their informal quality and emphasis on angles—suggested randomness of reality. Such artists ventured outside their studios to paint scenes. They especially sought to convey the impression of a view that the eye actually sees at first glance—the impression created by light reflected off a surface at a single moment—rather than what the knowing brain interprets from visual cues, hence the name **impressionism** for this school of painting. The French artist Claude Monet (1840–1926) (see Biography) described the way he painted: "Try to forget what objects you have before you—a tree, a house, a field, or whatever. Merely think, here is a little square of blue, here an oblong of pink, here a streak of yellow, and paint it just as it looks to you . . . until it gives your own naive impression of the scene before you."

Monet's *The Docks of Argenteuil* (**Figure 21.14**) is an example of many paintings of the suburban countryside—the places to which the urban bourgeoisie might travel on Sundays or vacations. In this scene near his home just outside of Paris, middle-class women carrying parasols stroll down a wide, tree-lined path bordering the Seine or wander over to a dock on the right where boats might be rented. Sailboats on the river suggest pleasure; a bridge in the distance implies that the city is not far away. The bourgeoisie purchasers of Monet's paintings would recognize this sort of place, where civilization and countryside meet under a broad sky.

Impressionists also painted psychologically subtle portraits, bedroom and dance-hall interiors, urban parks, and city streets. *Boulevard des Italiens, Morning, Sunlight* (**Figure 21.15**) by Camille Pissarro shows one of the straight, wide, tree-lined fashionable boulevards constructed in Paris during the Second Empire under Napoleon III. Pissarro, often regarded as the father of the impressionist movement, needed only a few brushstrokes to suggest people, buses, carriages, storefronts, and building details—the impression that one might get glancing out an upper-floor window at an anonymous but vibrant urban scene below.

FIGURE 21.14 Claude Monet, *The Docks of Argenteuil, 1872* This vivid impressionist painting shows an appealing suburban scene just outside Paris.

FROM OPTIMISM TO UNCERTAINTY

The impressionists' delight in the beauty and charm of modern life fit well with the continuing belief in reason, individual rights, and progress that marked the decades after 1850. Economic growth, improving conditions in the cities, and new conquests by science buoyed a broad sense of moderate optimism about the world. However, from the 1880s on, signs of a disturbing new undercurrent rose to the surface of Western culture. Some of the West's best intellectuals, writers, and artists injected themes of pessimism and painful introspection into their work. They emphasized how strongly irrational forces guided human behavior. Though still a minority, these thinkers and critics undermined rather than overwhelmed the prevailing certainty and optimism of the period. They added to the growing social and political tensions of the turn-of-the-century decades described in Chapter 20.

Everything Is Relative

In part, this disillusionment stemmed from the growing feeling of uncertainty creeping into elite scientific circles—the sense that the more people learned, the less solid [Einstein] and reliable the material world became. The work of Albert Einstein (1879–1955) exposed this uncertainty in physics. A German who later fled to America, Einstein assailed time-honored concepts about the stability of matter and the nature of the physical universe. In 1905, while still earning a living as a patent clerk in Switzerland, he proposed

BIOGRAPHY

Claude Monet
(1840–1926)

Impressionist

Painter

As a boy growing up in Le Havre on France's north coast, Oscar Claude Monet was rebellious and daring. "My youth was essentially that of a vagabond," he wrote. "Never would I bend to a rule."

That pattern of assertive rebellion would stay with him. In 1857, the 16-year-old Claude announced to his father, a prosperous merchant, that he was going to Paris to become a painter. His father refused to help him financially, but Claude left home anyway. In Paris, he rejected academic art training, instead working with other young artists such as Pissarro and Renoir, with whom he would remain connected for many years.

In 1864, he met the 18-year-old Camille Doncieux, and the two moved in together. That year, Claude had his first paintings accepted at the official Salon, where prominent artists entered their paintings to be judged and—if accepted—offered for sale. Success at the Salon meant the possibility of earning a living as an artist. Despite this triumph, financial problems plagued the young Monet. He often had to hide in Paris or flee to the suburbs to escape from creditors. He perpetually wrote letters begging his family, friends, and other artists for money.

In the following years, Monet enjoyed some successes but was disappointed whenever his paintings were turned down by the Salon. Depression often haunted him: "I am like a man going down the third time. . . . I see everything black. . . . Money is always lacking. Disappointments, insults, hopes, new disappointments." But in good times, he lived the bourgeois life and experienced private joys. In 1868, he wrote: "I am surrounded here by all that I love. I pass my time outdoors on the flint beach when the seas are heavy or when the boats go off to fish, or I even go into the country, which is so beautiful here. . . . I find in my tiny house a good fire and a good little family." Though he had a one-year-old son, Jean, with Camille, it took the prospect of money from an inheritance by Camille, guaranteed by a contract, before he finally married her in 1870.

In 1872, the Monets moved to Argenteuil, twenty minutes from Paris by train. Camille played the role of a middle-class housewife, rising early to serve breakfast to her husband and son, shopping, buying bread just before lunch, cleaning the house, preparing dinner, and reading the newspapers daily. Their son, Jean, dressed in long skirts, as was the style of the time and riding his tricycle with a stuffed horse mounted on its front end, appeared on several of Monet's canvases, as did Camille. Every day, Monet painted by the shore of the river, sometimes accompanied by other visiting impressionists.

By 1874, Monet had turned his back on the official Salon. That year, he and other artists formed a group and mounted their own exposition. Monet was at the head of the group, which included Renoir and Pissarro. Critics attacked the paintings at the exposition, particularly one by Monet titled *Impression: Sunrise*, for rejecting accepted standards of good art. Yet the group continued to paint and show together, earning a reputation for being rebellious artists and "bohemians" with inappropriate lifestyles.

In 1878, the ailing Camille gave birth to a second son. A year later she died. Soon Monet became involved with another woman, Alice Hoschede, already married to a successful merchant and the mother of several children. The couple soon moved in together.

Monet was happy living with Alice, and his paintings began to sell well. He stopped showing his paintings with the other impressionist painters and moved to Giverny, northwest of Paris. There he created a large garden and pond, which he would paint for the rest of his life.

Monet gained a public reputation for being both brilliant and unyielding. When the government tried to award him the Legion of Honor, he refused. By 1890, he was recognized as France's premier painter, far more popular than any of his colleagues. His paintings commanded high prices. Now sporting a long, white beard, he became a revered figure. Despite his failing eyesight, he painted almost up until his death in 1926.

Monet made the bourgeoisie both the subject and the assumed audience of his paintings. Many of his landscapes featured the suburban fields, gardens, walks, and riverbanks that the bourgeoisie loved to visit (see **Figure 21.14**). Even his landscapes of southern France or the north coast were presented from the point of view of a tourist. Monet always emphasized the "modern" in his work. There was no horror in his depictions of the city, only a celebration of its boulevards, railway stations, and parks.

Connecting People & Society

1. How do Monet's life, paintings, and popularity reflect European society during the second half of the nineteenth century?

2. Does this profile of Monet's life suggest that art was a business much like other businesses? Explain.

3. Why did Monet and other artists come to be viewed as "bohemians" with inappropriate lifestyles?

FIGURE 21.15 Camille Pissarro, *Boulevard des Italiens, Morning, Sunlight*, 1897 Impressionist painters such as Pissarro depicted city scenes such as this interpretation of a bustling boulevard in Paris.

what would become the seminal theory of relativity. According to this theory, time, space, and motion are relative to one another as well as to the observer—they are not the absolutes scientists had believed in for so long.

Building on the work of the German physicist Max Planck (1858–1947), who had shown that heated bodies emit energy in irregular packets (quanta) rather than a steady stream, Einstein also derived a ground-breaking formula, $E = mc^2$ (E = energy; m = mass; c = speed of light). This formula blurred the distinction between mass and energy and described the immense energy contained within each atom. The atomic energy in a lump of coal, for example, was revealed to be some three billion times as great as the energy obtained by burning the coal. This unsettling notion later contributed to the development of the atomic bomb. By showing that matter could be transformed into energy, Einstein again challenged Newtonian physics. More conservative scientists, wedded to time-honored Newtonian physics, dismissed his theories. Eventually, however, Einstein's views gained support, further undermining scientists' assumptions about the physical nature of the universe.

Sex, Conflict, and the Unconscious

Ideas about the human mind—the internal, mental universe—also took a disturbing turn in these years. Sigmund Freud (1856–1939), the Viennese neurologist, concluded that nervous disorders stemmed from psychological causes, not physiological sources as most doctors had believed. Basing his ideas on the words, experiences, and dreams of troubled patients, he founded psychoanalysis, which he described as "the scientific method by which the unconscious can be studied."

> Freud and psychoanalysis

Freud argued that much of human behavior was irrational, unconscious, and instinctual. Conflict, he claimed, was a basic condition of life, particularly when it occurred between people's innate biological drives (such as sex or aggression) and their social selves. According to Freud, these conflicts developed on a mostly unconscious level and in stages during childhood. At war within all people are what Freud called the id, the superego, and the ego. The id is the source of our basic desires, the most important and disturbing of these being sexual. The superego imposes socially acceptable standards of behavior on the individual. The ego tries to find ways to satisfy both the demands of the id and the restraints of the superego. Typically, the mind responds to this conflict by repressing the id's desires from consciousness. However, the unconscious psychic struggle continues, creating a mental life of great tension.

Freud added fuel to his already controversial ideas by emphasizing the importance of sexual conflicts originating in childhood. He argued that children inevitably come into conflict with their parents, competing with the same-sex parent for the love of the opposite-sex parent. At an unconscious level, he claimed, this competition for the parent of the opposite sex strongly shapes the development of an individual's personality.

Freud believed that much psychic pain and many emotional disorders stemmed from the suppressed and frustrated drives of early life—frustrations that then festered outside of people's awareness. He concluded that the correct therapy for such disorders was to make the sufferer conscious of the facts and circumstances of his or her original frustration. Hence, he encouraged patients to talk about their dreams, for by interpreting dreams the unconscious could be revealed.

Freud's controversial explanation of human behavior had several disturbing implications: Neither adults nor children are innocent beings after all; too few people lead happy lives; sex and aggression play powerful roles in children and adults alike; people cannot escape from internal conflict and frustration. Although he hoped that reason and understanding would ease humanity's psychological plight, Freud was far from an optimist. He eventually concluded that "the price of progress in civilization is paid in forfeiting happiness."

Fear of Social Disintegration

The French scholar Émile Durkheim (1858–1917), a founder of modern sociology, offered a different sort of warning about trends in modern

Durkheim

society. Though a strong believer in science, Durkheim argued that industrial society—especially with its competitive individualism and lack of collective values—was weakening the ties that connected people with one another. As people became more concerned with their own freedom and advancement, he believed, the restraints and the spiritual beliefs that held traditional societies together would break down. This

trend toward social disintegration, Durkheim warned, disoriented individuals, made them feel cut off from others, and left them without a sense of purpose. As a result, more and more people were experiencing despair, which in turn led to rising suicide rates. Like Freud, Durkheim believed that advancing civilization left psychic pain in its wake.

Disenchantment Sets In

Perhaps the deepest sense of disenchantment with the optimistic, bourgeois, urban society of the nineteenth century emerged in philosophy. Friedrich Nietzsche (1844–1890), a brilliant German philosopher, is one exam-

Nietzsche

ple. Reason could not solve human problems, Nietzsche concluded. Instead, he believed in "will," which in his view enabled people to survive and the strongest among them to achieve power. Great leaders, he argued, rose through strength, intelligence, and above all, "the will to power." Nietzsche further claimed that if a superior society were to emerge, it would have to come about through the efforts of gifted individuals who would rise to positions of leadership because of their superior strength, will, and intelligence. Anything that contributes to power is good, he explained—be it strength of will, boldness, cunning, or intelligence. Likewise, whatever leads to weakness is bad—be it gentleness, modesty, generosity, or compassion.

In Nietzsche's view, Christianity stood in the way of a better human society. "Christianity has taken the side of everything weak, base, ill-constituted; it has made an ideal out of opposition to the preservative instincts of strong life," he announced. "God is dead; we have killed him." For Nietzsche, the idea of the death of God was liberating: Now humans could cast off all conventions. Nietzsche also decried democracy for amounting to rule by the supposedly mediocre "masses . . . or the populace, or the herd, or whatever name you care to give them." He went on to attack many other accepted tenets of nineteenth-century civilization, such as liberalism, rationalism, and science. Although Nietzsche was not a nationalist or racist himself, others would later use his ideas to support militant nationalism and racism.

In France, the philosopher Henri Bergson (1859–1941) also questioned the limits of rational and scientific thinking. Gaining a large following by lecturing at the University of Paris, he argued that truth is best grasped

Bergson

through intuition and unconscious feelings rather than reason: "Science can teach us nothing of the truth; it can only serve as a rule of action." Society, Bergson said, needs the energy that only a spontaneous following of the "life force" can provide. His views, like those of Nietzsche and others, reflected a growing criticism of the dominant ideas of middle-class society in the West.

Art Turns Inward

Many talented artists also turned away from the mainstream of nineteenth-century civilization. Their work grew

| Expressionism |

more pessimistic and critical of middle-class life. The slogan "Art for art's sake" reflected the trend of various artistic movements, such as **expressionism** and symbolism. They self-consciously attacked social and artistic taboos in ways that mystified much of the public. Their often introspective works proved understandable mainly to themselves and a small artistic elite. The Russian abstract expressionist painter Wassily Kandinsky (1866–1944) spoke for many of his fellow artists when he explained that his work was not intended to represent how things looked. "Look at the picture as a graphic representation of a mood and not as a representation of objects," he suggested.

Many artists focused on peripheral members of a society that seemed to be disintegrating, painting prostitutes, solitary drinkers, blind beggars, and circus performers. Moreover, threatening symbols of science, machinery, and speed began to crop up on canvases. Photography had already displaced traditional representation art. The French poet Guillaume Apollinaire (1880–1918) explained that modern painters "avoid any representation of natural scenes . . . since everything is sacrificed by the artist to truth." Now avant-garde painters created distorted, subjective, and abstract images.

We can see evidence of these trends in expressionist paintings such as those by the Belgian artist James Ensor (1860–1949). In *Christ's Triumphant Entry into Brussels* in 1888 (**Figure 21.16**), Ensor shows a parade and a mob of people whose faces are in coarse caricatures or masks that reflect pretense and false smiles. Behind their masks lurk isolation and anxiety. They march under banners that cynically proclaim "Long Live Socialism," "Political Spectacles Always Succeed," and "Long Live Jesus."

Like Ensor, the Norwegian artist Edvard Munch (1863–1944) expressed a deep current of horror in middle-class life, but in a deeper, more personal way. In *The Scream* (**Figure 21.17**), a wide-eyed figure standing on a bridge lets out a terrified shriek. The land, water, and sky—all distorted and painted in alarming colors—echo the cry of the figure. Munch described the feelings that inspired the scene: "I was

FIGURE 21.16 James Ensor, *Christ's Triumphant Entry into Brussels,* 1888 Expressionist artists such as the Belgian painter James Ensor often attacked the pretenses of everyday life in their paintings.

FIGURE 21.17 Edvard Munch, *The Scream,* 1893 Much late-nineteenth-century expressionist art focused on themes of horror and anguish in middle-class life.

tired and ill—I stood looking out across the fjord—the sun was setting—the clouds were colored red—like blood—I felt as though a scream went through nature. . . ." In this painting, themes of death, anxiety, loneliness, and fear coalesce. Munch once exclaimed, "How much of my art I owe to suffering!"

Many other artists painted similarly anguished scenes, emphasizing social anxieties, urban loneliness, violence, horror, and a turning inward toward the unconscious. Their paintings penetrated through surface-level appearances into a deeper, disturbing psychic reality.

In music, expressionism also challenged artistic conventions and public tastes. The Russian composer Igor Stravinsky (1882–1971) led this movement in his music for the ballet *The Rite of Spring*. The premiere of the ballet on May 29, 1913, in Paris has been called the most notorious event of the twentieth century. Upon hearing the music—with its offbeat rhythm and unrestrained, dissonant sounds—the audience rose in outrage. Fights broke out, and many listeners stormed from the theater after complaining loudly. Yet among certain elites, Stravinsky became the leading composer of the day.

Like science and philosophy, art and music were slipping away from the grasp of ordinary people. The new understandings of modern life that had seemed so promising a few decades earlier now appeared shadowed by doubt and even foreboding.

Music

LOOKING BACK & MOVING FORWARD

Summary   By 1914, industrialization, urban growth, and the culture of progress had pulled much of the West into new territory. Life in large parts of Europe and North America had undergone a huge transformation. Someone who had lived during the late eighteenth century would have found virtually everything about the turn-of-the-century West strange or even shocking. Most of us, however, would readily recognize early-twentieth-century Paris, Berlin, or New York as modern. Those cities—like our cities today—were part of a widespread urban society and culture dominated by the middle classes and marching to the quickening pace of economic transformation. The variety of public and private life within those cities has persisted to the present day.

People have called the years 1850–1914 the Age of Progress. The reasons are clear. Income for most people rose at least a little, and for some quite considerably, while the machines of industry pumped out endless new products that promised to ease the burdens of everyday life. Science promised even more and delivered findings that seemed to unlock the mysteries of both the physical and social worlds. Many of the cultural forms of the period gazed directly at the modern world and embraced it. In the 1920s, the French would look back to the two decades surrounding the turn of the century as La Belle Époque—the beautiful era.

Yet, as we have seen, darker forces of change simmered below the optimistic surface during these same years. Just how much progress was achieved in politics is not so clear. Events in the summer of 1914 would expose that sense of dangerous uncertainty as all too well founded. Whether progress was made in the West's relations with the rest of the world is also in doubt. From outside the West, some observers questioned the very value of Western civilization. "In order to estimate the value of a civilization," explained a high Chinese official educated in European universities, "the question we must finally ask is not what great cities . . . it has built . . . what clever and useful implements . . . it has made . . . what institutions, what arts and sciences it has invested: the question . . . is what type of humanity, what kind of men and women it has been able to produce." These complex questions, too, would be immediately recognizable to us today. Modern times had arrived.

KEY TERMS

Victorian,   *p. 666*
psychoanalysis,   *p. 673*
Social Darwinism,   *p. 674*
positivism,   *p. 677*
realism,   *p. 679*
impressionism,   *p. 681*
expressionism,   *p. 685*

REVIEW, ANALYZE, & CONNECT TO TODAY

REVIEW THE PREVIOUS CHAPTER

Chapter 20—"Mass Politics and Imperial Domination"—traced the spreading demands for democracy and the West's imperial expansion during the second half of the nineteenth century.

1. How did politics adjust to the new industrial and urban realities of this period?

2. In what ways did imperialism support and reflect both the nationalism and industrialism of this period?

ANALYZE THIS CHAPTER

Chapter 21—"Modern Life and the Culture of Progress"—traces the changes stemming from new industrial transformations and urban growth, as well as the culture of the West.

1. Considering the material in this chapter and Chapter 17 (which focused on the industrial revolution), why do you think industrialization so quickly doomed traditional society in the West?

2. Analyze the impact of spreading industrialization on the various social classes during this period.

3. How did people adjust to the opportunities and pressures of life in the West's modernizing cities?

4. Do you think the title "Modern Life and The Culture of Progress" is an apt description of Western culture during this period? Why or why not?

CONNECT TO TODAY

Think about the new industrial transformation, urban growth, and cultural development between 1850 and 1914.

1. In what ways is the period of rapid industrialization we examined in this chapter similar to contemporary times?

2. In what regards is this historical period different from the experience of recent times?

3. Why do you think that so much of the culture—especially ideas, art, and literature—of the period 1850–1914 remains influential and popular in today's world?

BEYOND THE CLASSROOM

THE SECOND INDUSTRIAL REVOLUTION

Hobsbawm, Eric J. *The Age of Capital, 1848–1875.* New York: New American Library, 1979. Includes detailed sections on industrialism as well as its social consequences.

Ville, Simon P. *Transport and the Development of the European Economy, 1750–1918.* Houndmills, UK: Macmillan, 1990. A comparative study of the major forms of transportation from 1750 to 1918 and their relationship to economic development.

Williams, Rosalind H. *Dream Worlds: Mass Consumption in Late Nineteenth-Century France.* Berkeley: University of California Press, 1982. An exploration of the mental evolution of consumer society in late-nineteenth- and early-twentieth-century France.

THE NEW URBAN LANDSCAPE

Olsen, Donald J. *The City as a Work of Art—London, Paris, Vienna.* New Haven, CT: Yale University Press, 1986. A well-illustrated examination of nineteenth-century urban growth and design.

Pinkney, David. *Napoleon III and the Rebuilding of Paris.* Princeton, NJ: Princeton University Press, 1972. A classic study of one of the most important urban renovations of the nineteenth century.

GLOBAL CONNECTIONS

Chasteen, John Charles. *Born in Blood and Fire: A Concise History of Latin America.* New York: Norton, 2001. A useful survey covering the period.

CITY PEOPLE

Joyce, P. *Visions of the People: Industrial England and the Question of Class, 1848–1914.* Cambridge: Cambridge University Press, 1991. An examination of working-class culture and language.

Pilbeam, Pamela. *The Middle Classes in Europe, 1789–1914.* Chicago: Lyceum Books, 1990. A thorough treatment of middle-class life in the major European nations.

PRIVATE LIFE: TOGETHER AND ALONE AT HOME

Gay, Peter. *The Bourgeois Experience: Victoria to Freud,* 2 vols. New York: Oxford University Press, 1984–1986. Exhaustively researched volumes dealing with the varied experiences of middle-class life in America and Europe.

Perrot, Michelle, ed. *A History of Private Life, IV: From the Fires of Revolution to the Great War.* Cambridge, MA: Harvard University Press, 1990. Richly detailed and well-illustrated essays on the nineteenth century and its division between public and private life.

Peterson, M. Jeanne. *Family, Love, and Work in the Lives of Victorian Gentlewomen.* Bloomington: Indiana University Press, 1989. A portrayal that defies the stereotype that Victorian gentlewomen led productive lives, were well educated, and were sexually knowledgeable.

SCIENCE IN AN AGE OF OPTIMISM

Bowler, Peter J. *Evolution—The History of an Idea*, rev. ed. Berkeley: University of California Press, 2003. An outstanding survey of the subject that argues that the Darwinian revolution never really occurred.

Bynum, W.F. *Science and the Practice of Medicine in the Nineteenth Century.* Cambridge: Cambridge University Press, 1994. Examines the impact of the sciences on medicine.

Kern, Stephen. *The Culture of Time and Space, 1880–1918.* Cambridge, MA: Harvard University Press, 1983. A lively discussion of the impact of the new technology.

CULTURE: ACCEPTING THE MODERN WORLD

Dale, Peter A. *In Pursuit of a Scientific Culture: Science, Art, and Society in the Victorian Age.* Madison: University of Wisconsin Press, 1989. Examines the connections between science, culture, and society during the second half of the nineteenth century.

Thomson, Belinda. *Impressionism: Origins, Practice, Reception.* London: Thames and Hudson, 2000. A well-written study of the history of impressionism.

FROM OPTIMISM TO UNCERTAINTY

Burrow, J.W. *The Crisis of Reason: European Thought, 1848–1914.* New Haven, CT: Yale University Press, 2000. An excellent survey of the subject.

Gay, Peter. *Freud—A Life for Our Time.* New York: Norton, 1988. A standard biography of Freud.

Hughes, H. Stuart. *Consciousness and Society: The Reorientation of European Social Thought, 1890–1930.* New York: Vintage Books, 1979. A classic examination of the intellectual revolt against scientific certainty.

OTTO DIX, *WAR,* 1929–1932
The German expressionist painter Otto Dix (1891–1969) fought in the trenches of World
War I and was wounded several times. In this triptych he depicts the destructiveness of war. In
the panel on the left, soldiers march toward the bleak battlefront. Their fate is depicted in the
following panels: the gore and destruction of the front lines, trenches that serve as coffins for
the numberless dead, and the endless haunting nightmares of those who somehow survive. This
painting all too accurately captured the reality of the period as experienced by millions of people.

Descending into the Twentieth Century

World War and Revolution, 1914–1920

"Millions of men are going to be massacred in a War of the Worlds." As late as the first days of August 1914, only a few Westerners voiced such ominous warnings as these words by the French writer Marcel Proust. In 1917, the third year of the war that Proust had foretold, the young British poet and soldier Wilfred Owen became trapped in a hole on the still-raging battle lines with the shattered body of a fellow officer. As Owen put it, the officer "lay not only near by, but in various places around and about." Owen returned to England suffering from "shell shock," as nervous breakdowns were known. Yet, a year later, he chose to return to the front. In a letter to his mother, he explained why: "I came out in order to help these boys. . . ." He hoped "by watching their sufferings that I may speak of them as well as a pleader can."

Suffer the young soldiers did, and much of Western civilization agonized along with them. The Great War ended the era that had begun 125 years earlier with the French and industrial revolutions. It spawned a new round of revolution, destroyed several empires, and altered politics and society for the rest of the twentieth century. The consequences of this war even spread into the non-Western world, drawing in troops from Asia and Africa and changing how people around the globe viewed the West.

Why did entire nations send their people into this conflict? After all, the war was not inevitable, nor was it an accident. At the same time, some of the combatants reasoned that they had no choice in the matter. Indeed, the outbreak of the war seemed to pivot on something that happened one June day in 1914. By itself, that event would not have led nations to commit to such a costly endeavor. But people turned the event into a spark that ignited a deadly fire they could not put out.

ON THE PATH TO TOTAL WAR

On June 28, 1914, 19-year-old Gavrilo Princip, gun in hand, waited along a parade route in Sarajevo, the capital of the Austro-Hungarian province of Bosnia. Princip was a member of a Bosnian nationalist organization that had been trained by the Black Hand, a Serbian terrorist group. He was not alone. That day, Archduke Ferdinand, the heir to the Austro-Hungarian throne, was visiting Sarajevo. Princip, waiting with several conspirators, planned to kill the archduke to promote Slavic liberation from Austro-Hungarian control. As Ferdinand's open car passed by, Princip's co-conspirators lost their nerve and did not shoot. Then Ferdinand's driver took a wrong turn. Realizing his mistake, he stopped the car and, by chance, backed up to where Princip stood. Princip fired, killing Ferdinand and his wife.

In those years, several political leaders had been assassinated without great risk of war. Yet in just four weeks, this incident would lead Austria-Hungary, a second-rate power, to declare war on Serbia, a third-rate power in the southeast corner of Europe—the Balkans. Within one more week, most of Europe was engulfed by war. How could this incident in Sarajevo, far from the heart of Europe and not directly involving any of Europe's major powers, result in an all-out war that would end an era and transform Western society?

Rivalries and Alliances

Part of the answer lies in the national, economic, and imperial rivalry percolating in Europe at the time. Militant nationalism, intensifying since the mid-nineteenth century, encouraged countries to view one another as dangerous rivals in the struggle for power and prestige. Politicians used this nationalism to glaze over domestic problems and win public support. The growth of industrial capitalism created an environment of competitive economic struggle as nations tried to promote their industries and gain markets. The outburst of imperialism in the decades before 1914 pitted these rivals against one another in a race to acquire colonies and expand their arenas of influence around the world.

These rivalries fueled international affairs and pressured European states to form a system of alliances among themselves. The German statesman Otto von Bismarck initiated the alliances in the 1870s. Concerned about being <mark>The alliance system</mark> encircled by enemies, he allied Germany with Austria-Hungary and Russia to avoid any possibility of a two-front war—to the east against Russia and to the west against France. After forcing Bismarck's retirement, the new German kaiser—hoping to extend German influence over areas of concern to Russia—allowed the reinsurance treaty with Russia to lapse. This opened the door to major shifts in international relations. New alliances formed as European states tried to protect themselves and pursue their ambitions. Italy, looking for support against France in the competition for colonies, joined Germany and Austria-Hungary in 1882 to form the Triple Alliance. Russia, hoping to expand into southeastern Europe and gain access to the Mediterranean at the expense of the declining Ottoman Empire, came into conflict with Austro-Hungarian and German ambitions in the Balkans. By 1894, Russia had joined in a new alliance with France, which eagerly sought an ally in case of a clash with Germany. In 1904, Britain, threatened by the rise of Germany as a new naval, industrial, and imperial power, joined its old rival France in an alliance called the Entente Cordiale. In 1905 and again in 1911, German challenges to French sovereignty over Morocco in North Africa created international crises that drew France and Britain closer together.

By 1914, Europe had divided itself into two powerful alliance systems: the Triple Entente, comprising France, Russia, and Great Britain; and the Triple Alliance, made up of Germany, Austria-Hungary, and Italy. On the one hand, these alliances may have encouraged Europeans to believe that they could avert major wars. Between 1870 and 1914, a balance of power did generally prevail. Statesmen solved most conflicts diplomatically, and military scuffles remained brief and local. On the other hand, the alliance system gave smaller powers an opportunity to influence the decisions of larger powers; everyone feared that losing an ally—even a relatively weak supporter making decisions in its own interests—would upset the balance of power and make strong nations vulnerable.

Meanwhile, military might played a large part in politics in this world driven by competition and a struggle for international stature. Germany built a new navy; Britain kept ahead and in 1906 launched the *Dreadnought*, the first of a new class of battleships armed entirely with big guns; and most powers reinforced their armies. Between 1870 and 1914, France and Germany more than doubled the size of their standing armies by requiring citizens to serve for set periods of time. Politicians justified huge expenditures for the military buildup with nationalistic slogans and claims that military spending promoted industry, jobs, and trade. Military staffs made plans emphasizing quick offensive thrusts and drew up timetables for mobilizing their forces in case of war. Most people assumed that any war that broke out would be short, like the Franco-Prussian War of 1870 (see pages 614–615), and that their own nation would win it. This armaments race and military planning only heightened the suspicion and fear brewing between nations. It also made national leaders feel ever more dependent on their allies for support in case of war.

Military buildup

Crises in the Balkans

These rivalries and hardening alliances became enmeshed in a series of crises that exploded in the Balkans (see **Maps 22.1** and **22.2**). Why the Balkans? This was Europe's most unstable area—a land of strong nationalistic aspirations felt by several peoples who had been long dominated by the declining Austro-Hungarian and Ottoman empires. As the Ottoman Empire disintegrated during the late nineteenth and early twentieth centuries, various Balkan peoples, such as the Romanians, Bulgarians, and Serbs, had established independent nations. Peoples still under Ottoman or Austro-Hungarian rule agitated for their own independence or sought support from their linguistic kin—especially the Serbs—in these new Balkan states. The Ottoman Turks had long struggled to maintain what power they still retained in the area. Their efforts to modernize economically, reform the government, and maintain unity in the face of demands for a constitution failed to reverse the empire's decline. In 1908, a coup overthrew the sultan and brought the nationalistic Young Turks to power, but their efforts to make Turkish the official language in Balkan areas and to increase Turkish control made the region more volatile. The Austro-Hungarians feared dismemberment of their multinational empire by these nationalistic sentiments. They hoped to expand into the Balkans and thereby weaken any movements for independence among their own ethnic minorities. These hopes brought

Austria-Hungary into conflict with Russia, which had long hungered for influence and expansion in the Balkans and wanted to secure a port into the Mediterranean. Russia had fought two limited wars in pursuit of these aims during the second half of the nineteenth century. It also envisioned itself as the honorable, fraternal protector of Slavic peoples in the Balkans.

The first Balkan crisis erupted in 1908, when Austria-Hungary suddenly annexed two provinces, Bosnia and Herzegovina, which were home to Serbs, Croats, and others. Serbia had wanted to annex these territories, peopled by its own linguistic kin. Serbia appealed to Russia, and Russia threatened Austria-Hungary, whereupon Germany joined its ally and forced Russia to back down. The second Balkan crisis occurred in 1912–1913. The various Balkan states defeated Turkey in a war and then fought among themselves over the spoils. Victorious Serbia longed for more territory. Austria-Hungary thwarted the small country's expansion to the Adriatic Sea and threatened to annihilate Serbia. Again Serbia appealed to Russia, and again German pressure forced Russia to back down.

The assassination of Archduke Ferdinand on June 28, 1914, precipitated the third Balkan crisis. The government of Austria-Hungary, certain of Serbian involvement in the assassination, decided to crush Serbia and establish its own dominance in the Balkans once and for all. But this plan would require the backing of Germany, for Russia might come to the support of its Serbian allies and defend its own interests in the Balkans. At a fateful conference in Berlin eight days after the Sarajevo shooting, the German government encouraged Austria-Hungary's scheme with a "blank check" of full support. Emboldened by Germany's backing and advice to act quickly, Austria-Hungary presented Serbia with an ultimatum that Serbia could not hope to meet. The Austrians may not have wanted a Europe-wide war, but they felt they needed a war with Serbia. Upon hearing of Austria's demands on Serbia, Russia's foreign minister told Austria's ambassador, "You are setting fire to Europe." On July 28, even after Serbia had yielded on all but one of the ultimatum's terms (which would have allowed Austria to investigate Serbian involvement in the assassination plot), Austria-Hungary declared war.

Germany's blank check

To back Serbia against Austria-Hungary, Russia ordered its clumsy military establishment to mobilize. However, Russian military planning, which assumed a war against both Austria and Germany, did not allow for only partial mobilization against Austria. Russia's order of full mobilization on July 29 was almost the same as a declaration of war—especially to German military leaders.

Mobilization

MAPS 22.1 AND 22.2

The Balkans, 1878 and 1914

Map 22.1 shows the Balkans in 1878 and highlights fighting and territorial changes to 1913. **Map 22.2** shows the same region in 1914, after new warfare had resulted in further territorial changes.

Explore the Maps

1. What specifically do the red arrows in the two maps indicate about shifting alliances and battlefronts?

2. Who gained the most and who lost the most? Explain.

3. Why might this region have been such a complex political and military cauldron?

Germany's main war plan assumed a two-front war against Russia and France, requiring the German army to knock France out of the fighting before Russia could bring the weight of its slow-moving forces against Germany. Therefore, Germany mobilized and sent ultimatums to Russia, demanding demobilization, and to France, requiring a declaration of neutrality. When Russia failed to reply and France gave an unsatisfactory response, Germany declared war on Russia on August 1 and on France two days later. On August 4, when German troops violated Belgian neutrality on their way to attack France, Great Britain declared war on Germany.

Thus the great powers of Europe were sucked into a general war they did not want by the very alliances they had formed to protect themselves and feared to violate. The growing tensions in European societies—violent domestic politics, strikes, threats from the political Left and Right, and themes of uncertainty and disintegration expressed in the arts—all worsened matters.

One of the most ominous expressions of the growing tensions in the air came from German expressionist Ludwig Meidner (1884–1966). In his 1913 canvas *Apocalyptic Landscape* (**Figure 22.1**), the sky seems to explode as if under bombardment. Below, buildings shatter as the land quakes. People run in all directions over streets that echo the violence above. In the artist's words, this painting shows "big city life" where "life is lived at fever pitch" and reflects a time when "the great world storm was already baring its teeth and casting its harsh shadow over the whimpering land which was carrying my brush." These tensions made many Europeans, including many intellectuals and well-known observers, welcome war as a quick, all-encompassing relief. Facing these perils and tensions, Europe's stunningly inept political and military leaders made decisions based more on blind optimism and fear of humiliation than on reason and concern for their nation's well-being. That "great world storm" described by Meidner soon arrived. At the time, few Europeans guessed how long the brutality would last.

THE FRONT LINES

Off to Battle

Almost everywhere in Europe, people greeted the declarations of war with outbursts of nationalistic joy. As the Austrian writer Stefan Zweig (1881–1942), a volunteer himself, recalled, "There were parades in the street, flags, ribbons, and music burst forth everywhere, young recruits were marching

Celebrating war

triumphantly, their faces lighting up at the cheering." Young men volunteered in droves, "honestly afraid that they might miss this most wonderful and exciting experience of their lives; that is why they hurried and thronged to the colors, and that is why they shouted and sang in the trains that carried them to the slaughter." **Figure 22.2,** a photograph of German volunteers marching down a Berlin street during the first weeks of the war, reveals the enthusiasm, optimism, and naïveté of the young men. Well dressed and raising their hats, they announce their bravery and celebrate their good fortune at being able to fight for their nation.

Here, suddenly, was a way to end domestic divisions and renew one's sense of purpose in the world. Political opponents set their differences aside and came together to support the war effort. As Document 22.1 reveals, even socialists, long opposed to war and nationalistic calls, joined in the effort to promote national defense. In Germany, the socialists voted for war credits and agreed to suspend strikes until the end of the war. In France, socialists joined their old opponents to support a government of national defense, called the Sacred Union. Russia's leading socialist party proclaimed, "Our first duty is to preserve our nation's unity and integrity, and to defend her position as a world power." Most feminists also suspended their political demands and offered ardent support for the military cause. The troops, people assumed, would surely be home by Christmas. Indeed,

FIGURE 22.1 Ludwig Meidner, *Apocalyptic Landscape,* 1913
Disturbing social tensions during the years preceding World War I are captured in many works of the period, including this dark, chaotic urban scene.

the British government promised that life would go on as usual with no shortages and no new regulations. Each combatant expected to win.

Nations initially on the sidelines soon enlisted with one side or the other (see **Map 22.3**). Hoping to gain territory in a victorious fight, Turkey and Bulgaria joined Germany and Austria-Hungary to become the **Central Powers.** Italy, long a member of the Triple Alliance with Germany and Austria-Hungary, had declared its neutrality at the beginning of the war, claiming that Austria had violated the alliance by launching a war of aggression on Serbia. Italy shifted

DEVELOPMENTS LEADING TO WORLD WAR I

1882	Triple Alliance
1894	Franco-Russian Alliance
1904	Entente Cordiale
1905	First Moroccan crisis
1908	Revolt in Ottoman Empire
	First Balkan crisis
1911	Second Moroccan crisis
1912	Second Balkan crisis
1914	Assassination of Archduke Ferdinand

DOCUMENT 22.1

A Russian Socialist Supports the War Effort

At the beginning of World War I, there was tremendous popular enthusiasm and unity behind governments for the war effort. Even socialist parties—which had long argued that they would not support a nationalistic war entered into by a government dominated by capitalists—joined the effort. The following letter from V. Bourtzeff, a Russian socialist, appeared in the London Times *about six weeks after the outbreak of the war in 1914.*

To the editor of "The Times":

Sir—May I be allowed to say a few words in connection with the excellent letter by my compatriot, Professor Vinogradov, which appeared in your paper today (September 14)? Professor Vinogradov is absolutely right when he says that not only is it desirable that complete unity of feeling should exist in Russian political circles, but that this unity is already an accomplished fact.

The representatives of all political parties and of all nationalities in Russia are now at one with the Government, and this war with Germany and Austria, both guided by the Kaiser, has already become a national war for Russia.

Even we, the adherents of the parties of the Extreme Left, and hitherto ardent anti-militarists and pacifists, even we believe in the necessity of *this* war. *This* war is a war to protect justice and civilization. It will, we hope, be a decisive factor in our united *war against war,* and we hope that after it, it will at last be possible to consider seriously the question of disarmament and universal peace. There can be no doubt that victory, and decisive victory at that (personally I await this in the immediate future), will be on the side of the Allied nations—England, France, Belgium, Serbia, and Russia.

The German peril, the curse which has hung over the whole world for so many decades, will be crushed, and crushed so that it will never again become a danger to the peace of the world. The peoples of the world desire peace.

To Russia this war will bring regeneration. . . .

All the parties without any exceptions have supported the Government without even waiting for it to make any definite announcement about these crying needs. This is the measure of the belief of the people in the inevitableness of liberal reforms. The Government unfortunately still seems irresolute, and has up till now only done the minimum to justify the popular belief in it, but we are convinced that circumstances will develop in such a way that the Government will not be able to delay for long that which has become for Russia a *historical necessity.* And the sooner this happens the better.

SOURCE: Frank A. Golder, *Documents of Russian History, 1914–1917,* trans. E. Aronsberg (Prentice-Hall, 1927), pp. 38–39.

Analyze the Document

1. Why does Bourtzeff support the war effort?

2. How does Bourtzeff justify his opposition to the government's policies and his support for the government in the war?

3. What might this document suggest about the political advantages of going to war?

---

its loyalty to France and Britain after receiving better promises of victory spoils. This side, eventually joined by many other nations from the Americas and the non-Western world, became known as the **Allies.** The Allies had the advantage of sheer numbers, but the Central Powers were led by Germany's better equipped, well-trained army and could more easily move troops and coordinate military strategies.

> The Central Powers versus the Allies

The Schlieffen Plan

Anticipating a confrontation with both Russia and France, the German high command resorted to a military strategy known as the **Schlieffen Plan.** This plan called for a holding action against the slow-moving Russians while the main German forces thrust through neutral Belgium to knock out France. Then the Germans could concentrate on destroying Russia. Great Britain, her allies hobbled, would sue for peace, the Germans expected.

Day after day, the Schlieffen Plan worked. Four weeks after the outbreak of hostilities, German forces arrived just outside Paris ahead of schedule. Some

FIGURE 22.2 German Volunteers, 1914 This photograph shows German men optimistically celebrating as they march off to war.

MAP 22.3

World War I

This map shows the two alliances and the major fronts in World War I.

Explore the Map

1. What does this map reveal about the surrounded position of the Central Powers and the importance of Turkey during the war?

2. Locate the major areas of fighting on the western and eastern fronts. What do these reveal about the different natures of the wars on these two fronts?

3. Which areas in Europe were most directly affected by the fighting?

North Sea

NETHERLANDS

Ostend
Calais
Ypres
Lille
Arras
Amiens
Compiègne
Château-Thierry
Paris
MARNE
Soissons
Reims
CHAMPAGNE
FRANCE
Ghent
Antwerp
Brussels
BELGIUM
Liège
Cambrai
St. Quentin
ARGONNE
Aisne R.
Châlons-sur-Marne
Nancy
Cologne
Aix-la-Chapelle
Coblenz
GERMANY
ARDENNES
Sedan
LUXEMBOURG
Verdun
LORRAINE
Strasbourg
Epinal
ALSACE
Mulhouse
Basel
Besançon
SWITZERLAND

Rhine R.
Meuse R.
Moselle R.
Saar R.
Rhine R.
Marne R.

0   50 mi
0   100 km

- Germany 1914
- German Offensive, 1914
- Deepest German Penetration, Sept. 1914
- Front at Beginning of 1915
- German Offensive, Summer 1918
- Allied Offensive, Fall 1918
- Armistice Line, November 1918

MAP 22.4

The Western Front

This map shows the western front at various stages of World War I.

Explore the Map

1. How far did the Germans penetrate in their 1914 offensive?

2. How close did the Germans come to capturing the French capital?

3. Describe the location of the western front at the beginning of 1915—that line would change little over the next three years.

4. What countries were most directly affected by the fighting on the western front?

surprises, however, lay in store for them. Stubborn Belgian resistance had held up the Germans long enough for the French to redeploy their forces to the north and for the British to send their small army across the Channel. Germans suffered unanticipated casualties and transportation problems. At a critical moment, the German command detached 100,000 of

their best troops under generals Hindenburg (1847–1934) and Ludendorff (1865–1937) and sent them east to fight the Russians, who had invaded Germany with unexpected speed. Nearing Paris, the German First Army detoured from its planned route in order to concentrate its force on the French capital. This move opened a gap in the Germans' eastern flank and exposed its western flank. At this juncture, the desperate French armies seized the opportunity and turned on the Germans. Parisian taxicabs rushed army reserves to the front in the effort to save Paris. Units of Britain's army arrived to enter the fray at a crucial moment. In the bloody seven-day Battle of the Marne, the Allies at last halted the Germans, drove them back several miles, and shattered German hopes that the Schlieffen Plan would succeed. As **Map 22.4** indicates, both sides extended their lines more than 400 miles from the Swiss border to the North Sea and dug in for the winter. Germany was now stuck with what it had tried so hard to avoid—a war on two fronts.

Slaughter and Stalemate on the Western Front

The defensive lines proved superior to offensive thrusts. To the surprise of almost everyone, the armies on the western front fought a war of attrition from their networks of trenches protected by barbed wire, mines, and machine guns. The trenches became filled with mud, rats, human bodies, lice, waste, poison gas, and the stench of death. But they also served as homes and protection for troops under fire, as shown in **Figure 22.3.** Along with their rifles and grenades, soldiers carried wire cutters and gas masks. Between the trenches, mortar and massive artillery bombardments created a barren, pockmarked landscape of mud and death that few soldiers could cross and still hope to live. The British introduced tanks in 1916 but did not manage to use them effectively to cross trenches until the last year of the war (see Thinking About Science & Technology).

Trench warfare

Despite the defensive advantages of **trench warfare,** military commanders remained wedded to notions of an offensive breakthrough. Again and again, they sent troops scrambling out of their trenches, over the top and into no-man's-land, where enemy machine-gun fire mowed them down by the thousands. Fritze Franke, a German soldier, described his experience of trench warfare in a November 1914 letter: "Every foot of ground contested, every hundred yards another trench; and everywhere bodies—rows of them! All the trees shot to pieces; the whole ground churned up a yard deep by the heaviest shells; dead animals; houses and churches . . . utterly destroyed. . . . And every troop that advances in support must pass through a

FIGURE 22.3 Trench Warfare Rows of men in gas masks wait in trenches protected by barbed wire in this war of attrition on the western front.

mile of this chaos, through this gigantic burial ground and the reek of corpses." Fololiyani Longwe, an African serving in the British army on the western front, described how soldiers stood "buried in a hole with only your head and hands outside, holding a gun" for days with "no food, no water," and "only death smelling all over the place." Wilfred Owen, the British poet whom we met at the beginning of the chapter, related how the brutal reality of the war wiped out old images of its glory. Owen warned that anyone who saw the suffering

> . . . would not tell with such high zest
> To children ardent for some desperate glory,
> The old Lie: Dulce et decorum est
> Pro patria mori. ("It is sweet and proper
> to die for one's country.")

Military leaders failed to realize that machine guns, modern artillery, mass mobilization, and trenches had utterly changed the nature of warfare. Acting on old assumptions and oblivious to these new military realities, generals ordered offensives again and again. Each time the charges moved lines only yards, if at all, and

each time the human costs were staggering. "We lie under the network of arching shells and live in a suspense of uncertainty," wrote German war veteran Erich Maria Remarque (1898–1970) in his novel *All Quiet on the Western Front.* "Over us Chance hovers." The wartime life expectancy of a frontline officer such as Wilfred Owen was only two months. After a year and a half of this mutual slaughter, nothing had changed.

In 1916, the Germans tried for a draining victory by attacking the French fortress at Verdun (see **Map 22.3**). Their plan was, in the words of the German commander, to "bleed to death" the French by forcing them to sustain massive casualties defending this historic strongpoint. During the ensuing nine-month battle, the Germans sometimes fired as many as a million shells in one day. The French managed to hold off the Germans, but 700,000 men on both sides lost their lives in the effort. "You found the dead embedded in the walls of the trenches, heads, legs, and half-bodies, just as they had been shovelled out of the way by the picks and shovels of the working party," recalled one French soldier.

Great battles of 1916

That same year the British attempted a breakthrough in the Battle of the Somme in northeastern France (see **Map 22.3**). They suffered 60,000 casualties, with more than 20,000 killed in just the first day. "As far as you could see there were all these bodies lying there—literally thousands of them. . . . It didn't seem possible," wrote a British soldier. By fall, Britain had endured 400,000 casualties; France, 200,000; and Germany, 500,000, in this one battle. It ended in a stalemate. "Here chivalry disappeared for always," wrote the German Ernst Jünger. In the Passchendaele offensive (see **Map 22.3**), the British again tried to break through the German "crust," losing some 400,000 soldiers in the effort. Like other great battles in the west, Passchendaele scarcely moved the front lines at all.

Neither the politicians nor the generals found the will to call a halt to the slaughter. Anything short of complete victory, they feared, would mean that all the deaths and casualties were in vain. The troops were not so stubborn. Sometimes they agreed to avoid battles. They even occasionally fraternized across the trenches, sang together, and allowed each other to eat meals in peace or collect the bodies of fellow soldiers in no-man's-land. They also were capable of making their outrage known to their superiors. After a new, disastrous offensive ordered by France's commander General Nivelle in April 1917, mutinies broke out in almost half the French divisions on the front. Thousands of soldiers were court-martialed and more than 500 sentenced to death, although most executions were never carried out. New commanders and troops tacitly agreed to stop these hopeless offensive onslaughts.

thinking about
SCIENCE & TECHNOLOGY

FIGURE 22.4 British Mark 1 Tank, 1916

The Invention of the Tank

Efforts to build movable protective devices for use as offensive weapons in warfare go back thousands of years. A modern form of these devices is the tank, a vehicle first developed during World War I. Trench warfare created a demand for an armored, self-propelled weapon that could bridge trenches, maneuver across the cratered battlefields of the western front, and enable the infantry to break through enemy lines to victory.

The British and French led efforts to develop this weapon. Manufacturers' early models were unreliable, and the tank's use on the battlefield was questionable—and sometimes led to outright failure. Too easily, the vehicles became mired and exposed in difficult terrain. Moreover, the heat and fumes that built up inside often made crews sick—and even lose consciousness. But the British and French inventors persisted, modifying the vehicle's design and tactical features. They eventually came up with a practical tank that used iron armor for defense, an internal combustion engine for power, caterpillar tracks for mobility, and cannons and machine guns for weapons.

The British first employed these practical tanks at the Battle of the Somme in 1916 but with only limited success. The photo in **Figure 22.4** shows the British Mark 1 tank spanning a trench at that battle. The tanks proved to be of greater effect during the last year of the war. However, because the slow-moving vehicles were vulnerable to artillery and antitank weapons, they required support from accompanying infantry and ground-attack aircraft.

As we will see in Chapter 24, the tank would become a much more potent and decisive weapon in World War II.

Connecting Science & Society

1. In what ways is the invention of a practical tank an example of the industrialization of warfare?

2. What role did inventors, producers, and the government, working together, play in the development of the tank?

3. How might an earlier development of a practical tank have altered the nature and course of World War I?

Figure 22.5 illustrates how all means, old and new, were used to fight this war. Here soldiers with plumed helmets sit astride horses while an airplane, used for bombing and intelligence, flies overhead. Armies would use poison gas, flamethrowers, and tanks for the first time. Even dogs—75,000 of them—were employed to search for wounded men on the battlefronts.

On the seas, both sides in the war hoped for decisive victories. The British navy set up a blockade of Germany, and the Germans responded with the submarine. Germany and Britain never met in a conclusive naval showdown, however. In the Battle of Jutland, the only major naval battle of the war, the British fleet prevented the German fleet from breaking the blockade—but suffered serious losses as a result. Most of the massive struggle took place on the ground. After three years of fighting, neither side could break through on the western front. By then, the French alone had sustained more than 3.5 million casualties. Yet the war dragged on.

Victory and Defeat on the Eastern and Southern Fronts

As **Map 22.3** indicates, the war proved far more mobile and offensive on the eastern front than in the west. In eastern Europe, the terrain did not favor

Weapons of war

trench warfare, and in any case the Russians lacked the resources to sustain such a defensive effort. Initially, Russia, with its huge but inadequately supplied army, pushed into German and Austro-Hungarian lands. At the end of August 1914, however, the reinforced German armies, bolstered by their superior technology and leadership, trapped the Russians at Tannenberg and administered a crushing defeat. The Russian commander, General Samsonov, committed suicide on the spot. Farther south, the Russians defeated an Austro-Hungarian army at Lemberg only to bring in a German army that delivered a series of hammer blows to the Russians. The Germans drove deep into Russia and inflicted immense casualties, making Generals Hindenburg and Ludendorff heroes. In the Balkans, German, Austrian, and Bulgarian forces had eliminated Serbia from the war by the end of 1915. That same year, a disastrous Anglo-French effort to help the hard-pressed Russians by landing at Gallipoli and breaking through Turkish defenses at the nearby Dardanelles was beaten back by the Turks with heavy losses to the Allies (see **Map 22.3**).

FIGURE 22.5 Old and New Means of Warfare In World War I, all means, from the traditional cavalry horses to the new airplanes, were used on the battlefront, as this period photograph documents.

In 1916, Russia made one more great effort against the Austro-Hungarian forces in the south. Under General Aleksei Brusilov, Russian armies almost forced the Austro-Hungarians to withdraw from the war. The Austro-Hungarians resorted to recruiting men over the age of 50 into the

Russia's military collapse

army and, in the end, kept going only with German support. But the Russians could not sustain the effort. Lack of effective leadership, insufficient supplies, and desertions plagued Russia's armies. "Half of them have no rifles," Tsar Nicholas admitted, "the troops are losing masses and there is nobody to collect them on the battlefields." Germany's renewed push in 1917 resulted in massive Russian losses. These losses, along with internal strife that toppled the tsar, his government, and the succeeding provisional government (see pages 710–715), knocked Russia out of the war in December 1917. Nevertheless, for more than two years, the Russian effort had drawn German troops east, weakening the German forces in the west.

Meanwhile, in northeastern Italy, Austrian and German troops won some costly battles, but the

Southern fronts

Italian forces limited the Central Powers' advances (see **Map 22.3**). Farther south and east, Allied forces attacked the Ottoman Empire. In 1915, after an Anglo-French fleet failed to open the Dardanelles strait so that Russia could receive supplies in her Black Sea ports, a 400,000-man force of British, French, Australian, New Zealand, and other troops landed at Gallipoli. The invaders suffered terrible defeats at the hands of the Turkish defenders and were forced to evacuate. Even more crippling, malaria, cholera, dysentery, and other diseases spread among the troops fighting in the Middle East. Eventually, the British, most notably the charismatic officer and writer T. E. Lawrence (1888–1935), stirred up Arab resentment into a desert revolt against the Ottoman Turks in Palestine and Mesopotamia. Together, British and Arab forces gradually gained the upper hand against the Ottoman Turks.

The War Spreads Across the Globe

The war itself soon spread outside of Europe and the Mediterranean basin, in great part thanks to the West's colonies and imperial interests throughout the world. In the South Atlantic, British and German naval forces clashed off the Falkland Islands. In Africa, minor battles erupted around Germany's colonies. In East Asia, Japan joined the war on the Allied side and promptly seized German holdings in the Pacific and China. When Russia seemed on the verge of falling apart, Japan also sent soldiers into the tsar's far eastern provinces. Britain and France drew troops from Canada, Africa, Asia, and Australia to fight on several fronts. More than 1 million Indian soldiers served under the British, particularly in the Middle East campaigns, and hundreds of thousands of African soldiers from French colonies served in Europe. The Western nations also called on workers from these lands, including a 200,000-man labor battalion from China, to work in France and elsewhere in the war effort.

However, non-Western peoples often resisted the European powers' efforts to gain their support. Nomadic tribes fled Russia's central Asian provinces rather than serve in the tsar's army. In French West Africa, local tribes revolted when the French tried to mobilize labor brigades. Moreover, non-Westerners did not automatically favor the Allied cause. Most of those who followed the conflict in Asia viewed World War I as a European civil war. In addition, they were likely to favor Germany over France and Britain, two nations that had a tradition of Asian conquest. Indeed, for the most part, the first world war remained a European affair. Raging on year after year, the conflict shattered the lives of soldiers and civilians alike.

WAR ON THE HOME FRONT

No Western society could come through such a protracted war unscathed. As the toll on lives and supplies climbed, whole societies had to mobilize to support the military effort. In this sense, World War I became the first **total war,** blurring the traditional distinctions between combatants and civilians and between battle lines and the home front. The first world war transformed whole economies, societies, and governments, as well as the lives of soldiers.

Total war

Mobilizing Resources

After the first few months of hostilities, armies began to run out of ammunition, supplies, and troops. The French alone were firing more than 100,000 artillery shells a day—far more than their armaments factories could supply. Entire economies were reorganized to churn out huge quantities of bullets, guns, and machines in just days and weeks rather than the usual months and years. The war effort required untold quantities of other materials as well—everything from food and uniforms to trucks and coffins. Overall, the war demanded unprecedented industrial capability and organizational agility to produce and move supplies for the armed forces.

To varying degrees, the governments of the major powers took control of their economies. Government agencies, rather than the free marketplace, determined production, consumption, wages, and prices. In Germany, the War Raw Materials Board located, rationed, and distributed raw materials. To meet the need for products that Germany could no longer import, such as rubber, the board helped develop synthetic substitutes. In Britain, the Ministry of Munitions, led by David Lloyd George, supervised the armaments industry. The ministry's bureaucracy of 65,000 clerks controlled prices, supplies, and production of war materials.

Governments take control

This tightly controlled mobilization of resources also included people. Not only were men drafted into the armed services, but women and men on the home fronts were often required to work in accord with priorities determined by the government. Labor unions were brought into partnership with business and government. In addition, governments suspended laws limiting the length of the workday and controlling workplace conditions. People were thus forced to work longer hours under dangerous circumstances.

Demand for troops on the front lines and labor on the home front altered traditional social and national boundaries. Although the war did not eliminate class conflict, social distinctions blurred as people from all walks of society joined the war effort and worked or fought side by side. Conventional national distinctions were sometimes violated: For a while, the hard-pressed Germans forced thousands of Belgians to move and work in German factories. The war effort could even include children: Some German teachers organized their students to go through garbage and collect anything that might be useful. Perhaps most striking, officials challenged traditional gender roles by calling women into the labor force.

New Gender Roles

Gender roles changed radically under the pressures of all-out war. At first, many women were left on their own financially as their husbands marched off to battle. Later, when economies began straining with the war effort, women got new jobs previously reserved for men. **Figure 22.6** shows women working in a large British armaments plant, producing the huge quantity of shells needed on the battle lines. Such women participated in all aspects of the munitions industries. They became army clerks and streetcar conductors and drove taxis and ran farms. Some served as firefighters at home and as nurses at the front. Others gained entry into white-collar jobs in banks, commercial businesses, and urban offices. In Great Britain, the number of women working

KEY DATES

WORLD WAR I

1914	Battle of the Marne
1915	Italy joins Allies
1916	Battle of Verdun
1917	United States enters the war
1918	End of World War I
1919	Treaty of Versailles

outside the home had increased twentyfold to some five million by 1918. In Russia, women made up over 40 percent of the labor force. Similar patterns held in other European countries.

These shifting labor patterns created new tensions over women's roles as men began fearing they would lose their jobs to women permanently. "Workmen have to be handled with the utmost tenderness and caution lest they should actually imagine . . . that women could do their work equally well," wrote a female British munitions factory worker in 1916. Women themselves often had conflicted feelings about their new role. Many gained a new sense of independence from earning a paycheck. Some displayed their newfound freedom by living alone, going out socially on their own, wearing shorter dresses, cutting (bobbing) their hair, and smoking cigarettes. Others felt torn by the dual demands of service and family. "What exhausts women in wartime is not the strenuous and unfamiliar tasks that fall upon them, nor even the hourly dread of death for husbands or lovers or brothers or sons," recalled British writer Vera Brittain (1896–1970), who served as a nurse in France. "It is the incessant conflict between personal and national claims which wears out their energy and breaks their spirit." By no coincidence, several nations would grant women the right to vote at the war's end.

Maintaining the Effort

As the war persisted, governments became more involved in manufacturing consent and less tolerant of dissent. Propaganda specialists tried to inspire support for the war and hatred for the enemy. The more the propaganda succeeded in its aims, the harder it became for governments to compromise or withdraw from the conflict. Officials deliberately manipulated information and censored private letters to shape public opinion about the war. In particular, they tried to create the impression that their own country was completely virtuous and that it was the other nations that were committing crimes against humanity. To combat war weariness, governments painted the enemy as evil incarnate and whipped up people's sense of outrage. There was no way, political leaders declared, that "good" people could ever make peace with such diabolical opponents.

Figure 22.7, a cover from a French magazine, is an example of such propaganda. The image depicts Germans as having committed atrocities during their march through Belgium and northern France. Here an innocent, horror-stricken, assaulted woman kneels on a blood-soaked crib and cradles the body of her

Propaganda

FIGURE 22.6 Women War Workers   This interior view of a British armaments plant reveals how mass production, supported by women workers, created the huge quantity of materials needed for the war effort.

murdered child. The empty wine bottles and helmet scattered on the ground around her leave no doubt that immoral German soldiers have committed these acts. The illustrator also blames the Germans for setting the homes and church of this village on fire while passing through. The glaring headline exhorts people to "Let Us Never Forget."

Governments also tried to promote dissent among their opponents and turn neutral countries into allies. Germany supported the Irish in their 1916 Easter Rebellion in Dublin for Irish independence, which British forces brutally crushed. Germany also aided the Bolsheviks against Russia's government. The British promoted rebellion among the Arabs against the Turks and used propaganda to help bring the Americans in on their side.

Victories or defeats on the front lines reflected the abilities of civilian societies to mobilize effectively for the war effort—materially, politically, and psychologically. Those nations less able to develop and sustain this vast home-front effort—such as the Austro-Hungarian and Russian empires—faltered first. They lacked the solid industrial base and organizational strength of Germany, France, and Great Britain. Over time, however, even the strongest nations weakened under the strains of total war. Food shortages spawned malnutrition, disease, and high infant mortality, especially in Germany, which acutely felt the impact of Britain's naval blockade. Governments tried to pay for the war by printing more money, thereby creating an inflation of prices.

By 1917, hunger and war weariness were igniting strikes and domestic disorders throughout Europe. Beleaguered governments suspended civil liberties,

FIGURE 22.7

Let Us Never Forget

Numerous propaganda posters were produced on all sides of the war. This French poster depicts the fate of the Belgians when the Germans conquered the nation on the way to their main western adversary, France.

Connecting Art & Society

1. What kind of response do you think this scene was intended to stir in the viewer?

2. Why does the scene focus on a woman and her child rather than, for example, a battle scene?

3. In what ways has the artist used visual clues to prompt the viewer to read this picture as a dramatic series of events that have just occurred?

4. Why might propaganda posters such as this example be effective in influencing public sentiment?

ignored democratic procedures, and ruled by emergency police powers. In France, Georges Clemenceau (1841–1929) became a virtual dictator after November 1917. He sent troops against strikers and arrested those agitating for peace. "I wage war," he declared. "I wage nothing but war!" In Austria, political unity unraveled as different nationalities clamored for independence. In Germany, some socialist and Catholic legislators came out for peace, and Generals Hindenburg and Ludendorff assumed control over the German war effort. By the end of 1917, Russia's whole war effort had collapsed. Clearly, World War I would be won or lost on the home front as well as on the battle lines.

Rising dissent

TO THE BITTER END

Early in 1917, the German high command grew desperate to bring the draining war to a victorious conclusion. The generals decided to launch an unrestricted submarine campaign against enemy and neutral shipping alike. Germany's leaders knew this policy could bring the United States into the war. Up to that point, the United States had remained neutral but had become increasingly invested in the Allied cause through trade and loans. The sense that Germany and its partners were the aggressors, along with the 1915 sinking of the passenger liner *Lusitania* during a German submarine blockade of Britain, had also nudged American public opinion toward support of the Allies. Now Germany's high command gambled that they could defeat Britain and France before the Americans could send enough supplies and troops to Europe to make a difference. Indeed, Ludendorff and Hindenburg promised victory within only six months.

At about the same time, British intelligence turned over to the United States an alarming note that it claimed to have intercepted. In that document, called the Zimmermann note, Germany offered to grant U.S. territory to Mexico—the very territory lost by Mexico in the 1848 Mexican-American War—if Mexico agreed to attack the United States. When German submarines began sinking American cargo ships, U.S. entry into the conflict was ensured. On April 6, 1917, the United States declared war on Germany. President Woodrow Wilson promised to "make the world safe for democracy."

The U.S. enters the war

The Germans had good reason to think that they might prevail. At the beginning of 1918, the United States' contribution to the war was still relatively small. In addition, the Italians had suffered a disastrous blow at the Battle of Caporetto, almost putting them out of the war. Romania had been defeated, and Russia had withdrawn from the war. Now Germany could at last focus its efforts on a one-front war. In the

Atlantic, its U-boats (submarines) were sinking one-fourth of all ships taking supplies to Britain—350 ships went down in one month alone.

On the other hand, Germany's allies—the Austro-Hungarian and Ottoman empires—were teetering, and Germany was suffering from lack of materials and food, thanks to Britain's naval blockade. The British had also discovered a way to foil the U-boats by using heavily escorted convoys armed with depth charges. Now the race was between Germany and the United States. Germany transferred troops from the Russian front in an effort to overwhelm Great Britain and France before waves of American troops could arrive, while the United States struggled to raise, train, and transport sufficient forces to France to stem the German tide.

In March 1918, Field Marshall Ludendorff launched, on the western front, the first of a series of massive German blows designed to end the **Final battles** war. The British and French were driven back with heavy losses. Desperate, they finally agreed to a unified command under France's General Ferdinand Foch (1851–1929). By mid-June, after the fourth of the great drives, the Allied lines were so badly battered that when the climactic fifth drive began along the Marne River in mid-July, Ludendorff wired the kaiser: "If the attack succeeds, the war will be over and we will have won it." When Foch heard the opening German barrage, he wired his government: "If the present German attack succeeds, the war is over and we have lost it." The Allies stopped the Germans by a narrow margin. Foch, now receiving a swelling stream of fresh American soldiers—more than 250,000 soldiers a month—immediately ordered a counterattack. British tanks helped break through German lines. The balance shifted. Suddenly, the Germans were in retreat. German strength and morale waned rapidly. That spring and summer, Germans suffered more than 2 million casualties.

At the end of October, Germany's Bulgarian and Turkish allies surrendered. On November 3, Austria-Hungary, its ethnic minorities in revolt, also surrendered; a week later, the last Austro-Hungarian emperor abdicated. The next day, mutiny broke out in the German navy and spread to workers in German cities. Popular uprisings brought down the kaiser's government, and on November 9 he fled the country. On November 11, the new German Republic government accepted an armistice.

For many, however, even the last days of the war were too long. In Britain, Wilfred Owen's mother, like so many others, received news of her son's death (he was machine-gunned in a final attack) just as church bells began ringing for victory. Those last days would also leave a haunting legacy in Germany. German commanders manipulated reports from the front so that most of Germany's population remained unaware of the extent of their country's military collapse. The new civilian government of republicans and socialists in Germany would later be blamed by many Germans for the surrender. This development would in turn set the stage for future charges that Germany had not really lost the war but had been stabbed in the back by the very political forces that would rule Germany during the 1920s.

ASSESSING THE LOSSES

The war had shattered much of Europe. Some 10 million soldiers and perhaps another 7–10 million civilians had perished from the war and its hardships. Russia lost almost 2 million soldiers, as did Germany. Serbia lost some 15–20 percent of its population. All across northern France and Belgium, war cemeteries spread, many with unmarked graves, others with elaborate monuments to the fallen such as those in **Figure 22.8.** Europe lost the cream of a generation of its future leaders. Colonial troops from Asia and Africa also suffered. **Figure 22.9,** showing a Senegalese soldier learning to use artificial limbs with the help of a Red Cross nurse, indicates the price many such veterans paid for their service.

For those left behind, the hardships persisted. Many survivors would have to spend the rest of their lives in veterans' hospitals. In many places, mutilated people, widows, and spinsters seemed the rule rather than the exception. Many survivors would remain obsessed with the experience of this war, like the British poet Siegfried Sassoon, who wrote, "The rank stench of those bodies haunts me still, And I remember things I'd best forget" (see Document 22.2). In addition to all the death and misery, the fighting brought incalculable financial and material losses. The war laid to waste a tenth of the richest region of France and devastated the most developed part of Russia. It also saddled European nations with heavy debts, especially to a new international creditor—the United States. Finally, it was difficult not to merge the losses from the war with the tens of millions of deaths caused by the 1918 flu pandemic. That flu, which spread rapidly around the globe, was not *caused* by World War I, but the close quarters of troops and the mass movements of people spurred by the war probably added to the suffering and the staggering death toll.

THE PEACE SETTLEMENT

No peace settlement could make up for the losses of World War I. Nevertheless, delegates who gathered at Versailles near Paris in January 1919 and the people they represented expected a resolution that could somehow justify those losses. Other burdens

BIOGRAPHY

Käthe Kollwitz
(1867–1945)

By the eve of World War I, Käthe Kollwitz's prints, drawings, and posters had made her one of Germany's leading artists. "[M]y art has purpose," she said. "I want to be effective in this time when people are so helpless and in need of aid."

Käthe Schmidt was born in East Prussia in 1867. As a child, she often suffered from periods of depression, and these episodes continued well into her adulthood. Early on she learned to express her feelings in art. In 1891, Käthe married Dr. Karl Kollwitz, whom she would praise years later as her "life's comrade." Karl shared Käthe's socialist sympathies. That year, the couple moved to Berlin, where Karl took a job as a physician for a workers' health insurance fund and where Käthe gave birth to Hans in 1892 and Peter in 1896. Reflecting on the role of love in her life, she would later describe silently falling in love with women as well as men and the influence of bisexuality on the themes in her art.

Artist and Witness to War

Käthe earned her first public success as an artist between 1895 and 1898 with the publication of a series of prints, *The Weavers*. These images recorded a doomed revolt of handloom weavers in the 1840s. Indeed, most of her works explored the plight of victims of social injustice, the cause of peace, and the sufferings of war and death. Not surprisingly, her art often offended the authorities, including the kaiser.

In early August 1914, just after World War I broke out, the Kollwitz family heard German soldiers singing as they marched in the streets (see pages 695–696). Käthe wept in horror. During those same days, her youngest son, Peter, only 18 years old, volunteered for the army. On August 27, 1914, she wrote, "Where do all the women who have watched so carefully over the lives of their beloved ones get the heroism to send them to face the cannon? I am afraid that this soaring of the spirit will be followed by the blackest despair and dejection." A month later, she wrote, "It seems so stupid that the boys must go to war . . . how can they possibly take part in such madness?" Three weeks later, on October 22, 1914, Peter was killed in the war.

This loss of her son haunted Käthe for the rest of her life. In letters and diaries, she expressed endless grief for her fallen boy. She expanded her sorrow to embrace grieving mothers in all countries. Reflecting on the causes of the war, she described how Peter and others she knew had "subordinated their lives to the idea of patriotism. The English, Russian and French young men have done the same. The consequence has been this terrible killing and the impoverishment of Europe."

After her son's death, Käthe began a long struggle to create monumental sculptures in memory of Peter and other sons killed in the war. It would take her ten years to start work on the final forms for these sculptures and another eight years before the figures were completed in stone. **Figure 22.8** is a photograph of the two sculptures. At the opening ceremony, held in the Belgian cemetery where Peter was buried, Käthe stood before her stone figure of the mother: "I looked at her, my own face, and wept and stroked her cheeks."

When the war ended, she worried that "the peace will probably be very bad." For her the war, fought by Europe's youth, had destroyed "all that is most beautiful in Europe." In 1919, she became the first woman elected to the Prussian Academy of Arts. In 1928, she was further honored by being

---

weighed on the delegates as well. The end of fighting did not stop wartime hatred and suffering. Starvation threatened central and eastern Europe. In addition, a growing fear of revolutionary communism haunted the delegates, who primarily represented the forces of order and wealth in their nations. Already in power in Russia, communists had a real chance of triumphing in Germany and in the newly independent states of eastern Europe.

Gathering at Versailles

Although all thirty-two of the victorious Allies participated in the peace conference, the leaders of France, Great Britain, the United States, and Italy made the major decisions. Representatives of colonized peoples,

ethnic and religious groups, women's organizations, and various national groups went to Versailles hoping for a hearing but received none. The vanquished Germany and Austria-Hungary were excluded from the talks, as was Russia, which had dropped out of the war a year earlier.

Premier Georges Clemenceau, the aged Tiger of France, headed the French delegation. As host of the conference and leader of the nation that had done the most to defeat Germany, Clemenceau expected to dominate the decision making. The eloquent and fiery Prime Minister David Lloyd George led the British delegation. He also intended to dominate the conference. Premier Vittorio Orlando (1860–1952), head of the Italian delegation, wanted all the territory that the Allies had promised in the first place

FIGURE 22.8 Käthe Kollwitz, *The Mourning Father and Mother*

appointed head of a master class for graphic arts. In 1930, as the Nazis rose in strength, she wrote that "evil reaction is creeping into all areas." Käthe was forced to resign her prestigious position when Hitler came to power in 1933, and the Führer banned her work. In 1940 her grandson, Peter, the namesake of her son Peter killed in World War I, joined Germany's army as World War II erupted. He was killed on the Russian front in 1942. She continued her work almost until her death on April 22, 1945.

Like so many other people, Käthe Kollwitz had witnessed the great enthusiasm as soldiers first marched off to the Great War in August 1914. Also like countless millions of people, she had lost a loved one in that conflict. She, too, would live long enough to witness a terrible renewal of war. In her last letter, she wrote, "the war accompanies me to the end." She, along with far too many in the West, would never fully recover from the scars of World War I.

Connecting People & Society

1. How does Kollwitz's life reflect the impact of World War I on European society?

2. How does Kollwitz explain the causes and enthusiasm for the war?

3. What are your reactions to Kollwitz's sculptures?

to draw Italy into the war. The idealistic President Woodrow Wilson (1856–1924), expecting approval of his Fourteen Points as the basis for peace, led the American delegation. The United States had attained much prestige during the war and was the first non-European country in centuries to influence the fate of European nations.

A Victors' Peace

A fundamental and bitter clash immediately developed between Clemenceau, who wanted a "hard" peace that would render Germany harmless, and Wilson, who wanted a "just" peace free of vindictiveness. Wilson and his advisors feared that a harsh settlement would leave Germany resentful, eager for revenge, or ripe for takeover by extreme political forces. He also believed that secret diplomacy and the alliance system had caused the war in the first place, and urged "open covenants of peace, openly arrived at." In his Fourteen Points, Wilson also called for the self-determination of peoples, armaments reduction, and a "general association of nations" to guarantee the safety of "great and small states alike." Lloyd George often sided with Wilson but, like Clemenceau, wanted a victory worthy of the sacrifices made during the war.

Wilson's Fourteen Points

It took six months of hard work and wrangling to draw up the peace terms. Although the Treaty of Versailles reflected many of Wilson's ideals, it was more of a victors' peace reflecting France's desire

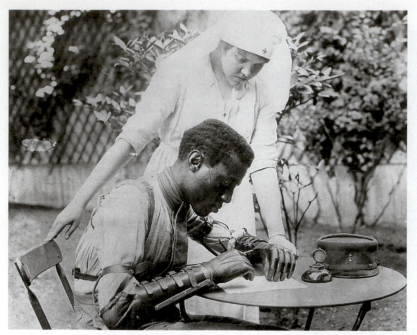

FIGURE 22.9 Casualty from the Colonies A nurse helps one of the many soldiers from Europe's colonies who became casualties of the war.

for security and an eagerness to punish Germany. In what came to be known as the **war guilt clause,** the agreement forced Germany and its allies to accept full responsibility for the war. Germany lost all its overseas colonies and concessions; several victorious nations gained control over these territories in Africa and the Pacific. France regained Alsace and Lorraine, lost in the Franco-Prussian War of 1870. In addition, the victors would occupy German territory on the west bank of the Rhine for the next fifteen years. The Polish-speaking areas of eastern Germany were ceded to the resurrected Polish state, and a "Polish corridor" was cut through German territory to give Poland an outlet at Danzig to the Baltic Sea. Germany's armed forces were limited to 100,000 soldiers and saddled with severe armament limitations. Finally, Germany was held liable for reparations that in 1921 were set at $33 billion.

Redrawing the Map of Europe

As **Map 22.5** reveals, the treaties dealt the harshest blow to Germany's allies because the territorial rearrangements were usually based on the principle of unifying national language groups. Austria-Hungary was cut down from a polyglot empire of 50 million—second in area only to Russia among the nations of Europe—to an Austria of 6.5 million German-speaking Austrians and a Hungary of 8 million Magyars. Many in Austria wanted their new country to merge with Germany, but the settlement specifically forbad this arrangement. The Czechs and Slovaks

were joined into the new state of Czechoslovakia, which included sizable German and other minorities. Serbs, Croats, Slovenes, Bosnians, and others populated the new state of Yugoslavia. The Ottoman Empire was dismembered, and parts of its Anatolian homeland were occupied by British, French, Italian, and Greek forces. Perhaps unavoidably, all these new national boundaries created many internal ethnic divisions and pockets of discontent that would breed future conflicts.

Woodrow Wilson had placed his chief hopes for peace in an association of countries—the **League of Nations**—that he expected would guarantee borders and peaceably settle the tensions and conflicts that were certain to arise in the future. The League was incorporated into the treaty with Germany but had no military forces at its command. Its only weapons were economic sanctions and moral condemnations. Though perhaps well intentioned, the League was doomed almost from the beginning. The exclusion of Germany and the Soviet Union from the association weakened its potential effectiveness. In addition, the self-righteous President Wilson—reluctant to compromise with political opponents back in the United States and physically weakening—failed to persuade the isolationist American Senate to ratify the peace accords and join the League. What little faith Great Britain and France had in Wilson's ideas quickly disappeared.

> The League of Nations

Legacy of the Peace Treaty

The peace settlement negotiated in Paris satisfied no one and left a legacy of deep resentments. France's Clemenceau considered the terms too lenient. Moreover, both Great Britain and the United States refused French pleas to join France in a defensive alliance. Not surprisingly, the French felt betrayed and abandoned. The Germans, for their part, considered the terms outrageous. Many Germans refused to believe that their armies had lost the war. The Germans also resented not being allowed to participate in the talks. Their representatives were presented with a humiliating settlement that they signed only after the Allies threatened to invade. Italy's leader, Orlando, walked out of the conference to protest broken Allied promises of more territorial gains.

Nationalists in Turkey, led by their wartime hero of Gallipoli, Mustafa Kemal (1881–1938), refused to accept the Treaty of Sèvres, which had been negotiated by the Allies and the sultan's tottering regime in 1920. That treaty allowed foreign powers to occupy eastern and southern Anatolia.

DOCUMENT 22.2

In the Trenches and Beyond

Some of the most poignant accounts of experiences on the front lines come from poets who have served in the military. Unlike many poets, such as Rupert Brooke and Wilfred Owen, Siegfried Sassoon (1886–1967) survived World War I. But the experience would haunt him for the rest of his life. The following are excerpts from "The rank stench of those bodies haunts me still" and "Does it Matter?"

The rank stench of those bodies haunts me still

The rank stench of those bodies
   haunts me still,
And I remember things I'd best forget.
For now we've marched to a green,
   trenchless land
Twelve miles from battering guns:
   along the grass
Brown lines of tents are hives for
   snoring men;

Wide, radiant water sways the
   floating sky
Below dark, shivering trees. And
   living-clean
Comes back with thoughts of home
   and hours of sleep.

To-night I smell the battle; miles away
Gun-thunder leaps and thuds along
   the ridge;
The spouting shells dig pits in fields
   of death,
And wounded men, are moaning in
   the woods.
If any friend be there whom I have
   loved, speed
God (send) him safe to England with
   a gash.

***

Does it Matter?

Does it matter?—losing your
   legs? . . .
For people will always be kind,
And you need not show that you
   mind
When the others come in after
   hunting
To gobble their muffins and eggs.

Does it matter?—losing your
   sight? . . .
There's such splendid work for the
   blind;

And people will always be kind,
As you sit on the terrace
   remembering
And turning your face to the light.

Do they matter?—those dreams
   from the pit? . . .
You can drink and forget and be
   glad,
And people won't say that you're
   mad;
For they'll know you've fought for
   your country
And no one will worry a bit.

SOURCE: Siegfried Sassoon, "The rank stench of those bodies haunts me still" and "Does it Matter?" in *The Penguin Book of First World War Poetry*, 2nd ed., ed. Jon Silkin (London: Penguin Books, 1979), pp. 124–125, 131–132.

Analyze the Document

1. Which images most vividly convey the war experience?

2. How does Sassoon describe the lives of maimed soldiers who return to society?

3. What do you think Sassoon means by "Does it Matter?"

Mustafa Kemal's national army drove out the occupying troops, toppled the sultan's regime, and established the Republic of Turkey—an act affirmed by the Allies in the Treaty of Lausanne (1923).

In areas of North Africa and the Middle East, Arabs were outraged by decisions of the Allied powers. Arab nationalists had been promised independence by the British and French during the war. Now mandates from the League of Nations authorized the French to exercise administrative control over Lebanon and Syria, and the British over Mesopotamia and Palestine (see **Map 22.6**). According to the League of Nations, these peoples were "not yet able to stand by themselves" and their "tutelage . . . should be entrusted to the advanced nations." Making matters worse, Britain had promised Jewish nationalists a homeland in Palestine.

China refused to sign because the Treaty of Versailles gave the Japanese rights in the Chinese mainland, and Japan left offended because the conference refused to declare formally the equality of all races.

Russia, which had suffered huge losses, had not even been invited to the conference, and the U.S. government failed to ratify the treaty.

John Maynard Keynes (1883–1946), an influential British economist who attended the talks, perhaps best summed up the flaws in the Paris agreement in his book *The Economic Consequences of the Peace* (1919) (see Document 22.3). "[T]he treaty," Keynes warned, "includes no provisions for the economic rehabilitation of Europe—nothing to make the defeated Central Empires into good neighbors, nothing to stabilize the new States of Europe, nothing to reclaim Russia. . . ."

World War I had unleashed passions and destruction of such magnitudes that possibly no settlement could have sufficed. Nowhere in the West did those passions rage stronger than in Russia, defeated by Germany in 1917 and still reeling from internal upheavals. There, revolution and civil war were forging a new union that would alter world affairs for the rest of the twentieth century.

MAP 22.5

Europe, 1923

This map shows Europe after the settlement that ended World War I.

Explore the Map

1. Notice the territorial losses suffered by the German, Russian, Ottoman, and Austro-Hungarian empires. Do these losses support the argument that the Versailles settlement was a harsh one?

2. What areas might suffer from instability stemming from these new territorial arrangements?

3. What strategic problems faced the new eastern European states that hoped for support from France and Great Britain?

REVOLUTIONS IN RUSSIA

In 1914, the Russian tsar Nicholas II and his advisors hoped that a short, painless war in the Balkans would overcome domestic divisions within Russia, strengthen the tsar's regime, and improve Russia's international stature. Instead, the "short, painless" fight turned into a massive conflagration that only compounded Russia's internal discord and revealed how far Russia had fallen behind other powers to the west. In addition, the greatest fears of the tsar, his government, and the aristocracy whose interests he

MAP 22.6

The Middle East, 1923

This map shows the Middle East in the years just after World War I.

Explore the Map

1. Notice what has happened to lands once ruled by the Ottoman Empire. How might Arab nationalists have reacted to these changes?

2. Consider the location of this region and its natural resources. Why might politics in this area of the world be so important?

thinking about
DOCUMENTS

DOCUMENT 22.3

Keynes Warns of the Economic Consequences of the Peace

The various parties involved in the peace treaty talks after World War I came to agreements only after painful, protracted negotiations. Much of the debate centered on how to deal with Germany. In the following excerpt from his influential book The Economic Consequences of the Peace *(1919), economist John Maynard Keynes—an advisor to British prime minister Lloyd George at the Versailles Conference—assesses the different attitudes toward the peace terms.*

By fixing the Reparation payments well within Germany's capacity to pay, we make possible the renewal of hope and enterprise within her territory, we avoid the perpetual friction and opportunity of improper pressure arising out of Treaty clauses which are impossible of fulfilment, and we render unnecessary the intolerable powers of the Reparation Commission.

***

It would be objected, I suppose, by some critics that such an arrangement might go some way in effect towards realizing the former German dream of Mittel-Europa.

***

If we take the view that for at least a generation to come Germany cannot be trusted with even a modicum of prosperity, that while all our recent Allies are angels of light, all our recent enemies, Germans, Austrian, Hungarians, and the rest, are children of the devil, that year by year Germany must be kept impoverished and her children starved and crippled, and that she must be ringed round by enemies; then we shall reject all the proposals of this chapter, and particularly those which may assist Germany to regain a part of her former material prosperity and find a means of livelihood for the industrial population of her towns. But if this view of nations and of their relation to one another is adopted by the democracies of Western Europe, and is financed by the United States, heaven help us all.

***

I pass to a second financial proposal. The requirements of Europe are *immediate*. The prospect of being relieved of oppressive interest payments to England and America over the whole life of the next two generations (and of receiving from Germany some assistance year by year to the costs of restoration) would free the future from excessive anxiety. But it would not meet the ills of the immediate present—the excess of Europe's imports over her exports, the adverse exchange, and the disorder of the currency. It will be very difficult for European production to get started again without a temporary measure of external assistance. I am therefore a supporter of an international loan in some shape or form, such as has been advocated in many quarters in France, Germany, and England, and also in the United States. In whatever way the ultimate responsibility for repayment is distributed, the burden of finding the immediate resources must inevitably fall in major part upon the United States.

SOURCE: John Maynard Keynes, *The Economic Consequences of the Peace* (Harcourt, Brace, and Howe, 1919).

Analyze the Document

1. What would be the consequences of high reparation payments from Germany, according to Keynes?

2. What role was the United States expected to play in the future?

3. Do you agree with Keynes that Germany should have been helped to "regain a part of her former material prosperity"? Why?

---

represented came true: World War I devastated Russia militarily and brought the centuries-old Romanov dynasty crashing down.

The First Warnings, 1905

Long-simmering discontent made Russia ripe for violent upheaval. This discontent had its roots in the Russian government's historical resistance to change. Throughout the nineteenth century, Russia's government had usually tried to ignore rather than adapt to the liberalizing movements that swept most of Europe. The tsar ruled autocratically, relying on the nobility, the church, the army, and the bureaucracy without allowing a hint of political participation to the vast majority of Russian society.

Industrialization, initiated in the 1880s and surging in the 1890s—encouraged by the aggressive policies of Sergei Witte (1849–1915), the finance minister, and an infusion of foreign capital into Russia—stimulated the growth of the middle and working classes in cities such as Moscow and St. Petersburg. These people chafed against Russia's traditional society and archaic government. Frustrated Russian intellectuals turned to revolutionary doctrines and even terrorism in an effort to promote rapid change. Others hoped for more moderate liberal reforms. Still the tsarist government, particularly under Nicholas II (1894–1917), refused to bend.

A turning point came with the embarrassing defeat of the tsar's army and navy by Japan in the 1904–1905 Russo-Japanese War. The various liberal and radical groups took advantage of the government's weakness and clamored for reform. The mounting pressures for change finally exploded early in 1905. On Sunday, January 22, thousands of workers gathered in front of the tsar's palace in St. Petersburg to protest economic hardships. "We have become beggars; we have been oppressed; we are burdened by toil beyond our powers; we are scoffed at; we are not recognized as human beings; we are treated as slaves who must suffer their bitter fate and who must keep silence," complained the petitioners. Marchers sang "God save the tsar," but the tsar's troops fired on them, killing and wounding hundreds of women, men, and children. The violent event, known as Bloody Sunday, was dramatically depicted by the Russian artist N. Vladimirov (**Figure 22.10**). On the right, a line of Tsar Nicholas II's troops shoot at the procession of workers. On the left, the unarmed workers, who sought to present peacefully a petition to the tsar at the Winter Palace in St. Petersburg, fall. Their blood darkens the snow as well as faith in the tsar as a protector of the people. In response, Father Georgi Gapon, a radical Orthodox priest, warned the tsar: "A sea of blood—unexampled—will be shed. Because of thee, because of thy whole family, Russia may perish."

FIGURE 22.10 N. Vladimirov, Bloody Sunday, 1905 On January 22, 1905, Russian soldiers opened fire on thousands of workers protesting economic hardships in front of the tsar's palace in St. Petersburg.

Demands for reform increased, and in October, a general strike paralyzed the country for ten days. In the cities, workers organized themselves into councils, or **soviets.** Sailors mutinied on the battleship *Potemkin*, as did soldiers in the army. At the same time, peasants in the countryside revolted and attacked wealthy landowners. Several officials were assassinated. With much of its army pinned down thousands of miles away in the Russo-Japanese War, the tsar's government wavered. Surrounded by dissension and revolt, Nicholas II yielded at last and issued a manifesto that promised civil liberties, a popularly elected Duma (parliament), and legalization of unions. These concessions had little lasting meaning, however. The return of the Russian troops from the Far East and a fresh round of governmental repression had restored order by 1907. The tsar and his advisors reduced the Duma to a nondemocratically elected body.

The Fall of the Tsar

The few halfhearted reforms were not enough, and discontent persisted in the years after 1905. In the months before the outbreak of World War I, strikes proliferated in Russia's cities. This turmoil probably encouraged the tsar to bring Russia into the war, for he immediately banned strikes and suspended the Duma, whose members still agitated for liberal reforms. As we saw earlier, Russia soon suffered staggering losses at the hands of the German armies. Its leadership, transportation facilities, supplies, and armaments simply could not withstand the demands of total war. Moreover, many non-Russian subjects living within the empire became more interested in establishing their own independent states than supporting the war effort.

In August 1915, a desperate Nicholas made a fatal mistake: He left the capital to take personal command of the army. The severity and depth of this error are revealed by the reaction of Russia's war minister. Reporting on the dire military situation to the council, the minister concluded, "Considering the present situation at the front and in the rear of the armies, one can expect an irreparable catastrophe momentarily." However, he added, "a far more horrible event threatens Russia." His stunned colleagues on the Council of Ministers waited for the grim news. "This morning, His Majesty told me of his decision to personally assume the supreme command of the army." As a result of Nicholas's actions, the Russian people blamed the tsar for their country's military losses. Equally problematic, the inept, unpopular government in the capital now fell under the sway of Nicholas's wife, Alexandra. When the tsarina came under the influence of Grigori Efimovich Rasputin (ca. 1871–1916), a corrupt Siberian mystic who claimed to have the power to heal the tsar's hemophiliac son, things took a more bizarre turn. Even the tsar's aristocratic supporters, a group of whom finally murdered Rasputin late in 1916, demanded fundamental change.

In early March 1917, the dam broke. The strains of war drove hungry workingwomen to initiate strikes and demonstrations. With industrialization, Petrograd (St. Petersburg), Moscow, and other Russian cities had grown rapidly. Women, who made up more than half of the labor force in Petrograd,

> **The March revolution**

The Provisional Government

Most members of the provisional government hoped that Russia would move toward constitutional parliamentary democracy. Led by moderate liberals Pavel Milyukov (1859–1943) and Prince Georgi Lvov (1861–1925), these politicians represented the upper classes. The provisional government enacted into law civil liberties, religious freedom, equality before the law, union rights, and other liberal reforms. They also promised more fundamental social reforms and a constitution.

However, in addition to its inexperience, its rival factions, and the intensifying pressures for change, the provisional government labored under three key burdens. First, it had to share power with the soviets—the political organizations of workers, soldiers, and radical intellectuals—particularly the strong Petrograd soviet. The soviets favored socialist self-rule and stood against the upper classes represented by the provisional government. Second, the government chose to continue Russia's draining involvement in World War I. The links between these first two burdens came to light with the Petrograd soviet's issuance of Order Number 1 on March 14. This significant mandate declared that military officers would be democratically elected by soldiers and that military decisions would be democratically made. Order Number 1 further unraveled authority and discipline within Russia's armed forces. Third, neither the provisional government nor the soviets could control the peasantry, which made up some 80 percent of the population. Peasants refused to wait for the land-redistribution legislation that the government had promised. They seized land and hoarded food for themselves, worsening hunger in the cities as prices rose and supplies became more scarce. The peasantry's defiance also attracted soldiers, who deserted the front to make land claims of their own.

The provisional government failed to satisfy many. The peasants wanted still more land, and workers demanded more bread. Russia could no longer support the unpopular war effort, yet the government could not find a way to withdraw gracefully from it. Again and again the provisional government tried to rally the Russian troops to victory. In desperation, it even created the Women's Battalion of Death in an effort to shame male soldiers into greater effort. More than 80 percent of these women became casualties. The desertions continued.

> **The soviets**

FIGURE 22.11 Demonstrations in Petrograd, 1917 Marches such as this one in March 1917 by Petrograd women led to the revolution that overthrew Russia's tsar and his government.

had to work long hours for low wages and then stand in long bread lines to buy food for their families. Rising prices and shrinking supplies, especially during the winters, translated into hunger and starvation. **Figure 22.11** is a photograph of one of these demonstrations. Here women march down a Petrograd street demanding an increase of rations to soldiers' families.

Women rightly blamed the government for Russia's continuing involvement in the war and for the food shortages. On March 8, in recognition of International Women's Day, they made their voices heard. That day, 10,000 women marched into Petrograd, shouting, "Down with war and high prices! Down with starvation! Bread for workers!" The protesters also demanded an end to the rule of Nicholas II. Thousands of sympathizers, both women and men, joined the demonstrations in the wintry days of March 1917. Yet police and troops were reluctant to fire on the crowds, especially because so many of them were women. Many troops actually joined the demonstrators. The French ambassador to Russia reported watching "a disorderly mob carrying a red flag" marching toward an oncoming regiment of troops. But instead of restoring order, "the army was fraternizing with the revolt." Too many people had lost their respect for the rigid, poorly led autocracy. As Russia's minister of foreign affairs put it, "The Emperor is blind!" Many of his colleagues agreed. On March 12, the Duma organized a provisional government, and three days later Nicholas II abdicated. Railroad workers took him and his family into custody.

In May, the liberal heads of the provisional government resigned and the moderate socialist Alexander Kerensky (1881–1970) became the leading figure in the government. Kerensky, however, faced new political divisions, for by this time many radical intellectuals had returned to Russia from the west, where they had fled from the tsar's repression, or rose from Russia's social ranks. They tried to push ideas and events in one direction or the other. Those who proved most influential came from a group of Marxist revolutionaries, the Social Democrats—in particular their minority faction, the Bolsheviks. This faction was led by Vladimir Ilich Ulyanov (1870–1924), known by his revolutionary name, Lenin.

Kerensky leads

The Rise of the Bolsheviks

Marxism had become influential among some Russian intellectuals, revolutionaries, and groups critical of Russia's tsarist autocracy toward the end of the nineteenth century. In 1898, Russian Marxists had formed the Social Democratic Party, whose principal leaders were Georgi Plekhanov (1857–1918) and his disciple Lenin. Repression by the tsar's government forced the Social Democrats into exile. At a London conference in 1903, the radical Bolshevik wing under Lenin split from the more moderate Mensheviks.

Until 1917, Lenin's **Bolsheviks** remained only a minor party within Russia. Its leaders were hunted down by the state police and shot, imprisoned, or exiled. For seventeen years, Lenin remained in exile in Switzerland, keeping his party alive from a distance and plotting the eventual overthrow of the tsar's government. During that time, he developed theoretical and tactical principles that the Bolsheviks would later use. Three of these principles set forth the most crucial guidelines and, for the most part, set Lenin's Bolsheviks apart from other Marxist organizations. First, the party should be an elite, highly trained, and constantly purged (cleaned of disloyal ideas and people) group of dedicated Marxist revolutionaries capable of instructing and leading the masses. This elite would not be seduced by short-term gains. Second, contrary to what Marx had argued, the socialist revolution need not include only the industrial working class. In Russia, it could be a dual revolution of workers and poor, land-hungry peasants—all part of an even broader socialist revolution that would sweep through other European countries. Third, the party should firmly oppose participation in the war, which Lenin considered a product of imperialist rivalries and a continuing civil war among capitalists.

Lenin's principles

In April 1917, the German government secretly transported Lenin from his place of exile in Switzerland to a Baltic port, from which he made his way to Russia, in an effort to worsen the chaos in Russia and remove Russia from the war. The Germans had good reason to consider Lenin a threat to stability in Russia. John Reed, a sympathetic American journalist and observer, described Lenin as "a strange popular leader—a leader purely by virtue of intellect; colorless, humorless, uncompromising and detached; without picturesque idiosyncrasies—but with the power of explaining profound ideas in simple terms, of analyzing a concrete situation." Back in Russia, Lenin refused to cooperate with the provisional government. Instead, he unleashed a barrage of compelling slogans, such as "Peace to the Army," "Land to the Peasants," "Ownership of the Factories to the Workers," and "All Power to the Soviets." He argued that the time was ripe for a socialist revolution against capitalism. To achieve this revolution, he urged his followers to gain control over the soviets, particularly the powerful Petrograd soviet.

When Kerensky failed to extract Russia from the war, Bolshevik influence grew, especially among the Petrograd workers and soldiers. In July 1917, a massive popular demonstration against the provisional government erupted in that city. Most members of the Bolshevik Party supported the demonstration, though in the end the leadership did not. In these bloody July Days, the provisional government put down the demonstrators with force. The Kerensky government arrested many Bolsheviks and impelled others, including Lenin, to flee to Finland.

Russia's July Days

Yet Kerensky soon suffered a fresh round of failures in the war as well as the threat of an impending coup d'état by General Lavr Kornilov (1870–1918). To avert disaster, in September the desperate Kerensky released the Bolsheviks and relied on the soviets to defend the capital against Kornilov. Kornilov's plans failed when most of his soldiers refused to follow his orders to attack Petrograd.

By October, many leading figures from larger socialist parties had become discredited through their association with the provisional government. This turn of events helped the Bolsheviks, under the leadership of Lenin and the brilliant Leon Trotsky (1879–1940),

THE RUSSIAN REVOLUTION

1904–1905	Russo-Japanese War
1905	General strike and revolution
1917	March revolution
	November revolution
1918	Treaty of Brest-Litovsk
1918–1920	Civil war

KEY DATES

finally gain control over the Petrograd and Moscow soviets. Bolshevik women created a network to call for demonstrations, organize women in factories, and do paramilitary work. Lenin judged the time right for his next move.

On November 6, he and Trotsky launched a well-organized seizure of power. His Red Guards (workers' militia units) took over crucial control centers and arranged for the transfer of power to the soviets and Lenin. Within just hours, the deed was complete. Kerensky, unable to reorganize his forces, fled. Although some of the fighting was violent, the success of the Bolshevik revolution stemmed mostly from the revolutionaries' organizational talents, a lack of effective resistance by the provisional government, and Trotsky's success in portraying the uprising as *defense* of the soviets rather than a Bolshevik *offensive*.

The November revolution

On November 7, the Bolshevik majority enthusiastically elected Lenin the head of the new government. The revolution won the endorsement of soviets throughout Russia. **Figure 22.12,** a painting by the Russian artist Vladimir Serov, shows Lenin, with Stalin standing behind him, proclaiming to the revolutionary forces the Bolsheviks' assumption of power in 1917. In this idealized re-creation of events, the artist has elevated Stalin to a prominent position just behind Lenin. The artist also portrays Lenin as a powerful orator towering above all others. The serious, impassioned crowd below, made up of women, sailors, soldiers, and workers, listens intently. The red flag of communism is held aloft in victory.

Communism and Civil War

The Bolsheviks, who now called themselves Communists, immediately moved to fulfill their promises and consolidate their power. In place of the old tsarist hierarchy, they set up a pyramid of people's soviets, or councils. These councils were elected by universal suffrage but were actually dominated by relatively few Communist Party members. When national elections failed to return a Communist majority to the Constituent Assembly, Lenin had armed sailors disperse that elected body. Capitalism was abolished outright. A barter system of exchange replaced money, the value of the ruble having been destroyed by inflation and devaluation. Committees of workers responsible to party commissars took over management of industry and commerce. The government nationalized the land and turned over its management to local peasant committees, who then distributed it to individual peasants to be worked by their own labor. All crop surpluses were to be given to the state. Finally, the state expropriated church lands and enacted laws to establish the legal equality of the sexes—the first Western government to do so.

To buy time and free the new regime for the enormous task of refashioning Russian society, Lenin immediately opened peace negotiations with Germany. The Germans, realizing Russia's helplessness, demanded the harshest of terms. Lenin attempted to stall them, but in March 1918, when the Germans threatened to attack Petrograd and Moscow, he signed the Treaty of Brest-Litovsk. Russia lost Finland, Estonia, Latvia, Lithuania, the Ukraine, Bessarabia, the Polish provinces, and some of the Trans-Caucasian territory. Lenin had paid a high price for peace. These lands contained one-third of Russia's European population, three-fourths of its iron, and nine-tenths of its coal. In addition, Germany compelled Russia to pay a heavy indemnity. Lenin gambled that a socialist revolution in Germany would reverse some of these losses and provide the support that the fledgling socialist system desperately needed to survive in Russia.

Nevertheless, these hard peace terms were not the worst of Lenin's woes. A bitter civil war broke out in Russia following the peace with Germany

FIGURE 22.12 Lenin Proclaiming Soviet Power This propagandistic painting by Vladimir Serov shows Lenin, backed by Stalin, announcing the Bolshevik victory in 1917.

thinking about

GEOGRAPHY

MAP 22.7

Civil War in Russia, 1919

This map shows Russia during the civil war.

Explore the Map

1. What different forces threatened the area controlled by the Bolsheviks?

2. Why might the Bolsheviks have emerged from this period with a sense of isolation from the West?

3. What strategy might have helped the forces opposing the Bolsheviks?

(see **Map 22.7**). The Russian aristocracy, including most of the higher army officers, launched a series of uncoordinated attacks against the Bolshevik regime. These "White" forces were aided by various other groups disaffected by the revolution. They also had the support of French, British, Greek, Polish, Japanese, Czech, and U.S. troops that were in Russia for various reasons, but in great part to oppose the anticapitalist Bolshevik government. For decades afterward, the Communists would remember how the outside world had turned against them during this vulnerable time.

Creating an emergency policy of "war communism," the Bolshevik government mobilized Russia's economy and society for the civil-war effort. Urban workers and troops swept through the countryside and confiscated grain from the peasantry to feed the cities and the army. The Bolsheviks sharply suppressed any internal opposition. A secret police force—the Cheka—unleashed the Red Terror to hunt down "class enemies" and ensure internal conformity to the Bolshevik regime. To avoid the possibility of White forces freeing the imprisoned Nicholas II and his family, the Bolshevik government ordered them executed. However, the Red armies faced numerous obstacles in their all-out effort to defeat the Whites. When peasants realized

that the government intended to seize their surpluses, for example, they resisted or refused to raise more crops than they needed for themselves. Moreover, the government had to contend with violent ethnic hatreds that further divided the country. Only with the greatest difficulty did the Red armies, well organized by Trotsky, finally defeat the Whites. In doing so, the Bolsheviks regained the Ukraine.

By 1920, World War I and the Russian civil war had ended. In addition to the two million Russian soldiers who died in the world war, some four to six million had lost their lives in the civil conflict. The once-powerful nation lay defeated, impoverished, and exhausted. Starvation hung like a specter over millions. The fighting was over, but Russia and other Western nations now faced the challenge of rebuilding social stability in an environment of continuing political and economic turmoil.

LOOKING BACK & MOVING FORWARD

Summary British historian Arnold Toynbee said that in the years before 1914, his generation expected that "life throughout the World would become more rational, more humane, and more democratic . . . that the progress of science and technology would make mankind richer . . . that all this would happen peacefully." World War I shattered that vision. The very technology and industrial prowess that had fueled the West's growth and sense of progress were turned to unimagined destruction. The war ended dreams of heroic battles and courageous military deeds: "Words such as glory, honor, courage, or hallow [became] obscene" in the face of how the war was fought and the carnage that resulted, wrote the American author and veteran Ernest Hemingway. Indeed, many survivors of World War I were haunted for the rest of their lives with a sense of belonging to a "lost generation."

Along with millions of human lives, the war destroyed or weakened European empires. The German, Austro-Hungarian, and Ottoman empires collapsed. Military losses and revolution ended the Russian empire, replacing it with the Soviet Union and Communist rulers who were transforming that society and would alter the political landscape throughout the world in the next decades. In the Far East, the Japanese gained lands and stature by expanding their empire at the expense of German colonies and China. In the Middle East, Africa, and Asia, the war and vague Allied declarations in support of national liberation stimulated struggles for national rights and independence. Even in the West, faith in imperialist ideals waned during and after the war. As one Indian diplomat explained, "there was no conviction left of the Europeans' superiority or sense of vision." From the outside looking in, Europe now seemed shrunken, vulnerable, and subject to unreasonable passions.

The calamities of those years were not limited to the war itself. In Turkey, the nationalistic government responded to Armenian demands for independence by deporting some 2 million Armenians from eastern Turkey. Probably one-third of these were massacred in what amounted to modern mass genocide; another third may have died during the forced march to Syria. In 1918, an influenza epidemic hit, killing some 50–100 million people worldwide. In central and eastern Europe, postwar starvation threatened millions despite relief efforts by the United States and the International Red Cross. The peace treaties "to make the world safe" and "to end all wars" left a legacy of disappointment and resentment. In the next two decades, these sentiments would draw Europe and the world once again into a maelstrom of violence.

KEY TERMS

Central Powers, *p. 695*
Allies, *p. 696*
Schlieffen Plan, *p. 696*
trench warfare, *p. 698*
total war, *p. 702*
war guilt clause, *p. 708*
League of Nations, *p. 708*
soviets, *p. 713*
Bolsheviks, *p. 715*

REVIEW, ANALYZE, & CONNECT TO TODAY

REVIEW THE PREVIOUS CHAPTERS

Chapter 20—"Mass Politics and Imperial Domination"—analyzed nationalism, the spreading demands for political inclusion, and imperialism during the second half of the nineteenth century. Chapter 21—"Modern Life and the Culture of Progress"—examined new industrial transformations and urban life during this same period.

1. In what ways did nationalism, industrialism, and imperialism create the forces underlying World War I?

2. After the experience of World War I, why might people have looked back on the decades preceding the war so longingly?

ANALYZE THIS CHAPTER

Chapter 22—"Descending into the Twentieth Century"—tells the story of World War I and the Russian Revolution.

1. How might it be argued that several nations should bear responsibility for plunging the West into World War I? Which countries, if any, do you think were most responsible?

2. Why was this war so devastating, physically and psychologically?

3. Analyze the role of the home fronts. How did problems at the home fronts relate to problems on the battlefronts?

4. It is perhaps easier to understand why there was a revolution in Russia that toppled the tsar than why the Bolsheviks came to power several months later in a second revolution. How do you explain this?

CONNECT TO TODAY

Think about the themes of war and revolution that are discussed in this chapter.

1. What insights from studying World War I might we use to analyze the potential causes of wars and to anticipate how a war, once started, unfolds?

2. Is one lesson from this chapter that any major war in modern times may result in a revolution that itself has unanticipated consequences? Explain.

BEYOND THE CLASSROOM

ON THE PATH TO TOTAL WAR

Ferguson, Niall. *The Pity of War: Explaining World War I.* New York: Basic Books, 1999. A thoughtful reassessment of the causes, course, and results of World War I.

Stevenson, David. *Cataclysm: The First World War as Political Tragedy.* New York: Basic Books, 2004. An excellent and comprehensive one-volume study of the war.

Strachan, Hew. *The First World War.* Oxford: Oxford University Press, 2003. A fine, very well written, up-to-date survey.

THE FRONT LINES

Ellis, John. *Eye-Deep in Hell: Trench Warfare in World War I.* New York: Pantheon Books, 1989. An examination of the daily experiences of the trench soldier.

Keegan, John. *The First World War.* New York: Knopf, 1999. A highly respected military historian examines the realities of warfare, stressing experiences on the western front.

WAR ON THE HOME FRONT

Brayborn, Gail, and Penny Summerfield. *Out of the Cage: Women's Experiences in Two World Wars.* London: Pandora Press, 1987. Analyzes women's experiences in the two world wars and finds that the wars were economically and socially liberating for women.

Coetzee, Frans, and Marilyn Shevin-Coetzee, eds. *Authority, Identity and the Social History of the Great War.* Providence, RI: Berghahn Books, 1995. A comparative study of the experience and significance of the war in people's lives, especially for those on the home fronts.

Williams, John. *The Homefronts: Britain, France and Germany, 1914–1918.* London: Constable, 1972. Studies the effect of the ongoing struggle on the British, French, and German populations.

TO THE BITTER END

Becker, Jean-Jacques. *The Great War and the French People.* New York: St. Martin's Press, 1986. An examination of the impact of the war on the French.

Schmitt, Bernadotte E., and Harold C. Vedeler. *The World in a Crucible, 1914–1918.* New York: Harper & Row, 1984. Analyzes World War I as a total war and traces its economic, social, cultural, and diplomatic consequences.

ASSESSING THE LOSSES

Fussell, Paul. *The Great War and Modern Memory.* Oxford: Oxford University Press, 1975. A fascinating study of the British experience on the western front from 1914 to 1918 and the literary means by which it has been remembered.

Winter, J.M. *The Experience of World War I.* New York: Oxford University Press, 1988. A well-written examination of how the war was experienced by the peoples of the belligerent nations.

THE PEACE SETTLEMENT

MacMillan, Margaret. *Six Months That Changed the World.* New York: Random House, 2002. A new, very comprehensive account of the talks and the settlement.

Sharp, Alan. *The Versailles Settlement: Peacemaking in Paris, 1919.* New York: St. Martin's Press, 1991. A balanced overview that stresses the difficulties facing participants at the conference.

REVOLUTIONS IN RUSSIA

Fitzpatrick, Sheila. *The Russian Revolution, 1917–1932,* 2nd ed. Oxford: Oxford University Press, 1994. A brief and insightful treatment of this complex subject.

Lincoln, W. Bruce. *Red Victory: A History of the Russian Civil War.* New York: Simon & Schuster, 1989. Examines the Bolshevik triumph over internal conflicts.

Pipes, Richard. *The Russian Revolution.* New York: Vintage Books, 1991. Argues that the Bolshevik revolution was an authoritarian coup d'état.

GEORGE GROSZ, *THE PILLARS OF SOCIETY*, 1926

In *The Pillars of Society*, German expressionist artist George Grosz (1893–1959) sarcastically and ominously depicted the leaders of Germany during the 1920s. The swastika on his tie, the sword in one hand and beer mug in the other, and the dreams of combat pouring out of his head identify the "old-guard" man in front as a Nazi. Behind him, in suits and ties, stand two other members of the dominant middle class. One, a dull journalist with a chamber pot on his head, holds a blood-stained palm leaf that suggests his hypocritical pacifism. The other, a parliamentarian with a head full of excrement, mindlessly clutches a German national flag. In the background, a corrupted military chaplain offers his blessings while murderous soldiers look on. The soldiers remind viewers of how violence and the catastrophic Great War provided a backdrop to German society in the 1920s.

Darkening Decades

Recovery, Dictators, and Depression, 1920–1939

"The Storm has died away," wrote French poet Paul Valéry in the years just after World War I, "and still we are restless, uneasy, as if the storm were about to break . . . we do not know what will be born, and we fear the future. . . ." Many in Europe shared Valéry's sense of "terrible uncertainty." The Great War was finally over, and people longed for the return of normal life. In 1919, almost any memory of the days before the war seemed rosy. Too much had changed, though; the pre–World War I era was gone forever.

In fact, the immediate postwar years would bring frustration and turmoil. In the victorious democracies, growing disillusionment and political bickering rather than dynamic action seemed the rule. Moreover, some of these nations faced dramatically rising resistance to foreign rule in their overseas holdings as colonial people, led by nationalistic intellectuals who combined Western ideas with their own cultural traditions, agitated for independence. Millions of people living in communist Russia still struggled just to survive, let alone transform that troubled nation. Elsewhere in the West, union, socialist, and communist movements alarmed those who feared change. As suggested by the painting on the facing page, many Europeans, especially in Italy, Germany, and east-central Europe, turned to right-wing leaders who attacked parliamentary government and raised the compelling banner of militant nationalism. Ahead, still unseen by most, lay the very dangers that people thought were over when the Great War ended.

TIMELINE

Fascism in Italy

Nazism in Germany

NEP in Soviet Union

Collectivization and Five-Year Plans in USSR

The Russian Revolution and Civil War

The Locarno Era

World War II

World War I

The Great Depression

1915 1918 1921 1924 1927 1930 1933 1936 1939 1942 1945

TRYING TO RECOVER FROM THE GREAT WAR,
1919–1929

In a haunting preview of troubles lurking over the era, Erich Maria Remarque, a German author and war veteran, described his life in Berlin during the early 1920s. "Prices have been soaring everywhere" and "poverty is greater than it was during the war." One afternoon he heard that demonstrations had been called for. In the streets, ominous rumors circulated that "troops have been concentrated at the barracks." Groups of strikers began marching through the streets. A disturbance broke out, people were yelling, and on corners speakers harangued small crowds. "Then suddenly everywhere is silence." A procession of maimed and wounded war veterans in the "faded uniforms of the front-line trenches" moved slowly toward him. Men with one arm carried white placards: "Where is the Fatherland's gratitude? The War Cripples are starving."

For Remarque and millions of others living in the post–World War I West, reality soon undermined the sense of liberation that the end of the war had brought. Families tried to care for their wounded sons, fathers, and brothers, and to endure the loss of those who had perished in battle. Many veterans came home angry. They had been promised moral purification during the war and compensation for their service after. Now they sensed that, in some ways, civilians did not fully appreciate their sacrifices. Too often, their old jobs had disappeared. For some, their wives or lovers had deserted them or developed a new, disturbing sense of independence. Many veterans, returning to homelands whose economies lay in ruins, struggled just to get enough food.

Indeed, economic uncertainty had settled like a pall over most of Europe. In the decades after the war, nations struggled to retool their economies from wartime needs back to ordinary requirements and to reestablish international trade. Enormous sums in veterans' pay, war-widow benefits, and unemployment insurance burdened government treasuries. In vain, the victors had hoped that high reparation payments from Germany would be enough to help them rebuild their economies or at least cover debts from the war. So, governments borrowed when they could and printed money that had no basis in actual wealth. The resulting inflation hurt the middle classes in particular. They watched in panic as rising prices drained away their life savings. Between 1914 and 1928, France's currency alone lost four-fifths of its value. Still more unlucky were the thousands of western European investors, especially in France, who had invested in Russian bonds and saw them turn worthless when the Bolsheviks came to power.

Economic uncertainty

Across Europe, recessions followed short periods of relative prosperity all too quickly. Unemployment persisted—in Britain, it remained above 10 percent in both good times and bad. Governments and employers pressured women to give up their wartime jobs or accept lower-paying positions so as to make way for men. Inflation and unemployment spun Germany's economy out of control. Among the Western powers, only the United States emerged from the war richer than ever. In Asia, Japan also emerged from the war stronger and richer—a new competitor looking to expand in East Asia and gain recognition as a great power. Europeans now looked to their governments for relief and leadership.

The Victors Just Hold On

Solutions to Europe's economic problems depended greatly on the politics of the postwar era. However, within the democracies, no one seemed to step forward with innovative ideas for change. Some people hoped that the addition of women to the voting roles in these countries (with the notable exception of France, Italy, and Sweden) would improve politics. In fact, however, women's suffrage seemed to change politics little, if at all. Most women voted as men did, and relatively few women gained political office.

International relations showed the same lack of innovation as domestic politics. Although the dominant military power on the Continent, France still feared a resentful Germany and defensively held on to what it had salvaged in the Versailles treaty following the war. The nation fiercely resisted

Defensive France any efforts by colonized people to move toward independence in its overseas holdings. Various conservative parties generally held power and domestic policies changed little from the prewar period. The conservatives concentrated on rebuilding France and trumpeting anti-German nationalism.

Great Britain might have worked with its ally France to find solutions to postwar problems, but each nation usually acted alone or in opposition to the other. Various political parties—Conservatives, Laborites, and Liberals—alternated in

Britain and its empire power in Britain. Sometimes they formed coalitions with each other, but none came forth with fresh solutions to the economic and diplomatic problems plaguing the British. Instead, Britain pulled away from extensive involvement in European affairs and tried to solve the Irish problem and to hold on to its restless colonies in Asia and Africa.

In the decades before World War I, British governments had attempted in vain to enact home rule for Ireland to quell growing demands for Irish independence. Leaders such as Constance Markievicz (1868–1926), a founder of republican and women's organizations, called on the Irish to "fix your mind on the ideal of Ireland free, with her women enjoying the full rights of citizenship in their own nation," warning that "our national freedom cannot, and must not, be left to evolution." In 1914, Parliament had finally passed the Irish Home Rule Bill, but it postponed the bill's implementation until after the war. In 1916, impatient Irish nationalists in Dublin rose up against the British but were crushed (see page 703). Executed leaders quickly became national martyrs, and the extremist organization Sinn Fein (Ourselves Alone) gained leadership in the nationalist cause. Its military wing became the Irish Republican Army. When the Sinn Fein Party declared Irish independence in 1919, fighting broke out between the IRA and the British army. With the British cast in the role of oppressors, the bloodshed persisted for two years. In December 1921, a treaty created the Irish Free State, although the six predominantly Protestant counties of Ulster (Northern Ireland) remained tied to Great Britain. Even then, a civil war broke out between protreaty and antitreaty forces. This legacy of violence would haunt the British and Irish again and again.

The British also faced nationalist problems elsewhere in the world. In West Africa, nationalistic leaders pressured the British to establish representative institutions; the British agreed to new constitutions in Nigeria in 1923 and the Gold Coast in 1925. In North Africa, opposition to foreign rule forced the British to grant independence to Egypt in 1923. In the Middle East, Britain faced uprisings in Iraq and conflicts in Palestine, where Zionist immigrants bumped up against native Arabs. In Asia, nationalist parties developed into powerful political forces. Perhaps the strongest movement for national liberation emerged in India. Many Indians, hoping they would be rewarded with self-government, had fought for Britain in World War I, and the Indian economy had grown with India's support of Britain's war effort. Indian leaders, such as Mohandas Gandhi (1869–1948) and Jawaharlal Nehru (1889–1964), who had been Westernized by education and experience while employed by British rulers, led the drive for independence. Gandhi used the tactic of civil disobedience—publicly and nonviolently breaking the law—to promote widespread sympathy for his cause. Even Britain's leaders, reacting to these pressures, began talking about granting self-rule to India.

The United States, for its part, could have taken a leadership role in international affairs. However, it refused to ratify the Versailles treaty, join the League of Nations, or involve itself extensively in tensions overseas. Europe's troubles came to center more and **The U.S. turns inward** more on events in Germany, an unstable nation that would soon become enmeshed in a round of political and international turmoil.

Continuing Crises in Germany

Germany emerged from World War I defeated and angry. However, it had the potential to regain its strength quickly. More populous than France, Germany still had an intact industrial infrastructure. It also occupied an advantageous position in the postwar rearrangement of the European map. On its eastern borders lay weak nations newly created at the end of World War I. Farther east, Russia was isolated and preoccupied with shoring up its struggling new communist society.

Soon after the war, the Germans set up the **Weimar Republic** (named after the city where its constitution was drawn up) as a model liberal democracy. Moderate Social Democrats led the republic, but they had **The Weimar Republic** inherited the taint of defeat from the outcome of the war. Moreover, many officials in the bureaucracy, judiciary, and army were the same people who had occupied these positions before 1918. They were not particularly dedicated to the new republic. Nationalists and right-wing parties looked on the new parliamentary system with contempt.

Challengers within Germany arose almost as soon as the Social Democrats came to power. From the Left, Rosa Luxemburg (1870–1919) and Karl Liebknecht (1871–1919) led an uprising of radical

Marxists (Spartacists). The government responded with repression, using the Free Corps—right-wing paramilitary groups made up mostly of veterans—to murder the two leaders and put down the communist threat. Nevertheless, communists continued to stir discord for several more years. In 1920, the German government faced a new threat, this time from right-wing nationalists under Wolfgang Kapp (1858–1922). A general strike by workers in support of the government paralyzed the economy and ended Kapp's effort to take over Berlin.

Then economic and international crises added to Weimar's political woes. In January 1923, after the German government defaulted on the huge war reparations bill, French and Belgian troops responded by occupying the Ruhr Valley, Germany's richest industrial area. The Germans struck back with passive resistance—opposing the occupiers in every way but with violence. Enraged, the French tried to create a secession movement from Germany in the Rhineland. Although the occupying forces failed to collect any reparations, the occupation paralyzed Germany's economy, and wild inflation swept the country. At the crest of the inflation wave, four trillion German marks were worth only one dollar. People literally took wheelbarrows full of money to go shopping. **Figure 23.1** reveals the extent of the inflation. Here children, apparently unaware of the economic turmoil throughout Germany, play with stacks of their nation's nearly worthless paper money. Within days, the inflation wiped out countless Germans' life savings. With a frightening hint of future events,

Wild inflation

FIGURE 23.1 German Inflation, 1923 In November 1923, these German children play with stacks of paper money made nearly worthless by ruinous inflation.

Document 23.1 reveals some of the fears and political turmoil engendered by this uncertainty.

Conciliation and a Glimpse of Prosperity

Germany's international and economic picture looked bleak in 1923. But near the end of that year, a series of events unfolded that held out hope for international cooperation and a return to prosperity, not only for Germany but also for other nations in the West. In August, Gustav Stresemann (1878–1929) rose to leadership in the German government and offered to reconcile the country's differences with France. Having lost more money and international standing than it had gained from its occupation of the Ruhr, France reversed its policy and agreed to cooperate with Stresemann. An international commission headed by Charles Dawes (1865–1951) of the United States drew up a plan for the occupying forces' withdrawal from Germany. The commission also arranged for international loans to Germany and set up a system by which Germany would pay lower reparations in installments. In 1925, Germany signed the Treaty of Locarno with France, Great Britain, Italy, and Belgium—an agreement that guaranteed Germany's existing frontiers with France and Belgium. Optimistic headlines in the *New York Times* declared, "France and Germany Ban War Forever." In 1926, the League of Nations admitted Germany and elected Stresemann its president. With inter-national relations apparently normalized, France retreated, hoping that alliances with smaller eastern European states and the **Maginot Line**—a string of defensive fortresses on the French/German border it began building in the late 1920s—would contain the economically revived Germany.

The Dawes plan

Most of the remaining Western economies also perked up after 1924. In several countries, automobile manufacturing, aviation, synthetics, and electronics took off. Vacuum cleaners, washing machines, refrigerators, and electric irons—now often purchased on installment plans—became the norm in middle-class homes. New production techniques spread, especially among big-business employers who began using the principles and methods of "scientific management" promoted by the American efficiency engineer Frederick W. Taylor (1856–1915). After conducting time and motion studies, Taylor and other industrial psychologists recommended a sharper division of labor and detailed control over every aspect of work in order to boost worker productivity. Taylor especially emphasized the division between thinking by managers and physical labor by workers: "We do not want any initiative [from workers]," he wrote. "All we want of them is to obey the orders we give them, do what we say and

Uneasy prosperity

DOCUMENT 23.1

Postwar Strains in Germany

Postwar dislocations and economic difficulties put enormous strains on European nations, particularly Germany. One of these hardships took the form of explosive inflation that struck Germany in 1923. This 1923 speech by Adolf Hitler—a minor but ambitious political figure at the time—reveals some of the anger and political uncertainty spawned by the inflation.

"Germany is a people of children; a grown-up people would say: 'We don't care a fig for your paper-money. Give us something of value—gold! What have you after all to give us? Nothing? Thus have you defrauded us, you rogues and swindlers!' An awakened people with its last thirty marks—all that is left of the millions of its glory—would buy a rope and with it string up 10,000 of its defrauders!" Even the farmer will no longer sell his produce, "When you offer him your million scraps of paper with which he can cover the walls of his closet on his dung-heap, can you wonder that he says, 'Keep your millions and I will keep my corn and my butter.'" "The individual and the nation are delivered over to the international capital of the banks; despair seizes the whole people. We are on the eve of a second revolution. Some are setting their hopes on the star of the Soviet: that is the symbol of those who began the Revolution, to whom the Revolution has brought untold wealth, who have exploited it until to-day. It is the star of David, the sign of the Synagogue. The symbol of the race high over the world, a lordship which stretches from Vladivostok to the West—the lordship of Jewry. The golden star which for the Jew means the glittering gold."

"And when the people in its horror sees that one can starve though one may have milliards of marks, then it will perforce make up its mind and say: 'We will bow down no longer before an institution which is founded on the delusory majority principle, we want a dictatorship.' Already the Jew has a premonition of things to come: . . . he is saying to himself: If there must be a dictatorship, then it shall be a dictatorship of Cohen or Levi."

SOURCE: Adolf Hitler, *The Speeches of Adolf Hitler*, vol. I, trans. and ed. by Norman Baynes (Oxford: Oxford University Press, 1942), pp. 72–73.

Analyze the Document

1. What explanation does Hitler offer for the painful problems confronting Germans?

2. What solutions does he suggest for those problems?

3. Are there any inconsistencies between this statement from 1923 and Hitler's later actions? Explain.

---

do it quick." These techniques may have made production more efficient, but for laborers, work became more mindless, dull, and repetitive than ever.

Outside of manufacturing, many people found jobs in the fast-growing service and housing sectors. Women in particular took positions as salesclerks, social workers, nurses, telephone operators, manicurists, hairdressers, and processors of convenience foods such as pudding mixes and dried cereals. Housing projects with indoor plumbing, electricity, and central heating sprang up throughout Europe—many of them boasted common-use day-care centers, laundries, and gardens. With all these developments, the West seemed to be back on the path of material progress that characterized the decades before World War I.

At the same time, several industries declined, unable to keep up with the new products, enhanced technology, and stiffer competition. Britain, especially, clung to its old expertise in metals and textiles and failed to invest in the rising new technologies. Its coal industry sank dramatically, sparking massive strikes that in 1926 turned into a general strike by miners and other industrial workers. The economies of nations outside of Europe—particularly in the United States, Canada, Australia, and Japan—benefited at Britain's and Europe's expense.

The Roaring Twenties?

The popular culture of the 1920s reflected these complex political and economic changes of the postwar era. This uneasy, worrisome time has been called the Jazz Age and the Roaring Twenties. Both terms convey the exuberance of the period's popular culture. They also hint at the superficial nature of the gaiety. This glittering culture had an edgy, frenetic quality that suggested a people haunted by a profound insecurity.

In **Figure 23.2,** a depiction of a cabaret scene, the German expressionist painter Otto Dix captures these contradictions of life during the 1920s. Berlin in particular became famous for cabarets such as this. In the painting, a couple dances to the music of a jazz band made up of black and white musicians, probably from America. European interest in American jazz and culture reflected the new international stature of the United States. To the right poses a "flapper," a fashionably thin woman whose dress and hair are cut short. She and the woman behind her smoking a cigarette stand alone, apparently independent. The scene suggests sexual abandon, yet the expressions on most people's faces are stiff, even apathetic. The picture conveys more of a sense of frenzy, decadence,

FIGURE 23.2 Otto Dix, *Grosstadt (Big Town)*, 1927–1928 These scenes from just outside (left) and inside (right) a Berlin cabaret show the contradictions of postwar life as impoverished, crippled veterans on the street look in on revelers frolicking on the dance floor. The painting suggests artificial celebration and underlying misery more than joy.

and artificial celebration than relaxed happiness. The artist's deeper message is especially clear in the left panel of this painting. In this smaller section, a crippled veteran leans on a crutch outside the cabaret and begs for assistance as the revelers pass him by with scarcely a glance in his direction. The canvas echoes a description of Berlin in that era by a leading German journalist, Hans Sahl: "It was a time of great misery, with legless war veterans riding the sidewalks on rolling planks, in a nation that seemed to consist of nothing but beggars, whores, invalids, and fat-necked speculators."

While millions of people read the proliferating practical books, popular fiction, and newspapers, no new forces of popular culture shaped and reflected national attitudes more than the radio and movies. In France, the first radio broadcast station opened in 1920. It transmitted poor-quality sound to a limited audience, but by 1939, the number of radios in France had reached almost five million. The movie industry also flourished, particularly in Germany, Russia, France, and the United States. More than 100 million people saw a film each week.

Filmmaking itself became an art form, a visual record of social attitudes, and an account of people's ambitions and dreams. Films were thoughtfully and cleverly edited to promote drama and show scenes from different perspectives. Increasingly, creating

movies involved specialized roles, such as producer, director, and editor. Marketed actors became envied celebrities, and millions followed the lives and careers of these movie stars. Many filmmakers projected their nations' self-images in stunning, creative ways—perhaps none more so than the legendary Russian Sergei Eisenstein (1898–1948). His epic films about the 1905 and 1917 revolutions in Russia represented the Soviet view of events in those "heroic" years.

Other films revealed deep-seated concerns about modern society. **Figure 23.3,** for example, shows an eerie, futuristic scene from the German director Fritz Lang's (1890–1976) film *Metropolis* (1925). This image emphasizes the overwhelming power of urban architecture and technology and demonstrates cinema's potential to serve as an artistic medium. Here a solitary airplane flies through the stark canyons of buildings in a futuristic city. Humans are dwarfed out of sight in the impersonal world they have created. The image seems to complement visually lines from "The Waste Land" (1922), a work by one of the period's leading poets, T. S. Eliot (1888–1965):

Unreal City,
Under the brown god of a winter dawn,
A crowd flowed over London Bridge, so many . . .
And each man fixed his eyes before his feet.

On another level, this scene also hints at other harbingers of modernity: the advent of skyscrapers,

The radio and movies

already rising in New York City, and the daring flights being made in small planes. Just two years after this film was made, the solo flight across the Atlantic of the American pilot Charles Lindbergh (1902–1974) won acclaim on both sides of the ocean. Americans and Europeans alike saw embodied in Lindbergh and New York the promise of something young, exciting, and dynamic that just might push the West forward into a bright future.

Indeed, throughout the West, cities such as Berlin, Paris, and New York became even more dazzling cultural centers than before. Office buildings and skyscrapers shot up, some of them displaying striking new trends in architecture. The most influential architect was the German Walter Gropius (1883–1969), who in 1919 founded the **Bauhaus** school of art in Germany. This school created new standards for modern architecture and for the design of ordinary objects, from chairs and lamps to dishes. In 1925, Gropius designed the building shown in **Figure 23.4.** Emphasizing clean, functional lines, this international style of architecture symbolized acceptance of the modern, industrial world. These buildings unabashedly displayed their efficient structure, prefabricated materials, and steel and glass features. Many architects would follow this new style over the next half-century in creating office buildings, workers' housing, and private homes.

| The Bauhaus school |

In addition to trends in entertainment and the arts, the phrase "Roaring Twenties" implied new attitudes toward sex. Especially in leading cities, clothing fashions, often popularized in movies, exhibited these changing attitudes. Women's clothing, featuring thinner fabrics, shorter skirts, and tight-fitting styling, became more revealing. Along with fashion, women's hairstyles grew progressively shorter as well. Women discarded confining corsets that had long been in fashion and even donned trousers for sporting activities. Bathing suits, too, became increasingly skimpy. The "flapper," whom we saw in **Figure 23.2,** was now the new symbol of the ideal, free, sexually liberated woman.

| New attitudes toward sex |

The new focus on body image and sexual appeal intensified concerns about hygiene. People began regularly using toothbrushes, deodorants, and cosmetics. In addition, they bathed more often than before and shaved more closely. Tanned, thin women and muscular men became the new standards of health and sexual attractiveness.

As sex became more openly discussed and encouraged, governments also searched for ways to revive declining birthrates and thereby replace the lives lost during the war. In France, for example, the government

FIGURE 23.3 Movies and Modern Life This scene from Fritz Lang's film *Metropolis* (1925) shows a plane flying through the canyons of a modern city. It suggests the power of the cinema to convey images and ideas about modern life.

made distributing birth-control information illegal and abortion punishable by death. The French proclaimed a new holiday, Mother's Day, an innovation that other Western countries soon copied. Many governments provided maternity benefits, and increasingly, births took place in hospitals under the control of specialized nurses and doctors. Separate rooms for testing, labor, delivery, and recovery made the process of giving birth almost factory-like. Doctors, nurses, and social workers told women the "best" way to care for their children, and child-rearing courses for girls became compulsory in some countries.

The Anxious Twenties

Of all the forms of culture that gained currency during these years, high culture most powerfully reflected the stressful undercurrents of the postwar period. Many writers, intellectuals, and artists emphasized the uncertainty of the era and explored the widespread feelings of insecurity that people harbored.

Several philosophers, reacting to the horrors of the Great War, attacked nineteenth-century optimism and rationalism. These thinkers expanded on the ideas set forth earlier by Friedrich Nietzsche in Germany and Henri Bergson in France (see page 684). The most widely read of the post–World War I philosophers was a German, Oswald Spengler (1880–1936). In his book *The Decline of the*

| Sense of decay and crisis |

FIGURE 23.4 The Bauhaus Building Designed in 1925, this building represented the new international style in architecture and symbolized acceptance of the modern industrial world.

West (1918), Spengler argued that all civilizations were like biological organisms, each with its own life cycle. Western civilization, he claimed, had passed its high point, and World War I signaled the beginning of its end. This sense of decay and crisis emerged in many other works, most notably in the Spanish writer José Ortega y Gasset's (1883–1955) *Revolt of the Masses* (1930). Gasset lamented the decline of liberal elites and the "accession of the masses to complete social power." The masses, he warned, were not equipped to lead, yet they now took control from qualified elites and demanded a dangerous conformity: "Anybody who is not like everybody, who does not think like everybody, runs the risk of being eliminated."

Sigmund Freud's ideas (see Chapter 21) about the irrational, unconscious, and instinctual aspects of human thought and behavior—which had first emerged just before World War I—gained more acceptance during the 1920s. The unconscious and irrational played particularly prominent roles in the most acclaimed literature of the postwar era. The Irish writer James Joyce (1882–1941), German author Franz Kafka (1883–1924), and French writer Marcel Proust (1871–1922) created disquieting, introspective works of literature that elevated personal psychological experience over reason. In *Ulysses* (1922), Joyce in particular mastered the stream of consciousness technique, which displayed to the reader the rambling thoughts, free associations, and erotic fantasies going on in the mind of a character. At first critics and the public dismissed the novel as "morbid," "nonsense," and "foul." Eventually, however, this book about a single day in the lives of a group of Dubliners, which also served as a commentary on the human condition, was hailed as one of the century's greatest works of literature. In her novel *Mrs. Dalloway* (1925), British author Virginia Woolf used similar techniques to describe one day in the inner life of a woman, including fragmented conversations, partial remembrances, and fantasies (see Biography).

Novels and memoirs of the Great War also proliferated during these years. As in *All Quiet on the Western Front* by the German author Erich Maria Remarque, these works emphasized themes of brutality and suffering, disillusionment with civilian life, and a sense that the war had spawned a generation of lost souls. At the same time, Remarque's and others' books revealed a longing for the sense of purpose and comradeship that so often arises during a war effort but subsides in times of peace.

Similar themes marked artistic styles of the day. The **Dada** movement stressed the absence of purpose in life. Surrealist painters explored dreams and the world of the subconscious. Other painters, such as Käthe Kollwitz (see the Chapter 22 Biography) and Otto Dix (**Figure 23.2**), created moving images of suffering, destruction, and social despair.

In the 1920s, then, Western democratic societies struggled mightily both to come to terms with the consequences of the war and to move on to better days. In the early postwar years, the difficulties seemed overwhelming. Even with the revival of healthier economies and easing of international tensions after 1923, underlying doubt and insecurity persisted and made themselves plain in the period's cultural expression.

TURNING AWAY FROM DEMOCRACY: DICTATORSHIPS AND FASCISM,
1919–1929

The sense of unease and the difficult realities clearly burdened politics in the Western democracies, but things were far worse on the political front elsewhere in Europe. Among the states of east-central and southern Europe, the strain of the postwar years became too much for the fragile democratic systems budding there.

Authoritarianism in East-Central Europe

In 1919, Admiral Miklos Horthy (1868–1957), the reactionary former commander of the Austro-Hungarian navy, led forces, aided by anticommunist Allies and ambitious Romanians, that overthrew the newly formed regime led by the communist Béla Kun (1885–1937) in Hungary. Horthy's rule, like other right-wing authoritarian regimes that followed in Poland (1926) and Yugoslavia (1929), amounted to a dictatorship backed by the nation's military and conservative forces—the bureaucracy, high church, and wealthy elites. Why did these east-central European

BIOGRAPHY

Virginia Woolf
(1882–1941)

In 1938, the British writer Virginia Woolf looked back on her life and described herself as "fundamentally an outsider." By then, however, literary critics and the public alike had accepted this sensitive author's extraordinary works and honored her widely.

Born in 1882, Virginia Stephens was raised and educated within the Victorian literary world by her scholarly, well-connected parents. "Think how I was brought up!" she said, describing her isolated childhood. "No school; mooning about alone among my father's books; never any chance to pick up all that goes on in schools—throwing balls; ragging; slang; vulgarities; scenes; jealousies!" In adolescence, the gifted Virginia suffered from depressions and endured the first of the nervous breakdowns that would haunt her for the rest of her life.

In 1912, she married Leonard Woolf, also a writer and intellectual. They remained close over the years, the patient Leonard taking care of Virginia when she fell ill. The two also founded the Hogarth Press, which would publish works by some of the most important writers of the twentieth century, including T. S. Eliot, Sigmund Freud, and E. M. Forster. Their house in Bloomsbury became a gathering place for an influential group of writers, artists, and intellectuals who came to be known as the Bloomsbury group. Woolf acquired a reputation as a bit of a social snob, admitting that she enjoyed rubbing shoulders with the aristocracy because "the aristocrat is freer, more natural, more eccentric than we are." Within this group of intellectuals and social elites, some of her closest friends and lovers were women.

Woolf began her career as a writer in 1905 and published her first novel in 1915. Over the next twenty-five years, her many novels and essays gained critical and public recognition.

Reflecting the growing interest in psychology and the life of the mind, she focused on England's intellectuals like herself, experimented with stream-of-consciousness narration in her novels, and emphasized the psychological and emotional underpinnings of her characters. After writing *Jacob's Room* (1922), she felt she had finally come into her own: "There's no doubt . . . that I have found out how to begin (at 40) to say something in my own voice." In some of her works, the action took place over just days. These included *Mrs. Dalloway* (1925), centering on a fashionable society woman, and *To the Lighthouse* (1927), her most autobiographical work of fiction. Other books, such as *Orlando* (1928) and *Between the Acts* (1941) covered large sweeps of English history. Woolf's characters embodied the traumas and challenges of the postwar years. For example, in *Mrs. Dalloway*, a shell-shocked war veteran, Septimus Smith, represents the millions of soldiers killed or maimed—in one way or another—in World War I.

Woolf's best-known nonfiction work, *A Room of One's Own* (1929), focuses

FIGURE 23.5 Virginia Woolf, 1925

on the role of women in literature, education, and twentieth-century society. "A woman must have money and a room of her own if she is to write fiction," she wrote. She went on to explore the hindrances faced by women writers and their need to depart from traditional literature "made by men out of their own needs for their own uses."

During the 1920s and 1930s, Woolf closely followed world events. Having lived through the Great War of 1914–1918 and anticipating the upcoming conflagration that would become World War II, she argued that men—with their power and need to demonstrate their masculinity—caused wars. As a pacifist and antifascist, she became disgusted with the rise of rulers such as Hitler and Mussolini: "His eyes glare," she wrote. "His body, which is braced in an unnatural position, is tightly cased in a uniform. Upon the breast of that uniform are sewn several medals and other mystic symbols. His hand is upon a sword. He is called in German and Italian Führer and Duce; in our language Tyrant or Dictator."

Writer and Self-Conscious Observer

Woolf's fears came true with the outbreak of World War II in 1939. She survived the terrifying bombing raids and threat of German invasion during the Battle of Britain. But she never broke free from her bouts of mental illness. On March 28, 1941, she filled her pockets with stones and drowned herself near her home. "I feel certain that I am going mad again," she had written in her suicide note. "And I shan't recover this time."

Connecting People & Society

1. Why do you think Virginia Woolf described herself as "fundamentally an outsider"?

2. Why do you think Woolf has won renown as a great writer and leading feminist?

3. What connections are there between Woolf's ideas and historical developments in the decades after World War I?

nations, most of which emerged from the dissolution of the Austro-Hungarian Empire during World War I with new democratic regimes, turn away from parliamentary democracy?

Part of the answer may be that the newly created nations in this area faced enormous economic problems. Although the old Austro-Hungarian Empire had suffered from ethnic and political divisions, it had functioned as an economic whole—its industrial areas trading with its agricultural regions. Now split up, the individual nations were mostly agricultural and too unproductive to create prosperity. Only Czechoslovakia, whose parliamentary system would survive the longest, boasted an advanced industrial economy.

Struggling with these problems, the new democratic regimes seemed divided and ineffective. Many conservative groups feared the kind of change represented by liberal democracy, socialism, and communism. Such changes promised to dilute conservatives' power, diminish their economic base, and undermine their beliefs in the traditional social order. This lack of experience with democracy and the strength of these conservative groups made these nations vulnerable to authoritarian men like Horthy, who promised order and advocated nationalism backed by armed force. One by one, the democratic governments fell to authoritarian takeovers. As in Horthy's regime, the new rulers sometimes used "White Terror" to silence opponents and often repressed Jews and other minority groups.

To the south, Turkey became a republic in 1923 under the leadership of the nationalist Mustafa Kemal and displayed some of the same authoritarian characteristics. Kemal soon became known as Atatürk (Father of the Turks). Theoretically, the nation was a constitutional democracy based on universal male suffrage, but in fact, Atatürk acted as an authoritarian ruler. He secularized Turkey completely, separating the state, legal system, courts, and schools from the Muslim religious establishment. In 1934, women gained the right to vote. Many of Atatürk's reforms, including the importation of the Roman alphabet and Western clothing, were based on European models. Yet, although Kemal was a modernizer, his regime became a one-party dictatorship that promoted Atatürk—a military man who was willing to use brutality to get his way—as the all-important nationalistic hero.

This rise of authoritarian governments during the 1920s spread to the West. The most dramatic and ominous move came in Italy. There, the charismatic Benito Mussolini (1883–1945) took power, bringing with him a new governance system and ideology: **fascism.**

The Rise of Fascism in Italy

At its core, fascism in practice meant dictatorship by a charismatic leader. However, it was more than that. It included a set of antidemocratic, anti-individualistic, and anticommunist ideas or attitudes. Fascist doctrine hailed the people while denouncing the principles of the French Revolution. Fascist leaders such as Alfredo Rocco (1875–1935) viewed the state as a living organism and rejected liberal democratic forms of government, complaining that the liberal state "is dissolving into a mass of small particles, parties, associations, groups and syndicates that are binding it in chains." The fascist call was to nationalism and military prowess. In Italy, people angry and dismayed by events following World War I heard this call and followed it.

Fascist doctrine

Italy had emerged from World War I a battered, disappointed victor. Its armies, on the verge of collapse, had nevertheless managed to hold on and ultimately contributed to the final Allied victory. However, the Treaty of Versailles denied Italy some of the territories on the Adriatic coast that the Allies had promised in return for Italy's contribution to the war effort. Many Italians felt that at Versailles, their nation lost its rightful status as a great power. All this left Italian nationalists bitter and convinced many more Italians that the war had not been worth the price Italy had paid.

Turmoil in Italy

Near chaos within this troubled nation multiplied these disappointments. Italy's already weak economy staggered under a huge national debt. Its inflated currency, together with a shortage of consumer goods, made prices skyrocket. Hundreds of thousands of veterans could find no jobs. In the summer of 1919, disorder spread. Farmworkers threatened property owners by joining unions called red leagues. Veterans and poor families began seizing idle lands. Banditry in the south grew out of control, and strikes plagued the cities. During the winter of 1920–1921, workers seized control of several hundred factories. Socialists

KEY DATES

FROM RECOVERY TO CRISIS

1919	Versailles treaty
1921	Irish Free State
1922	Mussolini's march on Rome
1923	Munich putsch
	Egyptian independence
	Occupation of Ruhr
1929	Stock market crash
1933	Nazis gain power
1935	Nuremberg Laws
1938	Kristallnacht

and communists gained strength within industrial and rural unions.

Italy's newly elected government, plagued by political divisions, seemed powerless in the face of these pressures. Frightened landlords and factory owners, along with thousands of veterans and a middle class ravaged by inflation and insecurity, longed for vigorous leadership and a strong, dependable government. The vigorous leader who stepped forward was Benito Mussolini. The strong government was his fascist dictatorship.

Mussolini was born into a family of socialist artisans; he received enough education to become a teacher and then a radical journalist. At

Mussolini takes power

the outbreak of World War I, he used the socialist paper he edited to advocate antimilitarism and to demand that Italy remain neutral during the war. A year later, he changed his mind, now convinced that "only blood makes the wheels of history turn." He broke from his socialist allies, started a new newspaper, and joined the army. After the war, he organized mostly unemployed veterans into the National Fascist Party—the term *fascist* alluding to Roman prowess, unity, and justice. His Fascist Party soon attracted enough support to bring down Italy's parliamentary government.

Why did Mussolini's political movement hold such appeal? The answer to this question is complex. Fascism attracted veterans hoping for a sense of renewal

The appeal of Fascism

after the disappointments of the war and the immediate postwar years and appealed to young men who felt they had missed out on the war experience and therefore responded to the call of wounded national pride. "When I returned from the war—just like so many others—I hated politics and politicians, who . . . had betrayed the hopes of soldiers, reducing Italy to a shameful peace," explained Italo Balbo, a future associate of Mussolini. These men became the members and muscle of the new party. Factory owners, merchants, and landowners also embraced fascism when Mussolini vowed to save Italy from communism. These groups provided Mussolini with money when he organized squads of black-shirted Fascisti to terrorize radical workers and their liberal supporters. Finally, those who blamed the parliamentary government for Italy's postwar woes warmed to fascist promises to act decisively and create unity through nationalistic policies. Fascism seemed to offer a third way—a path above socialism and conventional parliamentary democracy—to security and success for Italy.

Figure 23.6 reveals some of the qualities that made Mussolini's Fascist movement attractive. Mussolini

FIGURE 23.6 Mussolini and His Black Shirts Mussolini and his Black Shirt followers raise their arms in a military salute, capturing the flavor of Italian fascism.

stands on a platform dressed in a white paramilitary uniform, his arm raised in the Fascist salute of exaggerated bravery. Below him stands his bodyguard of black-shirted party members in their paramilitary uniforms, holding knives up in the disciplined salute. All are posing for the crowd of onlookers to the left and photographers. The whole scene has been self-consciously set up to present an image of strong leadership and military prowess, and it suggests the appeal of ritual and participation in a mighty movement. Similar scenes would become common as fascist movements and authoritarian governments spread across Europe.

In 1922, building on this support, squads of black-shirted Fascists marched on Rome under Mussolini's vow that "either we are allowed to govern or we will seize power." The indecisive Italian king Victor Emmanuel III (r. 1900–1946) buckled under the pressure and appointed Mussolini prime minister. With great speed, the Fascist leader acquired extraordinary powers.

Between 1924 and 1926, Mussolini turned his office into a dictatorship. Under his rule, only the Fascist Party could engage in organized political activity. Il Duce (the leader) **The Fascist system** sent his secret police everywhere. "Everything within the State," he demanded, and "Nothing outside the State." Mussolini next struck a deal with the powerful Catholic Church and signed the Lateran Treaty of 1929. In return for money and the right to teach religion in the public schools, the papacy finally recognized the existence of the Italian state. The agreement ended the sixty years of division between the church and the state since unification.

To guide Italy's economy toward self-sufficiency and industrialization while carefully protecting private property and profits, the Fascists worked closely with business leaders. They organized the different industries and trades into confederations, or corporations. Each corporation included a syndicate of workers and one of employers, each in turn headed by a Fascist official. The Fascists also abolished all independent labor unions, strikes, and lockouts. Instead, compulsory arbitration under the party's direction now settled issues of wages and working conditions and disputes between labor and management. The complicated economic and political machinery that Mussolini put in motion for these purposes became known as the corporate state, or corporatism.

Although the state would gain a controlling hand in several major industries, Mussolini's corporate state mainly enlarged the bureaucracy and hamstrung workers' unions. A few well-publicized achievements, such as new railroads, highways, building projects, and educational reforms, hid more fundamental deficiencies. His ambitious agricultural policies generally failed to improve per capita output. People of property fared well, but workers, especially women, suffered declining income. Even though women flocked to hear him, Mussolini cut their wages by decree and banned them from several professions. Those who did not heed his call to take up their maternal duties were pushed toward low-paying jobs. Nevertheless, growing numbers of Italian women still managed to enter universities and find positions in the world of paid work.

By 1929, Mussolini stood unchallenged. Using films, radio addresses, biographies, newspapers, and schools, he amassed a huge following of supporters who repeated his reassuring phrase "Mussolini is always right." Some artists and intellectuals supported at least his image of dynamic leadership. Mussolini also won a reputation among groups throughout Europe, South America, and the United States as someone who could "make the trains run on time," gain peace with the Catholic Church, and stand up to communist threats.

In reality, Mussolini—like many twentieth-century politicians—was more of an actor able to manipulate appearances than an effective ruler who could solve domestic or international problems. Many people immune to his charm saw him as merely a strutting, boasting carnival performer. Mussolini's vision of historical destiny—to create a Second Roman Empire and turn the Mediterranean into an Italian lake—perhaps most revealed a disturbing lack of touch with reality. Even with Il Duce in control, Italy was no major power.

To the east, the situation was entirely different. Russia had been a major power and might well rise again. Now transformed into a communist state and reformed into the Soviet Union by the Bolsheviks, its radical left-wing policies represented an even more frightening threat to capitalist democracies than the extreme right-wing politics of Italian Fascism.

TRANSFORMING THE SOVIET UNION, 1920–1939

In 1920, Russia's bloody civil war had finally ended. The suffering, however, dragged on. Industrial production sank to only 13 percent of pre–World War I levels. A famine struck, taking four to seven million lives. Countless thousands of veterans and city dwellers roamed the countryside in search of food, shelter, and employment. "Green Armies" of peasants revolted against forced requisitions of their crops and restrictions against selling products at market prices. Workers struck against declining wages and lack of control over the factories. Sailors at the Kronstadt naval base mutinied, demanding political liberty. Many Communist Party and union members called for more democracy. How could Lenin's still vulnerable Communist government survive?

Lenin's Compromise: The NEP

Lenin retreated. In 1921 he launched the **New Economic Policy (NEP)**, a "temporary" compromise with capitalism. This policy allowed peasants to manage their own land and sell their own crops. In addition, small-scale industries could operate under private ownership, and money and credit were restored. Although the state still supervised the economy, the NEP provided enough capitalist incentive to pull the Russian economy out of chaos.

Lenin's retreat did not extend to politics, however. Russia remained a "dictatorship of the proletariat," symbolized on Russia's flag by the red of socialism, the hammer of industrial workers, and the sickle of peasants. Lenin and the Communist Party elite maintained a tight grip on power and brutally suppressed any opposition. Local soviets submitted to the central government in Moscow, dominated by its 16-person Politburo and, above all, the secretariat of the Communist Party. The formal creation of the Union of Soviet Socialist Republics (USSR, or Soviet Union) in 1922 paid only lip service to desires for autonomy in "republics" such as the Ukraine, Armenia, and Georgia. Russia, home to four-fifths of the USSR's total population, dominated the Union.

Soviet society in the 1920s reflected its revolutionary origins as well as the temporary compromise with capitalism. The Communists had eliminated the old aristocracy, church, and traditional class distinctions. But party, military, and cultural elites enjoyed higher standards of living, better housing, and more educational opportunities than anyone else. Some peasants who took advantage of NEP opportunities also became relatively wealthy, as did their urban counterparts running small businesses.

Moreover, women enjoyed unprecedented legal equality. In addition to the right to vote, they received the right to equal pay, education, and professional opportunities. The government set up programs and agencies such as the Women's Bureau to promote equality, day care, housing, medical care, and information on birth control and divorce. Alexandra Kollontai (1872–1952), head of the Women's Bureau, urged collectivization of child rearing and a new family form: "The narrow and exclusive affection of the mother for her own children must expand until it embraces all the children of the great proletarian family. In place of the indissoluble marriage based on the servitude of woman, we shall see rise in the free union [of two people] . . . equal in their rights and in their obligations. . . ."

These new policies all showed promise, but in fact the burdens on Soviet women probably increased. Programs to help them lacked the resources to make a real difference. Greater access to jobs rarely translated into higher-level positions. Women were still expected to retain their traditional burdens at home, their "second shift."

Although the NEP was a retreat from strict Communist policies, Lenin's regime still envisioned itself as leading the world into modernity. The government turned churches and great mansions into museums and meeting halls. Cultural activities promoted proletarian pride, the benefits of technology, and the glories of the future. Avant-garde artists created utopian visions by connecting images of mass production and social justice.

The NEP may have encouraged the outside world to end its isolation of Russia. Between 1922 and 1924, all Western nations recognized the Soviet Union except the United States, which remained aloof until 1933. Indeed, to many socialists throughout the West, the Soviet Union stood as a source of hope and inspiration.

The Struggle to Succeed Lenin

Lenin would not live to witness the results of the NEP. After a series of paralytic strokes, he died in 1924. Three of his chief associates—Leon Trotsky (1879–1940), Nikolai Bukharin (1888–1938), and Joseph Stalin (1879–1953)—jockeyed to succeed him. Most observers assumed that the brilliant but arrogant Trotsky, who had led the Red Army during the civil war, would win. He argued that the Soviet Union must promote revolutions elsewhere in the West to survive and that the Soviet economy should

be tightly controlled and massively industrialized from above. By contrast, the popular Bukharin, who had been appointed by Lenin to lead the NEP, argued for socialism by slow, careful steps. The shrewd political manipulator Stalin claimed a middle-of-the-road position between these two but believed that Russia must survive alone—"socialism in one country." His opponents vastly underestimated him.

Stalin (a pseudonym meaning "man of steel") was born in Georgia the son of poverty-stricken ex-serfs. His mother managed to get him into an Orthodox seminary school, where he received a formal education. Expelled from the seminary because of his Marxist views, he joined revolutionary groups. Repeatedly arrested, he kept managing to escape. In 1917, he took advantage of the revolutionary turmoil and hastened to Petrograd from his exile in Siberia. A poor speaker and writer, he used daring and organizational talents to rise in the party. He played a prominent role in Russia's civil war and became executive secretary of the Communist Party. In this key position, he made himself master of the all-important party machinery and pursued his drive for power.

Toward the end of his life, Lenin warned that "Stalin is too rude" to lead. Nevertheless, after Lenin's death, Stalin cleverly played on the Soviet people's love of Lenin by posing as his heir and leading a movement to deify him. He also brought into the party new people, who thereby owed him a debt. Playing his rivals against each other, he used his control over the Central Committee of the Communist Party to edge the overconfident Trotsky and his supporters on the Left out of powerful positions and, in 1927, expel them from the party. The next year, he turned against Bukharin and the Right. Party members who had doubts about Stalin accepted the need for party loyalty. By the end of 1928, Stalin had maneuvered himself into a position of dominance over the Communist Party and of dictatorship over the Soviet Union. Now he set out to transform the nation.

Stalin's Five-Year Plans

By 1928, Soviet industry had probably attained little more than 1913 levels of production. Stalin and his party leadership wanted much more. That year, he ended the NEP and launched the First **Five-Year Plan**. The fundamental goal of the plan could not have been more ambitious: "We do not want to be beaten. . . . Old Russia . . . was ceaselessly beaten for her backwardness. . . . We are fifty or a hundred years behind the advanced countries. We must make good this lag in ten years . . . or they crush us." The plan called for the rapid, massive industrialization of the nation. Goals included more than doubling industrial production, increasing the generation of electric

Joseph Stalin

FIGURE 23.7 *The Five-Year Plan in Four Years,* **1930s** This propaganda poster portrays Stalin as leading efforts to industrialize the Soviet Union rapidly. He faces the old "enemies" of the Communist Party.

and livestock—some 50 percent of horses and cattle between 1929 and 1933. Officials terrorized such resisters into submission. "The expropriation of the kulaks is an integral part of the formation . . . of the collective farms," announced Stalin. The kulaks should be "eliminated as a class." Hundreds of thousands of peasants were killed and far more were exiled to Siberia, never to return. This violent battle of wills was accompanied by plummeting agricultural production and government pressure to increase agricultural exports at all costs to finance industrialization. The results were disastrous: Between 1930 and 1933, famine struck, taking the lives of four to six million people. An observer reported that in Ukrainian villages, peasants resorted to eating "dogs, horses, rotten potatoes, the bark of trees, grass—anything they could find . . . and no matter what they did, they went on dying, dying, dying." The effort to collectivize agriculture and the deadly hunger tore apart rural families, communities, and established ways of life. Nevertheless, Stalin finally got his way: More than half the land was collectivized within the first year, and over 90 percent after ten years. As one Communist Party worker put it, "It took a famine to show them who is master here. It has cost millions of lives, but the collective farm system is here to stay."

To industrialize the Soviet Union, planners had to start almost from ground level and build up. They concentrated on producer goods such as engines and tractors rather than consumer goods such as shoes and clothes. Gradually, steel mills, dams, power plants, foundries, mines, refineries, chemical factories, and railroads appeared all over the Soviet Union. Technocrats and officials faced pressure to produce targeted results. The government fostered a sense of emergency to inspire people, especially the young, to work hard. Presenting the effort as a great adventure, officials pointed out that those who most contributed to the industrialization drive could achieve a status similar to that of the heroes of the 1917 revolution. The government moved "shock brigades" of enthusiastic, efficient workers from factory to factory to stimulate production, while the press celebrated new "Heroes of Labor" who exceeded production targets. Officials encouraged women to work both on the collective farms and in factories; by 1940, women made up almost half the labor force.

Mobilizing for industrialization

All elements of Soviet society were mobilized to support the effort to make the USSR an industrial power. Schools, adult education classes, newspapers, union meetings, and youth associations became saturated with official doctrines of Soviet communism, efficiency, and class pride. "We must make every school child aware of . . . how the great people of

power almost fivefold, and building 1,500 new factories within five years. To achieve the goals, the State Planning Commission, or Gosplan, would strictly regulate all aspects of production, including targeting crucial industries such as steel, regimenting the industrial labor force, and hiring foreign engineers to help build the new factories. The 1930s Soviet propaganda poster shown in **Figure 23.7,** "The Five-Year Plan in Four Years," portrays the idea that Stalin will lead Soviet industrial development against the threatening reactionary forces of capitalism and religion. As if preparing for another war, Stalin ordered the USSR's entire society to mobilize for industrialization.

To help accomplish the Five-Year Plan's goals (which included doubling agricultural production), the state took agriculture out of the control of individual peasants by consolidating their lands into huge collective farms that used modern machines. Elected managers and party officials ran the farms. Individuals could own tools, keep small gardens for fruits and vegetables, and raise pigs and chickens for private use or sale. By determining prices and distribution of crops, the state expected to use agricultural "surpluses" to pay for industrialization—to buy the equipment to build factories, transportation facilities, and power plants. **Collectivization,** it was believed, would also push peasants to become industrial workers in the cities.

Collectivization

As Document 23.2 suggests, the process of collectivization proved ruinous. Hundreds of thousands of peasants, especially wealthier landowners derisively called kulaks, powerfully resisted the new policies. In protest, they even destroyed their own crops

DOCUMENT 23.2

Stalin Collectivizes Agriculture

As part of his campaign to collectivize agriculture, Stalin used massive coercion against the Russian kulaks (relatively rich independent peasants). Widespread destruction and death resulted. In the following excerpt, Lev Kopelev recounts his own participation in this collectivization drive.

A team consisting of several young kolkhozniks [collective farmers] and members of the village soviet . . . would search the hut, barn, yard, and take away all the stores of seed, lead away the cow, the horse, the pigs.

In some cases they would be merciful and leave some potatoes, peas, corn for feeding the family. But the stricter ones would make a clean sweep. They would take not only the food and livestock, but also "all valuables and surpluses of clothing," including icons in their frames, samovars, painted carpets and even metal kitchen utensils which might

be silver. And any money they found stashed away. Special instructions ordered the removal of gold, silver and currency. . . .

We were raised as the fanatical [believers] of a new creed, the only true *religion* of scientific socialism. The party became our church militant, bequeathing to all mankind eternal salvation, eternal peace and the bliss of an earthly paradise. It victoriously surmounted all other churches, schisms and heresies. The works of Marx, Engels and Lenin were accepted as holy writ, and Stalin was the infallible high priest.

. . . Stalin was the most perspicacious, the most wise (at that time they hadn't yet started calling him "great" and "brilliant"). He said: "The struggle for grain is the struggle for socialism." And we believed him unconditionally. And later we believed that unconditional collectivization was unavoidable if we were to overcome the capriciousness and uncertainty of

the market and the backwardness of individual farming, to guarantee a steady supply of grain, milk and meat to the cities. And also if we were to reeducate millions of peasants, those petty landowners and hence potential bourgeoisie, potential kulaks, to transform them into laborers with a social conscience, to liberate them from "the idiocy of country life," from ignorance and prejudice, and to accustom them to culture, to all the boons of socialism. . . .

SOURCE: Lev Kopelev, *The Education of a True Believer* (New York: Harper & Row, 1980), p. 123.

Analyze the Document

1. Why was this aspect of collectivization so devastating?

2. How does Kopelev justify his participation in the drive?

3. What insights into Soviet life during the early 1930s does this document provide?

---

our epoch—Lenin, Stalin, and their companions in arms—organized the workers in the struggle for a new and happy life," explained a Soviet text on teaching methods. Officials, minor bureaucrats, and members of the secret police ranged everywhere and monitored progress. Within families—the "school for socialism"—mothers were urged to raise their children to fit into communist society. Earlier policies supporting women's choices were reversed. The state made abortion illegal and promoted traditional marriage and relationships. In this more repressive era, homosexuality became a crime.

The state also tightened controls over cultural productions, ending the experimentation of the 1920s. The Central Committee of the Communist Party told publishing houses that "books must be an instrument for the mobilization of the workers for the tasks of industrialization and collectivization." A government ministry took control over filmmaking to make sure movies promoted revolutionary enthusiasm and favorable views of the communist state. Socialist realism became the required orthodoxy in art. In this style, approved murals, art, and literature portrayed realistic images of people carrying out the dreams of a communist society. **Figure 23.8** is an example of this effort

to make art relevant and compelling to the working masses. In this idealized image, an older man (reminiscent of an aged Lenin) shows a boy the achievements of Stalin's programs. Above the two smiling figures is a well-known nineteenth-century painting of poverty-stricken peasants and workers hauling a ship up a river by ropes. By contrast, the new social reality can be seen outside the window, where steamships haul barges up a river and in the distance modern facilities attest to the creation of modern industry. The eager boy, in a comradely embrace, wears the uniform of a Stalinist youth organization and represents the glowing future.

THE SOVIET UNION

1918–1920	Civil war
1920–1921	Famine
1924	Death of Lenin
1928	Beginning of First Five-Year Plan
1930–1933	Famine
1934	Beginning of Great Purges

KEY DATES

FIGURE 23.8 Promises of Soviet Society, 1930s This poster shows an idealized scene of Soviet accomplishments and announces, "People's Dreams Have Come True!"

СБЫЛИСЬ МЕЧТЫ НАРОДНЫЕ!

At the end of 1932, Stalin announced that all goals of the First Five-Year Plan had been accomplished several months ahead of time. He recited a list of accomplishments in iron, steel, tractors, automobiles, machine tools, chemicals, and aircraft production. "Our country has been converted from an agrarian into an industrial country," he proclaimed. These gains, however, came at a high price. For the hard-pressed workers, consumer goods beyond the necessities remained scarce. Clearly, some Soviet citizens—namely, party members—benefited more than others. One refugee cynically compared life before and after the Bolshevik Revolution: "In Tsarist times there were the rich and the poor; under Soviet power there were the party members and the nonparty members." Similar Second and Third Five-Year Plans would follow, this time with more emphasis on consumer goods and armaments. The terrifying Great Purges would also follow.

Blood and Terror: The Great Purges

In 1934, Leonid Nikolayev assassinated Sergei Kirov (1888–1934), a high Soviet official. Stalin used the murder as an excuse to eliminate potential rivals. The incident introduced a long period of party purges, marked by terror, house arrests, bizarre show-trials, torture, imprisonments, and executions—all approved by Stalin.

Historians still debate Stalin's motives for the **Great Purges.** Stalin and party officials blamed difficulties during the five-year plans on many—engineers, technocrats, army officers, older party members, regional nationalists, foreign conspirators, saboteurs—and purged the accused. Lower-level officials probably contributed to the waves of purges by trying to rise at the expense of higher-level officials. Stalin himself was extremely suspicious. He saw enemies everywhere. Certainly he worried about threats from within the party. He eradicated all potential opposition—real or imagined, and even on foreign soil. In 1940, Soviet agents assassinated Trotsky in Mexico.

By the time the Great Purges ended in 1939, authorities had killed some one million people. Another seven million died or languished in forced-labor camps; still more had been sent into exile. The terror spread throughout Soviet society, for everyone knew of someone accused and arrested. Almost all the original Bolshevik leaders and the Red Army's top officer corps were gone. New, younger figures beholden to Stalin now staffed the government, the Communist Party, and the military.

In the end, Stalin got most of what he wanted. By 1939, the Soviet Union had a fully planned economy, with the state determining production, prices, and distribution. Although officials announced successes whether they occurred or not, the USSR had in fact become the third-greatest industrial power in the world. More than 90 percent of peasants lived on collective, mechanized farms. Millions more had moved to the cities, where new housing, schools, libraries, and hospitals had sprung up. For the first time, most of the population could read. Within the Soviet Union, no one dared oppose Stalin, and now he had the armaments to face a new challenge already rising in the west. But the cost had been tremendous. Between 15 and 20 million people (some scholars argue that the figure might be much higher) had died from starvation, execution, or the harsh conditions in forced-labor camps, and far more had suffered as a result of Stalin's policies.

THE GREAT DEPRESSION,
1929–1939

The forces to the west creating that challenge to the USSR had begun to coalesce and gather momentum, and the Soviets were not the only ones threatened by them. As we saw earlier, authoritarianism and fascism—fierce opponents of communism—had already started to rise in the 1920s. In 1929, a new crisis struck the Western democracies: the **Great Depression.** Reeling from years of hard times and pulling much of the world with them, Western societies began edging toward a new darkness that would more than rival the horrors of World War I.

Crash!

In October 1929, the New York stock market crashed. In one month, stocks lost almost two-thirds of their value. The financial crisis quickly spread from the United States, the world's leading industrial nation and creditor, to Europe, where nations depended heavily on American loans and trade. The crash ended the relative prosperity since 1924 and provoked an unprecedented global depression. Within two years, thousands of banks and businesses throughout the West failed. Spending, production, employment, and income all dropped sharply. Plant closings, farm foreclosures, and joblessness haunted the Western nations. People's confidence in the economy died, and too often with it went their faith in themselves.

A complex series of events had led to the disaster. The postwar economic order was built on a fragile foundation of international credit, reparations payments, and foreign trade. Much of Europe remained dependent on the United States for credit. Germany in particular relied on American loans to support its reparation payments.

> Causes of the economic collapse

In 1928, American investors began pulling their money out of Germany and demanding repayment of loans to invest in the unregulated, soaring U.S. stock market. Credit dried up in Germany and in east-central European nations tied to the German economy. The 1929 crash sent people running to banks to withdraw funds, further undermining credit. Soon the West's entire economic house of cards collapsed.

The collapse took much of the globe with it. Over the years, non-Western lands had become important suppliers of raw materials—such as rice, cotton, cocoa, rubber, oil, copper, and tin—for Western industry and urban populations. With their economies more and more dependent on international trade, these regions were now tied to the economic fate of the West. Ties to the West particularly marked industrialized Japan's economy. The lure of increasing trade with the United States during the 1920s had persuaded Japan to halt its imperial expansion in Asia. The Great Depression—which quickly slashed exports to the United States in half and left three million people unemployed—brought an end to Japan's prosperity and revived its imperial ambitions.

> Effects in non-Western lands

Japan's leaders looked to make East Asian markets their own, by conquest if necessary.

In the Teeth of the Depression

By 1932, Europe's economies had shrunk to one-half their 1929 size. Unemployment in the West rose to a shocking 22 percent, leaving 30 million people out of work. Along with their jobs, people lost their savings, their farms, and their homes. In Germany, Heinrich Hauser described how "an almost unbroken chain of homeless men extends the whole length of the great Hamburg-Berlin highway." One British woman echoed the feelings of many: "These last few years since I've been out of the mills . . . I've got no spirit for anything." Masses of people sank into poverty, and malnutrition and diseases spread. Families suffered from new tensions as men lost their traditional role as breadwinners. "When he was out of work," lamented a woman from Liverpool, "we were always having rows over the children."

Scenes of despair could be found everywhere. **Figure 23.9**, a painting by Isaac Soyer, shows people in a New York employment agency. Their faces reveal little hope as they wait—reading a newspaper, looking away in distraction, or staring ahead in resignation. The dreary room offers no consolation, and the scene through the window suggests there is little to look forward to on the city streets.

In eastern and central Europe, hard-pressed farmers and unemployed workers looked for scapegoats. They blamed Jews, whom they saw as controlling the

FIGURE 23.9 Isaac Soyer, *Employment Agency*, 1937 Despair among unemployed workers such as these in the United States became common as the Great Depression wore on.

banks, bureaucracy, jobs, and policies responsible for the depression. People also pointed their fingers at socialists, communists, big business, and even modernity. Ethnic groups and major powers turned on one another, and throughout the West, popular protests by desperate, angry people spread.

Searching for Solutions

At first, governments met the depression the old way: by balancing the budget and increasing tariffs on imported goods. However, these policies just made matters worse by dampening spending and hindering trade. A moratorium on reparations and war debts in August 1931 came too late to do much good. Imperial powers such as Britain and France turned to their colonial holdings for secure trade and profits, only to meet rising demands for independence in India, Iraq, Vietnam, Algeria, and elsewhere. The British economist John Maynard Keynes (1883–1946) argued for new policies—more government expenditures financed by budget deficits to stimulate consumer spending and raise employment—but few listened to his still little-known ideas.

After 1932, new regimes in the United States, Britain, and Germany adopted policies to increase government spending and provide some relief. Similar policies had already enabled Scandinavian democracies to weather the depression with relative ease. However, even with these measures, most Western democracies recovered slowly and not fully until the late 1930s, thanks to spending for rearmament. **Figure 23.10** indicates that France and the United States in particular had difficulty raising industrial production to figures approaching pre-1929 levels. By then, these democracies faced new threats that made even the anxious 1920s look like "roaring"

good times. The most ominous menace came from Germany.

NAZISM IN GERMANY

In 1928, Germany's fascist party, the Nazis (National Socialists), won less than 3 percent of the vote in national elections. Five years later, the party and its leader, Adolf Hitler, gained power and ended German democracy—all through legal means. How did this happen?

The Young Adolf Hitler

The story of Nazism's rise begins with the life of Adolf Hitler (1889–1945). Hitler was born to a middle-aged Austrian customs official and his much younger wife. When his father died in 1905, Hitler quit school and traveled to Vienna, where he hoped to become an artist or architect. Denied admission to the art academy, he lived on his orphan's pension, selling postcards and hanging wallpaper. He compulsively followed daily routines and would do so for the rest of his life. He also picked up nationalistic, anti-Semitic, and racist ideas circulating in Vienna that he embraced with deadly seriousness.

When World War I broke out, Hitler "thanked heaven out of an overflowing heart." For this ardent German nationalist, here was a righteous crusade to end a life of drifting. He served as a courier in the German army and was decorated three times. War's end found him in a hospital recovering from a poison gas attack. He revered World War I as "the greatest of all experiences." As for Germany's defeat at the end of the conflict, he blamed Jews and Marxists, who he felt sure had "stabbed Germany in the back."

The Birth of Nazism in Germany's Postwar Years

Hitler spotted opportunities in Germany's turbulent postwar years. Several right-wing groups had formed that offered extreme solutions to Germany's problems and that threatened the newly formed parliamentary government of the Weimar Republic. In 1919, while working in Munich as an informer for the army, Hitler joined one of those groups—the German Workers' Party. A year later, he rose to leadership in the party and renamed it the National Socialist German Workers' Party, or the **Nazi Party** (despite the party's name, it was neither socialist in the traditional sense nor well supported by urban workers). Hitler also organized a paramilitary wing—the SA "stormtroopers"—to back the party. Copying Mussolini's techniques, the SA troopers wore brown shirts and carried pagan symbols (the swastika). They marched through the streets,

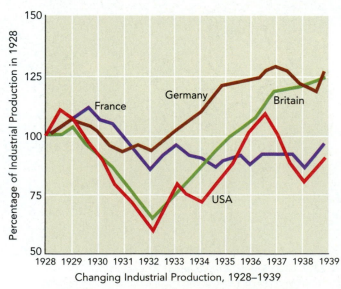

Changing Industrial Production, 1928–1939

FIGURE 23.10 Industrial Production, 1928–1939

sang patriotic songs, and beat up communists, socialists, and anyone else they considered their opponents.

Nothing yet marked this small group as destined for success. Nevertheless, in 1923 Hitler and the popular war hero Field Marshal Ludendorff made an ambitious grab for power. From a beer hall in Munich, the Nazis marched on the local government. Republican troops easily put down this "Beer Hall Putsch," and Hitler, after a highly publicized trial, spent nearly a year in jail. While in prison, he wrote *Mein Kampf* (*My Struggle*), a work that set forth the core of his Nazi doctrine.

Nazism, like other brands of fascism, assaulted the liberal, democratic tradition in the West. According to Nazi doctrine, the political order should be dominated by a single party headed by a dictatorial leader (Hitler) who appealed to the masses. In addition, the doctrine reflected the sense among many Germans of being haunted by defeat in World War I and "humiliated" by the settlement that followed, and it fostered the belief that Germany therefore should rearm and redress the "injustices" of the Versailles treaty. At the center of Hitler's beliefs lurked biological racism and anti-Semitism. He glorified the mythical German "Aryan race" as superior and destined to conquer all other peoples in the struggle for racial supremacy. He also condemned the Jews as corrupt, landless parasites who created Marxist communism, caused Germany's humiliating defeat in World War I, and propagated liberalism. Underlying this element of the Nazi doctrine was a sense that everything in politics and in life was a constant struggle between peoples. Perils and enemies—whether from Jews, Poles, Bolsheviks, or others—lurked everywhere, plotting Germany's destruction. These fears seemed to justify ambitions to conquer the Slavic people to the east, to gain living space (**Lebensraum**), and to follow policies to rid Germany of all opponents.

Nazi doctrine

The Growth of the Nazi Party

Hitler exited jail in 1924 determined to acquire power from within, legally. Between 1925 and 1929, the Nazi Party grew in numbers somewhat but still remained a small splinter group. Then in October 1929, Germany's foreign minister, Gustav Stresemann, whose effective leadership for five years held center parties of the Weimar Republic together, died. That same month, the New York stock market crashed. Soon the Great Depression had Germany in its grip. It spelled the end of American loans and ignited unemployment and panic. Internal divisions immobilized parliamentary government, and the political extremes on both the Left and Right rapidly gained strength.

In 1930, the aged president Paul Hindenburg, Germany's military commander during World War I and no friend to democracy, authorized rule by decree over Germany's unstable parliament. In elections held that year, the Nazis won a startling 18.3 percent of the vote—up from 2.6 percent in 1928. Hindenburg turned to conservative politicians to lead the republic, but they failed to govern effectively. The moderates, socialists, and communists, for their part, could not unify into a strong political force. In 1932, the Nazi Party became the largest political organization in Germany, winning an astonishing 37.3 percent of the vote. In elections for the office of president, Hitler gained 13.5 million votes against Hindenburg's 19 million.

The Appeal of Nazism

Nazism offered certainty to confused, frightened people; a sense of emotional belonging and unity in a time of crisis and anxiety; and action in a time of political immobility and conflict. Hitler and the doctrine of Nazism captured the imaginations of many Germans, especially young people and displaced veterans eager to achieve some measure of social stature in the new elite. Indeed, Hitler presented Nazism as "the organized will of the youth." For some, this included the appeal of being part of a street gang. He also appealed to the millions of Germans—the lower-middle class in particular—who had been traumatized by the Great Depression.

Much of Hitler's appeal stemmed from the alluring promises he made—promises that offered comfort and reassurance to a people in desperate need. He claimed that he would get rid of the despised war reparations, economic hardship, incompetent leadership, threats from the Left, and parliamentary government. In addition, he vowed to restore national unity and order in Germany and revive both the German people's shattered pride and their military might. Document 23.3 suggests how Hitler and the Nazi Party used nationalism and anti-Semitism to gain support.

To wealthy industrial leaders and landowners who feared the growing strength of unions, socialists, and communists, Hitler and his party held less of a personal attraction. Instead, Nazism represented the lesser of two distasteful options in the minds of these groups. Many such people who voted for the Nazis did so as a way to vote *against* the Weimar Republic, the terms of the Versailles treaty, and the communist path, rather than *for* the Nazi ideology. Indeed, most of these Germans probably would have preferred to elect more traditional conservatives, but none of the existing candidates passed muster.

Whatever the appeal, those drawn to Hitler and the Nazis either ignored the party's strident nationalism, racism, and anti-Semitic fervor or embraced those sentiments. After all, such calls had been heard throughout central and eastern Europe for decades.

DOCUMENT 23.3

Goebbels's Nazi Propaganda Pamphlet

Propaganda was strongly emphasized by the Nazis as a method of acquiring and maintaining power. Joseph Goebbels (1897–1945), an early leader in the Nazi Party, was made chief of propaganda in 1929, minister for propaganda and national enlightenment in 1933, and a member of Hitler's cabinet council in 1938. The following is an excerpt from a 1930 pamphlet, written by Goebbels, describing why the Nazis are nationalists and against Jews.

WHY ARE WE NATIONALISTS?

We are NATIONALISTS because we see in the NATION the only possibility for the protection and the furtherance of our existence.

The NATION is the organic bond of a people for the protection and defense of their lives. He is nationally minded who understands this IN WORD AND IN DEED.

Today, in GERMANY, NATIONALISM has degenerated into BOURGEOIS PATRIOTISM, and its power exhausts itself in tilting at windmills. It says GERMANY and means MONARCHY.

It proclaims FREEDOM and means BLACK-WHITE-RED.

WE ARE NATIONALISTS BECAUSE WE, AS GERMANS, LOVE GERMANY. And because we love Germany, we demand the protection of its national spirit and we battle against its destroyers.

***

WHY DO WE OPPOSE THE JEWS?

We are the ENEMIES OF THE JEWS, because we are fighters for the freedom of the German people. THE JEW IS THE CAUSE AND THE BENEFICIARY OF OUR MISERY. He has used the social difficulties of the broad masses of our people to deepen the unholy split between Right and Left among our people. He has made two halves of Germany. He is the real cause for our loss of the Great War.

The Jew has no interest in the solution of Germany's fateful problems. He CANNOT have any. FOR HE LIVES ON THE FACT THAT THERE HAS BEEN NO SOLUTION. If we would make the German people a unified community and give them freedom before the world, then the Jew can have no place among us. He has the best trumps in his hands when a people lives in inner and outer slavery. THE JEW IS RESPONSIBLE FOR OUR MISERY AND HE LIVES ON IT. . . .

WE ARE ENEMIES OF THE JEWS BECAUSE WE BELONG TO THE GERMAN PEOPLE. THE JEW IS OUR GREATEST MISFORTUNE.

It is not true that we eat a Jew every morning at breakfast.

It is true, however, the he SLOWLY BUT SURELY ROBS US OF EVERYTHING WE OWN.

THAT WILL STOP, AS SURELY AS WE ARE GERMANS.

SOURCE: From Louis L. Snyder, *The Weimar Republic.* Reprinted by permission of D. Van Nostrand Co. (New York, 1966), pp. 201–203. Copyright © 1966 by Litton Educational Publishing, Inc.

Analyze the Document

1. How does this document reflect the character of life in Germany during the 1920s?

2. To whom was this document designed to appeal? Give evidence for your answer.

3. In what ways might this excerpt be a convincing piece of propaganda?

However, many Germans failed to detect the especially virulent quality of the Nazis' version of these feelings. Even experienced politicians never saw the danger in the situation. In fact, some conservative leaders, such as Franz von Papen, supported Hitler under the assumption that they could control him. As they would discover, they were greatly mistaken.

Hitler Takes Power

In January 1933, President Hindenburg offered Hitler the chancellorship, and the Nazi leader accepted. Jubilant stormtroopers marched through Berlin's streets, holding their blazing torches high. In his new position, Hitler immediately called for another round of parliamentary elections. Now in official control of the state police and the agencies of information, the Nazis used propaganda and terror to confuse and frighten voters. As Hitler explained it, "Terror at the place of employment, in the factory, in the meeting hall, and on the occasion of mass demonstrations will always be successful."

Five days before the elections, Hitler discredited the communists by accusing them of burning the Reichstag building. He used the fire to justify the suspension of civil liberties and the arrest of many communists. On election day, the Nazis gained 44 percent of the vote; with their nationalist allies, they now had enough for a majority. The Reichstag quickly passed an enabling act granting Hitler the power to make laws on his own for four years. He soon outlawed all other political parties, and when Hindenburg died in 1934, Hitler became the sole leader of the German government. That same year, Hitler ordered Heinrich Himmler (1900–1945) and a handpicked private armed force, the elite **SS,** to "blood purge" his own paramilitary organization, the SA. Hitler saw the leader of the SA, Ernst Röhm (1887–1934) as a rival with plans to establish control over the army. That Night of the Long Knives eliminated potential opponents to Hitler within the party and the powerful SA as a rival to the reviving German army. Now the army swore allegiance to Hitler. The Nazi leader's dictatorship was complete.

Life in Nazi Germany

His power consolidated, Hitler proceeded to turn Germany into a police state. The government abolished freedom of speech, press, and assembly. An elaborate and all-powerful secret police, the Gestapo, uncovered and destroyed opposition. Nazi officials took over top positions in the government and pressured churches to conform to the new order. Professional organizations of doctors, teachers, lawyers, and engineers were transformed into Nazi associations. Officials even pushed people into joining Nazi leisure-time organizations.

The Nazis set out to bring family and private life under their control. As one step, the German Women's Bureau established guidelines for "proper" womanhood. Women, the bureau proclaimed,

Family and private life belonged at home, where they could fulfill their primary duties as homemakers, as subordinates to their husbands, and as producers of children. According to Guida Diehl, the leader of a pro-Nazi women's organization, "A woman's honor rests on the province specifically entrusted to her . . . love, marriage, family, motherhood. . . . The German man wants to know . . . that it is worthwhile to live and die for such German womanhood." Officials launched campaigns to honor and reward pregnant women, prevent birth control, and improve racial stock. The government provided subsidies for large, racially German families. Women who gave birth to more than four children received the bronze Honor Cross of the German Mother; more than six warranted a silver medal, and more than eight, the coveted gold. In 1937, the Nazi Art Council of the Reich demanded that painters cease depicting families with only two children. A new program in 1938 went so far as to encourage SS soldiers to breed children with "racially fit" women outside of marriage.

Nazi youth organizations such as the Hitler Youth and the League of German Girls expanded rapidly,

Nazi youth organizations absorbing the majority of teenage boys and girls by the late 1930s. Boys were molded into Nazi supporters with military values and sometimes encouraged to spy on their teachers and parents. "I don't want an intellectual education" for

FIGURE 23.11 Adolf Hitler at Buckeberg, 1934 Carefully organized mass rallies such as this one from the mid-1930s helped create a sense of belonging among the German people and increased Hitler's power.

boys, Hitler said. "They must learn in the face of the most difficult trials to conquer the fear of death for my sake." Girls were trained to become housewives and mothers, which the Nazis saw as the perfect complement to the loyal, fearless German soldier.

Hitler inspired and manipulated people with his stirring, inflammatory speeches, rallies, parades, and symbols. His organizers choreographed mass meetings such as the one at Buckeberg in 1934, shown in **Figure 23.11,** to whip up excitement and a sense of belonging among the populace. In

Promoting Nazism and Hitler this photograph, Hitler leads a procession of Nazi elites between two lines of honor guards and swastika banners. At such rallies, Hitler made a carefully staged, dramatic entrance and delivered a long, emotionally charged speech. "It is the belief in our people that has made us small men great, that has made us poor men rich, that has made brave and courageous men out of us wavering, spiritless, timid fold," he proclaimed at the Nuremberg rally in 1936. Listeners described feeling "eternally bound to this man." The ministry of propaganda, under Joseph Goebbels (1897–1945), reinforced the psychological power of the rallies by controlling information and spreading Nazi ideology through the press, radio, films, textbooks, pamphlets, and posters. For example, the ministry commissioned Leni Riefenstahl (1902–2003) to create the documentary film *Triumph of the Will* (1935), which portrayed the Nazis and their leaders as awe inspiring and gloriously on the march. Goebbels also painted an image of Hitler as the people's heroic leader, the one who could even be trusted to limit any

thinking about

ART

FIGURE 23.12

Felix Nussbaum, *Self-Portrait with Jewish Identity Card, 1943*

This painting depicts the German artist Felix Nussbaum within prison walls and holding up his Jewish identity card. Although this painting dates to 1943, the Nazis subjected Jews in Germany, such as Nussbaum, to increasingly harsh repression during most of the 1930s.

Connecting Art & Society

1. What do the yellow Star of David and the identity card indicate about the evolving Nazi policy toward Jews in Germany?

2. Why might the artist have portrayed himself looking out at the painting's viewers so directly?

3. What feelings might viewers of the times have experienced upon seeing this painting?

excesses by overzealous extremists within the Nazi Party itself.

In addition to promoting enthusiasm for their leader and ideology, the Nazis attacked "decadent" modern art and the popular culture of the Jazz Age. Only those whose works conformed to Nazi tastes—usually sentimental, pro-Nazi subject matter—could exhibit, publish, or perform. Officials promoted the burning of liberal books, sometimes even those of Germany's greatest literary figures of the eighteenth and nineteenth centuries, such as

Goethe and Schiller. The Nazi minister of culture told university professors, "From now on it will *not* be your job to determine whether something is true but whether it is in the spirit of the [Nazi] revolution." Although some intellectuals and artists supported these policies, many opposed them and left Germany.

Both to solidify their power and to carry out their racist ideas, the Nazis targeted many groups for repression. For example, they sent communists, socialists, resisting Catholics, Jehovah's Witnesses, and the Roma (Gypsies) to concentration camps. Mixed-race children, criminals, prostitutes, alcoholics—all considered genetically inferior or "community aliens"—became candidates for sterilization. Homosexuality warranted at least incarceration or castration. A frightening glimpse of the future for all these groups came in 1939 when the Nazis created euthanasia programs designed to eliminate the mentally ill, handicapped, aged, and incurably ill.

Nazi repression and persecution

No group, however, was more systematically repressed than the Jews. According to Joseph Goebbels, Jews had "corrupted our race, fouled our morals, undermined our customs, and broken our power." He blamed them as "the cause and the beneficiary of our misery." In 1933, the government excluded Jews from higher education and public employment. By 1935, most Jewish professionals in Germany had lost their jobs. That year the **Nuremberg Laws** took citizenship away from Jews and forbad marriage or sexual relations between Jews and non-Jews. In 1938, an episode of unrestrained violence revealed the mounting intensity of the Nazis' anti-Semitism. Incited by Goebbels, who blamed Jews for the assassination of a German diplomat in Paris, Nazi stormtroopers vandalized Jewish residences, synagogues, and places of business, smashing windows and plundering shops during the night of November 9–10. The troops then attacked Jews themselves, killing dozens and imprisoning tens of thousands in concentration camps. After this attack—known as **Kristallnacht**, or Crystal Night, for its images of shattered glass—the Nazi government increasingly restricted Jews' movements, eliminated their jobs, and confiscated their assets. By 1939, over half of Germany's Jews had emigrated, even though they had to leave their possessions behind, pay hefty emigration fees, and face rejection in other countries. Soon, though, it became too late to escape Germany.

Figure 23.12 depicts the repression closing in on the Jews. The man in this painting—a self-portrait of the German artist Felix Nussbaum (1904–1944)—grimly regards the viewer. In one hand, he holds up his identity card, which in red letters states that he is Jewish. The yellow Star of David on his coat also identifies him as Jewish to the public. The walls of a prison yard tower above him. Beyond the walls, barbed wire, a truncated tree, and a blackening sky all hint at the dark future facing this man and others like him. Nussbaum completed this painting in 1943 while in hiding from the Nazis; less than a year later the Nazis arrested, imprisoned, and then killed him, along with his parents and brother.

What did ordinary Germans think of this repression and persecution? Historians still debate this question. Although many people seemed to share Hitler's attitudes, at least to a degree, most people outside the persecuted groups may not have understood Hitler's extreme, ultimate purpose. Certainly some knew and many should have known. A few Germans objected. However, open resistance was dangerous. For those who disagreed with Hitler, it was much easier and safer to retreat into private life and apathy. Moreover, they, and many other Germans, found reason to overlook Hitler's repressive measures and support him in his efforts to revive their prostrate nation.

Rebuilding and Rearming the New Germany

Governmental expenditures fueled economic recovery, but Hitler's main goal was rearmament. Superhighways, hospitals, sports stadiums, and apartment houses sprang up all over Germany; so did rearmament plants that created jobs for millions. To make Germany self-sufficient in case of another war, the Nazis supported the development of synthetics for the manufacture of such items as rubber and petroleum that Germany would otherwise have to import. The planned conquest to the east, Hitler hoped, would provide needed raw materials and eventually pay for Germany's governmental expenditures.

For the most part, the Nazis left business organizations and the capitalist economy alone. However, big business, forced to bow to the will of governmental policy, did lose some freedom. The real assault was on independent labor unions, which the government abolished and replaced with the Nazi Labor Front.

All these efforts worked. Germany regained the economic and military strength to make it a great power. By 1935, Hitler had taken Germany out of the League of Nations and the Geneva Disarmament Conference. Unwilling to back the letter of the Versailles treaty with force, the Allies offered only muted opposition to Hitler's renunciation of the Versailles disarmament provisions. The next year, Hitler initiated a secret Four-Year Plan to prepare Germany for war. By 1939, the Nazis had increased armaments expenditures thirtyfold. Hitler felt ready to flex his newly developed muscles. His aggressive ambitions, combined with disturbing events outside Germany, were pushing the world toward war.

LOOKING BACK & MOVING FORWARD

Summary   During the 1920s, the West struggled to recover from the terrible World War I years. But any optimism generated by the end of the war was quickly tempered by problems such as inflation and unemployment in much of Europe. In southern, central, and eastern Europe, political turmoil created even more uncertainty. In the Soviet Union, crippled by the war and a devastating civil war, the Bolshevik regime faced an overwhelming task of rebuilding and creating a new kind of society. Even among the victors in western Europe and North America, the search for some return to "normalcy" brought frustrations and, at best, temporary moments of vibrancy, stability, and renewal. Most of the strong moments ended with the stock market crash of 1929, which ushered in the Great Depression.

By the early 1930s, the West had divided into three camps: the capitalist democracies, the fascist and authoritarian nations of central and eastern Europe, and the communist Soviet Union. As hardships from the Depression deepened and persisted, the capitalist democracies weakened, the authoritarian nations became ominously belligerent, and the communist Soviet Union under Joseph Stalin pursued—at terrible cost—its ambitious policies of agricultural collectivization and industrial five-year plans. But no country seemed to grow stronger, and for many in a more frightening way, than Germany under Adolf Hitler and the Nazis. The decade would not end before a return to the horrors that so many had hoped were behind them when that terrible storm lifted in 1918.

KEY TERMS

Weimar Republic, *p. 723*
Maginot Line, *p. 724*
Bauhaus, *p. 727*
Dada, *p. 728*
fascism, *p. 730*
New Economic Policy (NEW), *p. 732*
Five-Year Plan, *p. 733*
collectivization, *p. 734*
Great Purges, *p. 736*
Great Depression, *p. 736*
Nazi Party, *p. 738*
Lebensraum, *p. 739*
SS, *p. 740*
Nuremberg Laws, *p. 742*
Kristallnacht, *p. 742*

REVIEW, ANALYZE, & CONNECT TO TODAY

REVIEW THE PREVIOUS CHAPTER

Chapter 22—"Descending into the Twentieth Century"—told the story of World War I and the Russian Revolution.

1. In what ways were the forces unleashed by World War I responsible for the rise of authoritarian governments in Europe?

2. How might one argue that during the 1920s and the 1930s, the West never recovered from World War I?

ANALYZE THIS CHAPTER

Chapter 23—"Darkening Decades"—traces the rise of fascism, the development of the Soviet Union, and the trials of nations struck by the Great Depression.

1. Do you think the 1920s was a period of real recovery and cultural flowering or more of a haunted, anxious decade? Why?

2. Analyze the main qualities of German Nazism. How do you explain its rise and the acquisition of power by Hitler?

3. Why do you think Stalin initiated the Five-Year Plans? What were the purposes of those plans?

4. In what ways was the Great Depression much more than an economic downturn?

CONNECT TO TODAY

Think about the rise of fascism and Nazism, the transformation of the Soviet Union, and the hardships of the Great Depression.

1. In today's world, what might be some of the consequences of another serious economic depression?

2. What circumstances in the present day might facilitate the rise of regimes like the dictatorships or fascist governments of the 1920s and 1930s?

BEYOND THE CLASSROOM

TRYING TO RECOVER FROM THE GREAT WAR, 1919–1929

Kitchen, Martin. *Europe Between the Wars: A Political History*. London: Longman, 1988. An economic and political history of the interwar period.

Mommsen, Hans. *The Rise and Fall of Weimar Democracy*. Chapel Hill: University of North Carolina Press, 1996. Argues that Weimar collapsed because of a skewed political culture inherited from imperial Germany.

TURNING AWAY FROM DEMOCRACY: DICTATORSHIPS AND FASCISM, 1919–1929

Paxton, Robert O. *The Anatomy of Fascism.* New York: Knopf, 2004. A fine, comparative analysis of fascism and fascist movements.

Payne, Stanley G. *A History of Fascism, 1914–1945.* Madison: University of Wisconsin Press, 1995. Excellent in its European and global perspective on fascist movements.

Wasserstein, Bernard. *Barbarism and Civilization: A History of Europe in Our Time.* Oxford: Oxford University Press, 2007. An excellent survey emphasizing dark developments during the period 1914—2007.

TRANSFORMING THE SOVIET UNION, 1920–1939

Applebaum, Anne. *Gulag: A History.* New York: Doubleday, 2003. Vividly analyzes the Soviet Union's forced-labor camps.

Lewin, Moshe. *The Making of the Soviet System: Essays in the Social History of Interwar Russia.* London: Methuen, 1985. A thoughtful analysis by a noted scholar.

Thurston, Robert W. *Life and Terror in Stalin's Russia, 1934–1941.* New Haven, CT: Yale University Press, 1996. An attempt to revise accepted interpretations of Stalin and the Great Terror as the product of an evil mastermind.

Tucker, Robert C. *Stalin in Power: The Revolution from Above, 1928–1941.* New York: Norton, 1990. The second volume of an exhaustive and acclaimed analysis of Stalin, stressing the policies of collectivization and industrialization.

THE GREAT DEPRESSION, 1929–1939

Eichengreen, Barry. *Golden Fetters: The Gold Standard and the Great Depression, 1919–1939.* New York: Oxford University Press, 1992. Argues that the gold standard was the obstacle to financial stability and economic prosperity in the interwar period.

Kindleberger, Charles. *The World in Depression, 1929–1939,* 2nd ed. Berkeley: University of California Press, 1986. A wide-ranging account that argues that problems in the system of international exchange played the most important role in causing the Great Depression.

NAZISM IN GERMANY

Evans, Richard J. *The Third Reich in Power, 1933–1939.* New York: Penguin, 2005. An excellent examination of life in Nazi Germany during the 1930s.

Fischer, Klaus P. *Nazi Germany: A New History.* New York: Continuum, 1995. A highly regarded examination of Nazi Germany.

Kershaw, Ian. *The Nazi Dictatorship,* 3rd ed. London: Edward Arnold, 1993. A thoughtful examination of the historiography of Nazism.

Koonz, Claudia. *Mothers in the Fatherland: Women, the Family, and Nazi Politics.* New York: St. Martin's Press, 1987. Studies Nazi ideology regarding women as well as women's responses to it.

HORST STREMPEL, *NIGHT OVER GERMANY*, 1945

This 1945 painting by German artist Horst Strempel (1904–1975) depicts the fate of Germany in World War II. More broadly, it conveys the human suffering brought on by that horrendous conflict. In the left panel, a man huddles in terror and stares out from a confined space. Behind him mysterious figures loom in the darkness. In the right panel, a family peers out of a similar space, despair etched in their faces. The figures in the central panel mutely express that same despair, while the background hints at the misery and destruction of war. Below these individuals huddle more people, seemingly trapped but perhaps hoping for rescue. Strempel's painting, like World War II itself, has roots in World War I and echoes the stunning depiction of that conflict by Otto Dix, shown on page 690.

Into the Fire Again: World War II, 1939–1945

In September 1938, British prime minister Neville Chamberlain flew home from a conference with leaders of France, Germany, and Italy. At the airport north of London, he announced to cheering crowds that an agreement at that meeting, known as the Munich Conference, had achieved "peace for our time." British newspapers proclaimed him a hero.

Less than a year later, Chamberlain delivered another speech on the same topic. But this time, he made a painful admission to Britain's House of Commons. "This is a sad day for all of us, and to none is it sadder than to me," he confessed. "Everything that I have worked for, every-thing that I have hoped for . . . has crashed into ruins." The events that had devastated Chamberlain had just taken place in eastern Europe. On September 1, 1939, Germany had invaded Poland. Now Chamberlain was announcing Britain's declaration of war against Germany. He made his point clear: "I trust I may live to see the day when Hitlerism has been destroyed and a liberated Europe has been reestablished."

Chamberlain, who died in 1940, would not see that day. War raged in Europe and across the globe for more than five years. Some viewed this conflict as a chance to reverse the results of the Great War of 1914–1918. Others deemed it a dreaded return of that "war to end all wars." But for most, this new contest would prove unique in its horrors and far worse than World War I. Inhumanity—from indiscriminate bombing to programmed genocide—gained the upper hand in the West, Asia, and the Pacific between the late 1930s and 1945. In the end, the conflict would take the lives of tens of millions of people and leave lasting scars on many nations and individuals. The painting shown on the facing page not only echoes Otto Dix's image of World War I (see page 690) but also evokes the suffering of those who survived the violence and hardship inflicted by World War II.

TIMELINE

World War II

War in East Asia

Spanish Civil War

The Cold War

Nazism in Germany

Fascism in Italy

Decolonization

The Great Depression

Holocaust

1931   1933   1935   1937   1939   1941   1943   1945   1947

THE ROAD TO WAR,

1931–1939

"For us Germans the dictated Treaty of Versailles is not a law," announced Hitler to the German Reichstag on September 1, 1939. Throughout his speech—in which he sought to explain why German forces has just invaded Poland—Hitler jumped back and forth between the Great War of 1914–1918 and the present conflict, referring to himself as "the first soldier of the German Reich." He made clear his intent to reverse the results of World War I: "I have once again put on that uniform which was always so sacred and dear to me. I shall not lay it aside until after the victory—or I shall not live to see the end...." What happened in the West and the world that led to that moment?

As we saw in Chapter 23, in the tense years of the 1920s and 1930s a new wave of authoritarian governments had washed across eastern and southern Europe; by 1938, only Czechoslovakia remained a parliamentary democracy. Many of these regimes included elements of fascism, but most were simple dictatorships by royal or military figures. Fascist movements, such as the Cross of Fire organization in France and the "Rex" Party in Belgium, also sprouted up in western Europe.

The democratic nations turned inward as they grappled with the depression and political divisions within their own borders. After 1934, communists in those nations sought to form alliances with socialists and moderates against the growing strength of fascism. The **Popular Front** in France is an example of such a partnership. The Front governed from 1936 to 1938. It was unable to pull the nation out of the depression, however, and ultimately fell from power. Its defeat left France more politically divided and discouraged than ever.

International Affairs Break Down

For France and the other democracies, international affairs soon slipped out of control. Rearmament spread, aggression became the order of the day, and neither the democratic powers nor the League of Nations responded forcefully to stop it.

In 1931, Japan initiated the new pattern. Many in Japan had long viewed China as their immediate rival—an enemy with the potential to stand in the way of their ambitions for economic and political dominance in east Asia. On the orders of young officers, the Japanese army invaded Manchuria in northern China and began a drive for conquest. Crowds in Japan cheered the news of the Manchurian campaign, and a heightened sense of nationalistic militarism gradually pervaded Japanese political life. The League of Nations condemned Japan but took no action. By 1937, China had managed to shake off the most onerous Western controls over the country but still bore the scars of decades of a sporadic, bloody civil war. China's dominant Nationalist Party, under Jiang Jieshi (Chiang Kai-shek) (1887–1975), had expended much of its strength opposing the growing Chinese Communist Party, led by Mao Zedong (1893–1976). In the early 1930s, Jiang had almost vanquished the Communists, but Mao and the core of his movement held on.

In 1937, Japanese troops invaded China proper. Less than six months later, the Japanese Imperial Army captured Nanking, capital city of China's Nationalist government. Over the following six weeks, Japanese army officers gave their troops free rein of the city. An American reporter in Nanking described the Japanese victory as "accompanied by the mass killing of the defenders, who were piled up among the sandbags, forming a mound six feet high." Victory did not end the slaughter: "Thousands of prisoners were executed by the Japanese ... the killing of civilians was widespread ... Nanking's streets were littered with dead." In what probably amounted to a deliberate policy, the Japanese carried out mass killings and executions of up to 300,000 Chinese soldiers and civilians and raped thousands of women.

Appalled, the rival Chinese Communists and Nationalists finally forged an alliance against the Japanese, and the Soviet Union provided military assistance to China against its powerful rival in the east. Nevertheless, city after city in China fell to Japanese bombs and invading armies. With its expanding industrial economy hungry for new markets, Japan

Japan on the march

was determined to create "a new order in East Asia," under its domination. To secure its position, it moved to form an alliance with two other aggressive, authoritarian states: Italy and Germany.

In 1935, Mussolini ordered his troops to invade Ethiopia in East Africa, hoping to win popularity at home despite the unemployment

Italy invades Ethiopia and failing social policies there. Ethiopia appealed to the League of Nations for protection. The League condemned Il Duce's actions, but the democratic powers did not follow up with enough action to stop him. Indeed, these responses to his aggression only pushed Mussolini toward Hitler, and in 1936 the two leaders agreed to a friendship alliance—the Rome-Berlin **Axis.** In 1939, that alliance solidified into the military Pact of Steel. To show unity with Hitler, Mussolini promptly adopted anti-Semitic racial laws for Italy. To further his own military ambitions, he invaded Albania.

Civil War in Spain

In 1936, civil war broke out in Spain. Five years earlier, Spain had become a democratic republic for the first time. But when the Popular Front, made up of radicals, socialists, and communists, won election in 1936, a group of generals led by the conservative Francisco Franco (1892–1975) launched an armed rebellion against the new government. Franco's nationalist rebels enjoyed the support of the fascist Falange Party, the army, the church, and most of the wealthy elites; nevertheless, they could not easily overturn the popular Loyalists—the supporters of the Popular Front government.

The Spanish civil war soon became an international battlefield. Hitler and Mussolini, spotting an opportunity to advance the cause of fascism, gain an ally, and test their new weapons, sent arms and troops to aid Franco. At one point in 1937, Germans manning new airplanes on behalf of Franco's nationalists attacked the small Spanish town of Guernica, raining death on the civilian population there. The slaughter became the subject matter of one of the most haunting paintings of the twentieth century, *Guernica* (1937), by the Spanish artist Pablo Picasso (1881–1973). This 25-foot-long mural in black and white (**Figure 24.1**) captures the worst features of this war—terror, brutality, disjointedness, lack of direction, and despair. On the left, a woman shrieks while holding a dead child. In the center, a warrior and horse lie shattered into fragments as the wounded sorrowfully look on. On the right, a woman plummets from a burning building. The image expresses both a wailing lament and a warning: modern war not only kills indiscriminately but targets civilians in order to terrorize all into submission.

The Loyalists appealed to the other Western democracies for aid, but no help came. These nations hoped to maintain good relations with Italy and Germany and thus committed to a policy of neutrality, even though the fascist powers only pretended to agree. Unofficial Loyalist support came from some 40,000 idealistic volunteers, such as the Garibaldi Brigade and the Lincoln Brigade, who traveled to Spain from abroad and fought as individuals in the Loyalist cause. Otherwise, only the Soviet Union (until 1938) and Mexico provided assistance. The Loyalists also suffered from internal divisions between competing communists, anarchists, and liberals. In 1939, after three years of slaughter and atrocities on both sides, Franco's rebels finally beat down the last of the Loyalist resistance (see **Map 24.1**). The authoritarian Franco ruled Spain until his death in 1975.

Trying to Cope with Germany

In March 1936, Hitler gambled by ordering his armed forces into the Rhineland, that part of Germany on the west bank of the Rhine River that the Treaty of Versailles had deemed a demilitarized zone (see **Map 24.2**). France fretted and fumed but, lacking Britain's support, did nothing. Hitler's bold gamble paid off. With a new confidence, he turned to the three countries that bordered Germany to the east: Austria, Czechoslovakia, and Poland.

In 1938, the Nazis incorporated Austria without opposition, annexing the 6.5 million Austrians to the German Reich (empire) (see **Map 24.2**). Hitler then claimed a portion of Czechoslovakia—the Sudetenland—that included 3.5 million German-speaking people. The Czechs, however, surprised him by rushing to their defenses. For months, Hitler churned out a barrage of propaganda that painted the German-speaking Czechs as a persecuted minority. He threatened and roused his people to readiness for war, finally vowing to march if the Sudetenland was not surrendered to him.

A difficult question now arose for the rest of Europe as it watched Hitler's actions: What should be done? For complex reasons, no one opposed Hitler with force. For one thing, World War I had made many Europeans reluctant to risk general war again. In addition, disagreement swirled over the justice of Hitler's demands. Some people agreed with Germany that the Versailles treaty was too harsh and sympathized with those who wanted to appease Germany's injured feelings. Many other people saw Hitler as sometimes reasonable and as a force that at least might be used to stop the spread of communism. British prime minister Neville Chamberlain (1869–1940), aware of Britain's lack of armed forces and public support to halt Hitler, tried for a compromise with the German ruler.

FIGURE 24.1

Pablo Picasso, *Guernica*, 1937

Pablo Picasso's painting reveals the horrors of the Spanish civil war by focusing on a 1937 bombing raid on the town of Guernica. Here, Picasso uses symbols and images of people who are broken and suffering, with most of the faces looking up to the sky where destruction has rained down upon them.

Connecting Art & Society

1. What impressions of war was Picasso seeking to convey to viewers?

2. How does this painting differ from a traditional battle scene?

3. In what ways might details of this painting serve as a warning?

On September 29, 1938, the leaders of Germany, Italy, France, and Britain met in Munich to resolve the Sudetenland question. In the end, the two democratic powers chose **appeasement**—giving in to Hitler's demands in hopes of satisfying him. Hitler grabbed the piece of Czechoslovakia that he wanted. British and French leaders, underestimating Hitler's territorial ambitions and determination to go to war, felt pleased with the agreement. Their nations still suffered from the Great Depression and could not endure another conflict, they told themselves. Moreover, many Europeans—particularly the British and French—considered a renewal of horrors akin to those of the Great War of 1914–1918 unacceptable. However, the Czechoslovak and Soviet governments expressed outrage; they hadn't been invited to attend the conference. The agreement would force the Czechs to capitulate. For Stalin, the deal confirmed the continuing unwillingness of the Western democracies to unite with the Soviet Union against the growing fascist threat.

> **Appeasement at Munich**

Back in Britain, Chamberlain announced that the **Munich Conference** agreement had "saved Czechoslovakia from destruction and Europe from Armageddon." Across Europe, crowds cheered, celebrating what they saw as the preservation of peace. But a few months later, Hitler showed his true colors: With no warning, he sent forces to overrun the remainder of the Czechoslovakian Republic (see **Map 24.2**).

When Hitler next threatened Poland, Great Britain got tough and promised to come to Poland's aid. They turned to the Soviets for help, but it was too late. Isolated or excluded for too long from international affairs and disillusioned by France's and Britain's weak response to German aggression, Stalin stunned the world by signing a nonaggression pact with Hitler on August 23, 1939. In return for the Soviet Union's neutrality while Germany carved up Poland, Hitler gave Stalin a free hand to reannex territories in eastern Europe—including eastern Poland—that Russia

> **Nazi-Soviet nonaggression pact**

MAP 24.1

The Spanish Civil War, 1936–1939

This map shows the evolution of the Spanish civil war between 1936 and 1939.

Explore the Map

1. What was the route of Franco's forces? Where did they begin and end up? Why?

2. Why was France's unwillingness to help the Loyalist forces so important a factor in the war's outcome?

---

had lost during World War I (see **Map 24.2**). By making this cynical pact with his greatest ideological enemy, Nazi Germany, Stalin may have gambled that the Soviet Union could stay on the sidelines, growing in strength, while the fascist and democratic capitalists destroyed one another.

At dawn on September 1, the Germans launched an all-out attack on Poland by land, sea, and air. Hitler remained convinced that France and Britain would not go to war over Poland. He was wrong. Two days later, Great Britain and France declared war on Germany. In a poem titled "SEPTEMBER 1, 1939," poet W. H. Auden (1907–1973) moaned that

> *The unmentionable odor of death*
> *Offends the September night*

World War II had begun.

AXIS VICTORIES,
1939–1942

Perhaps the war initiated in 1914 never quite ended, and the 1920s were just a pause in three decades of fighting and crises after 1914. Maybe if the depression had not struck, Hitler and the Nazis would not have come to power, the democracies would have continued to grow, and war could have been averted. Tragically, the war that did break out in September 1939 would blaze six long years and encompass the globe as never before.

Triumph of the German Blitzkrieg

The German **blitzkrieg**—a "lightning war" of highly coordinated air strikes and rapid deployment of tanks and motorized columns—overwhelmed Polish forces.

MAP 24.2

German Expansion, 1936–1939

This map shows German expansion between 1936 and September 1939, as well as the territory annexed by the Soviet Union thanks to the Nazi-Soviet nonaggression pact of August 1939.

Explore the Map

1. In what ways did these developments leave Poland vulnerable?

2. What distinguishes the steps in Germany's expansion?

3. What nations might have felt most threatened by further German aggression?

But that did not end matters within Poland: German occupiers and Germans already living within Poland soon began destroying the Polish people, actions that would form a pattern to be repeated and magnified in the years to come. The French and British mobilized their armies along the German border, and the British fleet blockaded Germany by sea—all to no avail.

For the next six months, in what became known as the "phony war," almost no military action took place.

France and Great Britain seemed paralyzed. Meanwhile, the Soviet Union took advantage of its agreement with Hitler and reannexed territories in Poland and eastern Europe—including Estonia, Latvia, and Lithuania—that Russia had lost in World War I. When Finland refused to yield strategic territories, the Soviets attacked. The Finns put up a determined resistance, and it took several months for the Soviet army finally to defeat these stubborn soldiers.

In April 1940, the Germans suddenly overran both Denmark and Norway. German planes fended off Britain's fleet, inflicting heavy losses. The next month, German armies assaulted Luxembourg, the Netherlands, Belgium, and France. Tiny Luxembourg offered no resistance, while the Dutch fought heroically but fell after six days. To support the beleaguered Belgians, the British army and a large part of the French army moved into Belgium. The French trusted that their fortresses—the Maginot Line—would hold along the German border. However, the line proved useless against the highly mobile German tanks. The Germans skirted the fortresses to the north through the Ardennes Forest. German general Erwin Rommel recalled the breakthrough: "The tanks now rolled in a long column through the line of fortifications. . . . Our artillery was dropping heavy harassing fire on villages and the road far ahead. . . . Engines roared, tank tracks clanked and clattered . . . civilians and French troops, their faces distorted with terror, lay huddled in the ditches." And then, he noted, "the flat countryside lay spread out around us under the cold light of the moon. We were through the Maginot Line."

The German blitzkrieg drove quickly to the English Channel, cutting off Allied armies in Belgium and then trapping them at Dunkirk, a seaport in northern France. A flotilla of military and civilian ships, including fishing boats and pleasure craft, rescued 330,000 British and French troops off the beach at Dunkirk.

The Battle of France ended after only five weeks. Although almost equal in numbers to the Germans, the French seemed demoralized from the beginning of the war. According to one French journalist, they felt abandoned by the British, "who were ready to fight to the last French soldier." On June 16, 1940, the aged, right-wing Marshal Philippe Pétain became premier of France and quickly surrendered to Hitler. **Figure 24.2** shows triumphant German troops on the march through Paris that year. In the background stands France's Arch of Triumph, a reminder of past victories now vastly overshadowed by Germany's occupying forces. With the surrender, Germany took the northern half of France and the entire Atlantic coast. The new authoritarian French regime would govern the remaining unoccupied portion of France from the city of Vichy. French general Charles de Gaulle escaped to Great Britain and declared himself leader of the Free French government in exile.

The Battle of France

FIGURE 24.2 France in Defeat, 1940   In this stark photograph, German troops parade down France's celebrated Champs-Élysées boulevard after the fall of Paris in 1940.

France's collapse left Great Britain to face Germany alone. The audacious and eloquent Winston Churchill (1874–1965), who had replaced Neville Chamberlain as prime minister, warned his people of the serious struggle to come: "This is no war of chieftains or of princes, of dynasties or national ambition; it is a war of peoples and of causes." The Germans, determined to gain control of the English Channel and prepare for an invasion of Britain, unleashed massive air attacks against Britain in July 1940. As the Battle of Britain erupted, Churchill rallied his country, offering his "blood, toil, tears, and sweat" and vowing "we shall never surrender."

The Battle of Britain

For almost two months that fall, the Germans bombed London every night. A British civilian described some of the ordeal: "Bombs fell by day as well as by night. We became accustomed to the sudden drone of an airplane in the middle of the morning, the screech of a bomb, the dull crash of its explosion and the smell of cordite that filled the air a moment later." **Figure 24.3** reveals some of the effort involved in the Battle of Britain. A group of three women and one man pull in a barrage balloon. Weighted cables dangling beneath the balloon hinder low-level flights by German bombers. In the background are buildings destroyed by bombings, but numerous smokestacks in the distance indicate that Britain's ability to fight survives. In cellars and subway stations, the British people holed up while their planes and antiaircraft guns,

FIGURE 24.3 Laura Knight, The Battle of Britain, 1943 Women and men pull in balloons used to hinder flights by German bombers during the Battle of Britain.

Germany's Afrika Korps drove the British back into Egypt. Pro-German movements broke out in Iraq, Iran, and French Syria. At this point, however, Hitler hurled his main forces against the Soviet Union, giving the British a breathing spell to recoup their strength in North Africa and the eastern Mediterranean.

Operation Barbarossa: Germany Invades the Soviet Union

The eventual conquest of the Soviet Union had always been uppermost in Hitler's thoughts, despite his deceptive pact with the USSR. Even before that 1939 deal, Hitler had revealed his true intentions to a group of associates: "Everything I do is directed against Russia. If the West is too stupid and blind to understand that, I shall be forced to reach an agreement with the Russians and strike at the West. Once [the West] is defeated, [I shall] turn my concentrated forces against the Soviet Union." Conquest of the Soviet Union would bring Germany "living space" as well as vast industrial and agricultural resources. It would also eliminate any threat from Nazism's great ideological enemy. And it would afford Germany access to millions of Jews—Hitler's "blood enemy"—living in the Soviet Union. Still, the Nazi leader had hoped to subdue the British before turning to the Soviets. Failing that, he decided to invade the Soviet Union anyway.

In June 1941, the Germans launched Operation Barbarossa, sending more than three million soldiers, 3,700 tanks, and 2,500 planes against the USSR. Hitler expected to crush Soviet resistance in six weeks, well before the notorious Russian winter set in. "You only have to kick in the door, and the whole rotten structure will come crashing down," he claimed. But he also warned his generals, "The war against Russia will be . . . one of ideologies and racial differences and will have to be conducted with unprecedented, unmerciful and unrelenting harshness."

Stalin had long suspected that Hitler would someday turn against him, yet he believed that a German invasion was impossible before spring 1942, when Britain would be too crippled to constitute much of a diversion to German forces. Moreover, recent evidence suggests that Stalin himself may have planned to turn the tables on Hitler and launch his own full-scale pre-emptive attack on German forces in eastern Europe. In the days before the June invasion by Germany, Stalin refused to believe numerous reports from many sources that Hitler's forces were about to attack. He even ignored warnings from some of his top generals.

now aided by radar, fought off the Germans. Boosted by the high morale of the people, the increased output of aircraft factories, and Churchill's leadership, the island nation miraculously held. By November, the British had prevailed.

War in North Africa and the Balkans

Even though Italy was not yet ready to take on another major war, Mussolini did not want to miss out on the spoils of an easy victory. He, too, invaded France as it fell to the Germans. Then in September 1940, his armies in Africa moved east from Libya into Egypt. A few weeks later, they attacked Greece from Albania.

However, Mussolini's forces met disaster at every turn. Mobile British forces routed Italian armies in North Africa, and British planes crippled the Italian fleet in southern Italy. The Greeks also contributed to the rout, driving the Italians back into Albania.

In response, Germany's forces streamed into the Balkans and North Africa. Hitler had several goals in mind for this move. He coveted the Balkans for their rich supplies of raw materials, especially the Romanian oil fields. He also hoped to save the Italian forces in North Africa and take the Suez Canal, Britain's lifeline to its empire. Hungary and Romania yielded to Hitler's threats and joined the Axis alliance in November 1940; Bulgaria did the same in March 1941. Yugoslavia and Greece refused, and they were overrun by German forces within a few weeks.

On the morning of June 22, the Germans launched their assault. Caught off guard, Stalin delayed his response. For a few days, he disappeared from the public eye. Finally, he urged the Soviet people to rally to "the Great Patriotic War." Not everyone rose to the challenge. Indeed, the Ukrainians and some other Soviet groups initially greeted the Germans as liberators. The German forces quickly shattered Soviet armies. On July 3, the chief of Germany's General Staff wrote in his journal, "The Russian Campaign has been won in the space of two weeks." In just the first twenty days of the campaign, 600,000 Soviet soldiers lost their lives.

Even in the face of such destruction, most Soviet peoples put up a determined resistance. The weather worked against the enemy. The September mud season slowed German troops and tanks, and the unusually harsh winter that followed caught the invaders unprepared. Nevertheless, the German war machine crunched forward. By December 1, it had come within sight of Moscow and had nearly surrounded Leningrad (see **Map 24.3**). A confident Hitler announced the imminent, permanent destruction of the USSR.

Once again, the weather intervened. The winter tightened its grip, subjecting the lightly clothed and weakly supplied Nazis to frigid temperatures. Moreover, Japan's decision not to go to war against the USSR saved the Soviets from a disastrous two-front struggle. Stalin could now move troops from the Far East to the West. The combination of punishing weather and Russian counterattacks forced the Germans to halt and in some places even retreat—but only temporarily. By then, German forces had slaughtered more than three million Soviet soldiers and captured another three million. But the Soviet forces were not yet broken.

Japan Attacks

Farther east, events were brewing that would add yet another dimension to the war. Specifically, Western imperial presence in Asia and the Pacific had frustrated Japan's dreams of expansion. The resource-poor island nation depended on foreign raw materials and markets to fuel its industrial economy. During the 1930s, the Great Depression had weakened Japan's democratic regime and made the army a more potent political as well as military force. As military men gained control of the government, Japan's foreign policy shifted to expansionism (see Global Connections). By 1939, Japan had conquered the populous coastal areas of China and pushed Chinese forces well into the interior. When the war in Europe weakened European colonial powers—which controlled much of Southeast Asia, with its wealth of essential resources such as oil, tin, and rubber—Japan joined the Rome-Berlin Axis. It quickly occupied French Indochina and threatened the Dutch East Indies. The United States responded with a total economic embargo on all exports to Japan, threatening Japan's oil supplies in particular.

Hoping that the war in Europe would induce the United States to cede dominance to the Japanese in Southeast Asia, Japan struck. On December 7, 1941, Japanese air forces surprised the American fleet anchored in Pearl Harbor, Hawaii, crippling the U.S. naval and air forces. President Franklin D. Roosevelt (1882–1945) called it "a day that will live in infamy." The United States immediately declared war on Japan, and within days Germany and Italy declared war on the United States. Several Latin American nations joined the United States in the Grand Alliance against the Axis.

The U.S. enters the war

The long-isolationist United States had an army with limited capabilities. In addition, it had sent huge quantities of arms, equipment, and food across the Atlantic in its role as "the arsenal of democracy." Roosevelt agreed with Churchill to make the war in Europe the United States' first priority, and Americans started mobilizing their country's vast resources for the fight.

Meanwhile, the Japanese conquered a vast area in Southeast Asia and the Pacific (**Map 24.4**), creating The Greater East Asia Co-Prosperity Sphere. Japan claimed to be liberating Asia from the imperial West, but it dominated the new territories through nationalist leaders ready to collaborate with Japan's occupation forces and treated the conquered peoples as inferior subjects. Scoring victory after victory, the Japanese and Germans seemed to be winning the war.

BEHIND THE LINES: THE STRUGGLE AND THE HORROR

By 1942, Hitler ruled most of continental Europe from the English Channel to the outskirts of Moscow (see **Map 24.3**). In administering his lands, he pursued two primary goals. First, he hunted for ways to keep Germany supplied with war materials and maintain the standard of living for Germans without having to call on them to make unpopular sacrifices. Second, he sought to fulfill his racist agenda. To these ends, he implemented his "New Order," a program of economic exploitation and racial imperialism in the lands that he now controlled. He used conquered peoples according to their ranking in his racial hierarchy. Those most directly related to the Nazi conception of the Aryan race, such as Scandinavians, Anglo-Saxons, and Dutch, were treated well and might be absorbed into the Nazi

Hitler's "New Order"

Map legend:
- Hitler's Greater Germany
- Allied with Germany
- Occupied by Germany and Its Allies
- Grand Alliance
- Neutral Nations
- ★ Major Battles

MAP 24.3

World War II in Europe

This map shows Hitler's empire at its height in 1942, the front lines in the following years as the Allies closed in on Germany in 1945, and the major battles of the war.

Explore the Map

1. What does this map indicate about the military problems confronting Hitler after 1942?

2. Compare the eastern, southern, and western fronts. How might the fighting have differed in these three areas? Why?

3. Locate the western, Italian, and Russian fronts in February 1945, just a few months before the end of the war. What might these troop locations suggest about spheres of influence during the postwar decades?

empire as partners with the Germans. He considered the Latin races, such as the French, inferior but tolerable as supportive cogs in the New Order. Slavs ranked toward the bottom of Hitler's hierarchy; they were to be isolated, shoved aside, treated like slaves, or killed.

The Holocaust

Lowest on Hitler's racial scale were the Jews, and they fared the worst in Hitler's scheme. Nazis herded Jews into ghettos in German, Polish, and Russian cities. For a while, the Nazis envisioned forced

The Rise of Japanese Ultranationalism

During the 1920s, Japanese liberals who supported the international system established at the end of World War I held most of the power in the island nation's government. However, ultranationalists and militarists rejected the "Western" system and argued for an expanding Japanese empire in east Asia. These opponents of the system gained increasing power, especially after the Great Depression struck in 1929 and weakened Japan's economy.

During the 1930s, as some Western nations expressed alarm over Japanese expansionist moves, Hashimoto Kingoro, a leading ultranationalist, challenged them to reexamine their thinking. Western nations, Hashimoto proclaimed, were in no position to complain about Japan's desire to take territories it needed: "[W]e may wish to ask the white race just which country it was that sent warships and troops to India, South Africa, and Australia and slaughtered innocent natives, bound their hands and feet with iron chains, lashed their backs with iron whips, proclaimed these territories as their own, and still continues to hold them to this very day?" Okawa Shumei, another leading ultranationalist, built on Hashimoto's reasoning. A "struggle between the great powers of the East and the West," Okawa claimed, "which will decide their existence, is at present, as in the past, absolutely inevitable" if a better world for Asia was to come about. In Okawa's view, Japan's proper role in this new world was clear: "Heaven has decided on Japan as its choice for the champion of the East. Has not this been the purpose of our three thousand long years of preparation?"

Over the course of the 1930s, liberals lost ground to the ultranationalists and militarists, who increasingly took over Japan's government. In 1931, Japanese troops created an "incident" in Manchuria that ignited a war with China and led to the establishment by the Japanese of a puppet state, Manchukuo, in Manchuria. In 1937, Japan again attacked China, launching a full-scale but undeclared war against the beleaguered nation. Soon Japan had seized large areas of east and north China. In 1940, Japan allied itself with the two main ultranationalist powers in the West: Nazi Germany and Fascist Italy.

The following year, just a few months before the Japanese attack on Pearl Harbor, Japan's Ministry of Education distributed *The Way of Subjects*—required reading for all Japanese high school and university students. The pamphlet revealed the thinking behind Japanese ultranationalism. The document pointed to the harmful "influx of European and American culture into this country," by which the authors meant individualism, liberalism, and materialism. Thanks to these outside influences, "the traditional character of the country was much impaired and the virtuous habits and customs bequeathed by our ancestors were affected unfavorably." Japan's mission, the document continued, was "the emancipation of East Asian nations." Throughout Asia, "hopes to be free of the shackles and bondage of Europe and America were ablaze."

In 1942, at the height of its power, the Japanese government created a plan for the establishment of the Greater East Asia Co-Prosperity Sphere, which echoed ultranationalist thought. The plan asserted that "the Japanese empire is the center and pioneer of Oriental moral and cultural reconstruction." Moreover, Japan's mission was "to cause East Asia to return to its original form of independence and co-prosperity by shaking off the yoke of Europe and America." By this time, Japan controlled much of east and south Asia as well as the Pacific Basin. But this year also saw the beginning of the end of Japan's power, for U.S. military might had begun turning the tide against Japan. Ultranationalist dreams and policies finally collapsed in the summer of 1945. That year, American planes dropped atomic bombs on Hiroshima and Nagasaki, defeating Japan and ending World War II.

Making Connections

1. Why might the arguments of ultranationalists have appealed to various political and military groups?

2. How were Western imperialist practices used to justify Japanese expansion?

emigration of Jews, perhaps to the island of Madagascar off the east coast of Africa, to solve the "Jewish problem." In 1941, such ideas ended and Hitler initiated a policy of genocide, formally adopted in a January 1942 meeting, which came to be known as the **Holocaust.** Mobile SS squads under Reinhard Heydrich (1904–1942) and Heinrich Himmler began the wholesale killing of Jews, along with Slavic prisoners of war, in Poland and Russia. Firing squads shot victims en masse. Dissatisfied with the pace of the killings, the Germans began using mobile vans that murdered people by gas. Finally, when that

MAP 24.4

World War II in the Pacific

This map shows Japan's empire at its height in 1942 and traces the course of the Allied counteroffensive that led to Japan's defeat in 1945.

Explore the Map

1. What was the extent of Japan's territorial domination at this time?

2. What problems did the Japanese face in trying to control their far-flung territories?

3. Consider the Allies' strategy in their counteroffensive against the Japanese. Why did this strategy differ from that used in Europe?

method still did not seem efficient enough, the Nazis used large gas chambers that killed thousands at a time. Heydrich, the Plenipotentiary for the Preparation of the Final Solution of the European Jewish Question, promised that this campaign—"a historic moment in the struggle against Jewry"—would be carried out "effectively but silently." Heydrich charged Adolf Eichmann (1906–1962) with managing this task.

The Nazis built six huge death camps in what had been Poland. From gathering points all over Europe, unknowing victims were crowded into cattle cars, where they soon became dehydrated, disoriented, and terrorized; many died in transit. Upon their arrival, officials divided families, segregated people by sex, and made the first "selection." "Inside the camp, one's first view was fixed on a mountain of children's shoes," recalled a woman survivor. "To tell the truth I did not understand what that meant." Those who could not work as the Nazis wanted—therefore more women, children, and elderly—were sent to the "showers"— the Nazis' euphemism for the gas chambers. Officials especially targeted pregnant women to prevent the birth of more Jews. They sent the rest, now physically and mentally terrorized, to the work camps.

Death camps

The scale and depravity of this programmed inhumanity, torture, and death were unprecedented; thus the victims simply could not grasp what was happening until it was too late. Some Jews rebelled—in the Warsaw ghetto and the Treblinka camp, for example. They and others who fought back may have made important moral statements, but they stood no real chance against the Nazis. The masses of Jews trapped in ghettos or camps, their strength sapped by hunger and illness, had little choice. For many, the only way to maintain a shred of dignity against the degradation and death was silence. The Nazis had trapped these victims in a merciless, thoroughly organized system from which few escaped.

Struggling to survive in the camps, many people tried to help one another, though the desperate conditions at times also brought out the worst in people. In this surreal world, the Germans applied assembly-line methods to the destruction of millions of human beings. A French doctor described the killing process at the Auschwitz-Birkenau camp: Once prisoners were herded and forced into the gas chambers, "the massive oak double doors are shut. For two endless minutes one can hear banging on the walls and screams which are no longer human. . . . Five minutes later the doors are opened. The corpses, squashed together and distorted, fall out like a waterfall" (see Document 24.1). In a particularly brutal twist, the Nazis forced Jewish prisoners to carry out much of the dirty work of killing. Nazi guards subjected their captives to torture and abuse, and German doctors conducted gruesome experiments on camp prisoners.

In the end, almost all prisoners slaved in the camps on starvation rations until they died or were sent to the gas chambers when no longer useful to their captors. In Auschwitz alone, the largest of these camps, the Nazis murdered more than 12,000 people a day and more than one million Jews by the end of the war. Although Jews were the Nazis' main target, many people from non-Jewish groups—communists, gypsies, Jehovah's Witnesses, Soviet prisoners of war, Slavs, homosexuals—suffered the same fate. Moreover, the elite Nazis had other ominous plans—including an eventual genocidal "resettlement" to Siberia of more than 30 million people, mainly Slavs—if the Nazis should win the war in the East. Rudolf Höss, commander of the Auschwitz camp, would describe the order for mass killings as "something extraordinary, something monstrous. However the reasoning behind the order of this mass annihilation seemed correct to me . . . I wasted no thoughts about it." Ultimately

FIGURE 24.4 Nazi Atrocities, 1945 This grim photo taken in the Landsberg concentration camp is one of many that testify to Nazi atrocities.

these genocidal efforts took priority over even the war effort and continued right up until the last days of the war.

Figure 24.4 is a photograph taken after World War II ended. Here American officials force German civilians living near the Landsberg camp to stand witness to the Nazis' shocking atrocities. Who knew about the brutal realities of the camps during the war? The Nazis had gone to great lengths to cover up the process of killing, swearing everyone involved to secrecy and presenting more benign concentration camps outside Poland for international inspection. As reports of what really was happening filtered out, many people expressed disbelief. Atrocities on such a mass scale seemed impossible. But it had taken thousands of officials, bureaucrats, soldiers, police, and SS guards to carry out the murders. At least these thousands knew. Indeed, many concentration- and death-camp officials followed orders with enthusiasm, competing for approval from their superiors. Several large German companies, including the industrial giant I. G. Farben, benefited from contracts with the camps. Most German civilians may have been apathetic or may have chosen not to think about what was going on in the east, but information—from witnesses, from individuals indirectly involved, and by word of mouth—about the camps and massive killings was widespread. While perhaps not fully comprehended, the Final Solution had become an open secret in Germany by the end of 1942. Authorities on the outside who might have tried to help did nothing. At some point, British and American commanders probably

DOCUMENT 24.1

The Nazi Death Camps

In 1942, the Nazis began a new phase in their campaign to murder Jews and others. Their "final solution" took the form of death camps where Nazis could kill on a larger scale. Testimonies from witnesses paint vivid pictures of the horrors that occurred daily in these camps. The first account below is from Abraham Bomba, who in 1942 was transported with his family from a Polish ghetto to the Treblinka death camp, where his job was to cut women's hair before they were gassed. He escaped in 1943 and later described his experiences at the camp. The second account comes from a French doctor, André Lettich, whose job was to remove corpses from the crematoria at Birkenau.

1. Filling the Treblinka Gas Chambers

The gas chamber . . . was all concrete. There was no window. [It] had two doors . . . [and] the people went in to the gas chamber from the one side . . . [and] they pushed in as many as they could. It was not allowed to have the people standing up with their hands down because there was not enough room, but when the people raised their hand[s] . . . there was more room. . . . And on top of that they throw in kids, 2, 3, 4 years old. . . . The whole thing took . . . between five and seven minutes. The door opened up . . . from the other side. People working in Treblinka number two took out the corpses. Some of them dead and some of them still alive. They dragged them to the ditches . . . big ditches, and they covered them. That was the beginning of Treblinka.

2. The "Shower Room"

Until the end of January 1943, there were no crematoria in Birkenau. In the middle of a small birch forest, about two kilometres from the camp, was a peaceful looking house, where a Polish family had once lived before it had been either murdered or expelled. This cottage had been equipped as a gas chamber for a long time.

More than five hundred metres further on were two barracks: the men stood on one side, the women on the other. They were addressed in a very polite and friendly way: "You have been on a journey. You are dirty. You will take a bath. Get undressed quickly." Towels and soap were handed out, and then suddenly the brutes woke up and showed their true faces: this horde of people, these men and women were driven outside with hard blows and forced both summer and winter to go the few hundred metres to the "Shower Room." Above the entry door was the word "Shower." One could even see shower heads on the ceiling which were cemented in but never had water flowing through them.

These poor innocents were crammed together, pressed against each other. Then panic broke out, for at last they realised the fate in store for them. But blows with rifle butts and revolver shots soon restored order and finally they all entered the death chamber. The doors were shut and, ten minutes later, the temperature was high enough to facilitate the condensation of the hydrogen cyanide, for the condemned were gassed with hydrogen cyanide. This was the so-called "Zyklon B," gravel pellets saturated with twenty per cent of hydrogen cyanide which was used by the German barbarians.

Then, SS *Unterscharführer* Moll threw the gas in through a little vent. One could hear fearful screams, but a few moments later there was complete silence. Twenty to twenty-five minutes later, the doors and windows were opened to ventilate the rooms and the corpses were thrown at once into pits to be burnt. But, beforehand the dentists had searched every mouth to pull out the gold teeth. The women were also searched to see if they had not hidden jewelry in the intimate parts of their bodies, and their hair was cut off and methodically placed in sacks for industrial purposes.

SOURCES: (1) United States Holocaust Memorial Museum, "The Holocaust," in *Holocaust Encyclopedia*, www.ushmm.org/wk/index. (2) J. Noakes and G. Pridham, eds., *Nazism, 1919–1945: A Documentary Reader*, vol. 3, in *Foreign Policy, War, and Racial Extermination* (Exeter: University of Exeter Press, 1995), pp. 78–79.

Analyze the Document

1. Why did the Nazis use prisoners for these tasks?

2. How do you explain the reasons behind the procedures used in these camps?

3. What might be the significance of these actions, which occurred on such a large scale?

---

knew. While the full extent of the Holocaust may not have been clear, from almost the beginning Allied leaders had received information about the Nazi killing programs from various sources. After 1942, some Western newspapers published reports about mass murders and the death camps, though how much was widely understood or accepted before 1944 is unclear. Eventually, Jewish leaders pleaded to Allied governments to bomb the gas chambers and the railway lines leading to the death camps. But Allied officials claimed that other military targets were more important for the overall war effort.

Collaboration and Resistance

Collaborating governments often copied or cooperated with the Nazis. In some countries, such as Croatia, officials willingly rounded up Jews and carried out the killing themselves. The anti-Semitic government of Vichy France under Pétain transported thousands of Jews to Nazi death camps. In almost all conquered lands, the Nazis managed to find individuals who would collaborate with them.

However, many others resisted. The Danes saved most of the Jews living in their lands. In Italy, officials often ignored Nazi directives, despite Mussolini's alliance with Hitler. Numerous stories, such as the experience of the young Anne Frank hiding in the Netherlands, record individual heroism and tragedy. Resistance organizations rose in almost every occupied territory, particularly in France, Yugoslavia, and the Soviet Union. At great risk, men and women alike established underground networks, provided intelligence to the Allied forces, conducted guerrilla actions, aided escaping prisoners, sabotaged German military installations, and engaged Nazi forces that might have been used on the war fronts. Communists, such as those in Yugoslavia under the command of Josip Broz (Tito—see Biography), often formed the core of the most determined resistance movements. Tito's organization became one of the most effective resistance forces in Europe.

But the price of fighting back was high. The Germans infiltrated resistance groups and brutally crushed any hints of threats. Collective retribution for attacks against German leaders deterred many. In one case, the Nazis massacred 7,000 people in one town in retaliation for the killing of 10 Germans by Yugoslav partisans. In some places, such as Ukraine, Greece, and Yugoslavia, resistance groups with different political agendas fought among themselves, eroding their ability to oppose the Nazis.

Mobilizing the Home Fronts

Even more than in World War I, whole societies mobilized for the war effort in the 1940s. Governments controlled production and rationed goods. As labor shortages arose, women again assumed jobs normally reserved for men (see Document 24.2). Political leaders acquired unusual powers and discouraged dissent. Even outside the Nazi empire, some groups of citizens fell victim to the suspicion that the war engendered. In the United States, for example, government agents removed Japanese Americans living on the West Coast from their homes and businesses and placed them in camps. Propaganda on all sides painted distorted, racist pictures of the enemy and whipped up civilian support of the troops.

Britain, taking the brunt of German aggression early on, mobilized thoroughly. The government drafted men between the ages of 18 and 50 and women between 20 and 30 into military or civilian war service. Women accounted for most of the increase in Britain's labor force. The government also enlisted scientists to help break the German code and work on an atomic bomb.

The Soviet Union tried everything to brace itself against the Germans. Hundreds of thousands of Russian women served in the Soviet armed forces; millions took jobs, replacing men sent to the front. In October 1941, the Soviets managed an astounding feat: They dismantled more than five hundred factories in Moscow and elsewhere and reassembled them in the east, away from the encroaching German troops. By 1942, Soviet factories were producing far more tanks, guns, and combat airplanes than their German counterparts.

The United States, less threatened geographically by the war, mobilized unevenly; still, it boosted its wartime production by 400 percent in two years and sent large quantities of supplies to its British and Soviet allies. Germany was also slower to mobilize its citizens. In the early years, Hitler instead relied on quick victories and spoils from conquered lands to fulfill his nation's needs. Millions of conscripted foreigners and prisoners of war served as Germany's laborers. Only after 1942 did Hitler turn to full mobilization, multiplying Germany's production over the following two years despite concentrated Allied bombing.

TURNING THE TIDE OF WAR,
1942–1945

The now-global war was fought in three major theaters: the Soviet Union, the Mediterranean and western Europe, and the Pacific. The turning points in all theaters came between June and August 1942. The largest, bloodiest battles occurred in the Soviet Union and were fought by some nine million soldiers. The Germans had already conquered most of that nation's lands west of the Volga River, leaving nearly half of the Soviet people under German rule.

The Eastern Front and the Battle of Stalingrad

The Germans, refreshed and reequipped, resumed their offensive against the Soviet Union in June 1942, this time in the southern sector of the USSR. In July, one German soldier expressed confidence that "the Russian troops are completely broken," and "the Führer knows where the Russians' weak point is." The soldier recorded in his diary that he fully expected German forces to "take Stalingrad and then the war will inevitably soon be over." In early August, as German forces pushed forward, he and others anticipated the rewards of victory: "What great spaces the Soviets occupy, what rich fields there are to be had here after the war's over." By mid-August, they had reached the outskirts of Stalingrad on the Volga River. However, this soldier noted that the "doomed" Russian divisions "are continuing to resist bitterly."

BIOGRAPHY

Josip Broz (Tito)
(1892–1980)

Josip Broz was a hunted resistance leader for years. Born in Croatia in 1892 to a peasant family, the young Josip became an apprentice to a locksmith and then worked as a mechanic. In World War I, he served as a platoon leader in the Austro-Hungarian army, was severely wounded, and was taken prisoner by the Russians. Already a socialist, he joined Russia's Red Army during the revolution and civil war.

Communist Leader and Yugoslav Dictator

He also married a Russian woman, with whom he would have a son. In 1920, he returned to Croatia, became a trade-unionist, joined the Communist Party of Yugoslavia, and soon rose to a position of leadership. Eight years later, he was arrested

and imprisoned for six years for his communist activity—the police had discovered bombs in his apartment. He again traveled to the Soviet Union, where he rose through the ranks as a loyal Stalinist during the purges. In 1937, he became the head of Yugoslavia's Communist Party. During his underground party work, Josip assumed the pseudonym Tito.

When Hitler invaded Yugoslavia and the Soviet Union, Tito announced, "We do not recognize the various Fascist puppet governments." He called on the Communist Party of Yugoslavia to organize the "partisans," a guerrilla resistance movement against Axis forces. **Figure 24.5** shows Tito, standing on the far right, with his staff of fellow fighters. At the same time, he entered into a virtual civil war with a competing, more conservative resistance movement. Although Tito won this struggle between resistance movements, it may have cost more lives than the battle against the Nazis. While fighting occupying forces, he organized a provisional communist government that would stand ready to take over at the end of the war. With the help of Soviet troops, Tito's forces drove the retreating Germans from Yugoslavia.

FIGURE 24.5 Tito and the Yugoslav Resistance

In 1945, Yugoslavia became a federal republic, with Tito as its leader and virtual dictator. He turned the new republic into a one-party, communist state on the model of the Soviet Union. Eventually balking at Stalin's plans to purge Yugoslav leadership and undermine his authority, Tito led Yugoslavia on a separate course after 1948. Unlike Stalin, he emphasized more relaxed, decentralized control over his nation and its economy, yet he tolerated no opposition to his rule. In the 1950s and 1960s, he became a spokesperson for nations such as Egypt, Indonesia, and India who refused to align themselves with either the United States or the Soviet Union in the Cold War. He served as president of Yugoslavia until his death in 1980.

Yugoslavia would not long survive his passing. Conflict between ethnic groups had long plagued this region of Europe. Such tensions had helped ignite World War I, had contributed to the rise of authoritarian leaders of both the Right and Left during the 1930s and 1940s, and had taken thousands of lives during the resistance struggles of World War II. Now that conflict led to the undoing of the federation. Yugoslavia broke up in 1991 in a series of bloody civil wars that would drag on for years.

Connecting People & Society

1. How did Tito rise to power?

2. How does Tito's life reveal the ties among war, ideology, and politics during this period?

3. After reading this biography, what do you think of Tito?

The Battle of Stalingrad became the greatest of the war and raged for seven months. "Not a step backward," ordered Stalin. He spared no resource, including the many women who served on the front lines as combat soldiers, tankers, and snipers. Indeed, some airforce regiments were made up entirely of women. The most revered pilot, Lily Litvak, shot down twelve German planes.

Figure 24.6 provides a sense of the battle as well as the Soviets' use of propaganda. In this staged photograph, one Russian soldier has fallen for the cause. Two others, despite the danger, heroically fight on with their rifle, machine gun, and hand grenades. The photograph avoids the reality of how brutal and ignoble much of this battle was. It also suggests that these frontline soldiers willingly sacrificed themselves for

DOCUMENT 24.2

Women Go to Work in the Factories

In World War II, the major combatants recognized that victory hinged on the ability to increase industrial production. With so many men serving in the armed forces, nations called on women to work in jobs traditionally reserved for men. In this account, Elizabeth Hawes describes her experiences in an American airplane engine plant in 1943.

Now that I've worked a few months in a plant—on the graveyard shift too—the only wonder to me is that all the women in the USA aren't storming the factory gates. I'm convinced that any healthy woman can work in a factory—and like it. My biggest regret is that I had to leave because I'd agreed to do some writing. My biggest ambition is to get back.

It was a great pleasure to me that nobody gave a darn who anyone was. . . . Of course there are little discords. The foremen and subforemen are honestly scared to death of us women. When first you arrive they look at you out of the corner of their eyes. . . . Every woman machinist has to endure sheer torture from her fellow male employees at one point in her career. . . .

The men see that now you think you're a mechanic. Some honestly don't believe the Lord ever intended women to be mechanics. Others are infuriated by your presumption that you can do their work. . . . [The women] are working for money— money to feed their kids, money to keep their homes together—so their sons and husbands can fight. . . .

I want to go back to Wright's new plant because I think the women who work in war plants, and the men who first help them and then work with them are the luckiest people in the world. There's an equality developing there unlike any I've ever seen. Joe was an Italian—Nel, a Negro— Suzy, Irish—there were Germans, Poles, Hungarians, Gentiles, Jews.

Slowly you could see there was no difference between any two of us. Gradually everybody was beginning to work as one unit. When you see something like that happening you feel you're not just doing a job to help win the war. You also have the profound pleasure of seeing the future peace being worked out before your eyes.

SOURCE: Elizabeth Hawes, "My Life on the Midnight Shift," *Woman's Home Companion* (August 1943), pp. 24, 27.

Analyze the Document

1. What impresses Hawes most about her experience as a wartime factory worker?

2. How do men react to Hawes? Why do you suppose they react as they do?

3. What do you think were the longer-term consequences of such workplace experiences for women and other groups?

---

the cause and that all Soviets should make their own sacrifices for the war effort. While the scene omits the gore of the struggle, it reveals the close quarters, amid the rubble of a ruined city, in which the soldiers had to fight.

As the Russian winter again approached, Hitler ordered his army not to retreat. That decision took a huge toll on the German army. By the end of October, the German soldier's diary entries revealed a change in his optimistic attitude: "Who would have thought three months ago that instead of the joys of victory we would have to endure such sacrifice and torture, the end of which is nowhere in sight." The Germans mounted their final assault on November 11 and penetrated to the Volga. But a stalemate ensued, dragging on until November 19, when the Russians launched their long-planned encircling offensive. Though the Russian winter loomed, Hitler ordered his forces to stand firm. That decision took a huge toll on the German army. In December, the same German soldier complained, "Everybody is racked with hunger. Frozen potatoes are the best meal." Just before his death, he wrote, "The soldiers look like corpses or lunatics, looking for something to put in their mouths. They no longer take cover from

Russian shells; they haven't the strength to walk, run away and hide."

In January 1943, the Russians finally surrounded the remainder of the 300,000-man German army, now reduced by casualties to 80,000. German Sixth Army commander General Friedrich Paulus sent a note to the German high command: "Further defense senseless. Collapse inevitable. Army requests immediate permission to surrender in order to save lives of remaining troops." Hitler replied: "Surrender is forbidden. Sixth Army will hold their positions to the last man." A few days later, the German Sixth Army surrendered.

The Soviets lost one million soldiers in the bitter struggle over Stalingrad. And Germany never recovered from the massive loss of men and material, and morale suffered during the epic seven-month battle. Over the next two and a half years, Soviet forces slowly beat back the invaders (see **Map 24.3**).

The Southern Fronts

In North Africa the German general Rommel's (1891–1944) tough Afrika Korps fought to within 65 miles of the Egyptian coastal city of Alexandria.

FIGURE 24.6 The Battle of Stalingrad, 1942 In this staged photograph that exemplifies the use of propaganda during the war, Russian soldiers pose in ways suggesting the difficulty of this deadly battle.

firestorm in the German city of Hamburg. A survivor described what happened: The sky became "absolutely hellish" in minutes. "No noise made by humans—no outcry—could be heard. It was like the end of the world." The firestorm killed 40,000 people. **Figure 24.7,** a painting by British artist Leonard Henry Rosoman, suggests what civilians faced in cities subjected to heavy bombing. On the left, buildings that have stood for decades collapse in flames. Below, two firemen, armed with only a hose, fight a conflagration that is about to engulf them. While Rosoman set this in London, which endured indiscriminate rocket attacks until the last months of the war, similar and even worse scenes took place in Hamburg and many other cities.

The Western Front

On June 6, 1944 (**D-Day**), American, British, and Canadian forces under General Dwight Eisenhower (1890–1969) finally swept across the British channel to make a run at German forces holding France. Hitler, overextended in Russia and the Mediterranean, had to defend a 3,000-mile coastline in the west. Forced to gamble on where the Allies would invade, he bet on Calais, where the English Channel was narrowest. Instead, the invasion—supported by an armada of more than 6,000 vessels and 12,000 aircraft—came on the Normandy beaches. Hitler's "Atlantic Wall" of defenders took a huge toll on the invaders. In many cases, lead companies suffered 90 percent casualties; boats and tanks were often destroyed before their troops could even fire a shot. One American soldier reported that within the first ten minutes, "every officer and sergeant of the leading company had been killed or wounded. . . . It had become a struggle for survival and rescue."

Despite these losses, the Allies established a northwestern European front. Two months later, they opened a new front in southern France. Aided by French forces and resistance fighters, the Allies pushed the Germans out of most of France before year's end. Meanwhile, Allied bombs pulverized German cities and crippled Germany's transportation network.

Under the steady onslaught, Germany began running out of oil and soldiers. Early in 1945, American and British forces at last succeeded in crossing the Rhine into Germany. By that time, the Russians had swept | Germany defeated |

But in August 1942, at the Battle of El Alamein, the British forces, bolstered by supplies from the United States, held. Over the following months, British and newly arriving American forces managed to push the Germans back, and in May 1943, the cornered Afrika Korps surrendered.

| The Mediterranean |

The war-weary Stalin now urged Britain and America to open up a major western front in France to take the pressure off his forces. Instead, in an effort to protect British interests in the Mediterranean without risking a battle against major German forces, the Allies attacked Italy. First, they moved from the island of Sicily up into the southern Italian mainland. In July 1943, the Italian government arrested Mussolini, and two months later Italy surrendered. However, strong German forces still held most of the country. German commandos rescued Mussolini and set him up as the head of a puppet government in the north. The Allies' progress slowed through the Italian mountains, and the rest of the Italian campaign became a long and costly effort.

Meanwhile, Allied planes rained bombs on German targets. These dangerous missions took a heavy toll on both sides. In 1943, for example, only one-third of British crews flying planes across the channel would survive their first tour of duty. In late July of that same year, systematic bombing raids by British and American air forces set off a devastating through most of eastern and southeastern Europe. Along the 1,500 miles between Stalingrad and Berlin lay the wreckage of Hitler's once-mighty war machine. **Figure 24.8,** a painting by Canadian artist Charles Fraser Comfort, reveals the fate of so many combatants toward the end of World War II. Comfort, who accompanied Canadian troops in Europe, saw firsthand the horrors of war. In this haunting image, a German soldier lies dead among barbed wire on a desolate battlefield. His ravaged remains imply that the battle is long over and that his struggle was in vain. The image echoes scenes from World War I, suggesting ways in which the two wars were tragically related.

Still, Hitler would not give up. Even in the case of Berlin, he refused to evacuate civilians from the cities, despite the deaths and hardships that would result, so that his troops would feel compelled to fight even more desperately—a tactic Stalin had already used. On April 20, 1945, Berlin civilians heard the approaching Soviet troops. "Our fate is rolling in from the east," reported one woman in her diary. "What was yesterday a distant rumble has now become a constant roar. We breathe the din; our ears are deafened to all but the heaviest guns."

Germany finally surrendered on May 8, and the war in Europe ended. In what one survivor described as "the carcass of Berlin," Hitler, his wife, Eva Braun, and several other top Nazis committed suicide. In Italy, Italian partisans had already shot Mussolini and his mistress.

The War in the Pacific

In the Pacific, the turning point of the war came in the late spring of 1942 (see **Map 24.4**). American and Australian troops stopped the Japanese army in New Guinea, and the Americans turned back Japanese naval forces in the Battle of the Coral Sea, northeast of Australia. Soon, American ships, aided by intelligence from intercepted cipher transmissions, positioned themselves off Midway Island to ambush the incoming Japanese. At first, the Japanese fared well, destroying two-thirds of the American planes. Then, aided by luck, dive-bombers from American aircraft carriers spotted four Japanese carriers with their planes being refueled and rearmed. The encounter proved a disaster for the Japanese. In just five minutes, the course of the Pacific war was reversed. Three Japanese carriers went down, followed later by the fourth. The Japanese lost the advantage permanently. The U.S. arms industry was already on its way to outproducing the Japanese and creating an overwhelmingly strong fleet. The Battle of Midway

Battle of Midway

FIGURE 24.7 Leonard Henry Rosoman, *A House Collapsing on Two Firemen, Shoe Lane, London EC4,* 1940. Civilians suffered greatly from the heavy bombing of cities during the war, as suggested by this painting.

condemned the Japanese to fight defensively for the rest of the war.

In August 1942, the Americans attacked Guadalcanal in the Solomon Islands northeast of Australia. Capitalizing on their growing naval superiority and having broken the Japanese code, the Americans conducted an island-hopping campaign toward Japan. One American Marine described the "brutal, primitive hatred" that developed between the Japanese and American soldiers in this costly campaign, which "resulted in savage, ferocious fighting with no holds barred." As the battles raged on Pacific islands, "the fierce struggle for survival . . . eroded the veneer of civilization and made savages of us all."

In October 1944, the Japanese fleet made a final, desperate effort near the Philippines, but American forces annihilated it in the Battle of Leyte Gulf. However, as the United States and its allies closed in on the Japanese home islands, the most brutal land battles of the war lay ahead: Iwo Jima and Okinawa. During these

FIGURE 24.8 Charles Fraser Comfort, *Dead German on the Hitler Line*, ca. 1944 This painting of a single German soldier's remains stands for the loss of millions during this tragic, devastating war.

KEY DATES

battles, Japanese soldiers often fought to the death or took their own lives rather than surrender. During the battle of Okinawa, Japanese pilots volunteered to fly almost 2,000 **kamikaze** missions in which they dive-bombed their planes into Allied ships (see Document 24.3). The Allies lost dozens of ships and thousands of soldiers to these desperate tactics.

Isolated, exposed, and subjected to ceaseless air and sea attacks, Japan was doomed. In February 1945, the United States began massive bomb- **The atomic bomb** ing raids on Japan's home islands, igniting huge firestorms that destroyed vast sections of Japan's cities and killed hundreds of thousands of people. After Germany surrendered in May 1945, American and British troops rushed to the Far East. In mid-July, American and British scientists finished developing and testing the atomic bomb, a new, powerful weapon the two countries had been working on for several years. To avoid the heavy casualties that a direct assault on the Japanese home islands would cause, the United States decided to use the bomb to shock Japan into surrender—a decision that has sparked controversy ever since.

While some Japanese political leaders recognized the hopelessness of continuing the war and pressed the government to pursue a peace settlement, Japan's military leaders promised a bloody fight to the finish. The fighting on Okinawa had convinced many American soldiers that the enemy would not give up. As one survivor of that battle put it, "Japan would have to be invaded with the same gruesome prospects." At the same time, many of the scientists who developed the weapon opposed using it. So did General Dwight Eisenhower: "First, the Japanese were ready to surrender and it wasn't necessary to hit them with that awful thing. Second, I hated to see our country be the first to use such a weapon."

On August 6, 1945, a U.S. plane dropped an atomic bomb that destroyed the Japanese city of Hiroshima and some 80,000 of its inhabitants; tens of thousands more died later from the effects of radiation. One survivor, Yamaoka Michiko, described the horror: "There were people, barely breathing, trying to push their intestines back in. People with their legs wrenched off. Without heads. Or with faces burned and swollen out of shape. The scene I saw was a living hell." Three days later, a second atomic bomb demolished the industrial city of Nagasaki, killing an additional 50,000. On August 8, the Soviet Union declared war on Japan and sent troops into Manchuria. The Japanese surrendered on August 15, 1945.

DOCUMENT 24.3

"We Shall Plunge into Enemy Ships"

During the last year of the war in the Pacific, the Japanese responded to widespread losses by resorting to suicide attacks on U.S. ships. The Kamikaze Special Attack Corps carried out these attacks. Heiichi Okabe was a member of that corps, and on February 22, 1945, he wrote the following letter.

I am actually a member at last of the Kamikaze Special Attack Corps. My life will be rounded out in the next thirty days. My chance will come! Death and I are waiting. The training and practice have been rigorous, but it is worthwhile if we can die beautifully and for a cause.

I shall die watching the pathetic struggle of our nation. My life will gallop in the next few weeks as my youth and life draw to a close. . . .

The sortie has been scheduled for the next ten days. I am a human being and hope to be neither saint nor scoundrel, hero nor fool—just a human being. As one who has spent his life in wistful longing and searching, I die resignedly in the hope that my life will serve as a "human document."

The world in which I lived was too full of discord. As a community of rational human beings it should be better composed. Lacking a single great conductor, everyone lets loose with his own sound, creating dissonance where there should be melody and harmony.

We shall serve the nation gladly in its present painful struggle. We shall plunge into enemy ships cherishing the conviction that Japan has been and will be a place where only lovely homes, brave women, and beautiful friendships are allowed to exist.

What is the duty today? It is to fight.
What is the duty tomorrow? It is to win.
What is the daily duty? It is to die.

We die in battle without complaint. I wonder if others, like scientists, who pursue the war effort on their own fronts, would die as we do without complaint. Only then will the unity of Japan be such that she can have any prospect of winning the war.

SOURCE: Rihihei Inoguchi and Tadashi Nakajima, *The Divine Wind* (Annapolis, MD: United States Naval Institute, 1958), pp. 207–208.

Analyze the Document

1. How do you explain Heiichi Okabe's thoughts as expressed in this excerpt?

2. How does his "duty" compare to that of other soldiers?

3. Do you agree with his statement that he is "just a human being" and neither a hero nor a fool? Explain.

PEACE AND THE LEGACY OF WAR

In 1945, Europe lay prostrate as some 50 million refugees drifted across the land and countless people faced starvation and homelessness. Memories of lost loved ones and homes, the horrors of the concentration camps, the hardships of occupation, and the echoes of mass bombings would haunt people for the rest of their lives.

Europe in shambles

Outrage, fear, and violence continued to stalk Europe. Many resistance fighters and Soviet troops executed surrendering Nazi soldiers on the spot. Angry officials and ordinary people hunted down and punished collaborators after only summary trials. To shame women they suspected of sleeping with German soldiers, irate citizens shaved off women's hair and marched them through the streets. The Soviets, Poles, and Czechoslovakians pushed 13 million ethnic Germans out of homes in Eastern Europe toward the west. One eyewitness described how "families with children, packages, hand wheelbarrows, horse-drawn wagons, and bicycles were making their way, and were being assaulted" as they fled along the roads to Germany. Stalin's officials sent thousands of returning Soviet prisoners to forced-labor camps or to the executioner for being "contaminated" by dangerous, anti-Soviet ideas. Jews who had managed to survive often found their homes destroyed, and they still suffered from flagrant anti-Semitism.

With agricultural and nonmilitary industrial production at a fraction of their prewar levels, Western Europe looked to the United States for loans, relief, defense, and leadership. Eastern Europe, in even worse shambles, was falling under the dominance of the Soviet Union. Political leaders and diplomats involved in the peace settlement hoped this time to avoid the "mistakes" made at the close of World War I. The main challenge facing them was to find a way to deal with defeated nations without spawning new conflicts.

The Settlement

The leaders of Great Britain, the United States, and the Soviet Union shaped postwar Europe in two wartime conferences, at Teheran in December 1943 and Yalta in February 1945, and one postwar conference at Potsdam in July 1945. They agreed to accept only unconditional surrender by Germany and Japan and to require complete restructuring of the aggressors' governments. Germany, which had proved so powerful in two world wars, would be disarmed and divided. The Soviet Union, having suffered so much from Germany's massive invasion, demanded and received pledges of territories on its western border as well as reparations from Germany. To further weaken Germany and recognize the impact of the war, Poland's border with Germany was pushed westward. Finally, a **United Nations** organization was founded in 1945 by fifty-one nations to promote international peace and cooperation. **Figure 24.9,** a 1947 poster marking the second anniversary of the organization's birth, reveals the high hopes of its founders. Caring hands plant a tree of peace and union, each leaf representing the flag of a member nation. People hoped that as the "sapling" grew, new "leaves" and maturity would strengthen the young organization.

On other matters, however, discord among the wartime allies created a more ominous view of the future. The most crucial disagreements came over the fate of the Eastern European countries. Stalin argued that because the Soviet Union had endured invasions through these countries in both world wars, he needed them to serve as a buffer zone of states loyal to the USSR. The United

> **Discord over Eastern Europe**

States and Great Britain demanded complete independence and democracy for these countries. Concessions on both sides at the Yalta Conference in February 1945 left Eastern Europe vaguely democratic but "friendly" to the Soviet Union. This arrangement quickly proved unworkable. Two nations—Poland and Bulgaria—were already under communist control, and pro-Soviet "coalition governments" quickly formed in other Eastern European states.

At the final conference, at Potsdam in July 1945 (the war ended without a formal peace treaty), Stalin had the upper hand. President Roosevelt had died. Although the American president, Harry Truman, firmly demanded free elections in all of Eastern Europe, he had been in office only three months. Churchill might have been able to exert more pressure on Stalin, but the newly elected Clement Attlee replaced him during the conference. Stalin, insisting that the Soviet Union must obtain complete security against Germany and any potential Eastern European allies, refused to budge on the issue: "A freely elected government in any of these East European countries would be anti-Soviet," he admitted, "and that we cannot allow."

U.S. leaders had trouble swallowing the reality behind Stalin's words. In fact, Eastern Europe was already behind Soviet lines and occupied by Soviet troops by war's end, just as Western Europe remained behind Anglo-American lines and within the United States' and Britain's sphere of influence. "Everyone imposes his own system as far as his armies can reach," observed Stalin privately. "It cannot be otherwise."

The Legacy of War

Human beings have waged war on each other since the beginnings of civilization. But World War II, especially when viewed in connection with its twentieth-century predecessor, World War I, shook the West and the world as nothing before.

One crucial difference stemmed from technology. Bloody battles, massacres, torture, and cruelty were not new to the twentieth century. But for the first time, combatants had developed weapons to translate these acts into tens of millions of deaths on and off the battlefields. The use of chemicals, machines, and organizations to inflict a wide range of horrors on so many people so quickly was also unprecedented.

Certainly World War I set a well-remembered precedent for the decision makers of the Second World War. The 1914–1918 conflict had become a relentless mutual slaughter with single battles costing hundreds of thousands of lives and total deaths surpassing 20 million. Those years of war also carried in their wake genocidal actions by the Turks against the Armenians and Allied blockades for months after the

FIGURE 24.9 The United Nations, 1947 This period poster by Henri Eveleigh celebrates the founding of the United Nations and conveys the hopes of its founders for peace and international cooperation.

end of the war that inflicted widespread starvation on defeated nations.

The two decades after World War I brought to power regimes in Russia, Germany, and Japan that hinted at what a second world conflict might wreak on humanity. In Russia, transformed into the Soviet Union, Stalin inflicted a terror-famine on Ukraine, which cost millions of lives, and established the system of slave-labor camps (the Gulag) that also killed and imprisoned millions more. In Germany, the rise of the Nazis to power under Adolf Hitler in 1933 soon led to concentration camps, anti-Semitic terror, and policies of euthanasia. In Japan, the initiation of war against China in 1937 resulted in what is generally called the Rape of Nanking.

The outbreak of war in Europe in 1939 led to even worse acts and consequences. Violence raged across oceans and continents. The death toll alone was staggering. More than 60 million people—some scholars argue that the actual figure might be much higher—were killed during World War II.

Even more ominous, far more civilians than soldiers died, owing in part to the tactics and weapons of modern war. The drive to inflict massive damage led to indiscriminate carpet and fire bombings. These raids not only made little distinction between military and civilian targets but literally flattened German and Japanese cities such as Dresden and Tokyo. The search for revolutionary superweapons also bore frightening fruit. The atomic bomb—the weapon that finally ended the war in the Pacific—made it all too clear that human beings now had the ability to inflict unimaginable destruction with a single blow.

Meanwhile, the 11 to 12 million deaths resulting from the Nazis' genocidal program revealed a new capacity for bureaucratized and industrialized killing. Only a relatively few individuals survived the death camps to "tell the story, to bear witness." They and the rest of humanity have had to find ways to live with the realization, in the words of the Auschwitz survivor Primo Levi, "that such a crime should exist," and that it had been "introduced irrevocably into the world of things that exist."

More broadly, terror—of combatants and civilians alike—became a standard tactic during World War II. Officially sanctioned mass rape—in particular by advancing Russian forces in retaliation against the Germans and by Japanese soldiers against the Chinese—made the experience of war all the more vicious. Rape took tragic forms. For example, some 300,000 women, most of them from Korea, were forced to serve the Japanese military as "comfort women."

After World War II, it was clear that humans had acquired the capacity to annihilate peoples and civilizations. This realization called into question some of the very developments that had most characterized the West over the previous two centuries: science (used to destroy lives), industrialization (which made the war machines possible), nationalism (which mutated into militarism), ideological beliefs (which justified everything from sacrifice to terror and genocide), and humanism (which seemed irrelevant in the face of blatant inhumanity). In the European heart of the West, many people prayed that a conflict on the scale of World War II would never strike again. But even as they hoped, tensions between two countries that had once lain at the peripheries of the West—the Soviet Union and the United States—suggested that peace might prove short-lived.

LOOKING BACK & MOVING FORWARD

Summary World War II devastated much of Europe and left scars across the globe from North Africa and the Middle East to East Asia and the Pacific. The first battles erupted in Asia when the Japanese, eager to expand their empire, invaded China. Then Nazi Germany and Fascist Italy struck in Europe. The Axis powers piled up victories until the Allies, with their superior industrial might and manpower, finally turned the tide.

The war took a staggering toll. The Nazis not only waged war against the Allies, millions of European Jews, and other "undesirable" groups but also conducted nothing less than a campaign to destroy eastern European nations. Twenty-seven million Soviets, perhaps many more, perished in the struggle. Germans treated Soviet prisoners of war savagely—shooting, working, or starving to death some two million of them. The Soviets dealt with German prisoners only marginally better. German armies had left the Soviet Union's cities in smoking ruins and ravaged its countryside. Despite aid from the United States and Great Britain, the

KEY TERMS

Popular Front, *p. 748*

Axis, *p. 749*

appeasement, *p. 750*

Munich Conference, *p. 750*

blitzkrieg, *p. 751*

Holocaust, *p. 757*

D-Day, *p. 764*

kamikaze, *p. 766*

United Nations, *p. 768*

Soviets produced 90 percent of their supplies themselves. They had turned the tide against the Germans in Europe well before the Americans and British opened a western front in France. Understandably, the Soviets maintained that they had sacrificed more than any other nation to defeat Germany.

Other countries also sustained terrible losses. Some fifteen million Chinese died. Germany gave up six million lives; Japan almost two million. Poland suffered horribly: In addition to losing hundreds of thousands of ordinary citizens, its elites were systematically rounded up and executed by both the Soviets and the Germans.

At war's end, tens of millions of Europeans had been uprooted and were homeless. Western and non-Western societies, weary and bloodied, now faced an overwhelming task: to recover from the devastation of the war and regain some sense of order. The road ahead looked hard. In Asia, rumblings of national revolutions had already begun. There, the Japanese invaders had inadvertently emboldened nationalists by demonstrating that an Asian people could defeat Western overlords. Such developments all unfolded under the shadow of a sobering new realization: Through modern warfare and new technology, human beings now had the power to obliterate the entire world.

REVIEW, ANALYZE, & CONNECT TO TODAY

REVIEW THE PREVIOUS CHAPTER

Chapter 23—"Darkening Decades"—traced the rise of fascism, the development of the Soviet Union, and the trials of nations struck by the Great Depression.

1. How might one argue that World War II stemmed directly from World War I and the Great Depression?

2. What qualities of fascism and authoritarian governments fed the forces for war in the 1930s?

ANALYZE THIS CHAPTER

Chapter 24—"Into the Fire Again"—studies the causes, course, and consequences of World War II.

1. Analyze some of the thinking behind Japanese aggression during the 1930s and 1940s.

2. How was the Holocaust connected to Hitler's Nazi ideology and the course of World War II?

3. How did the Allies turn the tide and defeat the Axis powers in World War II?

4. What problems faced negotiators trying to design a settlement at the end of World War II?

CONNECT TO TODAY

Think about how World War II was fought and what happened during the war, both on the front lines and behind the lines.

1. In a major new war, what problems might there be in maintaining a meaningful distinction between civilians and combatants?

2. In today's world, how might propaganda be used to justify war and support a major war effort?

3. What communication channels that were not available during World War II do present-day propagandists use? For what specific activities do they—or might they— use them?

BEYOND THE CLASSROOM

THE ROAD TO WAR, 1931–1939

Crozier, Andrew. *The Causes of the Second World War.* London: Blackwell, 1997. A book with good detail within a world context.

Neville, Peter. *Hitler and Appeasement: The British Attempt to Prevent the Second World War.* New York: Continuum, 2005. Defends British efforts to avoid war and places "appeasement" in a broad context.

Watt, Donald Cameron. *How War Came: The Immediate Origins of the Second World War.* London: Heinemann, 1989. A helpful coverage of events directly leading to the war.

AXIS VICTORIES, 1939–1942

Keegan, John. *The Second World War.* New York: Viking, 1990. A book that is particularly good on battles and strategy.

Weinberg, Gerhard L. *A World at Arms: A Global History of World War II.* New York: Cambridge University Press, 1994. Excellent in its global perspective and its examination of the Nazi plan for world order.

GLOBAL CONNECTIONS

Irokawa, Daikichi. *The Age of Hirohito: In Search of Modern Japan.* New York: The Free Press, 1995. A broad study that covers the topic and more.

BEHIND THE LINES: THE STRUGGLE AND THE HORROR

Fritzsche, Peter. *Life and Death in the Third Reich.* Cambridge, MA: Harvard University Press, 2008. A well-argued interpretation.

Jackson, Julian. *France: The Dark Years, 1940–1944.* New York: Oxford University Press, 2003. A fine study of collaboration and resistance in France.

Kershaw, Ian. *Hitler, the Germans, and the Final Solution.* New Haven, CT: Yale University Press, 2008. A highly respected set of essays on the topics.

TURNING THE TIDE OF WAR, 1942–1945

Beevor, Anthony. *The Fall of Berlin 1945.* New York: Penguin, 2003. An effective narrative covering the final siege against Berlin.

Frank, R. B. *Downfall: The End of the Imperial Japanese Empire.* New York: Penguin, 2001. A balanced account of the end of the war in the Pacific.

Overy, Richard. *Russia's War: A History of the Soviet War Effort, 1941–1945.* New York: Penguin, 1998. A well-written account of the war on the eastern front.

PEACE AND THE LEGACY OF WAR

Glover, Jonathan. *Humanity: A Moral History of the Twentieth Century.* New Haven, CT: Yale University Press, 2000. A superb analysis of the grave challenges from the twentieth century that combines psychological, philosophical, and historical perspectives.

Winter, Jay, and Emmanuel Sivan. *War and Remembrance in the Twentieth Century.* Cambridge: Cambridge University Press, 1999. A series of interdisciplinary essays focusing on memory and loss in twentieth-century wars.

Forming the Present

The end of World War II marked the dawn of a new era that we can best understand by widening our focus from the West to the entire world. Between 1945 and the first decade of the twenty-first century, four key developments dominated interactions among civilizations around the globe. First, peoples throughout the world increasingly believed that being modern meant becoming Westernized. Second, more and more non-Western peoples agitated to free themselves from Western imperial control. Third, contradictory political beliefs emerged that pitted democratic capitalism against Marxist communism. And, fourth, a vast movement of ideas, technologies, labor, capital, and goods across borders further blurred lines between the West and the non-Western world.

The decades after 1945 witnessed an affirmation of the civilization located in the West and uncertainty about its borders and defining characteristics. In many areas of the world, Western civilization became a model for change and modernization. Indeed, some people used the term *modernization*—for example, the spread of cutting-edge science, technology, and industry—interchangeably with *Westernization*. The West's enduring power further affirmed its standing in the world. Despite the devastation in the European heartland wrought during World War II, the West had emerged

as the globe's politically, economically, and militarily dominant player. But with Europe prostrate, the West's centers of power shifted to what once had been its peripheries—across the Atlantic to the United States and east to the Soviet Union.

At the same time, what defined the West's borders and unique characteristics became less and less clear. Great numbers of people moved in and out of the West, carrying different ways of life with them. Meanwhile, elements of Western culture—liberalism and Marxism, sneakers and hamburgers, movies and the Internet—spread into and saturated other cultures. This mingling of culture, ideas, and institutions made it difficult to discern where the West ended and other civilizations began. Nevertheless, most historians think of the West at this time as consisting of Europe and those areas (such as the Americas, Australia, and New Zealand) where Europeans arrived, adapted, dominated, and almost crushed preexisting cultures and peoples.

Outside of the West, two main struggles dominated the decades after 1945. Both involved the West in one way or another. The first struggle was for national liberation, as peoples in Africa, Asia, and elsewhere threw off their Western colonial rulers. This process sometimes required extended armed combat; other times, it took the form of a peaceful transfer of power. Most such victories left problematic legacies that would plague the freed

countries for decades. For example, many newly liberated nations in Africa and Asia would experience great difficulty achieving political stability and developing the economic means to support their populations.

The second struggle that extended beyond the West came with a battle for political power and ideological control that pitted nations headed by the United States (with its system of democratic capitalism) against those allied with the Soviet Union (which had adopted state-directed communism). This complex conflict, known as the Cold War, spread to such far-flung places as Southeast Asia, Korea, Cuba, and Angola.

Connections between the West and the rest of the world became so extensive after 1945 that many call that period the age of globalism. But in reality, waves of globalism had struck earlier. The first began in the late fifteenth century, as Western powers moved out of Europe to establish imperial or commercial links across the seas. The second wave came in the nineteenth century. In those years, industrialism and imperial ambitions pushed Western nations to increase their influence and control over much of the world. People, goods, and ideas flowed between the West and other civilizations. World War I and the economic problems of the 1920s and 1930s dampened this second age of globalism. The new age that began after World War II renewed the flood

Earth from Space
This world map view of the Earth is a composite of many different NASA satellite images.

of ideas, trade, and peoples across borders, with technology bringing hourly if not instant communications around the globe. By the end of the century, for example, goods could be designed in one country, financed internationally, produced in yet another nation, sold in faraway markets, and serviced via phones and the Internet from still different points of the globe.

The West remained at the core of this new globalism. However, other areas of the world began coming to the fore. Some in parts of Asia took over industrial production and technology first developed in the West and successfully adapted it. Others in parts of the Middle East controlled crucial,

wealth-making assets such as oil. Still others, in parts of the Islamic world, reacted in a backlash against the West. In addition to these developments, all civilizations—Western and non-Western alike—would soon face challenges they could not have imagined previously. Perhaps none were more threatening to the entire human species than the spread of nuclear arms and such dramatic environmental changes as global warming.

Thinking Globally

1. Consider the four major developments on which this essay focuses. What other developments might be added to this discussion?

2. What areas of the world are generally considered to be of the West today?

3. In the satellite image above, identify areas that border the Pacific Ocean and that might be considered part of the modernized world. Refer also to the maps of Europe and the world at the back of this book for more detail.

4. Starting from Europe, scan the rest of the world, first to the south, then the east, and finally to the west. In what ways has the West touched and affected various parts of the globe over the three ages of globalism? How might our present age of globalism resemble previous ages of globalism? How might it differ?

DON EDDY, *NEW SHOES FOR H,* 1974

In this 1974 painting, Don Eddy uses the artistic style known as photo-realism to depict
a shoe-store display in New York City. Reflected in the store window are cars, buses, a
department store sign (S. Klein), office and apartment buildings, and a pedestrian
in blue jeans—all in all, a typically vibrant street scene in a leading Western city of the era.

Superpower Struggles and Global Transformations

25

The Cold War, 1945–1980s

In 1974, a retired Frenchwoman, Françoise Giroud, contrasted her early life as a stenographer in the 1930s with the lives of young women of the 1970s. "[T]here is simply no comparison. . . . A month of paid vacation, . . . organized travel, . . . paperback books, . . . blue jeans and the T-shirts, instant mashed potatoes, the transistor, . . . the boyfriend who has a [used car], . . . and the Pill! It's not a better world; it's another world altogether." This new world that Giroud described boasted unheard-of material well-being, international peace throughout most of the West, innovative day-to-day conveniences, and striking new medical knowledge. The painting on page 774 is an apt illustration of this new age. The image reveals a wealthy, commercial society awash in consumer goods. In effect, the painting offers a view of reality from different perspectives, paralleling the efforts that many Westerners made to understand their rapidly changing world.

Yet these decades also had their dark side. Nations around the world labored to recover from the devastation of World War II. As they did so, a new menace emerged—growing tensions between the United States and the Soviet Union that for decades would overshadow international relations and everyday life. At the same time, colonial peoples took advantage of Europe's weakness and changing attitudes toward imperialism and demanded their independence in ways the West could not ignore. New nations and international organizations soon emerged throughout the world, and global interactions grew so complex that the traditional lines between Western and non-Western societies blurred more than ever.

TIMELINE

Fall of Communism

The Cold War

Toward European Unification

Communism in China

Decolonization

World War II

Social Protests and Movements

Economic Reforms in China

1945   1950   1955   1960   1965   1970   1975   1980   1985   1990

PREVIEW

ORIGINS OF THE COLD WAR

"At the present moment in world history nearly every nation must choose between alternative ways of life," announced U.S. president Harry Truman on March 12, 1947. Ominously, he added, "The choice is too often not a free one," referring to what he termed the "coercion and intimidation" used to force "totalitarian regimes" on the peoples of several countries. Eight months later, his secretary of state, George Marshall, pointed to the heart of the problem: "The present line of division in Europe is roughly the line upon which the Anglo-American armies coming from the west met those of the Soviet Union coming from the east. . . . Developments in the European countries to the east of that line bear the unmistakable imprint of an alien hand." According to Truman and Marshall, the "alien hand" over Eastern Europe belonged to the Soviet Union, only two years earlier an ally of the United States in World War II.

The conflict over the fate of Eastern Europe drove a sharp wedge between the World War II allies. Long-standing antagonisms and new differences soon combined to break down further any cooperation between the Western democracies and the Soviet Union. Ever since the communists had come to power in 1917, they and the capitalist democracies had viewed each other as opponents (see Chapter 23). As ideologies, communism and capitalism had always been in direct opposition. As practiced in the Soviet Union under Lenin and Stalin, the political system of communism took a dictatorial form, in sharp contrast to the democracies of Great Britain and the United States. Hitler's invasion of the Soviet Union in World War II and the United States' entry into the war only temporarily united Great Britain, the United States, and the Soviet Union. The three powers joined as allies more in opposition to Nazi Germany than in agreement over principles or goals. Not surprisingly, when negotiations over war aims and settlement terms took place, the history of hostility, distrust, and fear between the capitalist and communist powers caused problems. After the war, when the threat of Nazi Germany no longer held the Allies together, tensions worsened.

In 1945, the U.S. cut off all aid to the USSR. The rhetoric of discord between the powers increased. The next year, Winston Churchill, speaking at a small college in Missouri, warned the world of an **Iron Curtain** descending from the Baltic to the Adriatic Seas, dividing Europe between communist East and capitalist West.

Churchill's warning proved apt. Within the next few years, Soviet-backed communist parties in Eastern Europe pushed their opponents aside and rose to power; only communist Yugoslavia and Albania would manage to follow independent courses. In Western Europe, despite the presence of popular communist parties, American-backed anticommunist politicians controlled the governments. In Greece, the two sides clashed as the British and the Americans supported the repressive anticommunist monarchy in an armed conflict against the Greek communists. The **Cold War** had begun.

The Heart of the Cold War

At the heart of the Cold War lay a troubled Germany. As **Map 25.1** indicates, the peace settlement had divided the aggressor nation into four occupation zones: American, Soviet, British, and French. The city of Berlin, in the Russian zone, was also divided into the same four sectors. Sharp disagreements soon surfaced among the occupiers. The Soviets alarmed their allies by grabbing valuable resources from Germany, including entire factories, and transporting them to the Soviet Union as reparations for war losses rather than waiting for cash payments. The Soviets also hoped to keep their old enemy Germany economically weak and fully divided. The United States and Britain, on the other hand, set out to restore and integrate economically the western sectors of Germany, seeing those regions as essential allies in the growing split with the USSR.

Matters came to a head in 1948 when the United States and Britain tried to spur economic recovery by introducing a new currency in the western zones of Germany despite Soviet opposition. Stalin countered by blockading the three western zones of Berlin. From

MAP 25.1

Europe After World War II

This map shows Europe after World War II and the dates that communists gained control of governments in Eastern Europe.

Explore the Map

1. Which territories were acquired by the Soviet Union?

2. Locate Berlin. Why was this city of such strategic, political, and symbolic importance?

3. What predicament arose for the western zones of Berlin when the Soviets cut off land traffic from the west?

4. How would you evaluate the size and potential importance of a unified Germany?

June 1948 to May 1949, the Soviets stopped all land traffic across their zone from the West to Berlin.

The Berlin blockade and the division of Germany

In response, the Western powers mounted a daring and continuous airlift that carried supplies to the city. If "Berlin falls," warned the American military commander General Lucius Clay, "western Germany will be next . . . if we withdraw, our position in Europe is threatened. . . . Communism will run rampant." The **Berlin airlift** eventually prompted the Soviet Union to back down.

In September 1949, the Western allies followed through on their plan to merge the three western zones of Germany and to create an independent West German state—the German Federal Republic. One month later, the Soviet Union established the German Democratic Republic in its eastern zone, completing the division of Germany into the capitalist West and communist East.

Meanwhile, the Cold War chill was already spreading across the rest of Europe. In 1947, U.S. president Harry Truman (1884–1972) initiated the Truman Doctrine, a policy that offered military and economic aid to countries threatened by a communist takeover. "The peoples of a number of countries of the world have recently had totalitarian regimes forced upon them against their will," he warned. "[I]t must be the policy of the United States to support free peoples who

The Cold War spreads

are resisting attempted subjugation by armed minorities or by outside pressures." His immediate concern was the civil war in Greece, where local communists aided by neighboring Yugoslavia were making gains against the royalist government. His larger goal was to create a military ring of "**containment**" around the Soviet Union and its satellite states.

That same year, Truman's secretary of state, George Marshall (1880–1959), launched the **Marshall Plan,** a package of massive economic aid to European nations designed both to strengthen them and to tie them to American influence. The Soviet Union forbad Eastern European governments to accept the aid and soon established the Council for Mutual Economic Assistance (COMECON), a Soviet version of the Marshall Plan for Eastern Europe.

In 1949, the United States organized the **North Atlantic Treaty Organization (NATO),** a military alliance among the United States, Canada, and most of the nations of Western Europe against the Soviet Union. Within a few years, Greece and Turkey had joined the alliance. After West Germany signed on in 1955, the Soviet Union countered NATO by creating its own military alliance in Eastern Europe, the Warsaw Pact. Now thousands of troops in each alliance—backed by the presence and might of the two superpowers—faced each other along a line

dividing Eastern and Western Europe. It had taken only a few years for each side in the Cold War to forge economic, political, and military ties among its allies and form two hostile camps (see **Map 25.2**).

The Cold War would color international relations and everyday life for more than four decades. Andrei Zhdanov (1896–1948), a powerful Soviet official, described the official Soviet view of the Cold War in 1947: U.S. goals were "domination in all countries marked out for American expansion" and "the creation in peacetime of numerous [military] bases . . . for aggressive purposes against the USSR." John Foster Dulles (1888–1959), President Dwight Eisenhower's secretary of state, presented the U.S. view in 1953: "Soviet communism . . . is the gravest threat that has ever faced . . . Western civilization, or indeed, any civilization . . . dominated by a spiritual faith." Compromise between such extreme, hostile views seemed impossible.

As Document 25.1 suggests, terror lurked just below the surface of the Cold War. By 1949, both superpowers had the atomic bomb; by 1953, the hydrogen bomb. Each country supported growing military

Cold War weapons

budgets and stockpiled huge caches of weapons, including intercontinental ballistic missiles (ICBMs) that could carry nuclear warheads. The danger rippled outward as other nations—Britain, France, India, China, Israel, and Pakistan—also developed nuclear weapons. As U.S. president John F. Kennedy (1917–1963) admitted in 1962, "The decision to use any kind of a nuclear weapon . . . presents such a risk of it getting out of control so quickly. . . ." In fact, the Cold War was fought in all ways except open military conflict between the United States and the Soviet Union. Networks of spies fanned out over the globe. Political struggles anywhere, even purely internal matters, became arenas for defining a victory or defeat in the Cold War. The competition expanded to include nonpolitical activities as well, such as space exploration and the Olympic Games.

Cold War posturing and imagery also saturated the media. In **Figure 25.1,** a 1948 poster created for the French Communist Party, atomic bombs hover over the prostrate victim, spreading death (the crosses in the background) and destruction (the burning buildings). The poster warns France against any form of alliance with Germany, which the communists claimed would amount to preparation for war against the Soviet Union. From the United States, the Voice of America radio station spread anticommunist messages throughout Europe, while the station's Soviet counterpart presented its own views. Most European governments controlled the news on their radio and television programs.

All this led to a pervasive sense of suspicion and fear. Novels, movies, and television shows featuring

thinking about GEOGRAPHY

MAP 25.2

Europe During the Cold War

This map shows how the Cold War had divided Europe by the 1950s.

Explore the Map

1. What connections between military and economic cooperation are revealed by this map?

2. Why do you think the Soviet Union was so anxious to maintain control over its Eastern European allies?

3. Why was Turkey such an important member of NATO?

4. Notice what nations are not a part of the alliance organizations. What are the possible reasons?

Map legend:
- NATO Alliance, 1955
- ★ Original EEC Members, 1957
- Communist Bloc (Members of Warsaw Pact and COMECON)

spies and international intrigue proliferated. In the United States, for example, Senator Joseph McCarthy (1908–1957) led a massive name-calling campaign between 1950 and 1954 "to uncover" communists and communist sympathizers; these "fellow travelers," McCarthy claimed, had infiltrated every aspect of American life, from the armed services to Hollywood movie studios. Atomic bomb drills in American schools and bomb shelters in city basements and suburban backyards completed the picture of a Western democratic nation menaced by communism and the Soviet Union.

The Global Impact of the Cold War

The Cold War quickly spread around the globe as each side searched for allies and victories wherever they could find them (see **Map 25.3**). No area escaped from the worldwide competition, but events in Asia and Latin America especially reveal the far-reaching impact of the Cold War. In both areas, the United States forged anticommunist alliances while the Soviet Union supported communist governments and revolutionary movements. More than once, the contest fueled crises and armed conflict in these areas.

Japan had emerged from World War II defeated on sea and land, the shocked victim of history's first two atomic bombs used for military purposes. Because the United States by far had played the major role in the defeat of Japan, it refused to share the occupation and governing of the Japanese islands with its former allies. The U.S. quickly promoted political democratization and used financial aid to help Japan rebuild and conform to U.S. policies. In this way, Japan, like West Germany, would become a link in the Cold War containment "chain" that the U.S. was forging around the Soviet Union. The strategy paid off handsomely. During the 1950s and 1960s, Japan became a firm ally and used its modern industries and skilled labor to make an astounding economic recovery that surpassed even that of West Germany.

The Cold War in Asia

China, just across the Sea of Japan, moved in a different direction. The civil war between Mao Zedong's zealous Communist forces and Jiang Jieshi's

The Cold War and Nuclear Weapons

The intensity of the Cold War and the existence of nuclear weapons on both sides spread fear throughout the West during the 1950s and early 1960s. Observers debated whether nuclear weapons would deter attacks from the opposing side, whether the contestants could agree to disarm, and whether unilateral destruction of nuclear weapons made the most sense. In the following selection from a 1956 debate, Philip Toynbee of Great Britain argues for the last position.

It is obvious, surely, that this is an issue which has nothing whatever to do with party politics and nothing whatever to do with our estimations of American and Russian society. In the terrible context of nuclear war even the vital differences between Communism and Western freedom become almost unimportant. We would infinitely prefer our Western system of freedom and privacy to prevail in the world; and if we are spared we shall have an opportunity of trying to ensure that it does so. But even if it didn't prevail *mankind* would still be given the opportunity of prevailing. Mr. Kennan has said that anything would be better than a policy which led inevitably to nuclear war. But surely anything is better than a policy which allows for the *possibility* of nuclear war.

The issue has nothing do to with politics. It has little to do with causes and highmindedness. Those who have had at least a partial vision of our destruction are like people who have leant out of the window of an express train and seen that a bridge is down a little further along the line. They are urging the driver and their fellow-passengers that the train should be stopped. But the others reply, many of them from behind their newspapers, that the train can't possibly be stopped because they have important engagements in the city. As for the bridge, it may not be down after all, and even if it is the train will probably manage to jump across it somehow. Besides, it does no good to the reputation of our railways if express trains are to be halted in this way. And finally, we ought surely to be aware that there is another express train coming in the opposite direction which will certainly fall down into the river just as soon as we do.

At the very least, then, let those who wish to continue with the arms-race be prepared with competent methods of killing off their mutilated families before killing their mutilated selves. Only when we see that they have made these preparations shall we be able to believe that they have faced the implications of their policy.

SOURCE: Philip Toynbee, *The Fearful Choice* (London: Victor Gollancz, 1956), pp. 21–22.

Analyze the Document

1. What does Toynbee's argument reveal about the level of fear during the Cold War?

2. How does Toynbee justify a policy of unilateral nuclear disarmament?

3. How might his opponents have responded to this argument?

---

conservative Nationalist forces was suspended during World War II. Mao's forces waged a more incessant guerrilla warfare against the Japanese than the Nationalists did and thereby gained a growing following among the Chinese people. After the surrender of Japan in 1945, the bitter, internal struggle for control of China began anew. The United States supported the Nationalists, while ever-increasing numbers of Chinese supported the Communists. In 1949, the victorious Communists swept over the entire Chinese mainland. Jiang's Nationalists fled to the nearby island of Taiwan, where they came under the protection of the U.S. navy. Mao promptly proclaimed the People's Republic of China and joined in an alliance with the Soviet Union. With Soviet aid, he began the daunting task of industrializing and communizing China.

Less than a year later, the Cold War merged with simmering internal forces in nearby Korea to produce a major conflict that embroiled both the new Chinese communist regime and the United States. At the end of World War II, in accordance with the Yalta agreements, Soviet troops occupied Korea north of the thirty-eighth parallel, while American forces controlled the south. The Soviets and Americans had withdrawn by 1949, leaving North and South Korea as armed client states rather than a united Korean nation. The new governments of the North and South, each ruled by dictators, talked loudly of conquering each other.

The Korean War

In 1950, the Soviet-backed North Korean communists—with the approval of both Stalin and Mao—suddenly invaded U.S.-backed South Korea. The determined, well-armed North Korean communists easily defeated the South Koreans. Supported by the UN, the U.S. quickly intervened. The American and UN forces soon overcame the North Koreans, but as their troops approached the Korean-Chinese border and threatened to bomb North Korean sanctuaries in China, the Chinese entered the fray. They pushed the U.S. and UN forces back to the thirty-eighth parallel, where a stalemate developed. By the time of the armistice in 1953, the war had cost some

La destruction de la France par l'alliance avec l'Allemagne. La guerre contre l'U.R.S.S. Voilà ce qu'on nous prépare.

ATOMIC BOMB

contre ça,

UNION et **ACTION**

il faut sauver la **PAIX**

LE PARTI COMMUNISTE FRANCAIS

FIGURE 25.1 *Peace Must Be Saved,* 1948 This French propaganda poster by André Fougeron, promoted by the French Communist Party, warns of the atomic destruction that would result from a French alliance with Germany.

1.5 million casualties on each side and had left much of Korea in ruins.

These experiences with Korea and China prompted the U.S. to involve itself in nearby Vietnam, Laos, and Cambodia. The U.S. feared that the fall of one nation in that region to communism would, as with a row of dominoes, lead to the fall of other adjacent nations. "Vietnam represents the cornerstone of the Free World in Southeast Asia, the keystone to the arch, the finger in the dike," warned Senator John F. Kennedy in 1956. "Burma, Thailand, India, Japan, the Philippines, and obviously Laos and Cambodia are among those whose security would be threatened if the red tide of Communism overflowed into Vietnam. . . ."

Accordingly, the U.S. helped the French fight against Vietnamese nationalists. Vietnam had been a French colony before World War II

The Vietnam War and, under the leadership of Ho Chi Minh (1890–1969) and his Vietnamese Communist Party, had fought for its independence from France in the years after World War II. After suffering a series of defeats, France finally agreed

to withdraw in 1954. The 1954 Geneva Accords provisionally gave Ho Chi Minh's Communists control of the nation north of the seventeenth latitude and provided for elections throughout the whole country in 1956. The U.S. refused to sign the accords, and Ngo Dihn Diem (1901–1963), who took power in the south where the remnants of the old French-supported Associated State of Vietnam had fled, refused to hold the elections. The nation was divided between the North, ruled by the victorious Ho Chi Minh, and the South, under an authoritarian, anticommunist government that tried to maintain the aristocratic society of a vanishing era (see **Map 25.4**).

The unpopular regime in the South relied for its survival on the economic and political support of the United States and its allies. Military aid and armed forces soon followed, as the United States sought to increase its influence not only in South Vietnam but also in Laos and Cambodia, which had gained freedom from the French. During the mid-1960s, the U.S. sent more than 500,000 troops to Vietnam. American planes dropped more explosives there than had been used by all combatants during World War II, pummeling the tiny nation. Still, the opposing North Vietnamese—helped by material aid from the Soviet Union and China—proved skilled and tenacious fighters, and the war dragged on.

Throughout the West, the United States drew harsh criticism from antiwar demonstrators for its relentless—and apparently futile—assaults on Vietnam. **Figure 25.2,** a 1968 collage titled *Miss America,* is one example of the reproach aimed at the United States. In this disturbing image, the well-known German artist Wolf Vostell uses photo-journalism to convey his message. In the center, a National Front for the Liberation of Southern Vietnam (contemptuously called the Vietcong by its enemies) suspect in South Vietnam is being executed. At the bottom, U.S. troops loom over crumpled corpses. Above is a mutilated image of a woman. The title of the work implies a mangling of American innocence, beauty, and honor by the daily, brutal realities of Vietnam published in newspapers and beamed into televisions around the world.

The cost, futility, and unpopularity of the Vietnam War put increasing pressure on U.S. leaders to end American involvement in the conflict. In 1973, after long negotiations, the U.S. and Vietnamese forces finally signed peace agreements, and the United States withdrew its forces. The civil war in Vietnam, however, persisted for another two years before the Communists swept to victory—not only in Vietnam but also in neighboring Laos and Cambodia.

The Cold War tide shifted in Asia several times. China, which had backed the Vietnam Communists, had continued in its own direction. During the 1950s, China was engaged in trying to meet overly ambitious

NATO 1949
BELGIUM
BRITAIN
CANADA
DENMARK
W. GERMANY
GREECE
ICELAND
ITALY
LUXEMBOURG
NETHERLANDS
NORWAY
PORTUGAL
SPAIN
TURKEY
UNITED STATES

SEATO 1954
AUSTRALIA
BRITAIN
FRANCE
NEW ZEALAND
PAKISTAN
PHILIPPINES
THAILAND
UNITED STATES

WARSAW PACT 1955
BULGARIA
CZECHOSLOVAKIA
EAST GERMANY
HUNGARY
POLAND
ROMANIA
SOVIET UNION

BAGHDAD PACT 1955
BRITAIN
IRAN
IRAQ
PAKISTAN
TURKEY

Map legend:
- North Atlantic Treaty Organization (NATO)
- Warsaw Pact Nations
- Middle East Treaty (Baghdad Pact)
- Southeast Asia Treaty Organization (SEATO)
- Asian Communist Nations Considered within "Soviet Sphere of Influence"
- ✦ Conflict Areas (with date)

MAP 25.3

Cold War Alliances and Conflicts

This map shows the Cold War alliances that spread across the globe during the 1940s and 1950s and the areas where conflicts related to the Cold War broke out.

Explore the Map

1. Which countries belong to anticommunist organizations?

2. What are the geopolitical advantages and disadvantages held by each side in the Cold War?

3. What areas of conflict suggest how worldwide the Cold War was?

goals in industry and agriculture. To that end, it communized its society even more completely than had ever been attempted in the Soviet Union. In a plan called the Great Leap Forward, China's huge and burgeoning population was set to building irrigation dams and ditches, steel mills, factories, railroads, schools, and hospitals at a frenetic pace. In 1959, an alternating cycle of droughts and flooding struck, producing one of the deadliest famines in history; some 20 million Chinese may have died of starvation and malnutrition over the next three years. Overzealous local party officials provoked resentment and resistance among the already harried populace, and for years the Communist Party hierarchy was wracked by a power struggle between moderates and radicals. In 1966, Mao tried to reignite the revolutionary spirit by launching the Great Proletarian Cultural Revolution. He empowered youthful zealots to cleanse China of those who did not enthusiastically support him. Over several years, millions of people suffered humiliation or death.

> China's Great Leap Forward

> Mao's Cultural Revolution

At the same time, relations between China and the Soviet Union began to cool. As early as 1956, China started criticizing the USSR, which that year under Nikita Khrushchev (1894–1971) began backing away from Stalin's harshest policies. Mao denounced Moscow for softening toward the capitalistic, imperialist West and for abandoning strict Marxist-Leninist principles. In 1960, the Soviet Union began to withhold promised economic and technological aid to China. When China exploded its first nuclear device in 1964, the two communist nations moved further apart, and by 1968, they were embroiled in border disputes.

> The Chinese-Soviet split

With the Soviet Union a common enemy, China and the United States tentatively looked to each other for support. During the 1970s, China normalized relations with the U.S., replaced Taiwan in the UN, and, after the death of Mao in 1976, initiated policies emphasizing economic decentralization and free-market activities. **Figure 25.3** symbolizes the new, assertive strength of communist China. In this striking photograph, a 90-foot statue of Chairman Mao Zedong towers over marchers celebrating the twenty-first anniversary of the communists' victory in China.

The Cold War soon took another turn in central Asia, where the Soviet Union became entangled in its own version of the Vietnam War. In 1979, Soviet troops intervened to support a communist coup in Afghanistan, a nation on the USSR's southern border that the Soviets considered within their own sphere

MAP 25.4

Vietnam and Southeast Asia

This map shows Vietnam and its neighbors during the 1950s, 1960s, and 1970s, when war wracked the area.

Explore the Map

1. Why might Cambodia and Laos have become involved in the conflicts?

2. Notice China to the north. Why were the U.S. bombings of Hanoi and Haiphong strategically risky?

Origins of the Cold War   783

thinking about

ART

FIGURE 25.3 Mao and Communist China, 1970 A statue of Mao towers over a 1970 victory parade in China, suggesting the growing strength and political will of that nation.

FIGURE 25.2

Wolf Vostell, *Miss America*, 1968

In this 1968 collage, German artist Wolf Vostell conveys impressions of the war in Vietnam. A female figure suggesting a fashion model or contestant from a Miss America pageant struts provocatively, but parts of her body are blotted with red. Below, photographic images of disturbing events during the war intrude. Much of the coloring suggests not only blood but also the American flag.

Connecting Art & Society

1. Why do you think Vostell titled this work *Miss America*?

2. What might the artist have intended the viewer to understand by superimposing photos of events in Vietnam over an image of this woman?

3. Should this collage be viewed primarily as a thoughtful, realistic depiction of the war or as a piece of propaganda? Why?

of influence. They promptly became locked in a ten-year war against tenacious guerrilla forces backed by the U.S. Central Intelligence Agency. In 1989 the Soviets finally withdrew, leaving Afghanistan in shambles and wracked by internal violence.

Soviets in Afghanistan

Even the Latin American countries, far from the conflicts in Asia and long considered "friends" by the United States, got pulled into the Cold War. At the end of World War II, the governments of independent Latin American states were republics in name. In reality, however, most of them were right-wing dictatorships, representing the interests of the well-to-do bourgeoisie, the landowning classes, and the professional military. The Roman Catholic Church, which had been a powerful conservative force in this region during the nineteenth century, had grown more liberal during the twentieth century. Sometimes it even exerted its influence in social and economic reform movements. In the years following World War II, the poor in Latin America became increasingly restless. Many of them turned to communism, encouraged by the Soviet Union. The United States, on the other hand, supported the conservative governments.

The Cold War in Latin America

Over the next four decades, the U.S. intervened in or invaded several Latin American nations to shore up conservative forces in its global struggle against communism. The Soviets, for their part, supported sympathetic revolutionary movements and regimes. Of all the Latin American countries, Cuba became the most volatile staging ground for the intensifying feud between the superpowers. In 1959, Marxist rebel leader Fidel Castro ousted the American-supported dictatorship in Cuba and launched a sweeping program of social and economic reforms. The new

Crisis in Cuba

program included the seizure of property owned by citizens and corporations of the United States. The U.S. government promptly terminated aid to the island nation, and Castro turned to the Soviets for help. These developments threatened the Americans in two crucial ways. First, a revolutionary, left-wing regime backed heavily by the Soviet Union had suddenly gained a beachhead in Latin America—a mere 90 miles from the U.S. mainland. Second, the Americans worried that Castro's success would embolden other opposition and revolutionary movements—also typically led by Marxists—throughout Latin America. Such uprisings would lead to more Cold War victories for the communists. Three years after the Cuban revolution, the U.S. government sponsored the Bay of Pigs invasion, an ill-fated attempt by Cuban refugees to topple the Castro regime.

Tensions soon reached a new high in the Caribbean. On October 12, 1962, a U.S. spy plane discovered Soviet missiles being installed in Cuba. Privately, President Kennedy admitted: "What difference does it make? They've got enough to blow us up now anyway. . . . This is a political struggle as much as military." Although the U.S. had missiles on Russia's border in Turkey, the Americans decided that Soviet missiles in Cuba were intolerable. With the USSR's ships steaming toward the Caribbean, the U.S. Navy under orders to intercept them to prevent the arrival of more missiles in Cuba, and American forces mobilizing, people around the world braced themselves for a possible nuclear war. On October 27, the U.S. Joint Chiefs of Staff urged an all-out attack on Cuba if the Soviets did not immediately remove the missile bases. Two days later, USSR leader Nikita Khrushchev backed down, and an agreement ended the crisis.

Détente

The two superpowers would not again come so close to war with each other. Indeed, at times Cold War tensions relaxed as each side backed away from the sort of conflict that promised to devastate each nation and much of the world. Nuclear test-ban treaties in the 1960s and strategic arms limitation talks in the 1970s eased fears of confrontation. The Helsinki agreement in 1975, confirming Europe's political frontiers and recognizing certain human rights, seemed to solidify a period of **détente**—growing cooperation between Cold War adversaries. But détente went only so far. The 1980s witnessed a return to combative rhetoric and policies with the Soviet invasion of Afghanistan and the tougher anticommunist policies of the Reagan administration in the United States. By the middle of that decade, few saw any end to the Cold War.

EAST AND WEST: TWO PATHS TO RECOVERY IN EUROPE

Under the long shadow of the Cold War, Europeans again tried to return to normal life after World War II. Beyond the astounding number of deaths and widespread destruction, whole cities—such as Berlin, in the heart of Europe—had been devastated. "Nothing is left in Berlin," wrote a reporter for the *New York Herald Tribune* in 1945. "There are no homes, no shops, no transportation, no government buildings. . . . Berlin can now be regarded only as a geographical location heaped with mountainous mounds of debris." Realists declared that economic recovery alone might take twenty-five years. Others wondered whether European society would ever recover.

European nations followed two main paths toward recovery that reflected Cold War differences and the politics underlying those differences. In the Soviet Union and Eastern Europe, communist governments promised clear planning and an unquestionable sense of direction under firm party direction. In Western Europe, the capitalist democracies relied on an alliance of the free market and governmental controls to transform their societies from the wartime devastation. Each path would have its successes and problems.

Tight Control in the Soviet Union and Eastern Europe

Nowhere was the damage and upheaval from World War II worse than in the Soviet Union and Eastern Europe. Soviet citizens longed for an end to wartime deprivations and Stalin's strict controls. Eastern Europeans living along the USSR's border wondered uneasily what to expect as their governments and economies came under the rule of communist parties controlled by Moscow.

Stalin refused to relax his grip over the Soviet Union. He asserted dictatorial control, crushing the merest hint of political dissent and purging those whom he perceived as potential threats. Prisons and forced-labor camps overflowed with his victims. Nor did his economic policies—tight planning and extreme sacrifice for heavy industrialization—change. To help rebuild what the war had destroyed in the Soviet Union, Stalin drained off economic resources from the Eastern European states.

Those countries under Soviet dominance—the "satellite" states—were required to cooperate with the Soviet Union. Single-party "people's democracies" in Poland, East Germany, Czechoslovakia, Hungary, Romania, Yugoslavia, and Albania initiated Soviet-style economic planning, nationalization, collectivization of agriculture, and industrialization. Officials allowed little contact with Western Europe.

Nevertheless, Eastern Europe refused to become a mere appendage to the Soviet Union. These nations harbored strong desires for national autonomy and they often resented Soviet restrictions. Within these states, discontent also rose over the persistent shortage of consumer goods, low wages, and poor working conditions. The Soviets and their followers often had difficulty maintaining control as resistance flared into open rebellions.

Yugoslavia snapped first. The Soviet Union had a weak foothold there because the Yugoslav resistance had liberated the nation from Nazi control almost on its own. In 1948, Yugoslavia's strong and popular dictator, Tito (see Biography in Chapter 24), stood up to Stalin's threats and headed his nation on an independent course. Tito's decentralized form of communism stressed more local control and worker participation in management than the Soviet model.

In 1953, Joseph Stalin, the man who had led the USSR for a quarter-century, died. In the Soviet Union, millions mourned Stalin as the leader who had saved them from Nazism. However, some Eastern Europeans saw his death as an opportunity to step up their demands for greater independence. Workers in East Berlin initiated protests against governmental efforts to increase workloads without raising wages. Crowds soon gathered in the streets, demanding political reform and a loosening of ties to the USSR. Police and Soviet tanks promptly crushed these uprisings.

The death of Stalin and new opportunities

In Moscow, potential successors to Stalin jockeyed for power. They quickly agreed to eliminate the dreaded head of the secret police, Lavrenti Beria (1899–1953), and restricted that organiza-

tion's terrorist activities. After two years of collective leadership, Nikita Khrushchev, the son of a miner, moved up from the party bureaucracy to emerge as Stalin's successor. In a 1956 unpublished speech to startled communist leaders, Khrushchev denounced the "cult of personality" fostered by Stalin. He also accused Stalin of using "the most cruel repression, violating all norms of revolutionary legality . . . mass arrests and deportations of many thousands of people, executions without trial." Khrushchev slightly loosened government control of Soviet cultural life; authors such as Boris Pasternak (1890–1960) even managed to publish works that implied some criticism of the Soviet regime. New policies also stressed the production of consumer goods, increased housing, and better health care. Workers throughout the USSR gained more freedom to move from one job to another.

Eastern Europeans hoped that this de-Stalinization would spell a relaxation of Soviet control over their nations. In Poland, worker strikes against wage cuts expanded into demands for political change in 1956, and the Soviets threatened to intervene. Nevertheless, Poland's Communist Party elected the moderate Wladyslaw Gomulka (1905–1982) instead of the Soviet candidate. Gomulka refused to cave in to Soviet demands but promised military loyalty. A compromise left Poland within the Soviet sphere of control while enjoying some new levels of economic and cultural independence—including increased toleration of the Roman Catholic Church.

Protests and uprisings in Eastern Europe

Next, Hungarians issued a challenging demand for independence. When Hungary's communist leaders called on troops to put down protesters in the streets, the troops refused to fire and instead switched sides. A new government under the reforming communist Imre Nagy (1896–1958) initiated major economic and political reforms that included the introduction of a multiparty system. Nagy even proposed to withdraw Hungary from the Warsaw Pact—Moscow's military alliance with its Eastern European satellites. The Hungarians had crossed the line. The Soviets sent in tanks and troops, slaughtering thousands and forcing hundreds of thousands to flee to the West. Nagy was hanged, and the lesson was made crystal clear: Cooperate with Moscow or pay the highest penalty.

In 1961, relations between East and West hit a new low. Under orders from Khrushchev, the East German government erected a 100-mile, heavily armed wall in Berlin to keep its citizens from fleeing to the West. Berlin had served as an escape route for 2.6 million people, especially professionals and the well educated who sought a higher standard of living in Western Europe. **Figure 25.4** shows a section of the **Berlin Wall** under reconstruction after it was

The Berlin Wall

FIGURE 25.4 The Berlin Wall Workers, soldiers, and onlookers gather on both sides as the wall dividing East and West Berlin is repaired.

rammed by an East German trying to escape into West Berlin. To the left, East German workers and machines build the heavy brick barrier. In the background, a fence topped with barbed wire extends into the distance. East German soldiers, such as those on the left side of the photo, will guard the wall; they have orders to shoot anyone between the fence and the wall trying to flee to the West. To the right, West German soldiers and citizens look on. The wall graphically marked the division of Germany and symbolized the hostility between Western and Eastern Europe.

In 1964, competitors within the Communist Party's Central Committee suddenly ousted Khrushchev, who had been weakened by foreign policy embarrassments such as the Cuban missile crisis, and installed the more conservative Leonid Brezhnev (1906–1982). The new Soviet leader took a firm line in dealing with Soviet satellites in Eastern Europe. Most of these states posed no problem for him. East Germany, for example, closely followed the Soviet line while developing its industrial capacity, and it became the richest nation in Eastern Europe. Hungary remained tranquil, orienting its economy toward consumer goods, loosening state control, and introducing limited capitalistic practices at the local level.

Other satellite states caused conflict—none more than Czechoslovakia. In 1968, reformers gained control of the Czechoslovak Communist Party and replaced the country's Stalinist leader with Alexander Dubcek, who believed that communism could be made compatible with internal party democracy and personal freedom. In this **Prague Spring** uprising, the Dubcek government initiated economic decentralization, greater national independence, democratic reforms, and elimination of censorship—"socialism with a human face." The reforms gained enthusiastic support within Czechoslovakia, especially among optimistic students and intellectuals thirsting for free speech.

Like Hungary in 1956, Dubcek's reforms went too far for the USSR's comfort. Especially fearful that the Prague Spring could inspire similar movements throughout Eastern Europe, the Soviets sent in Warsaw Pact troops to reverse Dubcek's policies and halt Czechoslovakia's steps toward independence. **Figure 25.5** shows Soviet tanks rumbling through Prague in August 1968. Czechoslovakian citizens stand on the sidewalks watching as the tanks overwhelm any potential resistance in the streets. Fire burns in the background, adding to this image of the Soviets using brute force to compel Czechoslovakia back into line. The Czechs reacted with passive resistance; they could do little more. The Soviets removed

The Prague Spring

FIGURE 25.5 The Prague Spring, 1968 Soviet tanks roll through Prague, Czechoslovakia, crushing a 1968 reformist uprising.

Dubcek and his liberal supporters from power, and Brezhnev established his "Doctrine": Soviet intervention is justified in order to ensure the survival of socialism in another state. The conservative Brezhnev would make sure that Eastern Europe, like the Soviet Union itself, would not stray too far from the tightly controlled communist path followed since the early post–World War II years.

Parliamentary Politics and Prosperity in the Western Democracies

Western European nations proceeded on a strikingly different course to recovery, dictated by both Cold War considerations and the internal histories of those societies. In 1945, most Western European nations quickly returned to prewar democratic forms of government, and political parties leaning toward the center of the political spectrum soon gained control. In some countries, one political party dominated for long stretches of time—the Christian Democrats reigned in West Germany for two decades, for example, and in Italy for four decades following World War II. In other countries, major parties alternated in power, as the Labor and Conservative parties did in Britain. Some governments lasted only months, as happened in France, though the same group of well-known politicians usually rotated into the high offices of new governments and worked with a stable bureaucracy that carried out policy.

Initially, communist parties also gained strength after the war, especially in France and Italy. In France, elections in 1945 resulted in a sweeping victory for parties of the Left, including the communists, as well as the retirement of the conservative general Charles de Gaulle, who had set up a government in Paris in 1944. In Italy, the communists also emerged from

World War II strong. For decades, the Italian Communists would command 25 to 35 percent of the vote and win local elections. But after 1947, when the Cold War heated up, these communist parties in France, Italy, and elsewhere were systematically excluded from participation in national governments.

In the struggle to repair their broken economies, European nations benefited greatly from U.S. aid. Having emerged from the war the world's preeminent economic power, the United States pumped almost $13 billion of Marshall Plan aid into Western Europe between 1947 and 1952. More than a sense of humanity motivated the Americans. The economic aid also served U.S. Cold War interests by supporting anticommunist forces. The aid came with strings attached: international cooperation and freer trade by the recipients. By demanding these conditions, the U.S.—now producing more than half the world's industrial goods—gained unprecedented access to large European markets.

U.S. aid and economic recovery

Europeans helped themselves as well. Drawing on lessons from the Great Depression, World War II, and the British economist John Maynard Keynes, governments adopted policies to dampen recessions by deficit spending (priming the pump) and to counter inflation by tightening expenditures and interest rates. Several European states, from France to Norway, went even further by engaging in economic planning. This typically included nationalizing certain industries. In France, for example, major banking and insurance companies, coal mines, and gas and electrical utilities came under government control. In such countries, technocrats—bureaucrats with technological or scientific expertise—made economic decisions that were once the province of business owners or parliaments. Other nations avoided such extensive planning. West Germany, for example, broke up prewar corporate cartels instead and pressured labor and management to cooperate for industrial peace.

At the same time, most European nations created social programs to protect citizens from severe hardship and to promote social peace. These **welfare state** programs had roots in the late nineteenth century, when governments had begun taking responsibility for the inequities of capitalism. Concerned about declining population growth, Europeans also wanted to encourage women to have more children. In the years after World War II, many governments followed Sweden's early lead and initiated programs providing health-care benefits and family allowances as well as prenatal care, maternity benefits, child care, and nursery schooling.

The welfare state

Nowhere was the welfare state more dramatically introduced than in Britain. Having shared the toil and suffering of World War II under the effective governmental direction of the economy, British citizens believed that everyone should get a piece of the prosperity that they expected would follow the war. In 1945, they elected a Labor government under Clement Attlee (1883–1967). The new government soon nationalized about 20 percent of Britain's economy and initiated what some called "cradle-to-grave" social-welfare policies. All British citizens could now look to governmental support during times of need—whether those times involved raising children, suffering job loss or an accident, paying for adequate housing, or ensuring adequate resources for retirement. Above all, Britain's National Health Service guaranteed free medical care to all.

Scandinavian countries continued to lead, going the furthest in ensuring a decent standard of living for everyone in both good times and bad. By contrast, the Americans swam against the tide. Prosperous, with its high-spending military in close alliance with big business, the United States strenuously resisted programs smacking of socialism. Not until the 1960s did it pursue moderate social reform, such as new educational programs, low-income housing projects, and limited governmental support of medical services.

Of course, all social programs came at a price. Taxes rose, particularly for the middle and upper classes, and government bureaucracies ballooned. Moreover, critics questioned the quality of the services provided, particularly medical care. Yet once established, most social programs served enough people and gained sufficient political backing to become permanent fixtures.

The nations of Western Europe recognized that cooperation offered the best hope for competing economically in a world of superpowers. Encouraged by the Marshall Plan, these countries moved toward economic integration. In 1950, France and West Germany created the French-German Coal and Steel Authority to remove tariff barriers and manage coal and steel resources regionally. Jean Monnet (1888–1979), the architect of this organization, held high hopes: "If only the French could lose their fear of German industrial domination, then the greatest obstacle to a united Europe would be removed. . . . It could, in fact, become the germ of European unity." In 1952, the organization expanded into the European Coal and Steel Community with the addition of Italy, Belgium, Luxembourg, and the Netherlands. Five years later, these same six nations signed the Treaty of Rome establishing the **European Economic Community** (the EEC, also referred to as the Common Market). The treaty proposed to eliminate tariff barriers, cut restrictions on the flow of labor and capital, and integrate the economies of the member nations.

Beginning European economic integration

The Common Market ended tariff and immigration barriers ahead of schedule, and its member nations

thinking about
DOCUMENTS

DOCUMENT 25.2

A Warning About the United States

By the mid-1960s, many Europeans sensed that the United States, although friendly, had grown overbearing in some ways. U.S. economic institutions, capital, and culture were invading Europe, even though Europe had recovered from the devastation of World War II. This sense was particularly strong in France, as evidenced by the following selection from Jean-Jacques Servan-Schreiber's The American Challenge. *This widely popular book was first published in 1967.*

Europeans can regain control over their destiny in this confrontation with the American challenge only by taking stock of themselves and, as we will now try to describe, by hard work and patience. What we must do is not so hard to explain, for the path of our counterattack can be clearly marked out.

1. Creation of large industrial units which are able both in size and management to compete with the American giants.

2. Carrying out "major operations" of advanced technology that will ensure an independent future for Europe.

3. At least a minimum of federal power to protect and promote European business.

4. Transforming the relationship between business, the university, and the government.

5. Broader and more intensive education for young people; specialized and continuing education for adults.

6. Finally, as the key to everything else, the liberation of imprisoned energies by a revolution in our methods of organization—a revolution to revitalize the elites and even relations between men. . . .

To build a powerful and independent Europe means strengthening the economic and political bonds of the Common Market. No single nation is strong enough to support efficient production in all areas of advanced technology, for the national framework is too narrow and cannot provide adequate markets for such products. Also, the growing diversification of these products demands a specialization that makes any attempt at national self-sufficiency virtually impossible. . . .

Our back is to the wall. We cannot have both economic self-sufficiency and economic growth. Either we build a common European industrial policy, or American industry will continue taking over the Common Market.

SOURCE: J.J. Servan-Schreiber, *The American Challenge,* trans. Ronald Steel (New York: Atheneum House, 1969), pp. 153–154, 156.

Analyze the Document

1. What does this document suggest about Europeans' perceptions of the United States?

2. How does Servan-Schreiber plan to confront the American challenge?

3. What do you think of Servan-Schreiber's ideas?

---

enjoyed increased trade, productivity, and industrial production. In 1967, the organization combined with other cooperative bodies to form the European Community (EC) to work toward even greater economic and political integration. As Document 25.2 indicates, optimistic supporters hoped that the European Community would make Western Europe an independent regional power that might economically and even politically challenge its superpower ally, the United States, as well as the opposing the Soviet bloc in Eastern Europe.

Assessing the Paths Taken

Throughout Europe, early fears about how long reconstruction would take proved unfounded (see **Figure 25.6**). The Soviet and East European economies expanded after the war, though not as rapidly as Eastern Europeans expected or hoped. The Soviets applied advanced science, technology, and engineering to establish a strong industrial

The Eastern-bloc nations

COUNTRY	1938	1953	1963	1980
Britain	181	258	330	441
France	74	98	194	362
Germany	214	224	416	747
West Germany		180	330	590
East Germany		44	86	157
Italy	46	71	150	319
Poland	19	31	66	169
Sweden	21	28	48	83
Soviet Union	152	328	760	1630

FIGURE 25.6 European Industrial Production, 1938–1980

Figures are a percentage of British industrial output in 1900.

base, support a huge military, and build large urban projects. Some Eastern European nations, such as East Germany and Czechoslovakia, also developed extensive industrial bases and even outperformed the Soviets.

East and West: Two Paths to Recovery in Europe   789

Although communism stood for the end to class differences, some citizens within each nation were, in the words of British author George Orwell, "more equal" than others. Certainly the Communist Party elite and professionals enjoyed better services and a higher standard of living than everyone else. But all citizens gained access to education, free medical care, and job security under communism. Subsidies made their usually overcrowded housing inexpensive, and unemployment and abject poverty virtually disappeared.

Women participated fully in economic life in these nations, often outnumbering men in the labor force. Moreover, a majority of doctors and teachers were women. Far more women engaged in manual labor such as logging and heavy construction work than their counterparts did in the West. They also received family allowances, maternity benefits, and child-care support. Outside the higher levels of government, Soviet women gained widespread political representation in parliamentary bodies, especially in local government. Nevertheless, women's pay lagged behind men's and women usually remained responsible for traditional domestic duties.

But even with all these improvements, Eastern-bloc nations could not keep up with their citizens' growing desires for a higher standard of living and more independence. Eastern Europeans had relatively few choices in consumer goods, food, and housing. In satellite nations, longing for autonomy from the Soviet Union persisted. Within each nation, Soviet-backed regimes—for the most part dictatorships—labored under questions about their political legitimacy. For many people, a sense of isolation from the West and a stifling of free expression within their own societies dampened cultural life in those nations.

In the capitalist democracies of Western Europe, government spending and welfare-state programs, as well as U.S. aid, fueled a strong revival (see **Figure 25.6**). Europeans used this money, their growing store of new technology, and their skilled workforce to rebuild factories and transportation networks into models of efficiency. Falling tariff barriers and a population enlarged by increased birthrates created new demand for consumer goods. Food and clothing prices declined, jobs abounded, and wages rose. By 1955, the standard of living for even those in the bottom half of society rose. In just a decade, Western Europe had recovered fully from the economic devastation of the war.

During the 1960s, some Western European nations achieved unimagined levels of prosperity. West Germany, Switzerland, and Sweden became the wealthiest nations in Europe. People in northern Italy spoke of their own "economic miracle." On the other hand, areas farther south still wedded to more traditional agricultural economies lagged behind, and once-mighty Britain—reeling from the loss of overseas trade and investments, and hampered by the antiquated state of most of its mines and factories—suffered a relative decline.

Overall, however, Western Europe took on the look and substance of wealth. Industries such as electronics, automobiles, plastics, petroleum, prefabricated housing, and airlines flourished. Newly restored city centers attracted hordes of shoppers, suburban commuters, tourists, and pedestrians. The number of cars on Europe's streets jumped tenfold from fewer than 5 million in 1945 to over 50 million by 1970. Stores overflowed with a cornucopia of foods and clothing. Electronic gadgets—from electric can openers to hand-held audiotape players—cropped up everywhere. The proliferation of restaurants, theaters, travel, and hotels reflected the affluence and the widespread standard of a forty-hour workweek and four weeks of paid vacation each year.

The good economic news outweighed almost everything else in Western Europe, and nothing helped its politicians more, for economic growth became the key measure of political success. Moreover, as observers and visitors looked at the paths to recovery taken in Eastern and Western Europe, the West's stunning prosperity clearly contrasted with the slower growth in the East. However, Western Europe also had problems that reflected its decline from the heights of power and certainty. Not only had these nations forfeited leadership to the United States, but they lost their colonial empires as well.

THE TWILIGHT OF COLONIALISM

Even before World War II, national liberation movements around the globe had gathered momentum. When Germany defeated imperial nations such as France and the Netherlands, and Japan conquered Western holdings in Asia and the Pacific, Europe's control over its colonial territories weakened. The United Status further undermined the imperial powers by pushing them to dismantle their empires at war's end. At the same time, the Soviet Union continued to spread its decades-old denunciation of Western imperialism throughout the world. In the United Nations, sentiment grew toward the view that colonial "subjugation, domination and exploitation constitutes a denial of fundamental human rights." In the colonies, people seethed with anger against the Europeans. "Leave this Europe where they are never done talking of Man, yet murder men everywhere they find them," wrote the French West Indian philosopher Frantz Fanon (1925–1961) in his widely read book *The Wretched of the Earth*. "For centuries they have stifled almost the whole of humanity. . . . Look at them today swaying between atomic and spiritual disintegration." The last emperor of Vietnam, Bao Dai, warned his French overlords about "this desire for independence which is in everyone's heart and which no human force can any longer restrain."

Despite the intensity of these sentiments, many European settlers felt they had lived in the colonies too long to cede control to the local populations. Several political leaders in Europe agreed with Winston Churchill's sentiments: "I did not become the king's first minister in order to preside over the liquidation of the British Empire." The French announced that "the attainment of 'self-government' in the colonies, even in the distant future, must be excluded." The struggle to end colonialism was on.

Revolts in Southern Asia

At the end of World War II, national liberation revolts threatened the huge British, Dutch, and French empires in southern Asia. Of the Western imperial powers, only the United States escaped direct embroilment in this revolt, by granting independence to the Philippines in 1946.

In India, the world's second most populous country, Mohandas K. Gandhi (1869–1948) led the independence movement. Educated in Great Britain, this astute middle-class Hindu used passive resistance and civil disobedience rather than direct violence to pressure British officials to grant Indian independence. In 1947, Britain's Labor government finally freed India, partitioned into the separate states of India and Pakistan because of growing political divisions between Hindus and Muslims. Great Britain also relinquished Ceylon (Sri Lanka), Burma (Myanmar), and Malaya.

India

Independence, however, did not end problems in this troubled region. Religious and national strife soon broke out between Hindu India and Muslim Pakistan. Gandhi tried to quell the hostilities, but a fanatical Hindu nationalist assassinated him in 1948. Open war between the two states erupted in 1949 over possession of the disputed state of Kashmir. The United Nations managed to stop the shooting but failed to resolve the dispute, which would simmer for decades. This conflict, as well as border clashes with China, persuaded India to accept military aid from both the United States and the Soviet Union. India and Pakistan also faced the huge tasks of unifying their populations—divided by languages, caste, and class—and helping their millions of poverty-stricken and illiterate citizens.

In the rich and populous Dutch East Indies, nationalist leaders had established underground organizations during the wartime Japanese occupation. These leaders now

Indonesia

stepped in and declared independence when the invaders left. The Dutch resisted fiercely for four years before yielding control. In 1949, they finally recognized the Republic of Indonesia as an independent nation.

A similar but more painful pattern emerged in France's Asian empire after the Japanese left Indochina in 1945. As we have seen (page 781), the popular Indochinese nationalists, led by Soviet-educated communist Ho Chi Minh (1890–1969), proclaimed the independent Democratic Republic of Vietnam. Heavy fighting between the French imperialists and communist nationalists ensued. In 1954, France finally admitted defeat, pulling out of Vietnam and freeing the neighboring countries of Laos and Cambodia.

Vietnam

Conflict in the Middle East

In the Middle East, Britain had been the dominant imperial power since World War I. However, under pressure from nationalists who had agitated for full independence since the first decades of the twentieth century, the British relaxed their control in the years before World War II. At the end of the war, British influence remained strong in several states, but only Cyprus, Palestine, and the Suez Canal were still official British possessions. Moreover, Britain was making a pronounced bid for Arab friendship and, to that end, helped to form the League of Arab States in 1945. Yet, the admission of tens of thousands of Jews into Palestine under the Balfour Declaration of 1917—a British promise to create a "national home" for Jews in Palestine—made Palestine a new trouble spot.

Palestine was the ancient home of the Jews—a people with a long history of being displaced by others. In the seventh century, the Islamic Arabs conquered Palestine and lived there until the twentieth century. In the late nineteenth century, a new movement— Zionism—emerged to restore Palestine as the national home for the Jews (see pages 637–640). During the anti-Semitic persecutions of the Hitler era, Jewish refugees poured into Palestine and bought land, enraging the dispossessed Arabs. The British were caught between their obligations to the Arab nationalists in Palestine and the Jewish settlers eager to reclaim Palestine as their homeland.

Palestine

In 1948, the beleaguered British finally turned Palestine over to the United Nations. The Jews immediately proclaimed the State of Israel and accepted the boundary lines that the United Nations drew up dividing Palestine between the Jews and the Arabs. However, the League of Arab States protested this arrangement, and fighting broke out between the

Israel founded

MAP 25.5

The Arab-Israeli Conflict, 1947–1982

This map shows some of the results of the various Arab-Israeli conflicts between 1947 and 1982.

Explore the Map

1. Which states in the area were most involved in these conflicts?

2. Who gained the most, and who suffered the greatest losses of territory?

3. Why were Jerusalem, the West Bank, and the Golan Heights of such importance to the parties involved?

two sides. Although outnumbered, the well-organized Jewish forces held on. After a year, the United Nations brokered a truce. During the conflict, Israel had gained some territory and had expelled more than a half-million Palestinian Arabs. Most of these refugees, not welcomed by neighboring Arab states, settled in rough camps just outside Israel's new borders. The vigorous new nation, with financial help from abroad and a social-democratic government at home, began building modern cities and a strong economy. The Arab nations, however, refused to recognize Israel, and Palestine nationalists, without a country of their own, continued to conduct border raids on the fledgling nation. Conflicts stemming from the birth of the Israeli state would drag on for decades (see **Map 25.5**).

These conflicts only compounded the broader anti-Western sentiment percolating in the region, especially in nearby Egypt, where Britain still controlled the Suez Canal. In 1952, a military coup in Egypt brought the dynamic nationalist leader Gamel Abdul Nasser (1918–1970) to **Egypt** power. Although Nasser kept much political power for himself, he promised parliamentary institutions, drew up a constitution guaranteeing individual rights, and distributed land to the poorer peasantry. In 1956, when the United States refused to support his plans to develop the Egyptian economy, he seized the Suez Canal. As he saw it, control of the canal would not only enrich Egypt but also symbolize Egypt's independence and Arab nationalism.

Nasser's bold action provoked a military attack by Israel, Britain, and France. Cold War rivalries quickly came into play when the Soviet Union threatened to intervene on the side of Egypt. At this point, the United States pressured the three invading powers to retreat. Though defeated militarily, Nasser ended up a national hero and the leader of the Arab world for standing up to Israel and the Western powers. Moreover, Britain lost the canal and soon its last holdings in the Middle East, and the Soviets gained influence in the region.

When war broke out again in 1967 and 1973—between Egypt (with its Arab allies) and Israel—the Soviet Union and the United States rushed billions more dollars of arms and advisors to their respective allies. The area had become another crucible of superpower competition that would continue to generate anti-Western resentment.

Liberating Africa

As in Asia and the Middle East, movements for national liberation stirred in Africa, where France and Britain held the most territory. France faced its greatest challenge in North Africa, where the largely Islamic population seethed with nationalistic unrest. In the face of this growing force, France granted independence to Morocco and Tunisia in 1956 but drew the line at Algeria. The imperial power had held Algeria for over a century and considered it part of France rather than just a colony. In addition, more than a million French settlers lived there. They feared loss of property and reprisals from the eight million Islamic Algerians in the case of France's withdrawal. Complicating matters, the French military was determined to hold Algeria so as to repair the damage that France's reputation had sustained in Vietnam. At the same time, Arab nationalists living in Algeria believed that, with enough resolve, they just might oust the colonialist regime.

The French in North Africa

A long, bloody stalemate resulted. As one French soldier noted, "There's this staggering fact: The entire Arab population is joining the resistance against us." When the French government eventually showed a willingness to compromise, disgruntled colonial army officers threatened to overthrow the government in Paris. In 1958, as France's government teetered on the verge of collapse, retired general Charles de Gaulle was recalled to power. The World War II hero alone had the stature and legitimacy to negotiate with the forces of Arab nationalism. He granted Algeria independence in 1962 and freed almost all the other remaining French colonies.

Britain experienced similar challenges to its authority in its African colonies. The Labor government tried to prepare for the gradual freeing of British territories by sharing power with Africans in the civil service and bolstering funds for educational and economic development. The experience with Nasser in Egypt and a rebellion in Kenya from 1951 to 1956 finally persuaded the British to hasten their departure from Africa. By 1965, Britain had formally dismantled its African empire.

Britain dismantles its empire

Yet even with most imperialists gone, trouble still brewed on the African continent. Sizable white minorities living in Rhodesia and South Africa clung desperately to their power over black majorities. In Rhodesia, despite persistent guerrilla attacks by angry members of the black majority, the exclusively white regime held on until 1980. In long-independent South Africa, the prosperous white minority held fast to its power over the nonwhite majority (see Global Connections). The white minority harshly suppressed the increasingly restless black majority and enforced **apartheid** (racial segregation). This policy earned the all-white South African government decades of heated protests from nonwhites and condemnation throughout the world. Only in the 1990s would the white government under F. W. de Klerk at last allow the popular African National Congress, headed by the venerated Nelson Mandela, to assume leadership. By then, all European powers had pulled out of Africa. As **Map 25.6** shows, their departure ended Europe's domination of Africa and Asia.

Rhodesia and South Africa

Decolonization did not end Western influence in the non-Western world or bring peace and prosperity to the previously subject peoples. Newly independent nations were often left with illogical borders drawn arbitrarily by nineteenth-century European imperialists, depleted economies, and internal political divisions that drew in Cold War agents from both sides to exploit the chaos. Especially in Africa, ethnic conflict sometimes flared up into bloody civil wars, such as in Nigeria, where the Ibos in

The legacy of colonialism

Apartheid in South Africa

In 1960, the United Nations formally recognized that "the people of the world ardently desire the end of colonialism in all its manifestations." Within a few years, most of Africa would be free from white control. However, events unfolded in a strikingly different way in South Africa. Marked by its unique history, that society still labored under apartheid.

Since its virtual independence from Britain and unification in 1910, the Union of South Africa had come increasingly under the political influence of Afrikaners. These whites traced their roots back to the seventeenth century, when their Dutch ancestors had established colonies in South Africa. They were committed to ensuring their own domination over black Africans. Meanwhile, as the political winds shifted, cheap labor, cheap energy, gold, diamonds, and governmental aid fueled the country's industrialization and urbanization.

These trends culminated in 1948 with the electoral victory of the radical Afrikaner National Party. Building on established policies, the party put into practice the officially sanctioned system of apartheid (which means "separation" in Afrikaans). Through apartheid, the National Party sought to rigidly segregate people by color in order to keep nonwhites (which included blacks, Indians, and people of mixed heritage) completely subordinated to whites. Apartheid dictated where people of different groups could live, work, and go to school. It determined whom people might marry and what lavatories they could use. After 1958, Afrikaner leader Hendrik Verwoerd created "grand apartheid," which sent black South Africans to live in a patchwork of small ethnic states. He claimed that the Bible justified this policy. "We have a very fine position in South Africa; we've got

land, we've got a country and we are obliged by the love commandment to provide exactly the same to black people." However, grand apartheid kept more than 85 percent of the land in the hands of the white minority and treated blacks in white areas as foreign migrant workers.

The African National Congress (ANC), founded in 1912 by black Africans "for the purpose of creating national unity and defending our rights and privileges," actively opposed apartheid. The South African government severely repressed the ANC and other black activist groups. In 1962, government forces captured one of the ANC leaders, Nelson Mandela (1918–). At his first trial in 1963, Mandela proclaimed, "I have cherished the ideal of a democratic and free society in which all persons live together in harmony and with equal opportunities. . . . It is an ideal for which I am prepared to die." During his second trial, in 1964, Mandela cited the English Magna Carta and the American Bill of Rights in support of his cause. He also castigated the apartheid system: "The lack of human dignity experienced by Africans is the direct result of the policy of white supremacy." That year, Mandela was sentenced to life imprisonment. He soon became an internationally recognized symbol of the struggle to end apartheid; his image could be found in homes from Africa to Europe and the Americas.

For a while, repression by the white regime quelled most black protests. However, in 1976, an 18-month uprising initiated by black schoolchildren in Soweto further spread South Africa's worldwide reputation for heartless repression. In 1978, the United Nations imposed a mandatory arms embargo against South Africa in an effort to weaken the

white regime.

Over the years, nation after nation cut economic ties with the country.

In 1989, National Party leader F. W. de Klerk (1936–) became president of South Africa and began dismantling apartheid. Ultimately, however many forces destroyed apartheid. Demographic trends shifted the balance of power: Though population growth tripled under apartheid, the percentage of white people declined from 21 to 14. Moreover, black African opposition movements sapped the white government's energy. International isolation also weakened the regime, and, as de Klerk explained, "the decline and collapse of Communism in Eastern Europe and Russia put a new complexion on things." In 1990, de Klerk released Mandela from jail and legalized the ANC. De Klerk, Mandela, and others created a new constitution, ending white minority rule, and in 1994, South Africa held open elections. Sally Motlana, long an ANC activist, spoke for many about her new freedom: "I never dreamt that one day I would be sitting here with other human beings and regarded as a human being. For all those years I've been made to feel that I was not part of the human race." Voters resoundingly chose Mandela, making him the first black president of South Africa. Still vital and determined despite twenty-seven years of imprisonment, the new president proclaimed his nation "free at last."

Making Connections

1. What was the nature of apartheid? What were its purposes?

2. What forces brought an end to apartheid?

3. What problems would still face South Africa after 1994?

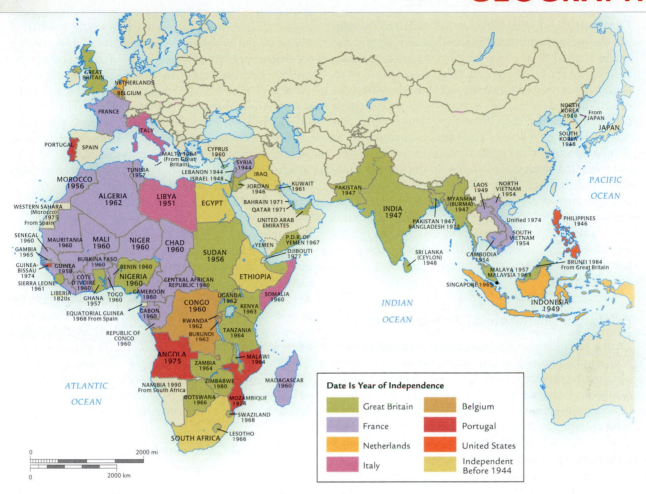

MAP 25.6

Decolonization

This map shows the colonial empires held by Western powers before World War II and the dates when the former colonies gained their independence.

Explore the Map

1. Which two nations had the most extensive colonial empires? Where were their holdings concentrated?

2. How did decolonization diminish the political reach of Europe?

3. Which former colonies became particularly volatile zones of conflict? How might that volatility have been related to decolonization?

the eastern region attempted to secede and set up the independent Republic of Biafra. Because the newly freed countries—especially in Africa—were generally left without internally generated political institutions, instability, bloodshed, and rule by military strongmen often resulted. In southern and southeastern Asia, religious and political differences broke out into wars in the years after liberation. Growing but impoverished populations lived under the threat of hunger and, in bad weather, starvation. Droughts, for example, in the huge sub-Saharan region of northern Africa during the 1970s, 1980s, and 1990s, brought famine and death to tens of thousands. Most former colonies remained "Third World" nations—relatively poor, supplying raw materials to industrialized nations and dependent on the wealthier countries' goods and aid. Interaction between Western and non-Western peoples had transformed life on both sides, and resentments nurtured by years of colonial suppression still lingered in many non-Western nations.

A SENSE OF RELATIVITY IN THOUGHT AND CULTURE

Decolonization forced Western Europeans to reevaluate themselves and their civilization. So did the rise of the United States and the Soviet Union as superpowers and the ensuing Cold War that quickly cast its shadow over the West and the world. In these decades of such accelerating change, thoughtful people struggled to understand and define their lives and the culture in which they lived. The idea of universal truths that had prevailed in earlier times gave way to a growing sense that truth was relative—to the individual, to time, and to place. Increasingly, intellectuals, scholars, and writers argued that values were defined by the cultures in which they arose, judgments stemmed from individual perceptions, and conclusions hinged on the evidence selected. In these subtle senses, the postwar decades stressed shifting meanings rather than certainties.

Existentialism: Responsibility and Despair

During the 1940s and 1950s, the philosophy of existentialism captured much attention in the West. Originating in an era marked by war, depression, mass death, and the decline of traditional standards of morality and religious beliefs, **existentialism** offered a stark interpretation of reality. France's Jean-Paul Sartre (1905–1980) (see **Figure 25.10**) became the most influential proponent of this body of thought. In novels, plays, and philosophical works, Sartre argued that there is no meaning to existence, no universal right or wrong. As he saw it, individuals are born and simply exist. They must make their own decisions,

Sartre and Camus

define their own purpose and values, and take responsibility for their actions. "Man cannot escape from the sense of complete and profound responsibility . . . one ought always to ask oneself what would happen if everyone did as one is doing." In the end, according to Sartre, one simply dies without there being any philosophical meaning to death. The French writer Albert Camus (1913–1960) also popularized existentialism, in novels and plays such as *The Stranger* (1942) and *The Plague* (1947). He stressed the plight of the responsible individual seeking understanding and identity in an amoral, purposeless world.

The sense of despair that existentialist assumptions often engendered came forth graphically in the Theater of the Absurd, which dispensed with linear plots, definable action, and conventional sets and costumes. Samuel Beckett's (1906–1989) plays are good examples of this genre. In *Waiting for Godot* (1952), two tramps wait for someone who never arrives. There is no purpose in what they do, for people in this culture no longer shared a sense of meaning. In Beckett's *Endgame* (1958), one character adrift in a world out of control describes his situation: "All life long the same questions, the same answers." In this absurd life, all responsibility rested with individuals, who had to make their own choices and decide how best to use their time on Earth.

Theater of the Absurd

A Culture of Contrasts and Criticism

The uncertainty and relativity implied by existentialism emerged not only in theater but also in other cultural forms. Writers, artists, and critics often disagreed with one another and with popular taste. In cinema, a stream of what critics dismissed as undistinguished movies nevertheless poured forth year after year. Yet cinema was perhaps the most original art form produced during the twentieth century. In the late 1940s and 1950s, several thoughtful movies, such as *The Bicycle Thief* by Italian filmmaker Vittorio de Sica, stressed the realistic struggles of ordinary people. During the 1960s and 1970s, the works of filmmakers such as Ingmar Bergman in Sweden, Federico Fellini and Liliana Cavani in Italy, Jean-Luc Godard in France, and Stanley Kramer in the United States exemplified the potential of cinema as a sophisticated, creative, artistic medium. These films contrasted sharply with the flashy artificiality of innumerable Hollywood movies—although many Hollywood motion pictures did feature stunning re-creations of the past, finely honed acting, and a creative mix of lighting, sound, and special effects.

Cinema

Many educators and commentators hoped that television would become a worthy cultural and educational medium as well. By the 1960s, people spent

KEY DATES

GLOBAL RELATIONS

1947	India gains independence
1948	Israel founded
1949	Indonesia gains independence
	Communist victory in China
1950–1953	Korean War
1954	France withdraws from Vietnam
1956	Egypt seizes the Suez Canal
1962	Algeria gains independence
1966	Mao's Cultural Revolution
1973	Oil crisis
1975	End of Vietnam War
1979	Invasion of Afghanistan

FIGURE 25.7 Jackson Pollock, *Convergence,* 1952
Paintings such as this work by American artist Jackson Pollock avoided realistic representations and seemed inaccessible to ordinary people.

on average fifteen to thirty hours per week watching television. To be sure, numerous situation comedies, adventure shows, dramas, and game shows celebrated the joys, anguish, and pains of everyday life—as well as violence, romance, and fantasy. Yet most television critics were disappointed. Like radio and newspapers, television crossed lines between serious news, politics, and entertainment alike. TV had an especially powerful impact on politics. Politicians sought or purchased TV exposure, shortened and simplified their messages, and cultivated an image created with the help of media and advertising professionals.

In the more traditional cultural fields, a similar pattern of conflict over new works emerged. Some of the most critically acclaimed works

Art seemed inaccessible to ordinary people. In art, abstract expressionistic paintings, such as those created by the American artist Jackson Pollock (1912–1956), who dripped paint onto canvases, drew attention but not crowds. **Figure 25.7** is one of Pollock's best-known works. Pollock explained why he avoided realistic representations of recognizable objects: "The modern artist is living in a mechanical age and we have a mechanical means of representing objects in nature such as the camera and photograph. The modern artist . . . is working and expressing an inner world . . . expressing his feelings rather than illustrating."

Pop art, with its images of everyday objects such as hamburgers in advertisements, also gained attention but bewildered audiences. **Figure 25.8,** by the American artist Andy Warhol (1928–1987), looks like nothing more than rows of soup cans. From another perspective, however, viewers might interpret it as an image of striking, colorful unity that reproaches our commercial, prepackaged society with its standardized tastes.

Such paintings sometimes drew popular ridicule. One American newsmagazine, *Time,* called Jackson Pollock "Jack the Dripper." On one level, this popular

rejection of bold new artistic forms was nothing new. Indeed, artistic styles that were once unpopular and considered avant-garde or elite—such as nineteenth-century postimpressionism and the twentieth-century paintings of Pablo Picasso—now attracted admiring crowds.

A related, but more puzzling, pattern emerged in literature and music. For example, the "new novel," which consciously avoided clear plots and well-defined characters, gained critical acclaim but attracted little popular attention. Yet other, hard-to-categorize novels that critics praised just as heartily—for example, works by German author Günter Grass, French author Marguerite Duras, and British author Doris Lessing—won wide popularity. In music, the dissonant, atonal music of Arnold Schoenberg (1874–1951) garnered few fans compared with the hugely popular rock and roll, whereas jazz—a creation of African-American culture that emphasized sophisticated improvisation and rhythm—enjoyed a large following.

Literature and music

Perhaps cultural products and tastes, like the civilization they reflected, were changing too fast for most people. To be sure,

Americanization

FIGURE 25.8 Andy Warhol, *One Hundred Cans,* 1962
Pop art painters such as Warhol created images filled with everyday objects that were not usually thought of as objects of art.

many Westerners worried about the speed of and the forces behind cultural changes. In Europe especially, people talked about maintaining their own cultural tastes and identities in the face of "Americanization." They complained about the Hollywood movies, blue jeans, Coca-Cola, hamburgers, and fast food that poured from the United States into Europe. They also bemoaned the drain of intellectuals and artists moving to the United States. However, they could do little about the rapid spread of ideas, tastes, talent, and culture across political boundaries. Western Europeans found themselves losing the control they once had, and even the relative stability and prosperity gained in the 1950s and 1960s came under attack.

PROTESTS, PROBLEMS, AND NEW POLITICS: THE 1960s TO THE 1980s

As the two postwar decades came to a close, the course of history in the West shifted. Events in the 1970s and 1980s unfolded in a context similar to that of the earlier decades: Cold War competition led by the United States and the USSR. Each side represented different political and economic systems that divided Europe and much of the world. Each side also marched to the beat of economic growth—more rapid in the capitalist West than the communist East. However, within this same context, economic and political trouble was afoot. During the late 1960s and early 1970s, the road to social peace grew bumpy.

A Flurry of Social Protests and Movements

During these years, the gap between the ideals and realities of democracy, equality, and prosperity became more obvious and irritating than before. In some cases, unprecedented access to education fueled a growing awareness of this gap, while in others prosperity itself gave people the confidence to demand change. Often the well-publicized efforts of one group to force change inspired similar efforts by others. Protest movements frequently began in the United States and attracted close attention throughout the West. These dissatisfied groups voiced their demands with an assertiveness that shook several Western societies and even threatened governments.

The first of the great social movements began in the United States during the 1950s. There, African Americans initiated the civil rights movement, which inspired several other protest and liberation efforts in the West. The civil rights movement stemmed from America's long failure to integrate its large black population. African-American veterans returning from World War II felt particularly

The civil rights movement

frustrated with the discrimination they again faced at home.

In 1954, the Supreme Court took a major step in the fight against discrimination by outlawing racial segregation in public schools. "Separate educational facilities are inherently unequal," the Court concluded. A year later, a quiet act by a courageous individual set a series of additional changes in motion. A black civil rights activist, Rosa Parks, took a seat in the white-only section of a bus in Montgomery, Alabama. A yearlong boycott of segregated public transportation by African Americans in Montgomery followed, the first of many mass actions throughout the United States in the 1950s and 1960s.

White resistance to the black struggle for equality flared up in the American South, and more than once the federal government had to send troops and marshals there to overcome white resistance. White opposition also mounted in the large industrial cities of the North. Many whites fled to the suburbs to avoid integration. In 1964 and 1965, Congress passed a series of civil rights acts that guaranteed voting rights for all and broadly outlawed racial discrimination. Still, the turmoil continued. Racially charged riots broke out in major cities. The violence reached a climax in 1968 following the murder of Martin Luther King, Jr. (1929–1968), the prominent African-American leader.

In the face of growing opposition and divisions within its own ranks, the civil rights movement lost steam in the 1970s, but not before inspiring other groups, such as Spanish-speaking Americans, Native Americans, young people, and women. The protests by youths became especially threatening. Like the civil rights movement, these protests began in the United States. Soon, however, they spread throughout the West.

College students, whose numbers in the West more than tripled during the 1950s and 1960s, created movements of their own. The sheer mass of this first postwar generation of students and the emergence of a separate youth culture helped give these young people an acute sense of their own power. The civil rights movement and growing opposition to the Vietnam War provided causes and experiences for many. In 1964, students at the University of California at Berkeley attacked the restrictive values, social inequities, and competitive impersonality of the university and the traditional society it represented. Students also decried racism, poverty, and the growing American participation in the Vietnam War. Sometimes the protests turned into riots when authorities used force. Similar demonstrations soon boiled up across the United States.

In 1968, the unrest spread to the campuses and streets of capitals from Tokyo and Mexico City to

Student movements

thinking about DOCUMENTS

DOCUMENT 25.3

An Oxford Student Explains Revolutionary Attitudes

The period between the mid-1960s and early 1970s was marked by intense political, social, and revolutionary activism. Perhaps most striking, university students throughout the West organized radical attacks on the status quo. The following selection by Tariq Ali, a student at Oxford and a leading revolutionary socialist, demonstrates the more extreme attitudes among these activists.

What is absolutely clear is that the revolutionary movement is in a period of upswing throughout the world. The war in Vietnam, the events of May 1968 in France and the invasion of Czechoslovakia symbolize this upswing.

Vietnam is at the moment the battle-front against imperialism. France showed the extreme vulnerability of monopoly capitalism and the strength of the working class. Czechoslovakia has initiated the struggle for political revolutions in Eastern Europe and the Soviet Union itself. . . .

Those of us who form the hard core of today's new revolutionaries are still Marxists, but we abhor Stalinism; we believe in Leninism but prefer the emphasis to be upon "democracy" rather than "centralism"; we are Guevarist but can appreciate and analyse the mistakes made by Che. We are puzzled by the tendency

among many Left factions in the developed countries to devote as much time and energy to attacking each other as to attacking capitalism. The new revolutionaries fight against sectarian tendencies. And what is most important of all, we are not to be bought off by the State. WE mean business.

SOURCE: Tariq Ali, *The New Revolutionaries* (New York: William Morrow, 1969), pp. 314–315.

Analyze the Document

1. In what ways are Ali's views revolutionary?

2. What developments of the 1960s does his analysis reflect?

3. What do you think Ali means by the last sentence?

London, Amsterdam, Milan, and Berlin. Even in Eastern Europe—especially in Czechoslovakia—youthful protesters added to dissident movements demanding social change and political democratization. "We are intensely aware, in a way perhaps not possible for the older generation, that humanity stands on the edge of a new era," declared students at the University of British Columbia in Canada. Document 25.3 reveals the views of some of the radical student groups. The most dramatic confrontations took place in Paris—the Days of May uprisings. Fed up with the rigid, overcrowded university system and fearing that many would miss out on France's new prosperity after graduation, Parisian students rampaged through the streets of the French capital. Charles de Gaulle, president of France since 1958, met the demonstrators with police repression. The students then gained the support of sympathetic workers, who in turn demanded higher wages and an end to police brutality. This alliance between students and workers paralyzed France and even threatened to overturn the government. But the danger was short-lived. Agreements to raise wages appeased workers and siphoned them off from the movement, and the government once more regained control. However, the protests provoked major reforms in higher education and probably played a role in de Gaulle's resignation a year later.

Like the civil rights movement, student activism waned in the 1970s. As universities adopted reforms that met many of the protesters' demands and the

war in Vietnam came to an end, the sparks of protest faded. Among women, however, an international feminist movement was still gaining momentum.

Although feminism had a lengthy history in the West, the traditionally defined domestic role of women still had not changed much, even as late as the 1950s. In most Western nations, the dominant message from pulpits, welfare offices, doctors, and governmental officials was the same: Women should stay at home and serve as the anchor of the family, defining their social identity through their husband and focusing on raising children. But that age-old message increasingly came under attack as women gained access to higher education, experience in various protest and liberation movements, and greater awareness of the social restrictions on their lives.

One key to this increasing awareness came from new books. In 1949, the French writer Simone de Beauvoir (1908–1986) (see Biography) published *The Second Sex*, the century's most pivotal analysis of the condition of women. In this powerful book, de Beauvoir uncovered the myths that had relegated women to second-class status relative to men. "There is an absolute human type, the masculine. . . . He is the Subject, . . . she is the Other." De Beauvoir argued that women remained in cultural and economic dependence to men and therefore did not live as free human beings. The passive role assigned to women, she explained, forced them to live according to

> The women's liberation movement

standards set up by men. De Beauvoir recommended a difficult but rewarding role for women: a life of work, self-definition, and independence.

The Second Sex became the fundamental text for feminist movements in the 1960s. Other writers, such as the American Betty Friedan, popularized de Beauvoir's ideas and added to them. In her widely read book *The Feminine Mystique* (1963), Friedan urged women to escape the confines of home, go back to school, get new careers, and become more independent.

These ideas struck a chord, especially among many middle-class women. Increasing life expectancy and fewer children meant that more of these women than ever were living longer and devoting less of their lives to raising a family. They now had the time and resources to seek fulfillment outside the home—if they could find a way to break down traditional barriers. As more women enrolled in universities and pursued careers, discrimination against them on the job because of their gender only heightened their sense of injustice and outrage.

Starting in the late 1960s, women in several Western nations founded organizations, conducted marches, held rallies, started journals, opened feminist bookstores, and pressured officials to recognize their needs. **Figure 25.9** shows one of many demonstrations. Women—many in slacks and jeans rather than traditional dresses—along with a few supportive men march through the streets of Paris. Carrying banners, signs, and balloons, they announce their purposes—equal pay with men for equal work—and unity. In 1969, an English women's group described the essence of the women's liberation movement: "We are economically oppressed: In jobs we do full work for half pay, in the home we do unpaid work full time. We are commercially exploited by advertisements, television and the press; legally we often have only the status of children. We are brought up to feel inadequate, educated to narrower horizons than men. This is our specific oppression as women. It is as women that we are, therefore, organizing."

Such efforts inspired a barrage of specific demands, including full citizenship in the political arena, equitable wages, and access to new careers. Despite opposition from conservative and religious groups, women pushed controversial issues such as day care, maternal leave, legalized abortion, and liberalized divorce into the spotlight of public discourse. They also protested stereotypical portrayals of femininity and widespread assumptions—among women and men alike—that raised the barriers facing them. Finally, they persuaded universities to introduce women's studies programs and prompted scholars in numerous academic disciplines to include feminist perspectives in their books.

By the early 1980s, the sharp edge of women's movements had dulled, but many long-term victories were already theirs. Women had gained greater control over

FIGURE 25.9 The Women's Movement in France During the late 1960s, women in many Western nations held rallies and demonstrations such as this one in Paris.

fertility and sexuality from governments, churches, and male-dominated medical establishments. Moreover, lesbians demanded and received some recognition of their rights. As French author Monique Wittig noted in 1979, without feminism, lesbian culture and society "would still be as secret as they have always been." More women than ever flocked to universities, began careers in law, medicine, education, government, and business, and won political office. "Every girl now thinks in terms of a job. This is progress," said one Swedish vocational counselor. "They don't intend to be housewives for some future husband."

Stagnant Growth and Rising Inflation

While the protest movements inspired optimism among their proponents and anger among conservative opponents, disturbing economic developments spawned worry and doubt. A new phenomenon that became known as "stagflation"—stagnant economic growth paired with rising inflation—spread in the West. The main culprit was oil and its central role in providing cheap energy for the Western economy. During the 1950s and 1960s, Western interests had kept oil prices low by expanding production and discouraging oil-producing countries in the Middle East, Africa, and South America from presenting a united front to raise prices. The low prices encouraged many users of coal to switch to oil and helped control inflation.

In 1973, a war broke out in the Middle East between Israel and its Arab opponents. Middle Eastern oil-producing states, now organized into the Arab-dominated **Organization of Petroleum Exporting Countries (OPEC),** began to punish the West for supporting Israel in this conflict. As they limited

The oil crisis

BIOGRAPHY

Simone de Beauvoir
(1908–1986)

Intellectual and Feminist

Simone de Beauvoir was born in 1908 to a devoutly Catholic mother and an intellectual father who practiced law. Later, after rebelling against her family's middle-class values, Simone wrote that her mother "held dear all those bourgeois, Catholic, pious, well-thinking ideas which I was learning to detest," while her father gave her "a taste for the intellectual life." World War I ruined the family financially. Realizing that she needed to support herself, de Beauvoir went to college. Reforms in 1924 gave women new access to higher education, and de Beauvoir, a brilliant student, seized the opportunity.

In 1929, while completing her degree in philosophy at the Sorbonne, Simone met and fell in love with Jean-Paul Sartre—a dazzling speaker and leader of a circle of rebellious intellectuals. "What is unique between Simone de Beauvoir and me," Sartre would later say, "is the equality of our relationship." The two vowed that "neither of us would conceal anything from the other." De Beauvoir had already concluded that "bourgeois marriage is an unnatural institution . . . that doubles one's domestic responsibilities and, indeed, all one's social chores." Neither did she want children: "I was too self-sufficient."

Through the 1930s, the couple's teaching careers in various parts of France kept them apart. De Beauvoir admitted that she and Sartre avoided getting involved in politics until 1939, when "history took hold of me and never let go thereafter." When the Germans invaded France the following year, de Beauvoir fled Paris along with thousands of others. Shortly thereafter, the Germans captured and imprisoned Sartre. Freed in 1942, he joined de Beauvoir, who had returned to Paris.

In 1944, de Beauvoir became a full-time writer. By then she had already published the successful novel *She Came to Stay* (1943), in which she discussed connections between personal life and existentialism—the philosophy she, Sartre, and their intellectual circle often discussed. Sartre had also published numerous well-received works. In 1946, the couple founded and edited the influential review *Les Temps Modernes*. Between 1946 and 1949, de Beauvoir researched and wrote her thousand-page study of women, *The Second Sex* (1949). By this time, de Beauvoir and Sartre had become France's—and perhaps the West's—leading intellectual couple (see **Figure 25.10**).

During the 1960s, de Beauvoir rejected formal participation in feminist groups, believing instead that socialism would lead women and men alike to full liberation. In the 1970s, disillusioned with socialism and impressed with the strength of the feminist movement, she changed her mind. She served as president of the French League of Women's Rights and editor of feminist journals and remained active in the feminist cause for the rest of her life.

In 1980, Sartre died. Their fifty-year relationship was not idyllic. Both had lovers, and their relationship was not equal. Much of the time, the companionship of Sartre and de Beauvoir had more of a verbal than physical intimacy. "That was why it lasted so long," said de Beauvoir just weeks before her own death in 1986.

Connecting People & Society

1. What does de Beauvoir's life reveal about the position and role of intellectuals during the twentieth century?

2. Do you think de Beauvoir should be considered one of the century's leading feminists? Explain.

3. Do you think de Beauvoir's relationship with Sartre should affect our evaluation of her as a historical figure? Why or why not?

FIGURE 25.10 Jean-Paul Sartre and Simone de Beauvoir

production and increased prices, the cost of oil rose sixfold between 1973 and 1975. Prices again surged in 1979, spurring global inflation that particularly distressed the poorer nations of Asia and Africa and sent Western nations into a downward spiral of debt. Western economies, also facing disruptions in the international monetary system and growing competition from Japan, fell into recession.

In Europe and the U.S., expectations of perpetual economic growth and limitless natural resources gave way to doubt. Indeed, the very forces that had brought prosperity for some threw others out of work. For example, the increased automation of industrial plants, the substitution of oil for coal, and the growing use of computers often eliminated more jobs than they created. The "green revolution" in agriculture boosted productivity but also forced people off the land and into the urban labor market. Equally alarming, large transnational corporations cut jobs as they moved their plants to regions offering cheap labor.

All these forces worsened unemployment, which by the early 1980s hit a whopping 10 percent and higher in many Western nations. In Britain—once an economic giant—unemployment stayed at more than 12 percent year after year through the 1980s. Unions weakened, unable to protect workers in this perilous economic climate. The gap between rich and poor widened, and for many people—especially lower-wage earners—the economic good times seemed over. Least able to protect themselves were immigrant workers.

Growing unemployment

As is common during periods of economic uncertainty, wealthier nations turned against "outsiders." During the prosperity of the 1950s and 1960s, Western Europeans had opened their doors to desperate immigrants from southern Europe, Turkey, North Africa, and former colonies lured north by the promise of work. Immigrants filled the jobs that British, French, German, and Swiss workers passed over—the hardest, lowest-paid work in factories and fields, undesirable night shifts, street cleaning, and garbage collecting. Immigrant women were particularly vulnerable to exploitation in these jobs and in positions as domestics. Immigrant workers also labored under obligations to send money back home. Many, having heard myths about "lands of plenty," assumed that some day they would return home rich.

Turning against immigrants

In fact, officials often denied them social services and discouraged them from settling permanently. West Germany refused to grant citizenship to even those "immigrants" born in Germany. In the 1970s and 1980s, many governments, fearing worsening unemployment in their own countries, slammed the door shut against immigrants. The millions of foreign-born residents or "outsiders" who managed to arrive in the West increasingly suffered racial and anti-immigrant attacks.

The New Political Landscape

Reacting to social movements and uneasy about their economic fate during the 1970s and 1980s, voters throughout the West turned to political parties that they had once ignored or even disdained. Socialists, who accommodated these voters by toning down their radical message, gained the most from this new development. In 1969, the Social Democrats in West Germany won control for the first time in almost fifty years. During the 1970s, under Willy Brandt (1913–1992) and Helmut Schmidt, they eased Cold War tensions by pursuing a policy of increased diplomatic and economic relations with Eastern Europe and the Soviet Union. By the late 1970s and early 1980s, Spain, Portugal, and Greece had also elected new Socialist governments that endured and led these nations into the European Common Market. In 1981, socialists under the leadership of François Mitterrand (1916–1996) came into power in France. They nationalized industries, shortened working hours, and enacted progressive social programs. However, persisting inflation and high unemployment soon led them to reverse some of these policies.

Turning to the Left

Communist parties in Western Europe also tried to adapt to voters' demands so as to garner popularity. In Italy, Spain, and France, the communists turned to "Eurocommunism," supporting more moderate policies and vowing to cooperate with other leftist parties. They even gave up the Soviet model and its call to worldwide revolution and promised to work within Western democratic institutions and economic systems that blended free enterprise and state planning. For a while during the late 1970s and early 1980s, communists gained strength in Italy and played roles in governments in Spain and France.

Britain turned the other way. In 1979, voters handed a sweeping victory to the Conservatives and their right-wing leader, Margaret Thatcher, Britain's first female prime minister. Thatcher initiated policies to diminish state control over the economy, crush union power, and cut spending for Britain's welfare state. Some state-owned and subsidized industries were "privatized"—sold to private enterprise. Thatcher also cut taxes on the wealthy, hoping to encourage investment and a "trickling down" of wealth to the rest of British society. Bitter strikes and urban riots by workers and the unemployed decrying her hard-line policies did not dissuade her.

Turning to the Right

Across the Atlantic, Thatcher found an ideological ally in Ronald Reagan, elected president of the United States in 1980. Reagan pursued similarly conservative policies, reversing some of the liberal social policies of the 1960s, moving against unions, privatizing governmental services, cutting taxes, increasing military spending, and reviving Cold War posturing against the Soviet Union. Thatcher's and Reagan's partially successful efforts in the 1980s to limit governmental spending on social programs marked the beginning of a gentle but broad turn toward conservative politics in the West.

Despite the changes, some groups still felt left out of politics. They demanded attention, even at the price of violence. In the 1970s and 1980s, political terrorism spread across the West, conducted by groups such as the Red Brigades in Italy, the Red Army Faction in West Germany, and the Palestine Liberation Organization (PLO). Many of these groups had radical political goals. Others, such as the militant Basque separatists in Spain and the Kurdish rebels in Turkey, demanded national liberation. All desperately wanted recognition and had concluded that only assassinations, abductions, and bombings would achieve their aims.

No area in Europe suffered more from terrorism than Northern Ireland. There the Roman Catholic minority struggled fiercely to gain equality with the Protestant majority. Many Roman Catholics demanded total separation from Britain and union with Ireland. The Provisional Wing of the Irish Republican Army (IRA) conducted a long campaign of terror to this end. As the Protestants fought fiercely to maintain their supremacy, violence begot even more violence.

Governments responded to terrorists, sometimes with violence and occasionally by making deals. Security measures increased, as did the presence of armed police, and occasionally governments were able to penetrate the urban anonymity of modern society to capture terrorists. For the most part, however, terrorism remained an exceptional means of protest that never gained enough support to threaten governments.

POSTINDUSTRIAL SOCIETY

The political fluctuations of the 1970s and 1980s reflected more than just economic ups and downs or politicians' efforts to garner popular support. Underlying many changes during this period was a fundamental development: The industrial societies of the West had begun transforming themselves into **postindustrial societies.** This term refers to a culmination of economic and social changes occurring in the West over several decades. Traditional manufacturing industries declined in importance as more competitive plants employing cheap labor opened outside of Europe and North America. In place of manufacturing, demand for financial, health, educational, informational, and consumer services mushroomed—all services at which the West excelled. Well-educated and handsomely paid professionals, managers, and financiers rose to prominent positions in corporations and government, joining or replacing property owners and entrepreneurs as key economic figures. The

bulk of the middle class—most of them well educated and with white-collar jobs—also grew in number and wealth. Industrial workers saw their jobs disappearing while demand for service employees expanded. Yet many of these service employees, who seemed white collar or middle class in their appearance or lifestyle, made the same income or even less than blue-collar workers. Traditional class lines were blurring.

Changing Fortunes in the Postindustrial Society

Some people gained more than others in this mobile society. The gap between rich and poor may have narrowed between the 1940s and 1960s, but that gap remained formidable and even increased in the 1970s and 1980s. Only the growing numbers of married women entering the paid workforce maintained or improved most families' standard of living after the early 1970s. Nor did overall prosperity solve problems of economic discrimination. Women generally received only two-thirds to three-fourths of men's salaries for the same work. Minority and immigrant groups still occupied the most poorly paid jobs. In many Western cities, a core of impoverished slum dwellers remained. Often without regular jobs and marked by their race or ethnic origin, they suffered the worst problems of urban life.

DEVELOPMENTS IN THE WEST

1947	Truman Doctrine
	Marshall Plan
1948	Berlin blockade begins
	NATO organized
1953	Death of Stalin
1954	Structure of DNA discovered
1955	Warsaw Pact
1956	Uprising in Hungary
1957	Common Market
1961	Berlin Wall built
1962	Cuban missile crisis
1964	Khrushchev falls from power
1968	Student uprisings
	Invasion of Czechoslovakia
1969	Americans land on the moon
1972	Britain, Ireland, Denmark join EEC
1975	Helsinki Agreement
1985	Gorbachev comes to power

KEY DATES

For most people in postindustrial societies, however, material life improved. Housing mushroomed, in France alone increasing to a half-million new units per year during the 1970s. New apartments had distinct rooms—bedroom, kitchen, living room, bathroom—and were not just for the middle class. Most homes boasted running water, indoor toilets, a bath or shower, and heating as well as an array of appliances. In the 1980s, one Italian woman reflected in amazement how her children "have grown up in a world in which washing machine, refrigerator, vacuum cleaner, and television set are taken for granted."

Daily patterns of life also changed as more and more people lived and worked in different parts of the cities and their expanding suburbs. People commuted on crowded trains or by car through traffic jams. The neighborhood cafés or pubs where people used to gather after work steadily lost customers, as did local, small stores where shoppers knew the merchants and each other. In their place, restaurants, supermarkets, and shopping malls sprang up, adding to the sense of urban anonymity.

The Baby Boom and the Booming Cities

Underlying the development of this postindustrial society were shifting populations that fueled economic growth and transformed patterns of life. Skyrocketing birthrates that had started during the war years led to the so-called **baby boom** soon after. An increase in life expectancy and the influx of immigrants added to the population growth. Europe's population, for example, increased from 264 million during the war to 320 million in the early 1970s. But the baby boom and the rapid jump in population did not last long. In the 1960s, birthrates began to decline as people returned to the long-term pattern of choosing to have fewer children. In the 1970s, these rates fell to less than half the pre–World War II figures in some areas.

Fewer of those populations lived on farms anymore. By 1955, less than a quarter of the population worked in agriculture. Over the next thirty years, that figure would fall to below 10 percent almost everywhere. Thanks to mechanization, fertilizers, pesticides, new seeds, and larger farms, dwindling numbers of farmers produced more than enough for everyone else, as well as surpluses for export. Rural economies could no longer offer employment to more than a small minority of the population. Once the heart of Western civilization, rural areas became places that city people traveled through and nostalgically imagined. Small country towns dominated by church steeples tried to stay viable by attracting tourists, people wanting second homes, or small industries looking to relocate. With the spread of highways, telephones, televisions, and computers, rural life retained only a hint of the isolation that formerly distinguished it from city life.

As they had for decades, people left rural areas and small towns in droves and headed for the cities. These migrations spread well beyond national borders. Wealthy northern European cities absorbed waves of newcomers from southern Italy, Greece, Turkey, and Africa, just as cities in North America took in Latin Americans and Asians. These immigration trends added to the traditional urban problems of congestion, overburdened transportation systems, pollution, and crime. Large parts of great cities deteriorated while the surrounding suburbs, with their own industrial plants, corporate offices, apartment complexes, and housing projects, expanded.

The Shifting Foundations of Family and Private Life

Along with this movement of people and transformation of cities, the very foundations of family and private life within postindustrial society began to shift. After the baby boom years of the 1940s and 1950s, families became smaller as people, aided by more widely available birth-control devices, chose to limit births. Families also became less stable, as married people used changing attitudes and laws concerning divorce to break apart more often. Many people decided to put off or avoid marriage altogether. Increasing numbers of single parents and same-sex partners now headed households.

The old family structure, in which the man wielded authority, weakened and began to be replaced by a sense of the family as a democratic partnership of equals. Married women streamed out of their roles as housekeepers, child rearers, and supporters of their "breadwinning" husbands. They now took paying jobs outside the home not only for the income but also for the equality and independence that paid employment offered. Especially within the middle classes, work outside the home became a sign of emancipation for women. With these changes, some homes became zones of domestic cooperation; others witnessed new battles between couples over household chores and child rearing. Overall, however, the burdens of housework and child care still rested primarily with women.

The process of raising children also changed. Children spent more years than ever in school to acquire the skills needed to excel in the competitive postindustrial society, a shift that made them financially dependent on their parents into their late teens and even early twenties. With nursery schools becoming standard, children now started school at age three rather than age six. More than ever, the socialization, training, and career choices of youths were taking place outside the home.

Within the home, an individual's private life became no longer secondary to family life. **Figure 25.11** presents the image of the small family together watching television. The television as much as the kitchen

FIGURE 25.11 Family Watching Television, 1950s
In mid-century, television viewing widely became the focal point of family gatherings and foreshadowed a continuing decline in family interactions.

Growing concern for private satisfactions

became a center of nightly family gatherings. But this image may also depict a decline of family interaction. Larger apartments and houses let family members spend more time than ever in separate rooms, coming together only for meals or TV watching. Much of home life became private, with individuals spending most time apart and alone rather than joining other family members.

This growing concern for private satisfactions, which fit so well with the competitive economic individualism of postindustrial society, also played a role in the frequent separation of families. More often than ever, the ties holding marriages together began breaking apart. With love as the primary motive for marriage, the declining intensity of love that often occurs with time seemed enough to warrant divorce. As the sexual satisfaction of both partners became a core purpose of marriage, trouble in this domain also became a volatile source of discord and divorce.

Legal changes and statistics reflected these new realities. The grounds for divorce eased in most places to the point where mutual consent was enough. By the 1980s, between 25 and 50 percent of those who married would eventually get divorced. The old image of the breadwinning father, the homemaking wife, and the dependent children bonded together in a lifelong relationship remained true for only a minority of the population.

The "Sexual Revolution" and the Youth Culture

Within or outside marriage, people gained new degrees of sexual freedom. Innovative methods of contraception, particularly the birth-control pill and the intrauterine device (and abortion, especially in Eastern Europe), achieved widespread acceptance in the 1960s and further separated sexual pleasure from reproduction. Manuals, sex education in schools, and the portrayal of sex in movies, books, magazines, and marketing materials became far more explicit than ever, reflecting the changing attitudes toward sex. Many conservative and religious groups strongly opposed these developments and the increase in premarital sex, though they were losing this battle by the 1970s. They also lost ground to gays, lesbians, and others who demanded respect and freedom.

Young men and women coming of age in the late 1950s and the 1960s, an era sometimes called the sexual revolution, led these widespread changes in sexual values. Their clothing—flowered shirts and beads for men, blue jeans and miniskirts for women—and long hairstyles symbolized their new sexual freedom as well as the wider challenge of their youth culture to the older generation.

Young people's taste in music and movies also announced a break between generations. In the United States, Elvis Presley led the explosion in rock and roll's popularity in the late 1950s. With his suggestive dancing, slicked-back hair, and devoted following of young, screaming fans, Presley embodied eroticism and sexual abandon. The Beatles and other popular rock groups had a similar impact. Social dancing evolved from a carefully choreographed, chaste ritual to a no-holds-barred celebration of the body and sexuality. In popular movies, brooding, sullen young actors such as James Dean and Marlon Brando portrayed rebellious youths and became icons of the expanding youth culture.

BREAKTHROUGHS IN SCIENCE

The postindustrial society and the changing patterns of urban life that characterized it owed much to the many scientific breakthroughs of the period following World War II. More than ever, science became linked to economics and the needs of large institutions—from governments and industrial corporations to universities. These links were particularly

The rise of big science

strong in "big science." Before World War II, most scientific research was carried out by individuals or small groups of scientists in a university setting. The application of their discoveries by engineers and technicians came later. After the war, funds for scientific research poured in from government and big business, forming what some called the military-industrial-university complex. With the influx of money and interest, the number of scientists jumped fivefold between 1945 and 1985, and the fields they entered divided into more and more subspecialties. Organized teams of scientists, technicians, and managers worked in large research laboratories, using expensive equipment and aiming for specific goals. The results were stunning.

From the Universe Above to the Universe Within

Cold War competition especially fueled the massive effort to put satellites and humans into space. By the 1960s, satellites spun around the earth, providing a steady stream of military surveillance, weather observations, communications, and scientific information. The "space race" between the United States and the Soviet Union climaxed with a televised walk on the moon's surface in 1969. While taking his first step, the American astronaut Neil Armstrong spoke his now-famous words: "That's one small step for man, one giant leap for mankind." **Figure 25.12** shows an American astronaut standing on the surface of the moon. One of the first things Armstrong did was to plant the U.S. flag and pose with it for a photograph. The image announced how daring and powerful the combination of government, science, and nationalism could be. Subsequent unmanned voyages carried spacecraft to planets throughout the solar system and beyond.

Government money funded other scientific and technological efforts as well. Teams of physicists used powerful particle accelerators to explore the subatomic world. From innovations in radar systems during World War II came microwave technology, which became central to the television and long-distance telephone industries. Work on the atomic bomb led to nuclear power plants.

Similar efforts by teams of scientists and individuals led to fundamental discoveries in fields such as genetics. In 1953, the structure of DNA, the material

FIGURE 25.12 Big Science, 1969 This photo of Americans on the moon serves to illustrate the combined power of large universities, big business, and governmental backing to carry out major scientific and technological projects.

in chromosomes that contains hereditary information, was discovered. This implied that the characteristics of all living things, including humans, could be controlled, and it opened the controversial possibility of tampering with this molecule to create new forms of life. Research into gene splitting and genetic engineering would turn this possibility into reality.

The Information Revolution

Much of the new scientific work depended on computers, which became the core of the "**information revolution.**" The computer first emerged in the 1940s as a tool for storing and manipulating information. Encouraged by business and government during the 1950s and 1960s, its scientific and economic impact widened. With miniaturization during the 1970s and 1980s, computers the size of a notebook could outpower their room-size predecessors. These new "personal computers" cropped up on desktops and in briefcases everywhere. Now most people involved in science, scholarship, and business relied on computers, and the new devices became the core of a booming, worldwide industry.

Transforming Medicine

In the decades after World War II, medicine also entered new territory—itself becoming a big business with strong links to science and economics. Long gone were the days of visits by horse-and-buggy doctors. Now most physicians saw patients in offices, clinics, and especially hospitals, which employed medical personnel working in coordinated teams with complex machines. The era of the family doctor also faded. Now patients consulted more prestigious specialists. Finally, doctors gained a new degree of power to battle medical problems. Whereas in earlier centuries physicians may have done more harm than good with their treatments, now medicine became a major lifesaver in the Western and non-Western world.

The keys to these changes were antibiotic drugs and vaccines. In the 1930s, researchers discovered that sulfa drugs could cure infectious diseases. Penicillin and other antibiotics soon followed. By the 1940s, once-fatal illnesses such as meningitis and pneumonia could be cured by antibiotic drugs. Tuberculosis, a disease so deadly that it was called the "white plague," was almost eliminated by a vaccine and antibiotics. In 1977, smallpox was literally eradicated throughout the globe. The spotlight on medicine shifted from traditional infectious diseases to cancer, heart disease, arthritis, and AIDS.

New surgical techniques also offered more hope than in previous centuries. Antibiotics let surgeons perform lung and other operations that had been too risky before because of the danger of infection. In the

1960s, open heart surgery and heart bypass operations became almost routine. Then organ replacement—first of kidneys and then even hearts—became possible. Surgery became more a process of continuous repair and replacement than cutting and removing.

Expensive new machines for diagnosis and treatment complemented all the new medical techniques. Ultrasound machines, CT scanners (which combined X rays with computer analysis), and MRI devices that used radio waves gave doctors a window into the body without having to open it up. Dialysis machines and pacemakers offered new hope to kidney and heart patients.

For those suffering from mental illnesses, effective medications emerged in the 1950s. Doctors prescribed a growing list of these psychotropic drugs for people with schizophrenic and manic-depressive conditions. Though the success of these drugs was far from complete, they contributed to the closing of many mental hospitals and asylums.

By the 1980s, medicine had become dominated by large hospitals, groups of doctors, insurance companies, and governmental agencies. Health "consumers" expected more and more from medicine—including cures for most ailments and what many saw as a right to live to retirement and a robust old age. Nations devoted more resources than ever to medicine—often more than 10 percent of the national income. Britain's minister of health once complained, "There is virtually no limit to the amount of health care an individual is capable of absorbing."

In several senses, then, the evolution of medicine since World War II reflected broader qualities of the era. Science, and especially big science, enabled doctors to expand and even revolutionize the field. Medicine also relied on the overall prosperity and governmental support of those decades, which enabled people to demand, and the health-care industry to provide, so many services. The very growth of this service industry as well as the high status and income enjoyed by its leading practitioners echoed the development of the postindustrial society, with its stress on services and technical expertise. Finally, like much else, Western medicine spilled across borders and into the non-Western world—though also in ways that highlighted the disparities of wealth between the Western and non-Western worlds and the conflicts that often arose when those different cultures met.

LOOKING BACK & MOVING FORWARD

Summary   The decades between 1945 and 1989 witnessed a quickening pace of change as more people than ever were drawn into the swirl of politics, economic development, and urban life. The Cold War, whose contours came into sharp focus after 1945, cast a pall over the entire era. Each side represented different paths to recovery after World War II and competitive ideologies that had their roots in the nineteenth century. Yet despite people's worst fears, the Cold War never ignited into an actual conflagration between the two superpowers. As we will see, it evaporated with surprising rapidity in the late 1980s.

During these decades, Western society became more technocratic, affluent, welfare oriented, and culturally open—characteristics that also had first come to light at the end of the nineteenth century. Western Europe, in particular, managed this transformation despite ceding leadership to the United States and losing its colonial empires. Although Western Europe's status in the world declined, it remained a strikingly prosperous, dynamic region.

As the final decade of the twentieth century approached, the West as a whole remained powerful and was often envied abroad. At the same time, it had become clear that the Western powers could no longer act without taking into account the concerns, power, and problems of the non-Western world. Soon, stunning developments in Eastern Europe would mark 1989 as the dawn of a new historical era.

KEY TERMS

Iron Curtain, *p. 776*

Cold War, *p. 776*

Berlin airlift, *p. 778*

containment, *p. 778*

Marshall Plan, *p. 778*

North Atlantic Treaty Organization, (NATO), *p. 778*

détente, *p. 785*

Berlin Wall, *p. 786*

Prague Spring, *p. 787*

welfare state, *p. 788*

European Economic Community, *p. 788*

apartheid, *p. 793*

decolonization, *p. 793*

existentialism, *p. 796*

Organization of Petroleum Exporting Countries (OPEC), *p. 800*

postindustrial societies, *p. 803*

baby boom, *p. 804*

information revolution, *p. 806*

REVIEW, ANALYZE, & CONNECT TO TODAY

REVIEW THE PREVIOUS CHAPTER

Chapter 24—"Into the Fire Again"—analyzed the devastating war that encompassed the world.

1. In what ways did World War II set the stage for the Cold War and the different paths followed by Western and Eastern Europe?

2. In what ways did World War II hasten decolonization in the following decades?

ANALYZE THIS CHAPTER

Chapter 25—"Superpower Struggles and Global Transformations"—traces the Cold War competition between the United States and the Soviet Union. Within this context, the recovery of the West and the end of colonialism are examined.

1. How did Cold War tensions influence international affairs in the Western and non-Western worlds?

2. In what ways did Western life during these decades represent a triumph of Western industrialization and political democracy? What sorts of problems persisted despite this triumph?

3. Compare and evaluate the two paths followed by Western and Eastern Europe during this period.

4. Evaluate the process of decolonization. What problems faced the newly independent nations of the non-Western world?

CONNECT TO TODAY

Think about the Cold War and the legacy of colonialism.

1. In what ways might international affairs in today's world reflect the end of the Cold War?

2. How might international politics in our times be different if the Cold War had *not* ended?

3. Even though colonialism has ended for the most part, how might its legacy still influence world affairs today?

BEYOND THE CLASSROOM

ORIGINS OF THE COLD WAR

Gaddis, John Lewis. *The Cold War: A New History.* New York: Penguin, 2005. An authoritative history of the Cold War.

Patterson, Thomas G. *On Every Front: The Making and Unmaking of the Cold War.* New York: W.W. Norton, 1992. Analyzes both the domestic and foreign policy aspects of the Cold War.

EAST AND WEST: TWO PATHS TO RECOVERY IN EUROPE

Judt, Tony. *Postwar: A History of Europe Since 1945.* New York: Penguin, 2005. Excellent, extensive treatment of the period, emphasizing how post–World War II Europe dealt with its own past and modernization.

Mazower, Mark. *Dark Continent: Europe's Twentieth Century.* New York: Knopf, 1999. A survey that emphasizes political developments.

THE TWILIGHT OF COLONIALISM

Ansprenger, Franz. *The Dissolution of the Colonial Empires.* London: Routledge, 1989. Stresses the legacy of inequality and cells of poverty created by imperialism but also asserts that imperialism helped to create a global economy.

Springhall, John. *Decolonization Since 1945: The Collapse of European Empires.* London: Palgrave Macmillan, 2001. A good overview with colony-by-colony coverage.

A SENSE OF RELATIVITY IN THOUGHT AND CULTURE

Maltby, R., ed. *Passing Parade: A History of Popular Culture in the Twentieth Century.* New York: New Oxford Press, 1989. Excellent in its breadth of coverage.

Stromberg, Roland N. *After Everything: Western Intellectual History Since 1945.* New York: St. Martin's Press, 1986. An excellent survey of ideas and ideology in the postwar period.

GLOBAL CONNECTIONS

Maier, Karl. *Into the House of the Ancestors: Inside the New Africa.* New York: John Wiley and Sons, 1998. A balanced and well-supported account.

PROTESTS, PROBLEMS, AND NEW POLITICS: THE 1960S TO THE 1980S

Caute, David. *The Year of the Barricades: A Journey Through 1968.* New York: Harper & Row, 1988. Examines the revolutionary upheavals in a period called "year one" of the revolution.

Lovenduski, Joni. *Women and European Politics: Contemporary Feminism and Public Policy.* Amherst: University of Massachusetts Press, 1986. Compares the movement for women's liberation in the 1960s with previous women's movements.

POSTINDUSTRIAL SOCIETY

Hoffman, Stanley, and Paschalis Kitromilides. *Culture and Society in Contemporary Europe.* London: Allen & Unwin, 1981. A wide-ranging, interpretative survey connecting cultural and social developments.

BREAKTHROUGHS IN SCIENCE

Ziman, John. *The Force of Knowledge: The Scientific Dimension of Society.* Cambridge: Cambridge University Press, 1976. A useful examination of connections between science and society during the postwar years.

CHINA, 2008

On an early morning in December 2008, the large steel mill in Baotou, China, is already in full production. The mill supports this rapidly expanding one-industry town, located just west of China's capital city, Beijing, and, along with similar cities, testifies to China's growing role as a leading industrial nation. The carbon-rich smoke pouring into the air and creating pollution that will spread east to Beijing and beyond also reveals the accelerating environmental problems—above all, global warming—facing China and the world in the twenty-first century.

Into the Twenty-First Century

The Present in Perspective

"The 20th century is now over." The historian John Lukacs made this announcement in a 1991 issue of the *New York Times.* By "20th century," Lukacs meant the 75-year era that began in 1914 and ended in 1989. The year 1914 marked the outbreak of World War I, which for most historians represented the beginning of the twentieth century. That conflict and World War II dominated the period. "The Russian Revolution, the atom bomb, the end of the colonial empires, the establishment of the Communist states, the emergence of the two superpowers, the division of Europe and of Germany—all of these were the consequences of the two world wars, in the shadow of which we were living, until now," wrote Lukacs. The year 1989 saw the nations of Eastern Europe break from their Soviet ties and from communism. In just two more years, the Soviet Union itself would fall apart.

Other developments, also with roots in the past, added to the sense that the world had just lived through the closing of one historical era and the opening of another. The movement toward economic integration in Western Europe, the growing strength of the newly unified Germany, and the changing position of the United States altered international relations. Beyond the West, the Pacific Rim—particularly East Asia—gained enormous economic clout. In the Islamic world, stretching from North Africa through the Middle East to Indonesia, mounting pressures posed a variety of threats to stability in those regions and beyond. From a global perspective, three regional power centers had emerged—Europe, North America, and East Asia. Almost everywhere, people, problems, cultures, and histories spilled across national borders, challenging those living in the Western and non-Western worlds to broaden their understanding of the world and their place in it.

TIMELINE

- The Fall of Communism
- German Reunification
- Disintegration of Soviet Union

Civil Wars in Former Yugoslavia

Growing Importance of Computers and "The Information Revolution"

The Cold War

Toward European Unification

1989   1990   1991   1995   1996   1997   1998   1999   2000   2004   2008   2010

THE COLLAPSE OF COMMUNISM

Of all these developments, the collapse of communism in the Soviet Union and Eastern Europe arguably had the most dramatic and far-reaching global impact. In a startling public announcement early in November 1989, East Germany's communist leader succumbed to months of growing pressure and ordered the Berlin Wall, the most powerful symbol of the Cold War, torn down. **Figure 26.1** shows Germans from East and West climbing over the Berlin Wall near the Brandenburg Gate. A reporter described the scene: "Nearby, before the Brandenburg Gate . . . people climbed up onto the rim of the wall during the night of November 9 . . . taking pickaxes to it." Then the cranes and bulldozers came. "People stared unbelieving, as East German cranes lifted away the slabs of concrete. ..." As the wall crumbled, another observer described the Berlin border crossings: "The streets were packed with people streaming past the East German border guards. . . . Cars from East Berlin slowed to a crawl alongside the crowds of West Berliners waiting just over the white stripe painted on the asphalt, cheering every car . . . handing cans of beer to the drivers." In those first heady days, millions of East Germans crossed the border, some to stay, others to return again and again "loaded down with full plastic shopping bags." The mayor of West Berlin declared, "This [is] the greatest historical event since the French Revolution."

Everywhere in Eastern Europe, communist governments were collapsing. The Soviet bloc, which had seemed so impenetrable, quickly dissolved. Soon the Soviet Union itself would break apart.

Undermining Communism in the Soviet Union

What explains this massive historical reversal? The story begins in the Soviet Union, where communist power was most firmly entrenched. During the two or three decades following World War II,

FIGURE 26.1 The Berlin Wall, November 1989
Demonstrators celebrate the fall of the Berlin Wall, which served as a barrier between Eastern and Western Europe. "In the Name of the People," written in English, credits popular will for tearing down the wall and announces the importance of the event to a watching world.

the Soviet Union, like other communist nations, enjoyed economic growth and relative prosperity (see Chapter 25). The USSR boasted impressive factories and elaborate technical projects such as dams, railway systems, military hardware, and manned rockets. Rapid industrialization, which pulled peasants and women into the urban workforce by the millions, boosted productivity.

However, during the 1970s and 1980s, central planning and collectivization—the hallmarks of the Soviet economic system—failed to match new consumer demands. Keeping up with the rapidly changing, technologically sophisticated economy of the 1970s and 1980s required flexibility, a willingness to experiment with new production methods, and local decision making—all of which the Soviet economic system lacked. Instead, economic decisions came from high officials more sensitive to political pressures than to economic realities. Central planners, pursuing out-of-date strategies or unaware of changes in grassroots needs, often ordered factories to produce goods that did not meet consumers' demands. Local plant managers, struggling to get needed materials and

Problems with central planning

labor, suffered long delays while distant officials made decisions. Workers, their jobs guaranteed, had little incentive to work hard or even show up consistently. Similar problems plagued agriculture, where collectivization discouraged effective decision making and hard work. As the rate of economic growth declined, embarrassed Soviet planners had to import grain again and again from the capitalist West. Government leaders worried that the Soviet economy would never catch up with formidable capitalist competitors such as the United States, Germany, and Japan.

Worse, everyday dissatisfactions spread. Soviet workers had money but not the selection or quality of goods that they wanted and that they knew were available to people in the West. Instead, they regularly stood in lines for as long as two hours a day just to buy basic supplies. Even urban professionals, managers, and technicians, although relatively wealthy and well educated, experienced similar frustrations. Far too obviously, only a small corps of Communist Party officials and privileged elites enjoyed access to the most desirable goods and services in this supposedly egalitarian society, fueling resentment. For everyone else, the only alternative was the thriving, but expensive and illegal, black market. Faith in the communist system, even among members of the Communist Party, began to evaporate. "I'm not a good Party member because I don't believe in Communism . . . nor do a lot of Party members," admitted one 40-year-old Communist in 1990. "Joining the Party was for me entirely a calculated way of furthering my career."

| Spreading dissatisfaction |

Three pivotal developments during the late 1970s and 1980s exacerbated the problems undermining the Soviet brand of communism. First, the spread of modern communications broke down the old Stalinist policy of enforced isolation from the rest of the world and fueled the growing dissident movement. By watching television, people saw for themselves the material wealth enjoyed by Western nations. They also perceived the swirling cultural and intellectual currents that officials tried to stifle within the Soviet Union. Yet photocopiers and computers spread information easily, making censorship difficult. Privately published manuscripts criticizing Soviet life circulated among the educated elite. The dissident movement grew, led by the Nobel Prize–winning physicist Andrey Sakharov (1921–1989) and others. Dissidents demanded more democracy, greater civil liberties, and some independence for nationalities within the Soviet Union. Although such demands earned Sakharov and others exile, the dissident movement persisted. Moreover, among many people not yet ready to join the dissident movement, the increasingly

| Growth of dissent |

obvious contradictions between the official party line and the harsh realities of Soviet life engendered cynicism and apathy.

Second, military and wartime expenditures increasingly burdened the Soviet economy. In the 1980s, the United States under President Ronald Reagan vigorously pursued the Cold War arms race, forcing the Soviets— with their fundamentally weaker economy—to struggle to keep up. At the same time, the 1979 Soviet invasion of Afghanistan turned into a costly military quagmire. The widely condemned conflict wore on for years, straining the USSR's economy and diminishing the Soviet leadership's popularity.

| Military burdens |

Third, the quality of the Soviet leadership declined in the 1970s and 1980s. Leonid Brezhnev weakened noticeably and repeatedly fell ill in the seven years before his death in 1982. Most of his colleagues were long established in their offices. Brezhnev's immediate successors, Yuri Andropov (1982–1984) and Konstantin Chernenko (1984–1985), each died shortly after assuming office. These older men were reluctant to alter the USSR's course or to make way for a younger generation of reformers. But in 1985, a new leader—Mikhail Gorbachev—was appointed head of the Soviet Union. Just 54 years old, he had very different ideas about how the Soviet Union should operate.

| Declining leadership |

Gorbachev Launches Reforms

Born into a peasant family, Mikhail Gorbachev (1931–) studied law as a youth at the University of Moscow. He moved rapidly up through the Communist Party ranks, eventually taking responsibility for agricultural policy. Charming and astute, he became a capable manipulator of people and events. Britain's prime minister, Margaret Thatcher, recognized him as a man "with whom we can do business." Gorbachev also had bold plans to lead the Soviet Union in new directions. Soon after assuming power in 1985, he replaced a third of the old party leadership with new supporters. By then, he shared the views of reformers who recognized the fundamental economic problems plaguing the Soviet Union. In his willingness to grapple with problems, Gorbachev echoed Khrushchev's attack on Stalinism some thirty years earlier. Nevertheless, he had no intention of loosening the party's hold on power.

Gorbachev embarked on a three-pronged policy: *perestroika* (restructuring), *glasnost* (openness to discussion), and disarmament. All three were intended to bring the Soviet economy up to the standard of Western capitalist societies. No one—not even

| Perestroika |

Gorbachev—imagined the consequences that would flow from these daring reforms.

Perestroika involved a thorough restructuring of the Soviet economy. The program's goals included decentralizing planning, allowing market forces rather than officials to set prices, and putting control of land and agricultural practices into the hands of families and cooperatives rather than large state farms. In short, *perestroika* would create a mixed economy featuring a blend of socialist planning and a capitalist, free market. Gorbachev knew that the transformation would take time and cause short-term pain, including further shortages of consumer goods, inflation, and unemployment. To gather the political backing and the financial resources he needed to carry out the program, he initiated *glasnost* and an arms-reduction plan.

Glasnost curtailed censorship, encouraged freer discussion of everything from culture to politics, and opened the doors to the partial **Glasnost** democratization of the Communist Party and the Soviet political system. Officials freed dissidents such as Andrey Sakharov. Some governmental proceedings were made visible to the public and even televised. In the spring of 1989, the government held the first open elections since 1917, which resulted in the defeat of numerous communist dignitaries. Gorbachev hoped that *glasnost* would elevate his prestige internationally, win him foreign political and financial support, and inspire intellectuals and workers at home to accept his bold restructuring of the Soviet economy.

His arms-reduction plan served the same ends. In meetings with U.S. presidents almost every year between 1985 and 1991, Gorbachev **Arms reduction** pushed for more and more reductions in both countries' military stockpiles. These meetings bore fruit: Both the USSR and the United States agreed to limit nuclear weapons and conventional forces not only on their own soil but also in Europe. At the same time, Gorbachev tried to extract Soviet forces from the war in Afghanistan. The effort took four years, but in 1989 the last Soviet troops finally came home. These feats burnished Gorbachev's reputation at home and abroad and promised to ease the USSR's heavy burden of military expenditures.

However, implementing *perestroika* proved more difficult than Gorbachev and his supporters expected. Entrenched officials resisted the changes, as did many Soviet individuals whose jobs and incomes were threatened by economic restructuring. Gorbachev's promises also raised the Soviet people's expectations to impossible heights. Some reformers even criticized him for moving too slowly.

To complicate matters, ethnic groups and republics within the Soviet Union began agitating for national autonomy and the freedom to express their own cultural beliefs. Peoples from central Asia and Armenia to the Baltic republics had long harbored resentments against the Soviet state. Most of these republics had been forced to join the Soviet **Demands for autonomy** Union during the devastating civil wars of 1917–1921. When Gorbachev weakened the monopoly power of the Communist Party, he undermined the principal institution holding the multinational Soviet Union together. Emboldened by Gorbachev's promised leniency in Eastern Europe, the republics took action. The greatest threat came from elites in Latvia, Lithuania, and Estonia on the Baltic coast, who led demands for political autonomy. As tensions mounted, events in Eastern Europe took a dramatic turn, overshadowing developments in the Soviet Union.

Revolutions in Eastern Europe

Ever since coming under the USSR's control, many people living in the communist nations of Eastern Europe had yearned to reclaim their national autonomy. Moreover, economic and cultural problems similar to those undermining communism in the Soviet Union plagued these societies and their governments. Though dissent did not always result in public protests, strikes, or demonstrations, it still simmered. In 1978, the Czechoslovakian playwright Václav Havel (see Biography) mocked the words of the *Communist Manifesto*: "A spectre is haunting eastern Europe: the spectre of what in the West is called 'dissent.'" Underground publications demanding honesty and civil rights circulated through intellectual and artistic circles in Poland, Hungary, and Czechoslovakia.

Two developments in the late 1980s strained the communist regimes trying to maintain control over these satellite states. First, economic difficulties mounted as Eastern European governments labored to **Economic problems** keep prices artificially low. To make matters worse, foreign loans from the West to Eastern European nations such as Poland became more expensive and began drying up. When those governments finally tried to increase prices without raising wages, public opposition mushroomed. Second, Gorbachev revoked the long-standing Brezhnev Doctrine. In 1989, he made his intentions clear: "Any interference in domestic affairs and any attempts to restrict the sovereignty of states, both friends and allies or any others, are inadmissible." Gorbachev had decided **Revoking the Brezhnev Doctrine** to let events in Eastern Europe unfold without Soviet intervention. For reformers and dissenters, this policy was a green light to action.

Poland led the way in the rush for liberation. This nation already had a history of protest movements that made it a weak link in the Soviet chain. In 1980, shipyard workers in Gdansk struck against rising consumer-goods prices. The strikers organized a noncommunist union, Solidarity, under the leadership of Lech Walesa. Support for Solidarity spread throughout the nation, forcing the government to recognize the new organization and accede to some of its demands. When the union pushed for more, resistance from Moscow and conservative elements in the Polish government stiffened. In late 1981, General Wojciech Jaruzelski, the new leader of the Polish Communist Party, declared martial law, arrested Walesa, and outlawed Solidarity.

Poland leads

However, the union survived these reversals. Early in 1989, with the Polish economy in crisis, negotiations began between Jaruzelski and Solidarity, still led by Walesa. The Polish Catholic Church, which had maintained a position in the nation and indeed enhanced its own prestige with the visit of Pope John Paul II in 1979, helped mediate discussions. The talks resulted in the legalization of Solidarity and, in June, new elections. Solidarity's stunning victory at the polls prompted Jaruzelski to ask the union to form a new government. A few months later, the communist leader stepped down, and the Communist Party gave up power in Poland without a fight.

Hungary soon followed suit. This satellite state already had a mixed economy, with almost one-third of its wealth coming from a private sector of small enterprises, crafts, and family agriculture. Reformers within the Hungarian Communist Party gained some power in 1988 and removed the old leader, János Kádár, from office. In the summer and fall of 1989, Hungary held elections, established a multiparty political system, and initiated economic reforms to open the country to private enterprise. **Figure 26.2**, a poster published by the Hungarian Democratic Forum, captures the sense of ushering out a bygone era. The poster announces the fall of communism in Hungary with the words "Comrades, It's Over," and with the depiction of the back of a departing man's head. The military hat symbolizes the confining authority of the old regime, and the wide neck perhaps represents the resentment against communist officials who had enjoyed special privileges.

Hungary

Next came Czechoslovakia. In the fall of 1989, student demonstrators took to the streets demanding academic freedom and human rights. When police responded with clubs and tear gas, the demonstrators turned against them and other authorities. Workers and employers alike joined the students in the streets of Prague and in the great St. Wenceslas Square in the city center. In November, the call went out for a general strike.

The "velvet revolution" in Czechoslovakia

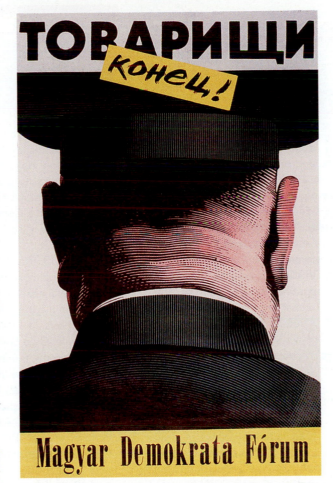

FIGURE 26.2 Istvan Orosz, *Comrades, It's Over*, 1989
This poster published by the Hungarian Democratic Forum announces the fall of communism in Hungary and elsewhere in Eastern Europe.

Within a few days, the hard-line Communist government resigned. Václav Havel, the playwright and dissident leader who had been imprisoned for his views, and Alexander Dubcek, who had tried to liberalize Czechoslovakia in 1968, quickly rose to power. As in Poland and Hungary, the fall of the communist regime in Czechoslovakia was bloodless—a "velvet revolution."

In East Germany, the wealthiest and most powerful of the Eastern European states, even people who did well under communism wanted to head west by the thousands. An American woman residing in East Germany described the growing dissatisfaction. "Too many . . . things were wrong. . . . Too much was missing from the shops. . . . There were no spare parts to fix home appliances or cars. Assembly lines were halted for want of supplies from auxiliary plants. It was the same on building sites, and the workers stood idle and furious. What good was this kind of socialism? Why did everything work so smoothly in the Germany next door?" When Hungary opened its borders with Austria in September 1989, tens of thousands of

East Germany

BIOGRAPHY

Václav Havel
(1936–)

Playwright,

Dissident,

and

Politician

In May 1989, Czechoslovakian authorities released the playwright and dissident leader Václav Havel from jail. Just seven months later, the nation elected him as its new president. The well-known American author Arthur Miller called Havel "the world's first surrealist president" in reference to his unusual literary and intellectual background. *Time* magazine described him as "the conscience of Prague." Havel referred to himself as a mere writer who lacked "any of the necessary qualities" of a politician. "I've always understood my mission to be to speak the truth about the world I live in, to bear witness to its terrors and its miseries— in other words, to warn rather than hand out prescriptions for change."

Václav was born in 1936 into a well-known, middle-class family of engineers. With the advent of the communist regime in 1948, the family lost much of their property and position. Havel thanked "the apparent disadvantage of coming from a bourgeois background and growing up in a Communist state" for enabling him to see "the world . . . as it really is."

At age 13, Havel began writing poetry and philosophy. Over the next several years, he developed an interest in the theater and started writing plays. In 1956, he met his future wife, Olga Splichalova, who would become the first person to read each of his manuscripts.

In the early 1960s, Havel wrote plays and articles while attending night classes at the Academy of Performing Arts. The boyish, blue-eyed writer often stayed up all night working or talking with friends in beer pubs. Soon he earned acclaim as one of Czechoslovakia's most successful playwrights. His best-known works included *The Garden Party, The Increased Difficulty of Concentration, The Memorandum,* and *Largo Desolato.*

Havel also acquired a reputation as a dissident in 1965 by publicly criticizing the Writers' Union for acting "as a broker between politics and literature" rather than "defending the right of literature to be literature." During the Prague Spring of 1968 (see Chapter 25), Havel published a bold article suggesting the end of single-party rule in Czechoslovakia. Warsaw Pact troops crushed that moment of liberation, and the new, repressive regime banned Havel's works.

In the 1970s, Havel helped establish an underground press that published many disapproved and hard-to-find works. He wrote several influential essays on totalitarianism and dissent, including "The Power of the Powerless." Further, he argued that the communist regime in Czechoslovakia was based on fundamental lies, though he had faith that truth could penetrate these lies. In 1977 he became a founding spokesman for Charter 77, signed by hundreds of Czechs, Slovaks, and intellectuals from other countries. The charter called for people to do

---

East Germans used that escape route to stream into the West. "They had been watching it longingly on West German television all their young lives. They knew from the commercials exactly how they would furnish their homes and make them shine."

In October 1989, antigovernment demonstrations spread throughout East Germany. People brandished signs proclaiming "We are the people." Long-suppressed criticism of the state's feared "security" forces surfaced. The hard-line communist leader was ousted from office. In November 1989, his communist successor bowed to the inevitable and ordered the Berlin Wall torn down. Joyful demonstrators celebrated for days. Soon, communists lost power, and within a year East and West Germany had reunified.

The rest of Eastern Europe also quickly followed. In Bulgaria, an internal coup deposed the Stalinist ruler. In Romania, the relatively independent but dictatorial communist leader Nicolae Ceaușescu ordered troops to fire on demonstrators, setting off a bloody revolution. His overthrow cost many lives and ended with the execution of Ceaușescu and his wife. The following year, Albania's independent but highly Stalinist regime also collapsed.

The freeing of Eastern Europe took less than a year. One after another, these nations cut the ties binding them to the USSR, enacted democratic reforms, and introduced capitalism into their economies (see **Map 26.1**). The repercussions of these events echoed throughout the Soviet Union, quickly pushing developments beyond the control of Gorbachev and his supporters.

The Soviet Union Disintegrates

The Soviet leader had managed only halting steps in his effort to restructure the Soviet economy— *perestroika.* High officials announced plans to move the economy away from central planning and then delayed the plans in the face of determined opposition by hard-liners. These officials

Problems with reform

all they could for human rights in Eastern Europe. Officials labeled the publication "reactionary," something "delivered to Western agents as instructed by anti-Communist and Zionist headquarters." Police quickly rounded up and interrogated signers.

Havel spent most of the period from 1977 to 1983 in prison for his human rights activities. Nevertheless, his wife, Olga, continued the underground publishing. Václav would later publish a book of his letters to her. Not long after his release, he reflected on his prison experience:

FIGURE 26.3 Václav Havel and the 1968 liberal leader Alexander Dubcek publicly celebrate the fall of Czechoslovakia's communist government.

"[A]ll that heroic time in prison was in fact one long chain of worries, fears, and terrors . . . and despite all this, I know that, if it were necessary, I would go back to prison again. …"

His words were prophetic. In February 1989, Havel once more languished in a prison cell for his criticisms of the communist regime. Yet his fortunes were about to change. Not far from the walls of his prison, student demonstrators marched angrily through the city streets. A petition campaign somehow persuaded authorities to release Havel in May. He soon took up his role again as a leader of the dissidents, circulating petitions demanding democratic reforms.

In November 1989, he helped found the Civic Forum, which led the opposition movement in Czechoslovakia. Before the end of the year, the Czech parliament elected Havel president, completing his

stunning transition from prison cell to the halls of government. **Figure 26.3** shows Havel in November 1989 at Sparta Stadium in Prague toasting the resignation of the communist politburo. He was soon elected to lead Czechoslovakia's new, noncommunist government. In his 1990 New Year's address, he announced, "People, your government has returned to you!"

Through the 1990s, the people again and again reelected Havel president. Some critics saw him as too much of an intellectual. Still, he gained a worldwide reputation as a moral spokesperson for Europe who stressed "the tolerant coexistence of different cultural identities" and the "ties that link everything in this world together."

Connecting People & Society

1. Why might intellectuals such as Havel have posed a threat to Czechoslovakia's authorities?

2. How did communist authorities try to maintain power during the 1960s, 1970s, and 1980s?

3. How does Havel's life reveal the forces behind the fall of communism in Eastern Europe?

---

also worried about the difficulties—including unemployment, inflation, and dislocation—that the transition would cause. Gorbachev watered down his reforms to the satisfaction of no one. The waffling and controversy only worsened the frustrations of hardliners and reformers alike. Reformers who wanted Gorbachev to move faster grew disgusted with the moderate pace of change, while the old communist guard became increasingly alienated. As the economy began to spin out of control, the Soviet leader's popularity dwindled.

Gorbachev tried pushing through promising political reforms as part of his *glasnost* policy, but, as with *perestroika*, each step taken to enact reforms opened the door further for new expressions of dissatisfaction. In 1990, he persuaded the Communist Party's Central Committee to eliminate the party's constitutional monopoly on political power. He created a new, strong presidency—an office separate from the Communist Party hierarchy. Equally daring, he called for new elections.

All these changes democratized Soviet politics and undermined the power of the Communist Party—in the process exposing the corruption of the old Soviet regime. Party members resigned in droves. These policies also facilitated the rise of Gorbachev's chief rival, Boris Yeltsin (1931–2007), the newly elected president of the Russian Republic. A charismatic, liberal reformer, Yeltsin publicly resigned from the Communist Party in July 1990. In another bold move, he declared the Russian Republic an independent state.

At the same time, movements for independence gained momentum within several ethnic groups and nationalities throughout the USSR. The Soviet Union contained more than a hundred ethnic groups, as well as some 50 million Muslims in central Asia. Many of these groups considered themselves separate nations and the Soviet Union as a collection of nations rather than a single whole. The republics of Estonia, Lithuania, and Latvia led in pressing Moscow for independence. In 1991,

Independence movements

thinking about

GEOGRAPHY

MAP 26.1

Eastern Europe, 1989

This map shows the upheavals that toppled the communist regimes in Eastern Europe.

Explore the Map

1. How widespread were the public protests and demonstrations of the times?

2. Which Western European states had the potential to gain more influence in Eastern Europe as Soviet control over the area waned?

3. Why might several of these states have been interested in joining Western European organizations such as NATO and the European Community?

★ Site of Popular Demonstrations
○ Capital Cities

the Ukraine joined the Russian Republic in declaring itself independent. Ethnic conflict and nationalistic demands spread in the Soviet republics of Armenia, Azerbaijan, Moldova, Georgia, and elsewhere. Though Gorbachev resisted these demands and tried to quell the ethnic conflicts, the situation had gone beyond anyone's control. In the spring of 1991, he proposed a compromise: the Treaty of Union, in which all the Soviet republics would be independent but held together as a confederation.

In August 1991, with the Treaty of Union about to take effect, communist hard-liners from inside the government and the KGB tried to oust Gorbachev. Within three days, the hard-liners' ineptitude and the opposition marshaled by Russian president Yeltsin doomed the coup to failure. Indeed, Gorbachev's authority was slipping away to Yeltsin even at this moment. In late 1991, after the two leaders stripped the Communist Party of much of its power, Gorbachev resigned.

Hard-liners' coup

In the end, no one, including the once-dominant Russians, wanted to save the old Soviet Union. Gorbachev had unleashed the forces of revolution, and he—along with the USSR itself—became

revolution's victim. The long Cold War was over (see Document 26.1). In 1999, Gorbachev would look back and explain, "Communism—as the inventors of the theory imagined it—never existed anywhere.... What did exist was Stalinist socialism. That system had exhausted itself and was doomed to disappear." **Map 26.2** shows what became of the former Soviet Union. Most of the republics within the old structure joined the new Commonwealth of Independent States, a loose confederation. A few republics, such as the Baltic states, broke away altogether.

Life After the Collapse of Communism

After the celebrations in the former communist bloc ended, people awoke to new, dismaying realities. In his 1990 inaugural address, Václav Havel had issued a warning that applied just as much to other nations in Eastern Europe as it did to Czechoslovakia: "Our

The End of the Cold War

In 1985, Mikhail Gorbachev rose to power in the Soviet Union and initiated the major reform policies of glasnost (political and cultural openness) and perestroika (economic restructuring). Major changes within the Soviet Union, in other Eastern European countries, and in international affairs streamed from these policies. By 1991, the Soviet Union had lost control over the states of Eastern Europe and was itself disintegrating—the Cold War was over. In the following selection, historian John Lewis Gaddis analyzes the causes of the Cold War's end.

Nevertheless, the upheavals of 1989, like those of 1789, caught everyone by surprise. Historians could of course look back, after the fact, and specify causes: frustration that the temporary divisions of the World War II settlement had become the permanent divisions of the postwar era; fear of the nuclear weapons that had produced that stalemate; resentment over the failure of command economies to raise living standards; a slow shift in power from the supposedly powerful to the seemingly powerless; the unexpected emergence of *independent* standards for making moral judgments. Sensing these trends, the great actor-leaders of the 1980s had found ways to dramatize them to make the point that the Cold War need not last forever. Not even they, however, foresaw how soon and how decisively it would end.

What no one understood, at the beginning of 1989, was that the Soviet Union, its empire, its ideology—and therefore the Cold War itself—was a sandpile ready to slide. All it took to make that happen were a few more grains of sand. The people who dropped them were not in charge of superpowers or movements or religions: they were ordinary people with simple priorities who saw, seized, and sometimes stumbled into opportunities. In doing so, they caused a collapse no one could stop. Their "leaders" had little choice but to follow.

One particular leader, however, did so in a distinctive way. He ensured that the great 1989 revolution was the first one ever in which almost no blood was shed. There were no guillotines, no heads on pikes, no officially sanctioned mass murders. People did die, but in remarkably small numbers for the size and significance of what was happening. In both its ends *and* its means, then, this revolution became a triumph of hope. It did so chiefly because Mikhail Gorbachev chose not to act, but rather to be acted upon.

SOURCE: John Lewis Gaddis, *The Cold War: A New History* (New York: Penguin Press, 2005), pp. 238–239, as excerpted.

Analyze the Document

1. According to Gaddis, what are the most commonly named causes for the upheavals of 1989?

2. What does Gaddis mean that the Soviet Union was a "sandpile ready to slide" in 1989?

3. What role did Gorbachev play in the upheavals of 1989?

country is not flourishing. . . . Entire branches of industry are producing goods which are of no interest to anyone, while we are lacking the things we need. A state which calls itself a workers' state humiliates and exploits workers. Our obsolete economy is wasting the little energy we have available. . . . We have polluted our soil, our rivers and forests. . . ." Leaders in Eastern Europe and the former USSR faced a crucial problem: how to institute capitalism and liberal democracy in nations with little experience of either.

The economic transition proceeded quickly in Poland and Hungary, but more moderately in Bulgaria, Romania, and Albania. Almost everywhere, however, it brought pain. When governments closed the doors of inefficient state industries or sold them, many workers lost their jobs. The removal of price controls also provoked instant inflation that especially hurt those living on fixed incomes. Some people took advantage of new opportunities that came with the transition; for example, former communist officials in particular benefited from lucrative insider deals. Several cities—such as Prague in the Czech Republic, with its domes, spires, cobblestone alleys, pubs, cafés, and secondhand bookstores—also fared well with heightened tourism. But too many people had let themselves expect more than the eradication of

Eastern Europe

FALL OF COMMUNISM

1980–1981	Solidarity union in Poland
1985	Gorbachev comes to power
1986	Chernobyl accident
1989	Soviet troops withdraw from Afghanistan
	Revolutions in Eastern Europe
1991	Disintegration of the Soviet Union
1993	Division of Czechoslovakia

KEY DATES

Population (in millions)

Estonia, Latvia, Lithuania	8.0
Georgia	5.5
Armenia	3.3
Turkmenistan	3.5
Moldova	4.3
Kyrgyzstan	4.3
Tajikistan	5.1
Azerbaijan	7.0
Belarus	10.2
Kazakhstan	16.5
Uzbekistan	19.9

Russia 147.4
Ukraine 51.7

Ethnic Groups

Other 8.2%
Russian 50.8%
Ukraine 15.4%

Kyrgyz	0.9%
Turkmen	1.0%
Lithuanian	1.1%
Moldovan	1.2%
Georgian	1.4%
Tajik	1.5%
Armenian	1.6%
Azerbaijani	2.4%
Tatar	2.4%
Kazakh	2.8%
Belarusian	3.5%
Uzbek	5.8%
Ukrainian	15.4%

RUSSIA	Republics Joining Commonwealth
GEORGIA	Not Joining

MAP 26.2

The Dissolution of the Soviet Union, 1991

This map shows the division of territory resulting from the disintegration of the former Soviet Union.

Explore the Map

1. Which states became the largest and potentially the most powerful in the former USSR?

2. Which areas had the greatest likelihood of being influenced by European states to the west, and which by Islamic states to the south?

3. Notice the ethnic divisions in the former USSR. What political and social problems did this ethnic diversity have the potential to cause after the USSR's breakup?

communism could deliver. In the face of widespread bitterness, governments struggled to gain stability and institute unpopular but apparently necessary economic policies such as closing state industries and allowing prices to rise.

In the former Soviet Union, people were unaccustomed to democratic politics, managers were unfamiliar with the market economy, and many officials resisted reform. The economy stumbled badly. Year after year, Russia's economic output decreased, as did its population. Removing price controls and privatizing industry had eliminated lines in front of stores and created economic opportunities for

The former Soviet Union

some. However, prices skyrocketed beyond the reach of average consumers, the Russian currency lost its value, and some 30 percent of the population struggled to subsist on approximately $1 per day.

The collapse of communism proved particularly stressful for Russian men. From Communist Party officials and generals to physicists and professors, men who had once enjoyed status, security, and relative wealth lost these benefits in the turmoil of the postcommunist era. Life expectancy for Russian men plummeted to fifty-eight years, a decline that was "the steepest and most severe ever documented anywhere in the world" according to one researcher. Alcoholism more than tripled in the years after the collapse.

For women, the story was different. Although many women suffered from unemployment when state industries folded, perhaps their losses were not so great and were eased by new opportunities. In any case, they seemed to manage the transition better than men, maintaining a life expectancy of seventy-three years. Indeed, a growing elite of women entered managerial positions and earned increasing salaries.

Boris Yeltsin retained a precarious hold on power as president of Russia and, despite illnesses, was reelected in 1996. But the Russian people resisted his inconsistent efforts at reform. In the parliament, with its tangled array of different political parties, fragmentation ruled. Moreover, "reformed" communists retained positions of power, as they did in Eastern European states such as Serbia, Bulgaria, and Lithuania. With control disintegrating, lawlessness—from street crime to organized crime—rapidly spread. By 1998, the fumbling Yeltsin had lost his popularity and much of his power as the Russian economy verged on collapse.

`Yeltsin's problems`

When he resigned on the last day of 1999, turning power over to Vladimir Putin, many Russians yearned for the power, order, and stability that communism had brought. While rich oligarchic figures and organized crime still sapped Russia's wealth, Putin, supported by an increasingly loyal bureaucracy and some genuine popularity, provided some functional stability and considerable respect within and outside Russia. He effectively supported Russia's evolving market economy and legal system. Although he moved against the independent media and undermined political opposition, he provided a welcome relief from Yeltsin, whose uneven and unpopular reign witnessed the collapse of basic industries and social services along with the growth of crime and widespread corruption.

In 2008, Putin gave up the presidency to his protégé, Dmitry Medvedev (1965–), and moved to the post of prime minister. By then, political stability and increasing wealth from oil and gas had propelled Russia's economy forward. While no longer a superpower, the country—described by Putin as a "managed democracy"—increasingly acted like a regional power ready to assert itself in disputes with neighbors.

Nationalism Unleashed

Despite its drawbacks, communism had provided many people with a sense of unity and security. Its fall opened a void that nationalistic sentiments rose to fill. As had often been the case in nineteenth- and twentieth-century history, nationalism provoked heated conflict along with a feeling of belonging. Ethnic and cultural struggles raged in several republics of the former Soviet Union. In Azerbaijan, the Azerbaijanis and Armenians clashed. The most violent outburst came in secessionist Chechnya, where Russians fought an unpopular war with Chechnyans demanding their independence. The indecisive two-year conflict cost some 80,000 deaths and 250,000 wounded, although the Chechnyans gained many of their goals. In 1999, another draining war broke out between Chechnyans and Russians.

In Eastern Europe also, nationalistic, ethnic, and religious rivalries opened old wounds and created new divisions. **Maps 26.3** and **26.4** reveal some of these problems. In 1993, the Slovak minority in Czechoslovakia, pushed by ambitious Slovak politicians, voted for independence. Czechoslovakia reluctantly agreed to divide itself into the Czech Republic and Slovakia. In Romania, ethnic friction between the Romanian majority and the Hungarian minority flared up.

The bloodiest conflicts broke out in Yugoslavia, where chaotic civil wars marked the disintegration of that country. **Figure 26.4,** a chart listing the many ethnic groups living in Yugoslavia, reveals the complexity of ethnic divisions in the country. In some regions, one ethnic group made up the vast majority of the population, but in other areas several ethnic groups lived as large minorities. The six republics that constituted Yugoslavia had been held together under communist rule since World War II (see **Map 26.4**). With the death of Tito in 1980 and the fall of communism in the rest of Eastern Europe in 1989, Yugoslavia began to crack. In 1991, Slovenians, angered by the refusal of the dominant Serbian communists to liberalize economic and political policies, detached themselves from Yugoslavia. Peoples in Croatia, Bosnia-Herzegovina, and Macedonia followed suit. War soon erupted between the religiously Orthodox Serbs, attempting to expand the territory they controlled, and their longtime Catholic Croatian rivals to the northwest. Trapped between the two antagonists were the mostly Muslim Bosnians and other peoples who lived as minorities in these areas.

`Civil wars in Yugoslavia`

The war for a Greater Serbia raged with appalling brutality. The worst fighting took place in Bosnia-Herzegovina. On this bloody battlefield, the Serbs initiated a policy of **ethnic cleansing,** driving Muslim Bosnians from their homes; placing them in concentration camps; and raping, murdering, and starving them. In 1992, a Serb guard at one concentration camp proudly explained, "We won't waste our bullets on them. . . . They have no roof. There is sun and rain, cold nights, and beatings two times a day. We give them no food and no water. They will starve like animals." A survivor reported seeing "corpses piled one on top of another. . . . The bodies eventually were gathered with a forklift . . . this happened almost every day." **Figure 26.5** shows some of the hastily created graves in Bosnia-Herzegovina's capital city, Sarajevo. Residents, still suffering from the ongoing struggle, search for the lost and visit the dead. Many

★	Capital
━━	Former Border of Yugoslavia
━━	Border of Bosnia-Herzegovina
━━	Dayton Agreement Inter-entity Boundary (November 1995)
🟩	Bosnian Serb Territory, After Dayton
🟨	Croat-Muslim Federation Portion of Bosnia, After Dayton

MAPS 26.3 AND 26.4

Disintegration of Czechoslovakia and Yugoslavia, 1991–2007

These maps respectively show the division of Czecho-slovakia into the Czech Republic and Slovakia and the disintegration of Yugoslavia.

Explore the Maps

1. Compare the maps. How do you explain the different paths to the breakup of these two nations?

2. Why did problems in this area of Europe lead to war at the beginning, as well as the end, of the twentieth century?

3. Why might so many people favor integrating these areas of Europe into the European Union?

more would be added to graves such as these during the following years.

The Bosnians, supported by aid from the Islamic world, fought back desperately for more than four years. Only a Western embargo and NATO interven-tion brought an uneasy end to the violence and peace accords in 1996. The conflict had killed 250,000 peo-ple, displaced three million, and left 800,000 antiper-sonnel mines embedded in the land. Moreover, peace still depended on the continued presence of interna-tional troops. In 1997, a NATO commander in Bos-nia warned that "if we withdraw our forces, there will be slaughter in the streets" and predicted that com-plete recovery would take decades.

Just two years later, brutality like that unleashed in Bosnia rose in nearby Kosovo—another region within Yugoslavia. Serbians, led by President Slo-bodan Milosevic, met rising demands for indepen-dence from the Albanian majority in Kosovo with

ETHNIC GROUP	PERCENTAGE
Serbians	36
Croatians	20
Bosnians (Muslim)	9
Slovenes	8
Albanians	8
Macedonians	6
Montenegrins	3
Hungarians	2
Others	8

FIGURE 26.4 Ethnic Groups in Yugoslavia, 1991

overwhelming military force. Renewing the practice of ethnic cleansing, Serbian troops slaughtered thou-sands of Kosovar Albanians and forced hundreds of thousands to flee to neighboring states.

After diplomacy failed, NATO unleashed its military resources for the first time in its fifty-year history. Member air forces, led by the United States, opened a three-month bombing campaign on Serbian forces and on Serbia itself. Milosevic finally agreed to terms and withdrew his forces. Protected by NATO troops, the Kosovar Albanians streamed back to their badly damaged land, bringing with them few hopes for ethnic cooperation in the region. In 2000, Vojislav Kostunica defeated Milosevic in Yugoslavia's presidential election, and soon Milosevic found himself standing trial for war crimes before an international tribunal in The Hague, Netherlands.

REPERCUSSIONS AND REALIGNMENTS IN THE WEST

Repercussions from the collapse of communism spread around the world. As communism lost its credibility, nations still committed to the Soviet model, such as Cuba and North Korea, were left isolated. Capitalism gained renewed respect and even inspired awe in both the Western and non-Western worlds. For many, the collapse of communism in Eastern Europe and the USSR signified the final triumph of capitalism. With the end of the Cold War, the contours of domestic and international politics began to shift.

The United States Unchallenged and Germany Rising

With the former Soviet forces in decline and the Warsaw Pact dissolved, the United States and Germany rose in stature. The United States emerged as the world's only military superpower. It flexed its military muscle in 1991 by leading a United Nations–authorized coalition that repelled Iraq's invasion of tiny, neighboring Kuwait. In the short war, the U.S.-dominated coalition easily defeated Saddam Hussein's forces. In 2001 and 2003, it again demonstrated its military might, in Afghanistan and Iraq (see pages 828–831). The U.S. also contributed to international peacekeeping efforts by sending forces to troubled areas such as Somalia, Haiti, Bosnia, and Kosovo. Despite years of large budget deficits and apparent decline, the U.S. economy rebounded in the mid-1990s to a position of leadership that inspired envy the world over.

Germany's influence and potential also rose. In 1990, German unification confirmed Germany as a European and world economic leader—in exports, in balance of trade, and in gross domestic product. Emerging victorious from the first national elections, the former West German chancellor Helmut Kohl and his conservative Christian Democrats vowed to bring eastern Germany's economy up to the high standard enjoyed in the West. The costs of the transition

FIGURE 26.5 Civil War in Bosnia-Herzegovina   The dead and the suffering from the civil war in Bosnia-Herzegovina mingle in a cemetery in January 1993.

mushroomed far beyond expectations; as state industries collapsed in the East, unemployment and the cost of welfare benefits shot up. Nevertheless, the reunified state still ranked as the top economic power in Europe. Clearly, Germany stood poised to exert new influence in Eastern Europe and the European Community.

Politics Shift to the Right

In the United States, Germany, and elsewhere in the West, politics shifted to the Right. The reasons behind this change were complex, but economic forces played a major role. Despite the continued overall prosperity enjoyed in the West, many nations suffered from high unemployment and declining growth rates during the 1980s and 1990s. In part, the free flow of trade and capital had created a new international labor market that operated outside the control of national governments and labor unions, resulting in the loss of many business opportunities and manufacturing jobs in the West. As global economic competition stiffened and nations struggled to stay in the game, many people blamed costly social programs—often supported by the political Left—for their nation's economic problems. The changes wrought by the postindustrial society, especially the shift from manufacturing to services, also weakened labor unions—the Left's traditional source of support. The previous sense that government was obligated to provide for rich and poor alike—a belief that had fueled the post–World War II welfare state—faded along with memories of those older times. Government regulation of economic affairs and the cost of social programs came under question everywhere.

Conservatives began scoring record successes at the polls. Citing the apparent triumph of capitalism, they attacked expensive programs and sometimes fanned the flames of anti-immigrant sentiments, playing on the popular perception that foreign-born newcomers took jobs. France's right-wing National Front, led by Jean-Marie LePen, attained particular prominence by blaming immigrants from North Africa and elsewhere for France's economic problems. The traditional communist parties in Western Europe declined, and socialist parties, whether in power or not, moderated their policies to shore up their popularity. In Austria, Italy, Germany, and Spain, conservative and right-wing politicians gained popularity. Even when traditional parties of the Left regained power, as they did in many countries during the late 1990s, their platforms were more muted and conservative than in the past. No other nation ventured as far down the conservative path as Great Britain and the United States. In Great Britain, the Conservatives led by Margaret Thatcher and her successor dominated throughout most of the 1980s and 1990s, cutting taxes, attacking social programs, and selling state-owned industries to private investors. When the Labor Party finally came to power in Great Britain in 1997, it pursued only mild changes. In the United States, Republicans rolled back liberal programs and Democrats scrambled to adopt more conservative platforms. The sharply conservative administration of George W. Bush came to power in 2001. Mostly in the name of economic development and the war against terrorism, it aggressively pursued many policies initiated by the Reagan administration in the 1980s, including loosening environmental protections, reducing social programs, lowering taxes in ways that favored the wealthy and corporations, increasing military spending, and cutting into the protection of civil liberties.

By the mid-1990s, this conservatism had merged with a broader questioning of traditional politics in the West. As anxieties over economic problems intensified and as scandals rocked governments, people voted for unknowns or stopped voting altogether. Especially in France, Italy, and Austria, candidates who voiced disenchantment with the standard politics of the Left and Right attracted popular support.

In 2008, elections swept Barack Obama into office as president of the United States. Backed by national and international popularity, as well as a more liberal administration, Obama promised to reverse some of his predecessor's conservative policies. Whether this new focus represents a broader political change in the West remains to be seen. All these shifts in domestic politics gained much attention. However, events beyond state borders would soon overshadow these internal concerns throughout the West.

Toward European Integration

The end of the Cold War may have left the United States the world's sole superpower, but it also strengthened the movement toward unity that had been unfolding in Europe since the 1950s. According to Michael Naumann, in 2002 the editor of a leading German magazine, the "huge influence of the world's single superpower, the United States, will push Europeans together." Moreover, many Europeans agreed with Michel Albert, a leading French official and industrialist, who in 1991 argued, "If the aim is to harness capitalism without impairing its efficiency, it is no longer to the nation-state that we must look, but to Europe."

In 1992, the 12 members of the European Community (EC) eliminated all major internal barriers to trade, the flow of capital, and the movement of people. That same year, the EC joined with the seven-member European Free Trade Association to form the European Economic Area, creating the world's largest trading bloc and paving the way for several new countries to seek full membership (see **Map 26.5**). Between 1999 and 2004, a number of Eastern European nations, such as Poland, the Czech Republic, Hungary, Lithuania, and Slovakia joined NATO and were accepted for membership in the European Union. Also in 1992, France and Germany formed a joint army corps, the European Corps, open to other participants in the European Union. With the Maastricht Treaty of 1992 (which changed the name of the EC to the European Union), most members of the **European Union (EU)** agreed to establish a common currency (the **Euro**) controlled by a central European bank by 1999. The plan required great economic discipline, above all controlling the large yearly budget deficits most nations ran. By 2002, people in most countries of the European Union carried Euros in their pockets, wallets, and purses.

The potential of the European Union seemed tremendous. In 2010, the twenty-seven member nations had more than 491 million inhabitants and a combined gross national product greater than that of the United States. Perhaps in response to the growing power of the European Union, the United States joined with Mexico and Canada in 1994 to create a new free-trade zone—the **North American Free Trade Agreement (NAFTA).** Not everyone embraced the idea of such alliances. Many Europeans opposed further integration, clinging to national preferences and warning against the dangers of giving up sovereignty to an international body of bureaucrats. To be sure, the European nations had great difficulty joining forces to put down the crisis in Bosnia, but their joint action as part of a NATO force to quell the violence in Kosovo in 1999 led to a vow by the leaders of fifteen European countries to make the European Union a military power for the first time. The Union adopted plans to build its own military of up to 60,000 troops. Moreover, by that same year, the European Union had opened its arms to possible membership for Turkey as

MAP 26.5

The European Union, 2010

This map shows the European Union in 2010 and identifies nations that have applied for membership.

Explore the Map

1. Notice how inclusive membership is. Which nations form the core of a potentially united Europe?

2. How economically and politically powerful might a united Europe be?

3. Why is it significant that several Eastern European nations have joined or applied for membership in this association?

Member of the European Union
Applied for Membership

well as virtually all of central and eastern Europe. Despite many reservations, most Europeans seemed willing to cooperate. The statement by a German woman early in 2002 reflected the sense of many: "I feel German, but also European."

In 2005, French and Dutch voters rejected a newly drafted constitution designed to strengthen the European Union. This outcome signaled the voters' broad ambivalence about taking further steps toward European integration and, in particular, their concerns about welcoming the populous, Muslim, and relatively poor Turkey into the Union—as well as their worries about a potential influx of immigrants and migrant workers. However, in 2009, member states finally ratified the Lisbon Treaty designed to streamline European Union institutions.

THE WORLD AND THE WEST FROM A GLOBAL PERSPECTIVE

As they took further steps toward unity, Europeans had more in mind than competing with the United States. They also knew that they had to meet the changes sweeping through much of the Western and non-Western worlds. Since the end of colonialism, European nations could no longer rely on colonies as controllable markets. By the 1990s, all nations faced a global economy marked by the presence of multinational enterprises beyond the command of individual states. Waves of huge corporate buyouts and mergers increased this concentration of economic power. By 2000, small handfuls of these corporations controlled more than half the global market in oil, automobiles, electronics, multimedia, and personal computers. Westerners also confronted new competitors, from Latin America to East Asia, who wielded growing economic and political clout. In addition, various international agencies and organizations, such as the International Monetary Fund, the World Bank, and the World Trade Organization, wielded great economic clout over financial aid and international commerce that affected governments, corporations, and ordinary people throughout the world. Finally, the pace of global economic integration and change had quickened, complicating international business for

Globalization

everyone. Certain technological advances, above all the development of the computer, the Internet, and genetic engineering, had the potential of creating the equivalent of a third industrial revolution.

By 2000, the mushrooming use of computers and the Internet in business and commerce had already transformed many economies. Increasingly, goods could be designed in one country, financed internationally, produced overseas, sold worldwide, and serviced through phones and the Internet from numerous locations. All these changes tended to blend local and national markets into global markets and called into question the very issue of national identity. Even in the poorest nations, signs of this **globalization** proliferated. As just one example, workers in new manufacturing plants owned by multinational corporations wore the same brand-name athletic shoes and drank the same beverages as their Western counterparts. Moreover, thanks to films, television, radio, computers, cellular phones, fax machines, satellites, and travel, ideas and images flowed across international borders as easily as money, goods, and services, further blurring the distinctions between cultures.

East Asia and the Rise of the Pacific Rim

The greatest challenge to the West's economic dominance came from East Asia. Since the 1960s, Japan had grown into a major economic power. Year after year, this island nation enjoyed the world's largest favorable balance of trade. By the 1980s, it boasted the world's second-largest gross domestic product. A giant in automobile production and electronics, Japan replaced the United States as the world's topmost creditor nation. Although reversals brought Japan's economic momentum to a virtual standstill during the 1990s, and even a decline during the 2001 and 2002 world economic slowdown, the nation still led the world in per capita gross domestic product.

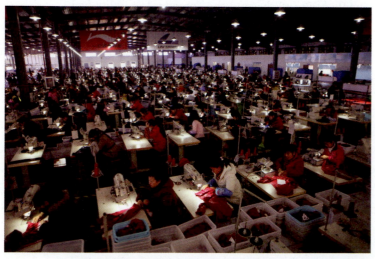

FIGURE 26.6 Factory Workers in China Row after row of women workers sew clothing for worldwide export.

In the 1990s, other regions on the periphery of the Pacific Ocean attracted wealthy investors with their political stability, cheap and disciplined labor force, and openness to capitalism. Multinational corporations opened offices and made investments throughout this so-called Pacific Rim. Hong Kong, Taiwan, South Korea, Malaysia, Indonesia, and Singapore all boomed, drawing manufacturing jobs away from Europe and the United States in industries such as electronics, textiles, plastics, metals, computers, automobiles, and leather goods. Visitors found thriving cities such as Kuala Lumpur in Malaysia—with the world's two tallest buildings marking its skyline and its high-rise apartment houses serviced by climate-controlled malls—"unrecognizable to anyone who knew it 30 years ago." On the outskirts of such glittering urban centers, satellite communities and industrial parks rose where jungles used to thrive. Similar developments transformed other great cities of East Asia, from Singapore and Bangkok to Jakarta and Hong Kong.

Yet no country experienced a more stunning economic transformation than China. In 1978, the successors to Mao, led by Deng Xiaoping (1904–1997), had initiated the Four Modernizations program to foster rapid economic development and greater productivity. The program departed dramatically from Mao's economic policies by decentralizing decision making and introducing a market-oriented economy into the countryside and, later, into some urban areas. By the mid-1980s, these policies had opened China to tourism and foreign investment, stimulated new economic growth, and created greater economic freedom within China. Agreements with Japan and the United States rapidly expanded trade as well. For the first time, Chinese farmers produced a surplus of food for export. In certain areas of the country, particularly the New Economic Zones in the southeast, capitalistic investments and manufacturing practices spurred high rates of growth. By the first decade of the twenty-first century, China had become the world's most important manufacturing nation and a major player in international finance. **Figure 26.6** shows one of the many new factories that fueled China's growing economic prowess. Here, women workers wearing coats in an unheated factory sew clothes that sport Western brand names and that are destined for export throughout the world.

Nevertheless, China made these economic reforms without corresponding political reforms. Whether that practice could continue was called into question in 1989, when students and intellectuals demanding political reform organized massive demonstrations in Beijing. After a brief standoff, the government, supported by China's rural population and most of the army, violently crushed the demonstrations and jailed the leaders. In the years that followed, as China's

> The economic transformation of China

leadership aged and pressures for political reform persisted, analysts watched carefully for change within the great Asian country. By the first decade of the twenty-first century, China stood as a rapidly growing economic power with tremendous political potential on the international stage.

The Challenge of Islam

Other areas of the world presented different challenges to the West. In particular, several Islamic nations in North Africa and the Middle East developed a new assertiveness and a willingness to make their dissatisfaction with Western ways known. They had long resented the former Western imperial powers' condescension toward them. The West's support of Israel only irritated an already raw nerve.

The emergence of combative leaders in states such as Libya, Syria, Iran, and Iraq—some of whom advocated Islamic or Pan-Arab unity against Israel and Western influence—stepped up tensions further. Moreover, in nations from Algeria and Turkey to Afghanistan and Pakistan, Islamic fundamentalists had gained strength. Western secular notions such as individualism, capitalism, materialism, commercialism, gender equality, and sexual freedom were flooding across airwaves and borders into the Islamic world. These notions seemed to insult and threaten fundamentalists' traditional and religious beliefs. Condemning Westernization and the secularization of life in their countries, they demanded a return to traditional symbols of their conservative views, such as the veil that they required women to wear in public. Iran's fundamentalist leader Ayatollah Ruholla Khomeini (1900–1989), who had come to power as the leader of a revolution in 1979, epitomized rejection of the West. "With the Qur'an in one hand and a gun in the other, defend your dignity and honor" against the "oppressive powers" of the West, he told his nation in 1980. He especially castigated the United States, labeling it the "great Satan" because it had supported Israel and had intervened several times in the region. Finally, many Middle Eastern Islamic states possessed the crude-oil reserves on which the West and Asia depended, and they used the precious resource to command international respect and attention. The potential of Middle Eastern states to pull Western nations into armed conflict was made all too clear in 1990 when Iraq invaded oil-rich Kuwait, prompting a UN-backed military response, in 2003 with the U.S.-led invasion of Iraq, and with the persisting violence in Afghanistan that threatened to spread into neighboring Pakistan.

International Terrorism and War

On the morning of September 11, 2001, coordinated teams of terrorists hijacked four U.S. American airliners. They slammed two of the planes into Manhattan's famed World Trade Center (Twin Towers) office buildings and a third into the Pentagon, headquarters of the U.S. Department of Defense in Washington D.C. Passengers apparently brought down the fourth plane before it could reach its target. Nearly 3,000 people lost their lives in the attacks, most of them perishing when the Twin Towers collapsed later that morning. Blame soon fell on the shoulders of a well-financed international terrorist group, **al-Qaeda,** which professed a radical version of Islamic fundamentalism, under the leadership of Osama bin Laden.

The forces behind this tragedy and the responses to it were complex, and historians can make only tentative analyses at this point. However, analysts point to the intensifying anger toward the West among radical Islamic fundamentalists as one major underlying force for the attack. Islamic fundamentalists had long lamented what they saw as the West's corruption of regimes within the Islamic world. Authoritarian governments that fundamentalists viewed as too secular and too connected to the West ruled most Islamic states. Fundamentalism found growing support among people who were outraged by this supposed perversion of Islamic law and who were enraged at the reality of masses of people living far below the wealthy elites in these countries.

Most Muslim leaders and clerics rejected violence and terrorism. But against the overwhelming military, political, and economic forces that Western nations and nonfundamentalist Islamic states could marshal, terrorism seemed a legitimate and even religiously justified way to assert some fundamentalists' point of view. For a group such as al-Qaeda, terrorism might catalyze widespread fundamentalist revolts that would bring down "corrupt" governments in the Islamic world.

A second force came in the form of the festering Israeli-Palestinian conflict. This struggle deepened Islamic fundamentalists' rage toward the West—in particular the United States. In various ways, Israel and the Arab world had been at odds since the mid-twentieth century (see Chapter 25). Moreover, Israel had long been perceived as a Western outpost in the Middle East. The close relationship between Israel and the United States encouraged that perception, and many held the United States partly responsible for the sufferings of Palestinians. For example, al-Qaeda's Osama bin Laden railed against "the crusader-Jewish alliance, led by the United States and Israel."

Fueled by these forces and religious enthusiasm, terrorist organizations grew in the 1980s and 1990s and adopted bolder tactics aimed at both military and civilian targets. Some of these groups gained strength and reach through financial support by wealthy

`Israeli-Palestinian conflict`

thinking about
GEOGRAPHY

MAP 26.6

Israel and the Occupied Territories, 2010

This map shows Israel, the occupied territories of the West Bank, and the Gaza Strip. It also identifies areas of varying Palestinian and Israeli control, as well as Jewish-Israeli settlements.

Explore the Map

1. Identify the location of settlements and the divided areas of Palestinian and Israeli control.

2. What difficulties do Palestinians and Israelis face in trying to establish a permanent peace?

3. How might any settlement affect surrounding states with large numbers of Palestinian refugees?

patrons. The growing availability of modern communications and military technology also enhanced their power.

During the first years of the new century, tensions grew. After efforts to forge a U.S.-sponsored settlement of the Israeli-Palestinian dispute collapsed in 2000, a new, more deadly round of violence erupted between Israelis and Palestinians (see **Map 26.6**). Day after day, pictures, reports, and stories of the conflict focusing on Palestinian deaths at the hands of the Israelis spread across the Islamic world. In Israel, suicidal terrorists bombed shopping centers, restaurants, and buses. Within Palestinian areas, the death tolls from missiles, planes, and guns fired by the well-armed and trained Israeli forces rose dramatically. By 2004, much of the violence had subsided, and in 2005 Israel unilaterally withdrew from the Gaza Strip. However, in 2006 an election gave the militant Islamic organization Hamas—considered a terrorist group by many in the West—governing power in Palestine, raising tensions again. That same year, a war broke out in Lebanon between Israel and Hezbollah, a radical Islamic organization apparently backed by Iran and Syria. In 2008, Israel, citing a growing number of rocket attacks on its territory, invaded the Gaza Strip, now controlled by Hamas.

The devastating attacks of September 11, 2001, against the United States were intended to strike at symbols of U.S. "imperial" power. The United States answered the attacks by declaring war against terrorism. President George W. Bush vowed to pursue terrorists wherever they lurked in the world and punish those who harbored them. Drawing on the sympathy and support of many nations, the U.S. military launched a massive aerial assault on al-Qaeda strongholds in Afghanistan, as well as on the Taliban, the radical fundamentalist regime that ruled the mountainous nation (see **Map 26.7**).

Afghanistan had a history of strife. During the 1980s, the Afghani people had endured a long, bloody war against Soviet invaders (see pages 783–784). The impoverished, war-torn country again suffered from the turmoil following the Soviet withdrawal in the late 1980s. In the mid-1990s, the Taliban seized power | War in Afghanistan | in most of Afghanistan, and there al-Qaeda found a home.

In 2001 and 2002, the U.S. military, using anti-Taliban Afghan forces for much of the campaign on the ground, crushed most of the al-Qaeda and Taliban forces harbored within Afghanistan. However, President George W. Bush declared the war on terrorism far from over, pointing to the possibility that other terrorists and regimes might acquire and wield weapons of mass destruction. He warned that other states might also feel the force of U.S. military power in the future.

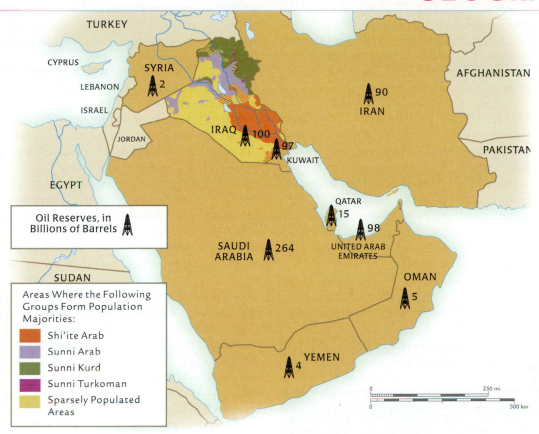

MAP 26.7

The Middle East and Iraq, 2003

This map shows the Middle East, estimated oil reserves in several nations, and ethno-religious groups in Iraq at the beginning of the U.S.-led invasion in 2003.

Explore the Map

1. Why is the Middle East of such strategic importance?

2. In what ways might the war in Iraq change this region?

3. What problems loom for Iraqis who are trying to establish a stable, unified nation?

In March 2003, the United States took another step in the name of its war on terror. The U.S. military, backed by British forces and the token support of other nations, attacked Iraq. During the months leading up to the war, the Bush administration, building on fears stemming from the September 11, 2001, terrorist attacks, cited the development and existence of terrifying weapons of mass destruction (chemical, biological, and nuclear) in Iraq that threatened the United States and the whole international community. Administration officials also claimed that Iraqi leader Saddam Hussein's dictatorial regime had links with international terrorist organizations such as al-Qaeda. The United States, officials said, had a duty to rid the world of Iraq's violent, brutal regime. Under these justifications for invading Iraq lay a vision

War in Iraq

within the Bush administration of aggressively and, if necessary, single-handedly reforming oil-rich Iraq. Other authoritarian regimes in the strategic Middle East, administration officials hoped, would then transform themselves into democracies or at least reform. These new regimes would become friends of the United States and its allies as well as stable sources of oil (see **Map 26.7**).

Within weeks, U.S. and British air and ground forces overwhelmed Iraqi defenders and toppled Saddam Hussein and the Baathist Party, which had ruled Iraq with an iron fist for more than twenty years. Although President Bush declared victory in June 2003, achieving peace, stability, or international acclaim in the months that followed proved daunting. The United States, backed by Great Britain, refused to cede authority over the stabilization and rebuilding of Iraq to the United Nations. Many potential allies who had opposed the war in the first place—including France, Germany, Russia, India, Turkey, and most Arab states—refused to lend a hand under those conditions. The cost and responsibility for the process fell squarely on the shoulders of the United States and Great Britain, though other allies provided some support. Within Iraq, guerrilla and suicide attacks steadily raised the death toll into the thousands each month. Looting and sabotage further undermined efforts to establish security and promote recovery. Some of these problems are suggested by **Figure 26.7.** The photograph shows a United States Marine sitting in a schoolroom below a damaged mural of the country he and his fellow soldiers are occupying and trying to pacify. He is part of a military operation in western Iraq, which in 2005 was still a stronghold of insurgent activities. In the following two years, violent insurgent attacks increased. By 2007, Iraq seemed on the verge of civil war.

Moreover, U.S. ambitions to usher in a new, democratic government met with mounting discord among factions within Iraq. Historic rivalries between majority Arabs and minority Kurds in the north, and between the majority Shi'ites and minority Sunnis in the center and south, stymied efforts to create a new,

FIGURE 26.7 The Occupation of Iraq A United States Marine rests below a map of Iraq in an Iraqi schoolroom.

effective government (see **Map 26.7**). Finally, despite the eventual capture of Saddam Hussein in December 2003 and extensive searches, U.S. investigators could find no weapons of mass destruction or links to the sort of international terrorist organizations that carried out the September 11, 2001, plot.

Only time will enable us to make firm judgments about the U.S. actions in Iraq and the policies underlying them. However, these actions and policies may prove to have greater historical significance than the toppling of Saddam Hussein's regime. First, the Bush administration set what many critics worldwide considered dangerous precedent by initiating a **preemptive war,** based on the *assertion* that Iraq had imminent plans to attack the United States, or, even worse, a "preventive war," based on the *possibility* that Iraq might attack sometime in the distant future. In these relatively nonthreatening circumstances, such a war violated long-established rules of international relations and dashed ambitions of those hoping to strengthen international barriers to the outbreak of wars.

> Preemptive war, unilateralism, and the occupation

Second, the Bush administration not only failed to win important UN and international support for the war but also appeared to punish those who disagreed with its foreign policies—including longtime major allies such as France and Germany. Indeed, the United States seemed to discard the principles of internationalism that had informed global diplomacy since the end of World War II. In place of those principles, it appeared to favor a kind of **unilateralism** in which the world's only superpower pursued its own interests regardless of its allies' views and interests. The administration's abandonment of the Kyoto Protocol, which sought to limit global-warming emissions; its plans to develop an antiballistic missile shield and a new class of nuclear weapons; its desertion of international efforts to strengthen rules against biological weapons, land mines, and small arms; and its attacks on the International Criminal Court all added to the impression that the United States had decided to go it alone.

Third, the way the U.S. government justified its invasion of Iraq and what many in the world saw as the destructive mishandling of the occupation that followed diminished the sympathy and support for the United States that had been offered after the September 11 attacks. Moreover, the bloodshed and political turmoil that reigned in Iraq year after year during the presence of U.S.-led coalition forces served to increase the regional influence of Iran, still ruled by a fundamentalist regime that now embarked on a policy to develop its own atomic resources. These developments, along with veiled threats by the U.S. government to launch strikes against Iran, cast a darkening shadow over the Middle East.

In 2008 and 2009, some of the violence within Iraq abated. The new president of the United States,

DOCUMENT 26.2

War in Afghanistan

After the attacks of September 11, 2001, the United States, supported by several other countries to various degrees, became deeply enmeshed in Middle Eastern affairs. By 2009, the United States had been fighting in Afghanistan for eight years, and that battle threatened to spill over into Pakistan. Some observers called for greater military commitments, while others argued for withdrawal. In 2009 Barack Obama, the recently elected president of the United States, announced his decision to send a limited number of additional U.S. troops into Afghanistan. The following are selections from Obama's December 2009 speech.

I have determined that it is in our vital national interest to send an additional 30,000 U.S. troops to Afghanistan. After eighteen months, our troops will begin to come home. These are the resources that we need to seize the initiative, while building the Afghan capacity that can allow for a responsible transition of our forces out of Afghanistan.

I do not make this decision lightly. I opposed the war in Iraq precisely because I believe that we must exercise restraint in the use of military force, and always consider the long-term consequences of our actions. We have been at war for eight years, at enormous cost in lives and resources. Years of debate over Iraq and terrorism have left our unity on national security issues in tatters, and created a highly polarized and partisan backdrop for this effort. And having just experienced the worst economic crisis since the Great Depression, the American people are understandably focused on rebuilding our economy and putting people to work here at home. . . .

This is not just America's war. Since 9/11, al Qaeda's safe-havens have been the source of attacks against London and Amman and Bali. The people and governments of both Afghanistan and Pakistan are endangered. And the stakes are even higher within a nuclear-armed Pakistan, because we know that al Qaeda and other extremists seek nuclear weapons, and we have every reason to believe that they would use them.

These facts compel us to act along with our friends and allies. . . .

SOURCE: Government document in public domain.

Analyze the Document

1. How does President Obama justify a new military effort in Afghanistan?

2. Why does he want to begin to bring troops home after eighteen months?

3. What do you think led Obama to emphasize connections between national security and the economy?

Barack Obama, riding a wave of national and international popularity, signaled changes in U.S. policy in Iraq and committed to the withdrawal of U.S. forces by 2011. But already, with U.S. troops and money diverted to Iraq since 2003, violence and instability were worsening in neighboring Afghanistan, where Taliban and al-Qaeda forces had gained new life and threatened the weak central government that relied heavily on financial and military aid from the West (see Document 26.2).

Terrorism and the war in Afghanistan also had implications for neighboring Pakistan. This predominantly Muslim nation had long-simmering problems with India, a primarily Hindu country, over Kashmir. These two nations' struggle for control over Kashmir (see **Map 26.8**) had sparked armed conflict several times over previous decades. The growing threat of terrorism made the area even more volatile. In 2002, the two sides again seemed on the verge of war. This time, however, both Pakistan and India had demonstrated to each other and the world their ability to use nuclear weapons. In 2008 a terrorist organization, apparently based in Pakistan, launched a deadly suicidal attack on one of India's major cities, Mumbai, an

Crisis over Kashmir

event that again threatened peace in the region. By the next year, the ability of Pakistan's central government to exercise control over the nation was in question, especially in its northern and western lands, where openly aggressive Taliban and pro-Taliban forces had found sanctuary and were gaining strength.

In various ways that drew the attention and involvement of the West, much of the Middle East, from the eastern shores of the Mediterranean to India, suffered from instability, threats of conflict, and outbreaks of violence. The turbulence was not simply about terrorism. Rather, the roots of these problems reach far back into the twentieth century and are entwined with the legacy of the West's imperialism, periodic wars within the region, the world's growing reliance on the area's oil deposits, and complex sectarian politics within Islamic states. But to many people around the world, it seemed clear that terrorism—and the conflicts, poverty, and political tensions that fueled it as well as reactions to it—had greater global significance than ever before. The images of peace and security that many people had envisioned after the fall of communism gave way to a new sense of vulnerability in a world that seemed to be slipping out of control.

MAP 26.8

Afghanistan, Kashmir, and South-Central Asia, 2002

This map shows Afghanistan, Kashmir, and the surrounding areas in 2002.

Explore the Map

1. What difficulties might there be in controlling conflicts in these areas?

2. What is strategically significant about this region?

3. Why might the conflict over Kashmir be of such importance to India, Pakistan, and the world community?

Across Borders: Cultural Conflict and Convergence

All these developments—in the Middle East, North Africa, and East Asia—revealed the West's inextricable ties with the non-Western world. They also posed new challenges to the dominance that the West had enjoyed for so long. Perhaps most important, they

illustrated a problem that spread well beyond any one region: the chafing of local cultures against global and even national influences. On one level, globalization meant the invasion of Western culture into centuries-old but vulnerable non-Western cultural legacies. **Figure 26.8** reveals this tenuous mixture and clash of cultures in Mexico. A descendant of the Olmecs, who once dominated parts of Mexico some three thousand years ago, prepares to dance as a jaguar to bring rain. The boy's clay-covered body is being stamped with ashes by an adult using a Coca-Cola bottle—one of the most recognized symbols of Western commerce. This image was soon transmitted by a Western photographer to a magazine with circulation in the millions, perhaps encouraging Western tourists and companies to invade this traditional culture even further. On another level, nationalism and religious fundamentalism revealed a deep resistance to globalization. The struggles of minorities to retain their own sense of identity in the face of demands for national and religious conformity within their own nations reflected a parallel resistance to

> Resistance to globalization

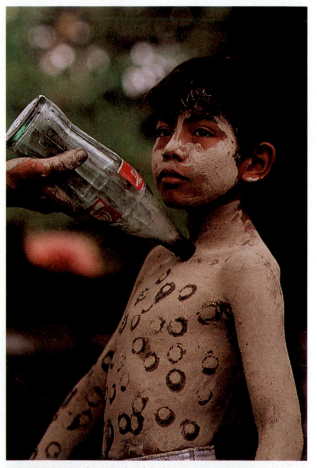

FIGURE 26.8 The Clash of Cultures In this striking photograph, a Coca-Cola bottle is used to prepare a boy, representing the ancient Olmec civilization, to dance as a jaguar to bring rain.

outside meddling. In one terrifying variation of this pattern, in the central African state of Rwanda, ethnic Hutu extremists slaughtered more than 500,000 ethnic Tutsi during the mid-1990s; fighting and civil war plagued the area for years. Another variation of this violence occurred in the western Sudan region of Darfur, where political disputes between Arabs and non-Arab rebels arose. Between 2004 and 2006, government-backed Arab militias carried out a systematic campaign that killed 300,000 non-Arab farmers and displaced two million people. In the West and elsewhere, these multilayered resentments and struggles formed a complex backdrop for other emerging developments.

While ethnic conflict and nationalism intensified in several parts of the globe, cultural differences among Western nations and between Western and non-Western peoples also softened with an increase in international contacts. People migrated in droves to the West and other wealthy areas of the world, such as the oil-rich Middle East, and crossed countless borders in the search for work. The new immigration opened doors for many people, but it also had its dark side. The opening of frontiers within Europe during the 1990s and the desperation of millions throughout the world made the movement of people difficult to control. Illegal immigration skyrocketed to more than 10 million people a year globally. For example, immigrants from Iran, Turkey, Iraq, Pakistan, Bangladesh, Albania, and elsewhere risked dangerous boat passages and expulsion to reach places such as Italy's long, exposed southern coast. "We lived like animals. . . . If we had not brought some biscuits and water, we would have starved," said a Kurdish immigrant in 1997. Some of the thousands who crossed North American borders each year—legally and illegally—told similar stories.

Germany in particular drew people from Turkey, Yugoslavia, Italy, Eastern Europe, and Russia and attracted asylum-seekers from many other parts of the world. In 1997, almost 9 percent of Germany's population were immigrants, many of whom remained unassimilated and yet alienated from their lands of origin. One Turkish woman who worked in her father's pizzeria in Berlin described the situation: "People like me are foreigners in Turkey. . . . There you are not a real Turk, and here you are not a complete German. We are somewhere in between." Her father agreed: "Even if I had a German passport, I would still feel like a foreigner and be regarded as a foreigner."

By 2010, some 20 million Muslims lived in Western Europe, many of whom were frustrated by bleak job prospects, outraged by discrimination, and yearning for a sense of respect. A French youth of Algerian descent living in one of the rough housing projects just outside of Paris explained: "You wake up every morning looking for work. But why? There isn't any." Like millions of other Arab and African immigrants and their French-born children and grandchildren, he had not been well integrated into French society. In 2005 and 2006, groups of young immigrants displayed their frustration in riots.

During these same decades, a common popular culture, especially among the youth in American, European, and non-Western cities, spread with increasing speed across all borders. The worldwide popularity of Hollywood movies, Disney products, soccer, Nintendo computer games, hamburgers, pizza, shopping malls, noodle soup, Nike shoes, Benetton clothes, TV series, and rock and roll all reflected this standardization of cultural tastes. The spread of English as the world's second language and the beaming of television shows across borders by satellite facilitated the convergence of cultures. No medium offered more potential for this crossing of cultural lines in the future than the Internet. Instantaneous electronic communication and access to burgeoning informational, commercial, and scientific resources on the World Wide Web seemed to have dissolved time and space as well as national borders, spawning what some observers called the "global village."

THE WEST AND THE WORLD

1991	Persian Gulf War
1992	Maastrich Treaty
1994	NAFTA created
	Mandela president of South Africa
1999	Euro introduced
2000	Palestinian uprisings
2001	Terrorist attacks in United States
	War in Afghanistan
2002	Kashmir crisis
	Terrorist bombing in Bali
2003	Invasion of Iraq
2004	Terrorist bombings in Madrid
	European Union adds ten new members
2005	Terrorist bombings in London
	Pope John Paul II dies
	France and the Netherlands reject new European constitution
2006	Israel invades Lebanon
2007	Power-sharing agreement in Northern Ireland
2009	Lisbon Treaty adopted

KEY DATES

FIGURE 26.9 Marco Ventura, *Mona Lisa Contemplating the Bust of Nefertiti as God Creates Order out of Chaos on a Starry Night on the Island of La Grande Jatte as the Infanta Margarita Looks On,* 1993 The artist used familiar masterpieces of Western art to suggest the blending of Western history and culture.

The easing of more traditional forms of travel also added to the meeting of cultures, particularly for middle-class tourists who journeyed throughout the world, visited museums, and absorbed at least visual images of different nations' cultural past and present. **Figure 26.9,** an illustration for the *Sophisticated Traveler* supplement to the *New York Times,* captures this sense of historical and cultural convergence. In this composite of six masterpieces of Western art, the artist makes a playful statement about the blending of Western cultures. Most of this image's components, which span three thousand years of Western history, are probably familiar to the millions of museum-going, "sophisticated" middle-class travelers for whom this magazine is intended.

Other cultural changes also set off the 1990s as unique. In the arts, what was once seen as modern in 1914 or even as late as mid-century—the glass skyscrapers and the abstract paintings of Mondrian and Pollock, for example—now seemed old and were taken for granted. Artistic and intellectual movements adopted the "postmodern" label. In the arts, followers of **postmodernism** became less concerned with austere principles. Architects, for example, rejected the pure forms and plain glass walls of the modern style in favor of buildings with elaborate shapes and ornamentation. Intellectuals and critics sympathetic to postmodernism attacked all ideologies—from liberalism to Marxism—and even the intellectual foundations of most academic disciplines as outmoded, oppressive distortions of the truth. Skeptical that

Postmodernism

objective truth was possible, they claimed that science itself was infected by the dominant values and beliefs of the culture that produced it.

Beyond Borders: Uncertainty and Opportunity in a Shrinking World

The spreading webs of communications and the goods and services radiating out from the West promised satisfactions galore for anyone who wanted to—and could afford to—participate. However, recessions during the 1980s and after 2000 reminded Westerners and non-Westerners alike that economic growth could not be taken for granted. Despite the West's overall prosperity, inflation and declining personal incomes for the bottom half of society spawned social discontent in these decades. In most of Europe, unemployment continued to hover above 10 percent and reached as high as 20 percent during the 1990s. Unions everywhere lost membership and clout, leaving more workers than ever without protection in a shifting, competitive marketplace.

In addition, with international economic ties proliferating, problems in one area of the world quickly made themselves felt in other regions. For example, the financial crisis and economic turmoil that struck Asia in 1998 spread rapidly, creating huge losses for investors and trading partners throughout the world. In 2008, another financial crisis, this time much more serious and combined with a collapse of real estate values, struck the United States. Repercussions quickly spread to Europe and around the globe, leading to what some economists have called the worst financial crisis, economic crisis, and recession since the Great Depression of the 1930s. Tens of millions of people lost their jobs, stock markets plunged, and bankruptcies felled large corporations and financial institutions. Trying to stem the losses, governments from the United States to Europe and China intervened massively in their economies.

Oil presented another long-term problem that spilled across borders in recent decades. Economic development in the West and elsewhere heightened demand for energy derived from oil and natural gas. Most Western nations consume far more oil than they produce, and nations with rising economies such as China and India want the oil-fueled wealth enjoyed in the West. In a competitive international arena, they vie for supplies from major producers such as Saudi Arabia, Iran, Iraq, Russia, Venezuela, and Nigeria. Webs of politics, arms, money, and influence surround this growing international need for oil. More insidiously, the divisions between rich and poor presented pressing across-borders dilemmas. The relatively affluent West, with its multinational corporations, could no longer ignore

Growing international economic ties

MAP 26.9

The Growth of Cities

This map shows those areas with the largest urban populations and the growth of population in the world's largest cities.

Explore the Map

1. Where has the greatest growth of large cities occurred?

2. What cities are expected to grow the most?

3. What problems might this growth in urban populations pose for the West and the world?

nations scourged by crushing debts, pressing economic needs, and unmet demands. The evolving global economic landscape added to the uncertainty. Despite the rise of East Asia and India, the gap between the affluent, industrialized nations of the northern latitudes and the poorer, developing nations of the south widened. Incomes in most nations in sub-Saharan Africa and Latin America actually declined from 1960s levels. In 2005, more than two billion people in the world subsisted on the equivalent of less than $1 per day.

As world population in 2010 approached seven billion—more than double that at the end of World War II—the poorer southern half of the globe carried the heaviest burden of population growth. **Figure 26.10** shows population changes for major areas of the world since 1900 and estimates population figures for the mid-twenty-first century. Europe, with declining birthrates, will experience a drop in population, while Asia and Africa will gain the most. Many Western nations—

particularly the United States—have relied on immigration to bolster population figures.

The distinction between Europe and the rest of the world in population trends is also reflected in the process of urbanization (see **Map 26.9**). Although the wealthy areas of the West once experienced the most rapid urban growth, other parts of the world gained the lead during the second half of the twentieth century. Moreover, in 1950, six out of the ten largest cities were in Europe and the U.S.; by 2000, most of the world's largest cities were in the non-Western world, a trend likely to grow in the future.

Economic growth, population increases, and urbanization created alarming environmental problems in the late twentieth century (see **Map 26.10**). The earth's air, water, and seas became more and more polluted, while acid rain, caused by smoke and fumes, damaged more than one-third of Germany's remaining forests. Great rivers such as the

Environmental costs

NORTH AMERICA

ATLANTIC OCEAN

EUROPE

ASIA

Unregulated industrial pollution in former communist nations of Eastern Europe.

Great Lakes

Black Sea *Caspian Sea*

AFRICA

EQUATOR

PACIFIC OCEAN

SOUTH AMERICA

ATLANTIC OCEAN

INDIAN OCEAN

EQUATOR

AUSTRALIA

Ozone depletion, caused by industrial and household chemicals, creates "ozone holes" over southern regions.

0 — 5000 mi
0 — 1000 km

ANTARCTICA

Overfishing leads to sharp drop in fish catch since 1970s

Clear-cutting of old-growth and tropical forests threatens ecosystems, increases risk of erosion

Areas at high risk of becoming desert

Areas where farmland might not supply enough food for growing population

Areas where acid in soil and water could damage the environment

Areas with too little wood for fuel

Coastal areas vulnerable to rising sea level from global warming

MAP 26.10

Global Environmental Problems

This map focuses on various widespread environmental problems confronting the world today, most of which stem from industrialization, the exploitation of natural resources, urbanization, and population increases.

Explore the Map

1. Which areas of the world are most affected by environmental problems?

2. How interconnected are these difficulties?

3. What environmental problems are not adequately revealed by this map?

4. What steps might world leaders take to diminish the present and future impact of these problems?

MAJOR AREA	1900	1950	2000	2050
		Population (in millions)		
Asia	947	1402	3672	5428
Africa	133	221	794	2000
Europe	408	547	727	603
Latin America	74	167	579	806
North America	82	172	389	438
Oceania	6	13	31	47
World (total)	1650	2522	6192	9322

FIGURE 26.10 Population Changes Across the Twentieth and Twenty-first Centuries

Rhine and the Danube became like sewers, and waters such as the Mediterranean and Black seas were fouled by runoff from industrial sites and cities. Even the monuments of ancient Greece and Rome were rapidly deteriorating and crumbling from the onslaught of fumes and vibrations of city life. In Eastern Europe and the Soviet Union, environmental problems had been virtually ignored for decades. The collapse of communism in those areas revealed staggering environmental degradation. In many Western countries, the growing importance of Green parties pushed environmental concerns into the political spotlight.

As **Map 26.10** shows, environmental problems extended well beyond the West. Thirteen of the fifteen cities with the worst air pollution in the world were in Asia. Of the estimated 2.7 million people worldwide who died each year from illnesses caused by air pollution, the majority were Asians. Each year, Asia lost 1 percent of its forests. As humanity consumed more and more resources and disrupted the globe's natural balance, thousands of plant and animal species became extinct each year. Humanity's need for more and more energy also led many nations to rely increasingly on nuclear power. The 1986 accident at the Chernobyl plant in the Soviet Union shed new light on the potential dangers of nuclear power—the accident released two hundred times the radiation of the two bombs dropped in World War II.

Many observers believe that **global warming** has become our most threatening environmental problem. Most scientists agree that in recent decades the Earth's atmosphere has heated up

Global warming

at an alarming rate, in great part thanks to the heat-trapping so-called greenhouse gases, such as carbon dioxide, that have been created through the combustion of coal and petroleum products. Factories, power plants, urban growth, and gas-guzzling motor vehicles in the West and in rapidly developing nations such as China and India add to those greenhouse gases every day. According to most scientists, the warming process is probably irreversible and, unless slowed by policies that crucial nations seem unwilling to adopt, could produce dramatic climate changes, resulting in the melting of ice sheets and glaciers, coastal flooding, widening droughts, worsening hurricanes, and rapid extinction of plant and animal species by the end of this century. **Figure 26.11** shows one example of the many glaciers that have been melting throughout the world. On the top is a photograph of the Muir Glacier in Alaska taken in August 1941. On the bottom is a photograph taken from the same vantage point in August 2004. The glacier had retreated more than seven miles, allowing ocean water to fill the valley. What remained of the glacier, now in the distance, had thinned by more than 875 yards. Some experts feel that such dramatic environmental developments will diminish or destroy our ability to sustain Earth's population. Climate-induced food shortages, mass migrations, and possible pandemics could destabilize entire regions of the world. Global warming is "the single biggest challenge facing the planet, the equal in every way to the nuclear threat that transfixed us during the past half-century and a threat we haven't even begun to deal with," warned one distinguished scientist.

People have turned to science and government to solve these environmental problems, but thus far the results have been mixed at best. On the one hand, scientists and governmental officials finally recognized the severity of these problems and have begun to address them by committing more funds to

FIGURE 26.11 Global Warming, 1941–2004 Two photographs of Muir Glacier, Alaska, in 1941 (top) and 2004 (bottom) reveal the signs of global warming.

research and coming to agreements on new regulations to minimize the damage (see Document 26.3). On the other hand, anxieties about the environment have often conflicted with a stronger desire of many people for continued economic growth. Businesses and governments, reflecting this desire, have often proved reluctant to commit to expensive environmental-protection programs.

Like the environment, health issues have also received an ambivalent response. In the last few decades of the twentieth century, many officials and commentators recognized that an aging population, particularly in the West, presented a growing health problem that would

AIDS

strain medical facilities and budgets, but they were unsure what to do. With certain health problems—the worldwide AIDS (acquired immune deficiency syndrome) epidemic is just one example—recognition of the dangers came too late. Even then, many efforts to address such crises proved halfhearted. Again, AIDS is an apt example. Between 1978 and 2006, 26 million people died from this disease. AIDS became the most deadly epidemic in recent global

FIGURE 26.12

Charles Michael Helmken, *Loveaidspeople*, 1989

This poster shows two figures lovingly aiding the Christian martyr Saint Sebastian as the saint, having been wounded by many arrows, looks up desperately for help. The poster was designed to increase public awareness of AIDS and to address negative attitudes toward individuals affected by AIDS.

Connecting Art & Society

1. How do you explain the meaning of the title *Loveaidspeople*? How has the artist interpreted the title in his depiction?

2. Why might the artist have chosen to feature the Christian martyr Saint Sebastian in this poster?

3. How, as a viewer, do you interpret the details and colors in this poster?

history, yet many people initially denied its existence or criticized those who had contracted it. The AIDS poster in **Figure 26.12**, *Loveaidspeople*, uses Renaissance painter Tanzio da Varallo's painting of the Christian martyr Saint Sebastian to protest these attitudes. In this poignant image, a modern-day AIDS victim has been wounded by the "arrows" of officials and social attitudes that condemn both the third-century martyr and the twentieth-century AIDS victim as morally dirty and sinful. The poster makes an urgent plea for assistance for AIDS sufferers. After several years, some help began to arrive, but not nearly enough. In 2006, the United Nations estimated that 40 million people in the world were living with AIDS or HIV, the virus that causes AIDS. In some sub-Saharan countries of Africa, one in four adults were infected.

In the face of frightening diseases, environmental degradation, economic uncertainty, and devastating weaponry, many people looked to the new century with cynicism or dread. Some found it all too easy to imagine even the violent destruction of all life on Earth, as **Figure 26.13** suggests. This painting, by American artist Jennifer Bartlett, shows a firestorm sweeping away everything in its path. Sculptural objects are dashed to the floor between the viewer and the canvas. In a world that still had unimaginably destructive weapons of war at its fingertips, this scene may well have offered a visual warning of the potential for holocaust that hung over the West and the rest of the world as the twenty-first century began.

Perhaps in response to these anxieties, the last two decades of the twentieth century saw a renewal of religious commitment among many people. In the United States and Europe, evangelical Christianity—with its emphasis on personal salvation and spiritual experience—became the fastest-growing religious movement. In Russia, an outpouring of religious sentiment within the Orthodox Church followed the collapse of communism. Islamic fundamentalism, calling for a return to traditional ways and a rejection of alien ideologies, intensified in lands from West Africa to East Asia. All of these movements reflected a hunger for a sense of meaning and a clarity of values by which to live in an uncertain time.

Movements of religious revival

Yet, despite these anxieties, there were also reasons to look to the coming century with hope and optimism. After all, the West had surmounted major obstacles. It had enjoyed more than sixty years of relative peace and had managed to avert the dreaded clash of superpowers during the Cold War. In Eastern Europe, most nations had gained their long-sought independence with a minimum of violence. In some areas, seemingly hopeless problems

Accomplishments and optimism

DOCUMENTS

The Copenhagen Accord on Climate Change

While many scientists have long warned about the dangers of global warming, only in recent years has the international community recognized the gravity of the problem. Building on earlier conferences, the United Nations organized a major conference on climate change in Copenhagen, Denmark, late in 2009. The following are excerpts from the resulting Copenhagen Accord.

We underline that climate change is one of the greatest challenges of our time. We emphasise our strong political will to urgently combat climate change in accordance with the principle of common but differentiated responsibilities and respective capabilities. To achieve the ultimate objective of the Convention to stabilize greenhouse gas concentration in the atmosphere at a level that would prevent dangerous anthropogenic interference with the climate system, we shall, recognizing the scientific view that the increase in global temperature should be below 2 degrees Celsius, on the basis of equity and in the context of sustainable development, enhance our long-term cooperative action to combat climate change. We recognize the critical impacts of climate change and the potential impacts of response measures on countries particularly vulnerable to its adverse effects and stress the need to establish a comprehensive adaptation programme including international support. . . .

Enhanced action and international cooperation on adaptation is urgently required, . . . especially in those [countries] that are particularly vulnerable, especially least developed countries, small island developing States and Africa. We agree that developed countries shall provide adequate, predictable and sustainable financial resources, technology and capacity-building to support the implementation of adaptation action in developing countries.

SOURCE: Governmental document in public domain.

Analyze the Document

1. What goals does this agreement set?

2. In what ways, and why, does the accord make distinctions between developed and less developed countries?

3. Many observers were disappointed with the results because the accord did not mandate change. Why might some countries be unwilling to accept legally binding actions to stem global warming?

---

showed signs of being solved. For example, in Northern Ireland, Protestants and Catholics created a power-sharing government, ending a decades-long bitter conflict.

For many people around the world, the standard of living had risen to unprecedented levels. In Asia, for example, increasing prosperity had lifted some 400 million people out of abject poverty. Between 1999 and 2008, the global economy doubled. Although social equality still remained only an ideal, the Western promise of continually improving well-being for everyone seemed to hold firm. The increasing human life span and rising numbers of elderly—in part thanks to the global increase in food production and better access to health care—attested to that well-being. Moreover, many women gained access to opportunities once available only to men: By the late 1990s, roughly equal numbers of women and men in the West received higher education and pursued paying careers. Women's presence in professional life and in politics continued to grow. True, traditionalists worried about the destruction of the family as an institution, citing the growing prevalence of two-career parents, a rise in cohabitation and single motherhood, and accelerating divorce rates. Nevertheless, family structures

FIGURE 26.13 Jennifer Bartlett, *Spiral: An Ordinary Evening in New Haven*, 1989 Contemporary artists have sometimes focused on the growing popular concern that all life on earth could be violently destroyed in the near future.

persisted, although many of them took new forms, such as "an emotionally bound partnership."

Continuing scientific discoveries suggested that the West and the rest of the world could look forward to dramatic developments in the future. Perhaps most

thinking about
SCIENCE & TECHNOLOGY

FIGURE 26.14 The CERN Hadron Collider

CERN

What gives matter its mass? What makes up the invisible 96 percent of the universe? These are two of the fundamental research questions being investigated by the European Organization for Nuclear Research (CERN). Located in Switzerland but spilling over the border into France, this is the world's largest particle physics laboratory. Ideas for the international organization first surfaced in the 1940s. Finally established in 1954 by eleven Western European countries, CERN now includes twenty European member states and many more observer nations. The organization employs some 8,000 scientists who split their time between the main CERN site and hundreds of universities and national laboratories in their home countries. The dual goals of projects such as those conducted by CERN are to advance knowledge and, in doing so, to set the stage for later practical applications to life.

One of CERN's best-known achievements was the invention of the World Wide Web in 1989. Originally designed to enable scientists in different institutes and universities to share information, the Web was expanded to a world audience in 1993. CERN's new, extremely expensive Large Hadron Collider, shown in **Figure 26.14,** is a current worldwide scientific cooperation project. Sixteen miles in circumference and buried 300 yards underground, the massive collider will be used to study the subatomic world and the nature of the universe in all its vastness. Computers around the world will process information from the Collider experiments, which perhaps will lead to yet-unimagined applications.

CERN represents another extension of the connections among science, universities, and governments we examined in Chapter 21, as well as the growth of big science, discussed in Chapter 25.

Connecting Science & Society

1. In what ways does CERN represent big science?

2. What are some effects that the World Wide Web has had on peoples around the world?

3. Do you think that projects as costly as those undertaken by CERN can be justified only if they lead to practical applications such as the World Wide Web? Explain.

4. How might the rise of organizations such as CERN reflect globalization?

stunning was the prospect of changes stemming from the decoding of the human genome—determining the chemical sequence of the DNA in every cell of the human body. In 2001, this costly, long-term project carried out by hundreds of scientists in six countries was completed. With this "blueprint" of human life, scientists hoped to revolutionize medicine and gain new insights into human nature. Another international organization, CERN (see Thinking About Science & Technology), has been conducting research into the nature of matter.

Overall, the West has gained a much needed appreciation of its place in the world, and human beings around the globe have new tools to understand themselves within a widening universe. Technology, trade, and instant communications provide growing opportunities for cooperation across national boundaries. As the second decade of the twenty-first century opens, life offers more options to more people than ever.

LOOKING BACK & MOVING FORWARD

Summary   In 1989, history in the West abruptly shifted course. The communist regimes in Eastern Europe fell, severing these nations' ties to the Soviet Union and sparking unprecedented political and economic reforms. Two years later, the Soviet Union itself disintegrated. The Cold War ended and along with it, a sharply defined historical era stretching back to 1914. The end of the Cold War renewed the commitment to democracy and capitalism in the West, accelerated the existing movement toward unification in Europe, and left the United States standing as the sole military superpower in the world.

But the collapse of communism did not end all the anxieties present during the Cold War era. The transition in Eastern Europe and the Soviet Union proved rocky, and Westerners realized that despite their lofty global position, they could no longer keep the rest of the world at arm's length. Indeed, the West's global status began to change, as statistics reveal. In 1950, some 30 percent of the world's population lived in Europe and North America. In 2010, that figure dropped below 15 percent. As peoples around the world interacted more and more, cultures mingled, producing both conflict and convergence; our time may mark the beginning of a new global society. The relentless human desire for limitless economic growth and material security also left its mark on the environment in ways that spread concern across national boundaries. Western civilization, so long centered on the western tip of the Eurasian continent, now seemed to be just one of many lights shining on this shrinking globe. As one era closed and another opened, great challenges faced all of humanity. Whether and how the West—and the world— would embrace these challenges remained to be seen.

KEY TERMS

perestroika,   *p. 813*
glasnost,   *p. 813*
ethnic cleansing,   *p. 821*
European Union (EU),   *p. 824*
Euro,   *p. 824*
North American Free Trade Agreement (NAFTA),   *p. 824*
globalization,   *p. 826*
al-Qaeda,   *p. 827*
preemptive war,   *p. 830*
unilateralism,   *p. 830*
postmodernism,   *p. 834*
global warming,   *p. 837*

REVIEW, ANALYZE, & CONNECT TO TODAY

REVIEW THE PREVIOUS CHAPTER

Chapter 25—"Superpower Struggles and Global Transformations"—analyzed the Cold War competition between the United States and the Soviet Union. Within the Cold War context, the recovery of the West and end of colonialism were analyzed.

1. How might you argue that developments since 1989 are not the begining of a new historical era and that, instead, they are a continuation of trends that first emerged in the post–World War II decades?

2. Do you think that the collapse of communism and the end of the Cold War should have been predictable by the early 1980s? Why?

ANALYZE THIS CHAPTER

Chapter 26—"Into the Twenty-First Century"—traces the collapse of communism and the intense interaction between the Western and non-Western worlds.

1. Analyze the consequences of the collapse of communism outside Eastern Europe and the Soviet Union.

2. In what ways has much of Europe become integrated, and what steps remain to achieve full integration?

3. What forces are pulling the world together? How do these forces compare with those dividing the world?

CONNECT TO TODAY

It is always difficult to predict the future, but history can sometimes provide grounds for reasonable guesses.

1. In the near future, what might be the consequences of continuing steps toward the unification of Europe?

2. From a historical perspective, what consequences might flow from the financial crisis and recession that began in 2008?

3. Judging from developments since 1989, which problems do you think will prove the most serious in the years to come? Why? Do you think there is good reason for optimism? Why or why not?

BEYOND THE CLASSROOM

THE COLLAPSE OF COMMUNISM

Garton Ash, Timothy. *In Europe's Name: Germany and the Divided Continent.* London: Jonathan Cape, 1993. Stresses the history of tensions between East and West Germany as background to their reunification.

Lucas, Edward. *The New Cold War: Putin's Russia and the Threat to the West.* London: Palgrave, 2008. A challenging interpretation of recent developments in Russia.

Remnick, David. *Lenin's Tomb: The Last Days of the Soviet Empire.* New York: Random House, 1994. Journalistic coverage of the final period before the collapse of the Soviet empire, stressing the role played by Yeltsin.

Service, Robert. *Russia: Experiment with a People.* Cambridge, MA: Harvard University Press, 2003. Solid, scholarly coverage of Russia from 1991 until the early 2000s.

Silber, Laura, and Allan Little. *Yugoslavia: Death of a Nation.* New York: TV Books/Penguin USA, 1996. An account of the nation's ethnic troubles.

Stokes, Gale. *The Walls Came Tumbling Down: The Collapse of Communism in Eastern Europe.* Oxford: Oxford University Press, 1993. Analyzes the decline and fall of communism in Eastern Europe between 1968 and 1991.

REPERCUSSIONS AND REALIGNMENTS IN THE WEST

Caplan, Richard, and John Feffer, eds. *Europe's New Nationalism: States and Minorities in Conflict.* New York: Oxford University Press, 1996. A collection of essays by scholars on the growth of nationalism in Europe after the collapse of communism.

Cheles, Juciano, et al., eds. *The Far Right in Western and Eastern Europe,* 2nd ed. London: Longman, 1995. A comparative study of fringe movements in these areas.

Dinan, Desmond. *Europe Recast: A History of the European Union.* New York: Lynne Rienner Publishers, 2003. A well-written overview.

THE WORLD AND THE WEST FROM A GLOBAL PERSPECTIVE

Cohen, Daniel. *Globalization and Its Enemies*. Boston: MIT Press, 2006. A brilliant discussion of the promises and problems of globalization in a broad historical context.

Friedman, Thomas L. *The Lexus and the Olive Tree*. New York: Farrar, Straus, Giroux, 1999. An engaging, boldly interpretive analysis of globalism.

Kolbert, Elizabeth. *Field Notes from a Catastrophe: Man, Nature, and Climate Change*. New York: Bloomsbury Publishing, 2006. A very well-written, well-documented account.

Mandelbaum, Michael. *The Case for Goliath: How America Acts as the World's Government in the 21st Century*. New York: Perseus, 2005. A sharp, challenging interpretation of America's changing role in world affairs.

McNeill, J.R. *Something New Under the Sun: An Environmental History of the Twentieth-Century World*. New York: W.W. Norton, 2000. An important union of historical and environmental perspectives.

Rashid, Ahmed. *Descent into Chaos: The United States and the Failure of Nation Building in Pakistan, Afghanistan, and Central Asia*. New York: Viking Penguin, 2008. A disturbing, critical interpretation.

Note to users: Terms that are foreign or difficult to pronounce are transcribed in parentheses directly after the term itself. The transcriptions are based on the rules of English spelling; that is, they are similar to the transcriptions employed in the *Webster* dictionaries. Each word's most heavily stressed syllable is marked by an acute accent.

A

Absolute monarch (máh-nark) A seventeenth- or eighteenth-century European monarch claiming complete political authority.

Absolutism (áb-suh-loo-tism) (Royal) A government in which all power is vested in the ruler.

Abstract expressionism (ex-présh-un-ism) A twentieth-century painting style infusing nonrepresentational art with strong personal feelings.

Acropolis (uh-króp-uh-liss) The hill at the center of Athens on which the magnificent temples—including the Parthenon—that made the architecture of ancient Athens famous are built.

Act of Union Formal unification of England and Scotland in 1707.

Afrikaners Afrikaans-speaking South Africans of Dutch and other European ancestry.

Age of Reason The eighteenth-century Enlightenment; sometimes includes seventeenth-century science and philosophy.

Agora In ancient Greece, the marketplace or place of public assembly.

Agricultural revolution Neolithic discovery of agriculture; agricultural transformations that began in eighteenth-century western Europe.

Ahura Mazda In Zoroastrianism, the beneficial god of light.

Ahriman In Zoroastrianism, the evil god of darkness.

Akkadian (uh-káy-dee-un) A Semitic language of a region of ancient Mesopotamia.

Albigensians (al-buh-jén-see-unz) A medieval French heretical sect that believed in two gods—an evil and a good principle—that was destroyed in a crusade in the thirteenth century; also called Cathars.

Alchemy (ál-kuh-mee) The medieval study and practice of chemistry, primarily concerned with changing metals into gold and finding a universal remedy for diseases. It was much practiced from the thirteenth to the seventeenth century.

Allies (ál-eyes) The two alliances against Germany and its partners in World War I and World War II.

Al-Qaeda A global terrorist network headed by Osama bin Laden.

Anarchists (ánn-ar-kissts) Those advocating or promoting anarchy, or an absence of government. In the late nineteenth and early twentieth centuries, anarchism arose as an ideology and movement against all governmental authority and private property.

Ancien régime (áwn-syáwn ráy-zhéem) The traditional political and social order in Europe before the French Revolution.

Antigonids (ann-tíg-un-idz) Hellenistic dynasty that ruled in Macedonia from about 300 B.C.E. to about 150 B.C.E.

Anti-Semitism (ann-tye-sém-i-tism) Prejudice against Jews.

Apartheid "Separation" in the Afrikaans language. A policy to rigidly segregate people by color in South Africa, 1948–1989.

Appeasement Attempting to satisfy potential aggressors in order to avoid war.

Aramaic (air-uh-máy-ik) A northwest Semitic language that spread throughout the region. It was the language that Jesus spoke.

Archon (áhr-kahn) A chief magistrate in ancient Athens.

Areopagus (air-ee-áh-pa-gus) A prestigious governing council of ancient Athens.

Arête (ah-ray-táy) Greek term for the valued virtues of manliness, courage, and excellence.

Arianism (áir-ee-un-ism) A fourth-century Christian heresy that taught that Jesus was not of the same substance as God the father, and thus had been created.

Assemblies, Roman Institutions in the Roman Republic that functioned as the legislative branch of government.

Assignats (ah-seen-yáh) Paper money issued in the National Assembly during the French Revolution.

Astrolabe (áss-tro-leyb) Medieval instrument used to determine the altitudes of celestial bodies.

Augury (áh-gur-ee) The art or practice of foretelling events though signs or omens.

Autocracy (au-tóc-ra-cee) Government under the rule of an authoritarian ruler.

Autocrat (áuto-crat) An authoritarian ruler.

Axis World War II alliance whose main members were Germany, Italy, and Japan.

B

Baby boom The increase in births following World War II.

Babylonian Captivity Period during the fourteenth century in which seven popes chose to reside in Avignon instead of Rome. Critics called this period the "Babylonian Captivity" of the papacy.

Bailiffs Medieval French salaried officials hired by the king to collect taxes and represent his interests.

Balance of power Distribution of power among states, or the policy of creating alliances to control powerful states.

Balkans States in the Balkan Peninsula, including Albania, Bulgaria, Greece, Romania, and Yugoslavia.

Baroque (ba-róak) An artistic style of the sixteenth and seventeenth centuries stressing rich ornamentation and dynamic movement; in music, a style marked by strict forms and elaborate ornamentation.

Bastard feudalism (feúd-a-lism) Late medieval corruption of the feudal system replacing feudal loyalty with cash payments.

Bastille (bas-téel) The royal prison symbolizing the old regime that was destroyed in the French Revolution.

Bauhaus (bóugh-house) An influential school of art emphasizing clean, functional lines founded in Germany by the architect Walter Gropius just after World War I.

Bedouin (béd-oh-in) An Arab of any of the nomadic tribes of the deserts of North Africa, Arabia, and Syria.

Berlin airlift The airborne military operation organized to supply Berlin's Western-occupied sectors during the Soviet Union's 1948 Berlin blockage.

Berlin Wall The wall erected in 1961 to divide East and West Berlin.

Bessemer (béss-uh-mer) **process** A method for removing impurities from molten iron.

Black Death Name given the epidemic that swept Europe beginning in 1348. Most historians agree that the main disease was bubonic plague, but the Black Death may have incorporated many other diseases.

Blackshirts Mussolini's black-uniformed Fascist paramilitary forces in the 1920s and 1930s.

Blitzkrieg (blíts-kreeg) "Lightning war," a rapid air and land military assault used by the Germans in World War II.

Boers (boars) Dutch settlers in south Africa.

Bolshevik (bówl-shuh-vick) "Majority faction," the Leninist wing of the Russian Marxist Party; after 1917, the Communist Party.

Bourgeoisie (boor-zhwa-zée) The middle class.

Boxers A nineteenth-century Chinese secret society that believed in the spiritual power of the martial arts and fought against Chinese Christians and foreigners in China.

Boyar A Russian noble.

Brezhnev (bréhzh-nyeff) **Doctrine** Policy that justified Soviet intervention in order to ensure the survival of socialism in another state, initiated by USSR leader Brezhnev in 1968.

Brownshirts Hitler's brown-uniformed paramilitary force in the 1920s and 1930s.

Burschenschaften (bóor-shen-shahf-ten) Liberal nationalist German student unions during the early nineteenth century.

C

Cabinet system Government by a prime minister and heads of governmental bureaus developed by Britain during the eighteenth century.

Caesaropapism (see-zer-oh-pápe-ism) The practice of having the same person rule both the state and the church.

Cahiers (kye-yéah) Lists of public grievances sent to the French Estates General in 1789.

Caliph (káy-liff) A title meaning "successor to the Prophet" given to Muslim rulers who combined political authority with religious power.

Capitalists Those promoting an economic system characterized by freedom of the market with private and corporate ownership of the means of production and distribution that are operated for profit.

Capitularies (ka-pít-chew-làir-eez) Royal laws issued by Charlemagne and the Carolingians.

Caravel (care-uh-véll) A small, light sailing ship of the kind used by the Spanish and Portuguese in the fifteenth and sixteenth centuries.

Carbonari (car-bun-áh-ree) A secret society of revolutionaries in nineteenth-century Italy.

Cartel (car-téll) An alliance of corporations designed to control the marketplace.

Cartesian (car-tée-zhen) **dualism** A philosophy developed by René Descartes in the seventeenth century that defines two kinds of reality: the mind, or subjective thinking, and the body, or objective physical matter.

Catacombs Underground burial places. The term originally referred to the early Christian burial locations in Rome and elsewhere.

Cathars (cáth-arz) A medieval French dualist heretical sect; also called Albigensians.

Central Powers World War I alliance, primarily of Germany, Austria, and the Ottoman Empire.

Centuriate (sen-chúr-ee-ate) **Assembly** An aristocratic ruling body in ancient Rome that made the laws.

Chancellor A high-ranking official—in Germany, the prime minister.

Chartists English reformers of the 1830s and 1840s who demanded political and social rights for the lower classes.

Checks and balances A balanced division of governmental power among different institutions.

Chivalry (shív-el-ree) Code of performance and ethics for medieval knights. It can also refer to the demonstration of knightly virtues.

Christian humanists During the fifteenth and sixteenth centuries, experts in Greek, Latin, and Hebrew who studied the Bible and other Christian writings in order to understand the correct meaning of early Christian texts.

Civil Constitution of the Clergy New rules nationalizing and governing the clergy enacted during the French Revolution.

Civic humanists Those practicing a branch of humanism that promoted the value of responsible citizenship in which people work to improve their city-states.

Classical style A seventeenth- and eighteenth-century cultural style emphasizing restraint and balance, and following models from ancient Greece and Rome.

Cold War The global struggle between alliances headed by the United States and the Soviet Union during the second half of the twentieth century.

Collectivization The Soviet policy of taking agricultural lands and decisions away from individual owners and placing them in the hands of elected managers and party officials.

Comecon (cómm-ee-con) The economic organization of communist eastern European states during the Cold War.

Committee of Public Safety Ruling committee of twelve leaders during the French Revolutionary period of the Terror.

Common law Laws that arise from customary use rather than from legislation.

Common market The European Economic Community, a union of Western European nations initiated in 1957 to promote common economic policies.

Commonwealth of Independent States A loose confederation of several former republics of the disintegrated Soviet Union founded in 1991.

Commune (cómm-yune) A medieval or early modern town; a semi-independent city government or socialistic community in the nineteenth and twentieth centuries.

Communist Manifesto A short, popular treatise written by Karl Marx and Friedrich Engels in 1848 that contained the fundamentals of their "scientific socialism."

Complutensian Polyglot (comm-plue-tén-see-an pólly-glàht) **Bible** An edition of the Bible written in 1520 that had three columns that compared the Hebrew, Greek, and Latin versions.

Compurgation (comm-pur-gáy-shun) A Germanic legal oath taken by twelve men testifying to the character of the accused.

Concert of Europe The alliance of powers after 1815 created to maintain the status quo and coordinate international relations.

Conciliar (conn-síll-ee-ar) **movement** The belief that the Catholic Church should be led by councils of cardinals rather than popes.

Concordat (conn-córe-dat) A formal agreement, especially between the pope and a government, for the regulation of church affairs.

condottieri (conn-duh-tyáy-ree) From the fourteenth to the sixteenth century, captains of bands of mercenary soldiers, influential in Renaissance Italy.

Congress of Vienna The peace conference held between 1814 and 1815 in Vienna after the defeat of Napoleon.

Conquistadors (conn-kéy-stah-doors) Spanish adventurers in the sixteenth century who went to South and Central America to conquer indigenous peoples and claim their lands.

Conservatism An ideology stressing order and traditional values.

Constitutionalism The idea that political authority rests in written law, not in the person of an absolute monarch.

Constitutional monarchy Government in which the monarch's powers are limited by a set of fundamental laws.

Consuls (cónn-sul) The appointed chief executive officers of the Roman Republic.

Containment The Cold War strategy of the United States to limit the expansion and influence of the Soviet Union.

Continental System Napoleon's policy of preventing trade between continental Europe and Great Britain.

Contra posto (cón-tra páh-sto) A stance of the human body in which one leg bears weight, while the other is relaxed. Also known as counterpoise, it was popular in Renaissance sculpture.

Copernican (co-pér-nick-an) **revolution** The change from an earth-centered to a sun-centered universe initiated by Copernicus in the sixteenth century.

Corinthian order One of three architectural systems developed by the Greeks to decorate their buildings. The Corinthian order is marked by the capitals of columns decorated with acanthus leaves.

Corn Laws British laws that imposed tariffs on grain imports.

Corporate state Mussolini's economic and political machinery to manage the Italian economy and settle issues between labor and management.

Corsair A swift pirate ship.

Cossacks The "free warriors" of southern Russia, noted as cavalrymen.

Cottage industry Handicraft manufacturing usually organized by merchants and performed by rural people in their cottages.

Coup d'état (coo-day-táh) A sudden taking of power that violates constitutional forms by a group of persons in authority.

Creoles (crée-ohlz) People of European descent born in the West Indies or Spanish America, often of mixed ancestry.

Crusades From the late eleventh century through the thirteenth century, Europeans sent a number of military operations to take the Holy Land (Jerusalem and its surrounding territory) from the Muslims. These military ventures in the name of Christendom are collectively called the Crusades.

Cult of sensibility The eighteenth-century emphasis on emotion and nature forwarded by several European artists and authors.

Cuneiform (cue-née-uh-form) A writing system using wedge-shaped characters developed in ancient Mesopotamia.

Curia Regis (kóo-ree-uh régg-ees) A medieval king's advisory body made up of his major vassals.

Cynicism (sín-uh-sism) A Hellenistic philosophy that locates the search for virtue in an utter indifference to worldly needs.

Cyrillic (suh-ríll-ik) **alphabet** An old Slavic alphabet presently used in modified form for Russian and other languages.

D

Dada (dáh-dah) An early twentieth-century artistic movement that attacked traditional cultural styles and stressed the absence of purpose in life.

Dauphin (dough-fán) Heir to the French throne. The title was used from 1349 to 1830.

D-Day The day of the Allied invasion of Normandy in World War II—June 6, 1944.

Decembrists (dee-sém-brists) Russian army officers who briefly rebelled against Tsar Nicholas I in December 1925.

Decolonization The loss of colonies by imperial powers during the years following World War II.

Declaration of the Rights of Man and Citizen France's revolutionary 1789 declaration of rights stressing liberty, equality, and fraternity.

Deductive reasoning Deriving conclusions that logically flow from a premise, reasoning from basic or known truths.

Deism (dée-iz-um) Belief in a God who created the universe and its natural laws but does not intervene further; gained popularity during the Enlightenment.

Demotic A form of ancient Egyptian writing used for ordinary life. A simplified form of hieratic script.

Détente (day-táhnt) The period of relative cooperation between Cold War adversaries during the 1960s and 1970s.

Devotio moderno (day-vóh-tee-oh moh-dáir-noh) A medieval religious movement that emphasized internal spirituality over ritual practices.

Diaspora The dispersion of the Jews after the Babylonian conquest in the sixth century B.C.E. The term comes from the Greek word meaning "to scatter."

Diet The general legislative assembly of certain countries, such as Poland.

Directory The relatively conservative government during the last years of the French Revolution before Napoleon gained power.

Division of labor The division of work in the modern process of industrial production into separate tasks.

Doge (dóhj) The chief magistrate of the Republic of Venice during the Middle Ages and Renaissance.

Domesday (dóomz-day) **Book** A record of all the property and holdings in England, commissioned by William the Conqueror in 1066 so that he could determine the extent of his lands and wealth.

Doric order One of three architectural systems developed by the Greeks to decorate their buildings. The Doric order may be recognized by its columns, which include a wide shaft with a plain capital on the top.

Drachma (dróck-mah) Hellenistic coin containing either 4.3 grams (Alexander's) or 3.5 grams (Egypt's) of silver.

Dreyfus (dry'-fuss) **affair** The political upheaval in France accompanying the unjust 1894 conviction of Jewish army officer Alfred Dreyfus as a German spy that marked the importance of anti-Semitism in France.

Dual Monarchy The Austro-Hungarian Empire; the Habsburg monarchy after the 1867 reform that granted Hungary equality with Austria.

Il Duce (ill dóoch-ay) "The Leader," Mussolini's title as head of the Italian Fascist Party.

Duma Russia's legislative assembly in the years prior to 1917.

E

Ecclesia (ek-cláy-zee-uh) The popular assembly in ancient Athens made up of all male citizens over 18.

Edict of Nantes (náwnt) Edict issued by French king Henry IV in 1598 granting rights to Protestants, later revoked by Louis XIV.

Émigrés (em-ee-gráy) People, mostly aristocrats, who fled France during the French Revolution.

Emir (em-éar) A Muslim ruler, prince, or military commander.

Empirical method The use of observation and experiments based on sensory evidence to come to ideas or conclusions about nature.

Ems (Em's) **Dispatch** Telegram from Prussia's head of state to the French government, edited by Bismarck to look like an insult, that helped cause the Franco-Prussian War.

Enclosure Combining separate parcels of farmland and enclosing them with fences and walls to create large farms or pastures that produced for commerce.

encomienda (en-koh-mee-én-da) A form of economic and social organization established in sixteenth-century Spanish settlements in South and Central America. The encomienda system consisted of a royal grant that allowed Spanish settlers to compel indigenous peoples to work for them. In return, Spanish overseers were to look after their workers' welfare and encourage their conversion to Christianity. In reality, it was a brutal system of enforced labor.

Enlightened absolutism (áb-suh-loo-tism) Rule by a strong, "enlightened" ruler applying Enlightenment ideas to government.

Enlightenment An eighteenth-century cultural movement based on the ideas of the Scientific Revolution and that supported the notion that human reason should determine understanding of the world and the rules of social life.

Entente Cordiale (on-táhnt core-dee-áhl) The series of understandings, or agreements, between France and Britain that led to their alliance in World War I.

Entrepreneur (on-truh-pren-óor) A person who organizes and operates business ventures, especially in commerce and industry.

Epic (épp-ik) A long narrative poem celebrating episodes of a people's heroic tradition.

Epicureanism (epp-uh-cúre-ee-an-ism) A Hellenistic philosophy that held that the goal of life should be to live a life of pleasure regulated by moderation.

Equestrians (ee-quést-ree-ans) A social class in ancient Rome who had enough money to begin to challenge the power of the patricians.

Essenes (Ess-éenz) Members of a Jewish sect of ascetics from the second century B.C.E. to the second century C.E.

Estates Representative assemblies, typically made up of either the clergy, the nobility, the commoners, or all three meeting separately.

Estates General The legislature of France from the Middle Ages to 1789. Each of the three Estates—clergy, nobility, and bourgeoisie—sent representatives.

Ethnic cleansing The policy of brutally driving an ethnic group from their homes and from a certain territory, particularly prominent during the civil wars in the Balkans during the 1990s.

Eugenics (you-génn-iks) The study of hereditary improvement.

Euro (yóu-roe) The common currency of many European states, established in 1999.

Eurocommunism The policy of Western European Communist parties of supporting moderate policies and cooperating with other Leftist parties during the 1970s and 1980s.

European Economic Community The E.E.C., or Common Market, founded in 1957 to eliminate tariff barriers and begin to integrate the economies of western European nations.

European Union (EU) The community of European nations that continued to take steps toward the full economic union of much of Europe during the late twentieth century.

Evolution Darwin's theory of biological development through adaptation.

Existentialism (ekk-siss-ténn-sha-lism) A twentieth-century philosophy asserting that individuals are responsible for their own values and meanings in an indifferent universe.

Expressionism A late-nineteenth- and early-twentieth-century artistic style that emphasized the objective expression of inner experience through the use of conventional characters and symbols.

F

Fabian (fáy-bee-an) **Society** A late-nineteenth-century group of British intellectuals that advocated the adoption of socialist policies through politics rather than revolution.

Factory system Many workers producing goods in a repetitive series of steps and specialized tasks using powerful machines.

Falange (fa-láhn-hey) A Spanish fascist party that supported Francisco Franco during the Spanish civil war.

Fascism (fáh-shism) A philosophy or system of government that advocates a dictatorship of the extreme right together with an ideology of belligerent nationalism.

Fealty (fée-al-tee) In the feudal system, a promise made by vassals and lords to do no harm to each other.

Federates In the late Roman Empire, treaties established with many Gothic tribes allowed these tribes to settle within the Empire. The tribes then became "federates," or allies of Rome.

Fibula (pl. fibulae) An ornamented clasp or brooch, favored by the ancient Germanic tribes to hold their great cloaks closed.

Fief (feef) In the feudal system, the portion—usually land—given by lords to vassals to provide for their maintenance in return for their service.

Five-Year Plan The rapid, massive industrialization of the nation under the direction of the state initiated in the Soviet Union in the late 1920s.

Forum The central public place in ancient Rome which served as a meeting place, marketplace, law court, and political arena.

Fourteen Points U.S. President Wilson's plan to settle World War I and guarantee the peace.

Frankfurt Assembly Convention of liberals and nationalists from several German states that met in 1848 to try to form a unified government for Germany.

Free companies Mercenary soldiers in the Middle Ages and Renaissance who would fight for whoever paid them. They were called "free" to distinguish them from warriors who were bound by feudal ties to a lord.

Free Corps (core) Post–World War I German right-wing paramilitary groups made up mostly of veterans.

Free trade International trade of goods without tariffs, or customs duties.

Fresco A technique of painting on the plaster surface of a wall or ceiling while it is still damp so that the colors become fused with the plaster as it dries, making the image part of the building's surface.

Fronde (frawnd) Mid-seventeenth-century upheavals in France that threatened the royal government.

Fundamentalists Those who believe in an extremely conservative interpretation of a religion.

G

Galley A large medieval ship propelled by sails and oars.

General will Rousseau's notion that rules governing society should be based on the best conscience of the people.

Gentry People of "good birth" and superior social position.

Geocentric Earth-centered.

Gerousia (gay-róo-see-uh) Ruling body in ancient Sparta made up of male citizens over age 60.

Gestapo (guh-stóp-po) Nazi secret police in Hitler's Germany.

Girondins (zhee-roan-dán) Moderate political faction among leaders of the French Revolution.

Glasnost (gláz-nost) Soviet leader Gorbachev's policy of political and cultural openness in the 1980s.

Globalization Twentieth-century tendency for cultural and historical development to become increasingly worldwide in scope.

Global warming The heating of the earth's atmosphere in recent decades, caused in part by the buildup of carbon dioxide and other "greenhouse gases" produced by burning fossil fuels.

Glorious Revolution In 1688, English Parliament offered the crown of England to the Protestant William of Orange and his wife Mary, replacing James II. This change in rule was accomplished peacefully and clarified the precedent that England was a constitutional monarchy with power resting in Parliament.

Gosplan The Soviet State Planning Commission, charged with achieving ambitious economic goals.

Gothic (góth-ik) A style of architecture, usually associated with churches, that originated in France and flourished from the twelfth to the sixteenth century. Gothic architecture is identified by pointed arches, ribbed vaults, stained-glass windows, and flying buttresses.

Grand tour An educational travel taken by the wealthy to certain cities and sites, particularly during the seventeenth and eighteenth centuries.

Great Chain of Being A traditional Western-Christian vision of the hierarchical order of the universe.

Great Depression The global economic depression of the 1930s.

Great fear Panic caused by rumors that bands of brigands were on the loose in the French countryside during the summer of 1789.

Great Purges The long period of Communist Party purges in the Soviet Union during the 1930s, marked by terror, house arrests, show-trials, torture, imprisonments, and executions.

Great Reforms Reforms instituted by Russia's tsar Alexander II in 1861 that included freeing Russia's serfs.

Great Schism (skíz-um) Period in the late Middle Ages from 1378 to 1417 when there were two (and at times three) rival popes.

Greek fire A Byzantine naval weapon made of combustible oil that was launched with a catapult or pumped through tubes to set fire to enemy ships.

Guild An association of persons of the same trade united for the furtherance of some purpose.

Guillotine (ghée-oh-teen) A device for executing the condemned used during the French Revolution.

H

Hacienda (ha-see-én-da) Large landed estates in Spanish America that replaced encomiendas as the dominant economic and social structure.

Haj (hodge) The Muslim annual pilgrimage to Mecca, Medina, and other holy sites.

Hasidim (hah-see-déem) Sect of Jewish mystics founded in Poland in the eighteenth century in opposition to the formalistic Judaism and ritual laxity of the period.

Heliocentric (hee-lee-oh-sén-trick) Pertaining to the theory that the sun is the center of the universe.

Hellenes (Héll-eenz) The name ancient Greeks assigned to themselves, based on their belief that they were descended from a mythical King Hellen.

Hellenistic Of or related to the period between the fourth century B.C.E. and the first century B.C.E.

Helot (héll-ots) A serf in ancient Sparta.

Heresy A religious belief that is considered wrong by orthodox church leaders.

Hermetic doctrine Notion popular in the sixteenth and seventeenth centuries that all matter contains the divine spirit.

Hieratic (high-rát-ick) A form of ancient Egyptian writing consisting of abridged forms of hieroglyphics, used by the priests in keeping records.

Hieroglyph (hígh-roe-gliff) A picture or symbol used in the ancient Egyptian writing system—means "sacred writing."

Hijra (hídge-rah) (also *Hegira*) Muhammad's flight from Mecca to Medina in 622 B.C.E.

Holocaust (hóll-o-cost) The extermination of some six million Jews by the Nazis during World War II.

Holy Alliance Alliance of Russia, Austria, and Prussia to safeguard the principles of Christianity and maintain the international status quo after the Napoleonic Wars.

Homeopathy (home-ee-áh-pa-thee) Medical treatment emphasizing the use of herbal drugs and natural remedies.

Hoplites (hóp-lights) Ancient Greek infantrymen equipped with large round shields and long thrusting spears.

Hubris Excessive pride, which for the ancient Greeks brought punishment from the gods.

Huguenots (húgh-guh-nots) French Protestants of the sixteenth, seventeenth, and eighteenth centuries.

Humanists Students of an intellectual movement based on a deep study of classical culture and an emphasis on the humanities (literature, history, and philosophy) as a means for self-improvement.

Hundred Years' War A series of wars between England and France from 1337 to 1453. France won and England lost its lands in France, thus centralizing and solidifying French power.

I

Icon (éye-con) A sacred image of Jesus, Mary, or the saints that early Christians believed contained religious power.

Iconoclasm (eye-cónn-o-claz-um) A term literally meaning "icon breaking" that refers to an eighth-century religious controversy in Byzantium that argued that people should not venerate icons.

Ideogram (eye-dée-o-gram) A hieroglyph symbol expressing an abstract idea associated with the object it portrays.

Ideograph A written symbol that represents an idea instead of expressing the sound of a word.

Ideology (eye-dee-áh-lo-gee) A set of beliefs about the world and how it should be, often formalized into a political, social, or cultural theory.

Imam Muslim spiritual leader, believed by Shi'ites to be a spiritual descendant of Muhammad who should also be a temporal leader.

Imperialism The policy of extending a nation's authority by territorial acquisition or by the establishment of economic and political control over other nations or peoples.

Impressionism A nineteenth-century school of painting originating in France that emphasized capturing on canvas light as the eye sees it.

Indo-European Belonging to or constituting a family of languages that includes the Germanic, Celtic, Italic, Baltic, Slavic, Greek, Armenian, Iranian, and Indic groups.

Inductive reasoning Drawing general conclusions from particular concrete observations.

Indulgence A certificate issued by the papacy that gave people atonement for their sins and reduced their time in purgatory. Usually indulgences were issued for performing a pious act, but during the Reformation, critics accused the popes of selling indulgences to raise money.

Industrial revolution The rapid emergence of modern industrial production during the late eighteenth and nineteenth centuries.

Information revolution A rapid increase in the ability to store and manipulate information accompanying the development of computers during the second half of the twentieth century.

Inquisition A religious court established in the thirteenth century designed to root out heresy by questioning and torture.

Intendant (ann-tawn-dáunt) A French official sent by the royal government to assert the will of the monarch.

Internationalism The principle of cooperation among nations for their common good.

Ionia (eye-ówn-ee-uh) Ancient district in what is now Turkey that comprised the central portion of the west coast of Asia Minor, together with the adjacent islands.

Ionic order One of three architectural systems developed by the Greeks to decorate their buildings. The Ionic order may be recognized by its columns, which are taller and thinner than the Doric columns and capped with scroll-shaped capitals.

Iron Curtain The dividing line between Eastern and Western Europe during the Cold War.

Islamic fundamentalism A movement within Islam calling for a return to traditional ways and a rejection of alien ideologies that gained strength during the second half of the twentieth century.

J

Jacobins (jáck-o-bins) A radical political organization or club during the French Revolution.

Jacquerie (zhak-rée) The name given to the peasant revolt in France during the fourteenth century.

Jansenism A religious movement among French Catholics stressing the emotional experience of religious belief.

Jesuits (jéh-zu-it) Members of the Catholic religious order the Society of Jesus, founded by Ignatius Loyola in 1534.

Jihad (jée-hod) Islamic holy war in which believers feel they have the authority to fight to defend the faith.

Joint-stock company A business firm that is owned by stockholders who may sell or transfer their shares individually.

Journeyman A worker in a craft who has served his or her apprenticeship.

Joust A medieval contest in which two mounted knights combat with lances.

Junkers (yóong-kers) Prussian aristocracy.

Justification by faith The belief that faith alone—not good works—is needed for salvation. This belief lies at the heart of Protestantism.

K

Kamikaze (kah-mih-káh-zee) Usually refers to suicidal attacks on Allied ships by Japanese pilots during World War II.

Kore (kóh-ray) (pl. *korai*) Greek word for maiden that refers to an ancient Greek statue of a standing female, usually clothed.

Kouros (kóo-ross) (pl. *kouroi*) Greek word for a young man that refers to an ancient Greek statue of a standing nude young man.

Kristallnacht (kriss-táhl-nahkt) The "night of the broken glass"—a Nazi attack on German Jewish homes and businesses in 1938.

Kulak (kóo-lock) A relatively wealthy Russian peasant labeled by Stalin during the period of collectivization as a "class enemy."

Kulturkampf (kool-tóur-kahmpf) Bismarck's fight against the Catholic Church in Germany during the 1870s.

L

Laissez-faire (léss-say-fair) "Hands-off." An economic doctrine opposing governmental regulation of most economic affairs.

Laudanum (láud-a-numb) Opium dissolved in alcohol, used as a medicine in the eighteenth and nineteenth centuries.

League of Nations A post–World War I association of countries to deal with international tensions and conflicts.

Lebensraum (láy-benz-rowm) "Living space." Hitler's policy of expanding his empire to the east to gain more land for Germans.

Legume (lég-yoom) A pod, such as that of a pea or bean, used as food.

Levée en masse (le-váy awn máhss) General call-up of all men, women, and children to serve the nation during the French Revolution.

Levellers Revolutionaries who tried to "level" the social hierarchy during the English civil war.

Liberalism A nineteenth- and twentieth-century ideology supporting individualism, political freedom, constitutional government, and (in the nineteenth century) laissez-faire economic policies.

Liege (léezh) **lord** In the feudal system, a lord who has many vassals, but owes allegiance to no one.

Linear perspective An artistic technique used to represent three-dimensional space convincingly on a flat surface.

Lollards Followers of the English church reformer John Wycliffe who were found heretical.

Long March An arduous Chinese communist retreat from south China to north China in 1934 and 1935.

Luddism The smashing of machines that took jobs away from workers in the first half of the nineteenth century.

M

Ma'at (máh-aht) An Egyptian spiritual precept that conveyed the idea of truth and justice, or, as the Egyptians put it, right order and harmony.

Maccabean (mack-uh-bée-en) **Revolt** Successful Jewish revolt led by Judas Maccabeus in the mid-second century B.C.E. against Hellenistic Seleucid rulers.

Madrigal Musical composition set to a short poem usually about love, written for several voices. Common in Renaissance music.

Magi (máyj-eye) Ancient Persian astrologers or "wise men."

Maginot (máh-zhin-oh) **Line** A string of defensive fortresses on the French/German border that France began building in the late 1920s.

Magna Carta The Great Charter that English barons forced King John of England to sign in 1215 that guaranteed certain rights to the English people. Seen as one of the bases for constitutional law.

Marshall Plan A package of massive economic aid to European nations offered in 1947 to strengthen them and tie them to American influence.

Marxism A variety of socialism propounded by Karl Marx stressing economic determinism and class struggle—"scientific socialism."

Megalith An archaeological term for a stone of great size used in ancient monuments.

Meiji (máy-jee) **Restoration** The reorganizing of Japanese society along modern Western lines; initiated in 1868.

Mendicant orders Members of a religious order, such as the Dominicans or Franciscans, who wandered from city to city begging for alms rather than residing in a monastery.

Mercantilism (mírr-kan-till-ism) Early modern governmental economic policies seeking to control and develop the national economy and bring wealth into the national treasury.

Mercator projection (mer-káy-ter) A method of making maps in which the earth's surface is shown as a rectangle with Europe at the center, causing distortion toward the poles.

Mesolithic Of or pertaining to the period of human culture from about 15,000 years ago to about 7000 B.C.E. characterized by complex stone tools and greater social organization. "Middle Stone Age."

Methodism A Protestant sect founded in the eighteenth century that emphasized piety and emotional worship.

Metics (métt-iks) Foreign residents of Athens.

Miasma (my-ázz-ma) Fumes from waste and marshes blamed for carrying diseases during the eighteenth and the first half of the nineteenth centuries.

Middle Passage The long sea voyage between the African coast and the Americas endured by newly captured slaves.

Minoan (mínn-oh-an) A civilization that lived on the island of Crete from 2800 to 1450 B.C.E.

Mir (mere) Russian village commune.

Missi dominici (mée-see do-min-ée-kee) Royal officials under Charlemagne who traveled around the country to enforce the king's laws.

Mithraism (míth-ra-ism) A Hellenistic mystery religion that appealed to soldiers and involved the worship of the god Mithra.

Mughals (móe-gulls) Islamic rulers of much of India in the sixteenth, seventeenth, and eighteenth centuries.

Munich Conference The 1938 conference where Britain and France attempted to appease Hitler by allowing him to dismantle Czechoslovakia.

Mycenean (my-sen-ée-an) A civilization on the Greek peninsula that reached its high point between 1400 and 1200 B.C.E.

Mystery religions Ancient religions that encouraged believers to cultivate a deep connection with their deity. Initiates swore not to reveal the insights they had gained during rites and ceremonies; the shroud of secrecy resulted in the name "mystery" religions.

N

Napoleonic (na-po-lee-ón-ik) **Code** The legal code introduced in France by Napoleon Bonaparte.

Nationalism A nineteenth- and twentieth-century ideology stressing the importance of national identity and the nation-state.

Natural law Understandable, rational laws of nature that apply to the physical and human world.

Nazi Party Hitler's German National Socialist Party.

Neolithic (nee-oh-líth-ik) Of or denoting a period of human culture beginning around 7000 B.C.E. in the Middle East and later elsewhere, characterized by the invention of farming and the making of technically advanced stone implements. "New Stone Age."

Neoplatonism (nee-oh-pláy-ton-ism) Views based on the ideas of Plato that one should search beyond appearances for true knowledge; stressed abstract reasoning.

New Economic Policy (NEP) Lenin's compromise economic and social policy for the USSR during the 1920s.

New imperialism The second wave of Western imperialism, particularly between 1880 and 1914.

Night of August 4 Surrender of most privileges by the French aristocracy at a meeting held on August 1, 1789.

Nominalism (nóm-in-al-ism) A popular late medieval philosophy based on the doctrine that the universal, or general, has no objective existence or validity, being merely a name expressing the qualities of various objects resembling one another in certain respects. Also called New Nominalism.

North American Free Trade Agreement (NAFTA) The 1994 agreement between the United States, Mexico, and Canada to create a free trade zone.

North Atlantic Treaty Organization (NATO) A military alliance against the Soviet Union initiated in 1949.

Nuremberg Laws Hitler's anti-Jewish laws of 1935.

O

Ockham's razor A principle that states that between alternative explanations for the same phenomenon, the simplest is always to be preferred.

October Revolution The 1917 Bolshevik revolt and seizure of power in Russia.

Old Regime (re-zhéem) European society before the French Revolution.

Oligarchy (áh-luh-gar-kee) Rule by a small group or by a particular social class—often wealthy middle classes, as in ancient Greek or medieval European cities.

Operation Barbarossa (bar-bar-óh-ssa) The German invasion of the USSR during World War II.

Optimates (ahp-tuh-máht-ays) The nobility of the Roman Empire. Also refers to the political party that supported the nobility. Contrast with the *populares*.

Ordeal An ancient form of trial in which the accused was exposed to physical dangers that were presumed to be harmless if the accused was innocent. Ordeals might include grasping hot pokers, trial by battle, immersion in water, and other similar challenges.

Organization of Petroleum Exporting Countries (OPEC) An Arab-dominated organization of Middle Eastern oil-producing states that became effective during and after the 1970s.

Ostracism (áhs-tra-sism) A political technique of ancient Greece by which people believed to be threats to the city-state were chosen for exile by popular vote.

P

Paleolithic (pay-lee-oh-líth-ik) Of or pertaining to the period of human culture beginning with the earliest chipped stone tools, about 750,000 years ago, until the beginning of the Mesolithic, about 15,000 years ago. "Old Stone Age."

Pantheon (pán-thee-on) A great temple in Rome built in 27 B.C.E. and dedicated to all the gods. In 609 C.E., it was rededicated as a Christian church called Santa Maria Rotunda.

Paris Commune The revolutionary government of the city of Paris, first in the 1790s and then in 1871.

Parlement (parl-máwn) A French court of law during the Old Regime.

Parliament Britain's legislature, including the House of Commons and House of Lords.

Parthenon (párth-uh-non) A famous Doric temple of Athena on the Acropolis in ancient Athens.

Patricians The ancient Roman aristocracy who populated the Senate and were particularly powerful during the Republic.

Pax Romana ("pocks" or "packs" row-máhn-ah) Literally, "Roman Peace." Two hundred years of relative, internal peace within the Roman Empire beginning with the rule of Caesar Augustus.

Peace of Paris The 1919 peace settlement after World War I.

Peers Members of the House of Lords in England.

Perestroika (pair-ess-trói-ka) Gorbachev's policy of "restructuring" the Soviet economy during the 1980s.

Petrine (pée-tryn) **doctrine** The belief that the popes, bishops of Rome, should lead the church because they are the successors of Peter, who many claim was the first bishop of Rome.

Phalanstery (fa-láns-ter-ee) The model commune envisioned by the French utopian socialist Fourier.

Phalanx (fáy-langks) An ancient Greek formation of foot soldiers carrying overlapping shields and long spears.

Pharaoh The title of the rulers of ancient Egypt. Also refers to the household and administration of the rulers.

Pharisees (fáir-uh-sees) Members of an ancient Jewish sect that rigidly observed purity laws, including dietary rules. They also believed in the resurrection of the just and the existence of angels.

Philosophes (fee-low-zóff) Leading French intellectuals of the Enlightenment.

Phonogram A character or symbol used to represent a speech sound used in ancient writing.

Physiocrats (fízz-ee-oh-crats) Eighteenth-century French economic thinkers who stressed the importance of agriculture and favored free trade.

Pictogram A picture representing an idea used in ancient writing.

Pietism (píe-uh-tism) An eighteenth-century Protestant movement stressing an emotional commitment to religion.

Plebeians (pleb-ée-an) The members of the urban lower classes in ancient Rome.

Plebiscite (pléb-uh-sight) A direct vote that allows the people to either accept or reject a proposed measure.

Pogrom ('puh-grúhm'; also 'póe-grom') An organized persecution or massacre of Jews, especially in eastern Europe.

Polis (póe-liss) (pl. *poleis* [póe-lease]) An ancient Greek city-state.

Poor Laws Eighteenth- and nineteenth-century British laws enacted to deal with the poor.

Populares (pop-you-lahr-ays) In Roman history, the political party of the common people. Also refers to the people themselves. Contrast with the *optimates*.

Popular Front The political partnership of parties of the Left, particularly in France and Spain, during the 1930s.

positivism A mid-nineteenth-century theory of sociology holding that scientific investigation could discover useful fundamental truths about humans and their societies.

Postindustrial societies Late-twentieth-century societies that moved from manufacturing to services led by professionals, managers, and financiers.

Postmodernism A late-twentieth-century approach to the arts stressing relativism and multiple interpretations.

Pragmatic Sanction The international agreement secured by the Habsburg emperor in the 1730s to ensure that his daughter would succeed him without question.

Prague Spring The brief period of democratic reforms and cultural freedom in Czechoslovakia during 1968.

Predestination Doctrine claiming that since God is all-knowing and all-powerful, he must know in advance who is saved or damned. Therefore, the salvation of any individual is predetermined. This doctrine is emphasized by Calvinists.

Preemptive War War initiated by one side on the justification that another side was on the verge of attack.

Prefect Powerful agents of the central government stationed in France's departments.

Preventive war War initiated by one side on the justification that another side might attack sometime in the future.

Principate (prínce-a-pate) The governmental system of the Roman Empire founded by Octavian (also known as Caesar Augustus).

Privateer An armed private vessel commissioned by a government to attack enemy ships.

Protestant Of or pertaining to any branch of the Christian church excluding Roman Catholicism and Eastern Orthodox.

Psychoanalysis Pioneered by Sigmund Freud, a method of investigating human psychological development and treating emotional disorders.

Ptolemaic (ptah-luh-máy-ik) **system** The traditional medieval earth-centered universe and system of planetary movements.

Ptolemies (ptáh-luh-meez) Hellenistic dynasty that ruled in Egypt from about 300 B.C.E. to about 30 B.C.E.

Purgatory In Roman Catholic theology, a state or place in which those who have died in the grace of God expiate their sins by suffering before they can enter heaven.

Purge Expelling or executing political party members suspected of inefficiency or opposition to party policy.

Puritans In the sixteenth and seventeenth centuries, those who wanted to reform the Church of England by removing all elaborate ceremonies and forms. Many Puritans faced persecution and were forced to flee to the American colonies.

Q

Quadrant An instrument for taking altitude of heavenly bodies.

Quadrivium (quad-rív-ee-um) The medieval school curriculum that studied arithmetic, music, geometry, and astronomy after completion of the trivium.

Quadruple (quad-róo-pull) **Alliance** Alliance of Austria, Prussia, Russia, and France in the years after the Napoleonic Wars to maintain the status quo.

Quietism (quíet-ism) A movement among seventeenth-century Spanish Catholics that emphasized the emotional experience of religious belief.

Qur'an (also Koran) The Muslim holy book recorded in the early seventh century by the prophet Muhammad.

R

Racism Belief that racial differences are important and that some races are superior to others.

Raison d'état (ráy-zawn day-táh) "Reason of state." An eighteenth- and nineteenth-century principle justifying arbitrary or aggressive international behavior.

Rationalism The belief that, through reason, humans can understand the world and solve problems.

Realism A medieval Platonist philosophy that believed that the individual objects we perceive are not real, but merely reflections of universal ideas existing in the mind of God. In the nineteenth century, this referred to a cultural style rejecting romanticism and attempting to examine society as it is.

Realpolitik (ray-áhl-po-lee-teek) The pragmatic politics of power; often a self-interested foreign policy associated with Bismarck.

Redshirts Garibaldi's troops used in the unification of Italy.

Reform Bill of 1832 English electoral reform extending the vote to the middle classes of the new industrial cities.

Reichstag (ríkes-tahg) German legislative assembly.

Reign of Terror The violent period of the French Revolution between 1792 and 1794.

Relativity Einstein's theory that all aspects of the physical universe must be defined in relative terms.

Relics In the Roman Catholic and Greek Orthodox churches, valued remnants of saints or other religious figures. Relics usually are parts of bodies but may also include objects that had touched sacred bodies or that were associated with Jesus or Mary, such as remnants of the True Cross.

Renaissance Literally, "rebirth." The term was coined in Italy in the early fourteenth century to refer to the rebirth of the appreciation of classical (Greek and Roman) literature and values. It also refers to the culture that was born in Italy during that century that ultimately spread throughout Europe.

Resistance movements Underground opposition to occupation forces, especially to German troops in conquered European countries during World War II.

Restoration The conservative regimes in power after the defeat of Napoleon in 1815 that hoped to hold back the forces of change or even turn back the clock to prerevolutionary days.

Risorgimento (ree-sor-jee-mén-toe) A nineteenth-century Italian unification movement.

Rococo (roe-coe-cóe) A style of art developed from the baroque that originated in France during the eighteenth century that emphasized elaborate designs to produce a delicate effect.

Romanesque (Roman-ésk) A style of architecture usually associated with churches built in the eleventh and twelfth centuries and that was inspired by Roman architectural features. Romanesque buildings were massive, with round arches, barrel vaulted ceilings, and dark interiors.

Romanticism A cultural ideology during the first half of the nineteenth century stressing feeling over reason.

Rosetta Stone A tablet of black basalt found in 1799 at Rosetta, Egypt, that contains parallel inscriptions in Greek, ancient Egyptian demotic script, and hieroglyphic characters. The stone provided the key to deciphering ancient Egyptian writing.

Rostra The speaker's platform in the Forum of ancient Rome.

Roundheads Members or supporters of the Parliamentary or Puritan party in England during the English civil war (1642).

Royal absolutism The seventeenth- and eighteenth-century system of elevated royal authority.

S

Sacraments In Christianity, rites that were to bring the individual grace or closeness to God. In Roman Catholicism and Greek Orthodoxy there are seven sacraments: baptism, confirmation, the Eucharist, penance, extreme unction, holy orders, and matrimony. Protestants in general acknowledge only two sacraments: baptism and the Lord's Supper.

Sadducees (sád-juh-sees) Members of an ancient Jewish sect that emphasized worship at the Temple in Jerusalem. They rejected new ideas such as resurrection, insisting on only those ideas that could be found in the Torah.

Saga A medieval Scandinavian story of battles, customs, and legends, narrated in prose and generally telling the traditional history of an important Norse family.

Salon (suh-láhn) Seventeenth- and eighteenth-century social and cultural gatherings of members of the upper and middle classes.

Sans-culottes (sawn-key-lóht) Working-class people of Paris during the French Revolution.

Sarcophagus (sar-kóff-a-gus) A stone coffin.

Satellite states Eastern European states under the control of the Soviet Union during the Cold War.

Satrap (sát-trap) An ancient Persian governor in charge of provinces called "satrapies."

Schlieffen (shléaf-en) **Plan** German military strategy in World War I that called for a holding action against Russia while German forces moved through Belgium to knock out France.

Scholasticism The dominant medieval philosophical and theological movement that applied logic from Aristotle to help understand God's plan. It also refers to the desire to join faith with reason.

Scientific Revolution The new sixteenth- and seventeenth-century methods of investigation and discoveries about nature based on observation and reason rather than tradition and authority.

Scutage (skyóot-ij) Medieval payment in lieu of military service.

Seleucids (se-lóo-sids) Hellenistic dynasty that ruled in Asia from about 300 B.C.E. to about 64 B.C.E.

Semitic (sem-ít-ik) Of or pertaining to any of a group of Caucasoid peoples, chiefly Jews and Arabs, of the eastern Mediterranean area.

Senate, Roman The deliberative body and influential governing council of Rome during the Republic and Empire. Composed of ex-magistrates with lifetime membership, the Senate did not legislate, but conducted foreign policy and warfare and authorized public expenditures.

Septuagint (sep-tu-eh-jint) A Greek translation of the Hebrew scriptures (the Old Testament), so named because it was said to be the work of 72 Palestinian Jews in the third century B.C.E., who completed the work in seventy days.

Serfs Medieval peasants who were personally free, but bound to the land. They owed labor obligations as well as fees.

Shi'ite (shée-ite) **Muslims** Those who accepted only the descendants of 'Ali, Muhammad's son-in-law, as the true rulers. It was not the majority party in Islam but did prevail in some of the Muslim countries.

Shire An English county.

Sinn Fein (shín féign) "Ourselves Alone." An extremist twentieth-century Irish nationalist organization.

Skepticism (skép-ti-cism) The systematic doubting of accepted authorities—especially religious authorities.

Second Reich (rike) German regime founded in 1871 and lasting until the end of World War I.

Sepoy (sée-poy) **Mutiny** The 1857 uprising of Indians against British rule.

Social Darwinism The effort to apply Darwin's biological ideas to social ideas stressing competition and "survival of the fittest."

Socialists Those promoting or practicing the nineteenth- and twentieth-century ideology of socialism, stressing cooperation, community, and public ownership of the means of production.

Socratic method The method of arriving at truth by questioning and disputation.

Solidarity A Polish noncommunist union that became the core of resistance to the communist regime during the 1980s.

Sophists (sóff-ists) Fifth-century B.C.E. Greek philosophers who were condemned for using tricky logic to prove that all things are relative and success alone is important.

Sovereignty (sóv-rin-tee) The source of authority exercised by a state; complete independence and self-government.

Soviet A workers' council during the 1905 and 1917 Russian revolutions and part of the structure of government in the Soviet Union.

SS The Schutzstaffel, Hitler's elite party troops of the 1930s and 1940s.

Stadholder (stáhd-holder) A governor of provinces in the Dutch United Provinces.

Statutory law Laws established by a king or legislative body. Contrast with common law.

Stoicism (stów-i-cism) A Hellenistic philosophy that advocated detachment from the material world and an indifference to pain.

Strategoi (stra-táy-goy) Generals in ancient Athens who eventually took a great deal of political power.

Struggle of the Orders The political strife between patrician and plebeian Romans beginning in the fifth century B.C.E. The plebeians gradually won political rights as a result of the struggle.

Sturm und drang (shtúrm unt dráhng) "Storm and stress." A literary movement in late eighteenth-century Germany.

Sumptuary (súmp-chew-air-ee) **laws** Laws restricting or regulating extravagance (for example, in food or dress), often used to maintain separation of social classes.

Sunna (sóon-a) A collection of sayings and traditions of the prophet Muhammad that delineates the customs adhered to by Muslims.

Supply and demand Adam Smith's liberal economic doctrine that demand for goods and services will stimulate production (supply) in a free-market system.

Surrealism (sur-rée-a-lism) A twentieth-century literary and artistic style stressing images from the unconscious mind.

Symphony A long sonata for orchestra.

Syncretism (sín-cre-tism) The attempt or tendency to combine or reconcile differing beliefs, as in philosophy or religion.

Syndicalism (sín-di-cal-ism) A late-nineteenth-century anarchist ideology envisioning labor unions as the center of a free and just society.

T

Taliban The strict, fundamentalist Islamic regime that ruled most of Afghanistan from 1996 to 2001.

Tennis Court Oath Oath taken by members of the French Estates General not to dissolve until they had created a constitution for France.

Tetradrachma (tet-ra-drák-ma) Hellenistic coin worth four drachmas.

Tetrarchy (tét-rar-key) The governmental system of the Roman Empire founded by Diocletian that divided the empire into four administrative units.

Theocracy (thee-áh-kruh-see) Government by priests claiming to rule by divine authority.

Theme A division for the purpose of provincial administration in the Byzantine Empire.

Thermidorian (ther-mi-dór-ee-an) **Reaction** The overthrow of Robespierre and the radicals in July 1794, during the French Revolution.

Third Estate Commoners, or all people except the nobility and clergy, in early modern European society.

Third French Republic The republican government established in 1871 and lasting until Germany's defeat of France in 1940.

Torah (tór-uh) The first five books of the Jewish sacred scriptures, comprising Genesis, Exodus, Leviticus, Numbers, and Deuteronomy.

Tories A conservative British political party during the eighteenth and nineteenth centuries.

Totalitarianism A twentieth-century form of authoritarian government using force, technology, and bureaucracy to effect rule by a single party and controlling most aspects of the lives of the population.

Total war A form of warfare in which all the forces and segments of society are mobilized for a long, all-out struggle.

Transubstantiation (trán-sub-stan-chee-áy-shun) In the Roman Catholic and Greek Orthodox churches, the belief that the bread and wine of the Eucharist were transformed into the actual body and blood of Christ.

Trench warfare An almost stagnant form of defensive warfare fought from trenches.

Triangular trade Trade pattern between European nations and their colonies by which European manufactured goods were traded for raw materials (such as agricultural products) from the Americas or slaves from Africa.

Tribune An official of ancient Rome chosen by the common people to protect their rights.

Triple Alliance Alliance of Germany, Austria-Hungary, and Italy in the years before World War I.

Triumvirate (try-úm-vir-ate) A group of three men sharing civil authority, as in ancient Rome.

Trivium (trív-ee-um) The basic medieval curriculum that studied grammar, rhetoric, and logic; after completion, students could proceed to the quadrivium.

Troubadour (tróo-buh-door) Poets from the late twelfth and early thirteenth centuries who wrote love poems, meant to be sung to music, that reflected the new sensibility of courtly love, which claimed that lovers were ennobled.

Truman Doctrine U.S. policy initiated in 1947 that offered military and economic aid to countries threatened by a communist takeover with the intention of creating a military ring of containment around the Soviet Union and its satellite states.

Tsar The emperor of Russia.

Twelve Tables According to ancient Roman tradition, popular pressure in the fifth century B.C.E. led to the writing down of traditional laws to put an end to patrician monopoly of the laws. The resulting compilation—the Twelve Tables—was seen as the starting point for the tradition of Roman law.

U

Ultra-royalism The nineteenth-century belief in rule by a monarch and that everything about the French Revolution and Enlightenment was contrary to religion, order, and civilization.

Unconscious According to Freud, that part of the mind of which we are not aware; home of basic drives.

Unilateralism Actions or policies taken by one nation in its own interests regardless of the views and interests of its allies.

United Nations (UN) An international organization founded in 1945 to promote peace and cooperation.

Universal A metaphysical entity that does not change, but that describes particular things on earth—for example, "justice" or "beauty." Explained by the ancient Greeks and examined by subsequent philosophers. (Also called "forms" or "ideas.")

Utilitarianism (you-till-a-táre-ee-an-ism) A nineteenth-century liberal philosophy that evaluated institutions on the basis of social usefulness to achieve "the greatest happiness of the greatest number."

Utopian (you-tópe-ee-an) **socialism** A form of early nineteenth-century socialism urging cooperation and communes rather than competition and individualism.

V

Vassal In the feudal system, a noble who binds himself to his lord in return for maintenance.

Versailles (ver-sígh) **treaty** Peace treaty between the Allies and Germany following World War I.

Victorian Referring to the period of Queen Victoria's reign in Britain, 1837–1901.

Vulgate (vúll-gate) A version of the Latin Bible, primarily translated from Hebrew and Greek by Jerome.

W

Wahhabism (wuh-háh-biz-uhm) An Islamic reform movement founded in the eighteenth century that stressed a strict, literal interpretation of the Qur'an.

War guilt clause Article 231 of the Treaty of Versailles that places all blame on Germany for causing World War I.

Warsaw Pact A military alliance in Eastern Europe controlled by the Soviet Union and initiated in 1955.

Waterloo Site in Belgium of a decisive defeat of Napoleon in 1815.

Weimar (wy'e-mar) **Republic** The liberal German government established at the end of World War I and destroyed by Hitler in the 1930s.

Welfare state Governmental programs to protect citizens from severe economic hardships and to provide basic social needs.

Wergeld (véhr-gelt) In Germanic law, the relative price of individuals that established the fee for compensation in case of injury.

Whigs A British political party during the eighteenth and nineteenth centuries.

Witan The ancient Anglo-Saxon men who participated in the Witenagemot.

Witenagemot (wí-ten-uh-guh-mote) Ancient Anglo-Saxon assembly of nobles.

Z

Zealots (zéll-ets) An ancient Jewish sect arising in Palestine in about 6 C.E. that militantly opposed Roman rule and desired to establish an independent Jewish state. The sect was wiped out when the Romans destroyed Jerusalem in 70 C.E.

Zemstva (zémst-fah) Municipal councils established in Russia in the second half of the nineteenth century.

Ziggurat (zíg-gur-raht) A pyramid-shaped Mesopotamian temple.

Zionism A late-nineteenth- and twentieth-century Jewish nationalist movement to create an independent state for Jews in Palestine.

Zollverein (tsóll-ver-rhine) Nineteenth-century German customs union headed by Prussia.

Zoroastrianism (zorro-áss-tree-an-ism) An ancient Persian religion that had a belief in two gods: a god of light named Ahura Mazda and an evil god named Ahriman.

PHOTOS

Chapter 13

p. 414: The Louvre Museum, Paris, France/Scala/ Art Resource, NY; p. 417: Erich Lessing/Art Resource, NY; p. 418: Bibliotheque nationale de France; p. 423: Réunion des Musées Nationaux/Art Resource, NY; p. 424: Erich Lessing/Art Resource, NY; p. 425: © National Gallery, London/Art Resource, NY; p. 431: Russian Historical Museum Moscow/Alfredo Dagli Orti/The Art Archive; p. 434: Dyck, Anthony van (1599–1641) *James Stuart (1612–1655), Duke of Richmond and Lennox.* ca. 1634–35. Oil on canvas, 85 × 50 1/4 in. The Metropolitan Museum of Art, Marquand Collection, Gift of Henry G. Marquand, 1889. (89.15.16). Photograph © 1998 The Metropolitan Museum of Art/Art Resource, NY; p. 438: The Granger Collection; p. 439: British Library, London, UK/ Bridgeman Art Library; p. 440: British Library/HIP/ Art Resource, NY; p. 443: National Portrait Gallery, London, UK/The Bridgeman Art Library; p. 446B: Bildarchiv Preussischer Kulturbesitz/Art Resource, NY; p. 446T: The Granger Collection, New York.

Chapter 14

p. 450: Houghton Library, Harvard University; p. 453: Charles Walker/Topfoto/The Image Works; p. 454: V&A Images, London/Art Resource, NY; p. 456: Erich Lessing/Art Resource, NY; p. 458: Snark/Art Resource, NY; p. 459: Image Select/ Art Resource, NY; p. 461: Réunion des Musées Nationaux/Art Resource, NY; p. 463: Houghton Library, Harvard University; p. 464: Fitzwilliam Museum, University of Cambridge/Bridgeman Art Library; p. 467: Private Collection/The Stapleton Collection/The Bridgeman Art Library; p. 471: Chateau, Coppet, Switzerland/Bridgeman-Giraudon/Art Resource, NY; p. 472: Réunion des Musées Nationaux/Art Resource, NY; p. 473: Musee des Beaux-Arts, Dijon, France/Erich Lessing/ Art Resource, NY.

Chapter 15

p. 478: Bristol City Museum and Art Gallery, UK/ Bridgeman Art Library; p. 485: Scala/Art Resource, NY; p. 488: Mary Evans Picture Library; p. 491: Harper Collins Publishers/The Art Archive; p. 492: National Maritime Museum, Greenwich, London, UK/The Art Archive; p. 494: © British Library Board. All Rights Reserved/The Bridgeman Art Library; p. 496: National Gallery of Ireland; p. 500B: The Granger Collection; p. 500T: Cheltenham Art Gallery & Museums, Gloucestershire, UK/Bridgeman Art Library; p. 502: Eigentum des Germanischen Nationalmuseums, Nuremberg; p. 504: Réunion des Musées Nationaux, Paris, France/Photo: Gérard Blot/Art Resource, NY; p. 505: Réunion des Musées Nationaux/Art Resource, NY; p. 506: Réunion des Musées Nationaux/Art Resource, NY; p. 507: © The Trustees of the British Museum/Art Resource, NY; p. 509: Spencer Collection, NYPL, Astor, Lenox and Tilden Foundations; p. 512–513: Sébastien Cailleux/ Sygma/Corbis.

Chapter 16

p. 514: Musee Carnavalet/Roger-Viollet/The Image Works; p. 518: Bettmann/Corbis; p. 520: Réunion des Musées Nationaux/Art Resource, NY; p. 522:

Réunion des Musées Nationaux/Art Resource, NY; p. 527B: Réunion des Musées Nationaux/Art Resource, NY; p. 527T: Erich Lessing/Art Resource, NY; p. 529: Musée des Beaux-Arts de Quimper, France/The Bridgeman Art Library; p. 531: Musée Carnavalet Paris/Gianni Dagli Orti/The Art Archive; p. 532B: Erich Lessing/Art Resource, NY; p. 532T: The Granger Collection; p. 536: Erich Lessing/Art Resource, NY; p. 539: The Granger Collection; p. 541: Erich Lessing/Art Resource, NY.

Chapter 17

p. 546: Lady Lever Art Gallery, National Museums Liverpool/Bridgeman Art Library; p. 549: The Royal Collection © 2003, Her Majesty Queen Elizabeth II; p. 553: Science Museum, London, UK/Bridgeman Art Library; p. 554: Musée des arts et métiers— CNAM, Paris/Photo: P. Faligot, Seventh Square; p. 556: New Walk Museum, Leicester City Museum Service, UK/Bridgeman Art Library; p. 557: Guildhall Library, Corporation of London, UK/ Bridgeman Art Library; p. 561: General Research Division/Print Collection/Science, Industry & Business Library. New York Public Library/Art Resource, NY; p. 563: Trade Union Congress, London, UK/Bridgeman Art Library; p. 566: The New York Public Library/Art Resource, NY; p. 568: Naudet, Caroline. *Voyage Et Conduite D'Un Moribund Pour L'autre Monde.* 1988-102-116. Philadelphia Museum of Art: The William H. Helfand Collection, 1988; p. 570: *Merrymakers*, 1870. Carolus-Duran. Founders Society Purchase, Acc. # 80.37. Robert H. Tannahill Foundation Fund. Photograph © 1989 The Detroit Institute of Arts/Bridgeman Art Library; p. 573: Courtesy of Cadbury Ltd.

Chapter 18

p. 576: Erich Lessing/Art Resource, NY; p. 579: AKG Images, London; p. 585: The British Library/ HIP/Art Resource, NY; p. 588: Bildarchiv Preussischer Kulturbesitz/Art Resource, NY; p. 589B: Bildarchiv Preussischer Kulturbesitz/Art Resource, NY; p. 589T: Yale Center for British Art, Paul Mellon Collection, USA/Bridgeman Art Library; p. 593: The Granger Collection; p. 594: Musée des Beaux-Arts, Bordeaux, France/Bridgeman-Giraudon/Art Resource, NY; p. 595: Chateaux de Versailles et de Trianon, Versailles, France/Bridgeman-Giraudon/Art Resource, NY; p. 599: Musée du Petit Palais, Paris, France/ Bridgeman-Giraudon/Art Resource, NY; p. 603: The Louvre Museum, Paris, France/Bridgeman-Giraudon/ Art Resource, NY; p. 604: Hamburger Kunsthalle, Hamburg, Germany/Bridgeman Art Library.

Chapter 19

p. 608: Bildarchiv Preussischer Kulturbesitz/Art Resource, NY; p. 613: Culver Pictures, Inc.; p. 617: Bildarchiv Preussischer Kulturbesitz/Art Resource; p. 618B: The Bridgeman Art Library; p. 618T: Image copyright © The Metropolitan Museum of Art/Art Resource, NY; p. 621: Staedtische Kunsthalle, Mannheim, Germany/Erich Lessing/ Art Resource, NY; p. 623: National Army Museum, London/The Bridgeman Art Library; p. 624L: The Granger Collection; p. 624R: Sovfoto.

Chapter 20

p. 628: Bildarchiv Preussischer Kulturbesitz/ Art Resource, NY; p. 631: Private Collection/

Photo © Christie's Images/Bridgeman Art Library; p. 632: Eugene Appert/Hulton/Getty Images; p. 634: Musée d'Orsay, Paris, France/Erich Lessing/ Art Resource, NY; p. 636: Branger/Roger Viollet/ Getty Images; p. 638: Gift of the Estate of Rose Mintz. The Jewish Museum, New York, NY, USA. Photo by Richard Goodbody, Inc./Art Resource, NY; p. 640: Culver Pictures, Inc.; p. 641: Royal Museum of Fine Arts, Antwerp. Image courtesy of Reproductiefonds Vlaamse Musea NV/Lukas Art in Flanders; p. 643: Mary Evans Picture Library; p. 651: Hulton/Archive/Getty Images; p. 654: Marine Corps Historical Society; p. 655: Keystone-Mast Collection (14757)/California Museum of Photography, University of California at Riverside.

Chapter 21

p. 658: Harrogate Museums and Art Gallery, North Yorkshire, UK/Bridgeman Art Library; p. 660: ullstein bild/The Granger Collection; p. 662: Tallandier; p. 665: Archives Charmet/ The Bridgeman Art Library; p. 667B: Archives Charmet/The Bridgeman Art Library; p. 667T: Cadbury Ltd; p. 668: Frederic, Leon (1856–1940) © ARS, NY. *The Ages of the Worker*, triptych. Oil on canvas, 1895–97. Musee d'Orsay, Paris, France Musée d'Orsay/Reunion des Musées Nationaux/ Art Resource, NY; p. 670: Magyar Nemzeti Gallery Budapest/Gianni Dagli Orti/The Art Archive; p. 673: Musée d'Orsay, Paris, France/Réunion des Musées Nationaux/Erich Lessing/Art Resource, NY; p. 675: Public Domain; p. 676: The Granger Collection, NY; p. 679: Allgemeines Krankenhaus (General Hospital), Vienna, Austria/Erich Lessing/ Art Resource, NY; p. 680: Bildarchiv Preussischer Kulturbesitz/Art Resource, NY; p. 681: Musée d'Orsay, Paris, France/Réunion des Musées Nationaux/Erich Lessing/Art Resource, NY; p. 683: National Gallery of Art, Washington/ The Art Archive; p. 685B: Munch, Edvard (1863–1944) *The Scream.* 1893 (Tempera and pastels on cardboard, 91 × 73.5 cm.) © Copyright ARS, NY. National Gallery, Oslo, Norway. Erich Lessing/Art Resource, NY; p. 685T: *Christ's Triumphant Entry into Brussels*, 1888 (oil on canvas), Ensor, James (1860–1949)/J. Paul Getty Museum, Los Angeles, USA. © ARS, NY. © DACS/Lauros/Giraudon/© 2010. ARS, NY/ SABAM, Brussels/The Bridgeman Art Library.

Chapter 22

p. 690: Dix, Otto (1891–1969) *The War.* Triptych, oil on wood, 1929–32. © 2010.ARS, NY/VG Bild-Kunst, Bonn. Staatliche Kunstsammlungen, Dresden, Germany. Erich Lessing/Art Resource, NY; p. 695: Meidner, Ludwig (1884–1966) *Apocalyptic Landscape*, 1913. Painting, Oil on canvas, 37 1/2 × 31 5/8 in. (95.25 × 80.33 cm). Gift of Clifford Odets (60.65.1b). Los Angeles County Museum of Art, Los Angeles, CA. © Ludwig Meidner-Archiv, Jüdisches Museum der Stadt Frankfurt am Main.Digital Image © 2009 Museum Associates/LACMA/Art Resource, NY; p. 696: Corbis; p. 699: Roger Viollet/ Getty Images; p. 700: Mary Evans/Robert Hunt Collection/The Image Works; p. 701: Imperial War Museum, London; p. 703: Imperial War Museum, London; p. 704: Mary Evans Picture Library; p. 707: Memorial depicting the artist and her husband mourning their dead son, Peter Kollwitz, dedicated in 1931 (stone), Kollwitz,

Kathe Schmidt (1867–1945)/Vladslo German Military Cemetery, Vladslo, Ypres, Belgium © 2010. ARS, NY/VG Bild-Kunst, Bonn. © DACS/© Paul Maeyaert/© 2010. ARS, NY./VG Bild-Kunst, Bonn./The Bridgeman Art Library; p. 708: Bettmann/Corbis; p. 713: Scala/White Images/Art Resource, NY; p. 714: Sovfoto; p. 716: © DACS/Archives Charmet/The Bridgeman Art Library.

Chapter 23

p. 720: *Pillars of Society*.1926. Grosz, George (1893–1959) Oil on canvas, 200,0 × 108,0 cm. © Estate of George Grosz/Licensed by VAGA, New York, NY. Stuetzen der Gesellschaft.Inv.: NG 4/58. Photo: Joerg P. Anders. Nationalgalerie, Staatliche Museen zu Berlin, Berlin, Germany. Bildarchiv Preussischer Kulturbesitz/Art Resource, NY. © Estate of George Grosz/Licensed by VAGA, New York, NY; p. 724: AKG Images, London; p. 726: Dix, Otto (1891–1969) © 2010.ARS, NY/VG Bild-Kunst, Bonn.*Grosstadt—Big town*, tryptich, left wing. 1927/28, wood, distemper 181 × 101 cm. Inv. 0-1890.Kunstmuseum, Stuttgart, Germany. Erich Lessing/Art Resource, NY; p. 727: UFA/ The Kobal Collection; p. 728: Michael Nicholson/ Corbis; p. 729: Mansell/Time Life Pictures/Getty Images; p. 731: AP Images; p. 734: Fotomas/ Bridgeman Art Library; p. 736: RUSU 2225, Poster Collection, Hoover Institution Archives; p. 737: Isaac Soyer, *Employment Agency*, 1937. Oil on canvas. 34 1/4 × 45 in. (87 × 114.3 cm.) Whitney Museum of American Art, New York; purchase. 37.44; p. 741: Heinrich Hoffmann/Timepix/Time Life Pictures/Getty Images; p. 742: Nussbaum, Felix (1904–1944) *Self-portrait with Jewish Identity Card*. 1943. Oil on canvas, 56 × 49 cm. © 2010.ARS, NY/VG Bild-Kunst, Bonn.Bildarchiv Preussischer Kulturbesitz/Art Resource, NY.

Chapter 24

p. 746: Strempel, Horst (1904–1975) © 2010. ARS, NY/VG Bild-Kunst, Bonn. *Night Over Germany*. 1945. Oil on canvas. Inv. A III 257. Photo: Joerg P. Anders. Nationalgalerie, Staatliche Museen, Berlin, Germany. Bildarchiv Preussischer Kulturbesitz/Art Resource, NY; p. 750: Picasso, Pablo (1881–1973) *Guernica*. 1937. © ARS, NY. Oil on canvas, 350 × 782 cm. Museo Nacional Centro de Arte Reina Sofia, Madrid, Spain. John Bigelow Taylor/Art Resource, NY; p. 753: Bettmann/Corbis; p. 754: Imperial War Museum, London. IWM ART LD 2750; p. 759: AP Images; p. 762: Bettmann/Corbis; p. 764: Archive Photos/ Hulton Archive/Getty Images; p. 765: Imperial War Museum/The Art Archive; p. 766: Canadian War Museum, Ottawa, Canada/Bridgeman Art Library; p. 768: Archives Charmet/The Bridgeman Art

Library; p. 772–773: KATIA CHRISTODOULOU/ Corbis; p. 773: NASA/Corbis.

Chapter 25

p. 774: Don Eddy (American, b.1944). *New Shoes for H*, 1973–74. Acrylic on canvas; 111.7 × 121.9 cm. © The Cleveland Museum of Art, Purchased with a grant from the National Endowment for the Arts and matched by gifts from members of The Cleveland Society for Contemporary Art, 1974.53.; p. 781: © DACS/Roger Perrin/ The Bridgeman Art Library; p. 784L: Museum Ludwig/Rheinisches Bildarchiv; p. 784R: Goksin Sipahiouglu/Sipa Press; p. 786: Bettmann/ Corbis; p. 787: Joseph Koudelka/Magnum Photos; p. 797B: © 2003 Andy Warhol Foundation for the Visual Arts/ARS, NY/TM Licensed by Campbell's Soup Co. All rights reserved. Albright-Knox Art Gallery, Buffalo, New York, Gift of Seymour H. Knox, Jr., 1963/Art Resource, NY; p. 797T: Pollock, Jackson (1912–1956) © ARS, NY.*Convergence*. 1952. Oil on canvas, framed: 95 1/4 × 157 1/8 × 2 7/8" (241.935 × 399.0975 × 7.3025); support: 93 1/2 × 155" (237.49 x 393.7 cm.). Gift of Seymour H. Knox, Jr., 1956. Albright-Knox Art Gallery, Buffalo, New York. Albright-Knox Art Gallery/Art Resource, NY; p. 800: Georges Pierre/Corbis SYGMA; p. 801: Gianni Giansanti/Sygma/Corbis; p. 805: Lambert Studios/Hulton Archive/Archive Photos/Getty Images; p. 806: NASA.

Chapter 26

p. 810: Ryan Pyle/Corbis; p. 812: © Régis Bossu/Corbis Sygma; p. 815: Musee d'Histoire Contemporaine, BCIC, Universite de Paris, France; p. 817: Peter Turnley/Corbis; p. 823: Antoine Gyori/ Sygma/Corbis; p. 826: China Photos/Getty Images; p. 830: Jehad Nga/Corbis; p. 832: Kenneth Garrett/ National Geographic Image Collection/Getty Images; p. 834: Marco Ventura; p. 837B: Bruce F. Molnia/USGS; p. 837T: William O. Field; p. 838: Courtesy of the National Library of Medicine; p. 839: Jennifer Bartlett. *Spiral: An Ordinary Evening in New Haven*, 1989. Painting: oil on canvas, tables: painted wood and steel, cones: break formed hot rolled welded steel painting: 108" × 192", tables: 30" × 32"× 35", 39"× 41" × 35" cones: 20" × 30" × 21", © J. Bartlett. Private Collection, Greenwich, CT. Courtesy of the Paula Cooper Gallery, NY; p. 840: Valerio Mezzanotti/The New York Times/Redux.

TEXT CREDITS

Chapter 13

J.B. Bossuet, Politics Drawn from the Very Words of Holy Scritpure, 1709 in Brian Tierney and Joan Scott,

Western Societies: A Documentary History, Vol II, McGraw-Hill, 1984, pp. 11–13. Used by permission of The McGraw-Hill Companies, Inc.

Chapter 14

Jean Antoine Nicholas Caritat Marquis de Condorcet, Sketch for a Historical Picture on the Progress of the Human Mind, tr. June Barraclough, Weidenfeld and Nicolson (Orion Books), 1955, pp. 236–237, 244.

Chapter 22

Frank A. Golder, DOCUMENTS OF RUSSIAN HISTORY 1914–1917, Peter Smith Publisher, Inc., Goucester, MA 1964. Reprinted by permission of Peter Smith Publisher, Inc.

"Does It Matter", from COLLECTED POEMS OF SIEGRRIED SASSOON by Siegfried Sassoon, copyright 1918, 1920 by E.P. Dutton. Copyright 1936, 1946, 1947, 1948 by Siegfried Sassoon. Used by permission of Viking Penguin, a division of Penguin Group (USA) Inc.; Copyright Siegfried Sassoon by kind permission of the Estate of George Sassoon.

Chapter 23

Adolf Hitler, The Speeches of Adolf Hitler, vol. 1, trans. and ed. by Norman Baynes, Oxford University Press, 1942, pp. 72–73.

Excerpt from page 123 from THE EDUCATION OF A TRUE BELIEVER by LEV KOPELEV and TRANSLAGED BY GARY KERN. English translation copyright © 1980 by Harper & Row, Publishers, Inc. Reprinted by permission of HarperCollins Publishers.

Chapter 24

Reproduced by permission of The United States Holocaust Memorial Museum.

Reprinted, by permission, from Capt. Rikihei Inoguchi and Cdr. Tadashi Nakajima with Roger Pineau, The Divine Wind: Japan's Kamikaze Force in World War II (Annapolis, Md: Naval Institute Press, © 1958).

Chapter 25

Philip Toynbee, The Fearful Choice, Victor Gollancz, Ltd., 1956. Used by permission of Victor Gollancz, Ltd., a division of The Orion Publishing Group.

THE AMERICAN CHALLENGE by Jean Jacques Servan-Schreiber. English Translation copyright © 1968 by Atheneum House. Originally published in French as Le Defi Americain Copyright © 1967 by Editions Denoel. Reprinted by permission of Georges Borchardt, Inc., for Editions Denoel.

Kirov, Sergei, 736
Knight, Laura: *The Battle of Britain, 1943, 754*
Knox, John, 435
Koch, Robert, 678
Kodak cameras, 670
Kohl, Helmut, 823
kolkhozniks, 735
Kollontai, Alexandra, 733
Kollwitz, Karl, 706
Kollwitz, Käthe, 728
    The Mourning Father and Mother, 707
    "The Weavers," 706
Kopelev, Lev, 735
Korea, 652, 655, 769, 772, 780–781
Korean War, 780–781
Kornilov, Lavr, 715
Kosovo, 822–824
Kossuth, Louis, 600
Koster, Henry, 495
Kostunica, Vojislav, 823
Kramer, Stanley, 796
Kristallnacht, 742
Kronstadt naval base, 732
Kropotkin, Pyotr, 635
The Krupp Steelworks, 1880, 660, 660
kulaks, 734–735
Kulturkampf, 632
Kun, Béla, 728
Kurds, 803, 830
Kuwait, 823, 827
Kyoto Protocol, 830

L

Labor Party, 635, 723, 787, 824
labor unions, 596, 599, 620, 667, 714, 732
    strikes of, 634, 636, 725, 802
Laermans, Eugène: *The Emigrants, 641, 641*
Lafayette, Countess de: *The Princess of Clèves,* 423
laissez-faire economics, 469, 583
Lamartine, Alphonse de, 599, 599, 603
land redistribution, 714
Lang, Fritz: *Metropolis, 726, 727*
Laos, 650, 781, 791
Large Hadron Collider, 840
Lateran Treaty, 731
Latin America, 540, 663, 779, 784, 835
Latvia, 716, 752, 814, 817
laudanum, 566, 571, 652
Law, John, 490
law codes
    equality under, 522, 524, 535, 537, 543,
        582, 602, 714
    Napoleonic Code of 1804, 535, 537,
        539–540, 570
    of Russia, 429, 482
law enforcement, 565–566
Law of the Maximum, 528
Lawrence, T. E., 701
laxatives, 567
League of Arab States, 791
League of German Girls, 741
League of Nations, 708–709, 723–724, 743,
    748–749
League of Women's Rights, 801
Lebanon, 828
Lebensraum (living space), 739, 754

LeBrun, Charles, *Chancellor Seguier,*
    ca. 1670, *414*
leeches, 567
Leeuwenhoek, Anton van, 458–459
legal codes. *See* law codes
Legion of Honor, 535, 682
Legislative Assembly, 524, 526
legitimacy, 578
Leibnitz, Gottfried Wilhelm, 466
Lemonnier, Anicet Charles: *An Evening at
    Madame Geoffrin's in 1755, 472, 472*
Lenin, Vladimir Ilich, 715–716, *716,*
    732–733, 735
Leningrad, 755
Leo XIII, Pope, 676
Leopold I, 427–429
Leopold II, 646
LePen, Jean-Marie, 824
Lespinasse, Julie de, 472
Lessing, Doris, 797
Lettich, André, 760
Levasseur, Thérèse, 470
levée en masse, 529
Levellers, 437, 443, 446
Levi, Primo, 769
Leyte Gulf, Battle of, 765
liberal democracy, in Western Europe, 630–632
Liberal Party, 631
liberalism, 582–585, 595, 835
    classic, 583
    in Great Britain, 630–631
    nationalism and, 603
    romanticism and, 589
"Liberty, Equality, Fraternity," 515, 520, 522
    "or Death," 530, *531*
La Libre Parole, 637
Libya, 654
lice, 698
life expectancy, 820–821
limited monarchy, 468
Lin Zexu, 652
Lincoln, Abraham, 617, 625
Lincoln Brigade, 749
Lindbergh, Charles, 727
Lisbon Treaty, 825
Lister, Joseph, 678
Liszt, Franz, 587, 589
literature
    classical style in, 423
    in Europe, eighteenth century, 503, 507
    of Europe, nineteenth century, 586–587
    "Storm and Stress" (Sturm und Drang)
        literature, 586
Lithuania, 433, 716, 752, 814, 817
"little ice age," 417
Litvak, Lily, 762
Liverpool, 493–494, 547, 556, 644
Lloyd George, David, 635, 702, 706–707, 712
Locke, John, 442–443, 446, 509, 582
    Essay Concerning Human Understanding,
        463–464
    The Second Treatise of Government, 443, 468
logic, 460
Lombardy, 579, 593, 600
"Long Parliament," 436
longevity, 501

Longwe, Fololiyani, 699
Lorraine, 615, 708
Lorraine, Claude: *The Marriage of Isaac and
    Rebekah (The Mill), 1640, 425*
Louis XIII, 420–421, 436
Louis XIV, 488
    death of, 480
    France under, 1661–1715, 426
    Louis XIV at Versailles, Seventeenth
        Century, *424*
    on monarchical rights and duties, 422
    outlawing Protestantism, 425, 441
    as Sun King, 420–427
    wars of aggression by, 425
Louis XV, 480, 489–490, 516, 518
Louis XVI, 490–491
    execution of, 526, *527,* 529
    financial crisis of, 516
    flight with royal family, 524
    taxes and, 516
Louis XVII, 592
Louis XVIII, 542, 592, 595
Louis-Philippe, 595, 598–599, 602
Loutherbourg, Philip James de: *The
    Coalbrookdale Ironworks at Night,* 553
L'Ouverture, Toussaint, 531
Louvois, Marquis of, 425
Low Countries, 444, *444*
lower middle class, 666–667
"loyal opposition," 491
Ludd, Ned, 563
Luddism, 563, 593
Ludendorff, General, 698, 701, 704–705, 739
Lueger, Karl, 637–638
Lugard, Lord, 644
Lukacs, John, 810
Lusitania, 704
Luxemburg, Rosa, 723
Lvov, Georgi, 714
Lyrical Ballads, 587

M

Maastricht Treaty of 1992, 824
Macartney, George, 550
Macaulay, Thomas Babington, 586, 596, 650
Macedonia, 821
machine guns, 645, 654, 698–700, 705, 762
Mackenzie, William Lyon, 617
magic, 453, 461
Maginot Line, 724, 753
Magna Carta, 439, 794
magnetism, 676
Magyars, 585, 600, 618, 708
Maier, Anna, 635
Maistre, Joseph de, 581
    *Essay on the Generative Principle of Political
        Constitutions,* 582
maize, 495
malaria, 646, 701
Malaya, 791
Malaysia, 826
Malthus, Thomas: *Essay on the Principle of
    Population,* 560, 583, 674
Manchester, 548, 549, 556, 564, 644
Manchukuo, 757
Manchuria, 655, 748, 757